**Nevill Drury** is the author or co-author of over sixty books and has been published in seventeen languages. His work includes writings on shamanism and the western magical traditions as well as contemporary art, holistic health and ambient music. He is well known both as a lecturer and for his workshops on magical visualization and shamanic drumming.

# The Watkins Dictionary of

# Magic

## 3,000 Entries on the Magical Traditions

### Nevill Drury

WATKINS PUBLISHING
LONDON

This edition published in the UK by

Watkins Publishing, Sixth Floor, Castle House, 75-76 Wells Street, London W1T 3QH
Distributed in USA and Canada by Publishers Group West

13579108642

Designed and typeset by Jerry Goldie

Printed and bound in India by Gopsons Papers Ltd., Noida

British Library Cataloguing in Publication data available



Library of Congress Cataloging in Publication data available

ISBN 1 84293 152 0

www.watkinspublishing.com

# Acknowledgements

I would like to acknowledge the pioneering work of scholars like A.E. Waite and MacGregor Mathers who began the considerable task of documenting the western magical tradition around a century ago. They were followed by other major writers like Lewis Spence, Israel Regardie, Dion Fortune and Gareth Knight – among many others – who then consolidated much of this earlier material. In our own time writers like Francis X. King, Stephen Skinner, Rosemary Ellen Guiley, Caitlin and John Matthews, Ronald Hutton, Vivianne Crowley, Margot Adler, Janet and Stewart Farrar, Starhawk, Dolores Ashcroft-Nowicki, Doreen Valiente, Kenneth Grant, Mircea Eliade, Gershom Scholem, Aryeh Kaplan, Lyndy Abraham, Z. Budapest and many others, have added enormously to our understanding of the western esoteric tradition. I salute them all for their tremendous insights and understanding. Finally, I would like to acknowledge the very helpful and well-informed comments provided by my editor, Peter Bently.

This book is dedicated to the memory of the remarkable trance occultist and artist **Austin Osman Spare** (1886–1956) who opened a new path to the visionary world of magic.

# ACKNOWLEDGEMENTS

# Preface

The world of magic and the esoteric traditions is a source of endless fascination and speculation although it invariably attracts a wide range of human responses. For some people – wary, perhaps, of the often sinister overtones associated with magic and the occult arts – this whole realm of enquiry can seem frightening, potentially demonic, or simply irrational. To others it may seem remote or irrelevant. The subject has attracted much shallow and sensational media coverage, with its more superficial aspects such as fortune telling, horoscopes, and superstitions receiving the most public attention.

However, in recent times there has been an increasing interest in alternative religious and spiritual perspectives and, with the exception of the Kabbalah, most of these alternatives have tended to lie outside the Judaeo-Christian tradition. While many in contemporary western society have found a sense of spiritual fulfilment in exploring eastern forms of mysticism and meditation, in the West these spiritual alternatives have included revivals of various forms of goddess worship, Celtic neopaganism, and shamanism, and metaphysical frameworks like Gnosticism, alchemy, and the Tarot. There has also been renewed interest in the mysteries of ancient Greece and Egypt and an ongoing focus on Jewish mysticism – since the Kabbalah and the Tree of Life provide a key spiritual framework for the expansion of magical consciousness.

There can be no doubt that in contemporary western society the rise of rational and scientific thought has challenged the "divine-authority" base of mainstream Christianity to such an extent that church attendance is now very much on the decline. Indeed, it would seem that our society is at a type of spiritual crossroads. Our western culture continues to perpetuate the enshrined belief systems of our formal religious institutions but for many people the prevailing religious orthodoxies have a hollow ring about them, and do not reflect deeply felt personal experience.

So where does this leave the elusive and much misunderstood world of magic and the occult? How do practitioners of magic, witchcraft, neopaganism, and goddess worship respond to the modern world?

Ironically, although they may be reviving archaic belief systems and practices, the majority of occultists today are supporters of the new technologies – especially if they are seen to be helpful to the community at large. A surprisingly high number of occult devotees and neopagans work in the computer industry or in other areas of communication and information technology. However, they tend to believe that the demands of urban existence should be complemented by a sense of spiritual attunement to the broader world outside. There is a general consensus that the cycles of nature and the universe as a whole provide a broader scope for meaning than can be found in the daily urban routines that most of us endure.

The perspective which emerges within this broad-based metaphysical movement is a type of spiritual humanism – an approach based on the belief that all human beings have within them an intrinsic spiritual connection with the cosmos, an innate potential divinity which can be brought through into conscious expression. The magical traditions recognize this potential, and invite us to explore the visionary realms within our own being.

Another interesting aspect of the "occult" is that, increasingly, its so-called magical "secrets" are no longer hidden. The really worthwhile aspects of occult belief and practice are now very much out in the open – as more and more people seek to explore the different potentials for visionary and spiritual expression. This book is just one small example of that new openness – that new and open access to previously "occult", or "hidden" information.

This dictionary seeks to provide a wide range of cross-referenced listings covering the diverse and exotic traditions that are now part of the magical world-view. These traditions include Wicca, western ceremonial magic, alchemy, astrology, Gnosticism, Kabbalah, Rosicrucianism, Tarot, shamanism, voodoo, Macumba, and Santería. I have also included specialist listings related to Enochian angelic magic, Goetia, and the left-hand path, and the Thelemic and the O.T.O. cosmologies associated with such figures as Aleister Crowley and Kenneth Grant. In addition there are listings for magical plants, stones, and perfumes as well as important figures from Celtic, Norse, Egyptian, Greek, and Roman mythology, and native and indigenous magical traditions. Finally, I have included some listings from eastern mysticism where they relate specifically to the western esoteric tradition – chakras, kundalini yoga, and the tattvas being examples of eastern concepts that have entered the realm of modern western magic.

Finally I must admit to writing this book as one who is basically sympathetic to the western esoteric tradition. I know that I myself have benefited enormously from its exploration over the last thirty years or so, and I value my personal contact with people all over the world who share a similar interest. I also believe quite strongly that at this time in our history – a time when many people are expressing feelings of personal despair, despondency, and aimlessness – that we can all learn from each other's individual quest for sacred visionary experience. In fact, one of the most relevant tasks now, it seems to me, is to explore the various pathways that lead to the transformation of human consciousness. The revival of magic in modern times is very much a response to this need.

*Sydney, January 2005*

# A

**A∴A∴.** The abbreviated form for Argenteum Astrum.

**Aah** In ancient Egypt, one of the names of the moon god. See **Thoth**.

**Aaskouandy** Among the Iroquois Indians, small magical **charms** believed to contain considerable supernatural power. The Iroquois relate to these charms as if they are human and believe that neglecting them can lead to them turning against their owners.

**Ab** The ancient Egyptian term for the heart. It was regarded as the source of life and the seat of the conscience; hence it was crucial that the heart be preserved in the tomb.

**Abaddon** The name given by St. John in the *Book of Revelation* to the chief of the demons of the seventh hierarchy. Abaddon is also known as the "king of the grasshoppers" and the "destroying angel".

**Abaris** The Sethian high priest of Apollo. Abaris claimed to be able to ride through the air on a golden arrow given to him by his god. The priest foretold future events, banished disease, and produced the so-called Palladium **talisman**, which he sold to the Trojans to protect their town from assault.

**Abbey of Thelema** The centre for practising sex magic established in a villa in Cefalu, Sicily, by the ceremonial magician **Aleister Crowley**. Crowley referred to it as his *Collegium ad Spiritum Sanctum* (College of the Holy Sprit), a temple of Thelemic mysteries, and daubed the walls with erotic and quasi-pornographic paintings. Crowley maintained that, by seeing sexually explicit paintings on the walls, visitors to the Abbey would come to view such images indifferently and would therefore lose any inhibitions about sex. The Abbey of Thelema attracted notorious coverage in the British press in 1923 and these media reports led to Crowley's expulsion from Italy.

**Aberdeen Witches** A group of witches in northeast Scotland who were persecuted at the Aberdeen Assizes during 1596 – 1597. The witches were organized in **covens** – groups of thirteen – and each member had a specific task in the magical arts. One of the accused, Helen Rogie, modelled figures of her victims in lead and wax; while another, Isobel Ogg, was said to be able to raise storms through **sorcery**. When the Assizes closed in April 1597, 24 people – 23 women and one man – were found guilty of witchcraft and executed.

**Abiger** A grand duke of **Hades** with a particular knowledge of matters pertaining to war. According to Wierius (**Johannes Wier**), he is a handsome, armoured knight with 60 of the "infernal regions" at his command.

**Ablution** In alchemy, the stage in the refining process after the blackened putrefied material of the metal – associated with **nigredo**, or death – was washed and purified into a state of whiteness or **albedo**.

**Abortion** In alchemy, the term used for any work, or opus, that failed to come to completion.

**Abracadabra** A magical **chant** or incantation. Quintus Serenus Sammonicus, the physician to Emperor Severus on the Roman expedition to Britain in 208CE, used this formula to cure fevers and asthma. Rows of the word were written in a triangular formation on a piece of paper, which was then worn for nine days and thrown into a stream. As the word shrank on the paper, the ailment was supposed to diminish. The word itself may derive from the **Gnostic** deity **Abraxas**.

**Abrahadabra** The so-called formula of the **Great Work** in the cosmology of Aleister Crowley – the formula of sexual **magick**. Crowley believed that Abrahadabra was the "Word of the New Aeon" and that it would unite the microcosm and macrocosm in the next stage of human evolution. Its magical number is 418. It is related to, but not to be confused with, the well-known magical mantra **Abracadabra; Aeon of Horus.**

**Abraham the Jew** (1362–1460) Abraham was probably born in Mainz, Germany, and travelled widely through Austria, Hungary, and Greece, finally proceeding through Palestine to Egypt. At Arachi, on the banks of the Nile, he met a sage named Abra-Melin, who initiated him into a range of magical secrets. Abraham returned to Würzburg in Germany, undertook alchemical research, and endeavoured both to apply the magical arts in politics and to convert his children to his occult philosophy. He compiled his famous work *The Sacred Magic of Abra-Melin the Mage* when he was 96 years of age, as a legacy for his son Lamech. He gave details of the **invocation** of angelic forces and presented a series of magical rituals which took six months to perform. His magical system greatly influenced the occultist **Aleister Crowley**; and as recently as 1976 the pseudonymous "Georges Chevalier" published a diary based on his experience with the ceremonial invocations. See also **Magic.**

**Abra-Melin** See Abraham the Jew.

**Abraxas** or **Abrasax** A Gnostic deity whose name in Greek letters had a numerical value of 365, thereby linking the god to the days of the year. An important deity in the **pantheon** of **Basilides**, Abraxas had historical links with the Greek god Aion (see **Aeon**); the Iranian god of time, **Zurvan**; and the Indian sky god, **Varuna**. He was often represented on talismans. The symbolic concept of Abraxas as a deity of good and evil in one form has been put forward by psychologist **Carl Jung** in *Septem Sermones ad Mortuos*, and also by the novelist Hermann Hesse in *Demian*. He is also sometimes spelled Abrasax. See also **Abracadabra; Gematria.**

**Absolute, The** A metaphysical term connoting the ground of all being, that which exists in and of itself. It is often used to describe the One God, or Creator, the Infinite and Eternal. As the supreme transcendent reality, it is the focus of many mystical traditions.

**Abulafia, Abraham ben Samuel** (1240–1291) A kabbalistic mystic born in Saragossa, Spain, who later represented himself as the Messiah, both to Christians and Jews. He decided to confront Pope Nicholas III, but when the Pope heard of this, an order was sent that the heretical mystic would be burned to death if he set foot in Rome. The Pope then died unexpectedly, just as Abulafia arrived at the city gate. The mystic was imprisoned, but was set free a month later, and he then travelled with a group of followers to Sicily. Abulafia's approach to mysticism was purposeful and orderly, placing more emphasis on mental and spiritual integration than visionary flights of the soul. He believed in the divine symbolism of the Hebrew alphabet, and produced many mystical tracts, including *The Book of the Righteous* and *The Book of Life.*

**Abyss** In magical and kabbalistic terminology, the gulf between the Trinity – represented by **Kether, Chokmah**, and **Binah** on the **Tree of Life** – and the remaining **sephiroth** of manifested existence. Occultists believe that only adepts can bridge this gulf to higher spiritual consciousness. The Abyss is sometimes associated with the so-called "eleventh sephirah", **Daath.**

**Achad, Frater** (1886–1950). The magical name of Charles Stansfeld Jones, who was adopted by **Aleister Crowley** as his "magical son". Achad, who lived in

Vancouver, gained occult respectability by interpreting the numerical keys to Crowley's *Book of the Law*. He also produced highly original and sometimes confusing interpretations of the **Kabbalah** and the interconnecting **Tarot** paths of the **Tree of Life**, which are described in his books *QBL: The Bride's Reception* and *The Anatomy of the Body of God*. Achad began to lose his mental stability after taking the magical grade of **Ipsissimus**, which implied that his every action had cosmic significance. Also known as Brother Unity.

**Acheron** In Greek mythology, one of the five rivers in **Hades**, specifically the river of woe. **Charon** ferried the souls of the dead across this river to the **Underworld**.

**Acronym** A word formed from the initial letters of other words. For example, "laser" derives from "*l*ight *a*mplification by the *s*timulated *e*mission of *r*adiation". In the **Kabbalah**, acronyms were said to have related symbolic meanings.

**Action de Grâce** In **voodoo**, the Roman Catholic ritual and litanies which precede a magical ceremony.

**Adam** In alchemy, another name for the *prima materia*. Adam's name is thought to be derived from the Hebrew word *adom*, meaning "red earth" and the alchemists sometimes referred to the *prima materia* as the "red earth" for this reason. It was said that the secret of the Philosopher's Stone was divinely revealed to Adam and then transferred from Paradise to the care of the holy patriarchs. Adam was regarded as hermaphroditic prior to the Fall and the hermaphrodite embodies the fusion of opposite polarities which in turn represents spiritual unity. See also **Hermaphrodite**, **Eve**.

**Adam Kadmon** The Judaic concept of the archetypal man, the primordial human being formed in the creation of the universe. Every human being is said to reflect this archetypal form. Adam Kadmon is also, metaphorically, "the body of God".

**Adams, Anton and Mina** An Australian Wiccan couple who together have produced several accessible books on the magical traditions. Anton and Mina Adams practise as solitaries and are not members of a larger coven. Their international publications include *The Learned Arts of Witches and Wizards*, *The World of Wizards*, and *The Wizards' Handbook*.

**Adept** An initiate or occult master; one who has gained profound magical powers and insights through **initiation**. In the theosophical system, adepts form part of the **Great White Lodge**, a group of mystical leaders who guide the world and its inhabitants through processes of spiritual evolution. The **Hermetic Order of the Golden Dawn** had four ceremonial grades of adept: **Zelator Adeptus Minor**, **Theoricus Adeptus Minor**, **Adeptus Major**, and **Adeptus Exemptus**, associated with grades of initiatory experience on the **Tree of Life**.

**Adeptus Exemptus** In the inner order of the **Hermetic Order of the Golden Dawn**, the ritual grade associated with the magical initiation of **Chesed** on the kabbalistic **Tree of Life**. See also **Kabbalah**; **Ordò Rosae Rubeae et Aureae Crucis**.

**Adeptus Major** In the inner order of the **Hermetic Order of the Golden Dawn**, the ritual grade associated with the magical initiation of **Geburah** on the kabbalistic **Tree of Life**. See also **Kabbalah**; **Ordo Rosae Rubeae et Aureae Crucis**.

**Adeptus Minor** In the inner order of the **Hermetic Order of the Golden Dawn**, the ritual grade associated with the magical initiation of **Tiphareth** on the kabbalistic **Tree of Life**. It was divided into two sub-grades, **Zelator**

**Adeptus Minor** and **Theoricus Adeptus Minor.** See also **Kabbalah; Ordo Rosae Rubeae et Aureae Crucis.**

**Adjuration** A form of command made by an exorcist to an evil spirit. The exorcist may command the spirit to depart from the body of the possessed person. See also **Exorcism.**

**Adler, Margot** (1946 – ). A noted American goddess worshipper, author, and radio journalist, Adler is the grand-daughter of the distinguished psychiatrist Alfred Adler and one of the leading spokespersons for **neopaganism** in the United States. Adler maintains that she has had a love of the pagan traditions since she was twelve, when she "fell in love" with the Greek gods and goddesses. In 1971 she was initiated into a **Gardnerian** witchcraft coven and she is now a priestess in her own coven. Her pioneering work *Drawing Down the Moon*, first published in 1979 and subsequently reissued in revised editions, is still the definitive overview of American **neopaganism**, goddess worship and Wicca.

**Adonai** The Hebrew word for "the Lord", used when speaking, reading about, or referring to Jehovah, the God of Israel. The awesome and mysterious sacred name of God was held in such respect that Jews avoided pronouncing it and substituted YHVH – the **Tetragrammaton** – in its place. In the magical ceremonies of the **Hermetic Order of the Golden Dawn**, it was used as a **god-name** in formulating the **Pentagram** of earth.

**Adonai ha Aretz** In the Kabbalah, the divine name associated with the sphere **Malkuth** on the **Tree of Life**. It translates as "Lord of the Land".

**Adoptive Masonry** See Co-Masonry.

**Adoration** In **voodoo**, the song which accompanies the money offerings at magical ceremonies. The coins are placed on a plate which in turn rests on the sacrificed animal and this money is sometimes buried as an offering to the **loa**.

**Adrop** In alchemy, the ore from which "philosophical mercury" was said to be extracted. Adrop was associated with Saturn (Arabic *usrubb*, meaning "lead").

**A.E.** See Russell, George.

**Aegle** See Garden of the Hesperides.

**Aeon** (1) An enduring period of time, from the Greek *aion*. Some magical groups, especially those influenced by **Aleister Crowley**, refer to aeons in terms of characteristic patterns of mythic and ceremonial worship: the Aeon of Isis (worship of lunar goddesses); the Aeon of Osiris (worship of solar gods); and the **Aeon of Horus** (worship of the magical child who combines male and female forces in the **androgyne**).

**Aeon** (2) A spiritual being in Gnostic and Mithraic cosmology. In Gnosticism, aeons were emanations of the **pleroma**, the fullness of the **godhead**. The Greek god Aeon (Aion) is related to the Gnostic **Abraxas** and was amalgamated into Mithraism in the second and third centuries CE. See also **Mithra; Valentinus.**

**Aeon of Horus** In the Thelemic cosmology of ceremonial magician **Aleister Crowley**, the "New Aeon", in which he himself would play a crucial role. Following a revelation from an entity named **Aiwaz** in Cairo in 1904, Crowley came to believe that he had been chosen to be the Lord of the New Aeon. This was the Aeon of Horus – the Aeon of the Crowned and Conquering Child – and it replaced the two earlier aeons, the matriarchal Aeon of Isis, characterized by the worship of lunar deities, and the later patriarchal Aeon of Osiris, which included the worship of incarnating demi-gods and divine kings. The Aeon of Horus would be based on the union of male and female polarities, and Crowley incarnated the "divine child",

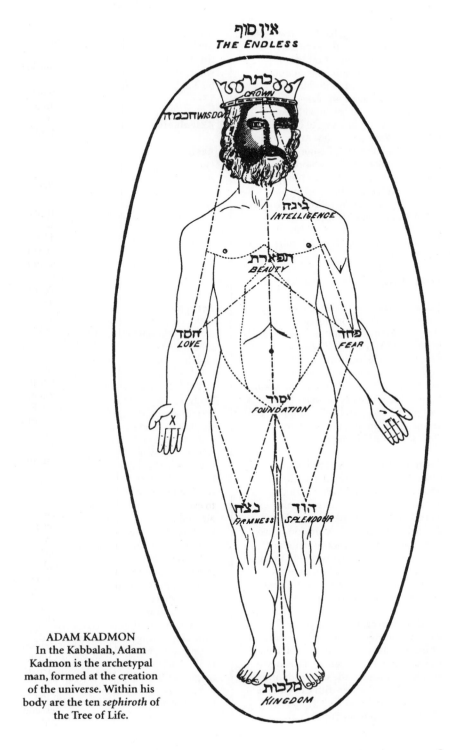

אין סוף
THE ENDLESS

כתר
CROWN

חכמה WISDOM

בינה
INTELLIGENCE

תפארת
BEAUTY

חסד
LOVE

פחד
FEAR

יסוד
FOUNDATION

נצח
FIRMNESS

הוד
SPLENDOUR

מלכות
KINGDOM

**ADAM KADMON**
In the Kabbalah, Adam Kadmon is the archetypal man, formed at the creation of the universe. Within his body are the ten *sephiroth* of the Tree of Life.

5

the offspring of the gods. The New Aeon would be characterized by spiritual freedom and all religious traditions which impeded freedom – including Christianity, Islam, and Buddhism – would be considered obsolete. For Crowley the basis of spiritual freedom was sexuality and he came to believe that the **Great Work** of the New Aeon would arise through the sexual union of the **Great Beast 666** and the **Whore of Babalon**, the Scarlet Woman (he spelt it Babalon rather than Babylon for numerological reasons). Crowley would spend much of his life from 1904 onwards seeking lovers and concubines who could act as his "Divine Whore". See also **Thelema**.

**Aeon of Isis** See Aeon of Horus.

**Aeon of Maat** In Thelemic cosmology, the **Aeon** which, according to tantric magician **Kenneth Grant**, will succeed the **Aeon of Horus**. Maat was the Egyptian goddess of truth and justice. According to Grant, the Aeon of Maat will be characterized by the elements **air** (representing space) and **water** (representing the deep) and will continue the sex-magic orientation of the **Aeon of Horus**. See also **Thelema**.

**Aeon of Osiris** In the Thelemic cosmology of ceremonial magician **Aleister Crowley**, an earlier period in human history characterized by the worship of incarnating demi-gods and divine kings who were "slain and raised from the dead in one way or another". According to Crowley, Osiris and the resurrected Christ both belonged to the Aeon of Osiris and were now declared obsolete. See also **Thelema**.

**Aesch Mezareph** An expression meaning "purifying fire" and the name of a medieval treatise linking the **Kabbalah** and **alchemy**. In this process alchemical metals are linked to the **sephiroth** of the **Tree of Life** (e.g. silver with **Chesed**, tin with **Binah**, and iron with **Tiphareth**). The French magician Eliphas Lévi believed *Aesch Mezareph* was one of the most important hermetic books. It was first translated into Latin by **Christian Knorr von Rosenroth** and forms part of his *Kabbala Denudata*, published in 1714.

**Aesculapius** See *Asklepios*

**Aesir** In Scandinavian mythology, a family of gods living in the stronghold Asgard, which was the equivalent of Mount Olympus. According to the writer Snorri Sturluson, **Odin** was the head of this community and **Thor** and the other gods were his "sons". The gods of the Aesir were locked in continual battles with another group of deities – the fertility gods of the **Vanir**, headed by Njord and **Freyr**.

**Aethyrs** "Ethers", a term used by the 16th-century astrologer **Dr John Dee** and his colleague **Edward Kelley**, and subsequently revived by **Aleister Crowley** and described in the latter's classic work *The Vision and the Voice*, written in Paris in 1929. The term relates to the angelic "calls" or "keys" obtained by Kelley from certain angels and spirits by employing a **skrying** method that involved the use of a **crystal ball** and a black obsidian mirror. Following a number of skrying sessions the "keys" were written down by Dee. Nineteen "keys" were obtained, the first eighteen of which could be used to evoke the elements **spirit, fire, water, air**, and **earth**. The final key could be modified to evoke any of the 30 so-called "Aethyrs", or "Aires". Aleister Crowley invoked the first two Aethyrs in Mexico in November 1900, and the remaining Aethyrs nine years later in the Sahara Desert, where he was accompanied by **Victor Neuburg**. The calls resulted in a series of extraordinary magical visions including a dangerous encounter with the spirit of chaos, **Choronzon**. In the Thelemic system of **Enochian magic** the 30 Aethyrs are arranged in ascending order from the lowest and most material to the highest and most spiritual, as follows: **Tex, Rii, Bag, Zaa,**

Des, Vti, Nia, Tor, Lin, Asp, Khr, Pop, Zen, Tan, Lea, Oxo, Uti, Zim, Loe, Ikh, Zax, Zip, Zid, Deo, Maz, Lit, Paz, Zon, Arn, and Lil (see individual listings). As a map of the magical universe the Aethyrs parallel the **sephiroth** and **Major Arcana** paths on the kabbalistic **Tree of Life** but, with one exception, there are no exact correlations. This exception is the tenth Aethyr, **Zax**, which corresponds to **Daath** (Knowledge) – the so-called eleventh sephirah on the Tree of Life, which corresponds to the **Abyss**, the bridge between the manifest realm of Creation and the realm of spiritual transcendence.

**Afreet** See **Efreet**.

**Agaberte** A daughter of the Scandinavian giant Vagnoste. A powerful enchantress with remarkable magical powers. Agaberte could change her form, appearing sometimes as a wrinkled old woman hunched over with age, and on other occasions as a tall, vibrant woman who could touch the sky. She was said to be capable of overturning mountains, ripping up trees, and drying up rivers, with consummate ease.

**Aganjú** See Orungan.

**Aganyú** See Oddudúa.

**Agapé** A Greek word for "love", and the name given to early Christian love-feasts combining a common meal with hymns and prayers. Because the numerical value of agapé is 93, followers of **Aleister Crowley** regard it as one of the key magical words of the **Aeon of Horus** and associate it with the deity **Aiwaz**, whose name adds to the same total.

**Agapé Lodge** Branch of the **Ordo Templi Orientis**, established in Los Angeles in 1930 by Wilfred Talbot Smith, an associate of **Frater Achad**. Lodge members included **Jack Parsons** and the actress Jane Wolfe – who had been with **Aleister Crowley** at the **Abbey of Thelema**.

**Agares** In the **Goetia**, the second spirit, a duke who is "under the power of the East" and who appears in the form of an old man, riding upon a crocodile and carrying a goshawk on his fist. Mild mannered, he nevertheless leads 31 legions of spirits. He teaches "all languages or tongues" and is also known as Agreas.

**Agla** A kabbalistic magical formula used to exorcise evil spirits. In modern magic it is one of the god-names of the banishing ritual of the Lesser Pentagram. It is made up of the initial letters of the Hebrew phrase *Athah gabor leolam, Adonai*, meaning "Thou art powerful and eternal, Lord".

**Aglaophotis** An Arabian herb used in sorcery to evoke demons.

**Agogô** In **Macumba**, a double bell made of metal which is hit with an iron rod to make the gods descend.

**Agotkon** Among the Iroquois Indians, shamans and sorcerers who use their magical powers to cast harmful spells on others.

**Agoué** See Agwé.

**Agreas** See Agares.

**Agrippa von Nettesheim, Heinrich Cornelius** (1486–1535). A German occult scholar and astrologer, born of noble parentage in Cologne. An attendant to Holy Roman emperor Maximilian I, he entered the imperial secret service and spied on the French while attending Paris University. Here he encountered mystics and **Rosicrucians** and developed an interest in the **Kabbalah** and Hermetic philosophies. In 1531 he published *De Occulta Philosophia* which dealt with divine names, natural magic, and cosmology. In this famous treatise, Agrippa divides the universe into the elemental world, the celestial world, and the intellectual world, each receiving influences from the one above it. The virtue of the Creator descends via the archangels to the intellectual world, is then transmitted to the stars in the celestial world, and finally filters down into the physical world where it permeates the elements – from which all things are created. *De Occulta Philosophia* is divided into three books. The first is about natural magic, or magic in the elemental world; the second is about the magic of the stars and how to utilize it; and the third is about ceremonial magic, that is to say magic involving angelic spirits. Knowledge of all three worlds involves a familiarity with the Hebrew alphabet, specific ritual formulae, and the sacred names of God. Agrippa was rumoured to possess a magic mirror in which he could divine future events, and he also dabbled in necromancy, believing he could conjure up the spirits of the dead.

**Aguet** See Agwé.

**Agwé** In **voodoo**, the spirit of the sea. He is married to **La Sirène**, the sea-aspect of the goddess of love, **Erzulie**.

**Aha** See Bes.

**Ahayuta** The twin war gods of the Zuni Indians.

**Ahriman** The Zoroastrian personification of **evil**. The antagonist of "Wise Lord" **Ahura Mazdah**, Ahriman was committed to perpetuating lies against the Holy Spirit. In the **Gathas**, he is described as being locked in eternal conflict with the forces of Light and Truth. Alternatively knowm as Angra Mainyu.

**Ahura Mazdah** The supreme god in Zoroastrianism. Aligned with the Holy Spirit, Ahura Mazdah – as the embodiment of Truth – was the sworn enemy of **Ahriman**, the personification of evil. In late Zoroastrianism, Ahura Mazdah became **Ohrmazd**, a fusion of the "Wise Lord" and the "Holy Spirit" in one being.

**Aidoneus** See Hades.

**Aiguillette** In medieval France, a knotted loop of thread which – according to folk-tradition – was used by witches to cause impotence and sometimes castration in men. The aiguilette could bind lovers together in illicit relationships and was also known as a ligature.

**Ailm** In the Celtic tree alphabet, the **ogham** representing the silver fir and pine and the letter "a". Ailm is also linked to the lapwing and the colour grey.

**Aim** See Aini.

**Ain** In the Kabbalah, the deepest of the three aspects of the unmanifested God. The Hebrew term translates as "nothing". Also known as Ayn.

**Ain Soph Aur** A Hebrew expression meaning "Limitless Light". In the Kabbalah, it represents the infinite and mysterious source from which all comes forth.

**Aini** In the Goetia, the 23rd spirit, a powerful duke who appears in the form of a three-headed man. The first head is like a serpent, the second is human, with two stars on the forehead, and the third is like a cat. Aini rides on a viper and carries a firebrand in his hand, which he uses to set fire to cities and castles. He provides truthful answers to private questions and imparts cunning and cleverness. Aini commands 26 legions of spirits. He is also known as Aim or Aym.

**Air** In alchemy, one of the four elements, the others being **fire, water,** and **earth.** The spirits of air were known as sylphs. The three astrological signs linked to air are **Gemini, Libra,** and **Aquarius.**

**Aires** See Aethyrs.

**Aires, Enochian** See Aethyrs.

**Aiwaz** or **Aiwass** The name of the deity from which **Aleister Crowley** received his transformational magical doctrine, formulated in *The Book of the Law*. Aiwaz communicated this doctrine to Crowley's wife, Rose, via trance state, while the couple were visiting Cairo in 1904.

**Aix-en-Provence Nuns** A classic example of the hysterical and tragic **witchcraft** delusion in France during the early seventeenth century. The events of the Aix-en-Provence nuns focus on two women, Sister Madeleine de Demandolx de la Palud and Sister Louise Capeau, who were members of the small, exclusive Ursuline convent in Aix. Madeleine, who had entered the convent at the age of twelve, became very depressed with her environment and was sent back home to Marseilles. Here she was housed by a humorous and somewhat carefree family friend, Father Louis Gaufridi, with whom she subsequently fell in love. The relationship with an older man – Gaufridi was 34 – was frowned upon by the head of the Ursuline convent in Marseilles and Madeleine was taken into this convent as a novice. Here she confessed that she had been intimate with Gaufridi; and, undoubtedly to keep Madeleine's lover at a distance, the head of the convent, Mother Catherine, transferred the young novice back to Aix. Madeleine soon began to develop dramatic shaking fits and severe cramps and had visions of **devils**. The hysteria soon spread to the five other nuns in the convent, one of whom, Louise Capeau, tried to rival Madeleine with the intensity of her visions.

The Grand Inquisitor, Sebastian Michaelis, now became involved in the case and arranged for the two young women to be taken to the Royal Convent of St Maximin to be treated by an exorcist. The demonic visions continued, with Louise claiming to be possessed by three devils and accusing Madeleine of being in league with Beelzebub, Asmodeus, Ashtaroth, and several thousand other evil spirits. Later, Father Gaufridi was called in to attempt an **exorcism**. Madeleine mocked him with demonic condemnations and insults, and at first his part in the hysterical outbreak was unproven. However, when Madeleine continued with her visions, neighed like a horse, and told fantastic tales of sodomy and witch sabbats, Gaufridi was interrogated by the **Inquisition** in more depth. Finally, in April 1611, he was found guilty by the court of magic, sorcery, and fornication, and was sentenced to death. His execution was especially barbaric; he was humiliated, tortured, and finally publicly burned. His demise led to a sudden reverse in the fortunes of Madeleine who, the following day, seemed free of demonic **possession**. Louise Capeau, however, continued to have visions of witches and devils, and similar outbreaks of witchcraft hysteria were reported at St Claire's convent in Aix, and at St Bridget's in Lille.

In 1642, Madeleine was again accused of witchcraft. She was cleared of this charge, but a further attack against her ten years later resulted in the discovery of **witch's marks** on her body. She spent the rest of her life in prison.

**Ajna Chakra** In **Kundalini** yoga, the occult power centre also known as the "third eye", situated just above and between the eyes.

**Akasha** From a Sanskrit word meaning "luminous", but referring to "essence" or "space", akasha is one of the five Hindu elements: the black egg of **spirit**. These feature in the **tattvas**, which have been incorporated into western **magic**. See also **Chakras**; **Quest, Quinary**.

**Akashic Records** A Theosophical concept for an astral memory of all events, thoughts, and emotions that have arisen since the world began. Psychics are said to be able to tune into this dimension and receive authentic impressions of past ages. Some theosophical descriptions of Atlantis derive from apparent Akashic memories and some magicians try to access these memories through skrying. See also Theosophy.

**Al** A Hebrew term for God, the Most Ancient One. See also El; Elohim.

**Al Azif** See *Necronomicon*.

**Alan, Jim** See Fox, Selena.

**Alastor** A cruel demon who, according to Wierius (Johannes Wier), was the chief executioner in Hades. The word "alastor" also has general usage, meaning an evil, avenging spirit.

**Albedo** In alchemy, the "white" stage of the work which is reached after the blackened putrified material of the metal – associated with nigredo, or death – is washed to a state of whiteness by the purifying mercurial waters or fire. See also Queen Luna; White Elixir.

**Albrerich** See Andvari.

**Albertus Magnus** (1206–1280). Born in the town of Lauingen in Swabia, Germany, Albertus Magnus, Count of Bollstadt, was highly regarded by his contemporaries as a philosopher, alchemist, and theologian. Although he claimed inspiration from the Virgin Mary, became bishop of Ratisbon (Regensburg), and was a mentor to St. Thomas Aquinas, Albertus was suspected by many of communicating with the Devil. However, he was more a philosopher than a magician, for he was essentially an observer of natural phenomena. A keen field botanist, he visited mines and mineral outcrops and was fascinated by the "marvellous virtues" of plants and stones – this type of enquiry would come to be known as "natural magic". Albertus believed that engraved gems had magical powers, and regarded astrology as the basis of all forms of divination. However, this was for the proto-scientific reason that, just as Aristotle had decreed, celestial bodies were seen to govern all things on earth.

Albertus similarly considered alchemy as a "true art" and championed the idea that gold could be produced artificially. According to popular tradition, he owned a precious stone that could produce certain marvels: "When William II, Count of Holland, dined with him in Cologne, Albertus had the table set in the garden of the convent in spite of the fact that it was midwinter. When the guests arrived they found a snow-decked table. But as soon as they sat down, the snow disappeared and the garden was filled with fragrant flowers. Birds flew about as if it were summer, and the trees were in bloom."

**Albigenses** or Albigensians A twelfth- and thirteenth-century French sect named after one of its main centres, the town of Albi. Associated with the Bogomils, Cathars, and Paulicians, the Albigenses were strongly opposed to the Roman Catholic Church, which in turn branded them heretics and persecuted them severely during the Inquisition. The Albigenses believed that God had created Lucifer as his firstborn, who in turn escaped with a band of fallen angels to create the world and all its inhabitants. Jesus Christ was God's second son, and his role was to re-establish spiritual order in a totally evil world. This doctrine was quite unacceptable to the established Church, particularly with its implication that the Church, and humankind generally, was essentially demonic. The Albigensian Crusade (1209–1229), and subsequently the Inquisition, dealt with the sect so severely that after 1330 there were no more Albigenses left to persecute.

**Alchemical metals** In alchemy, specific metals were associated with the astrological planets: Sun – gold; Moon – silver; Mercury – quicksilver; Venus – copper; Mars – iron; Jupiter – tin; Saturn – lead. Four of these (copper, iron, tin, and lead) were considered "imperfect".

**Alchemy** The ancient science of transmuting base metals into gold and silver.

**ALCHEMY Medieval alchemical apparatus. The flames from the furnace are clearly visible.**

The etymology of the word is uncertain, but it may derive from the Arabic *al-kimiya*, meaning "the (magical craft of the) Black Land", the ancient name of Egypt – a reference to the inhabited areas along the Nile, with its black, fertile soil, in contrast to the "Red Land" of the desert. The ancient Egyptians were master metalworkers and believed that magical powers existed in certain fluxes and alloys. After the Arabs conquered Egypt in the seventh century, they took alchemy with them to Morocco and Spain. From the ninth to the eleventh centuries, Seville, Cordova, and Granada were leading centres for alchemy; later, this esoteric science spread to France, England, and Germany.

The three main aims of alchemy were to attempt to make gold from base metals with the aid of the **Philosopher's Stone**; to search for an elixir that could prolong life indefinitely; and to acquire methods of creating life artificially. In the Middle Ages considerable fortunes were lost by wealthy patrons who financed alchemical experiments that came to nothing. Nicholas Flamel (1330–1418) claimed to have transformed mercury into silver and gold, but it is more likely that he acquired his wealth as the result of his moneylending business.

To a substantial degree, though, alchemy was also a metaphor for spiritual transformation, a process quite divorced from laboratory experimentation. The imperfect individual, leaden

11

and dark, could become pure and golden through gradual processes leading to spiritual illumination. Basil Valentine, a celebrated alchemist and Benedectine monk, described alchemy as "the investigation of those natural secrets by which God has shadowed out eternal things", and Jacob Boehme regarded the Philosopher's Stone as the spirit of Christ, which would "tincture" the individual soul. In this sense, alchemy was both a precursor of modern chemistry and also a complex spiritual philosophy – one of the major sources of medieval esoteric thought.

**Aldinach** An Egyptian **demon** given to causing earthquakes, hailstorms, and tempests. He sometimes masqueraded in the form of a woman.

**Alectorius** A magical stone, normally crystal-clear, but sometimes with pink, flesh-like veins through it. In the Middle Ages it was believed to have many occult properties, including the power to bring fame and love to its owner.

**Alectryomancy** A form of **divination** through observing the actions of birds, often a black hen or a gamecock. In Africa, where this form of augury is practised, the diviner sprinkles grain on the ground and allows the birds to peck at it. When the birds have finished, the seer interprets the patterns that remain.

**Alef** See Aleph.

**Alembic** In **alchemy**, the beaked vessel used as the upper part of the distillation apparatus. The beak of the alembic carried vapours through to a receiving vessel in which they were condensed. See also **Beak; Head; Helmet; Womb**

**Aleph** The Hebrew letter ascribed to the path linking **Kether** and **Chokmah** on the **Tree of Life**. Aleph has a numerical value of one. In modern magical visualization and **pathworkings**, the Tarot card associated with this path on the Tree is *The Fool*.

**Aleph of Unity** In the Kabbalah, the so-called "Small Face" of God – those aspects of God manifest in the **sephiroth** on the **Tree of Life**.

**Aleph Worlds** In the Kabbalah, the unmanifested states of the so-called "Vast Face" of God – those unknowable states beyond **Kether**, the Crown, on the Tree of Life.

**Aleuromancy** A form of **divination** with flour. Among the ancient Greeks, the procedure was as follows: sentences were composed, written on small pieces of paper, and rolled up in balls of flour. The balls were then mixed up nine times and distributed to those who were eager for information on their destiny. The god **Apollo** presided over this form of divination.

**Alexander of Abonotica** A second-century seer and oracle who established a shrine on the southern shore of the Black Sea. Possessed of good looks and a fine voice, Alexander announced that he was the prophet of Apollo and the healing god **Asklepios**, who would both manifest through his shrine. Alexander soon acquired a following and his fame spread as far as Rome; according to one tale, Emperor Marcus Aurelius consulted the seer of Abonotica before undertaking a military operation. Alexander liked to appear before the crowds with a large but harmless Macedonian snake coiled around his neck. The actual head of the snake would be concealed under his arm and an artificial head – which was supposed to be that of Apollo – was allowed to protrude. Alexander, through sheer showmanship, managed to convince the crowds that the snake deity could give mystic oracles relating to the cause of disease, and could also divine the future. Alexander's shrine and cult survived for many years after his death.

**Alexandrian Witches** In Wicca, witches initiated by the British witches Alex and **Maxine Sanders** or their successors. The term "Alexandrian" is a play on Alex Sanders' name.

**Alfheim** In Scandinavian and northern European mythology, the world of light and the beautiful elves.

**Algol** A bright star in the constellation of Perseus. Known variously as the Demon's Head by the Arabs, Lilith by the Jews, and Medusa's Head by the Greeks, it was regarded as evil. This may be because a dark star that revolves around it periodically dims its radiance, giving the impression of an evil, winking eye.

**Alhazred, Abdul** See *Necronomicon*.

**Alkahest** In alchemy, a term used by Paracelsus to denote the "universal solvent". See **Universal Solvent**.

**All Hallows' Eve** Also known as Halloween and Samhain, a pagan festival representing the change of season from autumn to winter, celebrated in the northern hemisphere on 31 October, the eve of the Christian feast of All Hallows (All Saints' Day). It was also a time when the souls of the deceased revisited their former homes and once again enjoyed the company of their kinsfolk and friends around an open fire. Bonfires are one of the symbols of All Hallows' Eve, perhaps intended to retain something of the light and warmth of summer and early autumn by contrast with the onset of chilly winter winds. In the United States, Halloween has become a special occasion for children, who dress up as ghosts or witches and go from door to door seeking a "trick or treat".

**Allocen** In the Goetia, the 52nd spirit, a mighty duke who appears in the form of a soldier riding on a horse. His eyes are blazing with fire, his ruddy face is like that of a lion and he speaks in a hoarse voice. Allocen can locate "good familiars" and is well versed in astronomy and all the liberal sciences. He rules over 36 legions of spirits and is also known as Alocas, Alloien, or Allocer.

**Allocer** See Allocen.

**Alloien** See Allocen.

**Almadel** In medieval magic, a wax talisman inscribed with the names of deities or spirits. It was made from wax so that it could be melted down, and the secret information inscribed upon it destroyed.

**Alocas** See Allocen.

**Alomancy** A form of **divination** by sprinkling salt. The diviner interprets future events by analyzing the patterns made by this action. Alomancy has probably given rise to the superstition that spilling salt is unlucky. Misfortune is averted by casting a small amount of the salt over the left shoulder.

**Alostrael** The magical name of Leah Hirsig, who served as Aleister Crowley's Scarlet Woman at the Abbey of Thelema in Sicily. She bore him a daughter, Poupée.

**Alphabet of Desire** In the trance magic of Austin Osman Spare, a sacred alphabet consisting of letters, planetary signs, and imaginary sigils which formed the basis of his magical will. Spare used these sigils and letters to awaken subconscious memories.

**Alrunes** In German and Norse myth, shape-shifting sorceresses or female demons who could foresee the future and who responded to questions by moving their heads in different ways. Statues of these sorceresses were clothed, served with food and drink, and highly respected. It was believed that the statues would cry out and bring catastrophe, if neglected. See also **Shape-Shifting**.

**Altar** In traditional forms of **religion** and also in the practice of **ceremonial magic**, an elevated place or structure on which sacrifices are offered or at which religious or magical rites are performed. In **Wicca**, the altar is a ceremonial table or flat surface where the working tools of the witch and appropriate images of the Goddess and the God are displayed and readily accessible. The altar faces the quarter assigned to the element earth – north in the northern hemisphere, south in the southern hemisphere – and is located either in the centre of the magical working space or close to the perimeter of the circle in the earth quarter. The tools and items on the altar will typically include the sword, athame, a white-handled knife, a wand, a pentacle, a censer of incense, a scourge, some ritual cords, a chalice of wine, a bowl of water, a dish containing salt, candles, and a bowl of anointing oil.

**Altar Cloth** In Wicca, a black or white cloth which rests on the **altar**. Placed on it are containers for the salt and water used to purify the magic circle with the elements earth and water.

**Altar, Live** In contemporary **Satanism**, which venerates carnal desire and hedonistic indulgence, naked women serve as "live altars" in ceremonial rituals. In a description of ritual practices in the **Church of Satan**, **Anton La Vey** has written: "The woman who serves as the altar lies on the platform with her body at right angles to its length, her knees at its edge and widely parted. A pillow supports her head. Her arms are outstretched crosswise and each hand grasps a candleholder containing a black candle. When the celebrant is at the altar, he stands between the woman's knees."

**Altered State** A state of consciousness different from normal, everyday consciousness, the latter sometimes being referred to as the "consensus reality" on which normal patterns of communication are based. Altered states exclude or minimize the external world, allowing subconscious imagery to rise into consciousness. Altered states include some types of dreams, trance states, out-of-the-body experiences, dissociation experiences, mystical states, and hallucinations associated with psychedelic drugs.

**Althotas** A mysterious occultist whom **Count Alessandro di Cagliostro** claimed to have met in Messina, Sicily. Althotas and Cagliostro allegedly travelled to Alexandria and Rhodes and then on to Malta, where they undertook a series of alchemical experiments under the sponsorship of Grand Master Pinto. The actual existence of Althotas has never been established, and some believe he was a figment of Cagliostro's imagination.

**Aludel** In alchemy, the pear-shaped bottle used as a condensing vessel to collect sublimates. It was referred to as the Hermetic Vase or the Vase of the Philosophy, and was the vessel in which the **Great Work** took place.

**Am Tuat** or Am Duat An important text of the **Egyptian Book of the Dead** describing the passage of the sun god through the twelve dungeons of the **Tuat**, or **Underworld** (the twelve hours of night). Taking the form of the Ram, Afu-Ra travels by boat through the waters of darkness, vanquishing his opponents with **hekau**, or magical words of power. The sun god gradually transforms, becoming **Khepera**, and is reborn from the thighs of the sky goddess **Nut**, as his boat floats forth on the ocean of New Day.

**Amalantrah** An extraterrestrial entity whom the ceremonial magician **Aleister Crowley** claimed to have contacted in 1918 through the mediumship of his Scarlet Woman, Roddie Minor.

**Amandinus** A coloured stone with mystical properties. It is said that whoever wears the stone has the power to interpret dreams and mysteries.

**Amanita muscaria** Also known as fly agaric, the beautiful red-and-white-capped mushroom of fairy tales, usually found growing in forests beneath birch, fir, and larch trees. This mushroom, one of the oldest hallucinogens known to humanity, was, until recent times, the focus of shamanic rites among the Siberian and Uralic tribesmen. The ethnomycologist R. Gordon Wasson linked *Amanita muscaria* to the sacred plant called **Soma** in the Indian *Rig-Veda*.

**Amaranth** A flower symbolizing immortality. Amaranths often have colourful foliage and decorative flowers, and in occult tradition a crown of amaranths bestows supernatural gifts upon those who wear it.

**Amber** In alchemy, a synonym for gold. Prized in ancient times, this pale yellow resin exuded by various trees (alder, pine, fir, poplar) was closely linked by the alchemists to both gold and the sun (Sol). It was regarded by some as a type of "vegetable gold".

**Ambrosia** In Greek mythology, the food or drink of the gods, which made them immortal. The gods were also able to use ambrosia to bestow the gift of immortality upon favoured human beings.

**Amdukias** See Amduscias.

**Amduscias** In the Goetia, the 67th spirit, a strong and powerful duke who appears first in the form of a unicorn but then assumes a human shape when so commanded. At the same time all manner of musical instruments will be heard but not seen. He can also cause trees to bend or incline, according to the magician's wishes, and is also able to supply "excellent familiars". Amduscias governs 29 legions of spirits and is also known as Amdusias.

**Amdusias** See Amduscias.

**Amesha Spentas** In Zoroastrianism, a group of benevolent spirits under the command of **Ahura Mazdah**. They represented his noble attributes.

**Amethyst** On the Kabbalistic **Tree of Life**, a magical stone assigned to the sephirah **Chesed**.

**Amiante** A type of fireproof stone recommended by the Roman writer Pliny as being useful to counteract magical spells.

**Amon** (1) or **Amun** The ancient Egyptian deity personifying the breath of life; also a god of fertility and agriculture. Amon was worshipped principally at Thebes (present-day Karnak and Luxor), where he was part of a divine triad – the husband of Mut and the father of Khons. Amon's temple at Karnak was the largest in Egypt. Amon came to be seen as a manifestation of the great sun god **Ra** of Heliopolis, and in the form Amon-Ra became the supreme national god of Egypt, with the title "King of the Gods". His name is also found as Amen and Amoun.

**Amon** (2) In the **Goetia**, the seventh spirit, a marquis "great in spirit and most stern". He appears in the form of a wolf with a serpent's tail. His head sometimes resembles that of a raven, and flames of fire "vomit out of his mouth". Amon reveals details of "all things past and to come" and he is able to resolve disputes between friends. He governs 40 legions of spirits.

**AMORC** The initials of the Ancient and Mystical Order Rosae Crucis, a modern American organization with its headquarters in San José, California. AMORC was founded in 1915 by H. Spencer-Lewis and claims authentic Rosicrucian origins, but this assertion is not universally accepted.

**Amoun Temple** See Stella Matutina.

**Amulet** A small object, worn or carried as a protection against misfortune or evil. Amulets vary considerably, ranging from a rabbit's foot or a coloured stone to an engraved and highly ornamented work in precious metal. The Egyptians had a wide variety of amulets, including motifs based on the eye of **Isis** and the backbone of Osiris. Among the Gnostics, amulets of **Abraxas** were popular. Today, astrological amulets are a continuing fashion.

**Amy** In the Goetia, the 58th spirit, a great president who appears first as a "flaming fire" and then adopts a human form. He offers perfect knowledge of astrology and the liberal sciences and is able to locate "good familiars". He can also locate treasure that is protected by other spirits. Amy rules over 36 legions of spirits and is also known as Avnas.

**Anahata Chakra** In Kundalini yoga, the occult power centre associated with the thymus gland and cardiac plexus. It is represented by the tattva **Vayu**, symbol of water.

**Anakua** Among the Eskimo, or Inuit, the visionary ability to see shamanically – to perceive spirits and interract with the hidden unseen world. See also **Shaman, Angakoq.**

**Ananse** In Ashanti legends, the spider who gave rise to the material from which **Nyame** – the supreme sky-god – created the first human beings. Occultists in the **Ordo Templi Orientis** have adapted the mythology of Ananse, using the spider's web as a visual image for magically exploring the dark, reverse side of the **Tree of Life.**

**Anathema** An offering to a deity, usually hung up in a temple; also, the word used in the Roman Catholic Church as part of the formula in the excommunication of **heretics.**

**Ancestor Worship** The worship of the spirits of deceased relatives, who are believed to witness and influence events on earth even after death. Prayers, supplications, and offerings are made by the descendants to appease the ancestor spirits and seek continuing goodwill.

**Ancient of Days** In the Jewish mystical tradition, a reference to the infinite and unknowable unmanifest God who is the source of all existence. See also **Vast Face.**

**Anderson, Victor** See Faery Tradition.

**Andras** In the Goetia, the 63rd spirit, a great marquis who appears in the form of an angel with the head of a black night-raven, riding on the back of a strong black wolf and flourishing a bright sword in his hand. Andras sows discord and the Goetia warns that Andras can slay the evoking magician himself, if he does not take care. Andras governs 30 legions of spirits.

**Andreae, Johann Valentin** (1586–1654) A Lutheran pastor and scholar who, in his youth, travelled to several European countries and eventually became a chaplain at the court of Württemberg. He published several short works aimed at social transformation – these included *The Tower of Babel* and *The Christianopolitan Republic* – but is best known for the allegorical alchemical novel attributed to him, *The Hermetic Romance,* or *The Chymical Wedding of Christian Rosenkreuz,* published in 1616. Andreae's coat of arms featured a St Andrew's cross and four roses, and it is now widely accepted that he played a central role in issuing a series of pamphlets in 1614 announcing the existence of the **Rosicrucians.** Indeed, many also believe that Johann Valentin Andreae and "Christian Rosenkreuz" were one and the same.

**Andrealphus** In the Goetia, the 65th spirit, a mighty marquis who appears first in the form of a noisy peacock but then assumes a human shape. He teaches perfect geometry and is skilled in all aspects pertaining to measurement and astronomy. He is also able to transform men into the likeness of birds. Andrealphus governs 30 legions of spirits.

**Andrews, Ted** A prolific American author whose specialist subject areas include the study of the Kabbalah, Tarot, psychic protection, music therapy, visionary magic and shamanism. A teacher and counsellor in the public school system for ten years, Andrews has explored holistic health, metaphysics and the occult for over thirty years, has worked as a holistic healer and conducts animal education and storytelling programmes throughout the United States. His many works include *More Simplified Magic*, *Psychic Protection*, *Animal-Speak*, and *Simplified Qabala Magic*.

**Androgyne** A hermaphrodite. In alchemy and **mysticism**, the androgyne is a sacred symbol, because male and female polarities are united in one being, which therefore represents totality, unity, and oneness. See also **Dualism**; **Harmony of opposites.**

**Android** An artificially created human being. The medieval magician **Albertus Magnus** was credited with having created such an entity, and there are many tales of the **golem** in Jewish mythology and legends. See also **Homunculus.**

**Andromalius** In the Goetia, the 72nd spirit, a mighty earl, who appears in the form of a man holding a great serpent in his hand. His special skill is to discover "all wickedness and underhand dealing", identifying thieves and retrieving stolen goods. He not only punishes thieves and wicked people but can also locate hidden treasure. Andromalius rules over 36 legions of spirits.

**Andvari** In Scandinavian mythology, a dwarf who jealously guarded the magic ring **Draupnir** and other precious belongings of the gods. When the ring was stolen by **Loki**, Andvari cursed the ring, causing grief and misfortune to befall all those who had anything to do with it. Also known as Alberich.

**Angakoq** The Eskimo, or Inuit, term for a **shaman** (plural *Angakut*).

**Ange** In **voodoo**, an angel or guardian **loa**.

**Angel** From the Greek word *aggelos*, meaning "messenger". In Christianity, Judaism, and Islam, angels are immortal beings who serve as intermediaries between God and human beings. Angels are often arranged in a hierarchy, but their significance varies greatly. *The Book of Enoch* identified the top seven archangels as follows: Uriel, Raphael, Ragual, Michael, Zerachiel, Gabriel, and Remiel. For St Ambrose (fourth century), angels were comparatively low in the celestial hierarchy, which consisted (in descending order) of Seraphim, Cherubim, Dominations (or Dominions), Thrones, Principalities, Powers, Virtues, Archangels, and Angels. This order differs slightly from the hierarchy generally accepted in the Middle Ages. In the medieval Christian cosmos each of the nine angelic orders was associated with a different heavenly sphere as follows: Seraphim (**Primum Mobile**); Cherubim (the **zodiac** or "fixed stars"); Thrones (**Saturn**); Dominations (**Jupiter**); Virtues (**Mars**); Powers (**sun**); Principalities (**Venus**); Archangels (**Mercury**); and Angels (**moon**). The months of the year and the astrological signs also have angels assigned to them. See also *Enoch, The Book of*; **Fallen Angels.**

**Angel's Trumpet** *Brugmansia*, also known as tree datura, a plant species widely used by shamans and healers in South America. No longer found in the wild, several species of *Brugmansia* are cultivated and grown in the Sibundoy Valley of Colombia and traded throughout the Amazon. The plant has beautiful trumpet-like flowers. The dried leaves, flowers, and seeds are smoked to assist asthma and coughs. Fresh leaves are applied to the skin to treat cuts and burns, and all parts of the plant are used by shamans to produce a narcotic beverage which induces visions.

**Angelica** *Angelica atropurpurea*, a herb whose aromatic root is widely used to treat cramps, urinary tract infections and stomach disorders. Among Native

American Indians in California it is commonly burned during a shaman's prayers in a healing ceremony. Among the Creek Indians it is known as *Notosa*.

**Angra Mainyu** The alternative name for **Ahriman** who, in Zoroastrian mythology, personifies evil and darkness. He is locked in conflict with the god of light and goodness, **Ahura Mazdah**.

**Angurvadel** The magical sword inherited by Frithjof, a hero in Icelandic mythology. Decorated with a golden hilt, the sword shone like the Northern Lights and glowed fiery red during times of battle.

**Anima Mundi** A cosmological concept of a **world soul** or governing force in the universe that allows divine thought to become manifested in laws affecting matter. According to the mystic **Marsilio Ficino**, the world soul is omnipresent, but cooperating star daemons assist in uniting spirit and matter. Ficino was influenced by **Plotinus** and other Neoplatonists who believed that the world soul established processes in the heavens that defined and influenced what occurred on earth. Philosophically, the world soul was midway between spirit and matter, a dimension of energy and vitality for the world below. See also **Daemon; Neoplatonism**.

**Animal ceremonialism** Rituals associated with slaughtered game in animism.

**Animism** The belief, common among many native peoples, that trees, mountains, rivers, and other natural formations possess an animating power or spirit. In spiritualism the term also refers to the concept that inanimate objects as well as animate ones have a life force or energy quite distinct from the physical form, which is capable of existing without the physical "shell".

**Ankh** An ancient Egyptian symbol resembling a cross with a loop at the top.

The ankh is a symbol of life, and every major Egyptian deity is depicted carrying it. It has been suggested by some that the symbol has a sexual origin, combining the penis and vagina in one motif; however, the Egyptologist **E.A. Wallis Budge** regarded this interpretation as "unlikely". The ankh is also known as the *crux ansata*.

**Ankh-f-n-Khonsu** The name of a high priest of Amon-Ra of the 26th Dynasty in ancient Egypt. The ceremonial magician **Aleister Crowley** claimed to be a reincarnation of this high priest.

**Anointing** In Wicca, the act of applying herbal or floral oils to the body, for ritual purposes or healing. Typically, anointing oils are rubbed into the palms or onto the chest or forehead, but they can also be applied to candles burned in spells and rituals.

**Anselm de Parma** (died 1440) An Italian astrologer and author of *Astrological Institutions*. **Wierius** (Johannes Wier) regarded him as a **sorcerer**, possibly because a sect known as the Anselmites claimed to be able to heal wounds and sores by the use of magic words. However, this latter sect probably derived its name from St. Anselm of Canterbury, who was known for spiritual healing.

**Ansuz** See Os.

**Anthony, St** A Christian ascetic saint, born in Egypt c. 250CE. He is best known for accounts of his demonic visions, which have inspired numerous artists. St Anthony lived on a minimal diet, fasted frequently, and lived in isolation in conditions that may well have caused his hallucinations. He believed he was tormented by devils because they were "jealous of all mankind and particularly of the monks, for they cannot bear to see heavenly lives led upon the earth". It has been suggested that St Anthony's visions may have also been caused by his eating bread infected by ergot – the fungus

from which LSD is synthesized.
See also **St Anthony's Fire**.

**Anthropomancy** A barbaric form of
**divination** using human entrails –
usually those of virgins or young
children. According to legend, the
magician-emperor **Julian the Apostate**
sacrificed a number of children during
his ritual workings, in order to evaluate
their entrails. Anthropomancy was also
practised in ancient Egypt.

**Anthropophagy** See Cannibalism

**Anti-Christ** An evil Messiah who
would work miracles, raise the dead, and
walk on the water in imitation of Christ,
but who in reality was his deadly
antagonist. The concept of devil
incarnate has recurred through Jewish
and Christian history, being fuelled by
such figures as the pagan Syrian King
Antiochus IV; the mythic Great Beast
666 in *The Book of Revelation*; and, in
modern times, by Kaiser Wilhelm II and
Adolf Hitler. Following his initiation
with *The Book of the Law* – a mystical
tract with distinctly blasphemous
elements – the ritual magician **Aleister
Crowley** also claimed to be the Anti-
Christ and "Lord of the New **Aeon**".

**Anubis** The Egyptian dog or jackal
deity associated with the Western Desert,
the home of the dead. A major figure in
the Osirian **Underworld**, Anubis was the
son of **Nephthys** and at times rivalled
**Osiris** in importance as a funerary deity.
In the Judgment Hall, Anubis had the
role of producing the heart of the
deceased person for judgment. He also
assisted in guiding the souls of the dead
through the Underworld.

**Apas** In the Hindu **tattvas** and western
magic, the element **water**, represented by
a silver crescent.

**Apep, Apepi** See Apophis.

**Aperfat** Among the Iglulik Eskimo, a
shaman's helper spirit.

**Aphrodite** The Greek goddess of love
and beauty, and one of the Twelve Great
Olympians. According to some legends,
she came forth from ocean foam near
Cythera. She was described as fun-loving
and beautiful, but was notoriously
unfaithful. Her lovers included Adonis
and Ares. The Romans identified
Aphrodite with **Venus**.

**Apo leo** Among the Kahunas of Hawaii,
a specific form of sorcery in which a
victim is suddenly unable to speak. Uli,
the god of sorcery and Hiiaka, sister to
Pele, goddess of fire, are responsible for
causing this type of magical condition.
See **Kahuna**.

**Apocalypse** From a Greek compound
root meaning "an unveiling of hidden
things", an esoteric or prophetic
revelation. Often used specifically to
refer to the last book of the New
Testament, *The Apocalypse of St John*, or
*The Book of Revelation*. There are also
several examples of apocalypses in
Gnostic literature, including the
*Apocalypse of Paul*, the *First and Second
Apocalypses of James*, the *Apocalypse of
Peter*, and the *Apocalypse of Adam*. These
form part of the **Nag Hammadi Library**.

**Apocrypha** From a Greek compound
root meaning "to hide away", secret
teachings not available to the uninitiated.
In Christian usage, the Apocrypha is the
collective name of several books not
included in the Jewish Bible but included
among the Christian scriptures with
semi-canonical status.

**Apocryphal** "Of unknown origin."
Sometimes used to mean "spurious". Also
used to refer to the Christian **Apocrypha**.

**Apollo** The ancient Greek god of the
sun, fertility, purity, and truth, and also
associated with healing, music, and
poetry. He was the son of **Zeus** and Leto
and the twin brother of **Artemis**, and
was one of the **Twelve Great Olympians**.
Among his other names are Helios,
Hyperion, and Phoebus. Apollo had

numerous shrines dedicated to him and was the chief deity of the oracles at Delphi, Delos, and Tenedos. His Colossus at Rhodes was one of the Seven Wonders of the ancient world. Perhaps the most famous of the statues of Apollo that have survived is the marble "Apollo Belvedere" in the Vatican Museum. Because he epitomizes light and therefore mystical illumination, Apollo's influence in esoteric literature, as well as in the arts generally, has been enormous. See also **Asklepios; Delphic Oracle.**

**Apollonius of Tyana** A first-century Greek philosopher and sage credited with supernatural powers. Apollonius was credited with a number of miracles, including raising a young noblewoman from death in Rome; saving a friend from marrying a vampire; and witnessing in his "spirit vision" the assassination of Emperor Domitian at Rome in 96CE while he, Apollonius, was in Ephesus.

**Apophis** Also known as **Apep** or **Apepi,** a huge serpent that lived in the Nile and would attempt to prevent the sun-god Ra from travelling across the **Tuat** in his boat. Apophis represents the powers of darkness and is one of several images from Egyptian mythology that have been incorporated into the magic of the so-called **left-hand path.**

**Apotheosis** The act of raising a mortal to the rank of the gods. In ancient Egypt, the pharaohs were regarded as god-kings, and pre-Christian Roman emperors were routinely deified. See also **Deification.**

**Apotropaic** Something which is capable of warding off evil or negative influences. See **Amulet.**

**Apparition** The appearance of someone living or dead in conditions that cannot be accounted for by a physical cause. Although apparitions are often thought of as ghosts, the term is also used in occult literature to describe human forms that appear to another person as the result of astral projection or clairvoyance. Here one person is "willing" his or her consciousness to appear to another person, for purposes either of observation or direct communication. Many accounts exist in parapsychological literature of a person appearing in spirit form at the time of death, as if wishing to communicate this fact to a friend or loved one some distance away.

**Apsara** In pre-Vedic Indian mythology, a water nymph who lived in a lotus pond or water tank. Sometimes associated with fertility rites, the apsaras also had some qualities in common with the classical **sirens,** who were also irresistibly beautiful and lured men to their deaths.

**Apuleius, Lucius** A second-century Roman philosopher and author. Apuleius was initiated into the mystery traditions. After practising as an advocate in Rome, he retired to northern Africa where he devoted his life to literature. His writings incorporate many ancient legends. His best-known work is *Metamorphoses,* a novel that describes how a man was transformed into a monkey.

**Aqua Fortis** In alchemy, nitric acid (Latin "strong water').

**Aqua Permanens** See Mercurius.

**Aqua Regia** or Royal Water. In alchemy, a mixture of nitric acid and hydrochloric acid that could dissolve gold.

**Aqua Vitae** See Mercurius.

**Aquarian Age** The astronomical epoch beginning with the entry of the vernal equinox into the constellation of **Aquarius** c. 2740CE. Each epoch lasts approximately 2000 years and, according to **astrology,** derives many of its dominant qualities from the **zodiac sign** associated with it. The present epoch is that of the constellation **Pisces**, the fish, identified symbolically with Jesus Christ – the "fisher of men". Many regard the Age of Aquarius as a new frontier in human spiritual evolution.

**Aquarius** In astrology, the sign of the zodiac for those born between 21 January and 19 February. Aquarius is the water carrier, and the astrological motif is of a man pouring water into a stream from a flask. Aquarius is an **air** sign and is ruled by Saturn. The "typical" Aquarius is quiet, shy, patient, intuitive, and confident that truth will prevail. He or she may at times seem lazy or distant, but this is really the cautious nature of Aquarius revealing itself.

**Aquino, Michael** See Temple of Set.

**Ara ben Shemesh** See Felkin, Robert William.

**Arabi, Ibn al-** (1164–1240) A Spanish Muslim mystic who lived in Seville for 30 years, devoting his time to law and Sufic poetry. While superficially his works often appeared as simple love poems, they concealed many complex esoteric ideas. He believed that essence and existence were one, and maintained that the task of the mystic was union with the Perfect Man, who was an emanation of Allah and personified by Mohammed. At the time of the mystic's union with God, the image of God became conscious of itself. In this sense, God needed man as much as man needed God. Many of Ibn al-Arabi's contemporaries denounced him as a heretic. See also **Sufism**.

**Aradia** In Tuscan witchcraft, the daughter of the lunar goddess **Diana**. Aradia was virtually unknown as a deity until the 19th century American folklorist **Charles G. Leland** learned about her from a hereditary witch named Maddalena. Leland's book *Aradia, or the Gospel of the Witches*, published in London in 1889, describes how Diana became Queen of the Witches. According to the legend

recounted by Maddalena, Aradia was said to have been born from the union of Diana and her "brother" Lucifer, the "light-bearer". Aradia lived for a time in heaven but later Diana despatched her to earth to teach the arts of witchcraft. When her work on earth was done, she was recalled to heaven by her mother.

**Arallu** In Babylonian mythology, the abode of the dead. Regarded as a dark, forbidding cave entered through a hole in the earth, this domain was ruled by **Ereshkigal** and her consort Nergal.

**Ararita** A sacred name in the **Kabbalah** made up of a Hebrew sentence that translates as "One is his beginning. One is his individuality. His permutation is one." Ararita is used as an invocation in modern western **magic**, for example in planetary hexagram rituals and in Aleister Crowley's ceremony of the **Star Sapphire**.

**Aratron** According to the **grimoire** *The Arbatel of Magick*, an Olympian spirit that governs all aspects of the universe associated with **Saturn**. Aratron is said to have many attributes. He can make people invisible, is a master of magic and **alchemy**, and is able to convert plants into stone and stone into treasure. Beneath him he has 49 kings, 42 princes, 35 presidents, 28 dukes, 21 ministers, fourteen familiars – and 36,000 legions of spirits.

**Aravot** In the Jewish mystical tradition, a sacred realm inhabited by the departed souls of saints and sages.

***Arbatel of Magick, The*** An important medieval work on ceremonial magic first published in Latin in Basle (1575) and subsequently translated into English by Robert Turner (London, 1655). The book names seven angels as spiritual beings for the aspiring magician to contact, and these angels are identified with celestial bodies. They are **Aratron** (Saturn); **Bether** (Jupiter); **Phalec** (Mars); **Och** (Sun); **Hagith** (Venus);

Ophiel (Mercury); and **Phul** (Moon). The *Arbatel* provides the magical **sigils** for these entities, and also describes their special powers and virtues.

**Arcana** The plural form of *arcanum*, a Latin word meaning "something hidden in a box or chest". The meaning has widened to suggest a secret or a mystery. The **Tarot** cards are divided into **Major Arcana** (the 22 mythic cards) and **Minor Arcana** (the 56 remaining cards divided into four suits: cups, wands, swords, and pentacles).

***Arcana Arcanissima (The Secret of Secrets)*** An allegorical alchemical work by **Michael Maier**, published in 1614.

**Arcane** From Latin *arcanum*, "something hidden". Anything hidden or mysterious, especially those things requiring a "key" to be understood. See also **Clavicle**.

**Archangel** In non-biblical Jewish and Christian tradition, a great angel. *The Book of Enoch* identified seven archangels: **Uriel, Raphael, Michael, Gabriel**, Ragual, Zerachiel, and Remiel. They were sometimes said to be seven archangels assigned to the seven heavens, named as Uriel, Raphael, Michael, Gabriel, Jophiel, Zadkiel, and Samael. Samael was identified as **Satan**. According to *The Book of Revelation*, because **Satan** desired to be as great as God, there was a war in the heavens and "Satan, which deceiveth the whole world, was cast out into the earth, and his angels were cast out with him". In the Jewish mystical tradition represented by the **Kabbalah**, the archangels attributed to the ten emanations on the **Tree of Life** are **Metatron (Kether)**, Ratziel (**Chokmah**), Tzaphqiel (**Binah**), Tzadqiel (**Chesed**), Khamael (**Geburah**), Raphael (**Tiphareth**), Haniel (**Netzach**), Michael (**Hod**), **Gabriel (Yesod)**, and **Sandalphon (Malkuth)**. Islam also recognizes four archangels: Gabriel, Michael, Azrael, and Israfil. The Islamic equivalent of the "fallen angel" is the devil **Eblis**, who, as

Azazil, was formerly close to God but fell into disgrace for neglecting God's command that he pay homage to Adam.

**Archetype** In the psychology of **Carl Jung**, a primordial image found in the **collective unconscious**. According to Jung, archetypes appear in mystical visions as sacred or mythic beings and have the power to "seize hold of the psyche with a kind of primeval force". Archetypes are often personifications of processes or events in nature (e.g. the sun-hero or lunar goddess), or universal expressions of family roles (e.g. the Great Father and Great Mother). Jung believed that mythic images have an "autonomous" existence in the psyche. This concept is important for religious, magical and mystical thought because, historically, archetypal visions have often been regarded by mystics as personal revelations from an external divine source. For Jung, however, such experiences could be regarded as an expression of the most profound depths of the psyche. See also **Myth; Solar Gods**.

***Archidoxes of Magic, The*** A work on magic, occult philosophy, **astrology**, and celestial medicines written by the medieval alchemist **Paracelsus** and first translated into English by Robert Turner in 1655. It provides fascinating insights into the "secrets of alchymy" and gives complete sets of zodiacal **lamens** and planetary **sigils** – with details about how to manufacture and consecrate them. It also provides descriptions of medical ailments like vertigo, gout, cramps, trembling of the heart, and ruptures of the bones, together with correlating **zodiac signs** and treatments, and includes a treatise on the "Magicke Art" and the exorcism of evil spirits. See also **Lamen; Sigil (2)**.

**Archon** In Gnosticism, planetary rulers who guarded the world collectively and who were assigned to certain "spheres". Some archons took their names from Old Testament designations of God (e.g. Sabaoth, **Adonai, Elohim, Iao**). When a person died, his or her soul would be barred from flying to God by archons who would not let the soul pass unless certain magical formulae were acknowledged. Sacred knowledge or gnosis provided direct access to the higher spheres.

**Argent Vive** In alchemy, another name for mercury or quicksilver – the "cold, moist, receptive seed of metals" – which had to be united with the hot, dry, active seed of sulphur in order to create the Philosopher's Stone.

**Argenteum Astrum** A magical order founded by the ceremonial magician Aleister Crowley after leaving the Hermetic Order of the Golden Dawn. Established in 1907, the Argenteum Astrum, or Order of the Silver Star, built on the ritual structures developed by MacGregor Mathers in the Golden Dawn and gradually transformed into a vehicle for Crowley's bisexual orientation. Members included Victor Neuburg, Captain J.F.C. Fuller, Frank Bennett, George Cecil Jones, Pamela Hansford Johnson, Leila Waddell and – for a brief period – Austin Osman Spare. The Argenteum Astrum (abbreviated A.·. A.·.) was later amalgamated within the Ordo Templi Orientis.

**Arianrhod** In Welsh mythology, the beautiful goddess of the dawn. She was the sister of Gwydion, and also the mother by him of Lleu Llaw Gyffes, whom she cursed at birth. See also *Mabinogion, The.*

**Aries** In astrology, the sign of the zodiac for those born between 21 March and 20 April. Aries the ram is a symbol of aggression and dominance, especially as a result of its association with the Roman battering ram. It is often associated with politicians and military leaders. Arians are typically assertive, somewhat self-centred, and find it difficult to compromise their viewpoints. However, for the same reasons they are often idealistic, ambitious, and pioneering in their chosen pursuits.

Aries is a Fire sign and is usually listed as the first figure in the zodiac.

**Ariolists** Magicians who used altars as part of their divination proceedings. In ancient times they were said to conjure demons through the altar and observe any "trembling" or other manifestation of occult forces at work. Ariolists were usually regarded as demonologists and idolators.

**Aristeas of Proconnesus** (c. 675BCE) A mystic mentioned in the writings of Herodotus, Pliny, Suidas, and Maximus of Tyre, credited with remarkable occult powers. Pliny says that Aristeas was able to leave his body by taking the shape of a raven; and Maximus records that Aristeas claimed to be able to "fly" in a trance state, observing distant rivers, cities, and cultures that he had not visited in his normal day-to-day life. His poem *Arimaspea* records how he became possessed by Apollo, journeyed beyond Scythia to the Issedonians, and later had an encounter with the mythical griffins, who were sacred to Apollo and guardians of the precious gold. Aristeas may have been the classical Greek equivalent of a native shaman.

**Arithmancy** An ancient Greek and Chaldean method of divination by numbers. The Greeks would analyze the names of warring opponents, seeking their numerical value and predicting the outcome of the contest. The Chaldeans divided their alphabet into three sections of seven letters and linked these symbolically to the seven planets. Arithmancy is a precursor of numerology.

**Arn** In Enochian magic, the second Aethyr. The meanings associated with Arn include intense joy and bliss, happiness, and harmony. Arn is associated with Taurus, Pisces, and Scorpio and its magical number is 156.

**Artemis** The Greek goddess of the moon and of hunting, whose Roman equivalent was Diana. Always chaste, she protected young maidens from over-zealous youths and was quick to punish transgressors with her bow and arrows. The hind and the cypress tree were sacred to her. As a lunar goddess she has been an influential archetype for practitioners of **witchcraft** and the contemporary goddess worship movement. Artemis became identified with **Luna, Hecate,** and **Selene.**

**Arts, Black** A general term, usually associated with **demonology** and **sorcery,** but sometimes extended to apply to the whole spectrum of occult subjects. Linked to the symbolic status of the **Devil** as a god of darkness, and antagonist of "light" and "truth". See also **Magic, Black; Satanism.**

**Ascendant** In **astrology,** the degree of the **zodiac** rising on the eastern horizon at the specific moment for which a **figure** is cast. The latter is also known as a **horoscope** and represents the 360-degree circle of the heavens. The ascendant at the point of birth is considered by many astrologers to be almost as important as the zodiac sign.

**Ascending Arc** In Theosophy, a "life-stream" of growing spiritual entities who pass upwards through a series of increasingly mystical planes of existence. May be contrasted with the so-called **descending arc,** where etheric beings descend towards the physical plane.

**Asclepius** See **Asklepies**

**Asgard** In Scandinavian mythology, **Odin's** citadel in the sky and the dwelling place of the **Aesir.** Asgard, which could only be reached by crossing the rainbow bridge, included **Valhalla,** the hall of heroes killed in battle, and was located at the crown of the World Tree, **Yggdrasil.**

**Ash** (1) A tree with mythological and magical associations. Magic wands are made of ash or **hazel,** and Yggdrasil, the World Tree of Norse myth, was an ash.

**Ash** (2) A term used by the medieval alchemist **Paracelsus** to describe **philosophical salt,** one of the three principles of matter (the other two being fat, or **philosophical sulphur,** and phlegma, or **philosophical mercury**).

**Ashcroft-Nowicki, Dolores** (1929– ) Successor to **W.E. Butler** and director of the magical order known as Servants of the Light (SOL), which has its headquarters in St Helier, Jersey, one of the English Channel islands. Ashcroft-Nowicki is of Welsh ancestry and was born into a family with an extensive esoteric lineage. Her great-grandmother was a full blooded gypsy and her grandmother practised gypsy magic. Both of her parents were also third degree initiates. Ashcroft-Nowicki was tutored in the **Fraternity of the Inner Light** by **C.C. Chichester** and W.E. Butler and is the author of over a dozen books, including *The Tree of Ecstasy, Daughters of Eve* and *Building a Temple.* See also **Servants of the Light.**

**Ashipu** Babylonian priests and sorcerers who performed magical ceremonies to counteract evil spells and control nature. They also exorcised evil spirits, returning the sick to health.

**Ashtaroth, Ashtoreth** See **Astaroth.**

**Ashwanni** Zuni Indian rain priests.

**Asiyah** See **Assiah.**

**Asklepios** A Greek demi-god famed for his powers of spiritual healing. The son of **Apollo** by the princess Coronis, Asklepios healed the sick through dreams and was also venerated at special shrines in his honour. Also known as Asclepius and Aesculapius.

**Asmoday** In the **Goetia,** the 32nd spirit, a strong and powerful king who appears with three heads. The first is like that of a bull, the second is human, and the third resembles a ram. He has the tail of a serpent and webbed feet like a goose, rides on a dragon and holds a lance bearing a banner. Flames issue forth from his mouth. According to **Johannes Wier**, he can only be evoked bareheaded and in a standing position, because otherwise he will prove deceitful. However he has many powers to impart: he can make men invisible, he can answer all conceivable questions, he is skilled in handicrafts, and he can teach the arts of arithmetic, astronomy, and geometry. Asmoday rules 72 legions of spirits. The demonographer Collin de Plancy, author of *Dictionnaire Infernal* (1863) quotes Jewish sources as identifying the well known evil spirit **Asmodeus** not with Asmoday but with **Samael**.

**Asmodeus** In demonology, the evil spirit who was king of the demons and who filled men's hearts with rage and lust. Asmodeus angered King **Solomon** by preying on one of his wives; and it was not until the archangel **Michael** intervened, offering Solomon a magic ring, that this mighty demon could be conquered. Asmodeus was credited with a knowledge of geometry and astronomy and could also locate buried treasure. Asmodeus is sometimes identified with Samael. See also **Goetia**.

**Asp** In Enochian magic, the 21st **Aethyr**. The meanings associated with Asp include cause, purpose, and significance. It is associated with **Taurus, Virgo**, and **Leo** and its magical number is 22.

**Aspects** In astrology, angular relationships between the earth and any two celestial bodies. Some angles are believed to be "positive" and harmonious, others "negative" and unfavourable.

**Assiah** In the Kabbalah, the "densest" of the four worlds of manifestation. In Assiah we see the final materialisation of God's Will in the sphere of **Malkuth**. This final emanation, the World, is represented by the Daughter – Shekinah – the personification of the Divine Feminine on earth. Assiah is linked to the last of the four letters of the

Tetragrammation, YHVH. See also Atziluth; Briah; Yetzirah; **Four Worlds**.

**Asson** In **voodoo**, the sacred rattle used by the **houngan**, or **mambo**. It consists of a calabash, or gourd, filled with seeds and covered by a web of beads and snake vertebrae.

**Astaroth** In the Goetia, the 29th spirit, a powerful duke and fallen angel who appears riding on a dragon and carrying a viper in his right hand. His breath is so offensive that the magician who evokes him must "defend his face with his magic ring". Nevertheless he provides truthful answers about the past, present, and future and is willing to disclose the reasons for his own fall from grace. He commands 40 legions of spirits. Astaroth is also known as Ashtaroth or Ashtoreth.

**Astarte** Phoenician fertility deity, worshipped at Tyre and Sidon. She was identified with the moon and depicted with crescent horns. The Greek identified her with **Aphrodite**. See also **Lunar Goddesses**.

**Astragalomancy** A form of **divination** using knuckle bones, stones, or small pieces of wood marked with letters or symbols. The diviner asks a question and interprets these letters depending on how the objects lie on the ground. The use of dice for divination is a form of astragalomancy.

**Astral Body** The "double" of the human body, usually regarded by occultists as the source of "consciousness". The astral body has a luminous, shining appearance, and is capable of passing through physical matter. The act of willed separation of the astral body from the physical is known as astral travel. Occultists believe that at death the astral body leaves its physical counterpart and finds a new existence on the astral plane. Some parapsychologists believe that ghostly apparitions are astral communications between persons who have just died and those who are dear to them. The astral body is often depicted as being joined to the physical body by a silver cord – an etheric umbilical cord – and some subjects who experience out-of-the-body dissociation report seeing this cord. See also **Astral Travel; Out-of-the-Body Experience.**

**Astral Plane** The occult concept of a plane of existence and perception paralleling the physical dimension, but one phase removed from it, and also containing imagery from the unconscious mind. Occultists believe it is the plane reached during **astral projection** and also the first of the spheres that the astral body reaches after death.

**Astral Projection** See Astral Travel; Out-of-the-Body Experience.

**Astral Shell** The personality in its phase of disintegration following the death of the physical body.

**Astral Travel** Sometimes known as the **out-of-the-body experience.** Astral travel is the conscious separation of the **astral body** from the physical body resulting in an **altered state** of consciousness, and sometimes different qualities of perception. Astral travel is achieved by a variety of trance-inducing methods and is sometimes referred to by occultists as "travelling in the spirit vision".

**Astrology** A system based on the belief that celestial bodies influence the characters and lives of human beings. Astrologers claim that individuals are affected by the cosmic situation existing at the time of their births, and therefore plot a map of the heavens at the time of birth – a **horoscope**, or **figure** – for purposes of interpretation. Individuals fall under the influence of the twelve signs of the **zodiac**, and insights into the person's character and personality may also be interpreted from the **ascendant.** There are two main types of astrology: mundane, which deals with large-scale phenomena (e.g. wars, natural disasters, political trends, and the destiny of

nations); and horary, which determines the implications of undertaking a particular action at a specific time. Astrology remains one of the most popular forms of **divination.** See **Astrology, Horary;** and **Astrology, Mundane.**

**Astrology, Electional** A branch of astrology that calculates appropriate days for such important undertakings as marriage, commencement of a business enterprise, purchase of a property or home, and the date for an important journey.

**Astrology, Horary** Because astrology deals with **aspects** governing the particular moment of time at which something comes into being, it is possible to determine aspects governing the time of future events. Horary astrology may thus be applied to gauge the appropriateness of taking a particular course of action at a particular time.

**Astrology, Inceptional** A branch of astrology that deals with the outcome of an event whose location, date, and time of occurrence are known.

**Astrology, Medical** A branch of astrology that correlates signs of the zodiac and planetary influences with diseases and malfunctions of bodily organs. Some of these traditional astrological correlations are as follows: **Aries:** diseases of the head and face, smallpox, epilepsy, apoplexy, headache, measles, convulsions. **Taurus:** diseases of the neck and throat, scrofula, tonsilitis, tumours. **Gemini:** diseases of the arms and shoulders, aneurisms, frenzy, and insanity. **Cancer:** diseases of the breast and stomach, cancers, consumption, asthma, and dropsy. **Leo:** diseases of the heart, the back and the vertebrae of the neck; fevers, plague, jaundice, and pleurisy. **Virgo:** diseases of the viscera or internal organs (e.g. the intestines). **Libra:** diseases of the kidneys. **Scorpio:** diseases of the sexual organs. **Sagittarius:**

ASTROLOGY Astrologers plot a map of the heavens at the time of birth in order to determine individual destiny. This illustration shows a medieval Jewish astrologer.

diseases of the hips and muscles, gout, and rheumatism. **Capricorn:** diseases of the knees and the surface of the skin. **Aquarius:** diseases of the legs and ankles, lameness, and cramps. **Pisces:** diseases of the feet.

**Astrology, Mundane** A branch of **astrology** that concerns itself with large-scale phenomena like wars, national political and social trends, and disasters. Mundane astrology is based on the premise that cosmic influences affect large groups of people and also the physical structure of the earth; but predictions made on this scale are necessarily less accurate than individual calculations based on the natal

27

horoscope. In mundane astrology, the planets are said to relate to different roles in society: **Sun** (executive heads and managers); **Moon** (the working classes); **Mercury** (the intelligentsia); **Venus** (ambassadors of good will); **Mars** (military rulers); **Jupiter** (judges and other officers of the law); **Saturn** (executives of state); **Uranus** (air, road, and rail transport); **Neptune** (social movements); and **Pluto** (organized labour groups). Compare **Astrology, Natal.**

**Astrology, Natal** A branch of astrology that focuses on the natal horoscope. See also **Horoscope, Natal.**

**Astrology, Predictive** A branch of astrology that deals with predicting future events in one's life on the basis of the natal horoscope. Modern astrology has moved away from the traditional preoccupation with prediction, and is now more concerned with the analysis of character traits and the link between astrology and personal self-development. See also **Horoscope, Natal.**

**Astromancy** An ancient system of divination by the stars.

**Asvamedha** A Hindu term for the ritual sacrifice of horses, associated with the Vedic period in India. Priests sacrificed horses on behalf of kings and chieftains to ensure an increased sense of power and also to renew fertility of crops and cattle.

**Atavism** The concept that a primeval force related to an earlier phase of one's evolution can reappear after many generations. The English occult artist **Austin Osman Spare** practised **atavistic resurgence,** a technique combining magical visualization and sexual magic, in order to manifest animal aspects of his personality that he believed derived from his earlier incarnations.

**Atavistic Resurgence** A method devised by the English trance magician

and visionary artist **Austin Osman Spare** to arouse primal energies from the cosmic life force, which he named **Kia.** Spare focused his will on magical **sigils** and directed instructions to his subconscious mind when it is was in a "void" or "open" state.

**Athame** A ritual sword or dagger used by a **witch** in a magical ceremony. It has a black handle and magic symbols engraved on its blade. See also **Boline.**

**Athanor** From the Arabic *al-tannur.* In alchemy, a calcinatory furnace in which the glass egg-shaped vessel known as the philosopher's egg was placed in a sandbath over a fire. This type of furnace allowed the coke to burn very slowly

**Athena** Also Pallas Athena or Athene. In ancient Greek mythology, the goddess of wisdom and one of the **Twelve Great Olympians.** She was born from the head of **Zeus.** Athena's Roman counterpart was **Minerva.**

**Atiqa** In the **Kabbalah,** "the Hidden One" – a reference to the unmanifested God. See **Vast Face.**

**Atlantis** A lost continent said to have sunk beneath the sea after a natural cataclysm. Legendary accounts of Atlantis derive from Plato's *Timaeus* and *Critias,* which describe conversations between Egyptian priests and the Athenian statesman Solon (c. 638–558BCE). Some archaeologists believe that the legend of Atlantis may derive from the violent volcanic eruption, c. 1470BCE, that devastated the island of Thera (Santorini), 75 miles north of Crete.

**Atlantis Bookshop** A meeting place for pagans, mystics, and occultists in London, including **Aleister Crowley, Gerald Gardner, Dion Fortune** and **Alex Sanders,** its influence in metaphysical circles extends to the present day. The Atlantis Bookshop was founded in 1922 by Michael Houghton and its basement was converted into a temple used by a private magical lodge called the Order of the Hidden Masters. Houghton published Gerald Gardner's novel *High Magic's Aid* in 1949 – two years before the Last Witchcraft Act was repealed.

**Atonement** The act of atoning, or making amends for an offence, for example by making a sacrifice to a god.

**Attis** The Phrygian god of vegetation and fertility, whose cult became popular in ancient Greece. Attis was the lover of **Cybele**, but deserted her for a **nymph**. Cybele became intensely jealous and aroused such a frenzy of madness in Attis that he castrated himself and died.

**Atu** An alternative name for a **Tarot** trump – a card in the **Major Arcana**.

**Atziluth** In the **Kabbalah**, the purest of the four worlds of manifestation, sometimes called the archetypal world. This is the level of existence which comes closest to the mysterious, unmanifested realm of **Ain Soph Aur**, and it contains just one sephirah, **Kether**. Kether has been described as "the hidden of the hidden. It is the emergence of God's Will, His creative urge. It is the infinite, the initiation of all that can and will be. It is infinity". Atziluth is linked to the first of the four letters of the **Tetragrammation**, YHVH. See also **Assiah; Briah; Yetzirah; Four Worlds.**

**Aufu** In ancient Egypt, the term for the physical body, which was regarded as one of the five bodies of human beings. The other bodies were **Ka**, the double; **Haidit**, the shadow; **Khu**, the magical body; and **Sahu**, the spiritual body.

**Augoeides** The ancient Greek name for the **Holy Guardian Angel**. Derived from *Augos*, meaning "the morning light", it was popularized by the novelist **Sir Edward Bulwer-Lytton** in his novel *Zanoni*, where he interpreted it to mean the **Luminous Self** or the **Higher Ego**. The term was also used by the

ceremonial magician **Aleister Crowley** to describe the holy guardian angel or higher self. Crowley devised several Augoeides **invocations.**

**Augur** or **Augury** In ancient Rome, a magician-priest who interpreted the flight of birds in order to prophesy future events. Signs on the augur's east side were favourable, those on the west unfavourable. The word "augury" is now used for all kinds of **divination.**

**Aura** In magical and occult terminology, the psychic energy-field that surrounds both animate and inanimate bodies. The aura can be dull or brightly coloured, and psychics – those who claim to perceive the auric colours directly – interpret the condition or state of the person or object according to the energy vibrations. Bright red, for example, indicates anger; yellow, strong intellectual powers; and purple, spirituality. Occultists generally believe that the halos depicted around the head of Jesus Christ and the saints are examples of mystically pure auras. Theosophists distinguish five auras: the health aura, the vital aura, the karmic aura, the character aura, and the aura of spiritual nature. See also **Theosophy.**

**Aureole** A circular or oblong **halo** said to surround the bodies of mystics and saints. The symbolism of the aureole is linked to that of the sun as a life-giving force, representative of spiritual energy. See also **Aura.**

**Aurum potabile** In alchemy, "drinkable gold" or medicine – "the pure love essence which fills the grail cup of the adept". It is another name for the **Philosopher's Stone** or **Elixir of Life**.

**Austromancy** A form of divination by means of interpreting the wind.

**Automatic Painting and Drawing** Artworks created during mediumistic trance. These artworks are sometimes produced at great speed and invariably without the conscious awareness of the seer. Among spiritualists, it is often thought that a discarnate entity or spirit is working through the body of the artist, while psychologists regard the phenomenon as a state of mental dissociation leading to manifestations from the unconscious mind. Examples in recent times include the automatic drawings of the celebrated trance magician **Austin Osman Spare** and surrealist works by such artists as André Masson and Max Ernst. See also **Automatism, Spirits.**

**Automatic Speaking** Similar to automatic painting and drawing, except that the medium speaks without conscious awareness, usually in a trance state. In the case of **oracles**, it is assumed that a god or goddess is speaking through the medium. See also **Automatism.**

**Automatic Writing** Similar to automatic painting and drawing, except that the medium writes without conscious awareness, usually in a trance state. The handwriting produced is often in an unfamiliar style, and often assumed to be that of a deceased person. See also **Automatism.**

**Automatism** A general term in **spiritualism** for automatic painting, drawing, writing, and speaking, performed in trance without the conscious awareness of the medium. The term is also applied to a particular method of automatic drawing used by **Austin Osman Spare.** Spare believed that inspiration always occurred when the conscious mind was side-stepped into inattention. See **Automatic Painting and Drawing.**

**Autumn Equinox** In Wicca, one of the so-called Lesser Sabbats representing the conclusion of the harvest and celebrated in the northern hemisphere from 20–21 September. In the United States it is sometimes referred to as Mabon.

**Avalon** The so-called Isle of the Dead associated with the Arthurian legends. It is linked to the town of Glastonbury in Somerset, England, and is said to be the final resting place of King Arthur.

**Avatar** In Hinduism, an incarnation of the god Vishnu. Used more generally by occultists and theosophists to denote any divine incarnation.

**Avesta** The sacred book of **Zoroastrianism**, said to have been written in gold ink on 12,000 ox hides. The work was destroyed by Alexander the Great in 330BCE, but one-third of the text was memorized by the priests and later transcribed. This part consists of 21 books and includes a collection of hymns known as the **Gathas**, allegedly written by **Zarathustra** himself.

**Avicenna** An alchemical philosopher, born at Bacara in Persia c. 980CE. Skilled in mathematics and medicine, he was appointed Grand Vizier by the Sultan Magdal Doulet, but fell from grace and died at the comparatively early age of 56. According to rumours, Avicenna was served by elemental spirits known as **djinn**, and he had a knowledge of powerful magical formulae and incantations. Several treatises on Hermetic philosophy are ascribed to him, including *Porta Elementorum* and *Tractatulus de Alchimia*. The latter describes **Mercury** as a universal spirit pervading nature, and combines knowledge, borrowed from the eighth-century Arab alchemist Geber (Jabir ibn-Hayyan), with metaphysical speculation.

**Avir** In the Kabbalah, the Hebrew term for "air" or "atmosphere". It is also the **element** corresponding to the letter Aleph.

**Avnas** See Amy.

**Avodah** In the Jewish mystical tradition, directed prayer, or worship.

**Awahokshu** Among the Pawnee Indians, the holy place where spirits reside.

**Axé** In Macumba, a powerful magical force associated with the blood of sacrificial animals. Also, objects sanctified by being immersed in this sacrificial blood.

**Axis Mundi** In mythology and shamanism, the "axis of the world", often symbolized by the **World Tree**, which spans the different worlds and allows the mystic or magician access from one plane of reality to another.

**Axogum** In Macumba, the magical initiate responsible for sacrificing animals.

**Ayahuasca** The tree-climbing forest vine known botanically as *Banisteriopsis caapi* is the pre-eminent sacred plant of South America. Its bark is brewed to make a beverage known as ayahuasca, which allows direct contact with the supernatural realm, enabling a **shaman** to contact ancestors or helper spirits and have initiatory visions. The word ayahuasca translates as "vine of the soul". Ayahuasca is used to recover the souls of sick patients, to ask the spirits about the cause of bewitchment, or – in the case of sorcery – to allow the black magician to change his form into that of a bird or some other animal in order to cause harm to someone. However, the sacred drug also has the role of allowing the shaman to participate in his own cosmology, to "become one with the mythic world of the Creation". See also **Banisteriopsis**.

**Ayahuasquero** In South American **shamanism**, a folk healer who treats illnesses by using a potion prepared from the ayahuasca vine.

**Ayida Wedo** In voodoo, the rainbow loa and partner of **Damballah Wedo**, the serpent loa.

**Ayin** The Hebrew letter ascribed to the path linking **Hod** and **Tiphareth** on the Tree of Life. Ayin has a numerical value of 70. In modern magical visualization and **pathworkings**, the **Tarot** card associated with this path on the Tree is *The Devil*.

**Ayizan** In voodoo, the loa who is the patroness of the marketplace. She is the partner of **Loco**, loa of vegetation.

**Aym** See Aini.

**Ayn** See Ain.

**Aza** In Gnostic cosmology, the "evil mother of all demons".

**Azael** In Jewish mysticism, one of the angels who rebelled against God. He is said to be chained to sharp stones in the desert, awaiting the Final Judgment. Also known as Asiel or Aziel

**Azoth** In alchemy, the Universal Medicine, which according to *The Book of the Wood of Life*, "contains within itself all other medicines, as well as the first principles of all other substances". Azoth is symbolically analogous to God in nature.

**Azure** In alchemy, the colour ascribed to the mercurial water and alchemical **quintessence**. The alchemist and Hermetic philosopher **Thomas Vaughan** compared the colour azure to "the body of heaven on a clear day".

# B

**Ba** In ancient Egyptian religion, the soul, represented as a bird with a human head. The ba would wing its way towards the gods after death, but could return to the body as long as the latter had not been destroyed. See also **Ka**.

**Ba'al Shem** The Hebrew for "Master of the Divine Name", a term used from the Middle Ages onwards among hasidists and kabbalists to describe anyone who possessed secret knowledge of the **Tetragrammaton** and other sacred names. The most famous bearer of this title was Eliezer Ba'al Shem Tov (died 1760CE), the founder of modern Hasidism. See also **Kabbalah**.

**Baaheamaequa** Among the Crow Indians, a vision which bestows power and thus enables a **shaman** to act as a healer.

**Baal** (1) In Phoenician mythology, the god of fertility and vegetation and associated particularly with the winter rains. Depicted as a warrior with a horned helmet and spear, he was second only to El. The word "Baal" itself means "lord", a title given by Semitic peoples to the ruling deity of each city.

**Baal** (2) In the Goetia, the first and principal spirit, a king who rules in the East. He governs 66 legions of infernal spirits and can appear in the form of a toad, a cat, or a man. He speaks in a hoarse voice and can confer the power of invisibility. He is also known as Bael.

**Baalberith** In demonology, the keeper of the archives of hell and official of the second order.

**Baalzephon** In demonology, the captain of the guard and sentinels of hell.

**Baba Nkwa** See **Nzame**.

**Babalaô** See Babalawo (1).

**Babalawo** (1) In Macumba, a Yoruba priest and oracle of the spirit Ifá. He is also the trustee of a body of knowledge known as the *odú*. The Babalawo has high spiritual authority and traditionally accepts no money for his divinatory services. He is also known as Babalaô.

**Babalawo** (2) In Santería, a priest. There are various grades of *babalawo*, all of them male. The *babalawo* has various roles including those of healer, sorcerer, diviner, as required.

**Babalon Working** See Parsons, Jack.

**Bacchanalia** The Roman festival in honour of Bacchus, the god of wine. The rites were originally performed by women, but later included men. With time, the ceremonies became excessive and were finally banned by the Roman Senate in 186BCE.

**Bacchanals** Worshippers of Bacchus, who indulged in drunken orgies.

**Bacchantes** Women dedicated to the worship of Bacchus. Euripides described them in *Bacchae* as revellers who dressed themselves in furs and skins and wandered through forests and mountains filled with the divine spirit of their god.

**Bacchus** The Roman god of wine, linked to the Greek deity Dionysus. He was the son of Zeus and Semele and the husband of Ariadne.

**Bacon, Roger** (1214–1294) A medieval English alchemist, born near Ilchester in Somerset. He studied theology and science at Oxford University and could write Latin, Greek, and Hebrew. He was credited with the discovery of gunpowder, probably as a result of his experiments with nitre. He also studied alchemy and came to believe in the Philosopher's Stone, by means of which it was thought that gold could be purified, base metals transformed, and the human body fortified against death. His works included *Opus Maius* and *The Mirror of Alchemy*.

**Bad** In Persian mythology, a djinn who had power over the winds and tempest and who could be summoned on the 22nd day of the month.

**Bael** See Baal.

**Bag** In Enochian magic, the 28th Aethyr. The meanings associated with Bag include guilt, doubt, mistrust and sin. It is associated with **Aries, Taurus,** and **Cancer** and its magical number is 19.

**Bag, Medicine** See Medicine Bag.

**Bahir** Literally, *The Book of Brilliance* or *The Book of Light*, the mystical text *Sefer ha-Bahir* was anonymously written and appeared in Provence, southern France, where there was a Jewish community, between 1150 and 1200CE. It is one of the earliest works of kabbalistic literature and includes meditative texts like the *Greater Hekhaloth* from the **Merkabah** school and other important meditative classics. Some ascribe the text of *Sefer ha-Bahir* to Rabbi Nehuniah ben HaKana, a Talmudic mystic of the first century, because he is the sage who opens the text, but this authorship is by no means certain.

**Baiame** Among the Wiradjeri Aborigines of western New South Wales, a sky god who appears to men in their dreams and initiates them, helping them become great shamans. Baiame is described as a very old man with a long beard. Two great quartz crystals extend from his shoulders to the sky above him. When Baiame appears to Aborigines in their dreams, he causes a sacred waterfall of liquid quartz to engulf their bodies. They then grow wings and learn how to fly. Later, an inner flame and heavenly cord are incorporated into the bodies of the new shamans. See also **Wireenum.**

**Bain-Marie** In alchemy, a water-bath or double boiler used for separation. It is believed that the bain-marie was invented by the third-century Graeco-Egyptian alchemist Maria Prophetissa.

**Baka** In **voodoo,** an evil spirit or **demon** who often takes the form of an animal.

**Balam** In the Goetia, the 51st spirit, a "terrible, great and powerful king" who appears with three heads. The first is like that of a bull, the second is human, and the third resembles that of a ram. He has flaming eyes and the tail of a serpent and rides upon an angry bear. Balam carries a goshawk on his wrist and speaks with a hoarse voice. He can make men invisible and can provide truthful information regarding matters past, present, and future. Balam commands 40 legions of spirits.

**Balche'** In the magic of the ancient Maya, a brew extracted from the bark of the Balche' tree, *Lonchocarpus violaceus*. When facing major environmental problems and outbreaks of serious illness, the Maya consumed the Balche' beverage in a ritual circle, believing that because this drink had first been conceived by the God of Creation, divinatory insights would be received to help them deal with their problems.

**Balder** or Baldur In Scandinavian mythology, the god of the sun and the personification of wisdom, goodness, and beauty. He was the son of **Odin** and one of the **Aesir.**

**Baldur** See Balder.

**Bali** In Indian mythology, a **demon** who became king of heaven and earth, but who was finally overcome by Vishnu, incarnating as a dwarf named Vamana. Vamana was granted a wish by Bali, and asked for as much land as could be obtained in three steps. Vamana covered the universe in two steps and with his third crushed Bali down into the Underworld.

**Balneum** See Sand Bath.

**Balor** See **Bel (1)**

**Balsam, Friar's** See Benzoin.

**Banishing Ritual** In ceremonial magic, a ritual designed to ward off negative or evil influences. The banishing ritual of the Lesser Pentagram is performed in a magical circle and commences in the East. The magician uses a sword to inscribe pentagrams in the air and invokes the archangels **Raphael, Gabriel, Michael**, and **Uriel** at the four quarters. The banishing also includes a ritual prayer known as the "Kabbalistic Cross".

**Banisteriopsis** A common ingredient in a number of psychedelic sacraments used by **shamans** in South America to contact the supernatural world. **Yagé**, caapi, and **ayahuasca** all contain banisteriopsis and produce remarkable effects, including the separation of the "soul" from the body, visions of predatory animals and distant locations, the experience of heaven and hell, and explanatory visions of thefts and homicides. The active ingredients of banisteriopsis are the alkaloids harmine, harmaline, and d-tetrahydroharmine.

**Banshee** In Ireland and Scotland, a nature spirit who takes the form of an old woman and wails mournfully under the windows of a house where a person will soon die. From Irish Gaelic *bean sídhe*, Scottish Gaelic *ban-sith*, "fairy woman". See also **Fairies**.

**Baphomet** A demonic deity represented by **Eliphas Lévi** as a goat-headed god with wings, breasts, and an illuminated torch between his horns. In 1307 the medieval Order of the **Knights Templar** was accused by King Philip IV of France of worshipping this god, but only a dozen of the 231 knights interrogated admitted to the practice. The name Baphomet may be a corruption of Mahomet (Mohammed). Eliphas Lévi

identified Baphomet with the Tarot card *The Devil*. The ceremonial magician Aleister Crowley adopted the name Baphomet after assuming the leadership of the British branch of the **Ordo Templi Orientis** in 1912.

**Baptême** In voodoo, a baptism. All sacred objects and spaces are consecrated by baptism.

**Baptism** Ritual immersion in water, based on the ancient concept that water is the source of life. In Christianity, it symbolizes membership of the Church and the repentance of sins. It was parodied in medieval **witchcraft**, where children and toads were allegedly baptized on behalf of the Devil during the witches' sabbath.

**Barbatos** In the Goetia, the eighth spirit, a great duke who appears only when the Sun is in **Sagittarius**. He locates hidden treasure, has a knowledge of all things past and future, and also understands the sounds and language of birds and animals. He rules over 30 legions of spirits.

**Bardon, Franz** (1909–1958) An influential modern ritual magician, Franz Bardon was born in Katherein, near Opava in the present-day Czech Republic. Bardon was the oldest of thirteen children and the only son of a devout Christian mystic, Viktor Bardon. According to a close friend of the family, Viktor prayed that his son might receive some form of spiritual initiation and he maintained that in 1924 the spirit of a high Hermetic adept entered the body of his 14-year-old son in order to bring about this initiation. In the 1920s and 1930s Bardon became a stage magician who gained fame in Germany under the stage-name "Frabato". However he was also exploring authentic forms of magic, and in due course developed a model of the magical universe which drew in part on Taoism and Hindu cosmology as well as Hermetic concepts of the five elements. There is some evidence that

Bardon was a member of the Fraternity of Saturn, an occult lodge which flourished in Germany in the early part of the 20th century.

Bardon's major work, *The Practice of Magical Evocation*, describes the 360 "spirits" of the **zodiac** and also provides their magical sigils. His other published works include *Initiation into Hermetics*, *The Key to the True Qabalah* and an "occult novel" entitled *Frabato the Magician*, said to be based on true events. During World War Two Bardon spent nearly four years in a concentration camp. After the war he practised as a naturopath and graphologist while also devoting himself to writing and research into the Hermetic traditions. However, his career was interrupted when he was arrested during a Communist purge. He died in unusual circumstances in a prison hospital in Brno, Czechoslovakia, in July 1958. See also **Sigil (2)**.

**Barley Moon** See Esbats.

**Baron Samedi** In voodoo, the **loa** who is lord and guardian of the cemetery – an aspect of **Guede**.

**Barren Signs** In astrology, those signs which indicate a tendency towards barrenness, specifically **Gemini**, **Leo**, and **Virgo**.

**Barrett, Francis** (c. 1784–?1830) An English occultist best known as the occult author of *The Magus*, published in London in 1801. The work includes sections on magical herbs and stones, alchemy, numerology, and ceremonial magic, and includes portraits of such demons as Theulus and **Asmodeus**. Barrett may have influenced the magical novels of Bulwer-Lytton.

**Bas** See Bes.

**Basilides** A Gnostic philosopher who lived and taught in Alexandria c. 125–140CE. A disciple of Glaucias – who had known the apostle Peter – Basilides wrote 24 commentaries on the gospels.

He also developed a complex cosmology of his own, which involved 365 heavens, each with its own angelic population. Only the last of these heavens, embracing the earth, was immediately accessible to ordinary people. According to Basilides, the last heaven was headed by the "God of the Jews"; but the supreme deity over all 365 heavens was **Abraxas**. Perhaps predictably, Basilides was condemned by Bishop Irenaeus as a heretic. See also **Valentinus**.

**Basilisk** Also known as a cockatrice, this legendary beast was said to be a small, deadly serpent, born from a cock's egg and hatched by a toad on a bed of dung. It was often represented as having the head of a cock, a feathered back, and four pairs of legs. In legends, the basilisk had a deadly breath that made it much feared; and in the Middle Ages if was assumed that if a knight on horseback were to spear the creature with his lance, the basilisk's poison would pass up through the spear, killing both knight and horse. The only sure way to overcome the basilisk was to confront it with a mirror: the creature would die by gazing on its own reflection.

**Bast** The Egyptian cat-headed goddess, daughter of **Isis**. She was worshipped at Bubastis in the Nile Delta and regarded as a goddess of fertility. As such, she is one of the most popular ancient Egyptian deities in contemporary witchcraft and sexual magic cults. See also **Pakht**.

**Bates, Brian** An English humanistic and transpersonal psychologist who has become well known for his exploration of Anglo-Saxon sorcery. After schooling in England, Bates studied at the University of California, Berkeley, and Stanford Research Institute, and later received his doctorate from the University of Oregon. He returned to England in 1970 to become a Research Fellow at Cambridge University before transferring to the University of Sussex, where he has been conducting research into the medical techniques of shamans, healers, and sorcerers. His best known book is the authentic fictional work *The Way of Wyrd*. See **Wyrd**.

**Bathin** In the Goetia, the eighteenth spirit, a strong and mighty duke. He rides a pale horse and sports a serpent's tail. Skilled in the virtues of herbs and precious stones, he also has the ability to transport the magician suddenly from one country to another. He rules over 30 legions of spirits and is sometimes also known as Bathym or Marthim.

**Bathym** See Bathin.

**Batsirápe** Among the Crow Indians, a shaman's helper spirit. Sometimes this spirit confers power by entering the shaman's body.

**Battérie Maconnique** In voodoo, a rhythmic beat produced either by clapping hands or beating drums. In magical ceremonies this is said to represent rapping on the door which leads to the **loa** realm.

**Batuque** An alternative name for **Macumba** in the southern Brazilian state of Rio Grande do Sul.

**Beak** In alchemy, the spout of the retort or still through which the vapour rising from the vessel then descends into the receiver to condense. See also **Alembic**.

**Bealtaine** See Beltane.

**Bear Doctors** Native American shamans in central California who receive their magical power from the grizzly bear. It is said that such shamans can transform into the shape of a grizzly bear in order to inflict harm on their enemies.

**Beast 666, The** See Great Beast 666; Crowley, Aleister.

**Beast gods** Among the Zuni Indians, supernatural masters of the various animal species. Poshayanki is the culture hero who heads the beast gods.

**Bechard** Described in the magical work *Grimorium Verum* as a spirit with power over winds, tempests, lightning, hail, and rain. Magicians could summon him with a magical **charm** bearing his **character**.

**Bed** In alchemy, the name given to the alchemical vessel during the union of **sulphur** (male) and **argent vive** (female). The bed is the place where the "chemical wedding" of sun (red) and moon (white) is consummated and their union produces the **Philosopher's Stone**.

**Beelzebub** Traditionally, one of the most powerful demons – ranking in importance with **Lucifer, Ashtaroth, Satan**, and Beherit – Beelzebub was originally Baal-zebub, the Canaanite god of Ekron in the ninth century BCE, and is mentioned in 2 Kings 1.2. The Canaanites worshipped him in a temple unpolluted by flies; hence his popular designation as "Lord of the Flies". Flies were regarded as unclean creatures that thrived on corpses, and Beelzebub in this regard was thought of as a demon of decay. Luke 2.15 describes him as "chief of the devils". See also **Goetia**.

**Behemoth** Described in the apocryphal *Book of Enoch* as a great monster and counterpart of **Leviathan**. In Jewish mythology, the two beasts – the first of them masculine, the second feminine – slay each other on the final Day of Judgment.

**Beithe** In the Celtic tree alphabet, the **ogham** representing the birch and the letter "b". Beithe is also linked to the pheasant and the colour white.

**Bel** (1) The Celtic god of light and fire. In ancient times "bel-fires" were lit on the hilltops to celebrate the return of life and fertility to the world. The Wiccan sabbat of **Beltane**, or **May Eve**, celebrated on 30 April, honours the mating of the

BELIAL   Belial and the mouth of Hell. Belial was known as the 'demon of lies'.

sun god with the fertile earth goddess. Also known as **Balor**. See also **Sabbats, Greater**.

**Bel** (2) In Babylonian mythology, one of the supreme triad of the gods, the others being Anu, lord of the heavens, and Ea, lord of the waters. Bel was the chief god and founder of the Babylonian empire – his name literally means "king". The spelling "Bel" is the Akkadian form; its Semitic equivalent is Baal. Bel derives from the Sumerian god **Enlil**.

**Beleth** In the Goetia, the thirteenth spirit, a mighty and "terrible" king who rides on a pale horse with all manner of trumpets and other musical instruments announcing his presence. He may be commanded by the magician to enter the ritual triangle of evocation, and to do this the magician must strike a triangular shape to the south and east with a hazel wand. Once he has entered the triangle, however, Beleth must be accorded

respect and courtesy. Beleth can summon the powers of love between a couple but to protect against his bad temper the magician should wear a silver ring on the middle finger of his left hand and hold it close to his face. Beleth governs 85 legions of spirits. He is also known as Bileth or Bilet.

**Bel-Fire** See Bel, Beltane.

**Belial** In the Goetia, the 68th spirit, a mighty king who, it is said, was created next after **Lucifer**. He appears in the form of a beautiful angel sitting in a chariot of fire. He speaks with an alluring voice but deceives all who summon him unless continually constrained by the Divine Names of God. According to the Goetia, Belial provides excellent familiars but must have offerings and sacrifices made to him. He rules over 50 legions of spirits. The distinguished occult historian **A.E. Waite** notes that Belial was one of a vast cohort of spirits shut up by King **Solomon** in a brazen vessel but released subsequently by the Babylonians. Belial was also one of the demons summoned by the notorious black magician and murderer **Gilles de Rais**. The name Belial possibly derives from the Hebrew expression *beli yaal*, meaning "without worth", generally applied to someone who was wicked and debased.

**Beliar** See Belial.

**Bell, Book, and Candle** A ceremonial act of excommunication whereby a priest reads a malediction from a book, tolls a bell as if for the dead, and extinguishes a candle to indicate that the soul of the offending person has been cast forth from the sight of God.

**Belladonna** In Italy, the popular name for **deadly nightshade**. It translates as "beautiful woman".

**Bellows** In alchemy, an instrument designed to produce a strong blast of air which then fans and increases the fire in the alchemist's **athanor**, or furnace.

**Belomancy** A form of **divination** that involves analyzing the path of arrows in flight.

**Belphegor** A demon who appears in the form of a woman, and whose name derives from a form of **Baal**, worshipped by the Moabites on Mount Phegor. Belphegor was a demon of discoveries and inventions.

**Beltane** Also Bealtaine. In Wicca, a greater sabbat, celebrated on 30 April. Beltane is a Celtic fertility celebration that may take its name from the Celtic deity **Bel** or Balor – god of light and fire – for in ancient times "bel-fires" were lit on the hilltops to celebrate the return of life and fertility to the world. Wiccans often celebrate Beltane by dancing round the maypole and celebrating the love between men and women. Mythologically, Beltane honours the mating of the sun god with the fertile earth goddess. Beltane is also known as May Eve.

**Bembine Tablet** A bronze and silver tablet allegedly bought by Cardinal Pietro Bembo (1470–1547) after Rome was plundered in 1527 by the army of Emperor Charles V. The tablet was engraved with Egyptian hieroglyphs and was said to hold the key to interpreting many sacred alphabets.

**Benjamin, gum** See Benzoin.

**Bennett, Allan** (1872–1923) A leading figure in the **Hermetic Order of the Golden Dawn**, Bennett tutored **Aleister Crowley** and later became a worshipper of the god **Shiva** in Ceylon. Bennett's **magical name** was *Frater Iehi Aour* ("Let there be light"). He engaged himself in ceremonial magic with such vigour that he rivalled **Samuel MacGregor Mathers** as a dominant figure among the English occultists of his time. He wrote the powerful evocation of Taphthartharath, used for visibly manifesting the spirit of **Mercury**. He also compiled part of the magical reference system known as *777*, later published by Crowley. In 1900 he left England and became a Buddhist monk. He assumed the title Bhikku Ananda Metteya, and was influential in founding the British Buddhist Society in 1908.

**Bennu** or Benu In Egyptian mythology, a legendary bird believed to be the reincarnation of the soul of **Osiris**. Like the phoenix, the bennu bird rose to new life amidst the flames and was closely linked to the sun. At Heliopolis, where it was worshipped as a form of **Ra**, the bennu bird was said to fly forth from the Island of Fire in the Underworld, announcing the rebirth of the sun.

**Benzoin** Also known as friar's balsam and gum benjamin, benzoin is a balsamic resin which is exuded from Indian, Thai and Indonesian styrax trees. It is one of the classic ingredients of

incense and in ancient times,was burnt
to drive away evil spirits. See also
**Magical Perfumes.**

**Beorc** In the Germanic **Elder Futhark**,
the rune letter representing the number
18. Beorc corresponds to the letter "b"
and is the rune of birth, rebirth, rites of
passage, and healing. Beorc is associated
with the birch tree and northern
European pagan rites included acts of
flagellation using bundles of birch twigs.
Accordingly it is also the rune associated
with acts of **atonement** for past
misdeeds. In the pagan tradition, flagellation was also regarded as a way of
promoting fertility. Also known as
Berkano.

**Berith** In the **Goetia**, the 28th spirit, a
"terrible duke" who appears in the form
of a soldier wearing red apparel and a
golden crown, and riding upon a red
horse. He has the ability to turn all
metals into gold and can only be evoked
by using a magical ring. He speaks with a
clear and subtle voice but according to
magical tradition he is renowned for his
duplicity and is not to be trusted. Berith
commands 26 legions of spirits. He is
also known as Bofi or Bolfry.

**Berkano** See **Beorc.**

**Bertiaux, Michael** (1935– ) An
American ritual magician and director of
the Monastery of the Seven Rays. A
former Anglican curate, Bertiaux moved
from Seattle to an Anglican church
college in Port-au-Prince, Haiti, and
made contact with a group of **voodoo**
practitioners who wished to introduce
their tradition to the United States.
Bertiaux was initiated into what he refers
to as the Gnostic-Voodoo mysteries in
1963 and subsequently resigned from the
Anglican Church. In the late 1960s
Bertiaux penetrated more deeply into the
voodoo magical tradition. He was also
consecrated as an adept in the Monastery
of the Seven Rays, which he has
described as "the magical offshoot of
Roman Catholicism". In 1973 the

Monastery of the Seven Rays accepted
Aleister Crowley's Law of **Thelema** and
this also aligned Bertiaux's organization
with the **Ordo Templi Orientis.**
  Nevertheless the role of the dead and
risen Christ remains central to Bertiaux's
cosmology and there is also a substantial
element of voodoo in his magical ·
practice. Bertiaux is skilled in transferring his consciousness into a form which
he describes as an "astral tarantula" and
he also invokes voodoo deities like the
witch-goddess Maconda and **Guede**, god
of the dead. By his own account, much
of Bertiaux's magical work is conducted
within the nether-regions of inner space.

**Bes** In ancient Egypt, an ugly, hairy,
bandy-legged dwarf deity widely
worshipped as the god of pleasure,
music, and fighting. Bes had the power
to ward off evil spirits. He was also the
god of fashion and marriage, and he
protected women in childbirth. Bes was
also known as Aha, Bas, and Besam Bisu.

**Besam Bisu** See **Bes.**

**Besom** In Wicca, a witch's broomstick,
made from six different woods – birch,
broom, hawthorn, hazel, rowan, and
willow. It is used to clean the ritual area.
See also **Broomstick, Witch's.**

**Bestiary** A medieval catalogue of tales
about animals, real and mythical, and
portraying an allegorical or moral
Christian theme. Bestiaries were often
beautifully illustrated.

**Bet** See **Beth.**

**Beth** The Hebrew letter ascribed to the
path linking **Kether** and **Binah** on the
Tree of Life. Beth has a numerical value
of two. In modern magical visualization
and **pathworkings** the Tarot card
associated with this path on the Tree is
*The Magus.*

**Bether** According to the medieval
grimoire *The Arbatel of Magick*, an
Olympian spirit that governs all aspects

of the universe associated with Jupiter. Bether is said to be a "dignified" spirit that can produce miraculous medical cures and is capable of prolonging human life to seven hundred years. He also "reconcileth the spirits of the aire". Bether has beneath him 42 kings, 35 princes, 28 dukes, 21 counsellors, 24 ministers, seven messengers, and 29,000 legions of spirits. See also **Grimoires**.

**Bewitchment** The act of gaining power over another person by means of **spells, incantations,** or **sorcery.**

**Bibliomancy** A form of divination by interpreting a passage picked at random in a book – often a sacred text. Also known as Stichomancy.

**Bicorporeal signs** An astrological term for signs that include two symbolic figures. See also **Astrology; Double-Bodied Signs.**

**Bifrons** In the Goetia, the 46th spirit, a mighty earl who appears in the form of a monster but who will assume human form when so commanded. He instructs in such subjects as astrology and geometry and all the other arts and sciences and also knows the special virtues of precious stones, herbs and woods. He can transport dead bodies to other locations and create phantom candles on the graves of the dead. He commands six legions of spirits and is also known as Bifrovs.

**Bifrovs** See Bifrons.

**Bilet, Bileth** See Beleth.

**Bilocation** The ability to appear in two places, far apart, at the same time. Compare **Apparitions; Astral Travel.**

**Bilongo** In Santería, an evil spell.

**Binah** In the Kabbalah, the third mystical emanation of the Tree of Life, following **Kether** and **Chokmah.** Occultists identify Binah with the Great Mother in all her forms. She is the womb of forthcoming, the source of all the great images and forms that manifest in the universe as archetypes. She is also the supreme female principle in the process of creation and, via the process of **mythological correspondences,** is associated with such deities as **Rhea, Isis,** and **Demeter** in other pantheons, and with the Virgin Mary.

**Binding** In alchemy, the act of "fixing" or "coagulating" the volatile and elusive spirit of **mercury.** The spirit Mercurius – referred to by the alchemists as "philosophical mercury" – was forever dissolving, and a key task was to contain and trap him in the alembic.

**Birch** In Scandinavian mythology, a tree sacred to **Thor,** and a symbol of spring. See also **Beorc.**

**Bird of Hermes** In alchemy, a term used to describe the creation of **philosophical mercury** at different stages of the work. It is the name of the "philosophical bird" who emerges from the vessel containing the philosopher's egg – the egg which is synonymous with the Philosopher's Stone.

**Birthstone** In astrology, gems ascribed to particular signs of the **zodiac.** They are diamond (**Aries**); emerald (**Taurus**); agate (**Gemini**); ruby (**Cancer**); sardonyx (**Leo**); sapphire (**Virgo**); opal (**Libra**); topaz (**Scorpio**); turquoise (**Sagittarius**); garnet (**Capricorn**); amethyst (**Aquarius**); and bloodstone (**Pisces**).

**Bitom** In Enochian magic, the sacred name of the spirit of fire. Bitom (pronounced *Bee-toh-meh*) is assigned to the South and is represented by the colour red. See also **Exarp, Hcoma, Nanta.**

**Bittul Ha-Yesh** In the Jewish mystical tradition, a Hasidic term for the self-annihilation of the ego in order to experience higher states of awareness. See also **Hasidism.**

**Bizango** In **voodoo**, the secret society where magical ceremonies are performed.

**Black** A colour traditionally associated with darkness, evil, and malevolence. In **alchemy**, it is the colour of death, signifying the onset of the process of **nigredo**. In the cosmology of the **Temple of Set**, a colour signifying infinite human potential. See also **Magic, Black**.

**Black Arts** See Arts, Black.

**Black Hellebore** See Hellebore.

**Black Magic** See Magic, Black.

**Black Mass** A satanic practice, deliberately parodying the central ritual of Roman Catholicism, in which the host (representing the body of Christ) is stolen from a church, consecrated by an unfrocked priest, and desecrated. The ceremony includes activities forbidden by the Church, including the alleged sacrifice of unbaptized infants and the recitation of the Lord's Prayer backwards. In the Middle Ages, the threat of **satanism** was greatly exaggerated by the Inquisition, although undoubtedly small groups of heretics and satanists did exist (see **Albigenses, Knights Templar, Witch**). In modern times there have been spasmodic outbreaks of satanism, the most visible of which is perhaps **Anton La Vey**'s **Church of Satan** established in San Francisco, California, in 1966.

**Black Pope**
See La Vey, Anton Szandor.

**Black Shuck** In medieval English folklore, black demon-dogs (with glowing red or green eyes) that roamed lonely regions of the countryside and were regarded as an omen of death. Seeing Black Shuck meant that a member of one's family would soon die. The name derives from the Anglo-Saxon term *scucca*, meaning "demon".

**Blackwood, Algernon** (1869–1951) One of Britain's most famous occult novelists, Blackwood grew up in the Black Forest, Germany, and later attended Edinburgh University. A one-time member of the **Hermetic Order of the Golden Dawn**, he was a journalist with the *New York Times* and a prolific writer of mystical and supernatural tales. His works include *John Silence, The Bright Messenger*, and *Pan's Garden*.

**Blake, William** (1757–1827) An English visionary artist, poet, and mystic who, like his father, was profoundly influenced by Emanuel Swedenborg. Blake was apprenticed to an engraver, began to exhibit at the Royal Academy in 1780, and devised new methods of printing. However, his inner world was populated by spirits and visions. As a child he communicated with angelic beings and later, as an engraver, he claimed that the spirit of his deceased brother Robert had shown him new printing techniques. Blake's poetry and art is profound and richly symbolic, and he was very much a mythmaker. His cosmology, while unique in many respects, resembles that of the **Kabbalah**. Blake's works include *Songs of Innocence, The Marriage of Heaven and Hell, Songs of Experience*, and *The Book of Urizen*.

**Blavatsky, Madame Helena Petrovna** (1831–1891) A Russian mystic and adventurer who co-founded the **Theosophical Society** in New York in 1875. As a child, she claimed to converse with invisible play-friends and was often frightened by phantoms. After an unsuccessful marriage at the age of seventeen, she travelled widely through Europe and the Middle East and claimed that she had been initiated by "Mahatmas", or Masters, into the secrets of esoteric mysticism. She believed that these Masters helped her to write many of her major works, which in turn provided the foundation for modern Theosophy. Her first book was *Isis Unveiled*, and this was followed by *The Secret Doctrine, The Key to Theosophy*, and *The Voice of Silence*.

Madame Blavatsky was a powerful psychic medium, but it is likely that many of the psychic powers she claimed were given to her by the Masters were clever deceptions. Her main contribution to mystical thought was the manner in which she sought to synthesize eastern and western philosophy and religion, thereby providing a framework for understanding universal occult teachings.

**"Blessed Be"** A phrase used by witches both as a greeting and as a farewell. See Witch.

**Blood** Synonymous in ceremonial magic with life-force, blood is used by some sorcerers and black magicians to inscribe magical names of power, and to sign magical pacts with spirits; it is also consumed by some ritual magicians as a power-bestowing sacrament.

**Blood Moon** See Esbats.

**Bloodstones** Semi-precious stones used as magical amulets to facilitate healing or for psychic protection. They include red and green jasper, red marble, cornelian, and heliotrope. See also Amulet; Magical Stones.

**Boann** In Celtic mythology, the eponymous goddess of the River Boyne in eastern Ireland. She united with the fertility god **Dagda** to give birth to several children, among them **Ogma**, creator of the famous **ogham** tree alphabet in which different letters of the alphabet are represented by various species of tree and shrub.

**Bocca** See Iboga.

**Bocor** See Bokor.

**Body** In alchemy, the body, soul, and spirit of matter – known respectively as **salt, mercury,** and **sulphur** – had to be freed from their primitive state and reunited in a state of harmony or balance. From an alchemical perspective,

every metal was made up of salt, mercury and sulphur in varying proportions. Gold had equal proportions of these three constituents and was therefore "perfect"; the other metals were out of balance and "imperfect".

**Body of Light** An occult term for the **astral body.** Magicians believe that the body of light takes the form conjured in the imagination and that they can transfer their consciousness to this form, bringing it to life on the **astral plane.**

**Body Soul** See Soul.

**Boehme, Jacob** (or Jakob; 1575–1624) A German shoemaker who, at the age of 25, experienced a mystical transformation that had a profound and lasting effect on his life. A devout Lutheran, Boehme believed that God was far away, in the distant reaches of the universe – although mystical visions brought this presence nearer. Nevertheless, life on earth was a constant struggle between good and evil. In many instances, Boehme felt, evil seemed to have the upper hand. He therefore felt constrained to "wrestle with the love and the mercy of God" in order to break through "the gates of hell". Like a true mystic, Boehme came to the view that the human will had to subjugate itself to God's will because the latter represented true Reality. Interested in astronomy and cosmology, Boehme equated God the Father with the sky, and Jesus Christ with the sun. The light from the stars represented the Holy Spirit. To achieve true union with God, a person had to go through a process of "spiritual birth", recognizing the divine essence that lies within. Like the kabbalists, who were an influence on his thought, Boehme believed in the concept of the **macrocosm and microcosm** – that people mirror the universe and are a reflection of God. Thus the mystic way is essentially a path to self-realization

**Bofi** See Berith.

**Boggart** In English folklore, a mischievous spirit, fond of **poltergeist** activities. The boggart had a semi-human appearance, with certain animal characteristics such as fur or a tail. Legends concerning boggarts abound in Yorkshire.

**Bogle** In Scottish mythology, a goblin or phantom that was harmful and had a frightening appearance. Variants on this theme can be found elsewhere (e.g. the Yorkshire **bug-a-boo**). The modern equivalent, which has a more colloquial and less supernatural connotation, is "bogeyman".

**Bogomils** A tenth-century Bulgarian sect, which maintained that there are two creative forces in the universe, good and evil. They believed the world was intrinsically evil and the **Devil** had assisted in creating Adam. They also claimed Christ's resurrection was illusory and the Holy Cross was a demonic symbol, detestable to God. See also **Albigenses**.

**Bokor** or Bocor In **voodoo**, a practitioner of magic who is not necessarily an initiate and is therefore distinguished from the **houngan** or priest.

**Bol** The Mayan god of inebriation. See Balche'.

**Bolfry** See Berith.

**Boline** In Wicca, a white-handled knife sometimes located on the **altar** but which is purely functional and not used in ceremonies. See also **Athame**.

**Bön** The pre-Buddhist shamanic tradition in Tibet, characterized by the animist belief in spirits. Monks don animal masks and ornate costumes and their sacred dances open a path to the spirit-world. Also known as Bön-Po or Pön.

**Bone, Eleanor** (1910–2001) A noted witch of modern times, and a spokesperson for the modern **witchcraft** movement. Together with **Patricia** Crowther and **Monique Wilson**, she was one of the heirs to the estate of the influential witch **Gerald Gardner**.

**Bonewits, Isaac** (1949– ) Allegedly the world's "first academically accredited magician", Bonewits was born in Royal Oak, Michigan. He graduated with a bachelor's degree in **magic** from the University of California in Los Angeles and went on to found the Aquarian Antidefamation League. He was associate editor of the now defunct *Gnostica* journal and is the author of *Real Magic*.

***Book of Dead Names, The*** See *Necronomicon*.

***Book of Shadows, The*** In witchcraft, the personal book of spells, rituals, and folklore that a witch compiles after being initiated into the **coven**. *The Book of Shadows* is kept secret and, traditionally, destroyed when the witch dies. See also Spell.

***Book of Splendour, The*** A literal translation of the title of the *Zohar*, the main work of the medieval **Kabbalah**, written c. 1280CE by the Spanish mystic Moses de León.

***Book of the Dead*** A type of writing that describes the after-death condition and provides guidance for the passage of the deceased soul through heaven and hell states. There are also descriptions of deities which the soul might expect to encounter on the post-mortem journey. The best-known examples are *The Egyptian Book of the Dead* and *The Tibetan Book of the Dead*. Other works include the Egyptian texts known as the *Am Tuat* and *The Book of Gates*, and *The Ethiopian Book of the Dead* (*Lefefa Sedek*), which combines Christian and Gnostic thought.

***Book of the Law, The*** In the Thelemic cosmology of ceremonial magician · **Aleister Crowley**, a text dictated by the semi-invisible Egyptian entity **Aiwaz** during Crowley's revelation in Cairo in

April 1904. The book proclaimed the advent of the **Aeon of Horus**, with Crowley as its representative. Crowley was now considered an incarnation of **Ra-Hoor-Khuit**, the divine child of **Nuit** or **Nut**, the sky goddess, and **Hadit**, a Chaldean counterpart to **Set**, the Egyptian god of darkness. This union of Nuit and Hadit also heralded the arrival of the Law of **Thelema**, the main dictum of which was "Do what thou Wilt, Love is the Law, Love under Will". *The Book of the Law* is also referred to in Crowleyian literature as *Liber Al vel Legis*.

**Book of Thoth, The** A modern term for the **Tarot**, based on the mistaken assumption that the Tarot had an ancient Egyptian origin. It derives largely from the theories of French occultist **Antoine Court de Gebelin**, who believed that the Tarot was part of an initiatory procedure in the Great Pyramid; and **Aleister Crowley**, who used this title for his own work on the Tarot.

**Botis** In the **Goetia**, the seventeenth spirit, a great president and earl. When evoked he appears initially as an ugly viper but he can be commanded by the magician to assume a human form. Even so, he will then appear with "great teeth and two horns, carrying a bright and sharp sword in his hand". Botis can provide information about the present, past, and future and is also able to reconcile friends and foes. He rules over 60 legions of spirits.

**Boucan** In **voodoo**, ceremonial bonfires lit just before the New Year. They honour **Legba** – loa of light, life, and the crossroads – and represent the symbolic "re-firing" of the sun.

**Boullan, Joseph-Antoine** (1824–1893) A defrocked Roman Catholic priest who became leader of the eccentric Church of Carmel in Lyons, France, after the death of its founder, Pierre Vintras. Boullan and his followers believed that since the Fall of Adam and Eve people could only be redeemed by sexual intercourse with superior celestial beings such as angels, archangels, and saints. How this was achieved is not immediately obvious, but on some occasions attractive young women took the place of archangels. Boullan came under attack from four rival occultists, **Stanislas de Guaita**, Oswald Wirth, Edward Dubus, and **Sar Josephin Peladan**, who he believed had cursed him to die as a result of **black magic**. The French novelist **Joris-Karl Huysmans** became involved with Boullan and represented his side of the magical battle in the French newspapers. Huysmans became convinced of the reality of the magical confrontation when he himself began to experience "astral attacks"– "fluidic fisticuffs" which would strike his face at night. The skirmishes became more intense on both sides. Huysmans wrote that Boullan would "jump about like a tiger…He invokes the aid of St **Michael** and the eternal justiciaries then, standing at his altar, he cries out: 'Strike down Peladan, strike down Peladan.'"

As it happened, it was Boullan who succumbed first, dying suddenly in January 1893. Huysmans was convinced that Boullan had died of supernatural causes. "It is indisputable that Guaita and Peladan practice black magic every day," he said in an interview. "Poor Boullan was engaged in perpetual conflict with the evil spirits they continually sent him from Paris…. It is quite possible that my poor friend Boullan has succumbed to a supremely powerful spell." Boullan's magical activities are described in Huysman's novel *La Bas*. See also **Magical Attack; Spell**.

**Boyle, Robert** (1627–1691) Born in Ireland, Boyle was a pioneering chemist. The first scientist to collect a gas and to discover that sounds could not traverse a vacuum, Boyle is also significant for his work with elements. He defined an element – in the scientific sense of the word – as a substance that could not be decomposed but which could enter into combination with other elements giving rise to compounds that in turn were capable of subsequent decomposition into their constituent elements. He classified the metals as elements because they had resisted all efforts to decompose them but he remained open to the idea that gold was a compound. This meant that transmuting gold from other base metals remained a theoretical possibility. With this idea in mind Boyle helped to persuade the British government to repeal the law against manufacturing gold. Boyle later associated with **Rosicrucians** and **Freemasonry** and undertook secret experiments inspired by the alchemical philosopher and scientist Francis Bacon. Historically Boyle bridges the eras of alchemy and scientific chemistry.

**Brasa, Exú** In Macumba a surrogate of Exú.

**Briah** In the **Kabbalah**, the second of the four worlds of manifestation. Briah contains two **sephiroth**, **Chokmah** and **Binah**, representing the Great Father and the Great Mother respectively. Briah reflects the highest levels of expression of the sacred male and female principles. Their sacred union gives rise to the third world, the World of Formation. Briah is linked by occultists to the second of the four letters of the **Tetragrammaton**, YHVH. See also **Assiah**; **Atziroth**; **Yetzirah**; **Four Worlds**.

**Bride** In Wicca, the **Mother Goddess**.

**Brisingamen Necklace** In Scandinavian mythology, a superb magical necklace created by four dwarves for **Freyja** – the goddess of love and fertility. In return for creating the necklace each of the four dwarves was allowed to sleep with the goddess for a night. According to mythic tradition, the mischievous **Aesir** deity **Loki** transformed into a flea, bit the sleeping goddess, removed the necklace, and then took it to his friend **Odin**.

**Broceliande** A mystic forest in Brittany where the legendary wizard **Merlin** courted the beautiful siren-maiden Vivian.

**Brodie-Innes, John William** (1848–1923) A prominent member of the **Hermetic Order of the Golden Dawn**, Brodie-Innes practised law in Edinburgh, Scotland, and was the first Imperator of the Amen-Ra Temple in that city. Even though many members of the Golden Dawn deserted its controversial leader, **MacGregor Mathers**, in 1903, Brodie-Innes remained loyal to Mathers and assisted in the formation of the second Alpha Omega Temple and the Cromlech Temple which attracted members from the Anglican Church and the Episcopalian Church of Scotland. Brodie-Innes was interested in hypnotism and the visionary aspects of magic and produced an Order paper (Flying Roll No. XXV) under his **magical name**, Frater Sub Spe, in which he explained how to transfer consciousness to the **astral plane** through an act of focused magical will.

**Broomstick, Witch's** According to tradition, **witches** rode through the air with broomsticks between their legs, en route to the witches' sabbath. It is now believed that the witches' flight was a hallucinogenic dissociation effect brought on by psychotropic flying ointment constituents like **henbane** and **belladonna** that were rubbed into the skin, and that the broomstick is a euphemism for the penis, in much the same way that the **maypole** is also a symbol of fertility.

**Brother Unity** See **Achad, Frater**.

**Brothers of the Shadow** In Theosophy, a term given to those who follow the path of **black magic**. Compare **Left-Hand Path**.

**Brujo, Bruja** In Peru and Mexico, a sorcerer or witch. The term has become more familiar as a result of **Carlos Castañeda's** descriptions of the Yaqui shaman Don Juan Matus.

**Buckland, Raymond** (1934– ) A British-born witch who moved to the United States in 1962. Born in London and educated at King's College School, Buckland is of half-gypsy descent but was raised in the Church of England. Introduced to **spiritualism** and the occult by his uncle, he subsequently developed an interest in the magical traditions. Buckland met witchcraft practitioner **Gerald Gardner** in 1964 and was initiated' by Gardner's high priestess, **Lady Olwen**, in Scotland in that year. He subsequently introduced the **Gardnerian tradition** of modern witchcraft to the United States, where he and his first wife Rosemary had their home. In 1973 Buckland left Gardnerian witchcraft and established **Seax-Wica**, a new organization based primarily on the Saxon magical tradition. Buckland has written numerous books and articles on **magic**, **witchcraft**, and psychic potential. They include *Buckland's Complete Book of Witchcraft*, *Buckland's Complete Book of Saxon Witchcraft*, and *Witch Book: The Encyclopedia of Witchcraft, Wicca and Neopaganism*.

**Budapest, Zsuzsanna Emese** (1940– ) One of the most influential practitioners of Goddess worship in the United States, Z. Budapest (as she is now generally known) was born in Hungary in 1940, the daughter of a psychic medium. Zsuzsanna's mother, Masika Szilagyi, composed poems and invocations while in trance, claimed an impeccable pedigree as a shamaness, and could trace her mystical lineage back to the fourteenth century. At the age of nineteen, Budapest emigrated to Illinois from Vienna, where she had been studying languages, and renewed her interest in German literature at the University of Chicago. Later she worked in theatre in New York, studying techniques of improvisation, before moving to Los Angeles in 1970. Soon after arriving in Los Angeles she opened what became a legendary occult shop, the Feminist Wicca, on Lincoln Boulevarde in Venice Beach. This store served as a "matriarchal spiritual centre", dispensing candles, oil, incense, herbs, jewellery, Tarot cards and other paraphernalia, and also emerged as a meeting place for women wishing to perform rituals together. Soon there were groups of neopagan women meeting for ceremonies on the equinoxes and solstices and Budapest proclaimed that "feminist spirituality had been born again".

Budapest's form of magical worship, which she calls **Dianic witchcraft**, excludes men altogether. She acknowledges that there are men who wish to discover the "inner woman" within themselves but maintains that there are other occult groups that cater for this need. According to Budapest, women's mysteries must be kept pure and strong, and men have no place in them. As she once explained during an interview: "We have *women's* circles. You don't put men in women's circles – they wouldn't be women's circles any more. Our Goddess is Life, and women should be free to worship from their ovaries." Budapest now favours an equal mix of lesbian and heterosexual women in her circles to "balance the polarities" in her rituals. She is a practising lesbian herself although she has not always been. Formerly married, with two sons – one a physicist, the other a fighter pilot in the U.S. Marines – she has since adopted a strongly feminist position and has chosen to deliberately avoid what she calls the "duality" of man and woman. Her emphasis on *women's* mysteries allows the different phases of womanhood to be honoured in their own right: the young, the mature, and the older woman each have much to offer, and in Budapest's group ceremonies are performed for each of these phases of life.

Z. Budapest is a noted Wiccan author and has produced several publications, the most important of which is *The Holy Book of Women's Mysteries* (revised edition, 1989).

**Budge, Sir E.A. Wallis** (1857–1934) A leading translator of ancient Egyptian texts, including *The Egyptian Book of the Dead*, Budge was keeper of Egyptian antiquities at the British Museum from 1892 to 1924. He is believed to have been associated with the so-called "Egyptian Temple" of the **Hermetic Order of the Golden Dawn**.

**Buer** In the Goetia, the tenth spirit, a great president who appears only when the sun is in **Sagittarius**. Skilled in the magical treatment of disease, Buer teaches moral and natural philosophy and also has a profound knowledge of the healing powers of plants. According to the Goetia he "giveth good familiars" and governs 50 legions of spirits.

**Bug-a-boo** See Bogie.

**Builders of the Adytum** See Case, Paul Foster

**Bull-Roarer** A piece of wood attached to a string, which produces a loud humming noise when spun around in the air. It is used in the ceremonial rites of the Australian Aborigines and other peoples.

**Bulwer-Lytton, Sir Edward** (1803–1873) An English novelist, best known for his novel *The Last Days of Pompeii*. Bulwer-Lytton regarded himself as an occult **adept** and considered his magical novels *Zanoni* and *A Strange Story* to be his main work, despite their less popular appeal. Bulwer-Lytton studied at Cambridge, and on several occasions entertained the French occultist **Eliphas Lévi** at Knebworth, his family residence. He was at one time the honorary grand patron of the **Societas Rosicruciana in Anglia**, a predecessor of the **Hermetic Order of the Golden Dawn**.

**Bundle, Medicine** See Medicine Bag

**Bune** In the Goetia, the 26th spirit, a strong and mighty duke who appears in the form of a three-headed dragon. The first head is like that of a dog, the second like a griffin and the third is human. Bune bestows riches, wisdom and the gift of eloquence and also gives "true answers to demands". He governs 30 legions of spirits.

**Burning Times** An expression used by Wiccans and neopagans to refer to the period of persecution of witches during the fifteenth, sixteenth, and seventeenth centuries. In all countries except England and its American colonies, where they were hanged, witches were executed by burning. In Italy and Spain they were burnt alive. In Scotland, Germany and France it was customary first to strangle the witch, by garrotting or hanging, before lighting the pyre, provided that the witch did not recant the confession made under torture. For uncooperative witches, the fire was laid with green wood to prolong the process of dying.
The number of victims of the Burning Times cannot be known for certain, with estimates varying from just 3,000 (in one Catholic source) to 9,000,000 (in some neopagan sources). Recent scholarship, since about 1975, is based on systematic examination of trial records (and estimates of lost records) and puts the number of executions from c. 1400 to 1700 at between 50,000 and 100,000 maximum. Most executions took place between 1550–1650 in eastern France and in Germany, in areas and at times of acute Protestant-Catholic conflict. It is undoubtedly true that many more women than men were executed. Most death sentences in these centuries were passed and carried out by civil courts, not the Church (although the civil courts were following Church doctrine).

**Butler, W.E.** (1898–1978) An English occultist and author who trained as a member of **Dion Fortune's Fraternity of the Inner Light**, and was also a protégé of the psychic Robert King. Butler established a magical order, **Servants of the Light** (SOL), which has its present headquarters on the island of

Jersey. The SOL has continued to develop modern techniques of visionary magic known as **pathworkings**.

**Buttons, Mescal** See Peyote.

**Buzios** In Macumba, cowrie shells used for **divination**.

# C

**Caacrinolaas** See Glasyalabolas.

**Caapi** See Banisteriopsis.

**Caassimola** See Glasyalabolas.

**Cabala** Alternative spelling for Kabbalah, Qabalah.

**Cabiri** or Kabiri Agricultural deities of Phrygian origin worshipped in ancient Greek religion, especially in Samothrace, Lemnos, Thebes, and Mania. The mystery rites were second only to those of **Eleusis**. The main deities worshipped were **Zeus** and **Dionysus**.

**Cabocio** In Macumba, spirits who "work" in the forest and know the secrets of plants and herbs.

**Cabot, Laurie** See Witchcraft as a Science.

**Cacodemon** An evil spirit capable of changing its shape so rapidly that it cannot be identified. In medieval **magic** it was sometimes identified with the evil **genius** inside each person, and in **astrology** it is linked to the twelfth house, the Sun.

**Caduceus** The staff carried by the Greek god **Hermes** and the Roman **Mercury**, represented as having two snakes curling around it, with wings at the top. Occultists sometimes compare the staff with the symbolism of the psychic energy currents **ida** and **pingala**, which are said to encircle the central nervous system in **Kundalini** yoga. See also **Middle Pillar**.

**Caecus** In Greek mythology, a fire-breathing monster, half-beast, half-human, who lived deep in a cave, away from the sun. He slaughtered people and kept their skulls to adorn his cave. Caecus was finally overcome by **Heracles**.

**Cagliostro, Count Alessandro di**
(1743–1795). Regarded by Thomas
Carlyle as the "Prince of Quacks",
Cagliostro was a traveller, self-claimed
**alchemist**, and occult opportunist. Born
in Palermo, his real name was Giuseppe
Balsamo. After misleading a goldsmith
named Marano into believing that
hidden treasures could be located by
**ceremonial magic**, he escaped to
Messina, where he made contact with an
alleged alchemical adept named
Althotas. They travelled together to
Alexandria and Rhodes and later
conducted alchemical experiments with
Grand Master Pinto on the island of
Malta. Pinto's sponsorship allowed
Count Cagliostro, as he now styled
himself, to live in great wealth and style.
Cagliostro married Lorenza Feliciani in
Italy and became a well-known figure in
many European courts, charming
princes, kings, and queens, and assuring
them that his alchemical secrets could
help them swell the royal coffers. He
became deeply interested in **Freemasonry**, and acquired a reputation as a
medium and faith healer. Cagliostro also
became involved in the famous Diamond
Necklace affair, and was charged by
Madame de Lamotte with stealing the
valuable jewellery. This was later
dismissed in court, but a more serious
charge was forthcoming. The Holy Office
ordered his arrest in 1789 on the grounds
that Freemasonry was a heresy. He spent
the rest of his years in the Castle of San
Leo near Montefeltro. See also **Alchemy**;
**Egyptian Masonic Rite**.

**Caim** In the Goetia, the 53rd spirit, a
great president who appears initially in
the form of a thrush or blackbird but
then changes into a man brandishing a
sharp sword. When he speaks he utters
not words but burning ashes. He understands the calls of birds, bullocks, dogs,
and other creatures and also the "voice of
the waters". He can see into the future
and was once a member of the Order of
Angels. He now governs 30 legions of
infernal spirits. Caim is also known as
Camio.

**Cake of Light** See Gnostic Mass.

**Cakes-and-Wine** See Sacred Food.

**Calcination** In alchemy, the conversion
of a metal or mineral to powder (**calx**)
through heating. Several different types
of furnace were used for calcination.

**Caliburnus** The magical sword of King
Arthur. See also **Excalibur**.

**Call** See Aethyr.

**Calling Down the Moon** See Drawing
Down the Moon.

**Calx** In alchemy, the product of
calcination.

**Camarinha** In Macumba, a small room
within the temple which is reserved for
initiates.

**Camelot** The name of King Arthur's
legendary court. Various sites in England
have been suggested for Camelot,
including Exeter and the pre-Roman
earthwork known as Cadbury Castle,
near Glastonbury.

**Camio** See Caim.

**Camomile** See Chamomile.

**Cancer** In astrology, the sign of the
zodiac for those born between 22 June
and 22 July. A water sign, ruled by the
moon, Cancer is symbolized by the crab
and is the fourth sign of the zodiac.
Those born under this sign are supposed
to be sensitive, sentimental, and impressionable. True to the symbol, they "float
with the tide". Cancer is also said to be
the most "maternal" sign.

**Candelabra, Three-Pronged** In
Wicca, a candelabra holding a white
candle (representing the **Great Goddess**
as Maid), a red candle (representing her
as Mother) and a black candle (representing her as Crone). The candelabra is
placed on the altar.

**Candlemas** In Wicca, one of the Greater Sabbats, celebrated on 2 February. Also known by its old Celtic name, **Imbolc**, Candlemas has been described as "the quickening of the year, the first stirrings of spring within the womb of mother earth". The name Imbolc means "in the belly" and this sabbat is very much a fertility celebration. The focus is on light and new life, as opposed to the darkness of winter, which has now receded. Candlemas is sometimes known as the Feast of Lights.

**Candomblé** In Brazil, a Yoruba-based tradition within **Macumba** in which devotees call on African deities like Ogum, Xangô, and Iemanjá and where the focus is more on spiritual healing than on gaining magical power. The spirit is healed when the devotee fuses his or her awareness with an **orìsà** during initiation. Candomblé ceremonies date back to 1830 in the city of Salvador, now the capital of the state of Bahia.

**Cannibalism** The act of eating human flesh, sometimes with a view to acquiring the special qualities and characteristics of the deceased. In many pre-literate societies the act of cannibalism is closely linked to "eating the god" and is a feature of magical initiations. The term apparently derives from the West Indian man-eating Caribs, but cannibalism has occurred in many cultures worldwide. It is also known as anthropophagy.

**Canzo** In voodoo, the ordeal by fire through which the candidate must pass in order to be initiated. A person who succeeds is known as **canzo**, or **hounsi canzo**.

**Cap, Friar's** See Monkshood.

**Capnomancy** A form of **divination** by means of interpreting patterns in smoke, often associated with sacrificial offerings and incense thrown onto hot coals.

**Capricorn** In astrology, the sign of the zodiac for those born between 22 December and 20 January. An earth sign, ruled by **Saturn**, Capricorn is symbolized by a goat or by a goat with the tail of a fish. The source of the latter sign is the Babylonian god **Ea**, a deity associated with rivers and seas; but the characteristics ascribed by astrologers to the sign owe more to the goat than to the fish. A typical Capricorn is "sure-footed" and clear-headed – possibly too serious – and sets high personal standards. There is also an economy of style in the actions and pursuits of Capricorns, which sometimes makes them appear self-centred.

**Capstone** See Megaliths.

**Caput Draconis** In astrology, the dragon's head, the north node of the moon – the point where the moon crosses the ecliptic to begin its northward journey.

**Cardinal Signs** In astrology, the zodiac signs **Aries, Cancer, Libra**, and **Capricorn**, whose cusps coincide with the four cardinal points as follows: Aries (east); Cancer (north); Libra (west); and Capricorn (south).

**Cargo Cults** The name given to practices among native islanders, especially the Melanesians, based on the belief that ships and aircraft can be summoned magically to provide "cargo" – goods and money. The practice seems to be based on the native perception of the "white man's power", and that ideally roles should be reversed allowing western wealth and material possessions to be redistributed. For example, inhabitants of Vanuatu believe that a white leader named Jon Frum will arrive, bringing "cargo" in a huge scarlet aircraft, and will drive all other white people from the island, helping the native inhabitants regain control. They also believe an army is waiting in the crater of a volcano to help him. In the magical rituals designed to summon him, Jon Frum is carved in wood and painted red, alongside a representation of his aircraft.

**Carmen** Literally "song" (plural carmina). In ancient Rome, a positive spell or healing incantation.

**Carrefour** In voodoo, the crossroads. It also refers to the loa associated with the Bizango and Petro rites.

**Cartomancy** A form of divination by means of cards, for example Tarot cards or the Zener cards used by parapsychologist Professor J.B. Rhine in testing precognition.

**Case, Paul Foster** (1884–1954) An American occultist who made a detailed study of the Tarot and founded an occult centre known as the Builders of the Adytum (BOTA) in Los Angeles. Case claimed to be the American head of the Hermetic Order of the Golden Dawn and to have received "inner plane" teachings from the spiritual masters of that order. Case also believed in the rather fanciful idea that the Tarot had originated c. 1200CE, when a group of scholars from around the world are said to have met in Fez, Morocco, and synthesized the universal mystery teaching into the pictorial form of the Tarot. This eccentric viewpoint notwithstanding, Case produced one of the best books on the symbolism of the cards, *The Tarot, A Key to the Wisdom of the Ages*, and also a book of Tarot meditations titled *The Book of Tokens*.

**Castañeda, Carlos** (1925–1998) A Peruvian-born anthropologist and author, whose real name is thought to have been Carlos Arana. Castañeda studied at the University of California in Los Angeles, and claimed to make the acquaintance of an old Yaqui Indian named Don Juan Matus, who allowed him to become his apprentice in sorcery and magic. Castañeda experienced new types of perception after ingesting datura and psychedelic mushrooms, had visionary encounters with the peyote god Mescalito, and underwent astral transformations into the form of a crow. Castañeda's first book, *The Teachings of Don Juan*, was published by University of California Press in 1968 and became a counterculture classic. It was followed by a number of volumes detailing Castañeda's magical experiences with don Juan and other sorcerers, such as Don Genero and La Catalina. Castañeda's third book, *Journey to Ixtlan*, earned him a Ph.D.

Castañeda has not been without his critics, including the eminent anthropologist Weston La Barre, who has described Castañeda's writings as "pseudo-profound, deeply vulgar pseudo-ethnography", and the psychologist Richard de Mille, who believes Don Juan is a fiction. Some critics claim that Castañeda has amalgamated tales of other Indian shamans into his accounts. For example, there is a strong resemblance between magical attributes of the Huichol shaman Ramon Medina Silva and those of Don Genero in *A Separate Reality*. However, Castañeda kept a low public profile and, while maintaining that his magical writings were factually based, did not allow himself to become the focus of the debate surrounding their authenticity.

**Casting a Horoscope** In astrology, the act of making a horoscope by incorporating basic data of time, date of birth, location, and so forth. Horoscopes can be cast for the day (when the sun is above the horizon), or for the night (when the sun is below the horizon).

**Castle of the Interior Man** A mystical term for the seven stages of spiritual growth through which the soul ascends towards the Divinity. These are (1) prayer and concentration on God; (2) prayer directed at obtaining knowledge of the mystical significance of manifested reality; (3) self-renunciation, or the so-called "dark night of the soul"; (4) surrender to the will of God; (5) a state of union with the Divinity so that one's will and the will of God become one; (6) a state of ecstasy where the soul is filled with love and joy; and (7) the mystic marriage, or mystic union, with God in which the inner being enters heaven.

**Cat** Animal with strong occult and magical associations. In ancient Egypt, there were cat-headed goddesses (e.g. **Bast** and **Sekhmet**) associated with fertility and sexual power. In the Middle Ages, black cats were regarded as incarnations of the **Devil** and gave rise to much popular **superstition**. Cats are also said to be popular **familiars** of witches: the modern witch **Rosaleen Norton** believed that cats had more integrity and sensitivity than human beings, and she claimed a special psychic rapport with them.

**Cathars** See Albigenses.

**Catoptromancy** Divination by means of a mirror. The ancient Greeks placed mirrors under water, or held them in a fountain, and would carefully observe and interpret the reflections. See also **Magic Mirror**.

**Cauda Draconis** In astrology, the dragon's tail, the south node of the moon – the point where the moon crosses the ecliptic to begin its southward journey.

**Cauldron** Ancient magical symbol connoting transformation and germination. It is an image signifying new life, and has a strong association, like the **cup**, with the element **water**. Medieval witches were said to stir their magical concoctions in a cauldron, and it is also found as a symbol on the important **Tarot** card *Temperance* in the Crowley-Harris pack. Here it represents the fusion of opposites, harmony, and synthesis.

**Cavendish, Richard** (1930– ) A leading contemporary authority on **magic** and **witchcraft**, he was educated at Oxford University and has lectured widely. He was the editor of the encyclopedic series *Man, Myth and Magic* (1970– 1), which brought many international authorities on magic and mythology together for the first time.

Among his best-known books are *The Black Arts*; *Visions of Heaven and Hell*; and *Encyclopedia of the Unexplained*.

**Cedar Oil** An antiseptic oil widely used in ancient Egypt to produce sacred perfumes, magical cosmetics, and incenses, and also to embalm mummies. Associated with **Osiris**, the cedar tree was a symbol of cyclic rebirth.

**Celestial** Literally "heavenly", also used of anything divine or blessed. The word is used in the magical traditions to describe the "higher spheres" of consciousness and cosmic intelligence.

**Celestial Magic** See Magic, Celestial.

**Celts** Ancient peoples who spread throughout Europe, settling in Britain, Ireland and France (Gaul) as well as much of central and eastern Europe by the seventh century BCE. Their religion was essentially a fertility and nature cult in which certain animals (such as the pig, horse, bull, and bear) and natural features (such as trees and rivers) were sacred. Worship took place in open groves. The scholars and priests among the Celts were **Druids**, and this class produced the judges, bards, and magicians. After about the fourth century CE, traditional Celtic religious practice fell into abeyance and was generally replaced by Christianity. However, the main Celtic seasonal festivals (**Imbolc, Beltane, Lughnassadh,** and **Samhain**) all survive to this day in one form or another, whether in Christianized form (such as **Candlemas**); as folk festivals (see **May Eve; All Hallows' Eve**), or as Wiccan and neopagan revivals. Celtic influences also remain in many folklore customs, especially in areas where Celtic languages are still spoken (Breton, Gaelic, Irish, and Welsh) or have been revived (Cornish, Manx).

**Cen** In the Germanic Elder **Futhark** the rune letter representing the number six. Cen corresponds to the letter "k" and is associated with the image of the torch, the light of inspiration and initiation. Cen refers directly to guidance and illumination and is the rune of creativity and self-knowledge. Also Kenaz.

**Censer** In Wicca, an important ritual implement. The censer allows incense to be burned during the ritual, the scent conjuring an appropriate magical atmosphere for the work at hand. In magical rituals incense represents the element **air**. See also **Thurible**.

**Centaurs** In Greek myth, hostile creatures, half man and half horse, which dwelt in Thessaly and worshipped **Dionysus**. The most famous (and peaceful) centaur was Chiron. He taught people how to use medicinal plants and herbs and also gave instruction to many of the Greek heroes, including Achilles, Aeneas, and Jason.

**Central Column** In the Kabbalah, the so-called **Middle Pillar** on the **Tree of Life**.

**Cerberus** In Greek mythology, an awesome three-headed dog that guarded the entrance to **Hades**, in order to prevent anyone living from entering. In Greek legends the heroes Aeneas, **Orpheus**, and **Odysseus** succeeded in passing Cerberus and visiting the Underworld. Cerberus was the offspring of Typhon and Echidna.

**Ceremonial Magic** See Magic, Ceremonial.

**Ceremonialism, Animal** See Animal ceremonialism.

**Ceres** The Roman equivalent of **Demeter** and mother of Proserpina (**Persephone**). Ceres/Demeter was goddess of agriculture – the grain, harvest, and fertility of the earth – and was a central figure in the mystery teachings at Eleusis.

**Cernunnos** The name by which many modern witches refer to the **Horned God**. Cernunnos was a Celtic god depicted as having the head of a bull, a man's torso, the legs made of serpents, and the tail of a fish. He was lord of the wild animals. Also **Kernunnos**.

**Ceromancy** A form of **divination** by means of inspecting melted wax. In the Middle Ages, the magician would melt wax in a brass vessel and then pour it onto cold water in another container. The congealed wax globules would then be symbolically interpreted.

**Cerridwen** or **Ceridwen** In Wicca, a Welsh goddess name frequently used to represent the **Crone**, the third of the threefold aspects of the **Great Goddess**. The Crone represents old age and wisdom. In the Celtic tradition, Cerridwen prepares the **cauldron** of knowledge from which the poet Taliesin drinks. Also Keridwen.

**Cervus Fugitivus** In alchemy, the "fleeing hart", or male deer – a reference to the elusive nature of **Mercurius**, the spirit of **philosophical mercury**.

**Ch'wl** See Cheval.

**Chabad** A mystical system developed by Rabbi Schneur Zalman (1747–1812) which influenced Hasidic thought. The term itself derives from the first letters of three emanations on the kabbalistic **Tree of Life**: Chokmah (wisdom), **Binah** (understanding), and **Daath** (knowledge). See also **Hasidism**.

**Cha-cha** In voodoo, a gourd rattle filled with seeds, used for percussion during dances.

**Chakra** In Kundalini yoga one of several spiritual energy centres that align with the central nervous column, sushumna. The yogi learns to arouse the kundalini energy through the chakras from the base of the spine to the crown of the forehead. The chakras, from lowest to highest, are **muladhara** (located at the perineum); **svadhisthana** (near the genitals); **manipura** (solar plexus); **anahata** (heart); **vishuddha** (throat); **ajna** (between the eyebrows); and **sahasrara** (crown of the head). The literal meaning of the Sanskrit word *chakra* is "wheel", but the symbolism implies a spiritual centre in the human body; the chakras do not correspond literally to any organ, and are mystical rather than biological in nature. Many magicians correlate the chakras on **sushumna** with the **sephiroth** on the kabbalistic **Tree of Life**. See also **Middle Pillar; Khu.**

**Chaldean Oracles** Oracles and mystical sayings allegedly deriving from the Chaldean **Magi** and **Zarathustra** (Zoroaster), but transcribed and translated by the Neoplatonists. Commentaries on the oracles were written by Psellus, Pletho, Iamblichus, and Porphyry. The oracles have much in common with **Gnosticism**. See also **Neoplatonism.**

**Chalice** In Wicca, a drinking vessel, usually without handles, consisting of a bowl, stem, and base. The chalice represents the element **water** and is used in Wiccan ritual to contain wine that has been blessed by the goddess and god before being consumed as a ceremonial blessing. The chalice may also be used ritually in the Great Rite which forms part of the **Third Initiation**. Together with the **pentacle**, which represents the element **earth**, the chalice represents the female polarity in ritual workings.

**Chalices** See Cups.

**Chamomile** Also camomile. There are several different varieties of chamomile, a plant known and valued for centuries for its medicinal qualities and mythic associations. Renowned for its excellent anti-inflammatory qualities, chamomile can be used to treat skin conditions, chronic gastritis, colitis and cystitis as well as certain kinds of asthma. In ancient Egypt chamomile was

considered a sacred flower and was used as an offering to the sun god **Ra**. Some Germanic tribes dedicated chamomile to their sun god **Baldur**, while in Prussia wreaths of chamomile were hung in houses as a **charm** to protect the occupants from lightning and thunder.

**Chams** An Indochinese ethnic group in Thailand and Cambodia famous for their sorceresses. The magical initiation rites involve cutting a cockerel into two halves and dancing with it, while uttering magical incantations. The Chams believe that the magical spells can transform the dead bird into a live crow, confirming that the initiation is successful. Cham sorceresses have an extensive knowledge of ritual spells for propitiating evil spirits. They also interpret omens favourable to harvesting the rice crop and other agricultural produce. See also **Incantation; Spell.**

**Changeling** A deformed or ugly child said to have been left by the **fairies** as a substitute for a healthy, attractive one. According to legend, the fairies could only snatch a baby away before it was christened. Changelings were often thought to be senile fairies disguised as infants; in comparatively recent times, both children and adults have been accused of being changelings and put to death. In 1894, a young woman living near Clonmel in Ireland was accused by her husband and family of being a changeling and was burned alive.

**Changing Woman** A popular Navajo deity. She was the consort of the sun and the mother of twin offspring, Monster Slayer and Child of the Water, who slew the monsters that threatened humanity.

**Changó** In Santería, the god of fire, thunder and lightning and the ruler of human passions. He is one of the fourteen children of **Yeramayá**. See **Oddudúa**. Compare **Xangó.**

**Chankpana** In Santería, the god of smallpox – flies and mosquitoes are his messengers. Compare the **Macumba** deity **Shapanan.**

**Channelling** A spiritual practice in which a person opens their awareness to inner-plane communications from a discarnate being, spirit helper, or guide. The person who is channelling serves as an intermediary during this process and is temporarily possessed by the other being or entity. Messages may be transmitted to others present, but here the voice heard will be that of the possessing entity. The channeller is unaware of the messages that are being communicated and only learns of them from others, after returning to a state of full waking consciousness. See also **Oracle; Medium.**

**Chanting** The rhythmic repetition of sacred words, sounds, or phrases either in conjuction with meditation or sacred dancing. In a magical context, chanting is intended to raise power and energy and transport the practitioner into an altered state of awareness. An excellent example of magical chanting in contemporary **Wicca** is the well known **Witch's Rune** which is accompanied by a ring dance in the **deosil** direction. This chant commences with the lines *Eko, Eko, Azarak, Eko, Eko, Zomelak* and is used by both **Gardnerian** and **Alexandrian** witches. It was written jointly by **Gerald Gardner** and **Doreen Valiente.** See also Circle.

**Chaos** (1) In Greek mythology, a deity, one of the oldest of the gods and father of **Erebus,** god of darkness.

**Chaos** (2) In **cosmology,** the amorphous mass that existed prior to the creation of the universe. Because there was no light, chaos could not be perceived. In **alchemy,** chaos was the formless and shapeless matter from which both the world and the **Philosopher's Stone** were thought to have been formed. Chaos contains all things without division. One of the central tasks of the alchemist was to differentiate chaos into the four **elements** – earth, air, fire and water – so that the work could proceed.

**Chaos Magic** A contemporary branch of magic which draws on the cosmology of **Austin Osman Spare** and his use of magical sigils to focus the magical will. Chaos magic has been described as "success magic" or "results-based magic" and grew out of a concern among some within the magical fraternity who believed that magic had drifted too closely towards meditation and celebration and away from specific results. Leading figures associated with Chaos magic include Peter J. Carroll, author of *Liber Null* and *Psychonaut,* Frater U.D., author of *Practical Sigil Magic* and Ray Sherwin, author of *The Book of Results.* See also **Sigil** (2).

**Character** See Sigil (2).

**Charge** In voodoo, magical power which enables the individual to achieve unusual results.

**Charge of the God** In Wicca, the words spoken by the high priest who performs the ceremonial act of **Drawing Down the Sun.** Because the high priest embodies the **Horned God** it is effectively the god himself whose words are spoken.

**Charge of the Goddess** In Wicca, the address by the high priestess to members of her coven. It follows the ceremonial act of **Drawing Down the Moon** in the opening ritual. Because the high priestess now embodies the goddess, it is really the goddess herself who speaks directly to her followers.

***Charioteer, The*** In the Tarot, a card in the **Major Arcana** that depicts the Charioteer riding through his kingdom and surveying the positive and negative aspects of the world around him. Occultists regard *The Charioteer* as the warrior-like aspect of the male archetype and the destructive face of the Great Father. He is the antithesis of the peaceful qualities symbolized by *The Emperor*. In western **magic**, which combines the Tarot paths of the Major Arcana with the ten **sephiroth** on the **Tree of Life**, the path of *The Charioteer* connects **Geburah** and **Binah**.

**Chariot, Heavenly** In the Jewish mystical tradition, the divine throne moving through heaven, described in the first chapter of *The Book of Ezekiel* in the Bible. It is sometimes referred to as the **Supernal Chariot**. See also Merkabah.

**Chariot of Phaethon** In alchemy, a name given to the **opus alchymicum** or **opus circulatorium** – the repeated process of dissolutions and coagulations which occurs as the base metal or matter is dissolved into the **prima materia** and then coagulated into a newer, purer form. This process was sometimes compared to wheels coursing through the heavens in the form of a sun chariot. In Greek mythology, Phaethon, or Phaeton, drove the sun chariot recklessly close to the earth and was destroyed by Zeus before he could do more harm. Phaeton's death became a symbol of mortification or **nigredo** – one of the key stages in the alchemical process.

**Charm** In magic, an incantation or object believed to have special supernatural power. The word derives from the Latin *carmen*, meaning "song". Compare **Talisman**.

**Charon** In Greek mythology, the boatman who ferried the souls of the dead across the Rivers of Death (**Acheron, Styx**). It was customary for the living to pay for Charon's services by placing a silver coin beneath the tongue of the corpse at the time of burial. The Greeks believed that a proper funeral was necessary before a spirit could be ferried across to the infernal regions. However, some of the Greek heroes managed to deceive Charon. **Orpheus**, for example, charmed him with his lyre, and Aeneas bribed him with the Golden Bough. **Odysseus** also passed by him and was able to converse with the ghosts of dead heroes in the **Underworld**.

**Chaste Moon** See Esbats.

**Chax** See Shax.

**Chayot** A Hebrew term for the "lightning flash" described by Ezekiel. It is commonly used by the **Merkabah** mystics to describe states of spiritual ecstasy. See also **Hayyoth**.

**Chayot ha-Qadesh** In the Jewish mystical tradition, the "Holy Living Creatures" described in chapter one of *The Book of Ezekiel* – Bull, Lion, Eagle, and Man.

**Chelidonius** A magical stone, said to be taken from the body of a swallow. A cure for melancholy and fever.

**Chemic** or Chymick In alchemy, a term used from the sixteenth to eighteenth centuries to denote an alchemist or to refer to matters alchemical.

**Chemical Wedding** In alchemy, the joining (coniunctio) of the male elements **fire** and **air** (represented by **sulphur**) and the female elements **water** and **earth** (represented by **argent vive** or quicksilver) in **philosophical mercury** – symbolized by gold (**King Sol**) and silver (**Queen Luna**) respectively – in the final phase of the magical opus. This is the fusion of opposites which produces the **Philosopher's Stone**.

**Cherub** Plural cherubim, cherubs. In Jewish and Christian tradition, a winged angel with a human head, probably descended from Mesopotamian depictions of winged creatures with animal bodies. In the Bible, cherubim are angels of light, who, according to *The Book of Revelation*, perpetually sing: "Holy, Holy, Holy, Lord God Almighty, who was, and is, and is to come." There are four of them around the heavenly throne – one like a man, one like a lion, one like an eagle, and one like an ox –

and each has six wings. In western art the cherub came to be represented as a beautiful winged infant.

**Chesed** In the Kabbalah, the fourth mystical emanation on the **Tree of Life**. Occultists identify Chesed as the ruler (but not creator) of the manifested universe; and he is characterized as stable, wise, and merciful by contrast with his more dynamic and destructive opposite, **Geburah**. By the process of **magical correspondences**, Chesed is associated with the Greek god **Zeus** and the Roman **Jupiter**. Also known as Hesed.

**Cheth** The Hebrew letter ascribed to the path linking **Geburah** and **Binah** on the **Tree of Life**. Cheth has a numerical value of eight. In modern magical visualization and **pathworkings** the Tarot card associated with this path on the Tree is *The Charioteer*. Also known as Het.

**Cheval** In voodoo, the horse, and, by extension, the person "mounted" by the spirit-deities for the journey into **trance**. The term therefore refers to voodoo possession. Also known as Ch'wl.

**Chimera** In Greek mythology, a fire-breathing monster combining the front of a lion, the body and head of a goat, and the head and tail of a serpent. The chimera was slain by Bellerophon riding on the winged horse **Pegasus**.

**Chirer Ayizan** In voodoo, a protection and purification ceremony which involves the shredding of palm leaves. It is performed under the patronage of Ayizan, the **loa** of the marketplace and partner of **Loco**.

**Chokmah** In the Kabbalah, the second mystical emanation of the **Tree of Life** following **Kether**. Occultists identify

**CHEMICAL MARRIAGE** Alchemical depiction of the 'chemical marriage' of King Sol and Queen Luna – the conjunction of opposites.

Chokmah with the Great Father, the giver of the seminal spark of life which is potent only until it enters the womb of the Great Mother, **Binah**. From the union of the Great Father and the Great Mother come forth all the images of creation. By the process of **magical correspondences**, Chokmah is associated with such deities as **Kronos, Saturn, Thoth,** Atum-Ra, and Ptah, in other pantheons. Also known as Hokmah.

**Choronzon** In Enochian magic, the demon of chaos and guardian of the **Abyss**. Aleister Crowley described him as "the first and deadliest of all the powers of evil". This point notwithstanding, Crowley invoked Choronzon while experimenting with the so-called 30 **Aethyrs** in a magical ritual on the top of an Algerian mountain in December 1909.

**Christian, Paul** (1811–1877) The pseudonym of J.-B. Pitois, a French occultist whose writings blend astrology, **Kabbalah, Tarot,** and **spiritualism**. His best known work is *A History of Magic* (1870).

**Chthonian** From the Greek *chthon*, "earth", deities or spirits from the earth or **Underworld**, often associated with the souls of the dead.

**Church of All Worlds** See Zell, Otter; Zell, Morning Glory.

**Church of Satan** Founded in 1966 by occultist **Anton La Vey**, the Church of Satan was located on California Street in San Francisco, and claimed an affiliated membership of 7,000 supporters. It encouraged the development of the animal instincts, self-indulgence, and free sexuality, and included in its rituals a satanic "mass". Male and female participants in the ritual wore black robes, with the exception of a naked woman who volunteered to be the "altar" during the ceremony. La Vey made invocations to **Lucifer, Belial,** and **Leviathan;** drank from a chalice which was then placed on the "altar"; and encouraged the congre-

gation to focus their mental energies on achieving their secret desires. The ritual ended with satanic hymns accompanied by an electric organ. The Church fragmented in 1975 with the establishment of the **Temple of Set,** and following the death of Anton La Vey in 1997 it now has a greatly reduced membership.

**Church of Wicca** The oldest recognized church of **witchcraft** in the United States, founded by Gavin and Yvonne Frost in 1965. The Church of Wicca gained federal recognition in 1972 and is located in New Bern, North Carolina. Gavin Frost was born in Staffordshire, England, in 1930, spent much of his childhood in Wales, worked for an aerospace company in Wiltshire and subsequently became fascinated with the megaliths at Stonehenge. Intrigued by Celtic traditions, he was then drawn into the **Craft**. Yvonne Wilson (later Frost) was born in Los Angeles in 1931, grew up in a Baptist family, trained as a secretary, and met Gavin Frost at the company where they were both employed, in Anaheim, California, in the 1960s. They later moved to St Louis, pursued the Craft together, and were initiated into the Celtic tradition. They married in 1970 and have authored several books together, including the *Witch's Magical Handbook* and the *Magic Power of White Witchcraft*. The Frosts are practising witches but do not consider themselves pagans. Their church supports the **Wiccan Rede** and a belief in **reincarnation**. It also supports the "law of attraction" ("What I do to other living creatures I will draw to myself") and the principles of gaining power through knowledge and living in harmony with natural rhythms and cycles. The church also runs the highly successful School of Wicca, which teaches Celtic **magic, sorcery, astrology, herbalism,** spellcraft and many other related subjects.

**Churingas** Among the Australian Aborigines, oval stones or pieces of wood bearing sacred inscriptions. They were not to be seen by women or uninitiated men, and were linked to animal totems.

**Chymia** In alchemy, a name for the alchemist's vessel and also for alchemy itself. Also Kemia.

**Chymick** See Chemic.

**Cicatrization** Literally, the act of producing a scar (Latin: *cicatrix*) on the body; but in many pre-literate societies a form of decorative embellishment on the skin associated with magical and religious beliefs.

**Cimejes** See Cimeries.

**Cimeries** In the Goetia, the 66th spirit, a powerful marquis who appears in the form of a valiant warrior riding an impressive black horse. He rules over all spirits in Africa and also teaches perfect grammar, logic, and rhetoric. In addition he can locate hidden treasure and items that have been lost. Cimeries rules over 20 legions of spirits and is also known as Cimejes or Kimaris.

**Circe** In Greek mythology, a sorceress banished to the island of Aeaea after poisoning her husband. She lived in a palace surrounded by woods and had magical spells that enabled her to transform men into wild beasts. Circe would attract men to her domain by beautiful singing. In *The Odyssey*, When Odysseus and his men landed on her island some of the band, headed by Eurylochus, were invited to dine with her. Eurylochus feared a trap, but many of the men accepted the invitation and dined with her, drinking wine that was drugged. Circe used her magic to turn them into hogs and Eurylochus hastily reported to Odysseus what had happened. The god Hermes gave him a herb called moly to counteract Circe's magic, and Odysseus was able to force the sorceress to change the hogs back into their original human form. In due course, Circe became an important ally of Odysseus and gave him valuable advice on how to descend into Hades, encounter ghosts, and avoid the snare of the Sirens.

**Circle** In world mythology, a symbol of totality and wholeness; and in western magic, an important symbol used in ceremonial workings within the temple. In the **Hermetic Order of the Golden Dawn**, the circle is inscribed on the floor of the temple and represents the infinite **godhead** and divine self-knowledge to which the magician aspires. **God names** are inscribed around the periphery and the magician traces the circle with a ritual sword as part of the ceremonial procedure. The circle may be circumscribed by an equal-sided geometrical figure whose number of sides corresponds with the sephirah associated with the god (e.g. a **hexagram** in a **Tiphareth** ritual invoking Osiris – Tiphareth is the sixth sephirah on the **Tree of Life** and is linked to gods of rebirth). See also **Sephiroth**.

**Circle Sanctuary** See Fox, Selena.

**Circumambulation** In ritual magic procedure, walking around an object or person three times in succession.

**Citrinitas** In alchemy, the third, or yellow, stage of the **opus alchymicum,** represented by the symbol of a golden flower, e.g. a golden rose.

**Clavicle** From the Latin *clavis* meaning "a key", the mystical key to "unlocking" an occult secret. Examples of clavicles from occult literature and **grimoires** include the medieval grimoire known as *The Key of Solomon* (*Clavicula Solomonis*) and **Eliphas Lévi's** *The Key of the Mysteries* (*La Cléf des Grandes Mystères*). See also **Arcane**.

**Clear Mirror** In the Kabbalah, a term for unmediated and direct communication with the divine on the **Middle Pillar** of the **Tree of Life.**

**Cloven Foot** Also, cloven hoof. The mark of the **Devil**, based on the superstition that the Devil, as an imperfect being, always exhibits a sign of his bestiality as a distinguishing mark.

**Clover** In its three-leafed form, a symbol of the Trinity and a Christian protection against witchcraft and the forces of evil. See also **Oxalis; Shamrock.**

**Clutterbuck, Dorothy** (1880–1951) The daughter of an officer in the British Indian army, Dorothy Clutterbuck – otherwise known as "Old Dorothy" – was the high priestess who initiated **Gerald Gardner** into Wicca. Her magical name was Daffo or Dafo. See also **Fellowship of Crotona, New Forest Coven.**

**Clymer, Reuben Swinburne** An American occultist who claimed to succeed **Pascal B. Randolph** as a magical adept and who headed a number of allegedly **Rosicrucian** organizations in the United States. These included the Sons of Isis and Osiris, the College of the Holy Grail, the Church of the Illumination, and the Rosicrucian Fraternity. Among Clymer's main books are *A Compendium of Occult Laws*, *The Rosicrucian Fraternity in America*, and *Mysteries of Osiris*.

**Coagulation** In alchemy, the act of converting or "crystallizing" a liquid into a solid form. Also known as congelation.

**Cochinada** In Peru, witchcraft potions made from the offal of vultures and river snakes. They are used to inflict bad luck or illness upon one's enemies.

**Cock and Hen** In alchemy, names given to **King Sol** and **Queen Luna** in the early phase of the alchemical work when they are portrayed as quarrelling copulators like beasts or birds, rather than as the noble lovers they later become.

**Cockatrice** See Basilisk.

**Coelus** In Roman mythology, the god who personified the "overhanging

heavens" (Latin *coelus*), the equivalent of the Greek Uranus.

**Coffin Texts** In ancient Egypt, inscriptions on the sides of coffins assuring the deceased that they would be sustained with good food and drink and confirming the immortality of the soul. The Coffin Texts were the successors of the earlier Pyramid Texts, which included spells and incantations for the safe passage of the pharaohs to the next world. The Coffin Texts extended these benefits beyond the exclusive domain of the pharaohs, to the Egyptian nobility. See also *Egyptian Book of the Dead, The.*

**Cohoba** A hallucinogenic snuff, made from the beans of *Anadenanthera colubrina* and *peregrina* (also known as yopo, vilca, and huilca). It was used by the pre-Colonial Incas to obtain a visionary hypnotic state and remains in use among the Mashco Indians of northern Argentina. Its use in the West Indies has died out. See also **Hallucination.**

**Coll** In the Celtic tree alphabet, the **ogham** representing the hazel and the letter "c". Coll is also linked to the crane and the colour tawny.

**Collective Unconscious** A concept proposed by psychologist **Carl Gustav Jung**, who believed that certain primordial images in the unconscious mind were not individual in origin, but "collective" – being symbolic expressions of the "constantly repeated experiences of humanity". In Jung's view, these collective images were mostly religious motifs, acknowledged almost universally as significant. An example would be the mythic image of the sun, represented in numerous legends as the sun-hero and worshipped in Greece as **Apollo**, in Egypt as **Ra**, and in ancient Persia as Ohrmazd.

**Collegium ad Spiritum Sanctum** See Abbey of Thelema.

**Co-Masonry** Also Adoptive Masonry. A term used in **Freemasonry** to allow for the admission and initiation of women. Traditionally, women were not allowed into the Order of Freemasons; but historically there have been exceptions. Count Cagliostro admitted women in the so-called Egyptian rite and the Duchess of Bourbon presided as grand mistress in the Grand Orient of France lodge (1775); the Rite of Mizraim established Masonic lodges for both men and women as early as 1819. In authentic Co-Masonic orders, the rites have the same structure as in orthodox Freemasonry and men and women hold corresponding ranks.

**Commanding Signs** In astrology, the signs **Aries, Taurus, Gemini, Cancer, Leo,** and **Virgo,** which are said to be "powerful" because of their proximity to the zenith.

**Compact** In satanism, an agreement by which a person renounces Christ, the apostles, the saints, and all Christian values, in order to follow **Lucifer** and his cohorts. In return, Lucifer bestows upon his followers worldly possessions or special powers. In an example that survives from the events associated with the **Aix-en-Provence nuns**, Father Louis Gaufridi offered himself to the **Devil** and allegedly received the following benefit: "I, Lucifer, bind myself to give you, Louis Gaufridi, priest, the faculty and power of bewitching by blowing with the mouth, all and any of the women and girls you may desire." Unfortunately, the compact was short-lived. Gaufridi was accused of sorcery and publicly burned at Aix in 1611.

**Condition of Fire** For the poet and ceremonial magician **William Butler Yeats**, a term used to denote the visionary source of creativity and inspiration. In his work *Per Amica Silentia Lunae* (1917) Yeats employed imagery derived from the kabbalistic **Tree of Life**, describing how the "Condition of Fire" gave rise to an inspirational **daimon** which coursed in a creative lightning path down the Tree into the psyche of the artist.

**Cone of Power** In Wicca, the ritual act of visualizing a "cone of energy" and directing it towards whatever goal or task is at hand. Witches with psychic vision claim it is perceived as a silver-blue light that rises from the **magic circle** in a spiral.

**Congelation** See Coagulation (Alchemy).

**Coniunctio** See **Chemical Wedding.**

**Conjunction** (1) In astrology, the situation when two planets occupy the same degree position on a **horoscope.**

**Conjunction** (2) In Neoplatonic magic, the act of invoking a number of gods collectively, or "in conjunction". According to Psellus, Julian the Chaldean summoned Aion, **Apollo,** and **Hecate** simultaneously in certain magical rites. See also **Neoplatonism.**

**Conjuration** The act of evoking **spirits** by means of ritual formulae or **words of power.** In ceremonial magic, these spirits are directed to manifest within a triangle inscribed on the floor of the Temple (the triangle being a symbol of manifestation). Usually incense, or smoke, or some other "manifesting medium" is provided so that the spirits can be conjured to visible appearance rather than remain unmanifested on the **astral plane.**

**Consecration** In Wicca and **ritual magic,** a ceremonial procedure which reinforces the perception that a ritual implement, object or space is both special and sacred.

**Constant, Alphonse Louis** See Lévi, Eliphas.

**Contagious Magic** See Magic, Contagious.

**Copal** A generic term for tree resins used to produce **incense**. The word is derived from the Aztec word *copall*. For the Aztecs, copal smoke was believed to provide a bridge to the gods, thus linking heaven and humanity.

**Coppell** See Cupel.

**Cord Magic** See Cords, Ritual.

**Cordovero, Moses** (1522–1570) A kabbalist of Spanish descent who lived in Safed, Palestine, and was a teacher of **Isaac Luria**. Drawing on the *Zohar*, Cordovero maintained that God was the transcendent First Cause and that the **sephiroth** of the **Tree of Life** were the instruments by which he gave life to the world. Cordovero's interpretation of the **Kabbalah** tends towards pantheism. His two main books are *Pardes Rimmonium* (Cracow, 1592) and *Elimah Rabbati* (Lvov, 1881).

**Cords, Ritual** In Wicca, cords of different colours are used in "binding" ceremonies. Often made of silk, and traditionally nine feet long, the cords have different symbolic applications according to their colour. White cords are used for ceremonies involving innocence and purity, red cords represent fire and vitality, and blue cords are used for healing and justice and to represent the sky goddess.

**Corn Dolly** In England, Scotland, and Germany, a human figure or animal shape fashioned from the last sheaf of corn from the harvest. It is kept to ensure that the next year's harvest will be bountiful, and undoubtedly represents a folklore custom based on fertility worship.

**Corn King** See John Barleycorn.

**Cornucopia** The "Horn of Plenty", a horn overflowing with flowers, fruit, and produce, symbolizing prosperity and abundance. It is named after the goat Amalthea, which suckled the infant Zeus.

**Corpus Hermeticum** See *Hermetica, The;* Hermes Trismegistus.

**Corruption** In alchemy, a term for **putrefaction**. See also **Nigredo**.

**Corybantes** Priests of the goddess Cybele, who performed Phrygian mysteries. The rites were characterized by orgies and self-mutilation. The cult spread to Greece, Rome, and Crete.

**Cosmic** Of or pertaining to the universe (Greek *kosmos*). The **Rosicrucians** define cosmos as "the divine, infinite intelligence of the supreme being, permeating everything, the creative forces of God".

**Cosmic Epochs** In astrology, the division of time into periods of approximately 2,000 years represented by different signs of the **zodiac**. The Age of **Pisces** is symbolically linked to Christ, the fish being a well-known motif of the early Christians; and the next epoch will be the **Aquarian Age**. Astrologers differ on when this epoch will commence. Some maintain that it began in 1948, others that it will not begin until c. 2400CE. The epoch takes its name from the constellation in which the sun appears at the spring equinox.

**Cosmic Mind** An occult and mystical term for "universal mind", or the "mind of God". Sometimes equated with cosmic consciousness, or mystical transcendence.

**Cosmic Picture Gallery** A colloquial occult term for the so-called **Akashic Records**, the astral memory of all events that have taken place in the world.

**Cosmogony** From the Greek *kosmos*, "the universe", a theory describing the origin and creation of the universe and its inhabitants.

**Cosmology** From the Greek *kosmos*, "the universe", the study of the universe and its perceived attributes, including space, time, change, and eternity. In mystical and esoteric literature, it is often used to denote the study of gods and goddesses, the process of creation, and speculations about the nature of ultimate reality. See also **Cosmogony; Magical Correspondences; Myth.**

**Council of American Witches** A **witchcraft** group based in St Paul, Minnesota, which practises rites celebrating the rhythms of life and nature, marked by the phases of the moon and the four seasons. Members value the symbolic power of sexuality and the special role of witchcraft in interpreting the laws of nature. The council has as its chairman Carl Weschke, an occult publisher and practitioner, who was initiated by the witch Lady Sheba.

**Counter-Charm** A magical **charm** used to negate the effect of another charm.

**Coup** In **voodoo**, a magical **spell**. See following entries

**Coup l'Aire** In **voodoo**, an "air spell" – one intended to cause misfortune or illness.

**Coup n'Ame** In **voodoo**, a "soul spell" – one intended to capture the individuality, character, and willpower of another person.

**Coup Poudre** In **voodoo**, a "powder spell" – one which utilizes magical powder to cause illness and sometimes death.

**Court de Gébelin, Antoine** (1725–1784) A French theologian and linguist who believed that the **Tarot** originated in ancient Egypt and formed part of an initiatory procedure associated with the worship of **Thoth.** Knowledge of these esoteric symbols was acquired by the gypsies and disseminated throughout Europe. Court de Gébelin's view expressed in his mammoth nine-volume work *Le Monde Primitif* (1775–1784), was typical of the romantic

obsession with lost cultures prevalent in the eighteenth century.

**Coven** A group of witches who gather together to perform ceremonies at **esbats** and **sabbats.** Traditionally, the number of members in a coven has been assumed to total thirteen. The earliest known reference to this is the claim of Isobel Gowdie in 1662 that the Auldearne witches had "thirteen persons in each coven". The famous scholar of **witchcraft, Margaret Murray,** reinforced the idea that a coven consists of twelve members plus a leader masquerading as the **Horned God,** but this is incorrect. Modern covens do not exceed thirteen members in total, but groups of witches may gather in various numbers according to the nature of the rituals to be performed. See also **Sabbats, Greater** and **Sabbats, Lesser; Wicca.**

**Coven Crystalglade** See De Angeles, Ly.

**Covenant of the Goddess** See Curott, Phyllis.

**Covenstead** In Wicca, the coven's regular meeting place.

**Cowan** In Wicca, a person who has not yet been initiated. Cowans are not allowed to attend magical circles or esbats – meetings where magical work is undertaken – although they are sometimes allowed to attend sabbats. See also **Sabbats, Greater** and **Sabbats, Lesser.**

**Coyote** The prairie wolf, a mythic culture **hero** and trickster among many Native American peoples.

**Crab** A creature depicted as the fourth sign of the **zodiac, Cancer.** The crab is often regarded as a dualistic symbol, because it is equally at home in the sea and on land. It is also shown in an "evolutionary" capacity on the **Tarot** trump of *The Moon.*

**Craft Name** In Wicca, the new magical name taken by a witch following initiation into the **Craft**. Some practitioners have both secret and public Craft names.

**Craft of the Wise** See Craft, The.

**Craft, The** In Wicca, a popular general term used to describe the various traditions of modern witchcraft. The expression "Craft of the Wise" is a variant.

**Creative Visualization** A technique of visualization which utilizes mental imagery in order to achieve specific goals or outcomes. Creative visualization is a central aspect of practical magic, where specific outcomes are sought in a ceremonial or ritual setting.

**Crescent** The shape of the waxing moon, symbolic of fertility and abundant growth. It is often depicted as an emblem on the heads of **lunar goddesses** and other lunar deities.

**Crimson Emptiness** See Mauve Zone.

**Crocell** See Procel.

**Cromaat** A salutation used in rituals of the **Rosicrucians**, deriving from the Egyptian word *maat*, "truth". In the Hall of Maat, in the Egyptian Underworld, the soul of the deceased was weighed against the "feather of truth" and the goddess **Maat** presided over this judgment.

**Cromlech** A circle of large, vertical stones associated with Celtic sunworship. Sometimes the circle surrounds one or more **dolmens**. See Megaliths.

**Cromlech Temple** An occult group founded in Britain during the period following the fragmentation of the **Hermetic Order of the Golden Dawn** c.1903. Cromlech Temple members were interested in esoteric interpretations of Christianity. The group did not practise ceremonial magic and insisted that all members proceeding beyond the first grade of initiation believe in the Christian faith. It encouraged those seeking practical magical techniques to join a later incarnation of the **Hermetic Order of the Golden Dawn** known as the **Stella Matutina**, but remained in itself sufficiently Christian to attract a number of Anglo-Catholic clergymen. See also **Brodie-Innes, John William.**

**Crone** In Wicca, the third of the threefold aspects of the **Great Goddess**. The Crone represents old age and wisdom. The two other aspects of the Great Goddess are the **Maid** (representing youth and enchantment) and the **Mother** (representing maturity and fulfilment). These phases of womanhood are particularly important in the "women's mysteries" of feminist Wicca groups.

**Cronus** See Kronos.

**Crosslet** or Croslet In alchemy, a crucible. See also **Cupel.**

**Crossroads** In ancient times crossroads were associated with **Hermes** (the god of travellers, transfer, exchange, and transformation) and were marked by herms, busts of the god. **Hecate**, who resided in the underworld, would sometimes appear on earth at night time, especially at crossroads, accompanied by baying hounds. In medieval witchcraft, a traditional meeting place. Probably as a result of the fear of persecution, crossroads were popular as places where witches could scatter quickly if apprehended.

**Crow** See Crow's Beak; Crow's Head.

**Crow's Beak** In alchemy, the neck of the **alembic**, the beaked vessel used as the upper part of the distillation apparatus.

**Crow's Head** In alchemy, a symbol of the first stage of the alchemical work, the stage of dissolution or "death" known as the **nigredo**. The Crow's Head was also referred to as the "Crow's Bill".

ALEISTER CROWLEY  A self-portrait by the famous – and infamous – ceremonial magician, Aleister Crowley. Note the phallic aspects of his signature – a reflection of his all-absorbing fascination with sex magic
(courtesy of Kenneth Grant).

**Crowley, Aleister** (1875–1947)
Probably the most famous – and notorious – occultist of the 20th century, Aleister Crowley was born at Leamington Spa in Warwickshire, England, on 12 October 1875, and raised in a fundamentalist Plymouth Brethren home. His father was a prosperous brewer who had retired to Leamington to study the Christian scriptures. Crowley came to despise the Plymouth Brethren, primarily on the basis of his unfortunate experiences at the special sect school in Cambridge which he was obliged to attend. But after he went up to Trinity College, Cambridge, in 1895 he was able to spend much of his time reading poetry and classical literature as well as confirming his reputation as a champion chess player. Crowley had an adventurous spirit and would later become an enthusiastic mountaineer, joining an expedition in 1902 to scale the mountain known as Chogo Ri ( Mount Godwin-Austin, also referred to as K2) – at the time the highest peak in the world open to European climbers.

Crowley's direct association with the

western esoteric tradition began in London in 1898 with his introduction to George Cecil Jones, a member of the **Hermetic Order of the Golden Dawn**. By the following year Crowley had also become a close friend of magical initiate **Allan Bennett**, who for a time rivalled **MacGregor Mathers** as a dominant figure among the English occultists of the period. Within the Golden Dawn, Bennett took the magical name *Frater Iehi Aour* ("Let there be Light") and he became something of a guru figure for the young Crowley. Bennett tutored Crowley in the diverse paths of magic – teaching him applied **Kabbalah** and the techniques of magical invocation and evocation, as well as showing him how to create magical talismans.

Crowley quickly grasped the fundamentals of magic – or magick, as he would later spell it in his own writings on the subject. In one of his most influential books – *Magick in Theory and Practice*, privately published in 1929 and frequently reprinted since – Crowley outlined the basic philosophy of magic as he had come to see it: essentially as a process of making man god-like, both in vision and in power. As Crowley wrote: "The microcosm is an exact image of the macrocosm; the Great Work is the raising of the whole man in perfect balance to the power of infinity."

Crowley was initiated as a **Neophyte** in the Golden Dawn on 18 November 1898. He soon came to appreciate that those with the loftiest ritual grades were able to wield profound spiritual influence over their followers while also claiming rapport with the **Secret Chiefs** whose authority emanated from higher planes of existence. Keen to ascend to as high a rank as possible, Crowley took the grade of **Zelator** and then those of **Theoricus** and **Practicus** in the following two months. Initiation into the grade of **Philosophus** followed in May 1899, and he also became the first of the Golden Dawn magicians to attempt the fifteenth-century rituals of Abra-Melin the Mage. Having attained the grade of Philosophus within the Golden Dawn,

Crowley contacted MacGregor Mathers, who was then based in Paris, and asked for ritual entry into the Second Order – the **Red Rose and the Cross of Gold**.

In January 1900, under Mathers' supervision, Crowley was admitted "to the Glory of Tiphareth" – the archetype of spiritual rebirth – and then returned to England. There, he challenged the authority of **William Butler Yeats**, who was now the leader of the Golden Dawn in England. Yeats was unimpressed by this effrontery, regarding Crowley as an "unspeakable mad person", and Crowley was unsuccessful in his bid for ritual supremacy. The dispute, however, caused a rift in loyalties among the Golden Dawn membership since Crowley had been sent by Mathers – and Mathers had claimed a spiritual autocracy and infallibility over the Order as his right. Nevertheless, having failed to dislodge Yeats as the head of the Golden Dawn, Crowley now suddenly switched course. Unpredictably, and apparently acting on pure impulse, he withdrew from the dispute altogether and in June 1900 embarked upon a series of travels through Mexico, the United States, Ceylon, and India before finally arriving in Cairo – a location which would facilitate the announcement of a completely new magical conception.

On 17 March 1904, in his apartment in Cairo, Crowley performed a magical ceremony invoking the Egyptian deity **Thoth**, god of wisdom. Crowley's wife Rose (they married in 1903 and divorced in 1909) appeared to be in a dazed, mediumistic state of mind and, the following day, when in a similar state of drowsiness, announced that Horus was waiting for her husband. Crowley was not expecting such a statement from his wife but according to his diary she later led him to the nearby Boulak Museum which he had not previously visited. Rose now pointed to a statue of **Horus** (in one of its several forms – this one being **Ra-Hoor-Khuit**) and Crowley was amazed to find that the exhibit was numbered 666, the number of the Great Beast in *The Book of Revelation*. Crowley regarded this as a portent and returned to his hotel, where he invoked Horus :

> *Strike, strike the master chord!*
> *Draw, draw the flaming sword!*
> *Crowning child and conquering lord,*
> *Horus, avenger!*

On 20 March Crowley received a mediumistic communication through Rose that "the equinox of the gods had come" and in the ensuing days he arranged for an assistant curator at the Boulak Museum to make notes on the inscriptions from Stele 666. Rose meanwhile continued to fall into a passive, introspective state of mind and advised her husband that at precisely noon on 8, 9, and 10 April he should enter the room where the transcriptions had been made and for exactly an hour on each of these three days he should write down any impressions received. The resulting communications, allegedly dictated by a semi-invisible Egyptian entity named Aiwaz (or Aiwass) – a messenger of Horus – resulted in a document which Crowley later titled *Liber Al vel Legis* (*The Book of the Law*), and this became a turning point in his magical career. In this communication Crowley was instructed to abandon the ceremonial magic he had learnt in the Golden Dawn.

Crowley now increasingly identified with the Horus figure Ra-Hoor-Khuit, whose statue he had seen in the museum. He came to realize that Aiwaz equated with Hoor-paar-Kraat ("Horus the Child", or Harpocrates, the god of silence) – an entity whose sacred origins lay above the Abyss. In terms of this new cosmological perspective, Crowley now considered himself to be the "divine child" who had been chosen by transcendent forces to bring through to humanity a consciousness of the union of Nuit and Hadit. Previously, according to Crowley, there had been two other Aeons – one associated with the moon and the other with the sun. The first of these – the Aeon of Isis – was a matriarchal age characterized by the worship of lunar deities: "The virgin," said Crowley, "contains in herself the principle of growth." The second epoch – the Aeon of Osiris – was a patriarchal age: "The formula of incarnating demi-gods or divine kings; these must be slain and raised from the dead in one way or another." Osiris and the resurrected Christ both belonged to this Aeon and both had now been superceded by the Aeon of Horus. The age of Horus would be based on the union of male and female polarities. According to tantric magician Kenneth Grant, who knew Crowley towards the end of his life, Crowley maintained that in the Aeon of Horus, "physical life is recognised as a sacrament. The sexual act of union for Crowley involved possession by the highest consciousness (namely Aiwaz)." Crowley would spend much of his life from this time onwards seeking lovers and concubines who could act as his Scarlet Woman, or Whore of Babalon (*sic*). And while he would be frustrated in his numerous attempts to find a suitable and enduring partner, there were many who filled the role temporarily. Crowley was thus proposing a very different form of magic from that advocated within the Golden Dawn. Mathers had considered Osiris a supreme symbol of spiritual rebirth and had included references to this deity in the Tiphareth ritual of the Second Order. Crowley, on the other hand, was proclaiming something much more controversial. As the new avatar, he could offer his followers transcendental consciousness through the sacrament of sex. Having received his authority from Aiwaz, Crowley now believed he could speak "with absolute authority". He now believed that the doctrine of Thelema implied "not merely a new religion, but a new cosmology, a new philosophy, a new ethics. It co-ordinates the disconnected discoveries of science. Its scope is so vast that it is impossible even to hint at the universality of its application.... We may then expect the New Aeon to release mankind from its pretence of altruism, its obsession of fear and its consciousness of sin."

Crowley's exploration of sex magic took a new turn on 1 March 1920 when he received a modest inheritance from a deceased aunt. Crowley consulted the *I Ching* – the ancient Taoist oracle – about where he ought to go to start the Great Work, the Law of Thelema. The oracle seemed to favour Cefalu, a small port in northern Sicily. So on 22 March Crowley set off to his new destination. With him was a French woman, Ninette Shumway, and her young son, and he would soon be joined by Leah Hirsig, who had already become his Scarlet Woman and had borne him a daughter, Poupée. In Cefalu Crowley learned there was a villa to rent and soon began the process of converting it into an **Abbey of Thelema**. At last he would have a sanctuary where he could explore sex magic in earnest. Crowley referred to it as his Collegium ad Spiritum Sanctum ("College of the Holy Spirit").There was a steady stream of visitors to the Abbey – among them American film actress, Jane Wolfe (who was much less glamorous than Crowley anticipated); Cecil Frederick Russell, a hospital attendant whom Crowley had met in New York and who had been thrown out of the navy for taking cocaine (Crowley enjoyed discussing different types of drug experiences with him); a Lancashire bricklayer, Frank Bennett (who was also a member of Crowley's **Argenteum Astrum** (A.·. A.·.) as well as the **Ordo Templi Orientis** (O.T.O.); the novelist Mary Butts and her lover Cecil Maitland; and Ninette's sisters Mimi and Helen. It was not long before Mary Butts and Cecil Maitland left for Paris. They were quite appalled by what they had seen at the Abbey – the main images engraved in their minds being the ritual "baptism" of a cockerel slain in honour of Ra-Hoor-Khuit, and the extraordinary spectacle of Crowley's Scarlet Woman endeavouring to copulate with a billy-goat.

Meanwhile, Crowley was awaiting the arrival of a new follower, Raoul Loveday, an Oxford history graduate who had studied *The Equinox* with great interest. Loveday would come with his wife, Betty May, an artist's model who had at one time posed for the famous sculptor Jacob Epstein. Crowley installed Loveday as high priest of the Abbey and was most impressed by his new recruit. Loveday, said Crowley, "possessed every qualification for becoming a magician of the first rank. I designated him from the first interview to be my magical heir." Crowley gave him the title of Frater Aud, meaning "magical light". Raoul and Betty soon settled into daily life at the Abbey. Like all male members of the Thelemic group Raoul had to shave his head, leaving a phallic forelock, and Betty, like the other women at the Abbey, was obliged to dye her hair either red or gold to symbolize the magical energy of Horus. Another of the practices promoted at the Abbey was that only Crowley was allowed to use the word "I". His followers had to learn to repress their egos and were supposed to slash their bodies with a cutthroat razor every time they used the offensive word. Loveday's body was soon covered with cuts and it is possible that this caused a serious blood infection. Loveday did not have a strong constitution and another factor that no doubt contributed to his rapid decline in health was the ritual sacrifice of the Abbey's cat, Mischette – Loveday drank some of its blood from a silver cup. Soon afterwards a Palermo physician diagnosed Loveday's condition as an infection of the liver and the spleen, and Betty understandably became very alarmed – she felt that her husband had been poisoned. By 14 February 1923 Loveday's state of health had declined still further – he was now diagnosed with acute enteritis – and two days later he died. Proclaiming the passing of a worthy follower of Thelema, Crowley and the other members of the Abbey presided at his funeral with appropriate magical rites and readings from *The Book of the Law*, and he was buried in the local cemetery.

Loveday's death precipitated a torrent of bad publicity for the Abbey of Thelema. Betty May returned to England – her fare paid by the British consul in Palermo – and was immediately interviewed by the *Sunday Express* newspaper.

On 25 February it ran an explosive headline across its front page: "New Sinister Revelations of Aleister Crowley". Gruesome details were included in the article; many of them inaccurate, but a tide of adverse publicity was building against the Great Beast. Crowley's *Diary of a Drug Fiend* had been released in England just four months earlier, and it too had attracted venomous coverage in the *Sunday Express* and other sections of the media. Mary Butts had also been interviewed, and had spoken of "profligacy and vice" at the Abbey of Thelema. *John Bull* magazine added salt to the wound by dubbing Crowley "the wickedest man in the world". In England, Crowley's name had became publicly synonymous with depravity. Back in Cefalu, on 23 April 1923 Crowley was summoned to the local police station and ordered to leave Sicily immediately. Italy now had a new leader – Benito Mussolini – who did not approve of secret societies. The Italian authorities had read about the A.˙. A.˙. and the O.T.O. in the London newspapers.

One can argue that with the demise of the Abbey of Thelema, Crowley's magical career was effectively over. It is true that two years later, in 1925, Crowley was invited by the German occultist Heinrich Traenker to become the international head of the O.T.O. (although a substantial minority of German members rejected both Crowley and *The Book of the Law*), and that the O.T.O. would subsequently take root in Britain and the United States, albeit with different figures in charge. It is also true that Crowley would assist **Gerald Gardner** in formulating a practical approach to contemporary **witchcraft** – like Crowley, Gardner was fascinated by sex magic rituals. But by the end of the 1920s Crowley's path as a magician was in steady decline. Most of his best writings and his most innovative ideas were now behind him – a notable exception being his work on the Tarot, *The Book of Thoth*, published in 1944, three years before his death.

Yet for all his notoriety, there can be

no denying that Crowley succeeded in making himself an icon of the modern magical revival. His place in occult history is assured – he remains much better known than MacGregor Mathers, whose works he copied and adapted, and he is certainly much more famous than his original teacher, **Allan Bennett**, who introduced him to practical techniques of magic and yoga. One can even argue that "Crowleyanity" has continued as a minor religion to this day. Kenneth Grant asserts the continuity of Crowley's occult vision in the "typhonic" tradition of the British O.T.O., and in the United States Crowley's influence has extended to the **Temple of Set**. Unlike Mathers and Bennett, Crowley left behind an enormous outpouring of magical writing. His most important occult books include *Magick in Theory and Practice*; *The Book of the Law*; *Book Four*; *The Vision and the Voice*; *The Book of Thoth*; *The Confessions*; and the *Qabalah of Aleister Crowley*.

**Crowley, Vivianne** A senior lecturer in the psychology of religion at King's College, University of London. Dr Crowley is also an initiated Wiccan priestess and a practising kabbalist. Her many books include *Wicca: the Old Religion in the New Age*; *A Woman's Kabbalah*, and several publications on the work of **Carl Jung**.

**Crown, Highest** In the Kabbalah, a reference to the first sephirah on **the Tree of Life, Kether**. In some kabbalistic texts all ten **sephiroth** are referred to as "crowns".

**Crowther, Arnold** (1909–1974) An English witch, artist, and stage magician, and husband of Gardnerian high priestess **Patricia Crowther**. While stationed in Paris during World War Two Arnold Crowther learned from a psychic medium that he had been a Tibetan monk in a past life. He also experienced vivid dreams in which he claimed to receive ancient magical secrets. Arnold Crowther was also a friend of **Gerald**

Gardner and introduced Gardner to Aleister Crowley in Hastings in 1946. This in effect provided a point of potential overlap between the British witchcraft revival and Crowley's cult of Thelema. Gardner and Crowley got on well together and had further discussions in which they shared magical insights and techniques. Crowley made Gardner an honorary member of the Ordo Templi Orientis and Gardner began using quotations from Crowley's writings in his ceremonial rites. Crowley's influence on Gardnerian Wicca was later pared back by Doreen Valiente.

**Crowther, Patricia** (1927– ) An English witch who, with Eleanor Bone and Monique Wilson, was heir to the estate of Gerald Gardner. She describes herself as high priestess of the Sheffield coven and "Queen of the Sabbat", and continues to attract attention for her views on magical initiation, pagan folklore, and cosmic symbolism. Her books include her autobiography *Witchblood* (1974) and *Lid off the Cauldron* (1981), a guide to witchcraft, planetary rituals, and magical spells.

**Crucible** In alchemy, an earthenware pot for melting metals. It had a narrow base which widened out into a triangular or round bowl.

**Crux Ansata** The Egyptian ankh, a cross with an oval loop replacing the upper vertical bar. Important in ancient Egyptian religion as the symbol of life.

**Crystal** A mystical symbol of the spirit. Its associations derive from the fact that crystal, though solid and tangible, is also transparent. Among many shamanic groups, natural crystals are regarded as power objects.

**Crystal Ball** A ball made of crystal or glass, used by clairvoyants for crystal gazing.

**Crystal Gazing** Popularly associated with fortune-telling, crystal-gazing is a form of skrying in which a medium stares fixedly into a crystal ball. In this technique, the clairvoyant uses the ball to focus the gaze and enter a state of trance reverie. Paranormal visions may then arise, which form the basis of the divination. The first impressions may be hazy, but according to many mediumistic accounts this effect clears away and specific visionary scenes then present themselves. Occultists believe that the crystal ball is a focus for the medium's psychic perception and that it does not, in itself, cause the visions to appear. See also Enochian Magic.

**Crystallization** In alchemy, the process of coagulation or congelation.

**Crystalomancy** Divination by means of a crystal ball or a mirror-like pool of water. See Crystal Gazing.

**Cthulhu** A mythic cosmology formulated by the American fantasy writer H.P. Lovecraft. Cthulhu is the "Great Old One" who lies sleeping beneath the sea in the sunken city of R'lyeh.

**Cube** A symbol of the four elements and identified with solidity and endurance. In occult symbolism, the thrones of sacred deities are often depicted as cubes (for example, the Ancient of Days, as depicted by *The Emperor* in the Tarot, sits on a cubic throne inscribed with the motifs of Aries). In the Hermetic Order of the Golden Dawn, the magical altar consisted of a double cube of wood and had ten exposed faces, representing the ten sephiroth on the Tree of Life.

**Cucurbite** From Latin *cucurbita*, "gourd". In alchemy, the glass vessel or pumpkin-shaped retort which formed the lower part of the distillation process. It was often referred to as an "egg" because it was the vessel in which the alchemical "work" was achieved.

**Culebra** In South America, a general term for a snake or boa constrictor. In some regions of the continent it is held that the boa constrictor is the mother-spirit of the hallucinogenic vine ayahuasca.

**Culling, Louis T.** (born 1893) An American occultist and member of the Great Brotherhood of God, who practised a form of ritual magic based largely on the teachings of **Aleister Crowley** and the **Ordo Templi Orientis**. He published a number of occult works, including *The Complete Magickal Curriculum of the Secret Order G.B.G.*, *The Incredible I Ching*, and *A Manual of Sex Magick*.

**Cult** A closed system of religious or magical beliefs. The term is also used to describe collectively the practitioners of such beliefs, their ceremonies, and their patterns of worship.

**Culture Hero** A mythological, legendary, or even historical figure who is revered as the originator or bringer of fundamental aspects of human culture, such as fire, agriculture, language, music, or religion. The accomplishments of such figures become idealized in the form of a myth and the culture hero then serves as an **archetype** for a culture or society. Examples of culture heroes exist in most traditions, for example Prometheus in Greek mythology and Raven in Native American traditions, both of whom stole fire from the gods and gave it to humans. See also **Deification**.

**Cunning Person** In medieval magic, a wizard, magician or healer who performed magical spells to hex other witches and recover stolen property, or who used herbal treatments to treat disease. See also **Hex**.

**Cunningham, Scott** (1956–1993) An American-born authority on natural magic, **Wicca**, and herbalism, Cunningham was introduced to the

Craft in 1971. In 1974, following in the footsteps of his father – who was also a prolific author – he enrolled in a course in creative writing at San Diego State University and decided to become a professional writer. His many works included *Magical Herbalism, Techniques of Natural Magic* , *Wicca: A Guide for the Solitary Practitioner*, and *The Truth About Witchcraft Today*.

**Cup** Also Coppell In **Wicca** and western magic, a ritual implement symbolizing the feminine polarity and the element **water**. See also **Chalice**.

**Cupel** Also Coppell. In **alchemy**, a crucible made of bone-ash or clay and used for testing or refining gold and silver. See also **Crosslet**.

**Cupid** The Roman god of love, associated with the Greek god **Eros**. Cupid was often depicted as a beautiful winged boy who would fire arrows from his bow. The arrows would bring love to those whom they struck.

**Cups** Also known as **Chalices**, one of the four suits of the **Tarot**, ascribed to the element **water**.

**Curandero, Curandera** In Mexico and Peru, a male or female folk-healer or **shaman** skilled in summoning spirits to heal the sick. One of the most famous contemporary healers in Peru is Eduardo Calderon, a shaman who uses San Pedro cactus in an all-night curing ceremony that combines Indian and Christian rituals and features a selection of power-objects. The anthropologist **R. Gordon Wasson** documented in several books the healing vigil, or **velada**, of the Mexican Mazatec shaman Maria Sabina, who made use of sacred mushrooms as a healing sacrament.

**Curott, Phyllis** An American lawyer, Wiccan high priestess and author. Curott founded the Temple of Ara, one of the oldest Wiccan congregations in the United States, and also the Temple of the

Sacred Earth. President Emerita of the Covenant of the Goddess and co-founder of the Religious Liberties Lawyers Network, she is the author of the influential *Book of Shadows* (1999) and *Witch Crafting* (2001). Curott has been widely profiled in the media and lectures frequently around the globe. She lives in New York City and on Long Island.

**Current 93** A term used by the followers of **Aleister Crowley** and the cult of **Thelema** to describe the magical energies associated with the **Aeon of Horus**, which Crowley is said to have initiated in 1904 when *The Book of the Law* was revealed to him. One of Crowley's main magical dicta was "love under will", and the Greek words *agapé* (love) and *thelema* (will) both had a numerical value of 93. So too did the mystical Egyptian entity **Aiwaz**, who was credited by Crowley with inspiring *The Book of the Law*.

**Curse** An evocation or magical oath made with evil intent. Curses are associated with black magic or **sorcery** and are intended to harm or destroy opponents or property. Cursing is probably based on the idea that sound vibrations have a causal result; in many religions the sounds uttered by the beneficent gods are said to give rise to the universe or sustain it. Sounds uttered in the name of evil forces have an opposite, destructive effect. Curses therefore often require the evocation of evil spirits. See also **Demonology; Magic, Black**.

**Curson** See Purson.

**Cusp** In **astrology**, the imaginary line that separates one **sign** or house of the **zodiac** from another.

**Cybele** A Phrygian fertility goddess who was linked symbolically to mountains and wild animals, and was represented in myth travelling in a chariot drawn by lions. Cybele was linked by the Greeks to the mother goddess **Rhea** as the cult of Cybele spread from Phrygia and Lydia to Greece. The priests of Cybele were known as **Corybantes**. Her worshippers offered her passionate and intense homage, bewailing the death of her lover **Attis** with solemn ceremonies, chanting, and prayers, and then indulging in frenzy, jubilation, and songs to herald his spiritual rebirth.

**Cyclops** One of a race of hideous creatures (plural Cyclopes) described in *The Odyssey* as monsters with a single eye in the centre of their foreheads. **Odysseus** was captured by the strongest of the Cyclopes, Polyphemus, but escaped by making him drunk and striking him in the eye with a fiery brand.

# D

**Daath** In the Kabbalah, "knowledge", the child of **Chokmah** and **Binah** on the **Tree of Life**. It is sometimes referred to as the "false" eleventh sephirah, because it is the seat of conceptual rather than absolute knowledge. See **Sephiroth**.

**Dactylomancy** **Divination** by means of rings. Sometimes the ring is held on a string and allowed to swing unassisted against the side of a glass, thereby indicating yes or no to questions asked. A ring may also be suspended over a round table inscribed with letters of the alphabet and used as a type of pendulum to produce a mediumistic "message". The use of wedding rings is popular in this divinatory art.

**Dactyls** Phrygian soothsayers, sorcerers, and exorcists who brought their magical skills to Italy, Greece, and Crete. They are credited with discovering minerals at Ephesus and bringing musical instruments to Greece.

**Dadahnesesgi** Among the Cherokee Indians, evil shamans or sorcerers.

**Dadouchos** A Greek term meaning "torch-bearer". The Dadouchos was a celebrant in the **Mysteries of Eleusis**. There was also a role for a Dadouchos in some of the rituals of the **Hermetic Order of the Golden Dawn**, especially for the **Neophyte** and **Zelator** grades.

**Daedalus** In Greek mythology, the architect of both the legendary labyrinth and palace of King Minos. It was Daedalus who gave Ariadne the thread to guide Theseus through the passages of the labyrinth. Imprisoned by Minos, Daedalus and his son Icarus made themselves wings from feathers and wax and escaped. However, Icarus perished when he flew too close to the sun, causing the wax to melt.

**Daeg** In the Germanic **Elder Futhark**, the **rune** letter representing the number 23. Daeg (or Dagaz) corresponds to the letter "d" and means "day". Daeg is known as the Dawn Rune – a reference to the time of day when the powers of light and darkness are equal – and the rune motif itself suggests both equivalence and duality. The purpose of this rune is to bring together extremes, enabling visionary consciousness to dawn through the synthesis of opposites – this synthesis itself being a catalyst for further growth and exploration.

**Daemon** From the Greek *daimon*, a spirit, an evil spirit, or demon. Also used as a term for beings at an intermediate level between God and humanity. The word *daemon* therefore becomes identified with the concept of an inspiring intelligence or **genius**. See also Daimon.

**Daffo** See **New Forest Coven**.

**Dagaz** See **Daeg**.

**Dagda** The "Good God", the father god of the **Tuatha De Danaan** and chief deity of the pagan Irish, among whom he was god of fertility and the earth. Known as the "Lord of Great Knowledge", he controlled life and death with a great club and had a **cauldron** with magical powers. An able craftsman and a famous player of the harp, he was also a fine warrior and defeated the powerful Fomorians in a mighty battle. See also **Morrígan**.

**Dagon** (1) The Phoenician god of the earth, and later of the sea. He also had the title **Baal**.

**Dagon** (2) In the *Necronomicon*, a god of the Deep Ones, closely associated with the cult of **Cthulhu**. His characteristics are reminiscent of the shadowy magical entities associated with the **Qlippoth**.

**Daimon** For the poet and ceremonial magician **William Butler Yeats**, the visionary vehicle of creativity and inspiration. In his work *Per Amica Silentia Lunae* (1917), Yeats employed imagery derived from the kabbalistic **Tree of Life** as he described how the inspirational daimon followed the lightning path down the Tree. In Yeats' account, the "descending power [of the daimon] is neither the winding nor the straight line but zigzag, illuminating the passive and active properties, the tree's two sorts of fruit: it is the sudden lightning, for all his acts of power are instantaneous". Yeats was was also especially fascinated by the **Tarot** card known as *The Tower*, which shows lightning that has originated in the lofty heights of the Tree of Life striking a crumbling stone tower from the heavens.

**Dakini** In Tibet, a witch or terrifying female **demon** that appears to the magician during his rituals. Sometimes used in India as a general term for earth-mother deities.

**Dalet** See Daleth.

**Daleth** The Hebrew letter ascribed to the path linking **Binah** and **Chokmah** on the **Tree of Life**. Daleth has a numerical value of four. In modern magical visualization and **pathworkings**, the Tarot card associated with this path on the Tree is *The Empress*.

**Damballah Wedo** In voodoo, the serpent **loa** and partner of **Ayida Wedo**, the rainbow **loa**. Damballah Wedo represents the ancestral knowledge of the voodoo tradition.

**Dana** or Danu A mother goddess in the Irish Celtic pantheon. Dana represented fertility and abundance and was said to be the mother of the later deities, the **Tuatha De Danann**, also known as the sídhe, or fairyfolk, of Irish folklore and legend.

**Danbhalah Wedo** See Damballah Wedo.

**Dance** Rhythmic bodily movements, often accompanied by music, chanting, and clapping, which – from an occult point of view – may result in an **altered state** of consciousness or **trance** state, especially when performed in a ritual setting. Dance has this function in many forms of worship in pre-literate and tribal societies, and is a characteristic of fertility rites and the ceremonies of the dervishes, **voodoo**, and **witchcraft**.

**Dance of Death** A popular theme in the Middle Ages, in which a skeleton led men and women to the grave – the final stage of life's journey. In the Spanish *danza macabra*, skeletons are shown carrying a scythe, a clock, and a banner; while in the medieval **Tarot**, the card *Death* shows a skeleton wielding his scythe through a field of bodies, levelling king and commoner alike.

**Daño** In Peruvian magic, harm inflicted through sorcery, resulting in different kinds of illness.

**Danse de Rejuissance** In voodoo, a religious dance of celebration, often following a ceremony.

**Dantalian** In the Goetia, the 71st spirit, a great and mighty duke who appears in the form of a man with many countenances – both male and female. He holds a book in his right hand and is skilled in all the arts and sciences. He knows the thoughts of all men and women and can change them at will, and he can also conjure the likeness of any given person in a vision, irrespective of where they are located in the world. Dantalian rules over 36 legions of spirits.

**Dante Alighieri** (1265–1321) Italian poet who was born in Florence and spent much of his life in political exile in northern Italy. Although he wrote works on politics and the nature of Italian dialects, he is best remembered for his remarkable poem *La Divina Commedia* (*The Divine Comedy*, 1300–1321), which describes a visionary journey through hell, purgatory, and paradise. Dante described the ten divisions of hell as regions where the unbaptized, the lustful, the gluttonous, the spendthrifts, the heretics, the violent, the fraudulent, and the malicious spent their days in torment. Lucifer was depicted as an icy monster among followers devoid of feelings. Dante also described the journey through the ten spheres of heaven, spanning from St Peter's Gate to the highest revolving spheres and the **Primum Mobile**, and thence to the Empyrean domain where human will and God's will became as one.

**Danu** See Dana.

**Daphnomancy** Divination using the laurel plant. A branch of laurel was thrown into a fire and, if it crackled in the flames, the tidings were favourable; if it burned quietly, the omen was negative.

**Dark Goddess** See Crone.

**Dashwood, Sir Francis** (1708–1781) A wealthy English aristocrat who combined a life of privilege with a taste for·the bizarre. He worked for Frederick, Prince of Wales, and met many leading figures of the day. His contacts allowed him the opportunity for numerous liaisons with aristocratic mistresses and an outlet for his promiscuous and voracious tendencies. Despite his marriage to the somewhat pious widow of Sir Richard Ellis, Sarah, he continued to gather like-minded friends around him and decided to form a group of initiates who would hold sexual orgies to worship the **Great Goddess**. He called his brotherhood The Knights of St Francis – naming it after himself, not the saint – and attracted a membership of thirteen, including the Marquis of Queensberry, the Earl of Sandwich, and the Prince of Wales. Meetings were held at Medmenham Abbey near Marlow on the River Thames, and employed the services of whores who were transported from London by coach. These sexual practices at the Abbey continued for around fifteen years, and it became known as the Hell-Fire Club after acquiring a reputation as a place of devil worship. Dashwood later moved the premises to West Wycombe, where he had underground tunnels and a central chamber excavated, allowing his group to continue to meet in secret.

**Datura, Tree** See Angel's Trumpet.

**Datura** Psychedelic plant with magical associations, especially among **shamans** in Mexico and South America. Pulverized seeds of datura are dropped into native beers and the intoxication that follows is accompanied by vivid hallucinations which may last up to three days. Jivaro shamans use the experience to diagnose disease and divine theft. Datura can also produce auditory hallucinations and may result in conversations with imaginary beings.

**Days of Creation** According to *Genesis*, God created the world and its inhabitants in six days and rested on the seventh. In the **Kabbalah**, which interprets *Genesis* symbolically, the "seven days of Creation" equate with the seven **sephiroth**, or emanations from God, depicted on the **Tree of Life** beneath the trinity of **Kether, Chokmah**, and **Binah**. These seven lower sephiroth collectively represent the realm of manifest Creation.

**Deadly Nightshade** *Atropa belladonna*, also known as belladonna, a perennial herb with shining black berries containing seeds and dark, sweet juice. All sections of the plant are poisonous but because the fruit resemble small cherries, deadly nightshade has had an enduring fascination through the ages – especially for children, who sometimes eat the berries by accident. The plant contains hyoscyamine as well as small amounts of scopalamine and atropine and causes dizziness, dryness of the throat and in extreme cases of poisoning, blindness, paralysis, and coma. It is thought that in ancient Greece, the orgies sacred to **Dionysus** utilized a wine which may have contained deadly nightshade as well as **Thornapple**. The **maenads** who attended these revelries and drank this potion had dilated, flaming eyes and are said to have attacked live animals in a wild frenzy, tearing them to pieces. In medieval witchcraft, because deadly nightshade was deemed to have aphrodisiacal properties as well as inducing frenzy, it was also an ingredient in witches' flying ointments. See also **Walkerbeere**.

**De Angeles, Ly** Formerly known as Ly Warren-Clarke, De Angeles is an influential Australian witch and **Tarot** consultant based in Byron Bay, northern New South Wales. An initiated magical practitioner for over thirty years, she is the high priestess of Coven Crystalglade and has been involved in the occult arts since being introduced to this field when she was eleven years old. De Angeles is the author of *The Way of the Goddess: A Manual for Wiccan Initiation* (1987) and *Witchcraft: Theory and Practice* (2000), and co-author with Kathryn Matthews of *The Way of Merlyn: The Male Path in Wicca* (1990).

**Death** In the Tarot, a card in the **Major Arcana** that depicts a skeleton figure wielding a scythe over a field of human bodies. A river flows through this macabre landscape and leads towards the sun. Occultists believe that death precedes rebirth, that the lower instincts need to "die" before spiritual illumination can be attained. In western **magic**, which combines the Tarot paths of the Major Arcana with the ten **sephiroth** on the **Tree of Life**, the path of *Death* connects **Netzach** and **Tiphareth**.

**Death Posture** Term used by the English occultist and artist **Austin Osman Spare** to describe a state of self-induced trance in which he would "open" his mind psychically to the formation of magical images. Spare would meditate on his reflection in a mirror until his body went rigid, while at the same time concentrating on a magical sigil. Once he had reached a state of "oblivion", Spare found that marvellous magical images would well up from his subconscious mind, some of which he linked to earlier personal incarnations. He produced automatic drawings using this technique. See **Automatic Painting and Drawing**; **Sigil** (2).

**Debility** In **astrology**, a term applied to a planet whose position in the **horoscope** weakens its influence.

**Decad** In **numerology**, the number ten.

**Decarabia** In the **Goetia**, the 69th spirit, a great marquis who appears in the form of a star in a **pentacle**, but who will assume a human shape when commanded to do so. Decarabia can help the magician discover the virtues of birds and precious stones and can conjure all kinds of birds to visible appearance, as required. He governs 30 legions of spirits.

**Decoction** An extract prepared by boiling a medicinal or magical plant.

**Dedication** See **Paganing**.

**Dee, Dr John** (1527–1608) English classical scholar, philosopher, mathematician, and astrologer who began his career as an academic at Cambridge University and then travelled widely in Europe. Following a meeting with Jerome Cardan in England in 1552, he became interested in the conjuration of spirits. When Queen Elizabeth I came to the throne in 1553, Dee was invited to calculate the most beneficial astrological date for her coronation. Dee's excursion into magic began in earnest when he met **Edward Kelley**, who was both a **medium** and a **skryer**, and who claimed to communicate with angels in his **spirit-vision**. Dee and Kelley made use of a **crystal ball** and wax tablets, or almadels, engraved with magical symbols and the sacred names of God. The tablet for a given invocation was laid between four candles and angels summoned as Kelley stared into the crystal.

In 1582 Kelley began to receive messages in a new angelic language called "Enochian". Dee was amazed by these events and wrote in his diary: "Now the fire shot oute of E.K., his eyes, into the stone agayne. And by and by he understode nothing of all, neyther could read any thing, nor remember what he had sayde." On occasions Kelley seemed to become possessed by spirits, some of which – according to Dee – manifested to visible appearance: "At his side appeared three or fowr spirituall creatures like laboring men, having spades in their hands and theyr haires hanging about theyr eares." The spirits wished to know why they had been summoned, and Dee bade them depart. They refused, nipping Kelley on the arm. Dee writes: "Still they cam gaping or gryning at him. Then I axed him where they were, and he poynted to the place, and in the name of Jesus commaunded those Baggagis to avoyde [depart], and smitt a cross stroke at them, and presently they avoyded."

The eighteen angelic messages, or "Enochian calls", received by Kelley and Dee were later used as conjurations by the English occultist Aleister Crowley while on an expedition in the Algerian desert with the poet Victor Neuburg. A dictionary of the Enochian language, edited by the Australian linguist Dr. Donald Laycock, was published in London in 1978 and further scholarly analysis of the Enochian magic has also been undertaken by Stephen Skinner and David Rankine. See also Aethyrs.

**Deer** In alchemy, a symbol of the elusive Mercurius, or philosophical mercury.

**Defensive Magic** See Magic, Defensive.

**Defixiones** In ancient Rome, binding or cursing tablets used to subject another person to one's will or desire. See Katadesmoi.

**Dehar** Among the non-Islamic Kalash Kafirs of Pakistan, the dehar is a shaman who is skilled in entering a state of trance. The dehar invokes supernatural beings, kills a sacrificial animal, and sprinkles its blood upon an altar and then onto a fire. He then rivets his attention upon the altar and becomes physically rigid. Soon a shivering sensation passes through his body, his muscles begin to tremble, and his jaw jerks violently. The dehar often begins to sway, and foam pours from his mouth. He gradually sinks into a deep trance and his soul goes on a spirit-journey. It is shamans of this type who have led some anthropologists to link shamanism with epilepsy and to identify the shaman as one who "can rescue himself from his own affliction".

**Deification** The act of elevating a human being or mortal to the status of an immortal god. Among the best examples are the ancient Egyptian Imhotep, and the Greek Asklepios, both of whom became healing divinities. In contemporary times the act of self-deification is also a stated aim of members of the Temple of Set.

**Deity** From the Latin *deus*, a god, or supreme being. In polytheistic religions there are many gods who rule the world collectively and preside over different aspects of life affecting people and Nature; in monotheistic religions there is one supreme deity who reveals different aspect of his being to the world, but is nevertheless One. In general terms, there are deities who create the world, deities who maintain or govern it, and lesser deities who serve the rule of humankind and usually have specified functions. The magical and occult traditions draw on both polytheistic religions (ancient Greek, Roman, Egyptian, Celtic, and Scandinavian) and monotheistic religions (Judaism, Christianity). Within the monotheistic tradition most occultists lean towards the esoteric schools of thought associated with the Kabbalah and Gnosticism. See also Monotheism; Polytheism.

**Delphic Oracle** An influential ancient Greek **oracle** who made pronouncements at the temple of **Apollo** at Delphi, beneath Mount Parnassus. Apollo's priestess was named the Pythia, a reference to the Python or giant serpent that Apollo had slain when he first came to Delphi. After sacrificing a goat, the Pythia would mount a tripod and squat there, breathing in intoxicating smoke – possibly from **henbane** seeds – and awaiting divine inspiration. As she entered a state of trance, priests would interpret the oracles from the Pythia, and relay her answers to the inquirers.

**Demeter** In Greek mythology, the goddess of corn and agriculture. Her name means "Mother Earth" and as such she sustained the people, who in turn revered her at festivals held in her honour. These depicted different agricultural activities such as ploughing, sowing, and harvesting. In the same way that the passage of seasons brought forth new produce, the cycles of life were seen as an omen for people and a promise of "new life". Accordingly, Demeter was an important deity in the **Mysteries of Eleusis**. She was also the mother of **Persephone**.

**Demi-God** Especially in ancient Greece, a figure half human and half divine, such as **Asklepios**, the son of Apollo and Coronis, a human princess.

**Demiurge** The creator of the world, from the Greek *demiurgos*, "fashioner" or "architect". For **Gnostics** he was not the supreme reality, but a middle-ranking deity who proposed laws for the world, which the initiated could transcend.

**Demogorgon** In Roman mythology, an **Underworld** deity who lived at the centre of the earth. An awesome, frightening god, he was associated with chaos and eternity. In the late Roman empire (fifth century), Demogorgon was often invoked in magical rites.

**Demon** From the Greek *daimon*, a devil or evil spirit. See **Daemon; Daimon; Demonology**.

**Demoniac** One possessed by a **demon** or evil spirit.

**Demonic Exorcism** See Exorcism.

**Demonology** The study of **demons** and evil spirits, and the rites and superstitions associated with them. Many deities associated with ancient Middle Eastern and Egyptian religions (e.g. **Baal, Ashtaroth, Bel, Apophis**, and **Set**) have become associated either with demonology or the gods of black magic and the **left-hand path**. See also **Magic, Black; Wier, Johannes**.

**Demonomancy** **Divination** by means of evoking demons. The magician seeks prophecies from evil spirits summoned in ritual. See also **Demon; Magic, Black; Magic, Ceremonial**.

**Dense Body** A Theosophical concept, also present in some forms of **Gnosticism**, which regards matter as the densest emanation from the realm of spirit. In mystical and occult belief, people have several bodies – for example, a spiritual, etheric, mental, or astral body – as well as a physical body. The last of these is regarded as the "densest" and the furthest removed from God and spirit. See also **Theosophy**.

**Deo** In Enochian magic, the seventh Aethyr. The meanings associated with Deo include freedom and love for other people. Deo is associated with **Virgo** and Libra and its magical number is 44.

**Deosil** In Wicca, the act of moving in the same direction as the sun in a magical ritual. Deosil is therefore clockwise in the northern hemisphere and anti-clockwise in the southern hemisphere. See also **Widdershins**.

**Des** In Enochian magic, the 26th Aethyr. The meanings associated with Des include logic, reason, intellect and rationality. It is associated with **Virgo** and **Gemini** and its magical number is 21.

**Descendant** In astrology, the degree of the ecliptic which is setting. In the same way that the sun rises on the eastern horizon, identifying the **ascendant**, the sun sets in the evening on the western horizon producing the descendant. The first house begins at the ascendant, the seventh house at the descendant.

**Descending Arc** In Theosophy, the descent of a procession of spiritual beings from ethereal and spiritual realms of being towards the physical plane of existence. Also Involution. See also **Ascending Arc**.

**Descension** In alchemy, the distillation process in which liquid flowed down into a receiver vessel.

**Descent into the Underworld** In many world mythologies, demi-gods and heroes have had the ability to descend into the **Underworld**, to glimpse the hereafter and return with sacred knowledge in order to guide and inspire humankind. Aeneas used the Golden Bough as his passport to Hades, and **Odysseus** visited the Underworld in order to hold discourse with the ghosts of dead heroes. Christ is said to have descended into hell for three days before "rising from the dead". Similarly, in Egyptian mythology, as represented in the *Am Tuat*, the sun-god Afu-Ra would descend each night into the Underworld – the twelve dungeons representing the twelve hours of the night – and would be reborn with the new day.

**Desert of Set** See Mauve Zone.

**Desire Body** Alternative term for the "astral" or "soul" bodies of man. See **Astral Body**.

**Despacho** In Macumba, a ritual offering – usually of a sacrificial animal.

**Dessounin** In voodoo, the ritual in which the dead person's individual will and spirit are separated from the body.

**Destiny** One's future. In Greek mythology, Destiny was personified as a god beyond Zeus's control, and, together with the three **Fates**, dared to oppose his will.

**Destructive Magic** See Magic, Destructive.

**Devas** In Zoroastrianism, evil genii or malevolent spirits ruled by **Angra Mainyu**, the god of darkness.

**Devekuth** In the Jewish mystical tradition, the inward state of remaining attached to divine consciousness.

**Devil** A demon or evil spirit. See also **Daemon**; **Daimon**; **Demonology**.

**Devil's Girdle** Allegedly worn by witches in the Middle Ages as a token of their allegiance to the **Devil**.

**Devil's Mark** In medieval **witchcraft**, a mark on the body said to be an initiation motif given by the **Devil**, and which was insensitive to pain. Inquisitors searched victims accused of witchcraft in order to locate any such marks and thereby prove their guilt. The practice of searching for the Devil's mark became illegal in England in 1662.

**Devil's Pillar** Three stones preserved in Prague, which, according to legend, are the remains of a pillar with which the Devil intended to slay a priest who had signed a diabolic **pact**. St Peter cast the Devil into the sea, the priest repented, and the Devil broke the pillar in rage.

**Devil, The** (1) The personification of evil, also called **Lucifer** or **Satan** in Christianity, **Eblis** in Islam, and **Ahriman** in Zoroastrianism. Many religious devotees, especially fundamentalists, believe that the Devil is still active in the world, luring people away from God and spiritual salvation. Those who approach mysticism and religious belief from a psychological viewpoint are more inclined to view the Devil as a negative archetype of the mind, personifying adverse and destructive human characteristics.

**Devil, The** (2) In the Tarot, a card of the Major Arcana that depicts the Devil, illumined by a torch, with a naked man and woman bound in chains to his throne. The Devil's goat-like form is a reminder of his bestiality and the inverted pentagram on his brow represents retrograde evolution. Occultists believe that the card of *The Devil* demonstrates that individuals should acknowledge and transcend their animal nature. In western magic, which combines the Tarot paths of the Major Arcana with the ten sephiroth on the Tree of Life, the path of *The Devil* connects Hod and Tiphareth. See Devil, The (1).

**Dew** In alchemy, the healing essence of the mercurial water which magically transforms the black nigredo – the old, putrefied form of the metal – into the white albedo.

**Dexter** In astrology, a right-handed aspect – the exact opposite of a sinister aspect. The concept derives from Ptolemaic astronomy, which assumed that the earth was at the centre of the universe, with the sun, moon, and stars revolving around it. The terms "dexter" and "sinister" are not used extensively in modern astrology, which nowadays follows the scientific system of astronomy.

**Diablero** Term used in Mexico to describe a black magician or sorcerer, especially one who has the magical ability to transform into the shape of an animal. The term is virtually synonymous with Brujo. Compare Lycanthropy; Nagual.

**Diabolism** Acts, rituals, and worship associated with the Devil. See also

Magic, Black; Sorcery.

**Diamond** On the kabbalistic Tree of Life, a magical stone assigned to the sephirah Kether.

**Diana** In alchemy, the stage of albedo in the alchemical process. Albedo, or the "white" stage of the work, was reached after the blackened putrefied material of the metal – associated with nigredo, or death – was washed to a state of whiteness by the purifying mercurial waters or fire. See also Queen Luna; White Elixir; Argent Vive.

**Diana** The Roman goddess of hunting and the moon, and the protector of women and animals, equated with the Greek Artemis.

**Dianic Witches** Contemporary practitioners of witchcraft whose covens are dedicated to the Roman goddess Diana and whose orientation is feminist and/or strongly matriarchal – many Dianic covens do not admit men. Dianic witchcraft is predominantly an American phenomenon, and one of its leading advocates is the California-based goddess worshipper Z. Budapest, whose Dianic coven consists exclusively of a mix of heterosexual and lesbian women.

**Dianism** In the sex magic practices described by Louis T. Culling, the act of withholding ejaculation, thereby retaining one's personal vital energy. Culling distinguished between Dianism and karezza, but does not provide an explanation for the origin of the expression itself. He may have derived the technique from the Ordo Templi Orientis.

**Diasia** In ancient Greece, a ritual offering to the gods of the Underworld.

**Dignification** In ceremonial magic, the practice of making oneself wholly prepared for the process of invocation. This might involve prayer prior to the commencement of ritual. As Cornelius Agrippa notes in his *De Occulta*

DEVIL   Eliphas Levi's rendition of the Devil – the Sabbatic Goat.

*Philosophia*, an important aspect in relation to **theurgy**, or spiritually oriented "high magic", is the "dignifying of men to this so sublime virtue and power". See **Magic, Ceremonial**.

**Dignity** In astrology, a situation where the position of a planet strengthens its influence in a **horoscope**; the exact opposite of **debility**.

**Dijina** In Macumba, the holy name given to those who have just been initiated.

**Dionysia** In ancient Athens, a festival characterized by orgies and revelry, held in honour of **Dionysus**.

**Dionysus** The Greek god of wine, fertility, and revelry who was worshipped in frenzied orgies, the most famous of which, the **Dionysia**, was held at Athens in the spring. Dionysus (or Dionysos) symbolized freedom and spontaneous impulses, and encouraged a distinct lack of reverence for the other gods. Dance, music, and wine were regarded by his followers as means of release, a real surrender to the pure, unfettered joy of being alive. The Roman equivalent of Dionysus was **Bacchus**.

**Directional Sephiroth** In the Sepher Yetzirah, the six **sephiroth** assigned to the directions of above, below, east, west, north, and south. They correspond to the sephiroth Crown (**Kether**), Foundation (**Yesod**), Wisdom (**Chokmah**), Glory (**Hod**), Understanding (**Binah**), and Victory (**Netzach**) in the *Zohar*.

**Directions, Four** See Four Directions, The.

**Dis** or **Dis Pater** The Roman name of **Hades**, ruler of the **Underworld**. Also identified with **Pluto**.

**Discarnate** Not living; without a physical form or body. See also **Spirits**.

**Discs** See Pentacles.

**Disease, Magical Origin of** In many pre-literate societies, illness is thought to be caused by the loss of one's soul or spirit, often as the result of **sorcery**. A healer or **shaman** may undertake a spirit-journey to recover the **soul** and restore good health to the patient. See also **Soul-loss**.

**Disembodied** Existing without a physical body. Often used to describe discarnate entities and spirits, or the mind in a state of **dissociation**.

**Dismemberment** In many native mythologies, the act of dismemberment may be symbolic of a death and renewal process leading to visionary rebirth. In some shamanic societies, the act of initiation includes dreams or trance journeys where the person involved is devoured by hostile adversaries or wild animals, but is restructured by the gods and given new spiritual powers. Several ancient mythologies refer to a similar process. Dionysus was formed from the heart of the dismembered Zagreus, and Isis restored the fragmented body of Osiris after he had been slain by Set

**Dispositor** In astrology, when a planet is located in a certain **house**, the ruler of the sign on the **cusp** is known as the dispositor of that planet.

**Dissociation** The act of separation. Used in occult terminology to describe the separation of the **astral body** from the physical. Compare **Out-of-the-Body Experience**.

**Distillation** In alchemy, the process of purification of a material whereby the "volatile spirit" was extracted from the "impure" substance through heat. Vaporization was followed by cooling and condensation. The process of vaporization was known as **sublimation** and this was followed by distillation.

**Dittany of Crete** An aromatic plant

found on Mount Ida in Crete: It was sacred to the lunar goddess and was said to cure somnambulism. Dittany was used in magical ceremonies as a sedative.

**Divination** The act of foretelling the future, often by interpreting omens. Among the many forms of divination are predictions based on the symbols of the **Tarot** cards; the fall of dice, yarrow sticks, or coloured beans; the configuration of such natural phenomena as clouds or the wind; and the movements of birds and other living creatures.

**Divine** Pertaining to, or having the nature of, God; something or someone who is sacred or holy. See also **Priest**.

**Divine Ape, Formula of the** A form of magical evocation in which one "apes" the **god-form** of bestial atavisms in order to acquire their specific powers. See **Atavism**.

**Divine Presence** In the Kabbalah, a reference to the sacred nature of the **Shekhinah**, the feminine aspect of the **godhead**, manifesting in the world (**Malkuth**, the kingdom).

**Divine Water** See Mercurius.

**Divis** A variant of **devas**. In Persian mythology, they were cat-headed devils with horns and hooves.

**Djinn** See Genii.

**Doctor, Leaf** See Leaf Doctor.

**Doctors, Bear** See Bear Doctors.

**Doctrine of Signatures** See Signatures.

**Doerg** See Daeg.

**Dogon** A pagan Sudanese people who dwell in the Republic of Mali and whose magical practices include rainmaking ceremonies and masked dances.

**Dogué** or Dogwé In **voodoo**, the ritual word for a sacrificial goat.

**Dokte Feuilles** See Leaf Doctor.

**Dolmen** From a Breton expression meaning "table of stone", a prehistoric megalith consisting of a large, unhewn stone resting on two or more uprights. Dolmens and other ancient **megaliths** were significant in Celtic religion and later folklore.

**Don Juan Matus** A Yaqui Indian **brujo** from Sonora, Mexico, who allegedly initiated the anthropologist **Carlos Castañeda** into **shamanism** and sorcery. The teachings and philosophy of Don Juan Matus are documented in Castañeda's popular books. Several critics, among them Richard de Mille and Weston La Barre, have doubted whether Don Juan ever existed; others believe him to be a fictitious composite of several shamans. Castañeda himself always maintained that Don Juan was a real and authentic shaman and other members of Castañeda's magical group, including Florinda Donner, have also confirmed his existence.

**Double-Bodied Signs** In astrology, signs whose symbols incorporate two figures: **Sagittarius** (half man, half horse); **Gemini** (twins) and **Pisces** (two fish). It does not include **Capricorn**, which is sometimes represented as a goat-fish.

**Dove** In alchemy, a symbol of the pure white stage of the alchemical operation, the **albedo**.

**Draci** According to the writings of the English-born medieval author Gervase of Tilbury, draci are evil water spirits that like to prey on women. According to a twelfth-century legend, the draci take the form of wooden plates floating on a stream. As women reach out to take the plates they are dragged down to the bottom of the stream to care for, and nurse, the demonic offspring of the water spirits. Gervase of Tilbury was an officer in service of Holy Roman Emperor Otto IV (1175–1218) and wrote about the draci in his *Otia Imperiala*, or *Notes from the Imperial Court*.

**Draconian Cult** The cult of the "Dragon of the Deep", associated with worshippers of **Apophis** in ancient Egypt and revived today by members of the **Typhonian Order of the Outer Ones**, the magical system developed by the tantric occultist **Kenneth Grant**. According to Grant, the Draconian Cult is named after Draco, the son of **Typhon** in Greek myth – the primeval mother. The magical energy that infuses the cult is known as the Draconian Current. See also **Grant, Kenneth; Tanith**.

**Draconian Current** See Draconian Cult.

**Dracula, Count** A character in a famous novel by the Irish writer Bram Stoker (1847–1912). Dracula is depicted as a seductive **vampire** who drinks the blood of beautiful women. The fictional Count Dracula is thought to have his origin in the fifteenth-century Romanian prince Vlad V, who tortured (by impaling) not only captured Turkish invaders in his country, but his own subjects as well. Vlad's father was known as Vlad Drakul – "the Devil". Castle Dracula, north of Bucharest in the Carpathian mountains, has become a tourist attraction, and there are now Dracula societies in both the United States and Britain.

**Dragon** A mythical creature that has appeared universally in legends and folktales and whose symbolism is very diverse. In western and Middle Eastern mythology, dragons were originally associated with water. Often they were said to dwell at the bottom of the sea, where they guarded precious treasure; they could also breathe thunder and lightning, causing rain to fall. In western cultures, the dragon has usually been regarded as hostile to people, and it is associated with dark and evil forces. Medieval sages tell of numerous battles between virtuous knights and hostile dragons, and in *The Book of Revelation*, St Michael casts a fearful and monstrous dragon out of heaven which had "ten horns and seven heads, with ten diadems upon its horns and a blasphemous name upon its heads". In the east, the symbolism of the dragon was more positive. It was usually benevolent, was especially friendly towards monarchs, and often guarded the royal treasures. In China, it became the symbol of imperial power; and, according to Zhuangzi (Chuang Tzu), it represented the cosmic vibrancy of life itself.

The colour of dragons varied considerably. In China, they could be red (associated with science) or white (representing the **moon**). The multi-headed dragon in *Revelation* was also red, but in Christian mythology it symbolized gross evil and the forces of chaos and destruction. In ancient Greek literature, the earliest mention of dragons occurs in *The Iliad*, where Agamemnon is described as having a blue dragon motif on his sword-belt and a three-headed dragon emblem on his breastplate. In other cultures, dragons can also be yellow, brown, or black.

Different societies tend to draw on familiar animals in formulating their dragons and, as a result, they are often composite creatures. In ancient Babylon, one particular dragon had the head and horns of a ram, the forelegs of a lion, a reptilian body, and the hind legs of an eagle. A dragon described by the ancient Chinese writer Wang Fu had the head of a camel, the horns of a stag, the eyes of a demon, the ears of a bull, the neck of a snake, the belly of a clam, the scales of a carp, the claws of an eagle, the soles of a tiger, and long whiskers on its face. The dragon Chimera, described by Homer, combined a lion, a serpent, and a goat. Medieval dragons often had huge jaws, luminous eyes, a forked tongue, eagle's feet, and bat's wings.

Wherever it is found, the dragon represents awesome power to be reckoned with. As a personification of primeval force, it may be hostile or friendly to people, but its supernatural and cosmic presence is universally acknowledged.

**Draupnir** In Scandinavian mythology, the magical ring made by the dwarfs for **Odin**, the king of the gods. When Odin's son **Balder** was slain, Odin placed the magical ring on the funeral pyre.

**Drawing Down the Moon** In Wicca, the ceremonial invocation of the Great **Goddess** into the high priestess. This invocation is performed by the high priest.

**Drawing Down the Sun** In Wicca, the ceremonial invocation of the sun god into the high priest. This invocation is performed by the high priestess.

**Dream Body** Theosophical and mystical term for the **astral body**, so named because many occultists believe that dreams are images that have a reality of their own on the **astral plane**. See also **Theosophy**.

**Dreamtime** In Australian Aboriginal mythology, the period during the creation of the world when heroes and totemic animals roamed the earth, establishing links with sites now regarded as sacred. For tribal Aborigines, the Dreamtime still continues as an ongoing sacred reality, and provides a sense of mythic identification and purpose. See also **Totem**.

**Druid's Weed** See **Vervain**.

**Druids** Celtic priests in pre-Christian Britain and Gaul (France). The Druids were skilled in astronomy and medicine, and worshipped the sun, making use of much earlier Neolithic **megaliths** e.g. **cromlechs** and stone circles. They believed in the immortality of the soul and in reincarnation, and regarded the **oak** tree and **mistletoe** as sacred. The centre of Druidism in Britain was on the Welsh island of Anglesey, but the Druids also raised monoliths at Aldborough and York and probably made use of Stonehenge as an observatory-temple. Although the conquering Romans destroyed the power of the Druid class, the Celtic pagan religion was tolerated and died out in Gaul and southern Britain only with the coming of Christianity in the late Roman empire. It lingered on in Scotland and Ireland, which were Christianized later. In recent times there has been a substantial revival of interest in the philosophy and rituals of the Druids.

**Dryads** In Greek mythology, nymphs who presided over woods and trees. The dryad living in a tree would die at the same time as her tree. Dryads often took the form of huntresses or shepherdesses, and the oak tree was sacred to them. See also **Hamadryads**.

**Duat** See **Tuat**.

**Duhisa** A term used by the Hopi Indians to refer to the art of sorcery or black magic. Duhisa derives from the magician's helper spirit. Hopi sorcerers employ little black ants, coyotes, wolves, owls, crows, cats, and dogs as helper spirits. See also **Magic, Black**.

**Duir** In the Celtic tree alphabet, the **ogham** representing the oak and the letter "h". Duir is also linked to the wren and the colour dark brown.

**Dunsany, Lord** (1878–1957) Anglo-Irish dramatist and novelist whose full name was Edward John Morton Drax Plunkett, eighteenth Baron Dunsany. Gifted with a superb facility for portraying myths and legends, Dunsany helped establish the fantasy genre made popular by later writers such as J.R.R. Tolkien. Among his most enchanting books are *The Gods of Pegana* (1905) and *Time and the Gods* (1906).

**Duppy** In West Indian folk-belief, the part of a person that survives death.

Ghostlike and evil, duppies can be awakened from the grave by their relatives and bribed to perform certain things – however, they are obliged to return to their graves by daylight. Compare **Zombies**.

**Dwarfs** Small, hairy men who, according to Scandinavian folk-legend, lived beneath the earth, were expert steelsmiths, and skilled in fashioning precious jewellery. Dwarfs made Odin's magical sword and **Freyja**'s beautiful necklace, and play a major part in Richard Wagner's three-opera cycle *The Ring of the Nibelung*. The English fantasy-book illustrator Arthur Rackham provided memorable depictions of dwarfs in his two-volume adaptation of Wagner's work, *The Rhinegold and the Valkyrie* and *The Twilight of the Gods*.

**Dweller on the Threshold** The concept of a hostile spirit entity representing the accumulated bad **karma** of an occultist and appearing to such a person on the **astral plane** as a force to be confronted and overcome. The concept of the Dweller on the Threshold is thought to derive from the mystical novel *Zanoni* written by **Sir Edward Bulwer-Lytton**.

**Dyad Moon** See Esbats.

**Dyad** In **numerology**, the number two.

# E

**Ea** In ancient Babylon, the god of water who was also "Lord of Wisdom", the patron of **magic**, arts, and crafts, and the creator of people. Ea had the gifts of **prophecy** and **divination**, and was often represented as having the body of a goat and the tail of a fish. It is thought that the symbolism of the **zodiac** sign Capricorn derives from him.

**Eagle** A bird with many magical and symbolic associations. In **alchemy**, the eagle represents **philosophical mercury**, the white mercury or white tincture which can transmute base metal into silver. The eagle is linked in **astrology** to Scorpio, which with **Taurus, Leo**, and **Aquarius** is one of the "fixed" signs of the zodiac. Occultists also identify these fixed signs with the four letters of the sacred **Tetragrammaton** YHVH, the eagle being associated with the first H. In general terms, because of its capacity for soaring flight, the eagle symbolizes transcendence, light, spirit, and the unfettered powers of the imagination.

**Ear of Corn** A mystical symbol of fertility and growth, also linked to the sun because of its golden colour.

**Earth** In alchemy, one of the four elements, the others being **fire, water**, and **air**. The spirits of the earth are gnomes and goblins. The three astrological signs linked to earth are **Taurus, Virgo**, and **Capricorn**. See also **Gnome; Goblin**.

**Earth Goddesses** See Dana; Demeter; Fertility Deities; Gaea; Great Mother; Isis; Persephone.

**East** The direction of the rising sun, and in western **magic** therefore associated with new life, light, spiritual **illumination**, and **initiation**. All **white magic** rituals commence with salutations to the eastern quarter, and in kabbalistic magic this direction is ruled by the archangel Raphael, symbolizing the element air. In alchemy, east is associated with philosophical sulphur and the red, dry, and coagulating aspects of the alchemical process. See also Solve et Coagula; West.

**Ebadh** In the Celtic tree alphabet, the ogham representing elecampane and aspen and the sound "ea". Ebadh is also linked to the colour pale yellow.

**Ebane** In Macumba, a term given to a recently initiated medium who has reached a higher level of spiritual awareness.

**Eblis** The Devil in Islam. The *Qur'an* describes Eblis, or Iblis, as an **angel** who originally dwelt in heaven and was once close to God. However, he fell from grace for disobeying God's command to bow down before Adam. Eblis is composed of the elements of fire and, according to Muslim belief, he will roam the world until the Last Judgment.

**Eboga, Eboka** See Iboga.

**Echidna** In Greek mythology, the fearsome daughter of **Tartarus** and **Gaea**. Half-human and half-serpent, she was the mother of the three-headed dog Cerberus, who guarded the entrance of Hades, and of the **Sphinx** (2). Echidna was finally slain by Argus, a monster with a hundred eyes.

**Eclipse** In alchemy, an image used to represent the process of **nigredo** when the body of the impure metal or material is dissolved and putrefied so that its essence can be released and a new state of purification attained.

**Ecstasy** A state of joy, rapture, or spiritual enlightenment in which a person can feel lifted up into a state of visionary transcendence. Ecstasy is a profound **altered state** of consciousness and is sometimes associated with trance. See also **Out-of-the-Body Experience; Shamanism**.

**Edadh** In the Celtic tree alphabet, the ogham representing the aspen and yew and the letter "e". Edadh is also linked to the swan and the colour red.

***Eddas, The*** The medieval Icelandic sagas that are the main source of our knowledge of Scandinavian mythology and pre-Christian religious beliefs. The so-called *Elder Edda*, in poetry, dates from around the twelfth century, and its authorship is unknown. The *Younger Edda*, in prose, was written by Snorri Sturluson c. 1230CE.

**Eehyom** Among the Cheyenne Indians, a **shaman** who can cause harm at a distance. Cheyenne shamans use an *oxzem* (spirit lance) or *nimahenan* (sacred arrows) to inflict injuries on their enemies. See also **Oxzem**.

**Effigy** Image or representation of a person, often used in magical ceremonies or spells. Sorcerers and black magicians may burn or stick pins into an effigy of a particular person in order to bring harm to them. See also **Magic, Black**.

**Efreet** A type of genii or djinn in Islamic cosmology. Also, afreet, ifrit, yfrit.

**Egg** In alchemy, the **alembic** or cucurbite in which the alchemical opus takes place. The alchemists compared the creation of the **Philosopher's Stone** to the birth of a chick from an egg, and the fire warming the vessel with gentle heat was like a hen providing warmth and protection by brooding on her eggs.

**Egg, Cosmic** In many world religions and mystical cosmologies, both the universe itself and also major deities are said to have been born from an egg. The Hindu cosmic egg was known as Hiranya-Garbha and, when it hatched, the sun god Brahma came forth. The Egyptian solar deity Ra was also born from an egg, as were the twins of Greek mythology, Castor and Pollux. According to the teachings of the **Orphic Cults**,

"God, the uncreated, created all things [and] the unshapen mass was formed in the shape of an egg, from which all things have proceeded."

**Egrigor** A thought-form created in psychic groups or magical ceremonies by the combined "will" or visualization powers of the participants. Magicians believe it is often more effective to work ceremonially with an egrigor since this provides a cumulative effect in terms of magical visualization and one can benefit from the residual energetic power of magical workings which have taken place at an earlier time.

**Egums** In Macumba, the souls or spirits of the dead.

***Egyptian Book of the Dead, The*** An ancient Egyptian account of the afterlife that was usually buried with the deceased. It included details of burial procedures and an account of the passage of the deceased through the Judgment Hall en route to the other world. Several examples of *The Egyptian Book of the Dead* survive, and they are often illustrated. See also *Book of the Dead*.

**Egyptian Masonic Rite** A magical ritual devised by **Count Cagliostro**. Cagliostro claimed that Egyptian Freemasonry held the key to the **Philosopher's Stone** and that participants in it could discover their "primitive innocence". Cagliostro admitted both men and women to his lodge, his wife assisting with the initiation of the female neophytes. She would breathe upon their faces and say: "I breathe upon you this breath to cause to germinate in you and grow in your heart the truth we process; I breathe it into you to strengthen in you good intentions, and to confirm you in the faith of your brothers and sisters." The women later donned white robes and took part in a ceremony where they were encouraged to cast off the "shameful bonds" imposed on them by their male masters. They were

subsequently led into a garden and later to a temple, where they had an "initiatory" encounter with Cagliostro himself. Naked, he would descend on a golden sphere through the roof of the temple and order his neophytes to discard their clothing in the name of truth and innocence. He then explained to them the symbolic nature of their quest for self-realization before once again mounting the golden ball and rising up through the temple vault. The intentions of Cagliostro and his wife in bestowing these gifts were not purely altruistic, for it seems that the women who were initiated paid large sums in order to participate. However, many of his clients came from the Parisian aristocracy and could no doubt afford it.

**Eh** In the Germanic **Elder Futhark** the rune letter representing the number nineteen. Eh (or Ehwis, Ehwaz) corresponds to the letter "e" and is the rune of self-control, trust, and partnership. The word "ehwis" means "horse" and this rune is associated with the Aclis – sons of the sky god – who were excellent horsemen. Sacred horses drew the solar wagon across the sky each day. The Aclis rode in pairs, and this rune also represents friendship.

**Eheieh** In the Kabbalah, the sacred God-name associated with the sphere of **Kether** on the Tree of Life. It translates as "I am".

**Eheyeh** See Eheieh.

**Ehwaz, Ehwis** See Eh.

**Eidolism** From the Greek term meaning "an image", the belief in ghosts, souls, and disembodied spirits.

**Eidolon** From the Greek term meaning "an image", the astral body, or phantom.

**Eight** In numerology, a number indicating strength of character and individuality of purpose. People whose birth dates reduce to eight are said to demonstrate independence of thought and a sense of coolness at home, and often find it difficult to express their inhibitions. **Hod**, the eighth sephirah on the kabbalistic **Tree of Life**, is associated with the rational intellect.

**Ein Sof** In the Kabbalah, the "Infinite". See **Ain Soph Aur**.

**El (1)** The supreme deity among the Phoenicians, and specifically the god of rivers and streams. El was the father of the other gods and was usually depicted as a very old man with a flowing beard.

**El (2)** In the Kabbalah, the divine name associated with the sphere of **Chesed** on the Tree of Life. It translates as "God".

**Elder Futhark** See Futhark, Elder

**Elders** In Wicca, third-degree and second-degree members of a **coven**. See Second Initiation, Third Initiation.

**Electional Astrology** See Astrology, Electional.

**Eleggua** In Santería, the god of entrances, doorways, and roads and the equivalent of **Legba** in Macumba. Eleggua is associated with the Holy Guardian Angel, St Michael, St Peter, and St Martin de Porres. Compare with Legba.

**Elementals** Spirit-creatures said by magicians to personify the qualities of the four **elements**. These creatures are salamanders (fire), mermaids and undines (water), sylphs (air), and gnomes and goblins (earth).

**Elements** In alchemy, the manifested world was divided into four elements: fire, air, earth, and water. These in turn were encompassed by the quintessence, or fifth element: spirit. The basic fourfold division of the elements is still an integral part of contemporary magical beliefs. Occultists divide the Tarot suits as follows: swords (air);

wands (fire); cups (water), and pentacles, or discs (earth). The Tetragrammaton, or sacred name of God (YHVH) is also divided into the four elements: Y (fire); H (water); V (air) and H (earth). In the Enochian magic of Dr John Dee and Edward Kelley, and utilized in modern times by Aleister Crowley, there are angelic names for the four elements: Bitom (fire); Hcoma (water); Exarp (air) and Nanta (earth). Occultists following the system of magic developed in the Hermetic Order of the Golden Dawn also used the Hindu tattvas (elements) as visualization symbols. The tattvas added spirit to the other four elements. The tattva symbols are tejas, a red equilateral triangle (fire); apas, a silver crescent (water); vayu, a blue circle (air); prithivi, a yellow square (earth); and akasha, a black egg (spirit). The Chinese tradition has five elements (air, earth, fire, water, metal) with their own range of correspondences.

**Eleusis, Mysteries of** In ancient Greece, famous religious and mystical ceremonies held at Eleusis near Athens. The ceremonies, which were founded by Eumpolus, included purifications and fasts, and were sacred to the fertility goddesses Demeter and Persephone. The mystery revealed to participants is thought to have concerned immortality and spiritual rebirth. Until recently, it was assumed that the rituals at Eleusis were theatrical in nature, although the archaeological remains in the initiation temple do not suggest this. According to the ethnomycologist R. Gordon Wasson, the mysteries at Eleusis were of a psychedelic nature, induced by the ergot that grew on the cereal crops in the nearby fields. Wasson proposed that participants in the mysteries may have consumed a drink that contained barley water, mint, and ergot, and were immediately transported into a spirit world. "What was witnessed there," he has written, "was no play by actors, but *phasmata*, ghostly apparitions, in particular the spirit of Persephone herself." Wasson's belief has been supported by Albert Hofmann, who synthesized LSD from ergot. The psychedelic explanation also appears to find support in *The Homeric Hymn to Demeter*, which describes how participants felt a "fear and a trembling in the limbs, vertigo, nausea, and a cold sweat" before the vision dawned in the darkened chamber.

**Eleven** In Christianity, eleven disciples' remained loyal to Jesus and therefore the number has come to symbolize spiritual strength, idealism, and moral virtue. As the first number after **ten**, it represents revelations and visionary insight. However, because it falls short of **twelve**, a number that denotes completeness, eleven is a transitional number. In the **Kabbalah**, which describes ten emanations on the **Tree of Life**, the so-called "eleventh sephirah", **Daath** (knowledge), is not normally ranked with the other ten **sephiroth**, and represents an intermediary stage bridging the **Abyss** between the three **sephiroth** of the Trinity and the seven "days" of Creation. To this extent the number eleven has an element of danger about it; it is sometimes associated with martyrdom. See also **Numerology**.

**Elf** See Elves.

**Elf Arrows** In medieval Britain and Europe, small flint arrowheads associated with the **fairies** and, peripherally, with **witchcraft**. People shot by an elf arrow allegedly contracted mysterious diseases and such magical attacks were connected with witchcraft accusations.

**Elfin** Elf-like, having similar qualities to **Elves**.

**Elhaz** See Eolh.

**Eliade, Mircea** (1907–1986) Romanian-born authority on comparative religion and mysticism who was professor of the history of religions at the University of Chicago. A remarkably prolific author, Eliade produced a number of scholarly works on a wide range of subjects. *Yoga: Immortality and Freedom*; *Shamanism*; and the multi-volume *A History of Religious Ideas* were among his major books, but he wrote widely on the nature of religious experience, the symbolism of the sacred, and patterns of initiatory experiences.

**Eligor** Also **Eligos** In the **Goetia**, the fifteenth spirit, a great duke who appears in the form of a knight, carrying a lance, an ensign, and a serpent. Eligor is associated with both loving allegiance and war. He understands military strategy but also "causeth the love of lords and great persons". Eligor also has a knowledge of hidden things and the future. He commands 60 legions of spirits.

**Elixir of Life** In alchemy, a drink said to restore youth or grant immortality. It was associated with the **Philosopher's Stone**, from which these life-giving properties derived. Also known as **Aurum Potabile**.

**Elohim** One of the sacred names of God in Hebrew scriptures and the Kabbalah, and used by magicians as a god-name in magical ceremonies. It is the plural form of **El** (2), meaning "God". See also following entries.

**Elohim Gebor** In the Kabbalah, the sacred **God-name** associated with the sphere **Geburah** on the **Tree of Life**. Also **Elohim Givor**.

**Elohim Tzevaot** In the Kabbalah, the sacred **God-name** associated with the sphere **Hod** on the **Tree of Life**. It translates as "God of Hosts".

**Elves** Spirit creatures said in Christian tradition to be descended from the children of Eve. They were hidden from the sight of God because there were unclean. In German and Scandinavian mythology, there were elves of light and elves of darkness. Black elves were comparable to dwarfs, but white elves resembled angels. In folk legend, elves are often depicted as small fairies who dance around flowers in the garden, leaving elf-rings and elf-mounds as tokens of their presence, and occasionally firing **elf arrows** at people to cause them harm.

**Elysian Fields** In Greek mythology, "the fields of the blessed". See Elysium.

**Elysium** In Greek mythology, the place where deceased heroes and virtuous people lived in eternal life. Originally, Elysium was located in the West, on the shores of Oceanus, the great river that was said to encircle the world. However, other classical writers located Elysium in the Underworld.

**Emanation** A vibration that issues forth from a single source. In **mysticism**, the world is sometimes considered to be the most physical, dense, or "gross" emanation of the **godhead**. The mystical cosmologies described in the **Kabbalah**, **Gnosticism**, and **Neoplatonism** conceived of the process of creation in this way. In the Kabbalah, for example, there are ten emanations, or **sephiroth**, which come forth from **Ain Soph Aur**, the limitless light. These emanations manifest through Four Worlds, which are successively more dense. They are named **Atziluth**, **Briah**, **Yetzirah**, and **Assiah**, respectively.

**Emancoll** See Phagos.

**Emerald** A precious stone with magical associations. The emerald is sacred to **Venus** and is also identified with the zodiac sign **Taurus**. The alchemical tablet of **Hermes Trismegistus** was said to have been fashioned of emerald, and the Egyptian Eye of **Horus** amulet was often of emerald colour. In Wicca, emerald is assigned to the ritual celebrations of **Beltane** and **Mabon**. On the kabbalistic **Tree of Life** it is assigned to the sephirah Netzach.

**Emerald Tablet** According to *The Hermetica*, the fabled tablet of emerald – *Tabula Smaragdina* – was found clasped in the hands of the corpse of **Hermes Trismegistus**, the mythic founder of the Hermetic tradition. This tablet is said to have contained the essential wisdom-teaching of the Hermetic and alchemical traditions – the tablet included a text upon which the principles of medieval alchemy are based.
See also **Emerald**.

**Emperor, The** In the Tarot, a card of the **Major Arcana** that depicts a benign and peaceful ruler seated on this throne and looking out over the mountains of his kingdom. Occultists regard *The Emperor* as a form of "The Ancient of Days", a wise and loving ruler who has compassion for the inhabitants of the universe and sustains them. He is the antithesis of the destructive qualities symbolized by *The Charioteer*. In western **magic**, which combines the Tarot paths of the Major Arcana with the ten **sephiroth** on the **Tree of Life**, the path of *The Emperor* connects **Tiphareth** and **Chokmah**.

**Empress, The** In the Tarot, a card of the **Major Arcana** that depicts the Great Mother seated on a throne in a field of wheat with the River of Life flowing beside her. Occultists regard *The Empress* as a representation of **Hathor**, the mother of the universe. She also resembles **Demeter**, goddess of the grain. In western **magic**, which combines the Tarot paths of the Major Arcana with the ten **sephiroth** on the **Tree of Life**, the path of *The Empress* connects **Binah** and **Chokmah**.

**Encausse, Dr Gérard** See Papus.

**Enchanted** One who is bewitched or caught in a magic **spell**. See also Bewitchment.

**Enki** The Sumerian counterpart of the Babylonian god **Ea**.

**Enlil** The Sumerian god of the air, wind, and storms. He was worshipped at Nippur, the sacred city of Sumer, and was later regarded as Lord of the Earth. He was adopted by the Babylonians as the deity **Bel**.

**Ennead** From Greek *ennea*, "nine". In **numerology** and Egyptian mythology, the number **nine** or a group of nine. In ancient Egypt there were cycles of nine gods, of which the Ennead of Heliopolis is one example.

**Enoch, The Book of** An apocryphal Jewish book that has influenced the kabbalistic tradition and is considered part of the **Merkabah** mystical literature. There are three versions of *The Book of Enoch*. The Ethiopian version, known as *The First Book of Enoch* (*Enoch I*) and first brought to the West by the Scottish explorer James Bruce in 1773, is the text most commonly republished. The second version, titled *The Book of the Secrets of Enoch* and known as *The Second Book of Enoch* (*Enoch II*) is a medieval Slavonic text that was found in the Belgrade public library by Professor Sokolov in 1886; an English translation appeared in 1896. A Hebrew *Book of Enoch*, referred to as *The Third Book of Enoch* (*Enoch III*), was translated by Hugo Odeberg in 1928. Some versions of *Enoch III* include lists of the magical names and magical formulae ascribed to the archangel **Metratron**, who is regarded by contemporary occultists as the ruler of **Kether**, the first sephirah on the kabbalistic **Tree of Life**. See also **Angel**; **Kabbalah**.

**Enochian Magic** See Magic, Enochian

**Enochian Tablets** See Tablets, Enochian.

**Ensalmo** In South America, a **spell**, enchantment, or magical charm, thought to have been brought to the continent by the Spanish conquerors at the end of the sixteenth century.

**Entered Apprentice** In Freemasonry, a person who has been given the first degree of initiation.

**Enti** Among the Chiricahua Indians of the southwestern United States, a term used to denote the harmful aspect of magical power. This power is considered potentially good or evil, but the outcome depends on the intention of the person who directs it.

**Entity** A discarnate or disembodied spirit, or "presence".

**Eoh** In the Germanic **Elder Futhark**, the rune letter representing the number thirteen. Eoh corresponds to the sound "el" and is specifically linked to the sacred yew tree – a symbol of immortality. It evokes the eternal cycle of death and rebirth and is connected with such themes as endurance, transition, and the quest for enlightenment. The Eoh rune represents the path of vertical ascent along the axis of the world tree **Yggdrassil** and assures us that death is not to be feared. Also Ihwaz.

**Eolh** In the Germanic **Elder Futhark**, the rune letter representing the number fifteen. Eolh corresponds to the letter "z" and is the rune of protection and guardian spirits, used to ward off magical attack. Eolh reminds us of the dangers that accompany the mystical quest and that negative forces can attempt to divert us from our goal. Nevertheless, this rune offers protection. Eolh is the rune of the guardian deity Heimdall and is associated with the sacred elk.

**Ephemeris** A reference work, used by astrologers, which lists the positions of the sun and planets on each day of the year, including details of longitude, latitude, and declination. It is used in constructing a **horoscope**. See also **Astrology**.

**Epopt** One who is instructed in a secret system of mystical knowledge. Epopt is the Fourth Degree in the magical system recognized by the magical **Fellowship of Kouretes** in California.

**Epstein, Perle** Born in New York City, Epstein is a leading contemporary writer on the **Kabbalah**. A descendant of the eighteenth-century kabbalist Ba'al Shem Tov, she is the author of several works on mysticism, including *Kabbalah: The Way of the Jewish Mystic*; *Oriental Mystics and Magicians*; and *The Way of Witches*.

**Equinox** The time at which the sun crosses the equator. This takes place on 21 March and 22 September each year, and on these days the length of day and night are equal.

**Equinox of the Gods** In the Thelemic cosmology of **Aleister Crowley**, a change in the celestial hierarchy resulting in a radical and dramatic shift in human awareness. Following a revelation from a semi-invisible entity named **Aiwaz** in Cairo in 1904, Crowley came to believe that he had been chosen to be the Lord of the New Aeon. This was the **Aeon of Horus** – the Aeon of the Crowned and Conquering Child – and it replaced the two earlier aeons, the matriarchal Aeon of Isis and the later patriarchal **Aeon of Osiris**. According to Crowley, Osiris and the resurrected Christ both belonged to the Aeon of Osiris and were now declared obsolete. See also **Thelema**.

**Equinox, The** A series of occult books compiled by **Aleister Crowley**, which he decided to publish twice a year, coinciding with the vernal and autumnal equinoxes. Ten issues appeared between 1909 and 1913. The so-called *Blue Equinox* was published in Detroit in 1919. Several of Crowley's most important writings, such as *The Vision and the Voice*, first appeared in *The Equinox*.

**Erebus** In Greek mythology, the god of darkness. His wife and sister was **Nyx**, goddess of the night.

**Ereshkigal** The Sumerian queen of the Underworld, sometimes linked to Hecate. She had a bizarre appearance, with a sharp horn extending from her forehead, the ears of a sheep, the body of a fish, and scales like a serpent.

**Ergon** In alchemy, the right eye of the soul, which is directed towards the eternal. The left eye of the soul – the **parergon** – looks towards time.

**Ergot** A parasitic fungus, *Claviceps purpurea*, which attacks barley, wheat, and rye. **R. Gordon Wasson** has suggested that the visionary experiences of neophytes in the **Mysteries of Eleusis** may have been caused by the presence of ergot in the sacred barley-water drink; and Linnda R. Caporael has similarly proposed that ergot poisoning at Salem village may have caused convulsions and hallucinations wrongly associated with **witchcraft**. LSD, one of the most powerful psychedelics known, was first synthesized from ergot by Dr Alfred Hofmann in 1943. See also **Flying Ointments**; **St Anthony's Fire**; **Salem Witches**.

**Erinyes** or **Erinnyes** The three Furies of Greek mythology, Tisiphone, Alecto, and Megaera. They were fearsome to behold and looked like old hags with snakes for hair, bats' wings, and bloodshot eyes. They killed their victims with scourges. The role of the Erinyes was to avenge wrongdoings and breaches of social custom. Each of the Furies had a different function. Alectro maintained Justice, Megaera punished jealousy, and Tisiphone avenged evil. They were also known by the placatory term Eumenides, or "Kindly Ones".

**Eros** The Greek god of love, the equivalent of the Roman **Cupid**. The birth of Eros is obscure. Some say he was the son of **Aphrodite** and **Zeus**, others maintain that Ares or **Hermes** was his father. However, it is probable that he actually predated Aphrodite as the personification of universal passion – the force that brought the cosmic gods together in order to create the universe in the first place.

**Erytheis** See Garden of Hesperides, The.

**Erzulie** In voodoo, the loa of love, beauty, wealth, and prosperity. She is the lunar wife of Legba, the sun god.

**Esbats** In Wicca, the thirteen so-called "lesser" celebrations (in comparison to the eight sabbats). There are thirteen months in the lunar calendar, and therefore there are usually thirteen esbats each year. Wiccans believe that esbats are marked by a sense of heightened psychic awareness resulting from the lunar energy of full moon, and many Wiccans like to perform their specific magical workings at this time. Esbats are a time for invocations, love magic and healing ceremonies but they are also a time for dancing, drinking and feasting – the word "esbat" itself is thought to derive from the Old French word *s'esbattre*, meaning "to frolic and amuse oneself". Traditionally, the esbat lasts from midnight till cock-crow.

Each of the esbats has its own name and this is linked symbolically to the time of the year in which it occurs. The first occurs in October just before the festival of **Samhain** (All Hallows' Eve, or Halloween ) and is called Blood Moon. It is traditionally associated with the slaughter of animals for food prior to the onset of winter and is therefore repre-sented by the colour red. Snow Moon rises in November and is associated with the first falls of snow. Oak Moon is the full moon in December. It is linked to the colour black and also to the oak – sacred symbol of the Dark Lord aspect of **Cernunnos** – since it is his wood which is burnt at Yule. Ice Moon, represented by the colour purple, comes in January, followed by Storm Moon in February – a time when the ice and sleet may turn to rain. This full moon is linked to the element water, and to the colour blue. March brings the Chaste Moon, the

return of spring from the depths of winter, and is represented by the colour white. In April, Seed Moon is a time when the seeds in the earth bring forth new life, and this esbat is represented by the colour green. Hare Moon rises in May and is dedicated both to the **Great Goddess** and to fertility. Its colour is pink, symbolic of love. June brings the Dyad Moon and, as American neopagan author Gwydion O'Hare has noted, this name alludes to "the visible presence of the God and Goddess reflected in the bright sun and green fields". The associated colour is orange, "the colour of the summer sun".

The Mead Moon comes in July and is a time for dancing and revelry. Traditionally this is the time when honey mead was made for the ensuing harvest celebrations and accordingly its symbolic colour is yellow. August brings the Wort Moon – a reference to the dark green abundance of harvest time – and September is the month of the Barley Moon. This is the season when grain is harvested: brown is the symbolic colour for this esbat. Finally, Wine Moon is the esbat which arises as a consequence of the difference between the solar and lunar calendars. Unlike the twelve-month cycle of the solar calendar there are usually thirteen full moons in any given year, and this esbat is the thirteenth. It honours the sacrament of wine and its colour is burgundy red. Wine Moon precedes Blood Moon, and so the lunar cycle continues.

As mentioned above, esbats are sometimes referred to as "lesser" Wiccan celebrations. As **Doreen Valiente** has noted, "the esbat is a smaller and less solemn occasion than the sabbat". The major sabbats, on the other hand, are cel-ebrations which link contemporary Wicca directly with festivals honoured by the **Celts** and **Druids**. See **Sabbats, Greater** and **Sabbats, Lesser**.

**Eschatology** Beliefs and doctrines relating to "the last things": i.e. death, heaven, hell, purgatory, and the final judgment. From Greek *eskhatos*, "last, final".

**Esh** In the Kabbalah, the Hebrew term for "fire". It is also the element corresponding to the letter shin.

**Esoteric** Term applied to teachings that are secret, and only for initiates of a group; mysterious; occult; "hidden".

**Esprit** In voodoo, the spirit or soul of a dead person.

**Estafu** An alternative name for a Pueblo kiva.

**Ethiopian** In alchemy, a symbol of the "black stage" of putrefaction, or nigredo. It represented impure or unclean matter.

**Etteilla** The pseudonym of Jean-Baptiste Alliette (1738–1791), a French follower of Court de Gébelin. In true esoteric tradition, Alliette felt that his name had more mystique if reversed. Etteilla maintained that the Tarot had been conceived by seventeen magi and written down 171 years after the Great Flood. Despite these unlikely claims, which were popular in France at the time, Etteilla produced one of the most beautiful Tarot packs – which he called *The Grand Etteilla*. These cards have since been published in facsimile form.

**Etz Ha-Chayyim** In the Kabbalah, the Hebrew term for the Tree of Life. This map of consciousness encompasses the so-called Four Worlds, the ten spheres or sephiroth, and the 22 interconnecting paths.

**European Hellebore** See Hellebore.

**Eve** (1) According to *Genesis*, the first woman, formed by God from one of Adam's ribs. The Hebrew name for Eve, Hawwah, means "the mother of all living things". To this extent Eve is one of the great female mythic archetypes.

**Eve** (2) In alchemy, the counterpart to Adam and the feminine aspect of the prima materia and philosophical mercury. In representing the moist, cold, white receptive aspects of the alchemical process, Eve is associated with both Queen Luna and Diana.

**Evil** That which is debased, wicked, and opposed to the principles of spirituality and goodness. Associated with darkness and personified in the form of devils, demons, monsters, and other images of depravity, bestiality, and vice. See also Devil, The; Satan.

**Evil Eye** The occult belief that certain people can inflict harm or cause bewitchment by just glancing at their victims. This superstition was noted by many classical writers, including Herodotus, Horace, Ovid, Virgil, Plutarch, and Pliny, although the definition of which eyes are "evil" varies from place to place. People with a squint are often accused of possessing the evil eye, as are dwarfs and hunchbacks. Certain popes – including Pius IX and Leo XIII – were accused of it, as were King Louis XIV of France and Emperor Wilhelm II of Germany. In Mediterranean countries it has been more common to accuse people with blue eyes, while in northern Europe dark-eyed people are more suspect. The various protections against the evil eye include bright ornaments designed to divert attention, and charms said to counteract the evil influence. The symbol of Mercury's caduceus, church bells, horseshoes, crescent symbols, silver rings, and knotted cords are also said to be powerful antidotes to the effects of the evil eye. See also Fatal Look.

**Evocation** In ceremonial magic, the summoning of a spirit into visible appearance using spells or words of power. In modern magical rituals, a triangle is used to contain the power of the spirit. The magician places a talisman in the centre of the triangle before evoking the spirit in ritual and then stands outside the area of evocation. Without these symbolic restraints, occultists believe they can lose control over the manifestations and become possessed. See also **Possession**.

**Evola, Julius** (1898–1974) A highly regarded Italian metaphysician who, together with other leading esotericists like Arturo Reghini, Giulio Parese, and Pietro Negri, founded the mysterious UR Group in Rome in 1927. The purpose of this magical group was to bring their individual identities into such a state of superhuman power and awareness that they would be able to exert a magical influence on the world. To do this they employed techniques derived from ancient tantric and Buddhist rituals as well as rare Hermetic texts. Evola's works published in English include *The Yoga of Power*, *The Hermetic Tradition*, *Eros and the Mysteries of Love*, and *The Mystery of the Grail*. An anthology of major writings by Evola and other members of the UR Group, *Introduction to Magic*, was published in the United States in 2001.

**Exarp** In Enochian magic, the sacred name of the spirit of **air**. Exarp (pronounced *ehtz-ar-peh*) is assigned to the **east** and is represented by the colour yellow. See also **Hcoma, Nanta, Bitom**.

**Excalibur** In the Arthurian legends, the magical sword of King Arthur. It was the sword drawn forth from the anvil in the castle of King Pendragon, which identified Arthur as the heir to the throne, and in other accounts it was the sword kept by the Lady of the Lake. Also known as **Caliburnus**, it is possibly linked to the magical sword Calabolg, which belonged to the Irish folk-hero Fergus.

**Exorcism** A ceremony at which evil or satanic forces are banished – either from a location or from within a possessed person. Many cases are cited in the New Testament where Jesus cast forth devils from afflicted people and urged his disciples to do likewise in his name. Modern Christian exorcism follows the same principle. The priest recites the Lord's Prayer, makes the sign of the cross with holy water upon the forehead of the possessed person, places his hands upon him, and orders the evil spirit to depart in Christ's name. Occultists also have their own type of exorcism, although it is intended more as a protective psychic barrier against harmful influences sent by a rival occult group. Different forms of banishing rituals are believed to ward off evil or demonic influences and are used in white magic to ensure that all rituals performed within the magic circle are of an untainted nature. See also **Possession; Psychic Attack**.

**Exoteric** The opposite of **esoteric**. Exoteric teachings are not reserved for initiates or occult groups but are available to the public at large.

**Exú** In Macumba, the god of intersections and magic, and an intermediary between the gods and human beings. Exú is derived from the Yoruba deity Eshu, who is regarded more as a trickster than the devil he became in Brazil. Exú (pronounced *eshu*) was originally considered a phallic god and in the thirteenth century human sacrfices were made to him. Later worshippers offered him chickens, goats, and bulls. In Brazil, King Exú has been confused with the Christian **Devil** and is regarded as too formidable to deal with. However he has several surrogates, among them Exú Manqueira, who can be called on to kill one's enemies; Exú Brasa, who can assist in planning adulterous affairs; Exú Pagao, who instigates quarrels and thrives on hatred; and Poma-Cira, a female Exú who possesses the bodies of men. The sect devoted to Exú worship is known as **Quimbanda**.

**Exú Brasa, Exú Manqueira** and **Exú Pagao** See Exú.

**Eye of Horus** A popular ancient Egyptian **amulet**, which could face right or left, depicting the left eye or right eye of the god **Horus**. According to the noted Egyptologist **Wallis Budge**, it represented either the sun (right eye) or moon (left eye). The amulets were usually made of gold, silver, granite, lapis lazuli, or ceramic.

**Eye Biter** A term used in Elizabethan England to describe a witch accused of causing blindness through evil magical spells. It is also a general expression used to describe the act of inflicting harm by using the evil eye.

# F

**Fachan** In Irish Celtic mythology, an evil spirit, who, like the Cyclops, had one eye in the centre of its forehead. A hand protruded from its chest and a leg from its haunch. Its body was covered with ruffled feathers. The fachan would leap out at unwary travellers and kill them.

**Faery** Alternative spelling of fairy. See Fairies.

**Faery Tradition** A branch of Wicca established in the United States by Victor Anderson and Gwydion Pendderwen. Emphasizing self-development and a pragmatic approach to magic, it reveres the deities which symbolize the forces of nature and is polytheistic in its focus. The American goddess worshipper Starhawk is one of its best known initiates.

**Fafnir** In Scandinavian mythology, the son of Hreidmar, who changed himself into a dragon and slew his father in order to gain the treasure which Loki had stolen from the dwarf Andvari. Fafnir was later killed by Sigurd, who roasted his heart.

**Fagil** In Celtic folklore, the "parting gift" of the fairies. It could be lucky or unlucky, depending on the circumstances.

**Fairies** Spirit creatures who could bring people good luck or evil through their spells and enchantments. In Ireland, the fairy-folk were traditionally known as the *sídhe* – pronounced "shee" – or **Tuatha de Danann**, and inhabited the hills and slopes as well as prehistoric burial mounds such as Newgrange. They were aristocratic, and lived in a beautiful, eternal land called the Land of the Ever Young (Tír na Nóg). They also had monarchs. For example, in County Galway, Fin Bheara and Nuala were king and queen of the Connacht fairies. In

Wales, the king and queen of the fairies – known there as the Tylwyth Teg – were Gwydion ab Don and Gwendhidw, while Shakespeare records the fairy-rulers in *A Midsummer Night's Dream* as Oberon and Titania. Wherever they were found, the fairies had their own domain, or "fairyland", and lived in small groups beneath trees or under the fairy knolls. Some fairies have been regarded as spirits of the streams, rivers, lakes, and woods, and to this degree resemble **elementals**. See also **Banshee; Dryads**.

**Fairyland** The domain of the fairies.

**Fairy Light** See Will-o'-the-Wisp.

**Fairy Ring** A circle of grass whose colour or texture differentiates it from the surrounding grass in a field: In folklore, fairies are believed to have held their nocturnal dances on these rings, especially on All Hallows' Eve and May Eve.

**Falin** In Scottish folklore, a demon said to haunt the highest crags of the mountains near Glen Aven. His head was twice the size of his body and he only appeared before daybreak. To cross his path before the sun had risen led to certain death.

**Fall** In the Kabbalah, the fall from unity or oneness into dualistic consciousness through the process of creative manifestation. In kabbalistic magical cosmology, the Fall is symbolized by the Abyss on the Tree of Life and is traversed during the visionary experience of the sephirah Daath (knowledge). See also **Sephiroth**.

**Fallen Angel** An angel cast forth from heaven for disobeying the commands of God. Fallen angels are associated with the powers of darkness and become known as demons, under the command of the chief fallen angel, the **Devil**, also called **Satan** and **Lucifer**, the "light bearer".

**Familiar** In medieval witchcraft, a spirit helper or demon, usually in the form of an animal, that accompanied a witch or warlock and provided magical powers. Sometimes a drop of blood from the witch was included in the animal's food, allegedly forming a psychic bond between the witch and the familiar. According to one seventeenth-century account, dogs, cats, foals, chickens, hares, rats, and toads were common familiars. Witches sometimes consulted their familiars when making predictions or seeking omens.

**Fang-Shih** A Taoist term for magicians who were skilled in producing magical spells and summoning spirits. In ancient China, such magic predated Taoism itself. The best known Fang-Shih magician was Li Shao-chun (second century BCE), who evoked the "demon" of a cooking stove in order to conjure up the spirit of a dead woman for the emperor.

**Fang-Shu** The Taoist term for magic, occultism, and divination. See also **Fang-Shih**.

**Farine Guinée** In voodoo, powdered ash that is used to produce vevers on the ground which in turn invoke the loa.

**Farr, Florence** (1860–1917) An actress and one-time mistress of George Bernard Shaw, Florence Farr was introduced to modern ceremonial magic by W.B. Yeats and joined the Isis-Urania Temple of the Hermetic Order of the Golden Dawn. Tiring of MacGregor Mathers' autocratic tendencies, she left the Golden Dawn to form her own group, the Sphere. In 1896 she published *Egyptian Magic* (republished 1982), which included extracts from the Gnostic *Bruce Codex*. In this text, Christ is portrayed as an initiator as well as a teacher, and provides his disciples with an understanding of the archons and aeons. Sacred names of power are also included in the text. See also **Aeon; Archon**.

**Farrar, Janet** (1950– ) and **Stewart** (1916–2000) Among the most influential practitioners of contemporary witchcraft in the 1980s and 1990s, the Farrars had already assumed a leadership role in London's neopagan community a decade earlier. Janet Farrar (née Owen) was raised in London in a strictly Christian family: her grandfather was a church councillor in their Anglican parish. However, she began to drift away from Christianity during her adolescent years and later became briefly involved in Transcendental Meditation. She worked for a while as a model and then became a secretary in The Beatles' London office. Around this time Janet visited **Alex Sanders'** and **Maxine Sanders'** London coven. She was impressed by **Wicca** as a spiritual path and decided to join the circle. It was here that she met her husband Stewart Farrar. Stewart had been raised as a Christian Scientist but later became an agnostic – a position he maintained until becoming a devotee of witchcraft. He studied journalism at University College, London, during the 1930s, served as an anti-aircraft gunnery instructor during World War Two, and later worked for several years as an editor for Reuters. He also produced several radio drama scripts for the BBC before becoming a feature writer for the weekly magazine *Reveille* in 1969. It was in his capacity as a journalist that Stewart Farrar had been invited to the Sanders' coven – he had come simply to write an account of a Wiccan initiation. He did not realize at the time that he himself would become a dedicated convert to **neopaganism**.

Despite the substantial difference in their ages – 34 years – Janet Owen and Stewart Farrar were drawn together as magical partners and in December 1970, a few months after taking their initiations, they left Sanders' group to form a coven of their own. They married five years later in a traditional Wiccan **handfasting** ceremony and in 1976 moved to Ireland, where Stewart was able to gain tax relief as an author of science fiction novels, his other major interest. For a time the Farrars ran a coven in a secluded farmhouse near Drogheda, north of Dublin. Like **Gerald Gardner** and **Alex Sanders** before them, the Farrars always emphasized that they were supporting an authentic Celtic tradition. They co-authored several major works on neopaganism, including *Eight Sabbats for Witches*; *The Witches' Way*; *The Witches' Goddess*; and *The Witches' God* – all of which were published both in Britain and the United States – and through their writings and advocacy strongly influenced neopagan thought and practice on both sides of the Atlantic. Following Stewart Farrar's death in 2000, Janet Farrar has continued to promote neopaganism internationally together with her partner Gavin Bone.

**Fascination** The act of using the **evil eye** to cause harm, or to induce a state of trance in victims so that one can cause illness or impotence to befall them. See also **Witch Ball**.

**Fat** A term used by the medieval alchemist **Paracelsus** to describe **philosophical sulphur**, one of the three principles of matter (the other two being phlegma, or **philosophical mercury**, and ash, or **philosophical salt**).

**Fatal Look** The belief that one's gaze can inflict death. A variant on the **evil eye**.

**Fat, Sorcerers'** In the Middle Ages, sorcerers and **black magicians** were falsely accused of using human fat in their spells and rituals – a belief derived from the popular superstition that black magic involved human sacrifice. See **Magic, Black**; **Sorcery**.

**Fate** One's destiny or pre-ordained future. Those who trust in fate believe that the pattern of their lives is fixed at birth and cannot be altered. See also **Fates, Three**.

**Fates** Known in ancient Greece as the Moerae and in ancient Rome as the Parcae, the three Fates were the daughters of **Zeus** and **Themis**, and determined the destiny of all mortal beings. Clotho presided at birth and spun the thread of life; Lachesis was responsible for measuring the length of the thread of life; and Atropos cut the thread with her shears.

**Father God** In many cosmologies, the overseer or ruler (though not necessarily the creator) of the universe is a paternal male deity on whom rests the fate of humankind. Such deities include Zeus (Greek); Jupiter (Roman); Ra (Egyptian); Odin (Scandinavian); and Yahweh/Jehovah (Hebrew). In the Tarot, the symbolism of the father god is personified in two trumps, *The Emperor* (passive/merciful) and *The Charioteer* (active/destructive). See also **Cosmology**; **Demiurge**.

**Fauns** In Greek mythology, creatures with bodies that were half goat, half human and who attended **Pan**, the god of nature. They were more youthful than **satyrs**, but somewhat similar.

**Faust** A legendary figure who is said to have made a pact with the **Devil** in the form of the demon **Mephistopheles**, in return for worldly goods and magical powers. The legend ends in Faust's destruction and damnation. Faust seems to be a composite persona, based in part on historical figures. **Johannes Wierius** believed that Faust was a drunken occultist who lived in Cracow and Germany and was regarded as a deceitful trickster. But there are other figures on whom the legends may be based. Dr Georg Faust was a German necromancer and astrologer who worked as a schoolmaster in Kreuznach in 1507. He may be the same as the Dr Georg Faust of Heidelberg who, in 1528, was banished from the town of Ingolstadt for soothsaying. A Johann Faust, meanwhile, obtained a theology degree from Heidelberg University in 1509. The occult authority **E.M. Butler** inclines to the view that the two Fausts, Georg and Johann, may have been brothers or twins. The story of Faust was famously dramatized by Christopher Marlowe (*Dr Faustus*) in the sixteenth century and later by Goethe (*Faust*).

**Fay** An alternative word for fairy, from Old French *fae* (compare modern French *fée*). The word in turn derives from the Latin *fata*, "fate". The original idea was of a being through whom the power of fate was exercised. The word has probably influenced the modern use of the adjective "fay" or "fey" – meaning whimsical, enchanted, supernatural or fairy-like – which has an entirely different origin.

**Fearn** In the Celtic tree alphabet the **ogham** representing the alder and the sound "f". Fearn is also linked to the gull and the colour crimson.

**Feast of Lights** See Imbolc

**Feather** In ancient Egyptian religion, the attribute of the goddess **Maat**, the personification of truth. In the Judgment Hall presided over by **Osiris**, the heart of the deceased was weighed against this feather and his or her fate decided accordingly.

**Fehu** See Feoh.

**Felkin, Robert William** (c.1858–1922) A prominent member of the **Hermetic Order of the Golden Dawn**, Felkin studied and practised medicine in Edinburgh before moving to London and joining the Isis-Urania Temple. After the split with **MacGregor Mathers**, Felkin rallied several Golden Dawn members to create the Amoun Temple of the **Stella Matutina**. In 1908 he was able to draw on the mediumistic abilities of his second wife, Ethel, to make psychic contact with a discarnate Arab who called himself **Ara ben Shemesh**; Felkin accepted this entity as his Secret Chief, or "inner plane" master. A year earlier Felkin had become a Freemason and in 1912 he visited New Zealand with his family – possibly on masonic business. He eventually settled permanently there and established a lodge of the **Stella Matutina** titled Smaragdum Thalasses, which he governed until his death. See also **Secret Chiefs.**

**Fellow of the Craft** In Freemasonry, one who has attained the second degree of initiation.

**Fellowship of Crotona** A theatrical group based in Hampshire, England, prior to the outbreak of World War Two. It was influenced by Rosicrucian principles and headed by two occultists, Brother Aurelius and Mabel Besant-Scott, daughter of the well-known Theosophist Dr Annie Besant. Some have suggested that the Fellowship of Crotona was a front for the **New Forest Coven** headed by **Dorothy Clutterbuck** – the last of England's **witchcraft** laws had not yet been repealed and secrecy was vitally important. **Gerald Gardner** made contact with the Fellowship of Crotona after retiring as a rubber planter in Malaya and it was through the Fellowship that he was introduced to Dorothy Clutterbuck, who initiated him into **Wicca.**

**Fellowship of Kouretes** A magical order in Tujunga, California, which combines ancient Greek mythology, modern witchcraft, and magical rituals. It recognizes six degrees: Hieros, which includes instruction in the Greek alphabet and trance magic techniques; Dadouchos, which involves "inner plane" astral projection and communication with god-forms; Mystes, which features astral projection, **divination**, and sexual magic; Epopt, which teaches communication with the **holy guardian angel;** Hierodule, which includes initiation as a priest or priestess; and Harcharios, an honorary degree in which the priest or priestess is reminded that there are still many esoteric secrets to learn.

**Feminine Planets** In astrology, the moon (associated with lunar goddesses of fertility); **Venus** (associated with goddesses of love and beauty); and **Neptune** (associated, like the moon,

with the element **water**).

**Feminine Polarity** See Feminine Principle.

**Feminine Principle** In mystical cosmologies there is often a specific relationship between masculine and feminine forces. The feminine principle is usually regarded as receptive (symbolizing the womb from which the universe is born), lunar (reflecting light rather than providing it), and intuitive (rather than intellectual). In patriarchal cosmologies it is often also regarded as negative. See also **Binah; Chokmah; Lunar Goddesses; Male Principle; Yin.**

**Feminine Signs** In astrology, the even-numbered signs of the zodiac: Taurus, Cancer, Virgo, Scorpio, Capricorn, and Pisces.

**Feminist Wicca** See Budapest, Zsuzsanna Emese.

**Fennel** *Foeniculum vulgare*, a hardy perennial herb whose remarkable properties have entered folklore as widely as Asia, Egypt, and Europe. In ancient Greek mythology, Prometheus hid the fire of the sun in a hollow fennel stalk when he first carried it down from heaven to earth. Greek athletes are said to have eaten fennel when competing in the Olympic Games, because they believed it strengthened their muscles without making them fat. The Roman scholar Pliny believed that fennel enabled the eye to see the beauty of nature with enhanced clarity, and it gained a reputation for improving eyesight. In medieval England, bunches of fennel were hung up to keep away evil spirits and witches, and fennel seeds were stuffed into keyholes to keep ghosts out of the house. Fennel does have proven medicinal qualities. It is mainly used as a digestive aid and a diuretic; a few fennel seeds chewed daily will guard against indigestion as well as winter colds and flu.

**Fenrir** or **Fenris** In Scandinavian mythology, the monstrous and ferocious wolf that was the offspring of **Loki** and **Angerboda**. Always hostile to the gods, it was set free during the final cataclysm of **Ragnarok** and swallowed both **Odin** and the sun. It in turn was slain by Odin's son **Vidar**, who survived Ragnarok and heralded the New Age.

**Feoh** In the Germanic Elder Futhark, the rune letter sacred to Frey, or Freyr, the Norse god of fertility and the harvest. Feoh represents the number one, corresponds to the letter "f", and is associated with energy, wealth (gold), and success.

**Fertility Deities** Gods and goddesses who symbolize the cycles of fertility in nature. Because of the cyclic passage of the seasons, they are often associated with myths of rebirth. In ancient Greece, among the most famous fertility deities were **Demeter** and **Persephone**, in whose honour the rites of Eleusis were celebrated. The goddesses **Aphrodite** (the Roman **Venus**) and the gods **Hermes**, **Dionysus**, and **Osiris** were all deities associated with fertility; other examples can be found in most of the world's cosmologies.

**Fetch** In Wicca, a witch – usually male – sent on a confidential mission by the **high priestess** of a **coven**. The fetch is also known as a **summoner** or **officer**.

**Fetish** Symbolic object or **talisman** regarded by an individual as having the magical power to ward off evil. Some fetish objects are believed to house protective spirits. Fetish objects are common in traditional west African religion. See also **Fetishism**.

**Fetishism** Especially in traditional African religion, the belief in, and worship of, guardian spirits that reside in fetish objects.

**Ficino, Marsilio** (1433–1499) Florentine philosopher and mystic who translated the works of **Plato**, **Plotinus**,

and **Proclus** and also the tracts ascribed to the legendary **Hermes Trismegistus**. He believed that the universe was an emanation of God, and that one could attract celestial influences by meditating on the symbols of the planets. His works include *Theologica Platonica de Immortalitate Animarum* and *Libri de Vita*.

**Fifth Element** In magic and alchemy, the element **spirit**, which encompasses the other four **elements**, **fire**, **air**, **water**, and **earth**. As the so-called "fifth element" it is known as the **quintessence**. Among the alchemists it was referred to as **azoth**.

**Figa** In Macumba, an ornamental charm consisting of a thumb between the middle and index fingers. It is worn to ward off evil forces.

**Figure** In astrology, the map of the heavens more popularly known as the **horoscope**.

**Fir and Pine** Evergreen coniferous trees belonging to the genus *Abies* of the family *Pinaceae* (pines). Pine and fir trees have many magical and mythic associations. In Phrygia it was sacred to **Cybele**, and in ancient Roman mythology, **Rhea** turned **Attis** into a pine tree to prevent his death. The Romans regarded unopened pine cones as symbols of virginity and these were accordingly sacred to **Diana**. The pine was also sacred to **Dionysus**, whose devotees often wore foliage from the fir tree. Sometimes the fir symbolizes the "axis of the world" and in **shamanism** serves as a bridge between the everyday world and the supernatural dimension. For some shamans the fir is the "universal tree" that grows at the "centre of the world". One Yakut legend mentions that the souls of the shamans were born in a fir tree on Mount Dzokuo; another that the great shamans are found in the highest branches of the fir tree and the lesser shamans lower down. See also **Nature Worship**.

**Fire** One of the four alchemical elements, the others being **earth, water,** and **air**. The spirits of fire are known as **salamanders** (a mythic variety not related to the actual small, newt-like amphibian). The three astrological signs linked to fire are **Aries, Leo,** and **Sagittarius**. See also **Alchemy**.

**Fire, St Anthony's** See St Anthony's Fire.

**Fire Temple** In Zoroastrianism, a temple for worship that includes a "fire sanctuary". It is sometimes accessible only to the priest. The fire itself – which represents **Ahura Mazdah** – is never allowed to go out.

**Firmament** In ancient cosmologies, the "vault of the heavens" invariably associated with sky deities. **Nut**, the Egyptian goddess of the sky, is a characteristic example: she was often represented with an elongated star-covered body that arched above the earth so that only her fingertips and toes touched the horizons.

**First Initiation** or **First Degree** In Wicca, an initiation intended to cast away the old persona that existed prior to the candidate joining the **coven**. Many Wiccan covens ask candidates for initiation to fast for several days and also to spend lengthy periods meditating on nature before the ceremony itself. Immediately before the First Initiation takes place, the candidate will be asked to bathe and will then be brought naked and blindfolded to the sacred circle. Usually the hands are bound with ritual cords. While the new initiate-to-be waits outside the circle the **Great Goddess** and **Horned God** are invoked into the high priestess and high priest respectively. For all new coven members, the **Charge of the Goddess** is spoken to open the initiation ceremony. At the outer rim of the circle the candidate is challenged at the point of a sword: this is intended to heighten the candidate's sense of vulnerability and exposure. However, once the new candidate has been accepted within the circle as a sincere seeker after truth, he or she is welcomed by the initiator – always a member of the opposite sex – who kneels and bestows blessings and kisses upon different parts of the candidate's body (the feet, knees, phallus/womb, breasts and lips). As Wiccan high priestess **Vivianne Crowley** has put it, "the body is honoured and reverenced" and the essential message of the First Initiation is one of acceptance. See also **Second Initiation; Third Initiation**.

**First Matter** In alchemy, the first manifestation of the godhead, perceived as a fusion of spirit and matter. The first matter – or **prima materia** – was essentially formless, and constituted the darkness from which the universe was subsequently born. The alchemist Thomas Vaughan describes it in his work *Anthroposphia Theomagica*: "I conceive it (to be) the effect of the divine imagination, acting beyond itself in contemplation of that which was to come, and producing this passive darkness." Vaughan goes on to say that the "splendour of the Word" cast the darkness down into an abyss of formless night and eventually the divine spirit produced light and life from that darkness.

**First Order** In the Hermetic Order of the Golden Dawn, the five grades of initiation preceding **Tiphareth** at the centre of the kabbalistic **Tree of Life**. These grades were **Neophyte** (a grade not ascribed to the Tree of Life); **Zelator** (**Malkuth**); **Theoricus** (**Yesod**); **Practicus** (**Hod**); and **Philosophus** (**Netzach**).

**Firth, Violet** See Fortune, Dion.

**Fisher King** In the Arthurian legends, the lord of the castle of the **Holy Grail** and keeper of the bleeding lance (a symbol linking the Grail legend to Christianity). The Fisher King was so-named because fishing was his only pastime. He was a cripple and could only be restored to health by a question put to him by the Grail hero.

**Five** In numerology, the number associated with versatility, restlessness, and adventure. People whose names "reduce" to five (when numerical values are assigned to each of the letters) are said to love speculation and risks, and a varied environment. They are fond of travel and resist responsibility or any other factors in their lives that would tend to tie them down.

**Fivefold Kiss** or **Fivefold Salute** In Wicca, the witches' ritual kiss, performed inside the magic circle and applied to five different parts of the body of another coven member. Kisses are applied in sequence on each foot, on each knee, on the lower belly, on each breast and on the lips. See also **First Initiation**.

**Fixation** In alchemy, the coagulation of the volatile spirit of **Mercurius** – the "converting of spirit into body so that it can endure the fire and not fly away".

**Flagae** Spirits or familiars that appear to the witch or magician in a mirror and reveal esoteric truths or obscure information.

**Flagellation** The act of whipping or scourging the body. Some ascetics inflict this punishment upon themselves as **atonement** for their sins. Certain occultists, among them **Aleister Crowley**, have practised self-flagellation to strengthen the magical will. See also **Scourge**.

**Flamel, Nicholas** (1330–1417) A French **alchemist** born of poor parents but who subsequently attained great wealth, allegedly by discovering the **Philosopher's Stone**, which could transmute base metals into gold. He claimed guidance from an angel named Bath-Kol, who showed him a book bound in copper with leaves of bark and characters inscribed in gold. Although this book was not bequeathed to him, Flamel maintained in an account written in 1399 that a comparable work – bound in brass and "graven all over with a strange kind of letters" – came his way for the modest price of two florins. The book contained symbolic statements relating to **alchemy** and contained hints on how the **Great Work** might be attained. Flamel says he sought guidance on how to interpret the book from one "Anselm, a practiser of physic", but disagreed with his views. He travelled to Spain in search of other opinions, but returned to France, where he resorted to prayer in order to gain the insights he required.

Flamel wrote enthusiastically that on 17 January 1382, with his wife Perrenelle, he successfully performed an experiment in which he transmuted a pound and a half of mercury into "pure silver", and that in the following April he transmuted mercury into gold. Historians have regarded Flamel's account with rather less enthusiasm, however, and believe his claim to be totally spurious. It is more likely that the wealth he did obtain resulted from his business as a scrivener and money-lender. The issue is complicated by the fact that many of the works ascribed to Flamel are of dubious authorship, so we cannot be sure of the authenticity of his claims.

**Flauros** In the Goetia, the 64th spirit, a great duke who appears first in the form of a strong and terrible leopard but who then assumes a human form when commanded. Even then his eyes continue to blaze with flames and he has a frightening appearance. Unless he is contained within the magical triangle of evocation, he will lie and deceive those who conjure his appearance, but he does have the power to reveal the secrets of creation and how he and other spirits fell from grace. Flauros can destroy the magician's enemies through the power of fire, if instructed to do so.

He leads 36 legions of spirits and is also known as Haures or Hauras.

**Flexed Signs** In astrology, the mutable or double-bodied signs.

**Flowers, Stephen Edred** A leading authority on **runes** and closely associated with the **Temple of Set**'s Order of the Trapezoid – which specializes in the rune magic of northern Europe – Flowers has written or translated nearly 40 books in this subject area. In 1980 he founded the Rune-Gild, the world's most influential initiatory organization dedicated to rune work on the Odian path, and in 1984 he received a doctorate from the University of Texas for a dissertation titled *Runes and Magic*. Founder of the Woodharrow Institute for Germanic and Runic Studies and owner of the Runa-Raven Press, Flowers lives in Austin, Texas.

**Fludd, Robert** (1574–1637) An English mystic, musician, astrologer, and occult artist who studied the *Hermetica* and Rosicrucian philosophy. Fludd believed in the kabbalistic cosmology in which the Absolute God or YHVH transcends good and evil. He was interested in the notion of cosmic harmony, emanations, and mystical hierarchies of spirit beings, and portrayed the Hermetic axiom, "as above, so below", in many of his symbolic compositions. Fludd's works, many of which included detailed cosmo-logical diagrams and "occult mandalas", were interpreted by many of the best engravers in Europe.

**Fluid Body** In occultism and Theosophy, a synonym for the **astral body**.

**Fly Agaric** See *Amanita muscaria*.

**Flying Ointments** Lotions rubbed on the skin and used by medieval witches to produce states of dissociation and trance, and the perception of having flown to the **witches' sabbath**. According to American anthropologist Michael Harner, European witches rubbed their bodies with hallucinogenic ointments made from such plants as **deadly nightshade** (*Atropa belladonna*), mandrake (*Mandragora*) and henbane (*Hysocyamus*); the psychedelic con-stituent, atropine, was absorbed through the skin. This produced the visionary sensation of going on a "trip" (on a broomstick) and meeting with other witches and demons at the Sabbath. In 1966 the German scholar professor Will-Erich Peukert mixed a "witches' brew" consisting of belladonna, henbane, and datura and rubbed it on his forehead. He also invited his colleagues to do the same. According to a report of the experiment, "they fell into a 24-hour sleep in which they dreamed of wild rides, frenzied dancing, and other weird adventures of the type connected with medieval orgies".

**Flying Slave** In alchemy, a term for quicksilver, or **argent vive**.

**Focalor** In the **Goetia**, the 41st spirit, a powerful duke who appears in the form of a man with the wings of a griffin. He slays men by drowning them in the sea and overthrows ships of war: his power is vested in the wind and ocean. However he will cease his destructive acts on the command of the magician. Focalor hopes to return to the Seventh Throne of King **Solomon** after 1050 years and rules over 30 legions of spirits. He is also known as Furcalor.

**Folklore** Popular superstitions and beliefs that develop into a tradition of legends and stories often involving gods, spirits, demons, and other supernatural beings. Oral folklore traditions are often passed from one generation to the next as a collection of tales and anecdotes.

**Fomorians** In Irish Celtic mythology, the fourth race of beings to inhabit ancient Ireland. A maritime group, they were defeated by the **Tuatha De Danann** in the battle of Mag Tuireadh.

**Food, Sacred** See Sacred Food.

**Fool, The** In the Tarot, the supreme card, which symbolizes "he-who-knows-nothing" – the person who therefore has knowledge of no-thing, "that which is unmanifest or transcendent". This realm lies beyond the created universe and no qualities or attributes may be ascribed to it. In western magic, which combines the Tarot paths of the Major Arcana with the ten sephiroth on the Tree of Life, the path of *The Fool* connects Kether and Chokmah.

**Foraii** See Morax.

**Foras** or **Forcas** In the Goetia, the 31st spirit, a mighty president who appears in the form of a strong and imposing man. He imparts a knowledge of the virtues of herbs and precious stones, can lengthen one's life, and can also render a person invisible. Foras can also locate hidden treasure and items that have been lost. He rules over 29 legions of spirits and is also known as Forcas.

**Forfax** See Morax.

**Forneus** In the Goetia, the 30th spirit, a powerful marquis who appears in the form of a sea-monster. He is very skilled in the art of rhetoric, teaches all languages, and can make men love their enemies. He commands 29 legions of spirits, some of them drawn from the angelic order of thrones, others from the order of ordinary angels. See also Angel.

**Fort** In voodoo, someone highly skilled in ritual procedures who therefore has the strength to command the loa.

**Fortified Sign** In astrology, a sign that is well positioned or well aspected in a horoscope.

**Fortuna** The Roman goddess of happiness and good fortune and the counterpart of the Greek goddess Tyche. She bestowed wealth on some lucky mortals, but poverty on those who had fallen from favour. Notoriously fickle, she was also regarded as the goddess of chance.

**Fortune, Dion** (1890–1946) Dion Fortune was born Violet Mary Firth on 6 December 1890 at Bryn-y-Bia, in Llandudno, Wales. Although details of her early professional life are scanty, it is known that she worked as a therapist in a medico-psychological clinic in London and later studied psychoanalysis in classes held at the University of London. In Carl Jung's thought, especially, she found correlations between the archetypes of the collective unconscious and a realm of enquiry which would increasingly fascinate her – the exploration of sacred mythological images invoked by occultists during their rituals and visionary encounters. Through her friend Maiya Curtis-Webb, Violet Firth was introduced to the Hermetic Order of the Golden Dawn in 1919. In the Temple of Alpha and Omega, Firth took the magical name *Deo Non Fortuna* – "by God and not by luck" – which happened to be the Latin motto on the Firth family crest. She now became known in esoteric circles as Dion Fortune – a contraction of her magical name – and in 1922 formed her own meditative group. It was originally known as The Christian Mystic Lodge of the Theosophical Society and would later become The Fraternity of the Inner Light.

Dion Fortune's unique contribution to esoteric thought really began with the establishment of the Inner Light. Here she increasingly engaged herself in the mythological dimensions of magic – venturing into what she now came to regard as the collective pagan soul of humanity, and tapping into the very heart of the ancient mysteries. Reversing the male-dominated, solar-oriented tradition which MacGregor Mathers had established in the Golden Dawn, Dion Fortune now committed herself completely to the magical potency of the archetypal feminine, and began exploring goddess images in the major ancient pantheons. Dion Fortune died in 1946 but the approach and techniques of the Fraternity of the Inner Light have continued through the auspices of the contemporary occult group **Servants of the Light**, at present headed by **Dolores Ashcroft-Nowicki.**

Dion Fortune wrote a number of important occult works, but her best-known and most enduring is *The Mystical Qabablah*, which is regarded by many occultists as one of the best textbooks on practical **Kabbalah** ever written.

**Fortune Teller** One who claims to predict the future through **divination**. Fortune telling may take different forms, but the most popular contemporary forms are **astrology, Tarot**, and, to a lesser extent, **numerology.**

**Fortune Telling** See Fortune Teller.

**Fortunes, Greater and Lesser** In astrology, two planets – **Jupiter** (associated with wisdom, wealth, and generosity) and **Venus** (associated with love) – are said to determine one's "fortune". Jupiter is sometimes termed the "Greater Fortune" and Venus the "Lesser Fortune". The other particularly favourable bodies are the **sun**, the **moon**, and **Mercury.**

**Fountain** In alchemy, an image relating to the so-called Mercurial water or aqua permanens. The alchemists believed that all metals came forth from the Mercurial fountain, the fountain of sacred knowledge – the source of life. See **Mercurius.**

**Four** In numerology, the number associated with hard work and practicality – and also unhappiness and defect. People whose names "reduce" to four (when numerical values are given to each of the letters) are said to be stolid and uninspiring, but often very methodical in routine work situations. Their rather plodding and unadventurous natures mean that they do not easily attain success.

**Four Directions** The directions **north, east, south**, and **west**, also called the Four Quarters. In western **magic**, the four directions are symbolized in ritual by the four archangels: **Uriel** (north); **Raphael** (east), **Michael** (south), and **Gabriel** (west); representing the four **elements** – earth, air, fire, and water respectively. According to the *Grimoire of Honorius*, the four directions also have four demons associated with them: Magoa (east), Egym (south), Baymon (west), and Amaymon (north). See also **Archangel; Demon.**

**Four Elements** See Elements.

**Four-Footed Signs** In astrology, the signs of the zodiac that represent quadrupeds: **Aries, Taurus, Leo, Sagittarius**, and **Capricorn.**

**Four Quarters** See Four Directions.

**Four Worlds** In the Kabbalah, the four distinct stages of creative manifestation. God is present in each of the "worlds" and these in turn reflect the sacred name of God – the **Tetragrammaton YHVH** (Yod, He, Vau, He ), usually translated as Jehovah or Yahweh. The Four Worlds are: **Atziluth**, the archetypal world, which contains the sephirah **Kether**; **Briah**, the world of creation, which contains the sephiroth **Chokmah** and **Binah**; **Yetzirah**, the world of formation, which contains the sephiroth **Chesed, Geburah, Tiphareth, Netzach, Hod**, and **Yesod**; and **Assiah**, the physical world, which contains the sphere of **Malkuth** and is associated with the **Shekinah.**

**Fox Fire** See Will-o'-the-Wisp.

**Fox, Selena** (1949 – ) An American high priestess of **Wicca** who is well known for her association with the Wiccan-pagan community known as Circle Sanctuary near Mount Horeb, Wisconsin. Fox was raised in a fundamentalist Southern Baptist family but had psychic and mystical experiences as a child and later became fascinated by the **Tarot**. Soon after graduating in psychology from the College of William and Mary she met a Prussian hereditary witch at an archaeological dig in Hampton, Virginia. Fox described their meeting as "like old sisters finding each other" and she subsequently entered the Craft. She has since been initiated as a high priestess in many different traditions. Fox and her partner at the time, Jim Alan, together with a group of neopagan friends, founded a **coven** named Circle in 1974. It was subsequently incorporated in 1978 as Circle Sanctuary and legally recognized as a church. Ceremonies performed at Circle Sanctuary do not feature the ornate ritual swords, cups, and daggers associated with contemporary British **witchcraft**, but make use of objects which come from the land itself – like rocks, twigs, flowers, and herbs. As Fox has said: "Circle Sanctuary is sacred land purchased to be held by pagans for use by pagans.... Mother Nature is the greatest teacher."

**Franck, Adolphe** (1809–1893) An orientalist and Hebraist who was professor of natural philosophy at the Collège de France and produced one of the earliest general works on the **Kabbalah**. Franck's *La Kabbale: ou la philosophie religieuse des Hébreux* was first published in Paris in 1843 and translated into English by I. Sossnitz for its American publication in 1926. Franck's interpretation of the Kabbalah focused especially on the system of emanations from the godhead and, according to the modern kabbalistic authority **Gershom Scholem**, placed too much emphasis on **pantheism**. This criticism notwithstanding, Franck's work did much to pave the way for later research into Jewish esoteric thought.

**Frankincense** See Olibanum.

**Fraternity of the Inner Light** An occult group formed by **Dion Fortune** and her husband Penry Evans in 1922. Dion Fortune had joined the **Hermetic Order of the Golden Dawn** three years earlier, but felt that the temple to which she belonged consisted "mainly of widows and grey-bearded ancients" and needed a new spark of life. The Fraternity of the Inner Light was established to recruit people interested in more esoteric work, especially goddess-oriented research into visionary magic.

**Fravashis** In Persian mythology, guardian spirits, or **genii**, who defended all living creatures in the eternal battle between good and evil. See also **Magi**; **Zoroastrianism**.

**Free Soul** See Soul.

**Freemasonry** or Masonry This international institution now has the nature of a benevolent, friendly society, but was originally an esoteric organization. It still has elaborate secret rites and ceremonies and a code of morals, and requires that its members believe in "the Great Architect of the Universe". Freemasonry may be descended, directly or indirectly, from a guild of stonemasons that existed in fourteenth-century England; but modern Masonry dates from the establishment of the Grand Lodge of London (1717). Freemasonry later spread to the United States and Europe. At times, in some countries, Freemasonry has been suppressed by the state. Traditionally, it has aroused the hostility of the Roman Catholic Church, but in recent years this antagonism has subsided. See also **Co-Masonry**.

**Frey** See Freyr.

**Freyja** or **Freya**. In Scandinavian mythology, the goddess of fertility, love, and marriage. She is the most important goddess of the Vanir deities and ruled them with her brother **Freyr**. The **Brisingamen** necklace – created for her by four dwarfs – symbolized her magical power over nature.

**Freyr** In Scandinavian mythology, the god of fertility and harvests, and controller of both the sun and rain. He ruled the **Vanir** with his sister **Freyja**.

**Freyr's Aett** In the Germanic Elder Futhark, rune numbers one to eight.

**Friar's Balsam** See Benzoin.

**Friar's Cap** See Monkshood.

**Frog** See Toad.

**Frost, Gavin** See Church of Wicca.

**Frost, Yvonne** See Church of Wicca.

**Frustration** In astrology, a situation where three planets present themselves in conflict and one of the planets frustrates the aspects arising from the other two.

**Fuath** An evil water spirit of Scottish folklore. It has yellow hair, a tail and mane, webbed feet, and no nose. The term fuath is sometimes used to describe nature spirits generally, without any evil connotation.

**Fulcanelli** (c. 1856–?) A mysterious and semi-legendary alchemist who is said to be one of the only serious researchers to have pursued the **Philosopher's Stone** in the 20th century. In the early 1920s, Fulcanelli gave a French student of **alchemy** named Eugène Canseliet a manuscript called *The Mystery of the Cathedrals*. It created a sensation when it was published in Paris in 1926, and included descriptions of the heretical, pagan, and alchemical motifs that embellished the masonry of Gothic cathedrals in Bourges, Amiens, and Paris. Fulcanelli then disappeared and for many years was seen by no-one. However, Canseliet claimed that when he saw him briefly, many years later – when Fulcanelli should have been around 100 years old – "he looked not older than I was myself" (around 50). Fulcanelli is regarded as a modern **Comte de Saint Germain**, who similarly claimed to have discovered the alchemical secret of eternal youth.

**Fuller, John Frederick Charles** (1878–1966) A British military historian and soldier who became a disciple of **Aleister Crowley** and produced a volume entitled *The Star in the West* (1907), which praised his magical philosophy. Fuller contributed to Crowley's journal *The Equinox* and is thought to have originated the term "Crowleyanity" to describe the teachings of the **Aeon of Horus**, outlined in *The Book of the Law* (1904).

**Furcalor** See Focalor.

**Furcas** In the Goetia, the 50th spirit, a duke who appears in the form of a cruel old man with a long beard and hoary head. He rides a pale-coloured horse and carries a sharp weapon in his hand. Furcas teaches philosophy, **astrology**, rhetoric, logic, chiromancy, and **pyromancy**, and commands 20 legions of spirits.

**Furfur** In the Goetia, the 34th spirit, a great and mighty earl who appears in the form of a red male deer with a fiery tail. He will refuse to tell the truth unless confined by the magician to the triangle of evocation, but once within the triangle assumes the form of an **angel** and speaks with a hoarse voice. He creates thunder and lightning and great, tempestuous storms but is also able to inspire love between men and women. Furfur rules 26 legions of spirits.

**Furies** See Erinyes.

**Futhark, Elder** The Germanic alphabet of **runes** used in pagan northern Europe between the fifth and eighth centuries CE and which consisted of 24 letters. The use of these runes continued until at least 1000CE. An Anglo-Saxon variant futhark used in Britain between the fifth and twelfth centuries CE had more letters (until c. 900CE it had 28 letters and later 33 letters). Among contemporary magical practitioners the 24-letter Germanic futhark remains the most popular. See also **Futhark, Younger**.

**Futhark, Younger** The Norse alphabet of **runes** associated with stone inscriptions found in Norway, Sweden, and Denmark. This has only 16 letters, compared with the so-called **Elder Futhark**, which has more. There are apparently still practitioners of stavecraft – rune **divination** – in Scandinavia today.

**Fylfot Cross** A symbol used in modern **ceremonial magic**. Resembling a **swastika** whose arms point to the left, the fylfot cross is divided into squares bearing the twelve signs of the **zodiac** and the signs of the four **elements**, with the motif of the **sun** in the centre.

# G

**Gabriel** A chief **archangel** and one of only two angels named in the Bible, the other being **Michael**. First mentioned in *The Book of Daniel* (Daniel 8 and 9), he plays a major role in the New Testament, for example appearing to Mary to announcing the birth of Jesus. Gabriel also features in apocryphal works such as *The Book of Enoch*, and is also important in Islam, where he is known as Jibreel, and in esoteric traditions. In modern western **magic** Gabriel is considered to be the archangel of the element **water** and is invoked in the West.

**Gad** In **voodoo**, a protective tattoo applied to the skin during a magical initiation. Acting like a **charm**, the tattoo protects the individual against evil forces.

**Gaea** or **Gaia** In Greek mythology, the earth goddess, who was born after **Chaos**. She united with her son **Uranus**, the sky, to produce the divine race of twelve Titans and was also the mother of the Cyclopes. See also **Cyclops**.

**Gagnin Loa** In **voodoo**, literally "to have a **loa** in one's head" – to be possessed by a loa.

**Gaia** See Gaea.

**Galactides** A magical stone, resembling an emerald, which is said to make ghosts visible and magical formulae audible. It also bestows love and friendship.

**Galgalim** See Gilgulim.

**Gallows Hill** The execution site where witches condemned in the Salem witchcraft trials (1692–1693) were hanged. The site is said to be still haunted by the spirits of the dead witches. See **Salem Witches**.

**Galvanic Mirror** A magnetized disc,

consisting of a concave copper section and a convex zinc section joined together. It is used for **skrying** and is a modern variant on the **crystal ball**.

**Gamygyn** or **Gamigin** In the Goetia, the fourth spirit, a great marquis who appears in the form of a small horse or donkey as well as in human shape. He teaches "all liberal sciences" and also "giveth an account of dead souls that died in sin". He rules over 30 legions of inferior spirits and is evoked in acts of **necromancy**. He is also known as Gamigin or Samigina.

**Gandareva** In Sumerian mythology, a **dragon**-like **demon** known as the "Master of the Abyss" who provided assistance to an evil dragon intent on devouring the world. After several hostile encounters, the dragon and the demon were slain by Keresaspa.

**Gander** In alchemy, another name for the **Bird of Hermes**.

**Gangan** In **voodoo**, another word for a houngan, or priest.

**Garde** In voodoo, a protective **charm** used to counteract black magic.

**Garden of the Hesperides** In alchemy, the place where the **Philosopher's Stone** could be found. In classical myth, this fabled garden contained a tree with golden apples – a reference to the gold created by the Philosopher's Stone through the process of transmutation. The **Hesperides** themselves were Aegle, Hespere, and Erytheis, and they were the daughters of **Nyx** and **Erebus**.

**Gardner, Gerald Brousseau** (1884–1964) One of the principal figures associated with the emergence of modern **witchcraft**, Gerald Gardner was born at Blundellsands, near Liverpool in England, and was of Scottish descent. He was a man of independent means, having made a fortune as a rubber planter in Malaya, and on his retirement, he and his wife settled in the New Forest area of Hampshire. Just before the outbreak of World War Two, he made contact with a group of local occultists who called themselves the **Fellowship of Crotona**. Some members of the Fellowship had links with an established witchcraft **coven**, and secret sabbat meetings were being held at that time in the New Forest. Gardner soon became an enthusiastic devotee of witchcraft, and claimed that he was initiated in 1939 by "Old Dorothy" – **Dorothy Clutterbuck**.

In 1946 Gardner and his friend **Arnold Crowther** called on **Aleister Crowley**, who had retired to lodgings in Hastings. Crowther had met Crowley during his wartime travels, and it was he who arranged for the two occultists to meet. The encounter is significant because modern **ceremonial magic**, as developed by **MacGregor Mathers** and Crowley in the **Hermetic Order of the Golden Dawn**, and the coven-based witchcraft of the New Forest were now crossing paths – perhaps for the first time. Gardner and Crowley had several discussions, and before Crowley died in December the following year, Crowley had made him an honorary member of his sexual magic order, the **Ordo Templi Orientis**.

Following the repeal of England's last anti-witchcraft law in 1951, Gardner left the New Forest group and started his own coven. He then moved to Castletown on the Isle of Man, where a Museum of Magic and Witchcraft had already been established by an occult enthusiast called Cecil Williamson. Gardner bought the museum from Williamson, became the "resident witch", and added his own collection of ritual tools and artefacts. While he was engaged in developing his own coven, Gardner began using quotations from Aleister Crowley's writings in his ceremonial rites. It is also likely that substantial sections of Gardner's magical credo were written by Crowley and then fused with a witch's book of spells and rituals. But while Gardner sought to fuse witchcraft and Crowleyian magic during the early 1950s, a significant modifying factor seems to have been provided by **Doreen Valiente**, who had been initiated by Gardner into his coven in 1953. She felt that some of the Crowleyian material which Gardner had incorporated was either too "modern" or inappropriate. Much of it was written out of the ceremonial procedures between 1954 and 1957, as Gardner and Valiente worked together preparing the rituals that would form the basis of the "Gardnerian tradition" in contemporary witchcraft.

From Gardner's perspective it was important for witchcraft to reclaim its place once again as an authentic, nature-based spiritual tradition. Although Gardner was not to see it in his own lifetime, **Wicca** has since positioned itself at the very centre of the contemporary occult revival. Gardner described his experiences in the New Forest coven in his novel *High Magic's Aid*, published in 1949. His first non-fiction book on the Craft, *Witchcraft Today,* appeared in 1954, followed by *The Meaning of Witchcraft* in 1959.

**Gardnerian Witches** In Wicca, witches initiated by the British witch **Gerald Gardner** or one of his high priestesses. The term is also applied to witches who practise in the Gardnerian tradition but whose initiation does not derive historically from Gerald Gardner's coven.

**Garlic** *Allium sativum*, a herb with a long and exotic history. Originating in Siberia, garlic became widely known throughout Asia and the Middle East. According to Herodotus, the builders of the Great Pyramid had been issued with a clove of garlic each day as a tonic. It is also mentioned several times by Homer, Virgil, and Horace as a popular panacea in ancient Greece and Rome. Hippocrates recommended it for indigestion and bowel complaints and Greek magicians evoked favour from **Hecate**, queen of the **Underworld**, by placing

bulbs of garlic at the crossroads at midnight. In ancient China, garlic was used to ease skin problems and circulatory disorders. Garlic contains allicin, which is effective against infections, and it is widely recognized as an excellent natural antiseptic. The sulphides in allicin lower cholesterol levels in the body and have a pronounced anti-clotting effect.

**Garter, Magical** In Wicca, a ceremonial object and also a badge of rank among women in the coven. Often worn only by the high priestess, the magical garter is traditionally made of green leather, buckled in silver, and lined with blue silk. When a high priestess has a coven hive off, or depart, from her original coven, she is entitled to add a second buckle to her garter, and she may add an additional buckle for any other coven that hives off. A high priestess whose garter has at least three buckles is referred to as a **Witch Queen**.

**Gate** In the Kabbalah, a passageway associated with one of the Hebrew letters that connects one sephirah to another on the **Tree of Life**. See also **Sephiroth**.

**Gate of Horn** In Greek mythology, one of the two Gates of Dreams in the Underworld. Through the gate made of horn authentic dream-oracles relating to future events came forth to the sleeper. Compare **Gate of Ivory** and see also **Hades**.

**Gate of Ivory** In Greek mythology, one of the two Gates of Dreams in the Underworld. Through it came misleading and deceitful dreams from the cave of **Hypnos**, the god of sleep. Compare **Gate of Horn** and see also **Hades**.

**Gates of Dreams** See **Gate of Horn**; **Gate of Ivory**; **Hades**.

**Gatha** In Zoroastrianism, a song or hymn in the sacred writings collectively known as the **Avesta**, which includes many of the myths and religious beliefs of ancient Persia.

**Gaufridi, Louis** See Aix-en-Provence Nuns.

**Gebo** See Gyfu.

**Geburah** The fifth emanation or sephirah on the kabbalistic **Tree of Life**. In western magic, Geburah is associated with Mars, the Roman god of war, and represents severity and justice. The destructive forces of the sphere of Geburah are intended to have a purging, cleansing effect in the universe. Geburah represents the creator god, who applies discipline and precision in governing the cosmos and removes unwanted or unnecessary elements after their usefulness has passed. The symbolism of Geburah is reflected in the **Tarot** card *The Charioteer*. See also **Kabbalah**; **Sephiroth**. Also Gevurah.

**Geh** In Zoroastrianism, prayers recited five times a day, commencing with sunrise. Devotees face the sun as they pray and each geh is believed to have an **archangel** associated with it.

**Gehenna** The Jewish hell, derived from the Hebrew *Ge Hinnom* – the Valley of Hinnom. This was the valley south of Jerusalem where the Israelites sacrificed their children to Moloch, god of the Ammonites, according to Jeremiah 19.6. Gehenna came to be regarded as a place of torment and abomination, and the hell-fire imagery of Gehenna reflects the fact that the Valley of Hinnom was also a place where refuse was discarded and fires lit to avoid the spread of deadly disease. All of these features influenced the development of the idea of a "bottomless pit of eternal fire", where the wicked are said to be punished when they die.

**Gematria** An occult method of turning words or phrases into a numerical equivalent by assigning numbers to letters. It was used by practitioners of the Kabbalah, for whom Hebrew words or phrases with the same numerical total are said to be symbolically related. For example, the Hebrew word Messiah – consisting of the four letters *m-sh-i-ch* – totals 358, as does the word nachash – *n-ch-sh* – which means the brass serpent of Moses. Some Christian kabbalists in the Middle Ages therefore believed that the image of the brass serpent was a prefiguration of Christ on the cross and, as a result, in medieval iconography Christ is sometimes depicted as a serpent entwined around a crucifix. See also **Great Beast 666**; **Notarikon**; **Temurah**.

**Gemini** In astrology, the sign of the zodiac for those born between 21 May and 21 June, and symbolized by the twins. Geminis are said to be imaginative but materialistic, and their intellectual attainments are often superficial. They can be rash, unstable, and "two-faced", but are also outgoing and like to express themselves. They make good actors and politicians. An **air sign**, Gemini is ruled by **Mercury**.

**Genie** See Genii.

**Genii** or **Genie, Jinni** (plural genies, djinn, genn, or jinn) A **daemon** or spirit of Arabian tradition, a higher order of being than humans, and formed of "more subtle" matter. According to Islamic belief, the genii ruled the earth before the creation of Adam and were regarded as an intermediate race of spirit beings between angels and people. They were believed to have special architectural skills and, according to the *Qur'an*, were employed by **Solomon** to assist in erecting his magnificent temple.

**Genios** In South American **shamanism** and folk healing, the spirit allies under the control of the **ayahuasquero**. These spirit allies may be used for either good or evil magical purposes, depending on the intent of the practitioner.

**Geniture** In astrology, the aspects and configurations of a person's nativity or natal horoscope.

**Genius** Plural, genii. In Roman mythology, a spirit said to be present at one's birth which guided and protected a person throughout their life. In this, sense the Roman genius resembles the Greek daemon. In occult belief, a person of "genius" is one who is in tune with his or her true will and who holds conversations with the holy guardian angel. To this extent one of the basic aims of modern western **magic** is the discovery of one's inner genius. The Romans, like the Celts and other pagan peoples, also believed that individual places, as well as people, had their own presiding genii, and when invading a new area they would make offerings to the local spirits to avoid offending them. The word genius is unrelated to the Arabian genii or genie.

**Genn** See Genii.

**Geomancy** A form of **divination** by interpreting the pattern of objects thrown on the ground. Gravel, small stones, sticks, seeds, or even jewels may be used. The practitioner holds the objects in cupped hands, concentrates on the divinatory request, and then allows the seeds or stones to drop. Interpretations are made intuitively on the basis of the patterns on the ground.

**Ger** Also Jera. In the Germanic **Elder Futhark** the **rune** letter representing the number twelve. Ger corresponds to the letters "j" and "y" and is the rune of growth, fertility, and regeneration – and especially the time of harvest. By extension it points to positive results and rewards, especially the sort of success won by working in harmony with nature.

**Germer, Karl** (1885–1962) A German occultist who became head of the sexual magic group **Ordo Templi Orientis** after the death of **Aleister Crowley** in 1947. Germer was a dedicated follower of Crowley and assisted in the publication of some of Crowley's more specialized writings, such as *Magick Without Tears*.

His magical name in the Ordo Templi Orientis was Frater Saturnus.

**Getal** See Ngetal.

**Gettings, Fred** (1937– ) A highly regarded English authority on the relationship between art and the western magical traditions. Gettings studied painting and literature and has spent many years teaching and writing about painting and drawing. His many works include *The Occult in Art*, *The Book of Tarot*, *Hermetic and Alchemical Sigils*, as well as a *Dictionary of the Occult* and *Dictionary of Astrology*. He also wrote an illustrated biography of the British fantasy illustrator, Arthur Rackham.

**Gevurah** See Geburah.

**Ghede** See Guede.

**Ghoul** A spirit or **demon** that feeds on the bodies of dead human beings. The word derives from the Arabic **ghul**.

**Ghuevo** In **voodoo**, a small chamber which contains an **altar**. It is consecrated to the worship of a **loa**.

**Ghul** The Arabic term for a terrifying being or entity which drives one insane. It is also used to describe the monsters and evil spirits said to haunt forests, cemeteries, and lonely places, which terrorize and kill the living and also dig up and devour the bodies of the dead. See also **Ghoul**.

**Giants** In Greek mythology, a group of monsters with serpentine bodies and the heads of men who made war on the gods of Olympus, hurling rocks and trees at their adversaries. The giants were finally defeated by **Heracles**. Giants also feature in Scandinavian mythology and European folklore as large, somewhat cumbersome creatures often given to evil and mischievous deeds.

**Gifu** See Gyfu.

**Gifuma** See Iboga.

**Giger, Hans Ruedi** (1940– ) A Swiss occult fantasy artist who created the space entity known as "the Alien" for the Oscar-winning film of the same name. Giger's paintings feature **Medusa**-like women with ghostly-pale skin and snakes in their hair, and draw strongly on the **left-hand path** of western **magic** as well as on fantasy and horror fictions like *The Necronomicon*. Claws, needles, machine guns, and barbs also feature strongly in his works. For many people the works themselves are simultaneously disturbing and fascinating and often exhibit a macabre beauty. However, his nightmare fusions of the human and the mechanical also evoke a sense of "no escape" – a sense that we are all trapped in a hell of our own making. Selections of Giger's work are now on permanent display at his museum in the castle of St Germain in Gruyères, Switzerland, which opened in June 1998.

**Gilbert, R.A.** A leading British scholar of the western **esoteric** tradition, Gilbert read philosophy and psychology at the university of Bristol and now works as an antiquarian book dealer. His works include *The Golden Dawn: Twilight of the Magicians*; *Revelations of the Golden Dawn*; and an authoritative biography of **Arthur Edward Waite** entitled *A.E. Waite: Magician of Many Parts*.

**Gilgulim** or **Galgalim** The Hebrew word for "wheels". In the Jewish mystical tradition, the Gilgulim are cycles or transformations which each soul undergoes on the path towards spiritual enlightenment. It is a concept which requires a belief in **reincarnation**.

**Gimel** The Hebrew letter ascribed to the path linking **Kether** and **Tiphareth** on the kabbalistic **Tree of Life**. Gimel has a numerical value of three. In modern magical visualization and **pathworkings** the Tarot card associated with this path on the Tree is *The High Priestess*. See also **Kabbalah**.

**Gimmel** See Gimel.

**Ginn** See Genii.

**Girtabili** In the Babylonian creation myth, a fearsome **dragon** in league with the sea goddess **Tiamat**, who took the form of a creature half man, half scorpion.

**Glastig** In Scottish folklore, a spirit creature who was half woman, half goat and was generally kind to elderly people, helping them with their housework and other menial tasks. On occasion, however, she was known to be mischievous and was fond of misguiding unwary travellers.

**Glasyalabolas** In the **Goetia**, the 25th spirit, a mighty president and earl who appears in the form of a winged dog. Glasyalabolas incites violence and bloodshed but can also unite enemies in love. He also has the power to make a person invisible. Glasyalabolas commands 36 legions of spirits. He is also known as Caacrinolaas or Caassimola.

**Glyph** A magical symbol that represents a person's name and birthdate. It is regarded as having strong magical powers and has a comparable role to a **talisman** or **amulet**. Some occultists believe that glyphs can be worn as charms to ward off misfortune or disease. See also **Sigil** (2).

**Gnome** In myth and folklore, an elf-like creature, said in folk legend to live under the earth. Gnomes are similar to **goblins** and are often associated with buried treasure. In the symbolism of western magic, gnomes are regarded as the spirits of the element **earth**. See also **Elements**.

**Gnosis** see Gnosticism.

**Gnostic** Pertaining to Gnosticism. As a noun, one who seeks *gnosis*, or hidden spiritual knowledge; a follower of Gnosticism. See also **Gnostic Mass**.

**Gnosticism** The general term applied to the belief systems of certain religious sects which emerged around the same time as early Christianity and which were condemned as heretical by orthodox Church Fathers like Irenaeus. The followers of these sects are known collectively as Gnostics – people who believed in and sought *gnosis*, the Greek term for "knowledge", but here meaning "hidden spiritual knowledge". *Gnosis*, from the Gnostic viewpoint, consisted of the esoteric truths underlying religious teachings and represented the initiatory pathway to illumination and wisdom. Although the Gnostic sects varied considerably – some of them specializing in **astrology** and **cosmology**, others offering esoteric interpretations of the teachings of Jesus Christ – the main factor that differentiated these Gnostic groups from mainstream Christianity was their emphasis on knowledge rather than faith. It seems clear that **Zoroastrianism** exerted a considerable influence on Gnosticism. As in Zoroastrian dualism, the Gnostics were inclined to reject the world – and matter – as evil, and focused their visionary techniques on attaining the world of spirit. One of the main Gnostic deities, **Abraxas**, had a Persian antecedent in **Zurvan**, the Zoroastrian god of time. The ancient library discovered at Nag Hammadi in Egypt in 1945 represents the most extensive source of Gnostic scriptures in existence. See also **Nag Hammadi Library**.

**Gnostic Mass** The ceremonial magician Aleister Crowley's magical alternative to the Roman Catholic Mass. It focuses on the priest, who bears the "sacred lance", and the priestess, who is dedicated to "the Service of the Great Order". The two figures partake of the sacred "cake of light" and "cup of wine". During the Gnostic Mass the priest parts the sacred veil with his lance and embraces the knees of the priestess, who has now removed her robes to reveal her nakedness. She embodies the Egyptian goddess **Nuit**, who features in Crowley's *Book of the Law* and who is central to the cosmology of the **Aeon of Horus**. The Gnostic Mass continues to be performed regularly by members of the **Ordo Templi Orientis** around the world.

**Goat** An animal with occult and pagan associations. According to Christian detractors, the **Horned God** was said to take the form of a goat when he presided over the **witches' sabbath**, although this demonstrates some confusion between the Christian **Devil** and the horned pagan god **Pan**, who was the lord of nature. The goat is also featured in the zodiac as the sign **Capricorn**, which also appears as a composite creature that combines a goat with a fish.

**Goat of Mendes** See Mendes, Goat of

**Goblin** A mischievous and ugly fairy creature, similar to a **gnome**. In western **magic**, gnomes and goblins are regarded as the spirits of the element **earth**. See also **Elements**.

**God** The supreme being. In the monotheistic religions he is the omniscient and omnipresent creator and governor of the universe, usually referred to as male, but otherwise said to be undescribable. In Judaism, his name, which may not be uttered, is Yahweh or Jehovah (YHVH) and in Islam it is Allah. In polytheistic religions he is the chief of the gods. Among the ancient Greeks he was called Zeus ("God"). The Romans knew him as Jove, or **Jupiter** ("Father Jove"); the Egyptians as Ra; and the Scandinavians as **Odin**. See also **Demiurge**; **Father God**; **Gods and Goddesses**; **Tetragrammaton**.

**Goddess, Dark** See Crone, Hag.

**Goddess, Great** See Great Goddess.

**Goddess, Triple** See Great Goddess.

**Godhead** The essential nature of God. See also **Deity**; **God**.

**God-Form** The image of a god. Ritual

magicians use the expression "taking the god-form" or "assuming the god-form" when they visualize themselves as gods (e.g. Thoth, Isis) in a ceremonial context.

**God, High** An omniscient deity or ruler god, invariably associated in world mythologies with the sky. High gods may be distinguished from lower ranking gods, angels, devils, and elementals. The term was coined by Scottish anthropologist and folklorist Andrew Lang.

**God, Horned** See Horned God.

**God-Name** A magical word of sacred power. According to esoteric tradition, knowledge of the secret names of a god bestows special benefits upon the occultist because, in uttering a god-name formula, the magician becomes that god by way of imitation. In kabbalistic magic, the various names of God (Adonai, Shaddai, El, Elohim, Jehovah, and so on) are regarded as powerful god-names, and are used in ritual invocations. See also Golem; Hekau; Kabbalah; Magic, Imitative; Words of Power.

**Gods and Goddesses** In polytheistic religions, magical powers are vested in a pantheon of male and female deities that are believed to hold sway over the universe. Each deity has different attributes, and each requires different rites of appeasement, veneration, and invocation. In contemporary western magic, Egyptian – and to a lesser extent Greek – polytheism has had a pronounced influence on the structuring of ceremonial rituals. Occultists often choose to focus their magical activities on acquiring specific attributes (e.g. love, wealth, peace, wisdom), and specific gods and goddesses are selected to personify these qualities in ritual.

**Goes** In ancient Greece and Rome, a ritual ecstatic healer or diviner, regarded as an intermediary between the gods and humanity. The term later gave rise to the word Goetia, which in the Middle Ages was specifically associated with black magic. See Magic, Black.

**Goetia** A tradition of black magic, including incantations, ceremonies, and techniques of sorcery, associated with medieval grimoires, which provide practical instructions for contacting demonic spirits. The term Goetia itself is thought to derive from the ancient Greek word *goes*, which in Plato's time denoted a diviner, magician, seer or healer. The Goetia, however, has a much darker connotation and is associated specifically with demonology. Many of the devils and demons in the Goetia derive from so-called "heathen" traditions, including Greek, Egyptian, Assyrian, and Persian sources. Some of these devils, like Beelzebub (Baal-zebub, god of Ekron in the ninth century BCE), Asmodeus, and Astaroth (Ashtaroth) are mentioned in the Bible. The Goetia includes such works as *The Key of Solomon*; *The Lemegeton*, or *Lesser Key of Solomon*; the *Grimorium Verum*, which is partially based on the *Key of Solomon*, and the *Grimoire of Armadel*. A.E. Waite's *The Book of Black Magic and of Pacts* (1898) – later revised and reissued as *The Book of Ceremonial Magic* (1911) – includes selections from several of the main grimoires. See also Magic, Black.

**Going of the Ways** Wiccan divorce, or handparting.

**Gold** In alchemy, a precious and "perfect" metal associated with the sun. Gold also represents the "inner light" of mystical illumination and to this extent gold is the supreme "spiritual" metal. See also King Sol.

**Golem** In Jewish folklore, a creature – usually a human being – made artificially by means of magic and sacred names. In the Kabbalah, there are many references to the creative power of the letters of the name of God (see Tetragrammaton); the idea emerged that through the use of holy names the magician could simulate God's act of creation and produce a subservient, robot-like being. According to the kabbalist **Moses Cordovero**, people had the ability to give "vitality" to the golem, but not **"soul"** or **"spirit"**. In seventeenth-century Europe the golem was recognized as a creature that could assist people in daily tasks, but it was feared that the creature could grow day by day and present a threat to its masters. To avert this danger it was considered that periodically the golem should be reduced to dust by removing the letter *aleph* (symbolic of creation) from its forehead. See also **Simulacrum**.

**Gomory** In the Goetia, the 56th spirit, a strong and powerful duke who appears in the form of a beautiful woman with a duchess's crown tied around her waist. Gomory is riding on a large camel. He has access to the knowledge of all things, past, present, and future, and knows how to procure the love of women, both old and young. He also knows the where-abouts of hidden treasures. Gomory rules over 26 legions of spirits and is also known as Gremory.

**Good, Sarah** (died 1692) A member of a **coven** in Salem, Massachusetts, who was arrested after being accused of **witchcraft** by two young children, one of whom was the nine-year-old daughter of a church minister. Sarah Good became a leading figure in the Salem witchcraft trials and was taken to **Gallows Hill** on 19 July, 1692. Here, the Reverend Nicholas Noyes urged her to confess her heresy; but in return she is alleged to have put a curse on him, saying: "If you take away my life, God will give you blood to drink." She was hanged shortly afterwards. See also **Salem Witches**.

**Gorgons** In Greek mythology, three winged monsters who had serpents for hair, fierce claws, and a stare that could turn men into stone. Their bodies were covered by scales and, according to Aeschylus, they had only one tooth and eye among them. The Gorgons – Euryale, Stheno, and Medusa – were the daughters of Ceto and Phorcys. The first

two sisters were immortal, but Medusa was mortal. Perseus cut off Medusa's head and placed it on the shield of his protector, the goddess **Athena** – Medusa's terrifying eye had the same power even after her death.

**Gort** In the Celtic tree alphabet, the **ogham** representing ivy and the letter "g". Gort is also linked to the swan and the colour blue.

**Govi** In voodoo, sacred red clay vessels used to house **loa** or spirits of the dead. Ordinary clay vessels are referred to as canari, to distinguish them from their sacred counterparts.

**Gowäli** A term used by the Cherokee Indians to refer to a shaman's formulas. These include formulas for attracting love, treating ailments, and also for hunting and fishing. Each formula includes appropriate prayers, songs and calls to the animal spirits required to effect a result or cure.

**Gowdie, Isobel** (died 1662) A Scottish farmer's wife who became celebrated for her spontaneous **witchcraft** confession in 1662. Isobel, who lived with her husband at Auldearne, near Inverness, claimed that many years earlier she had been initiated into a **coven** under the sponsor-ship of one Margaret Brodie. During the ceremony the master of the **coven** had bared her shoulder, cut it, and drawn forth some blood, which he then mixed with spittle in order to make a mark on her forehead. He then "baptized" her as a member of the coven. Isobel began attending coven meetings, learned certain "mating dances", acquired the magical knowledge to change into a hare and other animals, and described how she had sexual intercourse with **demons** and the **Devil**. She also confirmed that a coven normally consisted of thirteen people. Apparently, Isobel's husband had no knowledge of Isobel's involvement with witchcraft until, fifteen years after her initiation, she came forward to confess to the elders of the church at

Auldearne. Isobel named several other members of the coven and they were arrested shortly afterwards. Although Isobel repented her crimes, she was hanged and her body later burned – the traditional fate of a witch in Britain at that time.

**Gran Maître** In voodoo, the original creator deity, or supreme being, who made the world. He is now considered a remote god and has withdrawn from the world, so – unlike the **loa** – he is no longer actively worshipped.

**Grandier, Urbain** (1590–1634) A priest at Loudun in France, who was accused unfairly in 1633 of practising **magic** and causing nuns to be possessed by demons. Several nuns at the Ursuline convent at Loudon conspired to discredit Grandier after he had fathered an illegitimate child and taken a mistress. In order to claim that Grandier had "bewitched" them, they began exhibiting signs of hysteria that included exaggerated erotic behaviour, gasping fits, and convulsions. The mother superior, Sister Jeanne, named Grandier and the demons **Asmodeus** and Zabulon as the cause of "spirit possession" at the convent. A commission was subsequently established by Cardinal Richelieu to investigate the bizarre happenings at Loudon, and Grandier was sent for trial. A highly suspect document, purporting to be a pact between Grandier and the **Devil**, was brought forward as evidence. Grandier was found guilty of practising magic and was condemned to be burned alive.

**Grans Bwa** In voodoo, the loa of the forest.

**Grant, Kenneth** (1924– ) An English tantric magician who, after the death of **Aleister Crowley** in 1947, continued as one of his followers and established his own Isis Lodge in 1955. Grant claims to be the world head of the **Ordo Templi Orientis** (O.T.O.), although this claim is disputed by another branch of the O.T.O.

that currently operates from Berkeley, California. Grant has collaborated with **John Symonds** in editing and annotating several of Crowley's works, including the *Confessions* and *The Magical Record of the Beast 666*. He is also the author of several important works on modern western **magic**, including *The Magical Revival*, *Cults of the Shadow*, *Nightside of Eden*, and *Outside the Circles of Time*. He has also produced two definitive works on the English trance artist and occultist **Austin Osman Spare** *Images and Oracles of Austin Osman Spare* and *Zos Speaks* – the latter co-authored with his wife Steffi, a distinguished occult artist in her own right.

**Gray, William G.** A British ceremonial magician whose mother was an astrologer and whose father had links with **Theosophy**. Gray was the British delegate to the Spiritual Symposium held in Dallas, Texas, in 1970 under the auspices of the Sangreal Foundation, and was regarded by magical authority **Israel Regardie** as one of the foremost contemporary writers on the western magical tradition. Gray's many books on **magic** and the **Kabbalah** include *The Ladder of Lights* (1968), *Magical Ritual Methods* (1969), *Inner Traditions of Magic* (1971), and *The Talking Tree* (1975).

**Great Beast 666** The Anti-Christ described in *The Book of Revelation*, who was said to be identifiable by the number 666 (Revelation 13.18). This is widely assumed by scholars to refer to Emperor Nero, whose name in Greek **gematria** (*Kaisar Neron*) has this numerical value. There was apparently a belief around the time *Revelation* was written (late first century CE) that Nero, who had died in 69CE and was a notorious persecutor of Christians, would return to face Christ in a great final battle. **Aleister Crowley** identified with the Great Beast from an early age and it was an image which remained with him throughout his career. Some critics of Crowley have labelled him as a black magician and satanist as a consequence. When accounts of Crowley's **Abbey of Thelema** in Cefalu, Sicily, appeared in the British press – sensationalizing his practice of sex magic – he was labelled by *John Bull* magazine as "the wickedest man in the world". See also **Gematria**.

**Greater Hekhaloth, The** The Jewish visionary text of the **Hekhaloth** school dating from the early Talmudic phase of Jewish mysticism (first century CE). The Hekhaloth were different "chambers" or "halls", through which the mystic ascended in meditation. During this meditative journey, divine **God-names** would be repeated in a mantra and the mystic would project his consciousness into a spirit-vehicle that would journey to each hall in turn, presenting a sacred "seal" to the **angel** or **archon** guarding the chamber. Just prior to the seventh chamber the mystic entered a chariot and was then lifted up into a profound state of mystical ecstasy. This experience was called the Journey of the **Merkabah**. See also **Rising on the Planes**.

**Greater Sabbats** See Sabbats, Greater.

**Great Goddess** In Wicca, the personification of fertility and the regenerative powers of nature. In ancient and classical mythology, the Great Goddess, or Great Mother, had many different forms. For example, she was **Cybele** in Phrygia, **Astarte** in Phoenicia, **Isis** in Egypt, **Demeter** in the Greek mystery religion, and **Dana** among the Irish Celts. Contemporary Wicca emphasizes the threefold aspect of the Great Goddess in her role as **Maid** (representing youth and enchantment), **Mother** (representing maturity and fulfilment), and **Crone** (representing old age and wisdom). These phases of womanhood are particularly important in the "women's mysteries" of feminist Wicca groups.

**Great Mother** See Great Goddess.

**Great Old Ones** In *The Necronomicon*, mysterious beings who control the destiny of earth and other celestial

bodies. According to tantric magician **Kenneth Grant**, these entities manifest themselves periodically as a guiding presence behind various magical organizations like the **Argenteum Astrum** and the **Typhonian Order of the Outer Ones**.

**Great Rite** See Third Initiation.

**Great Work, The** Referred to in **alchemy** as the *summum bonum*, the Great Work represented mastery of the secrets of alchemical **transmutation**, especially the power to transform base metal into gold.

In the **Hermetic Order of the Golden Dawn** it was regarded as a metaphor for **self-initiation**. Here it was associated with the rituals of spiritual rebirth that focused on **Tiphareth** (the sun sphere at the centre of the **Tree of Life**), and with knowledge of the **Holy Guardian Angel**. In the cosmology of ceremonial magician **Aleister Crowley**, the term was used to designate the next stage of human evolution and was part of Crowley's conception of the New Aeon.

**Green Egg** See Zell, Otter; Zell, Morning Glory.

**Green George** See Green Man.

**Green Jack** See Green Man.

**Green Lion** In alchemy, the green lion represents the **prima materia** in the earliest stage of the alchemical work. The appearance of green particles in the **alembic** indicated that the infant Stone – the "unripe" or still developing material being refined and purified in order to produce the **Philosopher's Stone** – was "growing" to maturity. The symbolism of the colour green was significant because in nature green was a sign of fertility and new growth. The alchemical motif of the green lion swallowing the sun is a reference to **aqua regia** (a mixture of nitric and hydrochloric acids) dissolving gold.

**Green Man** In Wicca, the pagan spirit of trees, plants, and woodlands. He is horned and is often depicted wearing a green mask surrounded by foliage – usually oak leaves. He is sometimes referred to as Jack-in-the Green, Green Jack, or Green George.

**Green, Marian** An influential British magical practitioner and author, Green runs correspondence courses on ceremonial magic and natural magic and provides lectures and practical training throughout Britain and Europe. Since 1970 she has been the editor of the magazine *Quest*, which explores all aspects of the western esoteric tradition. Her books include *The Gentle Arts of Aquarian Magic*, *Magic for the Aquarian Age*, and *The Elements of Natural Magic*.

**Gremory** See Gomory.

**Grenier, Jean** (1589–1610) Often dubbed "the wolf boy", Grenier was said to be a werewolf. He was discovered by some village girls disturbing a flock of sheep and related to them how he sometimes wore a wolf skin and attacked sheep, dogs, and even human beings. Grenier claimed that his powers of bestial transformation were given to him after he had signed a pact with the Devil. The boy was imprisoned in the Franciscan friary of St Michael Archangel at Bordeaux, and convinced onlookers of his werewolf characteristics when he consumed a quantity of raw offal and ran around on all fours. He died after seven years of imprisonment. See also Lycanthropy.

**Griffin** A mythical creature with the head and wings of an eagle and the legs of a lion, the griffin was said to be the largest of all birds. When it spread its wings, it was capable of obscuring the rays of the sun. It was also the sun's guardian and was sacred to Apollo. The Greek epic poem *The Arimaspea* tells of battles between the griffins and the one-eyed Arimaspi tribesmen for ownership of the sacred gold. See also Aristeas of Proconnesus. Also spelled griffon, gryphon.

**Grimoires** Medieval collections of magical spells, rituals, and incantations, which invariably claimed classical Hebrew or Egyptian authorship. Among the best known are *The Sacred Magic of Abra-Melin the Mage*, *The Lemegeton* (or *Lesser Key of Solomon*), *Clavicula Salmonis* (or *Greater Key of Solomon*), *The Sworn Book of Honorius*, and the *Grimoire of Armadel*. See also Goetia; Incantation; *Key of Solomon*; Spell.

**Gris-Gris** Amulets worn by African tribesmen to protect them from sorcery and evil forces. The term is also used to describe a witch-doctor and magician who sends forth evil spells and cause bewitchment.

**Gros Bon Ange** In voodoo, the "big good angel" – the individual soul of a person. See also Ti Bon Ange.

**Grottos** The term used by members of the Church of Satan in San Francisco to refer to regional branches of the Church. In its heyday the Church of Satan had grottos in a number of cities across the United States, including New York; Denver, Colorado; Louisville, Kentucky; and Dayton, Ohio, as well as in Santa Cruz, San José, and Los Angeles in California. It is thought that the reach of the Church of Satan has diminished substantially following the death of its founder, Anton La Vey, in 1997. Grottos centre around charismatic individuals intent on spreading the satanic doctrine and the extent of their membership is not publicly revealed.

**Grounding** In Wicca, the ritual act of connecting the body's energy with that of the earth.

**Gryphon** See Griffin.

**Guaita, Stanislas de** (1861–1897) A French marquis who established a Rosicrucian lodge in Paris as a meeting place for occultists. Among his many magical associates were Gerard Encausse, Sar Peladan, and Oswald Wirth. Guaita learned from Wirth that a magical coven had been established by **Joseph-Antoine Boullan** at Lyons; and, for reasons which are not quite clear, Guaita decided that he would firmly oppose it. Guaita wrote to Boullan condemning his occult practices, and subsequently urged his Rosicrucian cohorts to curse Boullan with all the magical power they could muster. Over several years a "psychic battle" raged between Guaita in Paris and Boullan in Lyons, culminating in Boullan's death. Guaita was accused in the Paris press of causing Boullan's death "by black magic", and the matter was finally settled in a duel between the journalist who had made the charges – Jules Bois – and Guaita. Fortunately, neither man was killed but both were slightly wounded, and honour was restored. See also **Magic, Black; Magical Attack.**

**Guardian Spirit** A personal, protective spirit that is said to oversee one's day-to-day activities and provide warning of impending danger. For the Romans, the idea of the **genius** – as the protective spirit of a person or place – had this connotation. In spiritualism, the discarnate guide that communicates through a psychic medium has much the same role.

**Guede** In voodoo, the loa of the dead and "god of the grave". He is both the keeper of the cemetery and guardian of the past. One of his aspects is **Baron Samedi.**

**Guide Meditation** See Steinbrecher, Edwin.

**Guided Imagery** Technique used in psychotherapy and also in magical **pathworkings**, whereby a subject is asked to visualize specific images in sequence. In magical procedure, the subject is led along pathways of the **Tree of Life** into archetypal areas of consciousness. The **Major Arcana** of the Tarot provides an ideal framework for guided imagery work. Examples of Tarot visualizations for use in guided imagery are provided in the present author's *The Tarot Workbook* (2004); Ted Andrews' *More Simplified Magic* (1998); and **Dolores Ashcroft-Nowicki**'s *The Shining Paths* (1983).

**Guiley, Rosemary Ellen** A contemporary American metaphysical author currently based in Arnold, Maryland. Guiley specializes in works on dreams, intuition, and visionary experience. Among her best known books are *Breakthrough Intuition, Dreamwork for the Soul, The Encyclopedia of Dreams*, and *The Encyclopedia of Witches and Witchcraft.*

**Guinée** In **voodoo**, the mythical homeland of Africa, the land of the **loa.**

**Gum Benjamin** See Benzoin.

**Gundestrup Cauldron** A ritual cauldron made of solid silver dating from the first or second century BCE, unearthed near the village of Gundestrup in Jutland, Denmark, in 1891 and now held in the National Museum in Copenhagen. Regarded as Celtic in origin, the cauldron is engraved with various mythic images. One of these is an antler-headed god or **shaman** whom some have identified as **Cernunnos**, the Celtic **Horned God.** He is shown sitting amid a cluster of animals and holds a torque and serpent in his hands.

**Gusayn** See Gusion.

**Gusion** In the Goetia, the eleventh spirit, a great and strong duke who has knowledge of all things – past, present and future. Gusion can unite friends who have fallen into conflict and he grants honour and dignity to those who evoke him. Gusion rules over 40 legions of spirits. He is also known as Gusayn.

**Gwragedd Annwn** In Welsh folk legend, beautiful female water spirits resembling mermaids, found in lakes. They were said to sometimes marry mortals and live normal, happy lives.

**Gwydion** In Welsh mythology, a legendary bard and magician who learnt his wizardry from his uncle Math, a sorcerer and shape-shifter. Gwydion was the brother of **Arianrhod** and the father, by her, of **Lleu Llaw Gyffes**. Considered a folk hero and benevolent protector of his people, Gwydion tricked his sister by getting her to do three things she had sworn she would not do. In the first instance she gave her son his name after he hit a bird on a ship that Gwydion had created magically; secondly, she gave Llew some armour when she saw a fleet of ships approaching – an illusion created through Gwydion's **sorcery**. Thirdly she refused her son a wife of the earthly race, but Gwydion and his uncle Math created a woman from flowers. Some authorities have linked Gwydion with **Ogma**, since he fought in the Battle of the Trees. See also *Mabinogion, The.*

**Gyfu** In the Germanic **Elder Futhark**, the **rune** letter representing the number seven. Gyfu, sometimes spelt gifu, corresponds to the letter "g" and represents a gift. In pre-Christian northern Europe, giving gifts was associated with high social standing and being generous and hospitable was considered virtuous. In a ritual setting, offering gifts to the gods also implied sacrifice.

**Gypsies** Wandering nomadic groups, said to be of Indian origin, who travelled through Egypt in the fourteenth century and entered western Europe through the region of Bohemia. Their name derives from the word "Egypt."; they were also sometimes called "Bohemians", and the expression "bohemian" now has the connotation of one who is eccentric and unconventional. The gypsies spread through the Balkan peninsula and later travelled to Germany, France, and Italy before reaching Britain c. 1500. Gypsies have been traditionally associated with **fortune telling**, especially palmistry and **Tarot** card **divination**. Some gypsies, especially those who call themselves

Romanies, claim to be able to forecast the weather by interpreting the flight of birds and also maintain that they have the psychic power to predict events far into the future.

**Gyromancy** A form of **divination** whereby the diviner walks around a circle until he or she collapses. The diviner's position relative to the circle is interpreted to determine the outcome of future events.

# H

**Ha-Shem** In the Kabbalah, "the Name" – a shortened form of **Shem ha-Meforash** (literally "the Name of the Brilliant Fire"). See also **God-Name**; **Tetragrammaton**.

**Hades** The Underworld of classical Greek mythology. Hades (or **Aidoneus**) was the god of the Underworld, and the brother of **Zeus**. He snatched **Persephone** away from the Nysian Plain where she was picking flowers, and made her queen of the Underworld. Her mother **Demeter** went in search of her and in the end it was agreed that Persephone would live on earth for part of the year and with Hades during winter. In Roman mythology, Hades was called **Pluto** and the Underworld was called **Dis**.

**Hadit** The Chaldean form of the Egyptian god of darkness, **Set**. Aleister Crowley and his magical disciple **Kenneth Grant** have identified Hadit with **Satan**; however, they regard him as not so much an adversary of humanity but as the master of magical initiation. In Crowleyian cosmology there is a link between Hadit and the entity **Aiwass** that inspired *The Book of the Law*.

**Haegl's Aett** In the Germanic Elder Futhark, **rune numbers** nine to sixteen.

**Hag** In Wicca, the dark, destructive aspect of the threefold **Great Goddess**, expressed symbolically through the passing of the seasons. The **Maid** is transformed into the Hag with the death of the year in autumn but is in turn reborn as the Maid in the following springtime. The Hag is also connected in some traditions with the **Crone** and the figure of **Cerridwen**. The term probably derives from the Old English *haegtesse*, "witch", "soothsayer", which is related to the German Hexe. See **Hex**.

**Hagalaz** See **Hagel**.

**Hagel** or **Haeg** In the Germanic **Elder Futhark**, the **rune** letter representing the number nine. Hagel corresponds to the letter "h" and is the rune of frost, ice, hail, and winter. This rune is associated with the element **air**, because hail and snow sweep down from the sky. By extension the rune symbolizes adverse occurrences that arise without warning. It also refers to the stress associated with sudden change and urges us to reconsider our priorities in a time of crisis. Also Hagalaz.

**Hagenti** In the Goetia, the 48th spirit, a great president who appears initially in the form of a mighty bull with the wings of a **griffin** but who will assume a human shape when so commanded by the magician. Hagenti is able to bestow the power of wisdom and transmute all metals into gold. He can also change wine into water and water into wine. He governs 33 legions of spirits.

**Hagith** According to *The Arbatel of Magick*, there are seven different spirits of Olympus, appointed by God to rule the world. Hagith is the spirit of Venus and governs all aspects of beauty. He is said to be able to convert copper into gold and has 36,536 legions of lesser spirits at his command.

**Hag of the Dribble** In Welsh folklore, a banshee who carried stones in her apron and then let them shower down, making a "dribble". She flapped her raven wings against the windows of houses where people would soon die, and howled mournfully in the twilight.

**Hag-Ridden** Troubled by nightmares and "ridden" like a horse in the night by frightening and evil witches. See also **Hag**; **Incubus**; **Succubus**.

**Hag Seed** The child of a witch. See also **Hag**.

**Hag Stone** In medieval English folklore, a stone with a hole in it, hung in the home or in the stables to ward off hags, evil spirits or witches, during the night. The hag stone was hung on a bedpost to prevent nightmares – terrifying dreams associated with magical attack and the feeling of being suffocated by a female demon or succubus.

**Haidit** or **Khaibit**. In ancient Egypt, the term for the "shadow", one of the five human bodies. The Haidit equated approximately with what we know as the unconscious mind and was capable of taking an astral form. See also **Aufu**; **Ka**; **Kuh**; **Sahu**.

**Hakata** Pieces of wood, bone, or ivory used for **divination** by an African witch-doctor, or medicine man. The objects are inscribed with symbols resembling signs of the **zodiac** and are cast upon the ground where they are then interpreted. See also **Geomancy**.

**Halaait** Among the Gitksan Indians of the Canadian northwest, a term used for a **shaman**, especially one who performs healing ceremonies in which patients are treated in a group. Another term used by the Gitksan Indians is **swanassu**, meaning a **medicine man**.

**Haldawit** Among the Tsimshian Indians of the Canadian northwest, a term used for a **sorcerer**. The haldawit is frequently accused of causing illness or harm.

**Hall, Manly Palmer** (1901–1990) An American author and student of the western mystery tradition who founded the Philosophical Research Society in Los Angeles in 1936. A prolific and highly regarded author, his best-known books include *The Secret Teachings of All Ages*; *Man, the Grand Symbol of the Mysteries*; *Sages and Seers*; and *Codex Rosae Crucis*.

**Halloween, Hallowe'en** See All Hallows' Eve.

**Hallristinger** or **Hallristningar Script** An ancient script or system of symbols used primarily by the Bronze Age people of northern Europe c.1300–1200BCE. The script is of shamanic origin and includes references to solar worship, fertility, the cosmos and the stars. It is thought that some of its symbols were incorporated into the Runic Alphabet. See also **Futhark, Elder**; **Futhark, Younger**.

**Hallucination** A state of perception that is not compatible with familiar, everyday reality and which is regarded in some societies as providing access to the sacred world. Hallucinations are often brought on by the action of psychedelic drugs or by conditions of sensory deprivation. In some indigenous cultures, hallucinogenic plants are thought to provide a pathway to a magical reality. For example, among the Jivaro Indians of eastern Ecuador, **shamans** take a hallucinogenic beverage made from the **banisteriopsis** vine in order to gain access to the spirit world. In their visions they often report giant, mythic jaguars and writhing snakes, which they interpret in an initiatory way. The Cashinahua Indians of Peru similarly use hallucinogens to contact the *nixi pae* spirit beings which are accompanied by brightly coloured snakes, armadillos, and singing frogs. It has been suggested that the magical flight of witches to the **Witches' Sabbath** may have resulted from hallucinatory ointments rubbed into the skin. Here, atropine was the ingredient causing the sensation of flight and the visionary experience of dissociation. See also **Altered State**; **Ayahuasca**; **Flying Ointments**.

**Halomancy** or **Alomancy**. A form of **divination** by throwing grains of salt onto a flat surface and interpreting the forms and shapes that result.

**Halpas** In the Goetia, the 38th spirit, a great earl who appears in the form of a dove but speaks with a hoarse voice. His appearance is deceptive for he is an agent of war, despatching men to fields of battle and constructing towns which are then filled with ammunition and weapons. He rules over 26 legions of spirits. Halpas is also known as Malthas.

**Hamadryads** In Greek mythology, the spirit-nymphs of woods and trees. See also **Dryads**.

**Hambaruan** Among the Dayaks of Borneo, the **soul** or **spirit** of a person, which may leave the body when it wishes and undertake a journey. It then becomes vulnerable to sorcery and the clutches of evil spirits. Compare **Astral Body** and see also **Soul Loss**.

**Handedness** The distinction between left-handed and right-handed people has a magical connotation. Left-handed people are often thought to be **sinister** (the Latin word for "left") or are regarded as having unusual characteristics, such as the ability to cast the **evil eye**. In modern occultism, the spiritual path of white magic is said to be that of the **right-hand path**, whereas the path of black magic is referred to as the **left-hand path**. See also **Magic, White** and **Magic, Black**.

**Handfasting** In Wicca, a wedding ritual that commits two people to each other like a marriage, "for as long as love lasts". Sometimes the **Great Rite** is performed either symbolically or "in true" as part of the marriage ceremony. Handfasting is not recognized legally as marriage so Wiccans who wish to have their union confirmed in law are also required to attend a conventional wedding ceremony. See also **Handparting**.

**Hand of Glory** In medieval magic, a charm used in black magic spells. Made from the severed right hand of an executed murderer, ideally cut from the corpse while the body was still hanging on the gallows, the hand was squeezed of blood, pickled, and dried. Later the hand was fitted with candles between the fingers. The Hand of Glory was supposed to have the magical power to freeze people to the spot and was therefore considered a deterrent against thieves. See also **Spell**.

**Handparting** In Wicca, a ritual which marks the dissolution of a **handfasting**, or Wiccan marriage. It is the equivalent of Wiccan divorce and is also referred to as "**going of the ways**".

***Hanged Man, The*** In the Tarot, a card of the **Major Arcana** that was regarded at one time incorrectly as a parody of Christ's crucifixion. The figure is shown upside down because he is a reflection of the profound spiritual energies of the supernal realm above him. His head is sometimes depicted as a beacon, with light streaming forth to the world below. The source of his inspiration is the ocean of spirit, **Binah**, higher up on the **Tree of Life**. In western **magic**, *The Hanged Man* is ruled by the element water, which makes the symbolism of his "reflective" nature more apparent. *The Hanged Man* is assigned to the path between **Hod** and **Geburah** on the Tree of Life.

**Hanon Tramp** A German expression for a type of nightmare in which a **demon** is thought to suffocate people as they sleep. See also **Incubus; Succubus**.

**Harakhtes** A Greek name of a form of the Egyptian god **Horus**, especially with regard to the sun's path across the sky. As Ra became increasingly identified with Horus, the Egyptians referred to the deity as **Ra-Horakhte** ("Ra-Horus-of-the-Horizon"). The ceremonial magician **Aleister Crowley** identified with this aspect of Horus, regarding himself as "the Crowned and Conquering Child, Lord of the New Aeon". Crowley spelled the name Ra-Hoor-Khuit. Compare **Harpocrates; Hor-em-Akhet**.

**Hare Moon** See Esbats.

**Harmachis** See Hor-em-Akhet.

**Harmakhu** See Hrumachis.

**Harmony of Opposites** The mystical and occult concept that cosmic consciousness may only be attained by transcending duality, i.e. when such distinctions as "male" and "female" or "object" and "subject" cease to be real. Many cosmologies portray a dynamic interplay between opposites: the Chinese yin and yang; the yogic ida and pingala; and the distinction, in Jewish mysticism, between thrones (static) and chariots (mobile) as vehicles of God. In the Kabbalah there are three vertical columns on the Tree of Life. The outer two, located beneath Chokmah (male) and Binah (female), represent archetypal polar opposites; and these opposites are resolved, or harmonized, by virtue of the Middle Pillar, which stands between them and joins Kether and Malkuth – the first and last spheres on the Tree. See also Androgyne; Dualism; Individuation; Tiphareth.

**Harner, Michael J.** (1929– ) An American anthropologist who spent many years of field research in the upper Amazon, Mexico, and western North America learning techniques of shamanism from native Indians. Harner has now adapted the traditional shamanic techniques for western practitioners, using a method that combines drumming and visualization to allow people to enter "the magical reality". This "journey" entails visualizing the Cosmic Tree, entering its root system, and travelling through to the lower world, where one may make contact with a power animal or magical ally. A variant on this procedure is to ascend to the upper world through a tunnel of smoke. Harner has been a visiting professor at Columbia, Yale, and the University of California, Berkeley, and is at present chairman of the Foundation for Shamanic Studies in Mill Valley, California. He is the author of a practical book on shamanism titled *The Way of the Shaman* (1980), and has also published two academic books on the subject: *The Jivaro* (1972); and *Hallucinogens and Shamanism* (1973).

**Harpies** In Greek mythology, horrible winged creatures with the bodies of vultures and the heads of women. They contaminated food, gave off a disgusting odour, and snatched away the souls of the dead.

**Harpocrates** or **Harpokrates** The name given by the ancient Greeks to a form of the Egyptian deity Horus, Horpa-Khered or Horus the Child. Harpocrates was the god of silence and was depicted holding his finger to his mouth. In the cosmology of Aleister Crowley, Harpocrates (whom Crowley called Hoor-paar-Kraat) was identified with the mysterious entity Aiwass or Aiwaz, who dictated *The Book of the Law* and the Law of Thelema in 1904. Hoor-paar-Kraat is also the twin of Ra-Hoor-Khuit, with whom Crowley identified. See also Aeon of Horus; Harakhtes; Ra-Horakhte.

**Harsiesis** "Horus, the Son of Isis", a title of the Egyptian deity Horus that affirmed his legitimacy as the successor of his father Osiris. As a child, Horus was protected by his mother Isis from his evil uncle Set and grew up skilled in the techniques of warfare. He hoped to avenge Osiris's death by decapitating Set and bringing his head to Isis. However, Set recovered from his wounds and continued to be his sworn enemy until, after a lengthy confrontation, Horus was confirmed by the gods as "Lord of the Two Lands".

**Hartley, Christine (1897–1985)** A senior member of Dion Fortune's Fraternity of the Inner Light, Hartley was born Christine Campbell Thomson in London, the daughter of a prominent neurologist. She worked for many years as a literary agent and was introduced to the realm of magical ideas by Dr J.W. Brodie-Innes, who was a minor novelist as well as a ceremonial magician and a member of the Hermetic Order of the Golden Dawn. Thomson later met Dion Fortune and in her professional role as a literary agent helped shape many of her novels, like *The Goat-Foot God* and *The Sea Priestess*. Fortune invited her to attend a lecture on magic in 1932 and she subsequently joined a magical study group, taking the magical name *Frere Ayme Frere*. In 1937 she established a close psycho-spiritual connection with Colonel **Charles R.F. Seymour**, exploring techniques of magical visualization and connecting with him energetically on the **astral plane**. Together, over a period of several years, they explored a succession of past lives and richly detailed reincarnational memories, the transcripts of which are provided in Alan Richardson's *Dancers to the Gods* (1985). Seymour died unexpectedly in 1943 and Thomson subsequently married Henry Alexander "Dair" Hartley, an engineer interested in psychic phenomena. Christine Hartley was the author of several books, including *A Case for Reincarnation* and *The Western Mystery Tradition*, published in 1968.

**Hartmann, Franz (1838–1912)** A German occultist and Theosophist who for many years resided in the United States. He was the founder of the Order of the Esoteric Rose Croix and was also affiliated with a magical group that eventually became the **Ordo Templi Orientis**. His best-known publications are *Magic, Black and White* and *In the Pronaos of the Temple of Wisdom*. See also **Occultism; Theosophy.**

**Haruspex** In ancient Rome, a priestly office connected with **divination**. The haruspex inspected the liver, heart, and entrails of animals and also interpreted the movements of the flames in the altar fire during ritual sacrifices. See also **Augur; Hepatoscopy.**

**Harvest** In alchemy, the act of producing the **Philosopher's Stone.**

**Hashish** A hallucinogenic resin made from the flowers of Indian hemp. It has powerful visionary qualities and can produce a euphoric altered state of consciousness when smoked or eaten. It is regarded as sacred in Tibet and is widely used as a sacrament in Central America. The Cuna Indians of Panama and the Cora Indians of Mexico both use it in their religious ceremonies. See also **Hallucination.**

**Hasidism** A Jewish mystical movement founded in Poland by the Russian-born Israel ben Eliezer (c. 1698–1760), otherwise known as Ba'al Shem Tov, or "Master of the Good Name" (i.e. the name of God). A Hasid is one who places total faith and trust in God and who interprets the "inner meaning" of the Law. Ba'al Shem Tov believed in "serving God with joy" and his services were accompanied by wild, enthusiastic singing, frenzied dancing, and potent drink. The body of Ba'al Shem Tov was said to tremble as he recited his prayers, and this type of ecstasy was transmitted charismatically to the congregation who would shout and cry out in joyful communion with God. Hasidism draws heavily on the kabbalistic teachings of **Isaac Luria**, and still continues as a movement within Judaism. The main centres of Hasidism today are New York and Israel. See also **Ba'al Shem; Kabbalah.**

**Hat, Witch's** See Witch's Hat.

**Hathor** In ancient Egyptian mythology, the queen of heaven. As a mother goddess and cosmic deity, she personified love, beauty, and joy and was depicted in the form of a cow with the sun disc between her horns. Her sanctuary was located at Dendera. She was also universally revered as "The Lady of the West", the goddess who welcomed the souls of the dead into the afterlife. Hathor and Isis were the greatest and most popular of Egypt's goddesses, and became so closely linked as to be virtually one deity, Hathor-Isis. Eventually, Hathor was subsumed into the great international Isis cult, which rivalled Christianity for popularity in the early centuries CE.

**Hathors** In ancient Egypt, a group of women, usually numbering seven, who had the psychic gift of predicting the future of a newborn child. They took their name from the goddess **Hathor**.

**Hauras** or **Haures** See Flauros.

**Hayyoth** In the Kabbalah, the four angelic beings in the prophet Ezekiel's vision who carry the Throne of Glory. They are also described as being like spiritual flashes of lightning that burst in four directions from the **Merkabah** (the chariot-throne of God) and in turn give rise to whirlwinds. The hayyoth are the source of the four cardinal directions and the four elements. See also **Chayot**.

**Hazel** A tree with strong mythic and magical associations. In Roman mythology, **Apollo** was said to have given a hazel rod to **Mercury** to enhance human "virtues", and the rods of the biblical Moses and Aaron were also made of hazel. In the Middle Ages hazel rods were thought to be effective against mischievous **fairies** and demons and, as a result, white magicians have traditionally fashioned their wands from hazel. Forked hazel twigs are also used by dowsers. See also **Demon; Magic, White**.

**Hcoma** In Enochian magic, the sacred name of the spirit of **water**. Hcoma (pronounced *heh-koh-mah*) is assigned to the West and is represented by the colour blue. See also **Exarp; Nanta; Bitom**.

**Head** In alchemy, another term for the alembic, the beaked vessel used as the upper part of the **distillation** apparatus.

**Heathen** From the Old English *haethen*, one who has not been converted to Christianity. It particularly applies to cultures that worship a multiplicity of gods rather than one, and for whom ancestor **spirits** and idols also have special significance. From a Christian perspective it is virtually synonymous with **pagan**.

**Heaven** (1) In world mythologies and cosmologies, a blissful and paradisial region or condition which the **soul** or disembodied human consciousness enters after its final separation from the physical body. Heaven is thus a mirror image of the most attractive and positive aspects of a culture or society, and epitomizes the spiritual "rewards" earned while on earth. Heaven is often believed to be somewhere beyond or within the sky, but it may also be under the earth or beyond the ocean. See also **Hell** (1).

**Heaven** (2) In alchemy, a term sometimes used to describe the **quintessence** – the fifth element, **spirit** – because of its brilliant azure colour, which was like "heaven".

**Heavenly Chariot** See Chariot, Heavenly.

**Heavenly Man** In the Kabbalah, the archetypal spiritual being associated with **Kether**, the first sphere of the **Tree of Life**, which allows God to take a human form. Without the concept of the Heavenly Man, no attributes could ever be ascribed to God, for he transcends all limitations.

**Hecate** In Greek mythology, a goddess with magical powers who took different forms. As a lunar goddess she was identified with **Artemis**, and as a goddess of the **Underworld** she was closely associated with **Persephone**. She had a frightening appearance, with snakes in her hair, and was attended by howling dogs. Annual festivals were held in her honour on the island of Aegina; there sacrifices were made and sorcerers and witches sought her aid. See also **Crossroads; Hemlock; Lunar Goddesses**.

**Hedgewitch** In Wicca a practitioner of the **Craft** who has not been initiated and does not belong to a **coven**, and who works as a **solitary**.

**Hedonism** The belief that the pursuit of pleasure is the most important activity in life. **Pagan** worshippers who idolize sensuality and indulge in orgies personify the cult of hedonism. See also **Corybantes; Dionysus.**

**Hegemon** In the Hermetic Order of the Golden Dawn, a ceremonial role representing the goddess of truth and justice. The Hegemon presides over the admittance of new candidates for the grade of **Neophyte.**

**Heh** The Hebrew letter ascribed to the path linking **Chokmah** and **Tiphareth** on the **Tree of Life.** Heh has a numerical value of five. In modern magical visualization and **pathworkings** the **Tarot** card associated with this path on the Tree is *The Emperor.*

**Heikhalot** See Hekhaloth.

**Heindel, Max** (1862–1919) The pseudonym of the Theosophical writer Max Grashof. Heindel was influenced by **Rudolf Steiner** and claimed to be an authentic Rosicrucian. He founded the Rosicrucian Fellowship in California, which is unrelated to the **AMORC** Rosicrucian organization situated in San José. Heindel's principal publication was *The Rosicrucian Cosmo-conception.* After his death, his wife Augusta continued the Rosicrucian Fellowship and was a strong advocate of his teachings until her own death in 1938. See also **Rosicrucians; Theosophy.**

**Hekau** In Egyptian magic and mythology, sacred **words of power** used to dispel evil and darkness. In the *Egyptian Book of the Dead,* and specifically in the texts known as the *Am Tuat* and *The Book of Gates,* the sun god proceeds through the dungeons of the **Underworld** (the twelve hours of night) by uttering hekau that cast aside hostile forces. These include abysses of darkness, streams of boiling water, appalling smells and stenches, demonic serpents, and monsters of all shapes and sizes.

**Hekhaloth** The "heavenly halls" of God's palace, glimpsed in visions by Jewish mystics as they ascended from one sphere to the next. A major text associated with this visionary activity is *The Greater Hekhaloth,* which dates from the first century CE.

**Hel** In Norse mythology, an earth goddess who became the queen of the dead. She ruled over those who died of natural causes – for example, old age and disease – as distinct from those who were killed in battle and whose souls went to **Valhalla.**

**Hell** (1) The domain of the wicked after death. It is conceived variously as a ghostly **Underworld** (the Greek **Hades**); as a pit of fire and damnation (the Jewish **Gehenna**); or as a large communal grave (as in the Mesopotamian afterworld). The Christian hell appears to derive from the Jewish vision of eternal fire and torment, and the Islamic vision of hell similarly resembles it. Hell typically personifies the most negative and destructive images projected by a culture and is regarded by occultists as an accumulation of negative thought-forms or images within the mythic realms of the unconscious mind. See also **Heaven.**

**Hell** (2) In **alchemy,** a term occasionally applied to putrefying matter in the state of **nigredo,** when the "body" was being "tortured" by the alchemist's fire.

**Hellebore** *Helleborus officinalis* (black hellebore) and *Veratrum album* (white, or European hellebore) are plants with longstanding magical associations. Traditionally both types of hellebore have been used to treat demonic possession. White hellebore is an erect perennial with star-like flowers and is classified as a hypnotic – it contains veratrine. In ancient Greece it was referred to as "the seed of **Heracles**" and became a magical narcotic incense. The first-century physician Dioscorides, who worked as a surgeon in the Roman army, reports that black hellebore was strewn around dwellings as a purifying agent. Black hellebore contains toxic glycosides which induce sneezing and in Germany it is known as "sneezing spice".

**Hell Fire Club** An eighteenth-century satanic club in England, founded by **Sir Francis Dashwood**, whose members gathered at Medmenham on the Thames. The group sang blasphemous hymns and conducted orgies in chambers excavated beneath a hill, and within the ruins of a disused abbey.

**Helmet** In alchemy, the name for the **alembic**, the beaked vessel used as the upper part of the **distillation** apparatus.

**Hemaneh** A term used by the Cheyenne Indians to refer to a transvestite **shaman** – the word means "half man, half woman". The hemaneh wore women's clothing and were renowned for their healing abilities. There have been no known hemaneh among the Cheyenne since the late 19th century.

**Hemlock** *Conium maculatum*, a plant sacred to **Hecate**, the ancient Greek goddess of the **Underworld**, hemlock is perhaps best known as an ingredient in the poisonous drink consumed in 399BCE by the Greek philosopher Socrates, who had been sentenced to commit suicide – the fatal potion contained hemlock juice mixed with laudanum and wine. Allegedly used in ancient times in a paste to dry up the milk in women's breasts or to prevent a virgin's breasts from becoming too large, hemlock was also used medicinally in medieval Europe to treat **St Anthony's fire**, a condition caused by **ergot** poisoning.

**Hemp, Indian** A popular name for cannabis. It has been associated by some authorities with the mystical Indian sacrament **soma**, although the ethnomycologist **R. Gordon Wasson** believes that soma is in fact *Amanita muscaria*. According to Mahayana Buddhist tradition, Gautama Buddha lived on one

Indian hemp seed a day as he progressed towards spiritual enlightenment. He is sometimes depicted with "soma leaves" in his begging bowl. See also **Hallucination; Hashish**.

**Henbane** *Hyoscyamus niger*, a poisonous, narcotic plant associated with **witchcraft** and **sorcery**. Henbane contains alkaloids which can cause the illusion that one has transformed into an animal, and it has traditionally been regarded as the active component of **Circe's** magical potion. It is possible that the **Delphic oracle** made her prophecies after inhaling smoke from burning henbane seeds. See also **Circe; Flying Ointments; Hallucination; Lycanthropy**.

**Hepatoscopy** A form of **divination** in which the liver of a sacrificed sheep was inspected and diagnosed by a diviner or magician-priest. This was a common practice among the Etruscans, Hittites, and Babylonians. See also **Haruspex**.

**Heptad** In **numerology**, the number seven.

**Hera** In Greek mythology, the queen of the gods and heaven. Hera was both the sister and wife of Zeus and the daughter of Kronos and Rhea. Hera was a jealous wife and was hostile to Zeus's many mistresses and illegitimate offspring, such as **Heracles**. She was perceived as the goddess of women and childbirth, and especially of marriage. Her Roman equivalent was Juno.

**Heracles** or **Hercules** In Graeco-Roman mythology, a legendary hero who achieved great fame for his bravery and strength. The son of Zeus, Heracles had a mortal mother – Alcmene – and as a result attracted the jealous wrath of Zeus's wife **Hera**, who sent two serpents to destroy him when he was still an infant. Heracles survived by strangling them. Hera nevertheless persisted with her interference and one day, when Heracles had grown up and become a married man, she filled him with madness and rage, causing him to murder his children. Heracles consulted the **Delphic oracle** and was told to go into service with King Eurystheus to atone for this wicked deed. As a result, he performed the twelve "labours of Heracles", which included slaying the multiheaded monster **Hydra**. When Heracles died he was assumed into the heavens as a god.

**Herbal Medicine** A tradition of medicine linked at different stages of its development to **witchcraft, astrology,** and **alchemy**. Herbal medicine dates back at least as far as c. 3000BCE, when the legendary Chinese emperor Shen-Nung compiled a major work on herbs, titled *Pen Tsao*. In it he praised the healing properties of ginseng, cinnamon, and the bark of the mulberry tree. The ancient Egyptians valued olive oil, cloves, myrrh, and castor oil, and developed a wide knowledge of "essential oils" for curative and embalming purposes. The ancient Greeks also valued herbal medicines, and Pliny's *Natural History* records that herbalism was endorsed by the great physician Hippocrates. Possibly because of its pagan associations and frequent references to the healing deities **Apollo** and **Asklepios**, much of the herbal knowledge that filtered through to medieval Europe from ancient Greece was discarded as non-Christian and linked to witchcraft and magic. The Swiss herbalist and alchemist **Paracelsus** (1493–1541) classified plants according to the colour symbolism of the flowers. Paracelsus also believed in the curative properties of such metals as mercury and antimony. In England, Nicholas Culpeper (1616–1654) combined astrology, magic, and herbalism in his work *The English Physician Enlarged* (1653).

One of the most curious aspects of herbs in the Middle Ages is that some herbal concoctions were supposed to bestow magic powers. One herbal recipe dating from c. 1600 describes how olive oil, rose water, and marigolds could be mixed together and used to obtain a glimpse of the **fairies**: "The roses and the marigolds are to be gathered towards the east, and the water thereof to be made of pure spring water. Put the washed oil into a vial glass and add hollyhock buds, marigold flowers, wild thyme tops and flowers, young hazel buds, and the grass of a fairy throne. The thyme must be gathered near the side of a hill where fairies use to be. Set the glass in the sun for three days so that the ingredients can become incorporated. Then put away for use…" Modern herbalism has since become a systematic branch of naturopathy, and quaint folk-recipes like this no longer form part of herbal medicine. However, some contemporary herbalists believe that modern doctors are unjustly prejudiced against their traditional remedies, and periodic accusations of "witchcraft" and "superstition" are still made against herbal practitioners.

**Herb, Sorcerer's** See Thornapple.

**Hercules** See Heracles.

**Hereditaries** Witches who claim a lengthy family-based lineage in practising the Craft, long before the current revival of Wicca.

**Heresy** From the Greek *hairesis*, meaning "choice", a heresy is a religious teaching regarded as contrary to, or deviating from, the accepted and established form of doctrine. It is most frequently associated with the Christian religion, especially in regard to the Church's persecution of unorthodox groups of believers (Albigenses, Cathars, witches, etc.) during the Middle Ages. It also applies to the condemnation of **Gnostic** sects by orthodox Church Fathers such as Irenaeus. However, the term heresy may also be applied to other religions as well. In ancient Egypt, the pharaoh Akhenaten sought to suppress the established cult of Amun – thus making himself a heretic – and in Islam the Sufi mystic Mansur al-Hallaj was crucified in Baghdad in 922 for linking himself with God. See also **Inquisition**.

**Heretic** See Heresy.

**Hermaphrodite (1)** Literally, a bisexual human being or animal. The name comes from Hermaphroditus, the son of **Hermes** and **Aphrodite** in Greek mythology. He fell in love with a nymph who embraced him so closely that they became fused as one being. In **mysticism** and **occultism**, the symbol of the human hermaphrodite or androgyne has special significance because it represents the fusion of opposite polarities, and therefore characterizes a major development on the spiritual path to transcending quality. The **Tarot** card of *The Fool* shows a hermaphroditic figure walking over a cliff-edge – the cliff representing manifested reality – and embracing universal "space". The card thus symbolizes the mystical act of surrendering one's individuality, or self, in transcendental union with the **godhead**. See also **Harmony of Opposites**.

**Hermaphrodite (2)** In alchemy, a reference to the **Philosopher's Stone**, which contains both the red and white tinctures capable of transmuting base metal into gold and silver respectively. The red tincture represents the male principle symbolized by **King Sol** and the white tincture the female principle symbolized by **Queen Luna**. The "red and white hermaphrodite" was sometimes said to contain roses and lilies for this reason.

**Hermes** In Greek mythology, the messenger of the gods and the counterpart of the Roman **Mercury**. Hermes had many roles and attributes. He was god of the wind, athletics, oratory and trade affairs. He also conducted the souls of the dead on their passage to the **Underworld**, and was the protector of sacrificial animals. See also **Hermes Trismegistus**; **Thoth**.

**Hermes Bird** See Bird of Hermes.

**Hermes' Seal** In alchemy, the "hermetic" seal that closed the alchemical vessel and helped keep it airtight.

**Hermes Trismegistus** "Thrice-Greatest Hermes", the principal figure in the mystical literature collectively known as *Hermetica*, where he takes the role of a prophet or spiritual leader who can save the world from evil. He is thought to be a combination of the Greek god **Hermes** and the Egyptian god of wisdom, **Thoth**.

**Hermetica, The** A collection of mystical tracts and dialogues – primarily Greek in origin – that contain references to the healing gods **Asklepios** and **Imhotep** and also **Isis**, **Osiris**, and **Thoth**. The literature as it exists today consists collectively of fourteen sermons by **Poimandres** or Pymander ("the shepherd of men" and spiritual leader), the so-called "Perfect Sermon" of Asklepios, 27 excerpts from the collection of the fifth-century writer Stobaeus, and a selection of fragments from the Church Fathers relating to the mystery tradition. There are several translations of *The Hermetica* in English, including those of John Everard (1650), J.D. Chambers (1882), and G.R.S. Mead (1906).

**Hermetic Axiom** "As above, so below." A metaphysical axiom, ascribed to **Hermes Trismegistus**, which describes the relationship between **macrocosm** and **microcosm**.

**Hermetic Order of the Golden Dawn** A magical order founded in England in 1888 that has strongly influenced contemporary western magical beliefs and practices. The rituals of the order were based originally on five masonic grades discovered in the papers of a deceased English **Rosicrucian**. Dr Wynn Westcott, who was himself a **Freemason**, asked **Samuel MacGregor Mathers** to expand the material to form a more complete occult system. Mathers worked on the formation of a new body of rituals and chose as his basis the kabbalistic **Tree of**

Life, using its ten **sephiroth** – or levels of consciousness – as the basis of different ceremonial grades. Westcott, Mathers, and another occultist, Dr William Woodman, appointed themselves the heads of the Second Order of the Golden Dawn (known as the **Red Rose and the Cross of Gold:** *Rosae Rubae et Aurea Crucis*), which in effect governed the first seven grades on the Tree of Life. The other three grades, representing the **Third Order**, were symbolically linked to the Trinity and were said to be the domain of **Secret Chiefs** – spiritual masters who would guide the Order and provide Mathers, in particular, with magical inspiration.

The first Golden Dawn temple, Isis-Urania, was opened in London in 1888. By 1896 there was a temple of Osiris in Weston-super-Mare, Somerset, a temple of Horus in Bradford, a temple of Amen-Ra in Edinburgh, and a temple sacred to Ahathoor in Paris. The names of these temples indicate the strong influence of Egyptian mythology which, along with Rosicrucian, Greek, Celtic, Enochian, and some Hindu elements, characterized the rituals. The Golden Dawn attracted many notable occultists, including the poet **William Butler Yeats**; **A. E. Waite**, the originator of a popular Rider **Tarot** pack and the leading occult scholar of his day; and **Aleister Crowley**, the famous, and later notorious, ceremonial magician. As Mathers became increasingly autocratic, the order began to fragment and by the time of Mathers' death in 1918, the original Golden Dawn had fractured completely. However, other derivative groups emerged, including the **Stella Matutina**. Between 1937 and 1941, Israel Regardie, a one-time secretary to Aleister Crowley, published the complete rituals of the Stella Matutina in four volumes under the title *The Golden Dawn*. These books constitute the most complete magical system produced in modern times. See also **Magic, Ceremonial; Magic, Enochian**.

**Hermetic Society** An occult organization founded in London in 1884 by **Anna Bonus Kingsford** and Edward Maitland. Kingsford was president of the London Lodge of the Theosophical Society from 1883–1884 but eventually rejected the increasing emphasis on eastern mystical thought promoted by **Madame Helena Blavatsky**. The Hermetic Society sought to introduce western mystical and esoteric themes into a Christian context.

**Hermetic Teachings** The doctrines of *The Hermetica*. The term is also applied to the western mystery tradition in a general and non-specific way.

**Hermetic Vase** See Aludel.

**Hermit, The** In the Tarot, a card of the Major Arcana representing the lonely ascent of the mystic, who climbs the cosmic mountain following the lamp of his own inner light. Occultists regard *The Hermit* as a form of the "Ancient of Days", the wise, patriarchal figure who shuns outward appearances (he wears a dark cloak) in favour of the sacred, mystical reality. In western **magic**, which combines the Tarot paths of the Major Arcana with the ten **sephiroth** on the Tree of Life, the path of *The Hermit* connects Tiphareth and Chesed.

**Herne the Hunter** In English folklore, the horned phantom of Windsor Forest and leader of the wild hunt, associated in turn with the practice of **witchcraft**, and with the Celtic horned god **Cernunnos**.

**Hesed** See Chesed.

**Hespere** See Garden of the Hesperides.

**Hesperides** See Garden of the Hesperides.

**Hesperus** The name given to the planet Venus when it appears after sunset as the Evening Star.

**Het** See Cheth.

**Hex** In sorcery, a spell or curse inflicted upon a person or property. The term derives from the German *Hexe*, "witch" and *Hexer* "sorceror, wizard". The word is related to the English **hag**. In Pennsylvania, where the art of hexing became popular, there are still hexters who make amulets and talismans to ward off evil influences. See **Hexter**.

**Hexagram** In western **magic** and Jewish mysticism, a symbol known as "the Star of David". It consists of two superimposed triangles, one whose apex faces up, the other down. The hexagram thus embodies the principle expressed in the **Hermetic Axiom**: "As above, so below." The triangle that points upward is regarded as masculine, that which points down as feminine. In western magic many rituals involve the inscription of the hexagram with the magical sword. Hexagram rituals may be used to "invoke" or "banish" each of the planetary forces, and are regarded by occultists as having considerable magical power. The six points of the hexagram are sometimes shown surmounting the kabbalistic **Tree of Life**, with the uppermost point in **Daath** and the lowest in **Yesod**. The sacred god-name Ararita is often used in hexagram rituals.

**Hexenbanner** In medieval Germany, the equivalent of the wizard, hexer, and healer known as the **cunning person**. See also **Hex**.

**Hexter** A "hex-doctor": one who has magical antidotes for spells and curses. See also **Hex**.

**Hierarchy of Adepts** In many mystical and occult groups, the idea of a hierarchy of spiritual masters has been popular. In **Theosophy** these adepts are often thought to be discarnate Tibetan priests, skilled in esoteric lore. In western magic, some occultists, especially MacGregor Mathers, R.W. Felkin, and Aleister Crowley, have claimed privileged contact with inspirational "masters" or **Secret Chiefs**. Invariably,

recourse to an occult hierarchy is made when a particular mystical teaching is given to followers and requires endorsement from a "higher source".

**Hieratic** That which is consecrated by priests for sacred ritual use. The term also applies to the cursive writing employed by the priests of ancient Egypt.

**Hiereus** A ceremonial role within the **Hermetic Order of the Golden Dawn**, personifying the dark aspects of the ancient Egyptian god **Horus**. Hiereus is described in the order's rituals as representing "the terrible and avenging god at the confines of matter, on the borders of the **Qlippoth**". He guards the sacred mysteries from evil but is himself "enthroned-upon matter and robed in darkness". Hiereus thus defines the border between good and evil in magical rituals. See also **Magic, Ceremonial**.

**Hieroglyphs** From the Greek meaning "sacred carvings", hieroglyphs was the ancient Egyptian form of writing that consisted of pictorial motifs. Principally used for inscriptions on the walls of tombs and temples, the hieroglyphs were called "the speech of the gods" by the Egyptians themselves

**Hierophant** From the Greek *hieros*, meaning "holy", one who serves as a priest and interprets the sacred and divine mysteries. In the **Hermetic Order of the Golden Dawn**, the Hierophant is a member of the **Second Order.**

**Hierophant, The** In the Tarot, a card of the Major Arcana representing the divine authority of the priest, who personifies wisdom and mercy and acquires these qualities from mystical inspiration. In western **magic**, which combines the Tarot paths of the Major Arcana with the ten **sephiroth** of the kabbalistic **Tree of Life**, the path of *The Hierophant* connects **Chesed** and **Chokmah**.

**Higher Self** One's spiritual self, realized fully as the divine essence that links each human being to God. This spiritual self-knowledge is also referred to as cosmic consciousness.

**High God** See God, High.

**High Magic** See Magic, High.

**High Priest** In Wicca, the male leader of the coven and the partner or consort of the high priestess, who maintains overall leadership. A high priest must have attained the second or third degrees. See also **Second Initiation; Third Initiation.**

**High Priestess** In Wicca, the female leader and overall head of the coven. A high priestess must have attained the second or third degrees. See also **High Priest; Second Initiation; Third Initiation.**

**High Priestess, The** In the Tarot, a card of the **Major Arcana** representing the virginal lunar priestess who has had no union with a male deity. In a mystical sense, she has the potential for motherhood (manifestation and form), but has not yet realized the possibility of giving birth to myriad forms within the cosmos. Her virginity and innocence symbolize her purity and place her mythologically above the **Abyss**, which separates the Trinity and the manifested universe. In western magic, which combines the Tarot paths of the Major Arcana with the ten **sephiroth** of the Tree of Life, the path of *The High Priestess* connects **Tiphareth** and **Kether**. *The High Priestess* also reflects the transcendental aspect of the Roman goddess Diana. See also **Lunar Goddesses.**

**Hippomancy** Form of divination practised among the **Celts**, in which the gait of white horses was symbolically interpreted.

**Hirsig, Leah** Aleister Crowley's magical partner and **Whore of Babalon**, or Scarlet Woman, at the Abbey of Thelema in Cefalu, Sicily. Leah Hirsig bore Crowley a daughter, Poupée. See Crowley, Aleister.

**Hitlahavut** In the Jewish mystical tradition, the state of "burning enthusiasm" to experience the divine in all aspects of life.

**Hiving Off** In Wicca, covens must not exceed thirteen members in total. If this happens a new coven must be formed by two or more members of the original coven. Traditionally members of the new coven should move at least a league (three miles) from the original coven.

**Hobgoblin** A mischievous **imp** or goblin who produces fear and apprehension, especially in children.

**Hockley, Frederick** (d.1885) An English clairvoyant and occultist who was a member of the **Societas Rosicruciana in Anglia.** Hockley used a crystal ball and mirror for **skrying** in the spirit-vision and recorded thirty volumes of conversations with spirit entities. He was also a collector of ancient esoteric texts and transcribed many unpublished manuscripts on **magic** and **alchemy.** See also **Rosicrucians.**

**Hocus-Pocus** A derogatory term used to describe erroneous beliefs, also used with reference to sleight-of-hand deception. It is thought to derive from a eucharistic phrase in the Latin Mass, *Hoc est corpus*, "This is my body."

**Hod** The eighth emanation or sephirah on the kabbalistic **Tree of Life.** In western magic Hod is associated with the planet **Mercury** and represents intellect and rational thought. It also represents the structuring and measuring capacities of the mind as opposed to the emotional and intuitional aspects, which are ascribed to **Netzach.** Hod has no exact parallel in the **Tarot**, but is closely linked to the card *Judgement*, ascribed to the path between Hod and **Malkuth.** See also **Kabbalah; Sephiroth.**

**Hodos Chamelionis** In western kabbalistic magic, the "path of the chameleon" – a reference to the different colours assigned to the spheres on the kabbalistic **Tree of Life**. The magician ascends through these different spheres, or sephiroth, on the spiritual journey towards the godhead.

**Hokmah** See Chokmah.

**Holda** See Holle

**Holhkunna** or **Holhkunnda**. Term used by the Choctaw Indians to refer to a shaman. A related term is holkkunda, or sorcery – widely regarded as the cause of personal illness or disease.

**Holle** Also, **Holda**. In German folklore, the queen of the elves and witches who was also a goddess of the sky. She caused showers of snow by shaking her feather bed, and rain would fall when she washed her veil. Holle was often depicted as a wrinkled hag who rode in the sky during thunderstorms.

**Holly King** In Wicca, the god of the waning year. At summer solstice he ritually "slays" the **Oak King**, who is the god of the waxing year. At winter solstice, the Oak King "slays" the Holly King in turn. The Holly King and Oak King represent opposing aspects of an eternal process – the natural cycle of life, death, and rebirth.

**Holy** That which is sacred or divine, originates in God or a pantheon of deities, or is put aside for worship. It also has the connotation of being awe-inspiring and transcendent.

**Holy Ancient One** In the Kabbalah, a term for **Ain Soph** – the infinite godhead – manifesting through **Kether** at the peak or crown of the **Tree of Life**.

**Holy Grail** The cup used by Jesus Christ at the Last Supper and which, according to legend, was brought to Britain by Joseph of Arimathea. The quest to find the Holy Grail was central to the legendary exploits of the knights of King Arthur, although in this capacity it seems to have been a symbol of perfection and virtue.

**Holy Guardian Angel** In western magic, the spark of God that is the essence of every man and woman. Knowledge of the holy guardian angel is synonymous with cosmic consciousness.

**Holy Seal** The scar left on the body after the act of complete castration. In initiatory rites of **sexual magic** the Holy Seal may be accorded special significance.

**Homunculus** Latin, "little man". In alchemy, a creature comparable to the golem, which was artificially created by magical means. Sperm was placed in a sealed vessel together with other obscure ingredients and incubated by being buried in horse manure for forty days. At the end of this period the embryo would begin to appear. Medieval magicians believed one could obtain a child in this way, but at the most it would only attain twelve inches in height. It was advisable to keep the homunculus in a glass jar, for this was its familiar environment. The alchemist **Paracelsus** claimed that he had been successful in creating a homunculus.

**Honey** In alchemy, a term used metaphorically to describe the **Elixir of Life**.

**Hoodoo** Form of cult magic which originated in Africa and bears some similarities to **voodoo**. In hoodoo magic, which was popular among African Americans on the plantations in the southern United States, charms were worn to bring good luck. They could also be used to direct misfortune against an enemy.

**Hoor-paar-Kraat** An aspect of the Egyptian deity **Horus** accorded special significance by the occultist **Aleister**

**MATTHEW HOPKINS** The notorious 'witchfinder', Matthew Hopkins took it upon himself to purge East Anglia of witchcraft during the 17th century.

Crowley in his assumed role as Lord of the New Aeon. Crowley identified this form of Horus, the twin of **Ra-Hoor-Khuit**, as symbolic of the "solar sexual energies" that were part of his own idiosyncratic form of sexual magic. See **Harpocrates**.

**Hopkins, Matthew** (died 1647) The notorious self-styled "Witch-Finder General" of the English Civil War period. The son of a Puritan minister, Hopkins mounted witch hunts in Suffolk, Norfolk, Essex, and Huntingdonshire. His career began when he discovered members of a local **coven**, searched their bodies for the **Devil's Mark**, and realized that he could earn a living by reporting witches to the authorities. He subsequently decided to purge the whole of East Anglia of **witchcraft** and went from village to village seeking those accused of "bewitching" their neighbours. Hopkins employed the notorious technique of **swimming**. Because water was associated with Christian baptism, it was assumed that the pond would reject a witch and make her "swim" (float). A person innocent of witchcraft would sink – possibly drowning in the process. Hopkins was at his peak of activity between 1644 and 1646, but was finally forced by public pressure to desist from his brutal campaign. It is thought that he caused the deaths of at least 200 people.

**Hor** The name by which the ancient Egyptians referred to the god better known by his Latin name, **Horus**.

**Horary Astrology** See Astrology, Horary.

**Hor-em-Akhet** "Horus in the Horizon", the ancient Egyptian name for the famous Great Sphinx at Giza in Egypt; the Greek form of this name is **Harmakhis**. The sphinx, which combined a lion's body with a man's head, represented the mystical power of the pharaoh, Egypt's king. The Great Sphinx is fashioned in stone, dates from

c. 2900BCE, and measures 58 meters (189 feet) in length. See also **Sphinx**.

**Horned God** A symbol of male fertility in **witchcraft**. The Horned God is usually identified as the Greek god of nature, **Pan**, who presided over woods and forests and played his magical pipes. Part man, part goat, Pan was fond of lechery and frolicked with the wood nymphs. The Horned God is also identified by contemporary Wiccans as **Cernunnos**, a Celtic nature deity combining the attributes of a bull, a man, a serpent, and a fish.

**Horne, Fiona** An Australian celebrity **witch**, musician, and actor now based in the United States. A long-time practitioner of **Wicca**, Horne starred in the SCI-FI Channel's original reality show *Mad Mad House*, which premiered in March 2004 and attracted 1.57 million viewers. Her publications include *Witch*, *Life's a Witch*, and *Pop! Goes the Witch* – an international anthology of contemporary writings on **witchcraft**, Wicca and **neopaganism**.

**Horoscope** In **astrology**, a **figure** or map of the heavens, encompassing 360 degrees which, for a specific moment in time, identifies the positions of the planets and the sun in different signs of the **zodiac**. Astrologers interpret the relationships or **aspects** between the planets and the **earth** as favourable or unfavourable influences pertaining to the specific moment for which the horoscope is cast. While the most significant moment in a person's life is the time when he or she first draws breath, horoscopes may also be cast for occasions other than one's time and date of birth. Horoscopes may be drawn up to determine favourable conditions for important future events – a marriage, starting a new company, travel overseas – and may even be cast to determine the likely political future of a nation. In this instance, the date of birth of the nation dates from its independence or date of constitution.

**Horoscope, Natal** In astrology, a horoscope of the heavens for the precise moment when a person first drew breath. It is also known as a **nativity** or **geniture**.

**Horoscope, Progressed** In astrology, a horoscope cast on the basis of "one day for one year", so that it is drawn up for a date that is as many days after the person's date of birth as that person's age in years.

**Horoscope, Solar Revolution** In astrology, a horoscope cast for the moment in any year when the sun reaches the exact longitude it occupies in the **radix**.

**Horse Brasses** Amulets attached to the harness and trappings of a horse in order to ward off evil influences. Because they were shiny, they were said to deflect the hostile power of the evil eye.

**Horseshoe, Lucky** A good-luck charm, often nailed above doorways to ward off evil forces. It is made of iron, traditionally regarded as a powerful protection against **witchcraft**. Its crescent shape is reminiscent of lunar worship.

**Horse-Whisperer** In traditional witchcraft, a person thought to possess the magical ability to communicate with horses and make them do one's bidding. The **words of power** and magical **charms** used to bring about these results have always been jealously guarded secrets.

**Horus** The latinized form of the Egyptian god Hor, who originally was a falcon-headed deity with the sun and moon as his eyes. As the pharaohs came to identify themselves with **Ra**, Horus became associated with the sun. At different times, Horus was considered to be the son of Atum, Ra, and **Osiris**. He is best known for his role in Osirian mythology, where he avenged the death of his father by finally overcoming Set. He had many aspects: see also Harakhte; Harpocrates; Harsiese; Hor-em-Akhet;

Hrumachis; Ra-Hoor-Khuit.

**Hotokeoroshi** In Japan, a ritual whereby a dead ancestor is summoned to descend into the body of a trance medium and speak through her mouth. See also Ichiko.

**Hounfor** In voodoo, the temple of the priest, including the ritual paraphernalia of the service and the acolytes who serve there. When contrasted with the peristyle, the roofed unwalled area where most ceremonies take place, the hounfor also refers specifically to the inner sanctuary containing the **altar**. Also Humfo; Hunfor; or Oum'phor.

**Houngan** In voodoo, a priest. The word derives from *gan*, "chief", and *houn*, "of the spirits", in the language of the Fons people of western Africa. Also Hungan.

**Houngenikon** In voodoo, the assistant to the **houngan**. The houngenikon is usually responsible for leading the singing during the ceremonies.

**Hounsi Çanzo** See Canzo.

**Hounsis** In voodoo, members of the hounfor, at various stages of initiation. Also Hunsis.

**Hountor** In voodoo, the spirit of the drums. The word is sometimes used to refer to the **loa** who possesses the drummer and in northern Haiti it is also the term for a sacrificial goat. Also Huntor.

**Hours** In astrology, each hour is important because planetary positions vary as the earth rotates on its axis and moves around the sun. In a **horoscope**, each two-hour period of the day is known as a different **house** and attracts different aspects. See Astrology, Horary.

**Hour, Witching** See Witching Hour.

**House** In astrology, one-twelfth of the

total circle of the heavens. This section – or arc – of the **horoscope** spans 30 degrees and covers two hours in time as the earth rotates on its axis. The term "house" is differentiated from **sign**, which refers to the specific twelvefold division of the **zodiac** commencing with **Aries** and culminating with **Pisces**.

**Hru** According to tantric magician and author **Kenneth Grant**, the angel who presides over the **Tarot**. Grant maintains that Hru was an inspirational presence behind the tarot images in **Aleister Crowley's** Thoth deck.

**Hrumachis** The Greek form of the Egyptian god-name Harmakhu, which translates as "Horus of the Star". See also **Horus**.

**Hsiang-Ming Shih** In Taoism, a soothsayer or fortune teller who divines the future by means of the hexagrams of the *I Ching*.

**Huathe** In the Celtic tree alphabet, the **ogham** representing the hawthorn and the letter "h". Huathe is also linked to the crow and the colour black.

**Hubbard, Lafayette Ronald** (1911–1986) The American founder of Scientology and Dianetics, Hubbard claimed extrasensory powers, including knowledge of past incarnations, and appears to have derived many of his Scientology principles from occultism, magic, and science fiction. In the late 1930s and early 1940s he wrote a succession of serials for the pulp magazine *Astounding Science Fiction* under both his own name and as "Rene Lafayette." He was also involved with the Los Angeles lodge of the **Ordo Templi Orientis** and worked ritually with one of Aleister Crowley's followers, Jack Parsons, in the so-called **Babalon Working**.

**Huldra** In Norse mythology, a wood nymph or **fairy** who appeared in the form of a beautiful woman, but had a concealed tail. Huldras were said to play enchanting music that had an air of melancholy.

**Human Signs** In astrology, those signs of the **zodiac** whose motifs have a human form: **Gemini**, **Virgo**, and **Aquarius**. **Sagittarius** is sometimes also included.

**Humfo, Hunfor** See Hounfor.

**Hungan** See Houngan.

**Hunsis** See Hounsis.

**Huntor** See Hountor.

**Hun-Tun** In ancient Chinese cosmology, the force of **chaos** – personified as an emperor-god who presided in the universe before the orderly and dynamic forces of **yin** and **yang** came into being.

**Hutin, Serge** (1929– ). A French occult author, born in Paris, who has written widely on alchemy, secret societies, **Gnosticism**, **Freemasonry**, reincarnation, and **astrology**. One of his best known books is *Astrology: Science or Superstition?*, published in Belgium in 1970 and translated into English in 1972.

**Hutton, Ronald** Professor of history at the University of Bristol, England, Hutton is the author of *The Triumph of the Moon* (1999), internationally acclaimed as the definitive study of the history of modern pagan **witchcraft**. His other books include *The Pagan Religions of the Ancient British Isles*, *The Rise and Fall of Merrie England*, *Stations of the Sun* and *Shamans: Siberian Spirituality and the Western Imagination*.

**Huysmans, Joris-Karl** (1848–1907). A French novelist of Dutch ancestry who wrote a number of "decadent" novels including *A Rebours* and *La Bas*, which includes a description of a **black mass**. He was fascinated by the satanic crimes of **Gilles de Rais**, and also became involved in the magical feud between **Joseph-Antoine Boullan** and **Stanislas de Guaita**. Boullan features in *La Bas* as the character Dr. Johannes.

**Hydra** In Greek mythology, a monster born of Typhon and Echidna. It took the form of a water snake with nine heads, one of which was immortal. The Hydra caused widespread havoc and destruction around Lerna, and **Heracles** was sent on his second labour to destroy it. Every time a head was cut off it would grow back, but Heracles succeeded in the task by having his assistant Iolaus cauterize the heads of the Hydra as Heracles struck them off with his club. The immortal head was buried beneath a rock pile.

**Hydrolith** In alchemy, the "waterstone", a reference to the mysterious and often elusive qualities of the **Philosopher's Stone** – the "stone that is no stone".

**Hydromancy** Form of **divination** in which the colour and patterns of flowing water are studied and interpreted. Sometimes ripples are counted as stones are dropped in a stream. See also **Lecanomancy**.

**Hypnos** In Greek mythology, the god of sleep. He was the father of **Morpheus**, god of dreams, and the twin brother of **Thanatos**, god of death. The Roman counterpart of Hypnos was Somnus.

**Hypocephalus** In ancient Egypt, a disc of bronze inscribed with **magical formulae** or **words of power**. It was placed beneath the heads of mummies, apparently to ensure warmth for the corpse.

**Hyssop** *Hyssopus officinalis*, an aromatic herb which has been used for over 2,000 years as a culinary seasoning and also for medicinal purposes. Some believe that modern hyssop is the same plant known to the ancient Hebrews as *ezob*, mentioned in Psalm 51.9: "Purge me with hyssop and I shall be clean."

Because of its deodorant properties it was one of the herbs used to purify sacred temples, and the Hebrews used bunches of it for the ritual cleansing of lepers.

**Hysteria, Witchcraft** A medieval European phenomenon associated with **witchcraft persecutions** and cases of alleged **satanic possession**. The classic cases of hysteria include those of the **Aix-en-Provence Nuns** and the so-called incident of the "Devils of Loudun", in which **Urbain Grandier** was unjustly condemned to death. **Isobel Gowdie** is an example of a witch whose magical fantasies and decadent activities led to her execution. Many modern authorities on medieval witchcraft hysteria interpret it as symptomatic of mental illness and sexual repression. Some outbreaks of witchcraft hysteria may also have been caused by **ergot poisoning** in the local bread, leading to unsettling and misunderstood visionary states comparable to those experienced under LSD. See also **Burning Times**.

# I

**Ialdabaoth** According to the Gnostic text *The Apocryphon of John*, an archon or spiritual ruler created from the "shadow" of chaos by **Sophia**. Ialdabaoth then created the heavens and the earth. According to various tracts, Ialdabaoth was arrogant and androgynous, and took the form of a boastful lion. See also **Androgyne; Gnosis**.

**Iamblichus** (250–325CE) Neoplatonic mystic and philosopher who, together with Psellus, Pletho and **Porphyry** wrote commentaries on the spiritual tracts known collectively as the **Chaldean Oracles**, which are thought to have been authored by Julian the Theurgist. Iamblichus was a practitioner of **theurgy**, or sacred magic, and believed that the soul could be lifted up to the domain of the gods through incantations and prayer. Iamblichus wrote the classic mystical work *On the Mysteries* (translated into English by Thomas Taylor in 1821), and was regarded by the Emperor **Julian the Apostate** as a finer intellect than **Plato**. See also **Neoplatonism**.

**Iansã** In Macumba, the goddess of the River Niger and also goddess of the wind. She is the consort of **Xangô**, god of fire and thunder, and is sometimes associated with St Barbara or Joan of Arc.

**Iao** A god-name equivalent to the **Tetragrammaton** among certain Gnostic groups, for example the followers of the Valentinian teacher Marcus, who lived in Gaul in the latter part of the second century. It is also the sacred name which, according to Clement of Alexandria, was worn by initiates of the mysteries of Serapis. The ceremonial magician **Aleister Crowley** ascribed special significance to the name, regarding it as the "formula of the Dying God" and relating it to sacrificed male deities – **Dionysus, Osiris, Balder, Adonis**, and Jesus Christ. See also **Gnosis; Valentinus**.

**Ibeji** The sacred twin children of the Yoruba religion who, in **Macumba**, are known as St Cosmas (São Cosme) and St Damian (São Damião).

**Ibimorphic** In the form of an ibis – the bird sacred to the Egyptian god **Thoth**.

**Ibis** In Egyptian mythology, a bird sacred to **Thoth**, the god of wisdom and magic. One theory behind the association of the bird with the gods is that the ibis's long, curved bill resembles the crescent moon – Thoth was a lunar deity. According to another theory, as proposed by the second-century Greek scholar Aelian, the author of *On the Nature of Animals*, the ibis was selected because it tucks its head under its wing when going to sleep. When it does this it resembles the shape of the heart – the seat of wisdom in Egyptian belief. Thoth was commonly portrayed in Egyptian art as an ibis or as an ibis-headed man.

**Iblis** See Eblis.

**Iboga** *Tabernanthe iboga*, a plant which grows in the tropical forests of west and central Africa. Magicians in these regions chew the root or boil decoctions to extract its juices. It is used to contact ancestor spirits, recover lost objects, and to provide strength. Iboga is also known as Eboga, Eboka, Bocca, Libuga, Mbasaoka, Moabi, and Gifuma.

**I.C.** See Imum Coeli.

**Icaros** In South American **shamanism** and folk healing, icaros are magical or healing exorcisms, orations and songs. They can be performed to ensure that one's friends do not betray secrets and so on, or to protect against **daño** inflicted by one's enemies.

**Ice Moon** See Esbats.

**Ichiko** In Japan, a shamanic medium who produces **oracles** while in a state of trance.

**Ichthyomancy** A form of divination in which the entrails of fish are inspected and interpreted.

**Ida** In Kundalini yoga, the negatively charged lunar current that circles around the central axis of the nervous system, **sushumna**. It counterbalances the positively charged solar current known as **pingala**. Compare **Middle Pillar**.

**Ido** In the Celtic tree alphabet, the **ogham** representing the service tree and the letter "i". Ido is also linked to the eagle and the colour pure white.

**Idol** An object or image representing a god or spirit, and regarded as possessing divine or magical powers. Idols often form part of ceremonial worship and are characterized as belonging to heathen or pagan ritual practice. One who worships an idol or idols is known as an idolater; in the monotheistic traditions the term is used almost exclusively with negative connotations.

**Iemanjá** In **Macumba**, the highest ranking female deity. The daughter of **Oxalá** and **Odudua**, she is the goddess of salt water and is known as "Our Lady of the Sea". She is identified with the Virgin Mary.

**Ifreet** or **Ifrit** See Efreet.

**Ihwaz** See Eoh.

**Iilápxe** A term used by the Crow Indians to refer to a shaman's helper spirits. They could appear in the form of an animal – like an eagle, otter, or buffalo – or in the shape of a rock or star. See **Spirit Helper**.

**Ikh** In Enochian Magic, the eleventh **Aethyr**. The meanings associated with Ikh include anticipation, hope, readiness, and expectation. Ikh is associated with **Sagittarius**, **fire**, and **air** and its magical number is 361.

**Ile Ife** See Oddudúa.

**Ilisitsut** A term used by the Inuit of the Arctic Coast of eastern Greenland to refer to a **sorcerer** who is able to steal a person's **soul** and cause illness. See also **Free Soul; Soul Loss**.

**Illuminati** A term used by occultists from the late fifteenth century onwards to describe spiritual adepts who had received mystical insights or "illumination" from a transcendent source. The Order of the Illuminati was founded by **Adam Weishaupt**, a Bavarian law professor, in 1776, but this was hardly esoteric in any mystical sense and based most of its "secrets" on the work of Voltaire and the French Encyclopedists. Weishaupt and another enthusiast, Baron Adolf Knigge, later adapted the order's teachings in order to infiltrate **Freemasonry**. A decree in Bavaria in 1784 banned all secret societies – including Freemasonry – and the order declined. However, it was revived around the turn of the 20th century by the occultists Leopold Engel and **Theodor Reuss**. In recent times the idea of a secret brotherhood of adepts or Illuminati has been popularized by fantasy occult writer **Robert Anton Wilson** and New Age spokesman Stuart Wilde.

**Illumination** Mystical or spiritual enlightenment. One who attains this level of consciousness is variously said to be an **adept**, a **Master**, a Buddha, or a saint, and so on, depending on the tradition. See also **Illuminati**.

**Image Magic** See Magic, Image.

**Image Taking** Term used by modern trance occultists to describe a situation where a hostile or paradoxical image presents itself during a magical **pathworking**. After the pathworking is complete, the occultist then "takes the form" of the paradoxical image by re-conjuring it into consciousness while other members of the group ask questions to try to discover its source or meaning. See also **Creative Visualization**.

**Imaging** The act of producing mental images and retaining them in consciousness. The technique is a form of mental concentration used in guided imagery work and in magical **pathworkings**.

**Imbibation** In alchemy, the return of distilled liquid at the bottom of the alembic to the "earth". This liquid was subject to further **distillation**.

**Imbolc** or **Oimelc** In Wicca, one of the Greater Sabbats, held in the northern hemisphere on 2 February. This is "the quickening of the year, the first stirrings of spring within the womb of Mother Earth". Imbolc means "in the belly" and in origin is an ancient Celtic fertility celebration dedicated to the ancient **mother goddess** Brigid or Bride and coinciding with the lactation of ewes. The focus is on light and new life, as opposed to the receding darkness of winter. Imbolc is sometimes known as the "Feast of Lights".

**Imitative Magic** See Magic, Imitative.

**Immanent** "Dwelling within", a term used in mysticism, **pantheism**, and western **magic** to describe the idea that the essence of God pervades the universe in all its manifested forms. It is the opposite of **transcendent**, in which God is regarded as having an existence beyond the confines of material creation.

**Immortal** One who will live forever. The term is especially used with reference to the gods of Greek and Roman mythology, and also in the context of Taoism, but also arises as a claim among certain occult adepts. The **Comte de Saint Germain** claimed to his followers that he would live forever, and his true dates of birth and death have never been ascertained.

**Immortality** The state of eternal life or unending existence.

**Immortals, Eight** In Taoist mythology a group of figures who were all said to have attained eternal life in one way or another. The pursuit of immortality was a central concern of Taoist alchemists.

**Immutable** In astrology, the "fixed" quality ascribed to certain signs of the zodiac. These signs, which are said to be "acted upon" rather than to "instigate action" in the cosmos, include **Aquarius** (fixed **air**); **Scorpio** (fixed **water**); **Taurus** (fixed **earth**); and **Leo** (fixed **fire**).

**Imp** A small demon, sometimes retained in a bottle by a magician. The French eighteenth-century **grimoire** *Le Secret des Secrets* describes how an imp can be trapped in a bottle by appealing to the Holy Trinity and then reciting sacred words of Moses: *Io, Zati, Zata, Abata*. The alchemist **Paracelsus** is said to have trapped an imp in the pommel of his sword; and the nineteenth-century Frenchman Alexis Berbiguier allegedly devised a variety of methods for trapping the imps he believed were persecuting him. Berbiguier concocted "anti-demonic" soups, stupefied imps with tobacco, and trapped them inside bottles. Others he "pinned" to his clothes and bed and kept captive. The term "imp" is sometimes used to refer to a witch's **familiar**.

**Imperfect metals** In alchemy, those metals afflicted with the "disease", or "leprosy", of imperfection. These were iron, copper, tin, and lead – which the alchemists associated with the astrological planets **Mars, Venus, Jupiter,** and **Saturn** respectively.

**Imum Coeli** In astrology, the lowest heaven – the lowest point of the ecliptic. It is the cusp of the fourth **house**, and is often abbreviated to IC.

**Inanna** In Sumerian mythology, a war goddess who was associated with the sky. She also personified the power of love and in due course became closely identified with the Babylonian goddess Ishtar.

**Incantation** From the Latin *incantare*, "to enchant", magical words of power recited in a ceremony or ritual. In many mythologies, the utterances of a creator deity are said to have given rise to the universe and provide a sacred vibration that sustains it. In ceremonial magic, the magician – by assuming a cosmic role through ritual – uses sacred formulae or incantations in order to obtain the supernatural power ascribed to God (or the gods). This power may be used by the magician for his or her own spiritual growth and development (white magic) or to bring harm to enemies (black magic). See **Magic, Black; Magic, White.**

**Incarnate** Having a physical, bodily existence, as opposed to **discarnate** or **disembodied.** In mysticism and occultism it is assumed that a spirit or soul animates the physical body, bringing it to life. See also **Incarnation; Reincarnation.**

**Incarnation** One's present life. Many mystics, witches, and magicians believe that the spiritual evolution of the soul occurs as the self passes through many incarnations, acquiring self-knowledge and insights from each successive lifetime. When mystical enlightenment and true self-realization are attained, further incarnations become unnecessary. See also **Reincarnation.**

**Incarnations, Divine** In many world religions and cosmologies, the concept exists that the godhead incarnates in the form of an **avatar** or enlightened spiritual leader who subsequently gives rise to a new religious mode of expression. In ancient Egypt the pharaohs incarnated the gods **Ra** and **Horus.**

**Incarnations, Satanic** A term sometimes applied to political tyrants and dictators who have inflicted such terror, misery, and bloodshed that some people have presumed them to be incarnations of **Satan** or the **Devil.** Examples from world history include Attila the Hun, Adolf Hitler, Joseph Stalin and, more recently, Saddam Hussein.

**Incense** From the Latin *incendere*, "to set on fire", a substance used in ceremonial worship which, when burned, gives off a pleasant aroma. The fumes of incense are believed by some to please the gods and ward off demons. Ceremonial magicians also believe that the smoke of incense may be used to manifest **spirits** and **elementals** and, in this regard, the magical entity summoned to visible appearance may be either good or evil. See **Magic, Ceremonial; Perfumes, Magical.**

**Inceptional Astrology** See Astrology, Inceptional.

**Incest** In alchemy, the mystical union of the **philosophical sulphur** (the male seed) and **argent vive** (the female seed) was sometimes considered incestuous because in alchemy all forms came from the same "family" or universal substance – the **prima materia.** See also **Chemical Wedding.**

**Incommunicable Axiom** See Ineffable Name.

**Inconjunct** In astrology, a term used to describe a planet that does not present an aspect with another planet. See also **Horoscope.**

**Incubus** A menacing male **spirit** or **demon** who is believed to visit women during the night and who subjects them to sexual depravity, lust, and terrifying nightmares. In medieval accounts this "demon lover" invariably appeared to a woman in the form of her normal partner or lover, but the act of lovemaking was always unpleasant. During the medieval witch trials, it was often maintained that a **demon** or devil had an ice-cold penis or one made of steel. The female equivalent of the incubus is the **succubus.** See also **Nightmare; Hanon Tramp.**

**Individuation** In the analytical

psychology of Carl Jung, the concept of "making the self whole". for Jung, this process includued harmonizing the forces of one's external life with the events of both the personal unconscious and collective unconscious. Jung was interested in mystical systems – especially in alchemical imagery and Gnostic cosmologies – which provided Pathways to spiritual transformation.

**Ineffable Name** Also Incommunicable axiom In Jewish mysticism, the name of God, deemed too sacred to be pronounced. See also **Tetragrammaton**.

**Ineffable One, The** In the Kabbalah, Ain Soph – the Infinite. See also **Ain Soph Aur**.

**Inferior Planets** In **astrology**, those planets whose orbits are within that of the **Earth**: **Venus** and **Mercury**. Sometimes the hypothetical planet Vulcan, said by some astrologers to orbit between Mercury and the sun, is also included.

**Infernal Court** Dignitaries and officers forming a hierarchy within the kingdom of **Satan**, or the **Devil**. Within the infernal regions, there are said to be dukes, ambassadors, ministers, and so forth, who promulgate evil in the world. The sixteenth-century demonologist and physician **Dr Johannes Wier** – also known as Johan Weyer or Wierius – chronicled the hierarchy of hell in his extraordinary work *Pseudomonarchia Daemonum*. Wier's demonic hierarchy includes such figures as Beelzebuth, Moloch, Baalberith, Astaroth, Baal, Behemoth, Dagon, and Asmodeus and is derived in part from works of **Goetia** like the *Lemegeton*, or *Lesser Key of Solomon*.

**Infernal Regions** The Underworld. See also **Gehenna**; **Hades**; **Hell**.

**Infinite Light** A mystical term for the godhead. It is the name given to the "Source of All Being" in the **Kabbalah**, where it is known as **Ain Soph Aur** – the

supreme cosmic reality that transcends all attributes and limitations.

**Inflowing** For the poet and ceremonial magician **William Butler Yeats**, a term used to describe the energy transmission that animates matter, facilitates inspiration and brings the creative **daimon** to the artistic imagination.

**Ing** In the Germanic **Elder Futhark**, the rune letter representing the number 22. Ing corresponds to the sound "ng", as in "ring". This rune literally means "the people" and refers to the community. The deity Ing was the male consort of the northern European fertility goddess and earth mother, Nerthus, who travelled through the countryside in a wagon dispensing peace, prosperity, and happiness. Accordingly, this rune is associated with collecting resources, conserving or storing energy, and more generally with harmony, balance, and completion.

**Ingwaz** See Ing.

**Initiate** One who has successfully passed through a ritual of initiation. In occultism and the magical traditions generally, an initiate is regarded as one who possesses superior esoteric knowledge.

**Initiation, Magical** A magical ceremony involving a sense of transition or self-transformation. The subject may be shown new symbolic mysteries, given a secret name or words of power, or granted a higher ceremonial rank. In the **Hermetic Order of the Golden Dawn** system of magic, from which most forms of modern western occultism have evolved, there were different grades of initiation for each level of the kabbalistic **Tree of Life** leading up to the experience of spiritual rebirth in **Tiphareth**. A candidate attaining the grade associated with Tiphareth would then proceed to membership of the **Inner Order**. In many occult traditions magicians take a new magical name or motto to reflect their new state of attainment. Magical initiation may not be formally acknowledged unless the candidate has a particular visionary experience that confirms his or her new magical status. In **Wicca** there are three initiations, culminating in the **Great Rite**. See **First Initiation; Second Initiation; Third Initiation.**

**Initiation, Progressive** See **Periplus.**

**Inner Chiefs** or **Secret Chiefs** In the Hermetic Order of the Golden Dawn, the Inner Chiefs or Secret Chiefs were thought of as transcendental beings on the inner planes who provided spiritual guidance to the leaders of the order. They were the magical counterpart of the Theosophical "Masters" or "Mahatmas" referred to by **Madame Helena Blavatsky** and were considered by **MacGregor Mathers** to be the source of his authority. The poet **William Butler Yeats**, also a leading member of the Golden Dawn, sometimes doubted their existence.

**Inner Guide** A helper figure from the inner realm who can be contacted via a state of visionary consciousness. Meditators and those who practise **channelling** or shamanic visualization often make contact with inner guides. See also **Spirit Helper; Steinbrecher, Edwin.**

**Inner Light** In mysticism and occultism, the light of God within. The experience of the "inner light" is equated with cosmic consciousness and represents a profound level of mystical attainment. Sometimes the expression is used to indicate that every person is potentially divine, and contains the spark of godhead. This view, sometimes characterized as the **microcosm** within the **macrocosm**, reflects the Hermetic axiom, "As above, so below" – God is in us, we are in God.

**Inner Light, Fraternity of the** See Fraternity of the Inner Light.

**Inner Order** See Red Rose and the Cross of Gold, The

**Inquisition** The Roman Catholic tribunal instituted by Pope Gregory IX in 1227–1231 in the wake of the crusade against the **Albigenses**, in order to suppress heretical movements deemed to be hostile to Christianity. This was expanded in 1320 to deal with cases of witchcraft where heretical beliefs and practices were involved. In 1252 Pope Innocent IV officially approved the use of torture to extract confessions. However, according to modern scholars, the Inquisition's standards of justice were relatively humane compared with those of most other medieval courts. Those who willingly confessed and repented were generally freed after performing a suitable act of penance. Penalties for less serious cases included public scourging, fines, obligatory pilgrimages, or the wearing of a cross. In serious cases, the guilty faced the confiscation of property or prison, including life imprisonment. As a Church body the Inquisition did not itself impose the death penalty, but when it handed a guilty person over to the civil authorities it was effectively a request for capital punishment. Those found guilty of making false or malicious accusations were made to wear two tongues of red cloth for all to see and in serious cases could have their property confiscated or face imprisonment.

The Inquisition was less active in the 1300s and 1400s after the suppression of the Albigenses, but it was revived in 1542 as the Holy Office, primarily to counter the spread of Protestantism and other heretical ideas (such as the scientific discoveries of Galileo). It eventually became a rather academic institution aimed at preserving Catholic doctrine. Since 1965 it has been called the Congregation for the Doctrine of the Faith.

The Spanish Inquisition, established with papal approval in 1478, was a separate and effectively independent institution. In the wake of forced conversions and expulsions of Jews, and later Muslims, from Spain, the Spanish Inquisition sought to root out those believed to be insincere converts to Christianity. With strong state support, Tomás de Torquemada, the first and most notorious Grand Inquisitor, executed thousands of reputed heretics. The institution later turned its ruthlessly efficient methods on "sorcerors" – traditional practitioners of native religion – in Mexico and Peru and other colonies, and on suspected Protestants in Europe. The Spanish Inquisition was abolished in 1834.

**Inspiration, Magical** In western magic, the act of allowing one's personal **daemon** or guiding **genius** to direct one's thoughts and intentions. The magician believes that he or she can also be inspired by opening themselves to channels of sacred knowledge through communication with angels, archangels, and God. See also **Magic, High; Theurgy.**

**Insufflation** According to the French occultist **Eliphas Lévi**, an important practice in the occult application of medicine. Insufflation is the act of breathing on another person and, in certain circumstances, it restores life. Warm insufflation, according to Lévi, aids the circulation of the blood and eliminates gout and rheumatism; cold insufflation soothes pain. Lévi considered that the two methods should be used alternately, and seems to have believed that the healing technique activated magnetic forces. To this extent it can be compared with the theories of Anton Mesmer. Candidates in **Count Alessandro di Cagliostro's** Egyptian Masonic Rite were also breathed upon as part of their initiation.

**Intelligence** In occultism and ceremonial magic, a supernatural force or power – usually regarded as discarnate – which serves as an inspirational force for an individual magician or a magical group. The mysterious entity **Aiwaz** (who, according to the ritual magician **Aleister Crowley**, inspired *The Book of*

*the Law*) is an example of a supernatural "intelligence". So too was **Lam**. See **Aiwaz; Lam.**

**In Token** and **In True** See **Third Initiation.**

**Intrusion, Spirit** See **Spirit Intrusion.**

**Invisibles, Les** In voodoo, a general term for all invisible spirits, including the **loa** and the souls of the dead.

**Invocation** In ceremonial magic, the act of invoking or summoning an **angel** or deity for a positive or beneficial purpose using sacred **god-names** or words of power. In western magic, the formulae of invocation often involve Hebrew names ascribed to God (e.g. **El, Jehovah, Adonai, Shaddai**) or the names of archangels – especially those associated with the four **elements:** Raphael (**air**); Michael (**fire**); Gabriel (**water**); and Uriel (**earth**). Magical invocations take place within the magical circle, which is regarded within the ritual as a sacred space, distinct from the profane, unsanctified territory which lies outside it. Compare **Evocation.**

**Invoke** In ceremonial magic, to call a spirit or deity into oneself or into the magical circle – in which case participating members of the group are considered as a "collective energy". See also **Invocation.**

**Involution** See **Descending Arc.**

**Ipes** See **Ipos.**

**Iphin** In the Celtic tree alphabet, the ogham representing the gooseberry and pine and the sound "io". Iphin is also linked to the colour whitish grey.

**Ipos** In the Goetia, the 22nd spirit, a mighty earl and prince who appears in the form of an angel with a lion's head, the webbed feet of a goose, and a hare's tail. He can impart a knowledge of all things past, present and future and also makes men "witty and bold". Ipos, also known as Ipes, governs 36 legions of spirits.

**Ipsissimus** In the **Hermetic Order of the Golden Dawn** system of western magic, the supreme ritual grade of the **Third Order**, indicating that the magician had attained the state of consciousness symbolized by **Kether** on the kabbalistic **Tree of Life**. In specific terms, the Golden Dawn grades covered the first four spheres of the Tree of Life, and the **Rosae Rubae et Aurae Crucis** grades the next three. The Third Order grades comprised Magister Templi (**Binah**), Magus (**Chokmah**), and Ipsissmus (**Kether**).

**Iron** A metal with magical associations. In the Middle Ages, iron was regarded as a powerful protection against witches and the damaging influence of the **evil eye**. A horseshoe was considered lucky because it was made of iron, and was believed to ward off evil forces.

**Is** In the Germanic **Elder Futhark**, the **rune** letter representing the number eleven. Is corresponds to the letter "i" and is the rune of ice, which is cold and slippery and impedes our progress. The is rune demands stillness and concentration and requires us to summon our inner resolve so we can focus on what lies ahead.

**Isa** See Is.

**Isagoge, The** The only published volume in the projected nine-volume series known as *The Arbatel of Magick*, first issued in English translation in 1655. *The Isagoge* is an introductory volume, or beginner's text, consisting mostly of magical aphorisms.

**Ishtar** In Babylonian mythology, a fertility goddess and mother goddess who personified the planet **Venus**. She had two aspects: one was warlike and aggressive, the other gentle and loving. Ishtar is associated with the Sumerian goddess **Inanna** and the Phoenician **Astarte**.

**Isis** In Egyptian mythology, the wife of the fertility god **Osiris** and the mother of **Horus**. Isis was a great goddess of magic and enchantment and succeeded in piecing together the fragments of Osiris's body after he had been murdered by **Set**. She also tricked **Ra** into revealing his secret, magical name. Isis was also a fertility goddess and at times was identified with **Hathor**. By the early centuries CE, Isis had subsumed the cult of Hathor and had become the focus of a great international cult that for a time seriously rivalled Christianity. There was even a temple of Isis in Roman London.

**Isle of the Dead** See Avalon.

**Ithyphallic** A term meaning "with erect phallus", used in reference to fertility cults and deities and phallic worship. Many prehistoric cave paintings depict ithyphallic figures and are believed to represent the regenerative powers of nature.

**Iynx** A Chaldean cosmic entity comparable to the **archon** of the **Gnostics**. The Iynx beings were described as "free intelligences" that transmitted cosmic energy from one plane of existence to another and were depicted as living spheres or winged globes.

**Izzekloth** Sacred cords worn by Apache Indian shamans. It was said that wearing these cords could protect the **shaman** from bullets and could also enable him to locate stolen ponies. Placing the cords upon the head relieved aches and pains.

# J

**Jabulon** In Freemasonry, the long-lost sacred word of the Master Mason, known to King **Solomon** and King Hiram. It consists of the names Jah, Bel, and On, respectively Hebrew, Assyrian, and Egyptian names of the sun.

**Jackdaw** In alchemy, the stage of putrefaction known as **nigredo**. It was also referred to as the **crow's head**, crow or raven.

**Jack-in-the-Green** See Green Man.

**Jack-o'-Lantern**, See Will-o'-the-Wisp.

**Jacob's Ladder** In the Bible (Genesis 28.12), a ladder that appeared to Jacob in a dream. The ladder spanned heaven and earth, and angels would use it to descend from heaven. Medieval Hermeticists interpreted the ladder as a symbol of the alchemical process of transformation and compared Jacob's ladder to a rainbow incorporating all the "colours" spanning spirit and matter. See also **Alchemy**; *Hermetica*.

**Jade** In China, a stone with occult and magical significance. Here it was said to possess the quality of immortality, and as such played an important role in traditional burial rites where it was often placed beside the orifices of a corpse to prevent bodily decay. Jade is also associated with Chinese **necromancy** and is normally associated with the masculine principle, yang, in Chinese cosmology. In Wicca, jade is a magical stone assigned to the ritual celebrations of **Beltane** and **Mabon**.

**Jaguar** A large feline of the Americas with magical significance, especially in South American **shamanism**. In Brazil, the jaguar is thought to be the form that the sun takes during the night; and among the Jivaro Indians of Ecuador – as with other native South American peoples – the jaguar has an initiatory function. When the Jivaro take **datura** near the sacred waterfall, it is often reported that a pair of giant jaguars appear, fighting with each other and rolling towards the shaman. The latter has to prove his courage by reaching forward to touch the visionary creatures. This act of bravery bestows strength and supernatural power upon the shaman.

**Janus** A distinctive Roman deity who had two faces, each looking in opposite directions. Janus was god of doorways and he has given his name to January, the first month of the year. In this respect, Janus looks forward to the events of the new year, and back upon the old.

**Jehovah** A form of Yahweh, the personal name of the biblical God. In Jewish tradition, the name is sacred and never uttered. See also **Tetragrammaton**; **YHVH**. In the **Kabbalah**, Jehovah is the divine name associated with the sphere of **Chokmah** on the **Tree of Life**. See also **God-Name** and the following entries.

**Jehovah Eloah va Daat** In the Kabbalah, the divine name associated with the sphere **Tiphareth** on the **Tree of Life**. It translates as "Divine All-Knowing One". See also **God-Name**.

**Jehovah Elohim** In the Kabbalah, the divine name associated with the sphere of **Binah** on the **Tree of Life**. Elohim is the plural form of El ("God"). See also **God-Name**.

**Jehovah Tzevaot** Meaning "Existance of Hosts". In the **Kabbalah**, the divine name associated with the sphere **Netzach** on the **Tree of Life**. See also **God-Name**.

**Jera** See Ger.

**Jet** In Wicca, a magical stone assigned to the ritual celebration of **Yule**.

**Jettatura** An Italian term for casting the **evil eye** upon a victim. See also **Bewitchment**; **Spell**.

**JHVH** See Tetragrammaton.

**Jimson Weed** See Thornapple.

**Jinni, Jinn** See Genii.

**Jinnistan** A mythic country believed in Persian folk legend to be the home of the genii or djinn who served King Solomon.

**John Barleycorn** In Wicca, a seasonal figure of the harvest related to **Cernunnos**, the so-called **Horned God** and lord of wild animals, who is also associated with fertility. John Barleycorn has tufts of corn sticking out of his clothing. Because he represents the harvest he has to be sacrificed – cut down by the goddess of death wielding her scythe. John Barleycorn is sometimes referred to as the Corn King.

**Jones, Charles Stansfeld** See Achad, Frater.

**Jotunheim** In Scandinavian mythology, one of the **Nine Worlds** located on the World Tree, **Yggdrasil**. Jotunheim is the world of the giants.

**Journey of the Soul** In shamanism, the "journey" undertaken by a **medicine man** or healer in order to recover the **soul** of a person who is bewitched or inflicted with disease; or, alternatively, in order to communicate with the gods. The journey occurs in a state of trance-dissociation and often employs the use of drum rhythms and the ingestion of psychedelic sacramental plants. See also **Trance, Shamanic; Soul Loss**.

**Jove** A Roman name for **Zeus**. Jove was normally referred to as **Jupiter** ("Father Jove").

**Joy** In astrology, a term used to describe the harmonious situation where planets have a strong affinity with the signs of the zodiac in which they are located. The sun in **Leo** is a classic example.

**Judgment Hall** In Egyptian mythology, the hall in the **Underworld** where **Osiris** and 42 other deities presided over the judgment of the dead. Osiris sat beneath a canopy and a balance was placed before him. The heart of the deceased was now weighed against a feather – the symbol of truth – and the subject's fate decided accordingly. If the heart and feather were in equilibrium, the deceased entered paradise as an akh, or blessed spirit. But if the heart was heavy with sin it would tip the scales and be devoured by a monster, consigning the deceased to oblivion. **Anubis**, the jackal-headed god, stood nearby, as did a number of other deities, including **Bast, Kenemti, Neba,** and **Khemi**. see also **Elysian Fields; Maat**.

**Judgment** In the Tarot, the card that shows naked figures rising out of their coffins and embracing the "light" of new life. Their upstretched arms make the shape of LVX (Latin: "light") as the archangel **Gabriel** revives them, and a trumpet sounds in triumph. *Judgment* is regarded by occultists as one of the three initial paths on the inner magical journey (the others being *The World* and *The Moon*), and its path links **Hod** and **Malkuth** at the base of the kabbalistic Tree of Life. See also **Pathworkings**.

**Ju-Ju** Name given to African magical rites which involve secret societies, witch-doctors, magical **amulets, curses,** and **exorcisms**. Ju-Ju men are able to cast out **demons** and rid the client of disease or the effects of a curse. They are also said to have telepathic powers, which enable them to identify the source of the bewitchment and overcome the sorcery of evil spells.

**Julian the Apostate** (331–363CE) A Roman emperor who was a nephew of Constantine the Great and raised as a Christian. However, in his youth he converted to pagan beliefs. After a period as governor of Gaul he succeeded Constantius as emperor in 361CE and began reviving pagan worship and persecuting Christians. Julian had been introduced earlier to initiatory rites sacred to **Mithra** and after his accession he began to introduce the Persian cult to Constantinople, the new imperial capital, and Athens. It is thought that Julian had a desire to conquer Persia in the belief that Mithra would protect him, but this proved not to be the case. He was slain in battle during the Persian expedition.

**Jumala** In traditional Finnish mythology, the name of the supreme God. The **oak** tree was sacred to him, and he was often depicted holding a **gold** cup filled with precious coins.

**Jung, Dr Carl Gustav** (1875–1961) A founder of analytic psychology and pioneer of the exploration of mythic symbolism as a function of human consciousness, Jung is also remembered for his study of **alchemy** and ancient cosmologies. Born at Kesswil, in Thurgau, Switzerland, Jung studied medicine in Basle and Paris. He later worked with Sigmund Freud for a number of years, but began to differ in his interpretation of the functions of the unconscious mind. Jung believed that there was a stratum in the unconscious that included a vast source of images and symbols which transcended the individual experience. The study of these images led Jung to formulate the concept of the **collective unconscious** and the theory of **archetypes** – profound, primordial images that presented themselves in the myths, folklore, and legends of different cultures and which symbolized universal, cosmic processes. In his later years, Jung became absorbed with ancient cosmologies and spent a considerable time analzying **Gnostic**, alchemical, and mystical systems of thought. He provided commentaries for Richard Wilhelm's translations of the *I Ching* and *The Secret of the Golden Flower*, and wrote many major works on spiritual dimensions in psychology. Among his most important mystically oriented books are *Aion* (1951); *Symbols of Transformation* (1952); *Mysterium Conjunctionis* (1955); and *The Archetypes and the Collective Unconsciousness* (1959). Jung's autobiography, *Memories, Dreams, Reflections* – which includes references to Gnostic aspects of his own visionary process – was published posthumously in 1963. See also **Alchemy; Gnosis.**

**Juno** In Roman mythology, the sister and wife of **Jupiter**. She reigned as queen of the gods and was the equivalent of the Greek **Hera**.

**Jupiter** In Roman mythology, the brother and husband of **Juno**, and the father of the gods. Jupiter, or Jove, was regarded as wise, all-knowing, and merciful, but was also the god of thunder and lightning. In **astrology**, the planet Jupiter inspires optimism, happiness, and abundance. See also **Zeus**.

**Jurupari** Among the Tupi and Guarani Indians of Brazil, a demonic spirit, hostile to women, who resides in the woods and guards animals. He is the principal deity of these tribes.

**Justice** In the **Tarot**, a card of the **Major Arcana** that depicts a female deity seated on a throne, holding a pair of scales and a large, fearsome sword. Occultists regard *Justice* as the path on the kabbalistic **Tree of Life** where one faces one's accumulated **karma** and learns to overcome the negative and hostile visions of one's own wrongdoings. *Justice* thus demands balance, adjustment, and total impartiality in assessing one's true spiritual direction. The card is ruled by Venus, goddess of love, but owes most of its symbolism to the Egyptian concept of the **Judgment Hall**, and the goddess depicted on the card has the same role as **Maat**, goddess of truth. *Justice* is the path linking **Tiphareth** and **Geburah** on the Tree of Life.

**Juturna** In Roman mythology, a **nymph** with whom **Jupiter** fell in love. She became a goddess of lakes and springs and had a fountain in the Roman Forum dedicated to her.

# K

**Ka** In Egyptian mythology and magic, the human double. The ka – often translated as "soul" – was the vital energy or life force, created with an individual at birth and remaining with them after death, when it continued to reside in the mummy or a special "ka statue". Occultists compare the ka to the **astral body**, which can be projected into a mental or imaginal realm and act as a vehicle for exploring the more subtle planes of consciousness. See also **Aufu; Ba; Haidit; Khu.**

**Kab** In Enochian magic, the angelic word for a ritual wand. It is pronounced *kah-beh*.

**Kabbalah (Qabalah, Cabala)** The esoteric and mystical aspect of Judaism, from the Hebrew word QBL meaning "oral tradition". Although the central book of the Kabbalah, the *Zohar*, was not written down until c. 1280CE – probably by **Moses de León** – the tradition has links with **Gnosticism** and other early mystical cosmologies. The Kabbalah presents a symbolic explanation of the origin of the universe, the relationship of human beings to the **godhead**, and an emanationist approach to Creation whereby the Infinite Light – **Ain Soph Aur** – manifests through different sephiroth on the **Tree of Life**. In the Kabbalah, all manifestations are said to have their origin in Ain Soph Aur and the successive emanations of the godhead reveal aspects of its divine nature. The emanations, as they proceed from the godhead to the manifested world, are: **Kether** (the crown); **Chokmah** (wisdom); **Binah** (understanding); **Chesed** (mercy); **Geburah** (power); **Tiphareth** (beauty and harmony); **Netzach** (victory); **Hod** (splendour); **Yesod** (foundation); and **Malkuth** (the kingdom). Kabbalists also conceived of four distinct stages of creative manifestation known as the

**Four Worlds**. These are **Atziluth**, or the archetypal world; **Briah**, or the world of creation; **Yetzirah**, the world of formation; and finally **Assiah**, the physical world. According to the Kabbalah, God is present in each of the four worlds and these worlds in turn are a reflection of the **Tetragrammaton** – the sacred divine name JHVH (also rendered as YHVH, YHWH) – usually transliterated as **Yahweh** or "Lord".

Occultists in the **Hermetic Order of the Golden Dawn** used the kabbalistic Tree of Life as a matrix for comparing the archetypal images of different mythologies that could be employed in ceremonial magic. For example, the merciful father (**Chesed**) has parallels in other pantheons, namely **Odin** (Scandinavia), **Zeus** (Greece), **Jupiter** (Rome), and **Ra** (Egypt). This system of comparisons became known as **magical correspondences**. It has also become common in the western magical tradition to link the ten sephiroth of the Tree of Life with the 22 cards of the **Major Arcana** of the **Tarot**, a concept first proposed by the nineteenth-century French magician **Eliphas Lévi**.

**Kabbalist** A practitioner of the Kabbalah. The term is also used generally to mean an occultist or a follower of the esoteric traditions.

**Kabiri** See Cabiri

**Kachina** Among the Hopi Indians of the southwestern United States, ancestral spirits and gods of the clouds who are impersonated by masked dancers in ritual ceremonies. The principal Kachina dances are held in February and relate to the fertility of crops. Beans and corn are given to the people to show that the gods and spirits of the Kachina cult can sustain the supply of food through the winter months. The Kachina ancestor spirits are also represented by ornately carved and coloured dolls.

**Kadaitja Man** Among the Australian Aborigines of the Central Desert region, a sorcerer or medicine man who can see spirits, heal the sick, and perform acts of magic. The kadaitja is said to be able to fly through the air in the form of an eaglehawk and dig his claws into his victim. See also **Shamanism**.

**Kadath** In *The Necronomicon*, the primal creative energy which resides in the "Cold Waste".

**Kaf** See Kaph.

**Kahuna** A Hawaiian **shaman**. The term is also used to describe a "master" or expert in a given field, like wrestling or building canoes. A *kahuna lapaau laau* specializes in herbal medicine, a *kahuna hoonoho* specializes in trance mediumship and a *kahuna hoonohonoho* specializes in sorcery.

**Ka-Ka** or **Koko** The Zuni Indian term for a kachina.

**Kakodemon** A Gnostic term used to describe an evil inspirational **genius**. See also **Daemon**.

**Kalah** In the Jewish mystical tradition, a synonym for **Shekhinah**, the Bride of the Lord, and the female aspect of the **godhead**. See also **Kabbalah**.

**Kali** A fearsome Hindu **goddess** personifying the dark and terrifying forces of nature. The word kali means "black", and the goddess is portrayed with dark skin, bulging bloodshot eyes, and protruding fangs. She wears a string of human skulls around her neck and is often depicted mutilating her victims. Kali is said to be the cause of disease and fevers, and blood sacrifices are still made to her to appease her wrath.

**Kamea** See **Magic Number Square**.

**Kami** In Shinto, a spirit or god. The term is used to describe both high gods and nature spirits. According to Shinto belief, after death a person's soul becomes a kami.

**Kamigakari** A Shinto term for divine spirit possession – the entry of a spiritual being into a human body.

**Kaph** or **Kaf** The Hebrew letter ascribed to the path linking **Chesed** and **Netzach** on the **Tree of Life**. Kaph has a numerical value of 20 (and as a final letter, 500). In modern magical visualization and **pathworkings** the **Tarot** card associated with this path on the Tree is *The Wheel of Fortune*.

**Kaplan, Aryeh** (died 1983) A leading author on the **Kabbalah**. His major work, *Meditation and Kabbalah*, was the first text in English to provide a coherent translation of important visionary texts of the **Hekhaloth** tradition. His other works include *Meditation and the Bible* and *Jewish Meditation*.

**Kappa** In Japanese folk legend, a river goblin with scaly limbs, the body of a tortoise, and a head like an ape. Hostile to humans, it could be overcome by acts of politeness because a life-sustaining substance would drain from its head if it bent over to return a bow.

**Kardec, Allan** (1804–1869) The penname of French spiritualist Denizard Rivail, who studied animal magnetism and later worked extensively with psychic mediums. Kardec was a strong supporter of the doctrine of **reincarnation** and derived his assumed name from beings whom he claimed were his former incarnations. Largely uninfluential in Britain and the United States, his biggest following has been in France and Brazil. For example, he has been a strong influence on practitioners of **Umbanda,** a movement linked to **Macumba**. Umbanda is a form of Brazilian white magic which contains many Yoruba elements, correlating African deities with Christian saints. Kardec's books include *The Spirits' Book, The Medium's Book,* and *Spiritualist Initiation*.

**Karezza** A **sexual magic** technique advocated by Thomas Lake Harris

(1823–1906), who derived it from tantric yoga. Energy is aroused through erotic stimulation, but the semen is not discharged. The energy is said to give birth instead to magical forms which may be directed for an occult purpose. See also **Tantra; Dianism.**

**Karma** A Sanskrit word meaning "action". Karma is a Hindu and Buddhist belief, embraced by many in the West, that all intentional actions are inevitably followed by consequences. A person who lives a virtuous life builds up merit, or "good karma", while a person committed to wrongdoing accumulates demerit, or "bad karma". According to Hindu and Buddhist tradition, the circumstances of one's present life are a consequence of karma established in former lives, so it follows that the development of good karma is central to the process of spiritual growth. **Sir Edward Bulwer-Lytton's** figure of the **Dweller on the Threshold** can be considered as the embodiment of "karmic" consequences. See also **Reincarnation.**

**Katadesmoi** In ancient Greece, binding or cursing tablets used to subject another person to one's will or desire. Consisting of thin sheets of lead on which the victim's name had been scratched, they were thrown into graves, pits, or wells, with the intention of consigning the victim's fate to various demons or the ghosts of the dead. The corresponding Roman term for these cursing tablets was **defixiones.**

**Kavvanah** In the Jewish mystical tradition, a rabbinical term for mental concentration or focused intention within the context of spiritual practice. It is a Jewish equivalent to the eastern concept of "one-pointedness" required to attain higher states of consciousness.

**Kavvanoth** In the kabbalistic tradition, the technical term for meditative exercises developed by practitioners in **Safed** in the sixteenth century. These included visualization exercises based on the ten **sephiroth** on the **Tree of Life**.

**Kegey** Among the Yurok Indians of the Oregon seaboard, a **shaman** or healer. Most Yurok shamans are women.

**Kelipot** See Qlippoth.

**Kelley** or **Kelly, Edward** (1555–1595) An English **alchemist**, magician, and skryer. Born in Worcester and educated at Worcester College, Oxford, Kelley worked with **Dr John Dee**. Together they summoned angelic spirits in trance and evolved what is now known as **Enochian magic**. Following a meeting with a magician named Jerome Cardan in England in 1552, Dee had become interested in the conjuration of spirits, but this exploration of the magical realms began in earnest when he met Edward Kelley, who claimed to communicate with angels in his **spirit vision**. On occasions Kelley seemed to become possessed by the spirits, some of which – according to Dee – manifested visibly. In order to summon these angelic spirits, Dee and Kelley made use of a **crystal ball** and wax tablets, or **almadels**, engraved with magical symbols and the sacred names of God. The tablet for a given invocation was laid between four candles and the angelic spirits summoned as Kelley stared into the crystal. In 1582 Kelley began to receive messages in a new angelic language he called "Enochian", and Dee transcribed the letters as Kelley called them out. The so-called "Enochian calls" were subsequently utilized in the **Hermetic Order of the Golden Dawn** and form the basis of Enochian magic. See also **Aethyr.**

**Kellner, Karl** (1851–1905) A German occultist who claimed to have made contact with three adepts – two Arabs, the other a Hindu – while travelling through India and the Middle East in 1896. Kellner was given certain sexual yoga secrets and decided to form an esoteric society. In a reference to the **Knights Templar,** whom he believed possessed comparable knowledge, Kellner named his new institution the **Ordo Templi Orientis** (O.T.O.), or **Order of Oriental Templars**. The journal of the O.T.O., *Oriflamme*, proclaimed in 1912 that the Order possessed "the key which opens up all Masonic and Hermetic secrets, namely, the teaching of sexual magic". Kellner was succeeded by **Theodor Reuss** who, in 1912, invited the English ceremonial magician **Aleister Crowley** to join the Order. Crowley became head of the organization in 1922. See also **Adept; Grant, Kenneth; Magic, Ceremonial; Magic, Sexual**.

**Kelpie** In Scottish folklore, a water spirit that took the form of a horse. Usually grey or black, its hooves pointed backwards and it had a mischievous nature. Kelpies would lead travellers astray as they mounted to cross a river or stream, and sometimes they would devour them as well.

**Kemia** See Chymia.

**Kenaz** See Cen.

**Keres** In ancient Greek mythology, evil spirits associated with violent death. They were the offspring of **Nyx** (Night), and were sometimes connected with the Furies.

**Keridwen** See Cerridwen.

**Kernunnos** See Cernunnos.

**Kerotakis** A three-legged alchemical brazier, thought to have been invented by the third-century Graeco-Egyptian alchemist Maria Prophetissa. She is also credited with the invention of the bain-marie.

**Kerux** In the magical system practised in the **Hermetic Order of the Golden Dawn**, a ceremonial role in the probationary grade admitting new candidates. Kerux personified the "reasoning faculties" – i.e. mental intelligence.

**Kether** or Keter In the **Kabbalah**, the first mystical emanation on the **Tree of Life**. Occultists identify Kether as the state of consciousness where creation merges with the veils of non-existence associated with **Ain Soph Aur**, the limitless light. Kether lies on the **Middle Pillar** and transcends the duality of **Chokmah** (male) and **Binah** (female), which lie immediately below it on the Tree. It is therefore symbolized in the mystical tradition by the heavenly **androgyne**, and represents a state of mystical transcendence and union with the supreme One Reality.

**Key** In the western magical tradition, a symbol indicating access to a secret or mystery: something normally "hidden". The medieval **grimoire** known as *The Key of Solomon* and Eliphas Lévi's *Key of the Mysteries* are examples of magical books employing this symbolism. See also **Clavicle**.

***Key of Solomon, The*** The title given to two famous medieval grimoires: *The Greater Key of Solomon* and *The Lesser Key of Solomon*, or **Goetia**. The *Greater Key* contains magical instructions, prayers, conjurations, and pentacles for each of the planets. *The Lesser Key* contains detailed commentaries on the nature of the spirits summoned in ceremonial magic, including those associated with medieval **witchcraft** and necromancy. See also **Grimoire**.

**Keys of the Tarot, The** A term used to describe the 22 cards of the **Major Arcana** of the Tarot, which have a self-initiatory function when viewed as a sequence of meditative archetypes. See **Tarot, Major Arcana**.

**Khabs** An ancient Egyptian word meaning "a star". See also **Khabs Am Pekht**.

**Khabs Am Pekht** In the Hermetic Order of the Golden Dawn, a magical phrase derived from ancient Egypt and used as a magical proclamation and statement of spiritual purpose. It translates as "Light in Extension".

**Khaibit** In ancient Egyptian magic and mythology, "the shadow". See Haidit.

**Khepera** or **Kheperu, Khepry** In ancient Egyptian magic and mythology, the sun god in his form as a deity of rebirth. Khepera emerges at dawn from the dungeons of the **Tuat**, or **Underworld**, and prepares to float forth on the ocean of the sky. He takes the form of a scarab beetle and is received by **Nut**, the sky goddess.

**Khr** In Enochian Magic, the 20th Aethyr. The meanings associated with Khr include cycles in nature, spirals, repetition, and destiny. It is associated with **fire**, **air**, and **Pisces**, and its magical number is 401.

**Khu** In Egyptian mythology and ritual, the "magical body". Occultists believe that the khu can be awakened once a person has learned to distinguish physical sensations and conscious and unconscious thought processes. The use of ritual mantras or magical formulae, sacred postures and gestures, and the internal activation of inner spiritual centres or chakras, are all ways of developing the khu. See also **Aufu**; **Chakra**; **Haidit**; **Ka**.

**Khubilgan** In traditional Buryat shamanism, an animal spirit helper, or familiar, which guarded the shaman and was essential to his healthy life. Loss of the khubilgan would invariably lead to the shaman's death.

**Khunrath, Henry** (1560–1601) A German alchemist who studied medicine at the University of Basle and later practised in Hamburg and Dresden. A follower of **Paracelsus**, he composed a mystical tract that described the seven steps leading to enlightenment. This book, titled *Amphitheatrum Sapientae Aeternae Solius Verae, Christiano Kabbalisticum*

*Divino Magicum* (*Christian-Kabbalistic, Divine-Magical Amphitheatre of the Eternal Wisdom*), was published after his death, in 1609. It identified Christ as the means of attaining perfection, and described the Ruach Elohim – the spirit on the face of the waters of creation – as the **Philosopher's Stone**, the very source of life itself.

**Kia** In the magic of trance occultist **Austin Osman Spare**, the primal cosmic life force. According to Spare, Kia contained spiritual and occult energies that could be channelled into the human organism. He used magical **sigils** to evoke and direct these magical energies to powerful effect and also incorporated them into many of his visionary paintings and drawings.

**Kimaris** See Cimeries.

**King, Corn** See John Barleycorn.

**King, Francis X** (1938–1994) An English occult historian who was one of the first writers to document the contemporary magical revival. His principal books include *Ritual Magic in England* (1970), *Sexuality, Magic and Perversion* (1971), and *The Secret Rituals of the O.T.O.* (1973). He also co-authored, with **Stephen Skinner**, an important introductory text on western magic, *Techniques of High Magic* (1976), and produced a sequel to *Ritual Magic* titled *The Rebirth of Magic* (1982) with Isabel Sutherland. Francis King is credited, together with **Israel Regardie**, Ellic Howe, and later R.A. Gilbert, as one of the main writers to revive interest in the Hermetic Order of the Golden Dawn.

**King, Holly** See Holly King.

**King, Oak** See Holly King.

**King of the Wood** In ancient Rome, the priest who oversaw the outdoor sanctuary of **Diana** at Nemi. This shrine was in a sacred grove and the priest was regarded as Diana's representative on earth.

**Kingsford, Anna Bonus** (1846–1888) English theosophical mystic and occultist who was especially interested in what she referred to as "esoteric Christianity". With Edward Maitland she formed the **Hermetic Society**, an organization contemporaneous with the **Hermetic Order of the Golden Dawn**. She was friendly with **MacGregor Mathers** but **Madame Helena Blavatsky** came to regard her as a potential competitor and threat. Kingsford's best-known work is *The Perfect Way*, first published in 1882.

**King Sol** "King Sun", the embodiment, in alchemy, of the active male qualities of "hot and dry" associated with the sun, sulphur, and gold. The king unites with the receptive, "cold and moist", female principle – the queen, or **Queen Luna** – in the **coniunctio**. In the process of becoming the **Philosopher's Stone**, the king must undergo death and resurrection, suffering putrefaction and becoming dissolved within the original matter of creation, the **prima materia**. The term "king" was also applied to the Stone itself – in its various states of transition from imperfection to perfection. After being cleansed and purified, King Sol becomes the "red stone" or "mighty king" who, according to alchemist **Edward Kelley**, can transmute all base metals into pure gold.

**Kiss, Fivefold** See Fivefold Kiss

**Kiss of Shame** In satanism, the act of ritually kissing the Devil on the buttocks. Sometimes known by its Latin name *Osculum Infame*.

**Kiva** Among the Pueblo Indians of the southwestern United States, a ceremonial chamber, often partially underground. The kiva can be square or round, covered or open. Those with a roof have a hole in the middle for entry called the sipapu.

**Knight, Gareth** (1930– ) Pseudonym of Basil Wilby, a leading contemporary authority on the magical applications of the **Kabbalah**. Knight was born in Colchester, England, in 1930 and in 1953 enrolled in the study course of the Society of the Inner Light, a group founded by **Dion Fortune**. In 1962 he began editing the occult magazine *New Dimensions* and three years later cofounded the publishing company Helios Books. Knight later founded his own esoteric school based on the principles of the Society of the Inner Light and this has since given rise to two further offshoots, the Avalon Group and the Companions of the Inner Abbey. Knight's main books include *A Practical Guide to Qabalistic Symbolism*, *The Experience of Inner Worlds*, *A History of White Magic*, and *The Magical World of the Tarot*. Knight is currently working on a series of books based on Dion Fortune's archive material.

**Knights Templar** A medieval order of knights – in full, the Order of the Temple of Jerusalem – founded in 1118, initially to protect pilgrims travelling to the Holy Land. Originally, the knights were very poor and two knights had to ride on one horse. However, they became a wealthy order after King Alfonso of Aragon and Navarre bestowed wealth upon them, and by the end of the twelfth century they had 30,000 members – most of them French. In 1307, at the instigation of King Philip IV of France, the French Templars were accused of heresy, and in particular of denying Christ, the Virgin, and the Saints. They were described as worshipping the Devil in the form of **Baphomet**, roasting the bodies of dead Templars, spitting on the crucifix, and engaging in unnatural sexual acts. Many confessions were extracted under torture and a number of knights, who later retracted their confessions, were burned to death. An investigation ordered by Pope Clement V found little evidence of heresy or wrongdoing in other countries, but the order was abolished in 1312. While the true nature of the Knights Templar may never be known with certainty, it is likely that many knights in the Order were influenced by the esoteric traditions of **Manicheism**, the **Albigenses**, and the **Cathars**. To this extent some members may have been continuing the mystical Gnostic philosophy, which the orthodox Church, since the earliest times, had sought to eradicate.

**Kobold** In German folk belief, a **gnome**, or spirit that haunts houses or underground mines.

**Koko** See Ka-Ka.

**Komselha** In Enochian magic, the angelic word for the **magic circle**. It is pronounced *koh-mess-el-hah*.

**Kotodama** A Japanese expression which translates as "the soul of words". It refers to the magical power that is innately present in certain sounds.

**Kraig, Donald Michael** (1951– ) Born in Chicago, Kraig is a philosophy graduate of the University of California, Los Angeles, and an accomplished author and journalist in the fields of **magic**, **Kabbalah**, psychic research, paranormal phenomena and New Age spirituality. A former editor of *New Times* and *Fate* magazines, he has been practising western magic for over 20 years and is the author of several books, including *Modern Magick: Eleven Lessons in the High Magickal Art*; *Modern Sex Magick*; and *Evocation of Spirits*.

**Kramer, Heinrich** (1430–1505) The co-author, with **Jacobus Sprenger**, of the notorious *Malleus Maleficarum*, a work that fuelled the Inquisition's campaign against **witchcraft** and **heretics**. Kramer was an experienced Dominican inquisitor and first aroused fear and hostility in the region of the Tyrol. He had a major ally in Archduke Sigismund, who rewarded him for his efforts, and is regarded as the major contributor to the *Malleus*. He died while on an apostolic mission to Bohemia.

**Kronos** or **Cronus** In ancient Greek mythology, the god of time, who existed before the creation of the world. In other versions he was one of the **Titans** – the youngest son of **Uranus** and **Gaea** and the husband of **Rhea**. Kronos swallowed each of his children, but the last-born, **Zeus**, was saved and later rescued the others. After a fight with the Titans, Zeus then deposed Kronos and gained supremacy over the world. In Roman mythology, Kronos is identified with **Saturn**.

**Kteis** The ancient Greek term for the female sexual organs. In the **Ordo Templi Orientis** the kteis and **phallus** form what tantric magician **Kenneth Grant** has described as "the physiological basis of the **Ophidian Current**".

**Kuf** See Qoph.

**Kulabel** The name of the Rainbow Serpent among the Djerag and Djaru Aboriginal tribes of the East Kimberleys in northwest Australia. The Djerag and Djaru **medicine man** is "killed" by the serpent at a waterhole and the serpent enters his body, making him "sick and mad" before then bestowing magical powers upon him.

**Kundalini** From a Sanskrit term meaning "coil" or "spiral", a spiritual and psychical energy that may be aroused systematically by techniques of yoga and can be channelled through the chakras from the base of the spine to the crown of the forehead. Kundalini is often symbolized as a coiled serpent and is sometimes associated with the goddess **Kali**. Kundalini yoga principles are utilized in the sex magic practices of the Ordo Templi Orientis. See also **Chakra**; **Ida**; **Pingala**; **Sushumna**; **Tantra**.

**Kwacmin** A term used by the Coast Salish Indians of the American northwest to refer to the rattle-stick carried by shamans during Spirit Dance healing ceremonies. Made of wood, it was highly decorated and had an animal or human head carved on top.

**Kyteler, Dame Alice** A fourteenth-century Irish aristocrat accused of **witchcraft** and **demonology**. Dame Alice lived in Kilkenny in southeast Ireland and practised fertility rituals with Sir Arnold le Poer, a relative of her fourth husband. Alice would sacrifice red cockerels at different times of the year, and Sir Arnold participated in ceremonies wearing a horned mask. These strange practices came to the attention of the Bishop of Ossory, Richard de Landrede, who was determined to stamp out witchcraft in Ireland and earn favour with the Pope. Dame Alice escaped to Dublin and later travelled to England, where she lived for the rest of her life. Others in Alice's circle were not so lucky. Her friend and servant Petronilla de Meath was cast into a dungeon and later burned alive in front of the bishop in November 1324.

# L

**Laboratory** In alchemy, the place where operations were undertaken. The alchemist's equipment included a furnace, or **athanor**; a **retort**; an **alembic** or glass vessel with a beaked neck; a **crucible** or earthenware pot for melting metals, and a circulatory still – also known as a "**pelican**" – with a dome at the top of its belly and tubes leading back into the bottom of the still allowing distilled liquid to be retained.

**Labyrinth** (1) In ancient Greek legend, a huge underground maze built by the master craftsman **Daedalus** for King Minos at the palace of Knossos in Crete. Minos confined the **Minotaur** in the centre of the Labyrinth and it was fed on human sacrifices – seven boys and seven girls sent each year from Athens – until it was slain by the hero Theseus.

**Labyrinth** (2) In alchemy, a term used to designate the difficult and, at times, confusing terrain negotiated by the practitioner in undertaking the **opus alchymicum**.

**Ladder of Life** A mystical symbol of ascending stages of consciousness. The ladder appears in the Bible (Genesis 28.12) as the bridge between heaven and earth, and in the **Kabbalah** as the **Tree of Life** or "Ladder of Lights". The rungs of the ladder represent different **emanations**, or levels of existence, in the cosmos.

**Lady Olwen** See **Wilson, Monique.**

**Lagu** or **Laguz** In the Germanic **Elder Futhark**, the **rune** letter representing the number 21. Lagu corresponds to the letter "l". The word "laguz" means "lake" and this rune is closely associated with the element water, and specifically with water as an essential to life. But as the seafaring Vikings well knew, the ocean was also fraught with danger. Accordingly, this rune is associated with the idea of accepting life's challenges, and also with the transition from life to death. Interestingly the sea god Aegir was not only a devourer of ships but also a brewer of beer, so this rune is also associated with companionship gained through beer drinking.

**Lam** An "extraterrestrial intelligence" contacted on the **astral plane** by ceremonial magician **Aleister Crowley** while he was in the United States. Crowley produced a drawing of Lam and it was exhibited in Greenwich Village, New York City, in 1919. Magical practitioners working in the **Typhonian tradition** claim that they have continued to maintain contact with Lam.

**Lambi** In **voodoo**, a conch shell that is used as a horn or trumpet.

**Lamed** The Hebrew letter ascribed to the path linking the **sephiroth Tiphareth** and **Geburah** on the **Tree of Life**. Lamed has a numerical value of 30. In modern magical visualization and **pathworkings** the **Tarot** card associated with this path on the Tree is *Justice*.

**Lamen** A magical pendant worn around the neck and positioned so that it hangs upon the breast, over the heart.

**Lamia** (1) In ancient Greek mythology, Lamia was the daughter of **Poseidon** and a mistress of **Zeus**. **Hera** was so jealous of her that she destroyed Lamia's children and deformed her appearance so that she took the hybrid form of a woman with the body of a serpent. Lamia lured victims to her domain and devoured them. In ancient Rome she became identified as a blood-sucking witch. See also **Lamia** (2).

**Lamia** (2) A general term, derived from the Lamia of Greek myth, for a female **demon** that might take many forms. As mermaids, lamias (or lamiae) could lure boats to destruction; but on other occasions they resembled goats, with horses' hooves. Lamias were said to hiss like serpents and feed on the flesh of corpses. See also **Lamia** (1) and compare **Ghoul**; **Siren**.

**Lammas** In Wicca, one of the Greater Sabbats, also known by its Celtic name of **Lughnassadh** and celebrated in the northern hemisphere on 1 August. The word "Lammas" literally means "loaf-mass" and this is the time of year when the first corn is harvested. In the Celtic tradition, the festival of Lughnassadh marks the approach of autumn and in ancient times was probably a celebration in honour of Lugh, the Celtic sun god. Lammas/Lughnassadh is associated with the waning power of the sun – in mythic terms the god has begun to die – but it is also a time when one can reflect upon the fruits of the earth. Wiccans gather at this sabbat to celebrate the gifts of abundance which have come forth from the womb of the goddess. Symbolically, the festival represents fulfilment – the reaping of all that has been sown. See also **Sabbats, Greater**.

**Lampadomancy** A form of **divination** using the flame of a lamp or torch. The actions and movements of the flame are interpreted as an oracle. See also **Pyromancy**.

**Lapidary** A book classifying and describing precious stones. Medieval lapidaries included *The Book of Stones*, attributed to Aristotle, *The Flowers of Knowledge of Stones* by Egyptian alchemist Shihab al-Din al-Tifashi, the *Lapidario* of King Alfonso X of Castile and León, and the *Gemmarum et Lapidum Historia* by **Anselmus Boetius de Boot**, who served Emperor Rudolf II, king of Bohemia.

**Lapis Exilis** A mythic stone that enabled the **phoenix** to regain its youth. This stone is regarded by some authorities as synonymous with the **Holy Grail**.

**Lapis Judaicus** Identified to some degree with the Lapis Exilis, this mystical stone is said to have fallen from the crown of **Lucifer** and was retained by the angels of the air. It is also called Theolithos.

**Lapis Philosophorum** See Philosopher's Stone.

**La-Place** In voodoo, the apprentice or assistant to the houngan, or priest.

**Lares** Ancient Roman household gods and spirits that protected the family, property, and servants. They also guarded the farmlands and sometimes whole cities. Shrines to the lares (singular, lar) would be found in most Roman homes and also at various crossroads. See also Penates.

**La Sirène** In voodoo, the sea goddess who is a form of the goddess of love, Erzulie. She is married to Agwé, the loa of the sea.

**Latona** or **Latten** An alloy of gold and silver, resembling bronze. The German alchemist and Rosicrucian Michael Maier described it as "an imperfect body composed of Sol and Luna" and emphasized that it needed to be purified by washing away its blemishes and making it "white".

**Laurel** A tree with magical and mythic associations. The Greek nymph Daphne was pursued by Apollo and prayed to be changed into another form. Athena transformed her into a laurel, or daphne, and this tree thereafter became sacred to Apollo. The leaves of the laurel were also chewed by the Delphic Oracle to induce visionary powers of prophecy, and were hung over doorways to send ghosts away.

**Laver Tête** In voodoo, the act of ritually washing the head of a person in order to baptize the loa located there.

**La Vey, Anton Szandor** (1930–1997) A renowned American satanist, also known as the Black Pope. According to his authorized biography, La Vey was born in Chicago on 11 April 1930 and was of French, Alsatian, German,

Russian, Romanian, and gypsy descent La Vey was attracted to the occult from an early age, and learnt about vampires from his Romanian maternal grandmother. He immersed himself in occult and fantasy literature, such as Bram Stoker's *Dracula* and the popular magazine *Weird Tales*. At the age of twelve he was familiar with medieval magical grimoires and the writings of Albertus Magnus. At age sixteen, La Vey left his home in Oakland, California, to join the Clyde Beatty Circus as a cage boy. He later worked for travelling shows on the Pacific coast, playing a calliope or a Wurlitzer or Hammond organ. LaVey was inspired by his first wife to study criminology at San Francisco City College, and for a brief period became a photographer with the San Francisco Police Department. Here he was exposed to the gruesome side of urban life. He concluded that violence was a part of the divine and inscrutable plan of God, and he turned away from God altogether as a source of inspiration and benevolence. LaVey went back to playing the organ, immersing himself further in his study of the occult and parapsychology. Soon he was holding weekly classes on various esoteric topics, attended by a diverse range of people, including novelist Stephen Schneck and avant-garde film producer Kenneth Anger. The so-called Magic Circle meetings were held in his tightly shuttered house at 6114 California Street, and included lectures on vampires, werewolves, haunted houses, extrasensory perception, and zombies. LaVey also lampooned the Catholic Church with a "Black Mass" which involved desecrating the host, using an inverted cross and black candles, and reciting prayers backwards. In an act of bravado, LaVey shaved his head and announced the formation of the Church of Satan on the most demonic night of the year, Walpurgis Night – traditionally associated with the ascendancy of the powers of darkness. He declared 1966 to be Year One, *Anno Satanas* – the first year of the reign of Satan. LaVey announced at this time that

"Satanism is the only religion in which a person can 'turn on' to the pleasures around him without 'dropping out' of society." This was an emphatic rephrasing of the hippie dictum, "Turn on, tune in and drop out," then being advocated by counterculture guru Timothy Leary. LaVey was opposed to any notion of drug-based escapism: instead he emphasized sensual indulgence and personal empowerment. LaVey believed, essentially, that man is God and God is man. The ceremonies of the Church of Satan would become a means for channelling magical power into a full expression of human carnal desire. Membership numbers in the Church of Satan remained a closely guarded secret throughout La Vey's magical career. The Church of Satan has continued, but in a very much diminished form, since his death in 1997. La Vey's books include *The Satanic Bible* (1969) and *The Satanic Rituals* (1972). See also **Church of Satan.**

**Law of Retribution** A popular term for the law of **karma.**

**Lea** In Enochian magic, the sixteenth **Aethyr.** The meanings associated with Lea include foreknowledge, adjustment, spiritual impulse, and an ability to change for the better. Lea is associated with **Cancer, Virgo,** and **Taurus** and its magical number is 24.

**Lead** In alchemy, the imperfect heavy metal which the alchemists maintained could be transmuted into pure silver or gold by the **Philosopher's Stone.** The alchemists associated lead astrologically with the Roman god **Saturn.**

**Leading Houses** In astrology, the cardinal signs – **Aries, Cancer, Libra,** and **Capricorn** – that are assigned to the first, fourth, seventh, and tenth houses respectively. See also **House.**

**Lead, Philosophical** See Philosophical Lead.

**Leaf Doctor** In Haiti, a herbal practitioner who treats minor medical conditions like colds, headaches, intestinal complaints, and aching joints. The leaf doctor does not have access to supernatural powers and must therefore be distinguished from the **voodoo** practitioner.

**Lecanomancy** A form of **divination** in which a stone or similar object is thrown into a basin of water. The image of the object in the rippling water, and the sound it makes dropping to the bottom, are interpreted as having divinatory significance. An alternative method is to drop oil on the surface of the water and interpret the shapes that form there. See also **Hydromancy.**

**Leek, Sybil** (1923–1983) An English-born witch who went to live in the United States in 1964 and began to attract widespread media coverage for her pagan beliefs and practices. Sybil Leek claimed to trace her **witchcraft** ancestry back to the twelfth century. Well known for her radio programmes on witchcraft, she opened an occult restaurant ("Sybil Leek's Cauldron") and wrote several books, including *Diary of a Witch, The Sybil Leek Book of Fortune-Telling,* and *Cast Your Own Spell.*

**Left-Hand Path** From the Latin *sinister,* "left", the path of black magic and **sorcery.** Practitioners in this tradition seek to use magic to acquire personal power, rather than to gain spiritual transcendence. See also **Brothers of the Shadow; Magic, Black.**

**Legba** In voodoo, the **loa** of light, life, and the crossroads. He is also referred to as the "guardian of the gates". As the sun god, Legba is the husband of **Erzulie,** goddess of the moon. See also **Papa.**

***Legend of the Descent of the Goddess, The*** In Wicca, a mystery play titled *The Legend of the Descent of the Goddess* forms a central part of the second initiation. This rite is essentially a journey into the depths of the mythic unconscious and an exploration of sexual polarities within the psyche. In this play the second-degree candidate and other **coven** members enact the descent of the **Great Goddess** into the **Underworld**. Here the goddess encounters the God in his role as the Dark Lord of Death.

**Leland, Charles Godfrey** (1824–1903) An American folklorist and authority on **witchcraft**. Leland went to college in the United States and later studied at the universities of Heidelberg and Munich and at the Sorbonne in Paris. After fighting on the side of the rebels in the 1848 revolution, he returned from Paris to the United States and took up a career as a journalist. A few years after marrying he was again involved in a military campaign, this time the American Civil War. After fighting at the Battle of Gettysburg, Leland left with his family for London to begin a new life and acquire new interests. He began to study folklore and gypsy legends, taught himself Romany – the language of the gypsies – and after ten years in England moved to Florence, Italy. There Leland became friendly with a young woman called Maddalena, who told him that the old gods were still being worshipped in secret, and Leland discovered to his surprise that there was still a cult of **Diana** in the guise of **Aradia**, Diana's daughter. Leland described in his book *Aradia, the Gospel of the Witches* how ritual offerings were made to Diana each month when the moon was full, and he provided a detailed description of a **coven** meeting. Leland's writings influenced **Gerald Gardner** and have had a strong effect on contemporary witchcraft.

**Lemegeton** A title given to the medieval work of black magic or **goetia** known as *The Lesser Key of Solomon*. It was translated from French, Latin, and Hebrew manuscript copies by the occultist **MacGregor Mathers**. According to A.E. Waite, the most complete extant copy is in French and dates from the seventeenth century; however, the medieval demonologist **Johannes Wier** refers to it, so other versions must have existed at an earlier date. See also *Key of Solomon, The.*

**Leo** In astrology, the sign of the zodiac for those born between 23 July and 22 August. A fire sign, ruled by the sun, Leo is symbolized by a lion and is the fifth sign of the zodiac. Those born under this sign are said to be proud, ambitious, generous, friendly, and practical; they can also be obstinate and boastful. Leos are supposed to be good managers and organizers.

**León, Moses ben Shem Tov de** (c. 1240–1305). A Spanish Jewish mystic who was born in the town of León. He became a member of the local community of kabbalists and was influenced by Todros Abulafia and Joseph Gikatilla. By about 1286 he had compiled a major work in Aramaic, which he called a "mystical midrash"; such commentaries form a major part of the *Zohar*, one of the principal works of the **Kabbalah**. Moses de León lived for some time in Guadalajara and later in Avila, although in the 1290s he also spent much of his life wandering and meeting other mystics. He was the author of over 20 works, many of which survive only as fragments. Moses de León died in Arevalo.

**Leprechauns** In Irish folklore, small dwarfs or elves who were said to haunt wine cellars and to guard mounds of hidden treasure. See also **Dwarf; Elves; Fairies.**

**Leprosy** In alchemy, a reference to the impurities, or "disease", afflicting certain metals in the earth. The so-called "imperfect metals" were iron, copper, tin, and lead.

**Lerajie** Also known as **Leraje** or **Leraikha** In the **Goetia**, the fourteenth spirit, a great and powerful marquis who appears in the form of an archer, clad in green and carrying a bow and quiver. Associated with the astrological sign of **Sagittarius**, Lerajie initiates battles and contests and the wounds caused by the arrows of his warrior-archers putrefy and fester. Lerajie governs 30 legions of spirits and is also known as Leraje or Leraikha.

**Leshy** In the traditional mythology of the Slavic peoples, a wood spirit or **satyr** with both human and animal characteristics. Traditionally, the Leshy was said to have a green beard and a blue skin. The Leshy inhabited the forests and lured unwary travellers into caves, but was fortunately alive only during the spring and summer months.

**Les Invisibles** See Invisibles, Les.

**Lesser Sabbats** See Sabbats, Lesser.

**Leviathan** According to the Bible, a monstrous fish or sea serpent formed on the fifth day of creation. For the Jews, Leviathan was a symbol of God's awesome power and as such he also features in the Day of Judgment. As a symbol of chaos and destruction, he was incorporated into medieval demonology. Leviathan is regarded by occultist **Kenneth Grant** as the negative or Qlippothic equivalent of the **Tarot** image *The Hanged Man*, which is ruled by the element water. See also **Qlippoth**.

**Lévi, Eliphas** (1810–1875) The magical name of Alphonse-Louis Constant, the son of a poor Parisian shoemaker. Lévi studied for the priesthood, but was asked to leave on account of his sexual permissiveness. He worked for a time as a political caricaturist and then turned to magical and Hermetic philosophy. He produced a number of books that have since become occult classics, despite their shoddy scholarship. Lévi's best work is contained in *The Mysteries of Magic*, an anthology of his writings edited by A.E. Waite. His other books include *Le Dogme et Ritual de la Haute Magie*; *Histoire de la Magie*; and *La Clef des Grandes Mystères*, which are available in a variety of

English-language editions. From an occult viewpoint, Lévi is remembered mainly for two things: he made the important observation that the 22 cards of the **Major Arcana** of the **Tarot** appear to correlate symbolically with the paths on the kabbalistic **Tree of Life**; and the fact that the magician **Aleister Crowley** claimed to be Lévi's reincarnation and occult successor. See also **Hermetica**.

**Leys** Alignments of ancient megaliths, dolmens, and stone circles, whose patterns are said to constitute grids of "power", or ley-lines. The English amateur archaeologist Alfred Watkins first brought attention to these alignments in 1921, and psychical researchers and mediums have since claimed that patterns of psychic energy emanate from the leys. Some ufologists believe that the ley-lines are "power grids" used to guide extraterrestrial visitors, who have allegedly contacted human civilization since earliest times and have profoundly influenced various myths and legends relating to the origin and cultural development of the human species.

**Libation** In Wicca, an offering of drink made to the goddess and god of wine and blessed within the magical circle.

**Libellus Merlini** "*The Little Book of Merlin*", a Latin tract ascribed to the twelfth-century author Geoffrey of Monmouth, which describes the supernatural prophecies of "Ambrosius Merlin" relating to the symbolic vision of the battle of the white and red dragons – said to represent the Saxons and Britons respectively. See **Merlin**.

**Liber Al vel Legis** See *Book of the Law, The*.

**Liber Lapidum** A medieval lapidary written c. 1123 by Bishop Marbod of Rennes, France. It ascribes symbolic properties to several stones. For example, onyx is supposed to induce nightmares; a sapphire may be used to protect oneself from fear; and the sardonyx represents the inner mystical self.

**Libra** In astrology, the sign of the zodiac for those born between 23 September and 22 October. An air sign, ruled by **Venus**, Libra is symbolized by a pair of scales and is the seventh zodiac sign. Those born under this sign are said to be intuitive, artistic, and charming. They are given to making comparisons and can therefore become quarrelsome; they may also be moody and whimsical. Librans are said to be ideally suited to careers in the arts, antiques, and the theatre.

**Libuga** See Iboga.

**Licking a Charm** A phrase used to describe a remedy for counteracting a spell inflicted on a child. The method was to lick the child's forehead in an upward direction, then across, and up again. The taste of salt on the tongue was taken as a sure sign of enchantment.

**Life Soul** See Body Soul.

**Life, Tree of** See Tree of Life.

**Ligature** See Aiguillette.

**Light** A universal symbol of illumination and transcendence, equated with the spirit and with the **godhead**. In the Kabbalah the supreme reality is **Ain Soph Aur**, "the Limitless Light", and mystics universally describe light filling their souls, or sweeping their minds into a state of transcendent bliss. White light contains all colours and also all "virtues". It therefore symbolizes totality and oneness. Many cosmologies, especially those of ancient Persia and Egypt, describe illumination and initiation in terms of the forces of light conquering the forces of darkness. In the Bible, the creation of light is the first divine act of creation.

**Light, Collector of** In astrology, a term used to describe a situation where a planet receives aspects from two other significators which are in a position of **dignity**. The collector of light is then seen as a mediating influence and is said to bring a harmonious outcome to quarrels, disagreements, and lawsuits. See also **Significator**.

**Lightness** A quality ascribed to the element air, also associated with spontaneous dance and the urge to rise above oneself. It is thus linked to ecstasy, and is a quality described by those who have the **out-of-the-body experience** or claim the paranormal faculty of levitation.

**Light Planets** In astrology, a reference to those bodies that are swift in motion and have a "light" gravity (the **moon**, **Venus**, and **Mercury**).

**Lights** In astrology, a term applied to differentiate the **sun** and **moon** from the other planets in the horoscope.

**Lil** In Enochian magic, the first and most sublime **Aethyr**. The meanings associated with Lil include purity, innocence, completeness, wholeness, and satisfaction. Lil is associated with **Cancer** and **Sagittarius** and its magical number is 76.

**Lilith** (1) According to Jewish tradition, the first wife of Adam. Probably of Babylonian origin, the figure of Lilith is a "dark" form of the goddess, identified as being vengeful, hostile to childbirth, and demanding of human sacrifice. Lilith's name means "night monster" and she was sometimes characterized as a night-demon or phantom who, like **Hecate** and **Lamia**, personified evil and darkness. In the magical tradition of the **Hermetic Order of the Golden Dawn**, Lilith was described as "Queen of the Night and of Demons" – one of the **Qlippoth**, the negative form of **Malkuth**.

**Lilith** (2) In the Ordo Templi Orientis, a vampire force which, if projected beyond the aura of the magician, can obsess the object of its attention.

According to **Kenneth Grant** it represents the "sexual shadow, or *succuba*, formed of uncontrolled desire".

**Lily, White** In alchemy, the pure white elixir associated with the **albedo** – the lunar phase of the alchemical opus.

**Limbeck** See Alembic.

**Lin** In Enochian magic, the 22nd Aethyr. The meanings associated with Lin include meditation, ideas, music, and transcendence. It is associated with Cancer, Sagittarius, and Scorpio and its magical number is 118.

**Lines of Power** See Leys.

**Lion** (1) In alchemy, a reference to **gold** or the sun – **King Sol**.

**Lion** (2) An animal with many mythic and magical associations. The lion symbolizes both **gold** and the **sun** and in ancient Egypt devotees of the goddess **Sekhmet** worshipped her in the form of a lion-headed woman. The lion was also sacred to the followers of the cult of **Mithra**. As **Leo**, the lion is the fifth sign of the **zodiac** and is identified in this capacity as one of the three **fire** signs (the other two being **Sagittarius** and **Aries**). The lion is also featured in the symbolism of the **Major Arcana** of the Tarot. On the card of *Temperance*, the lion symbolizes fire and is counterbalanced by the **eagle** (**air**). On the card *Strength*, however, it represents brute force that yields to intuition with the evolution of spiritual consciousness. In **alchemy**, the lion is a symbol of **sulphur**, and in different contexts may be a symbol of both fire and **earth**. As a symbol of strength, dignity, and power, the lion is also a common motif in heraldry.

**Lion, Green** See Green Lion.

**Lit** In Enochian magic, the fifth **Aethyr**. The meanings associated with Lit include truth and success. It is associated

with **Cancer, Sagittarius,** and **Caput Draconis** and its magical number is 77.

**Litha** In Wicca, the midsummer solstice. See Sabbats, Lesser.

**Lithomancy** A form of **divination** by means of precious stones. One method is to take stones, each of which has a planetary or symbolic significance, and scatter them on a dark surface. The stone that reflects the most light provides the **omen** in divination. See also **Birthstones; Stones, Magical.**

**Ljossalfheim** In Scandinavian and northern European mythology, one of the Nine Worlds located on the World Tree, Yggdrasil. Ljossalfheim was the realm of the elves.

**Lleu Llaw Gyffes** In Welsh Celtic mythology, "Lleu of the Skilful Hand" – the son of **Gwydion** and his sister **Arianrhod**. When he was born, his mother laid a triple curse on him, depriving him of a name, arms, and a wife. However his father, who was a sorcerer, used his magic to circumvent the curse. Lleu was murdered by his wife and lover and changed into an eagle, but Gwydion later found his son and changed him back into human form. The figure of Lleu is related to the Irish deity **Lugh**.

**Lo** In the **Kabbalah**, a synonym for **Ain**, the mysterious unknown which lies at the source of all existence (from the Hebrew, "not").

**Loa** In voodoo, deities that possess the practitioner while the latter is in a state of trance. There are two main groups – the Rada gods, of Dahomean origin, and the Petro gods, of Caribbean origin. Loas are evoked at ceremonies by **vevers**, magical **sigil** designs drawn on the ground.

**Loco** In voodoo, the **loa** of vegetation. He is the partner of the female loa Ayizan, patroness of the marketplace.

**Loe** In Enochian magic, the twelfth

Aethyr. The meanings associated with Loe include compassion, love, sacrifice, and dedication to others. It is associated with **Cancer**, **Libra**, and **Virgo** and its magical number is 48.

**Logos** A Greek term meaning "word" or "thought", used to refer to the divine creative utterance. In both magic and religion, the vibrational quality of sound and the power of utterance have always been regarded as of the utmost importance. In the gospel of John (1.1), it is written: "In the beginning was the Word [Logos], and the Word was with God, and the Word was God…all things were made through him and without him was not anything that was made." Similarly, in the Kabbalah, the world is said to have been formed by the utterance of the sacred Name of God – a 42 letter extension of **Tetragrammaton**. A similar emphasis pertains in ritual magic. In his book *The Key of the Mysteries*, **Eliphas Lévi** writes: "All magic is in a word, and that word pronounced kabbalistically is stronger than all the powers of heaven, earth, and hell." In Gnostic terminology, Logos refers to the sacred **god-name** of a deity in the manifested universe. See also **Hekau**; **Words of Power**.

**Loki** In Scandinavian mythology, the god of fire, who was originally a member of the **Aesir**. Loki guided the mistletoe that killed the sun-god **Balder**, and as a consequence the other gods bound Loki to a rock, with a snake dripping poisonous venom over him. Loki was saved by his wife and joined the evil monsters and giants as the sworn enemy of the Aesir.

**Lokoala** Among the Kwakiutl Indians of the Canadian northwest, a term used to describe the act of receiving magical gifts from **spirits**.

**Lord** In astrology, a term used as a synonym for **ruler**. It is customary to use the expressions "ruler of a sign" and "lord of a house".

**Lord of the Flies** Title given in medieval **demonology** to **Beelzebub**, whose name is a combination of **Baal** (a Phoenician deity) and *zebub* (a fly). Beelzebub claimed to be the first angel in the first heaven, but he had wings because he was a fly, not because he was a "fallen angel".

**Lord of the Year** In astrology, an expression most commonly used to describe the planet that has the most dignities, or strongly favourable aspects, in a solar revolution **horoscope**. See also **Dignity**.

**Lorelei** In German folk legend, a beautiful maiden who sat on a steep rock near St Goar on the Rhine, luring boatmen to disaster on the dangerous rocks. The Lorelei would sit combing her hair and singing beautiful songs, and in many respects resembled the **Sirens** of classical Greek mythology.

**Loudun, Devils of** See **Grandier, Urbain**.

**Loup Garou** In voodoo, an individual who has transformed into a **werewolf**.

**Lovecraft, Howard Phillips** (1890–1937) An American occult and horror-fiction author who became a cult figure in underground literature in the 1960s and whose creative imagery has inspired members of the **Ordo Templi Orientis** as a focus for magical exploration. Lovecraft developed a mythology around "the dread Cthulhu", in which powers of evil and darkness threatened to break through to control the world, and he was obsessed with the theme of global threat (*The Colours out of Space, The Dunwich Horror, The Shadow over Innsmouth*). Lovecraft invented the concept of the "legendary" occult text – *The Necronomicon* – and at least two versions of this text now exist, both purporting to be authentic. Lovecraft's supernatural tales have been collected into a number of volumes, including *The Tomb, At the Mountains of Madness, The*

*Haunter of the Dark,* and *The Lurker at the Threshold.*

**Love Potion** In witchcraft and herbalism, an aphrodisiac said to cause a person to fall in love with someone else – often simply the next person who happens to appear before them. Some traditional herbal or aphrodisiac recipes draw on foods that appeared to resemble the human sexual organs – asparagus, oysters, cucumbers, bananas, and so on. Certain herbs, such as mint, mandrake, and verbena, have also been used in love potions. Very often an incantation is performed as part of the magical conjuration. The American herbalist Jeanne Rose describes a traditional Egyptian love potion in her book *The Herbal Guide to Inner Health.* The recipe calls for one pint of water; one ounce each of mashed licorice root, mashed sesame seed, and bruised fennel seed; and some honey. The ingredients are boiled in a pot, allowed to simmer for five minutes and are then cooled, made into a infusion, and strained. The potion is taken twice a day with locks of the desirable person's hair entwined around the fingers, and a powerful magical formula of love and passion is recited at the same time.

***Lovers, The*** In the Tarot, a card in the **Major Arcana** that depicts two naked figures standing in the Garden of Eden – personifying innocence regained. The holy guardian angel towers over them, bestowing grace. The card symbolizes the gradual fusion of sexual polarities and the mystical transcendence of duality. It is also reminiscent of the Greek myth of Castor and Polydeuces (Pollux), who were placed in the sky by Zeus as solar and lunar opposites with a common destiny. The pathway of *The Lovers* links **Tiphareth** and **Binah** on the kabbalistic **Tree of Life,** spheres which in themselves represent the divine son and the great mother respectively. See also **Androgyne; Dual Signs.**

**Lucifer (1)** One of the many names for the **Devil.** Lucifer means "Light Bearer", and originally meant the planet Venus as the morning star. In the Bible (Isaiah 14), the name was given to a king of Babylon who boasted that he could ascend to the heavens and make himself God's equal, but who in fact was fated to descend hell. Later, St Jerome and other Church Fathers gave the name Lucifer to Satan, who was said to have fallen from heaven for his rebellious pride. He was classified among medieval demons and devils. In the Theosophical tradition, Lucifer has been looked upon more kindly and is regarded as a personification of the independent and self- conscious mind, which desires to evolve through many lifetimes towards the **Light.**

**Lucifer (2)** In **astrology,** the name given to **Venus** as the morning star.

**Luck** Good fortune. Occultists have traditionally believed that luck can be evoked through rituals, by heeding omens and portents, by using divinatory oracles, and by wearing or displaying lucky charms and amulets. See also **Amulet; Divination; Fortune Teller; Horseshoe; Lucky Charm.**

**Lucky Charm** A small object worn to bring good luck. For example, in Asia and many parts of Africa, **turquoise** is prized as a "lucky stone" that can ward off the evil eye, and it is worn in rings, necklaces, and bracelets as a protection. A lucky charm can also be an **incantation** or **spell** designed to summon the powers of good fortune.

**Lugh** or **Lugh Lamh Fada** In Irish Celtic mythology, the hero who was placed in command of the forces of the **Tuatha De Danann** in the victorious battle at Mag Tuireadh against the **Fomorians.** The name Lugh, like that of his Welsh counterpart Lleu, means "Shining One" and he is regarded by many as an ancient solar deity, who was known in ancient times as Lugus. The old Celtic festival (and modern Wiccan sabbat) of Lughnassadh, held on 1 August in the northern hemisphere, is traditionally linked with Lugh. See also **Lammas**; **Lleu Llaw Gyffes**.

**Lughnassadh** or **Lughnasadh** See Lammas

**Luis** In the Celtic tree alphabet, the **ogham** representing the elm and rowan and the letter "l". Luis is also linked to the duck and the colour dark grey.

**Lully, Raymond** (Ramon Lull) (c. 1235–1315). A Spanish-born Christian mystic and prolific traveller, who spent much of his early life at court, pursuing the favours of aristocratic ladies. It is said that his conversion to mystical affairs stems from an affair involving Signora Ambrosia Eleonora de Genes, to whom Lully was greatly attracted, despite the fact she was in love with, and married to, another man. The Signora, tiring of his amorous pursuits, called Lully to her in private and exposed her cancerous breast to him, at the same time urging him to transform his "useless and criminal passion into holy love" and direct his affections to the creator. Ashamed of his blatant passion, Lully withdrew to his home, cast himself beneath a crucifix, and dedicated himself to Christ. In subsequent years Lully became a fervent evangelist and travelled widely – in Italy, France, Cyprus, and northern Africa – his main quest being to prove the "errors" of Islam. He died in Tunis. Lully has been described in occult tradition as a great **alchemist** as well as a noted mystic, and a legend claims that he transformed a large quantity of quicksilver, tin, and lead into **gold** at the request of King Edward III of England. It is generally thought, however, that this tale was concocted by the English alchemist Sir George Ripley, who popularized Lully's works. As far as is known, Lully never visited England.

**Luminaries** In astrology, the sun and moon.

**Luminous Arc** In Theosophy, a term synonymous with **ascending arc**.

**Luminous Body** A term sometimes used by occultists as a synonym for the astral body.

**Luminous Paths** In western magic, a term used to describe the 22 **Tarot** paths of the **Major Arcana**, when used for visionary **pathworkings**. See also **Tree of Life**.

**Luminous Self** In the esoteric conception of novelist **Sir Edward Bulwer-Lytton**, a reference to **Augoeides**, or the Higher Self.

**Luna** (1) In alchemy, the female principle of the opus associated with argent vive, Diana, and "philosophical silver". Luna was also the name of the pure white elixir that could transmute base metals into pure silver. See also **Albedo**; **Argent Vive**; **Diana**.

**Luna** (2) In ancient Rome, the goddess of the moon. She was identified with **Selene** and also with **Diana**. See also **Diana**; **Lunar Goddesses**.

**Lunar** Pertaining to the **moon**.

**Lunar Goddesses** Traditionally, the **sun** has been regarded as a masculine force and the **moon** as feminine. Consequently, the moon has often been personified as a moon goddess and worshipped in this form. Many ancient pantheons featured lunar goddesses. They include: **Isis** and **Hathor** (Egypt); **Astarte** (Phoenicia); **Ishtar** (Babylonia); **Artemis**, **Hecate**, and **Selene** (Greece); **Diana** and **Luna** (Rome). In China the moon is the force behind all things that are **yin**, or feminine. See also **Feminine Principle**.

**Lunar Gods** Although lunar deities are traditionally thought of as feminine, there are many exceptions. Best known among these are the ancient Egyptian god of wisdom and magic **Thoth** and his Theban counterpart Khonsu, or Khons. Other examples include the Babylonian and Assyrian deity **Sin** (also called **Nanna**), the Slavic triple-moon god Myesyats (husband of Dennitsa), the Vedic god Soma and his son Budha, the Chaldean god Nebo, the minor Roman deity Virbius (consort of **Diana**) and the Lithuanian moon god Menuo, who was traditionally depicted wearing a starry robe and travelling across the sky in a chariot drawn by grey horses. See also **Eye of Horus**.

**Lunation** In **astrology**, a term used to describe the exact moment of the moon's **conjunction** with the **sun** – the time of new moon.

**Lupercalia** In ancient Rome, a fertility festival sacred to **Lupercus** and held annually on 15 February. It included purification ceremonies, which were believed to aid the renewal of life and nature, and also featured rites to protect domesticated animals from wolves. During the festival men known as Luperci ran around the Palatine Hill wearing only goatskins, and would strike women with goatskin thongs to enhance their fertility.

**Lupercus** A Roman fertility god, sometimes identified with **Pan** and Faunus. Lupercus protected the flock from wild ravenous wolves and was celebrated in the festival of the **Lupercalia**.

**Luria, Isaac** (1534–1572) An influential kabbalist and poet who grew up in Egypt and studied under David ben Solomon ibn Abi Zimra. Luria was well versed in rabbinical literature and the non-mystical study of Jewish law, but finally decided on a life of esoteric pursuits. He retired to an island on the Nile near Cairo and studied the kabbalistic writings of **Moses Cordovero** and the texts of the *Zohar*. It was during this period that he wrote his commentary on *The Book of Concealment*. Luria continued to read the **Kabbalah** in earnest and, after settling in **Safed** with his family in 1570, studied for a short while with Cordovero himself. After Cordovero died that same year, Luria

replaced him as a central figure and became the focal member of a group of distinguished kabbalists, including Hayyim Vital. Luria soon acquired the status of a great spiritual teacher and master – one in possession of "Holy Spirit". He taught the Kabbalah orally to his disciples and instructed them in the **kavvanah** – meditation and prayer techniques based on the **sephiroth**. Luria left no major writings, but it is known that he believed in the mystical concept that God's "self-limitation" gave rise to light and made the creation of the finite universe possible. This light flowed from God and in due course would return to him. Luria believed, however, that some of the light became diffused, giving rise to the "evil" of the lower worlds.

**Lycanthropy** From the Greek *lukos*, "wolf", and *anthropos*, "man", the belief among practitioners of **witchcraft** and **sorcery** that a human being may transform into a wolf. In Europe the wolf was traditionally regarded as the most ferocious animal, and in this regard the sorcerer capable of such transformation personified bestial power and terror – hence the many legends of the **werewolf**. The term is also used generally to describe the magical act of changing into any wild animal, for example a hyena or tiger, and there are examples of "leopard men" in Africa and "jackal men" in the Congo. Some legends relating to lycanthropy may have their origin in the psychedelic experience, since it is now considered that hallucinatory **witchcraft** potions are responsible for the legend of witches travelling through the air to the **witches' sabbath**, riding on their broomsticks. Many shamans – some of whom use psychedelic sacraments – similarly believe themselves capable of self-transformation, and assume the form of a **power animal**. See also **Hallucination**; **Shamanism**.

**Lyon-Poisson** A heraldic monster, half lion and half fish.

# M

**Ma'aseh B'reshith** In the Kabbalah, secrets regarding the process of creation subject to divine will. From the Hebrew for "work of creation".

**Ma'aseh Merkabah** In the Kabbalah, a general term for esoteric speculations. More specifically it refers to secrets relating to the Tree of Life as the divine throne-chariot or Merkabah.

**Maat** In ancient Egyptian mythology, the goddess of truth, whose symbol was a feather. In the Judgment Hall of Osiris, the heart of the deceased was weighed in the scales against a feather, and the person's fate decided accordingly. Those who were judged to be *maa kheru* ("true of voice") were allowed to enter the Underworld, the kingdom of Osiris or the Elysian Fields.

**Maban** Among the Aborigines of South and Western Australia, a "life-giving" shell that is placed in the ears to enable a person to hear and speak to the spirits.

**Mabinogion, The** A collection of eleven old Welsh mythological tales translated and compiled by Lady Charlotte Guest and first published in 1838. The collection, which is divided into four parts or "branches", is the chief source of the stories of such figures as the magicians Math and Gwydion and Gwydion's son, Lleu Llaw Gyffes, and contains some of the earliest Arthurian material. *The Mabinogion* represents a rich source of ancient Celtic mythology, folklore, magic, and daily life.

**Mabon** See Autumn Equinox.

**Mabza** In Enochian magic, the angelic word for a magical robe. It is pronounced *mah-beh-zodah*. See also Robes.

**Macaiyoyo** Among the Zuni Indians, the term for a divining crystal that enables a shaman to see "anything, everywhere". The crystal can be used to find the magical object in the patient's body that is causing sickness or malaise, or to locate the sorcerer who has sent this object to harm the victim. The shaman dips his crystal into a ceremonial medicine bowl known as a **waititcani** and then rubs his eyes with it. See also Spirit Intrusion.

**Machen, Arthur** (1863–1947) A Welsh mystic and author whose novels and short stories often allude to a supernatural, pagan reality beneath the veneer of familiar appearances. Machen was born at Caerleon-on-Usk and developed a profound fondness for the Welsh countryside, which, for him, was imbued with Celtic mystery. In 1880, after his education at Hereford Cathedral School, he went to London and worked for a book publisher and also as a cataloguer and translator. In 1901 he joined Sir Frank Benson's Shakespearean Company and later worked with Sir George Alexander at the St James's Theatre. For a brief period Machen was a member of the Hermetic Order of the Golden Dawn, although he quickly came to prefer mystics to ritual occultists. Machen's most accomplished novel is *The Hill of Dreams* (1900), but many of his short stories, including "The Great Return", "The Happy Children", "A Fragment of Life", and "The White People", are equally impressive. His personal reminiscences, *Far Off Things*, *Things Near and Far*, and *The London Adventure* were published between 1915 and 1923.

**Mackenzie, Kenneth R.H.** (1833–1886) A Freemason, occultist and member of the Societas Rosicruciana in Anglia. Mackenzie claimed that he received initiation into the brotherhood of Austrian Rosicrucians from Count Apponyi, for whom he worked as an English tutor. In 1861 Mackenzie also visited the famous French kabbalist Eliphas Lévi and discussed a broad range of esoteric subjects in depth – an account was published in *The Rosicrucian and Red Cross* journal in May 1873. Mackenzie is thought to have helped Robert Wentworth Little adapt the Scottish grades used as the basis for the **Societas Rosicruciana in Anglia**. Mackenzie joined the Society in 1872 but resigned in 1875 after an argument with Little. In 1877 Mackenzie published the work for which he is best known, the *Royal Masonic Cyclopaedia*. See also **Freemasonry**.

**Maconha** A Brazilian name for *Cannabis indica*, a form of **marijuana** sometimes used in **Macumba** ceremonies.

**Macrocosm and Microcosm** From the Greek *makros kosmos*, "great world", and *mikros kosmos*, "little world", the concept that the world, and in turn every human being, are copies in miniature of God's universe. This view was advocated by the theologian **Origen** and taken up by such Renaissance occultists as **Paracelsus** and **Heinrich Cornelius Agrippa**. Similarly, in the medieval **Kabbalah**, the primordial or archetypal man, **Adam Kadmon**, is regarded as reflecting the image of God the father, and thereby provides the necessary link between humankind and the creator of the universe. See also **Hermetic Axiom**.

**Macroprosopus** In the **Kabbalah**, the so-called Greater Countenance of God, which symbolizes the harmony in the universe following the act of creation. The Greater Countenance is forever concealed, while the Lesser Countenance, or manifested God, reveals himself through the sacred name of the **Tetragrammaton**.

**Macumba** A form of magical religion and spirit worship practised in Brazil. Related to Haitian **voodoo**, Macumba is an umbrella term for a variety of practices which are by no means identical. It encompasses African animism and the worship of Yoruba deities; blends spiritism with folk-belief; and also takes in elements of Christianity, correlating Christian saints with African deities. The African slaves who were taken to Brazil in the sixteenth century chose to follow their indigenous spiritual traditions in secret rather than accede to Roman Catholicism and in doing so, they transformed the worship of their African deities, or orìsàs, into the veneration of Catholic saints in order to avoid persecution. In this way **Oxalá** came to be identified with Jesus Christ, **Iemanjá** with the Virgin Mary, and **Oxum** with St Catherine, to give just three examples.

Some of the terms associated with Macumba include **Quimbanda**, **Umbanda**, and **Candomblé**, and these must be distinguished from each other, although there are points where the traditions overlap. Quimbanda is generally associated with black magic and the worship of the dark trickster god **Exú** and his evil surrogates – entities like Exú Manqueira, Exú Brasa, Exú Pagao, and Poma-Cira. Umbanda, by way of contrast with Quimbanda, refers specifically to a form of white magic influenced by the French spiritualist **Allen Kardec** but nevertheless containing many Yoruba elements, correlating African deities with Christian saints. **Ogun** is associated with St George, **Oxóssi** with St Sebastian, **Omulu** with St Lazarus, and **Xangô** with St James. Most practitioners of Umbanda insist on avoiding the Exús altogether, although some call on them to protect their temples.

Finally, Candomblé refers to ceremonies in the Yoruba tradition which focus on healing the spirit – this takes place when the devotee fuses his or her awareness with an orìsà during initiation. Candomblé ceremonies date back to 1830 and the city of Salvador, the former capital of Brazil and now the capital of the state of Bahia. Umbanda, on the other hand, is more recent and dates back only to 1904.

**Macumbeiro** A believer in, or devotee of, **Macumba**.

**Maddalena** A Tuscan-born witch who met American folklorist **Charles Godfrey Leland** in Italy in 1886. Leland described her as a hereditary witch and learned various **Craft** secrets from her, including a number of spells and incantations. It was from Maddalena that he learnt about **Aradia**, the goddess of the witches. See **Leland, Charles Godfrey**.

**Madimi** In Enochian magic, a female angel who appears during the call of the seventeenth **Aethyr, Tan**. The Elizabethan magician **Dr John Dee** who, with **Edward Kelley**, first transcribed the angelic Enochian alphabet, named one of his daughters after her.

**Mae de Santo** In Macumba, a high priestess and head of a **terreiro**, or temple. She is known as the "Mother of the Gods".

**Maenads** Also known as **Bacchantes**, the female devotees of Dionysus, who roused themselves into a great frenzy and celebrated with ecstatic dance and song, killing live animals and devouring their flesh.

**Maestro** In South American shamanism and folk healing, a term of respect used to address an **ayahuasquero**.

**Magen David** The "Star of David" in Judaism. Also known as the "Jewish Star", it is a **hexagram** made up of two intersecting triangles which, in the **Kabbalah**, symbolize the interrelatedness of matter and spirit. See also **Seal of Solomon**.

**Maggid** In Jewish mysticism, a spiritual entity that communicates through an adept while the latter is in a state of trance. The term is also used to describe a person of high spiritual attainment.

**Magi** The legendary "wise men" of the East, from whom the term **magic** is derived. In ancient Persia, the Magi (singular, Magus, in Greek Magoi, singular Magos) were a priestly caste, and were one of the six tribes of Medes –

a powerful ancient Iranian people – described by Herodotus. Responsible for royal sacrifices, funeral rites, the interpretation of dreams, and divining the future by the stars, the Magi were regarded with great awe. Their beliefs intermingled with the doctrines of **Zoroastrianism** and may actually have preceded it. In due course the Magi penetrated into the Greek world and India, and possibly also China. They feature in the New Testament narrative as the "three wise men" or "kings" – to whom later legend gave the names Caspar, Melchior, and Balthasar – who brought gold, frankincense, and myrrh as gifts for the baby Jesus. The term magus at this time had also begun to acquire the more general sense of a magician or sorceror. See **Simon Magus**.

**Magic** The overarching name given to the body of techniques and ritual practices used to harness the secret powers of nature and to influence events for one's own purpose. If the purpose is beneficial it is known as white magic, but if it is intended to bring harm to others, or to destroy property, it is regarded as black magic. Magicians employ a variety of ritual procedures. Sometimes, as in imitative magic, they seek to imitate the desired end result by using models of real people or objects, or by dressing in ceremonial regalia in order to identify symbolically with a particular deity. In certain black magic procedures, it is believed that harm can be inflicted upon a person by burning a wax doll or sticking pins into it, as if it were the real person. Sometimes "positive" effects are sought by similar procedures: *The Magus* – a classical textbook of magic written by Francis Barrett – includes a "scapegoat" ritual for transferring illness and pain from a sick woman to an unsuspecting frog: "Take the eyes of a frog, which must be extricated before sunrise, and bind them to the breasts of a woman who be ill. Then let the frog go blind into the water again and as he goes so will the woman be rid of her pains." Here, removing the eyes of the frog confirms the magician's mastery over the animal, which can no longer jump to freedom. The woman's breasts, with their life-giving milk, represent health, and the casting of the frog into water is a ritual act of cleansing. Taken overall, the frog literally carries the disease away.

Modern western magic, especially as practised in groups that follow the tradition established by the **Hermetic Order of the Golden Dawn**, has as its main function the self-initiation of its members into grades of visionary awareness associated with the spheres of consciousness on the kabbalistic **Tree of Life**, and must be regarded primarily as a form of white magic. However, there have been cases of alleged magical attack and ritual practices that summon bestial or demonic forces, which clearly are more related to black magic. White magicians seek to activate the spiritual **archetypes** in the unconscious mind by identifying with such life-sustaining deities as **Osiris, Thoth, Apollo, Ra**, and **Horus** (male); and **Isis, Hathor, Aphrodite, Demeter**, and **Persephone** (female). Black magicians, their intent generally being to harm others through **sorcery** and malevolent spells, focus more on archetypes associated with bestiality, degradation, aggression, and violence. See also **Magic, Black; Magic, Imitative; Magic, White; Magick**; and other entries below.

**Magical Ally** See **Familiar; Power Animal**

**Magical Almadel** A term used to describe the magical mirror used by occultists for **skrying** in the spirit vision.

**Magical Attack** The alleged ability of magicians to harm one another, especially by adopting hostile **thought-forms** on the **astral plane**. Magical attack does not take place on a physical level, but depends on the assumption that all living beings share a common and universal life force that can be summoned, guided, and directed by visualization and ritual procedures. There are two celebrated cases of magical attack in recent occult history. The first involved the conflict between two occult groups in the late nineteenth century in France, one headed by **Stanislaus de Guaita** and **Sar Peladan** and the other by **Joseph-Antoine Boullan** – for details see separate entries. The second involved **Dion Fortune**, who, at the time of the incident in 1922, had recently established the **Fraternity of the Inner Light** and was drawing members away from the **Hermetic Order of the Golden Dawn** (specifically from the Alpha and Omega Temple headed by Mrs **Moina Mathers**). Dion Fortune believed that Mrs Mathers (Soror Vestigia) launched a magical attack against her as a result of this rivalry. During the episode, which is described in Dion Fortune's book *Psychic Self Defence*, she was subjected to a vision of a huge cat, "twice the size of a tiger. It appeared absolutely solid and tangible. I stared at it, petrified for a second, and then it vanished. I instantly realized that it was a simulacrum, or thought-form, that was being projected by someone with occult powers." Soon afterwards, Soror Vestigia began to appear to Dion Fortune in her dreams, and a nightmare attack followed in which she was "whirled through the air". Dion Fortune summoned the **inner chiefs** to protect her, and the vision ceased; but when she awoke she discovered that "from neck to waist I was scored with scratches as if I had been clawed by a gigantic cat".

**Magical Child** In the Thelemic cosmology of ceremonial magician Aleister Crowley, a reference to Harpocrates, a name given by the ancient Greeks to the Egyptian deity Horus, son of Isis and Osiris. Harpocrates was the god of silence and was depicted holding his finger to his mouth. In Thelemic cosmology Harpocrates is identified with Hoor-paar-Kraat and the mysterious entity Aiwaz, who dictated *The Book of the Law* in 1904, identifying Crowley as Lord of the New Aeon. **Hoor-paar-Kraat** is also the twin of **Ra-Hoor-Khuit**, with whom Crowley personally identified. See also **Aeon of Horus; Law of Thelema.**

**Magical Correspondences** In modern western **magic**, a system for comparing the gods and goddesses of different pantheons in terms of their symbolic roles and attributes. In 1909, a list of correspondences developed by **MacGregor Mathers** and later supplemented by **Aleister Crowley** was published under the title *777* (it is also included in *The Qabalah of Aleister Crowley*, New York, 1973). Using the kabbalistic **Tree of Life** as a matrix, for example, it becomes possible to compare mother goddesses (**Demeter, Hathor, Sophia, Rhea**); warrior gods (**Mars, Horus**); solar gods/rebirth deities (**Apollo, Ra, Osiris**); and lunar goddesses (**Isis, Ishtar, Artemis, Hecate, Selene, Luna,** and **Diana**); as well as the precious stones, perfumes, sacred plants, and animals ascribed to them. See also **Archetypes; Kabbalah.**

**Magical Current** In magic, a visionary source of wisdom, knowledge, and inspiration. Some magicians have regarded supernatural entities and powers as their source of magical authority. The ceremonial magician **Aleister Crowley** regarded the mysterious Egyptian entity **Aiwaz** – the source of his magical revelation in Cairo in 1904 – as his "guardian angel". The magical number of Aiwaz is 93, and followers of Crowley, who refer to themselves as Thelemites, refer to the magical current stemming from Aiwaz as the "93 Current". See also **Aeon of Horus; Current 93; Thelema.**

**Magical Formulae** Conjurations, invocations, spells, or magical prayers, regarded by ceremonial magicians as powerful and effective for a given ritual purpose. One of the best sources for the formulae of western magic is **Israel Regardie**'s four-volume work *The Golden Dawn*. Another is A.E. **Waite**'s *Book of Ceremonial Magic*. See also **Goetia;**

**Hermetic Order of the Golden Dawn; Magic, Ceremonial.**

**Magical Name** A special name taken by a ritual magician to confirm membership in a particular magical order or to reflect newly won status following an initiation. The following are the magical names of some well-known occult figures who belonged to the **Hermetic Order of the Golden Dawn: Arthur Edward Waite** (Sacramentum Regis); **William Butler Yeats** (Daemon Est Deus Inversus); **Arthur Machen** (Avallaunius); **MacGregor Mathers** (Deo Duce Comite Ferro); **Aleister Crowley** (Perdurabo), and Violet Firth (Deo Non Fortuna). The last of these explains the origin of Violet Firth's pen-name, **Dion Fortune,** by which she is much better known.

**Magical Numbers** In magical cosmology, certain gods have been ascribed numerical values. The Gnostic deity **Abraxas** was regarded by Basilides and his followers as a personification of time; and in both Greek and Hebrew gematria the letters of his name added to 365, the number of days in a year (in Greek: alpha 1, beta 2, rho 100, alpha 1, Xi 60, Alpha 1, Sigma 200 = 365; in Hebrew: aleph 1, beth 2, resh 200, aleph 1, qoph 100, aleph 1, samekh 60 = 365). In *The Book of Revelation*, the number of the Great Beast, or Anti-Christ, was 666; and it was this name and number that the magician **Aleister Crowley** identified with after assuming the role of Lord of the New Aeon in 1904. See also **Great Beast 666.**

**Magical Perfumes** In Wicca and ceremonial magic, essential oils, resins and gums whose fragrances and odours are associated with different ritual and mythic activities and also with the planetary signs and sun signs of the zodiac. Essential oils are derived from flowers, fruits, herbs, seeds, roots, beans, pods, twigs, bark, moss, and lichens. Examples include jasmine, neroli, narcissus, rose, violet, and ylang-ylang (derived from flowering plants and trees); eucalyptus, patchouli, and **tobacco** (derived from leaves); aloe, **birch**, camphor, **cedar**, sandalwood, and sassafras (derived from wood); cinnamon (derived from bark); bergamot, citron, lemon, and tangerine (derived from fruits); lemongrass and citronella (derived from grasses); clove and juniper (derived from berries); and basil, **chamomile**, dill, lavender, thyme, verbena, and wormwood (derived from herbs). Magical odours are also derived from gums and resins – examples include **benzoin**, galbanum, mastic, **myrrh**, storax, and olibanum (also known as frankincense) – and from animal sources (ambergris, civet, and musk). See also the following two entries.

**Magical Perfumes and Astrology** The French ceremonial magician Eliphas Lévi (1810–1875) correlated the traditional astrological planets with the following perfumes: Sun: olibanum (frankincense), saffron, red sandalwood; Moon: white sandalwood, camphor, amber, aloe; Mars: no perfume specified; Mercury: benzoin, mace, storax; Jupiter: ambergris, saffron; Venus: rose, myrtle; Saturn: alum, sulphur. Later, the English witch Sybil Leek (1923–1983) suggested the following correlations between magical perfumes and the signs of the zodiac: Aries: cedar, pine, cypress, attar of roses; Taurus: musk, rose, carnation, honeysuckle, violet, saffron, and satinwood: Gemini: bayberry, mastic, sandalwood; Cancer: aloe, bay leaves, camphor, cedar, myrtle, cinnamon, sandalwood, poppy; Leo: red sandalwood, olibanum, camphor, cassia, clove; Virgo: bayberry, cinnamon, citron peel, mace; Libra: jasmine, musk, rose, violet, satinwood, sandalwood; Scorpio: pine, yucca, rosemary, cypress, briar rose, dogwood; Sagittarius: nutmeg, saffron, clove; Capricorn: olibanum, khus khus; Aquarius: olibanum, pine, pepperwort; Pisces: clove, nutmeg.

**Magical Perfumes and the Kabbalah** The magical correspondences listed in Aleister Crowley's *Liber 777* – itself sub-

stantially derived from **MacGregor Mathers'** work in the **Hermetic Order of the Golden Dawn** – allocate the following magical perfumes to the sephiroth on the kabbalistic **Tree of Life**: Kether: ambergris; **Chokmah**: musk; Binah: myrrh, civet; **Chesed**: cedar; Geburah: tobacco; Tiphareth: olibanum (frankincense); Netzach: benzoin, rose, red sandalwood; Hod: storax; Yesod: jasmine, ginseng; Malkuth: dittany of Crete. More recently the American authors Richard Allan Miller and Iona Miller, who specialize in the magical use of perfumes, have suggested the following additions to this list: Binah: madonna lily; Chesed: oakmoss; Geburah: leather; Tiphareth: angelica; Hod: amber, spikenard; Yesod: orris; Malkuth: poppy, patchouli.

**Magical Reality** In shamanism, the magical dimension that becomes experientially real to the shaman or trance visionary while in an altered state of consciousness. The shaman may enter the magical reality by journeying to the upper or lower worlds through the Tree of Life, or by consuming a hallucinogenic sacrament which then opens a path to the spirit world. Drumming and chanting are also powerful techniques for entering this state.

**Magical Snuffs** In South American shamanism and natural healing, plant-based snuffs are used to induce a visionary state of awareness. Such states are used by practitioners of natural medicine to diagnose the source of illness or by shamans to contact their spirit guides. Various plants are used to prepare magical snuffs, including angel's trumpet, ayahuasca, coca, and tobacco. It is the tryptamine content of magical snuffs that makes them effective.

**Magical Stones** Stones that have magical and mythic associations, usually because of their colour. In Wicca, specific stones are assigned symbolically to different ritual sabbats through the cycle of the Wheel of the Year. In the practice of ceremonial magic, certain stones are also correlated under the system of **magical correspondences** with the **sephiroth** on the kabbalistic Tree of Life. Magical stones with symbolic associations in either Wicca or western kabbalistic magic include **amethyst, diamond, emerald, jade, jet, moonstone, obsidian, onyx, pearl, quartz crystal, ruby, star sapphire, topaz,** and **turquoise** as well as the various **bloodstones.** See also **Magic, Ceremonial; Sabbats, Greater** and **Sabbats, Lesser;**

**Magic, Black** Magic performed with evil intent. Traditionally the black magician, or **sorcerer,** calls upon the supernatural powers of darkness – devils, demons, and evil spirits – and performs ceremonies invoking bestial or malevolent forces intended to harm another person. Black magic invariably involves imitative magic, in which there is said to be a link between a person or an object and something, such as a wax figurine or doll, resembling it. Injuries ritually inflicted upon the figurine with pins or nails are intended to have a harmful effect upon the person represented. Some magicians claim that the technique is only effective when the sorcerer has enough willpower to use the ritual figure as a focus for inflicting negative **thought-forms** on the person under attack. See also **Grimoires; Magic, Image; Magic, Imitative; Spell; Talisman.**

**Magic, Candle** In Wicca, the use of different coloured candles in spells and rituals. *White* candles symbolize spirituality, peace and purification; *red* – strength, energy, courage, and sexual passion; *pink* – love, tenderness, and romantic affection; *orange* – health, ambition, and matters pertaining to the law; *yellow* – intellect, memory, and the mind; *green* – harmony, abundance, good fortune, and fertility; *blue* – inspiration, wisdom, and devotion; *purple* – heightened psychic and spiritual awareness; *silver* – intuition and psychic inspiration; *gold* – wealth, abundance, and prosperity; *brown* –special favours

and an end to sorrow; and *black* – old age and wisdom.

**Magic, Celestial** The belief that the planets are ruled by spirits that in turn influence human beings. For example, in kabbalistic magic, the planets are ruled by the following **archangels:** Tzaphkiel (**Saturn**); Tzadkiel (**Jupiter**); Kamael (**Mars**); Raphael (**sun**); Haniel (**Venus**); Michael (**Mercury**); Gabriel (**moon**); Sandalphon (**earth**).

**Magic, Ceremonial** Magic that employs rituals, symbols, and ceremony as a means of representing the supernatural and mystical forces linking the universe and humanity. Ceremonial magic stimulates the senses – sight, hearing, smell, taste, and touch – by including in its rituals ceremonial costume, dramatic invocations to the gods or spirits, potent incense, and mystic sacraments. The aim of ceremonial magic in its "highest" sense is a transcendental experience, transporting the magician beyond the limitations of the mind towards mystical reality. However, as a term, it is also associated with medieval magical grimoires, which describe procedures for summoning spirits. These books, which are designed to confer power rather than transcendence on the magician, include *The Key of Solomon,* the *Grimoire of Honorius,* and the *Grand Grimoire.* In modern times the most extensive system of ceremonial magic has been the body of rituals formulated and practised in the **Hermetic Order of the Golden Dawn** and its offshoots. See also **Grimoire.**

**Magic, Chaos** A contemporary branch of magic which draws on the cosmology of **Austin Osman Spare** and his use of magical sigils to focus the magical will. Chaos magic has been described as "success magic" or "results-based magic" and grew out of a concern among some within the magical fraternity who believed that magic had drifted too closely towards meditation and celebration and away from specific results.

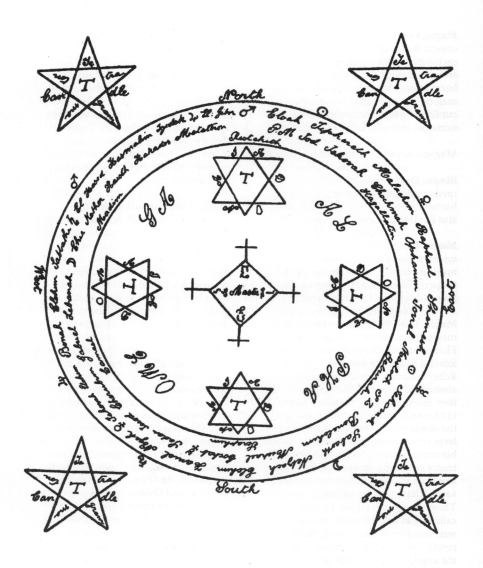

**MAGIC CIRCLE** The magic circle defines the 'sacred space' used in rites of ceremonial invocation.

Leading figures associated with Chaos magic include Peter J. Carroll, author of *Liber Null* and *Psychonaut*, Frater U.D., author of *Practical Sigil Magic* and Ray Sherwin, author of *The Book of Results*. See also **Sigil (2)**.

**Magic Circle** A circle inscribed on the floor of a temple for magical ceremonial purposes. It is "activated", or rendered sacred, through various ritual procedures.

**Magic, Contagious** The belief that objects that have been in contact with each other retain a link when separated, and that this link can be used to inflict harm magically – for example, by a magical rite performed over a person's cut fingernails, hair clippings, or possessions. See also **Magic, Sympathetic**.

**Magic, Cord** See Cords, Ritual.

**Magic, Defensive** Magical rituals and spells used to defend oneself from harmful **sorcery** or evil influences. See also **Banishing Ritual**.

**Magic, Destructive** Virtually synonymous with black magic, any magical act intended to destroy people, property, or crops, or to affect people's lives in a harmful way. See **Magic, Black**.

**Magic, Enochian** A system of angelic magic derived from the work of the Elizabethan occultists **Dr John Dee** and **Edward Kelley**, who met in 1581. Dee and Kelley made use of wax tablets called **almadels** engraved with magical symbols; they also used a large number of 49-inch (122.5cm) squares filled with letters of the alphabet. On his table, Kelley had a large crystal stone upon which he focused his concentration and entered a state of trance reverie. In due course, "angels" would appear, and they would point to various letters on the squares in turn. These were written down by Dee as Kelley called them out. When these invocations were completely transcribed, Kelley then reversed their order, for he believed that the angels communicated them backwards to avoid unleashing the magical power which they contained. Dee and Kelley considered that the communications formed the basis of a new language, which they termed "Enochian". These magical conjurations were later incorporated into magical practice by the ritual magicians of the **Hermetic Order of the Golden Dawn**, who used them to evoke specific angelic spirits and to induce trance visions on the **astral plane**. See also **Aethyr**; **Pathworkings**.

**Magic Herb** Any herb believed to possess magical properties. Several hallucinogenic herbs, including **deadly nightshade, mandrake, henbane**, and **thornapple**, have been used by witches in their **flying ointments**, and other herbs are used magically as sexual stimulants (damiana, yohimbe) or to induce vivid dreams (wild lettuce).

**Magic, High** Magic intended to bring about the spiritual transformation of the person who practises it. This form of magic is designed to channel the magician's consciousness towards the sacred light within, which is often personified by the high gods of different cosmologies. The aim of high magic has been described as communication with one's **holy guardian angel**, or higher self. It is also known as **theurgy**.

**Magician** One skilled in the arts of magic. The term is generally applied to ceremonial or ritual magicians who invoke deities or evoke spirits; make use of such symbolic regalia as cloaks, swords, cups, daggers, and wands; and claim special powers and supernatural insight. The word is also used by non-occultists as a synonym for one skilled in conjuring, although strictly speaking this is "stage magic" and has nothing to do with ceremonial workings or the magical states of consciousness stimulated by ritual. See also **Magic, Ceremonial**.

**Magician, The** See **Magus, The**.

**Magic, Image** The use of a magical image – a doll made of wax, clay, and so on – in magical spells. In black magic harm may be inflicted upon a victim by forming the magical image and then pricking it with pins, breaking its limbs off, or consigning it to a fire. This practice is thought to originate in ancient Mesopotamia. See also **Magic, Black**; **Magic, Imitative**.

**Magic, Imitative** A form of magical practice in which the anticipated or desired outcome is mimicked, or imitated, in ritual. The most common form is through image magic, in which an image of a real person may be subjected to hostile acts (pins, burning, and so on) in the hope that real injury and misfortune will befall the victim. The technique can also be applied to mental images. For example, a phobia could be visualized as a hostile creature (e.g. a spider, snake, or dragon) and "shrunk" in the imagination in the hope that the symptoms of fear would disappear with it. This technique is used in some forms of psychotherapy that involve techniques of "active imagination". For example, in guided-imagery techniques used in cancer treatment, the patient may be asked to visualize the cancerous growth as a "dragon" that is gradually overcome by the patient in the form of a "knight in armour". These treatments are often remarkably successful. The practice of "assuming the god-form" – identifying with the form and essence of a deity – is another type of imitative magic. See also **God-Form; Magic, Black; Magic, Image**.

**Magick** The archaic spelling of magic preferred by **Aleister Crowley**. Crowley defined magick as "the science and art of causing change to occur in conformity with Will" (*Magick in Theory and Practice*, 1929). See also **Will**.

**Magic Letter Square** A square arranged so that the letters of the words may be read in either direction, both vertically and horizontally. Such squares are believed to have magical properties and may form the basis of an incantation. The most famous example is the so-called "Sator" square:

```
S A T O R
A R E P O
T E N E T
O P E R A
R O T A S
```

This was interpreted by **MacGregor Mathers**, a leading figure in the **Hermetic Order of the Golden Dawn**, to mean, in Latin, "The creator (*sator*), slow-moving (*arepo*), maintains (*tenet*)

his creations (*opera*) as vortices (*rotas*)," although this is only one of several possible meanings. See also **Abracadabra**.

**Magic, Low** Magic intended to produce a utilitarian, material, or domestic effect. Examples would include attracting an influx of sudden wealth, a new lover, a change of occupation, or a resurgence of good fortune. Compare **Magic, High**; and see also **Magic, Chaos**.

**Magic Mirror** A mirror used for mystical or divinatory purposes, to foresee the future, to reveal secrets, or as a meditative aid allowing the magical practitioner to enter a state of trance. The Elizabethan astrologer and magician **Dr John Dee** had a polished black obsidian mirror that was used to contact angelic spirits. This mirror had been brought back from Mexico by the Spanish conqueror Hernando Cortés. It is also said that in ancient Greece, the witches of Thessaly showed **Pythagoras** how to divine the future by holding a magic mirror up to the moon.

**Magic, Mortuary** Magical rites and ceremonies performed in order to ensure that the deceased person will have an enjoyable life in the world beyond death. Mortuary magic was highly developed in ancient Egypt.

**Magic Mushrooms** See Psilocybe Mushrooms.

**Magic, Natural** Magical spells, enchantments, and conjurations believed to have an effect on nature (e.g. bringing much needed rain or thunderstorms, affecting the wind or other aspects of the weather, contacting nature-spirits, or influencing cycles of fertility). **Shamans** perform this function in tribal and aboriginal societies around the world.

**Magic Number Square** A square arranged so that the numbers in each row of the square have the same total when added in any direction. In ritual magic, the number square appropriate to each

planet is known as its **kamea**.
The following are examples:

| 4 | 9 | 2 |
|---|---|---|
| 3 | 5 | 7 |
| 8 | 1 | 6 |

Saturn

| 4 | 14 | 15 | 1 |
|---|----|----|---|
| 9 | 7 | 6 | 12 |
| 5 | 11 | 10 | 8 |
| 16 | 2 | 3 | 13 |

Jupiter

| 11 | 24 | 7 | 20 | 3 |
|----|----|---|----|---|
| 4 | 12 | 25 | 8 | 16 |
| 17 | 5 | 13 | 21 | 9 |
| 10 | 18 | 1 | 14 | 22 |
| 23 | 6 | 19 | 2 | 15 |

Mars

Magic number squares are an important feature in the medieval **grimoire** *The Sacred Magic of Abra-Melin the Mage*, the squares being regarded as sources of magical power. See also **Abraham the Jew**.

**Magic, Protective** Spells, rituals, and enchantments designed to counter the evil effects of black magic. See also **Amulet; Charm; Magic, Black; Spell**.

**Magic, Results** See **Magic, Chaos**.

**Magic Rings** In myth, folklore, and legend, magic rings are portrayed as **amulets** of power and protection. They are sometimes said to render their owners invisible, they can be blessed in order to produce a state of personal good health and wellbeing, and they can also be inscribed with magical **names of power**. It is said that King **Solomon** had a magic ring etched with a **hexagram** and the sacred name of God, and that this enabled him to conjure **genies**, or spirit helpers. According to the **Qur'an**, genies helped Solomon erect his magnificent temple.

**Magic Seal** A magical motif produced by drawing the kamea or **magic number square** of a planet and then connecting the numbers in the square by a sequence of lines. The following diagrams are the kamea and seal for the planet Saturn;

*kamea*

*seal*

**Magic, Sexual** Magical rituals and ceremonies that involve the sacred energies associated with sexual polarity, and which usually involve sexual acts that simulate the procreative union of the gods and goddesses. See also **Crowley, Aleister; Great Rite; Neuburg, Victor; Ordo Templi Orientis; Tantra**.

**Magic Square** A square arranged to include words or numbers in such a way that the words may be read horizontally or vertically in both directions (a **magic letter square**), and the numbers have the same total when added in any direction (a **magic number square**).

**Magic, Success** See **Magic, Chaos**.

**Magic, Sympathetic** An expression coined by the anthropologist Sir James Frazer (1854–1941), author of a famous work on magical philosophy, *The Golden Bough*. For Frazer, the concept of "like affecting like" – a principle often found in magical ceremonies – owed its meaning to the concept of a magical "sympathy" between two objects, or beings, separated by distance. The act of mimicry through ritual served to produce a cause-and-effect relationship, thus making magical acts apparently "effective". See also **Magic, Contagious**.

**Magic, White** Magic performed for a spiritual, healing, or generally positive purpose, as distinct from black magic, which is performed for self-gain, to inflict harm or injury, or for other evil purposes. See also **Magic, Black; Theurgy**.

**Magisterium** or **Magistery** In alchemy, a term used for any potent medicine but also applied to the entire alchemical process – the **opus alchymicum**.

**Magister Templi** Latin for "Master of the Temple." In the system of modern western **magic** developed by members of the **Hermetic Order of the Golden Dawn**, the third highest ritual grade attainable on the kabbalistic **Tree of Life**.

It equates with the sphere of Binah and is represented symbolically as 8° = 3°. See also Ipsissimus; Magus (2).

**Magna Mater** Latin for "Great Mother", a term used in ancient Rome to describe the Mother Goddess, especially with reference to Rhea and Cybele.

**Magnum Opus** Latin for "Great Work", a term used in alchemy to refer to the task of transmuting base elements into gold and, by extension, to the process of achieving spiritual rebirth. It is therefore a synonym for illumination.

**Magoi** See Magi.

**Magus** (1) See Magi.

**Magus** (2) In the system of modern western magic developed by members of the Hermetic Order of the Golden Dawn, the second highest ritual grade attainable on the kabbalistic Tree of Life. The grade of Magus equates with the sphere Chokmah and is represented symbolically as 9° = 2°. See also Ipsissimus; Magister Templi.

**Magus, The** (1) In the Tarot, the card of the Major Arcana which symbolizes the virginal, or "pure", male energy in the cosmos, and which is the direct counterpart of *The High Priestess* – the virgin goddess. *The Magus* represents the path from Binah to Kether on the kabbalistic Tree of Life. Residing above the Abyss on the Tree, the path of *The Magus* (also called *The Magician*) stands above the realm of manifest creation in an archetypal sense. The magician raises one hand aloft to draw down the creative energies of Kether, which may then be transmitted further down the Tree. Designs in some of the various Tarot packs show the magician standing in a paradise-garden, again symbolic of purity. *The Magus* is linked mythically to Thoth in his capacity as the Logos of the universe and is a higher form of Hermes/Mercury associated mythologically with Hod, lower down the Tree.

**Magus, The** (2) The title of an occult work on kabbalistic magic, numerology, alchemy, and magical stones written by Francis Barrett and published in London in 1801. It included illustrations of such devils as Theulus and Asmodeus, and has been reissued in several facsimile editions.

**Maid** In Wicca, the first of the threefold aspects of the Great Goddess. The Maid represents youth and enchantment. The two other aspects of the Great Goddess venerated in Wicca are the Mother (representing maturity and fulfilment) and the Crone (representing old age and wisdom). These phases of womanhood are particularly important in the "women's mysteries" of feminist Wicca groups.

**Maiden of the Coven** In Wicca, the high priestess or assistant high priestess of the coven.

**Maier, Michael** (1568–1622) A German alchemist and philosopher, born in Rendsberg, Holstein. He became a successful physician and served Rudolf II in Prague, who subsequently ennobled him. He later turned his attention to alchemy and travelled widely in Germany and other parts of Europe seeking adepts skilled in the spagyric art. A Lutheran who also claimed to be a member of the Rosicrucian fraternity, Maier interpreted the Christian eucharist as a type of alchemical transformation. He was also inclined to interpret the ancient fables of the Greek gods and heroes as allegories of the alchemical quest and presented his views in a work titled *Arcana Arcanissima (The Secret of Secrets)* published in 1614. His *Subtle Allegory concerning the Secrets of Alchemy* is included in the *Hermetic Museum*, together with another work titled *The Golden Tripod*.

**Ma-Ion** According to the magical cosmology of Frater Achad, the so-called "Aeon of the Daughter", which he regarded as a counterbalance to Aleister Crowley's Aeon of Horus. Achad maintained that the Aeon of the Daughter commenced on 2 April 1948 at 1.11 p.m. and marked the true beginning of the **Aquarian Age.**

**Major Arcana** In the Tarot, the 22 "mythological" cards, or trumps, which are assigned by occultists to paths on the kabbalistic **Tree of Life.** In sequence from **Malkuth** at the foot of the Tree to Kether at the crown, they are: *The World, Judgment, The Moon, The Sun, The Star, The Tower, The Devil, Death, Temperance, The Hermit, Justice, The Hanged Man, The Wheel of Fortune, Strength, The Charioteer, The Lovers, The Hierophant, The Emperor, The Empress, The High Priestess, The Magus,* and *The Fool.* For their symbolic ascriptions, see individual listings.

**Mala Carmina** Literally "evil songs". In ancient Rome, harmful **spells** or **curses** directed against one's enemies. See also Carmen.

**Malaphar** See Valefor.

**Male Principle** See Masculine Principle.

**Malefics** In astrology, planets said to cause a negative or harmful influence – especially **Mars** and **Saturn.**

**Malkuth** The tenth emanation or sephirah on the kabbalistic **Tree of Life.** In western **magic,** Malkuth is associated with goddesses of the earth, especially **Persephone** (Greece), **Proserpina** (Rome), and **Geb** (Egypt). Malkuth is the domain of the manifested universe – the immediate environment, the plane of physical reality. As a consequence, all "inner journeys of consciousness" begin symbolically in Malkuth. It is particularly appropriate, for example, that the myth of the rape of Persephone confirms her both as queen of the **Underworld** and as a **lunar goddess.** From an occult point of view, the Underworld equates with the unconscious mind, and the moon, represented by the sphere of

**Yesod,** is the first sephirah reached on the mystic inner journey up the Tree of Life. Malkuth is closely linked to the Tarot card *The World.*

***Malleus Maleficarum*** A famous medieval book on **witchcraft** whose title translates as *The Hammer of the Witches.* First published in 1486, the *Malleus* was written by two Inquisitors, **Heinrich Kramer** and **Jacob Sprenger,** and includes details of the spells and enchantments of witches as well as a section on the torture of witches which is so horrific that it is abbreviated in most modern editions. The most common edition of the *Malleus* in English is that translated by **Montague Summers,** which first appeared as a limited edition in 1928 and has since been reprinted many times.

**Malpas** In the **Goetia,** the 39th spirit, a powerful president who appears in the form of a crow but who will assume a human form on the bidding of the magician. Malpas speaks with a hoarse voice, destroys the hopes and desires of one's enemies, provides "good familiars", and can erect wonderful houses and high towers. Malpas deceives those who offer him sacrifices, although he accepts these offerings willingly. He commands 40 legions of spirits.

**Malthas** See Halpas.

**Mambo** In voodoo, a priestess – the counterpart of the male **houngan.**

**Man** In the Germanic **Elder Futhark,** the **rune** letter representing the number 20. Man (or manu, mannaz ) corresponds to the letter "m" . The word "manu" means "man" – both individually and collectively – and this rune draws on perceptions relating to kinship and family. While family ties are enormously important, every individual engaged on the path to self-knowledge has to cut these ties if he is to gain further life-experience. For this reason "man" is the rune of human potential and awareness.

**Mandeans** A Palestinian **Gnostic** sect, dating from the first or early second century CE. Their cosmology included a strong emphasis on the duality of light and darkness, and the formation of the universe by creator gods who emanated from the **godhead**. Like many Gnostic sects, the Mandeans regarded the physical world as the antithesis of the spirit and described the **soul**, or spirit of life, as being lost in an alien world. One Mandean tract includes the lines: "My eyes, which were opened from the abode of light, now belong to the body-stump… How I must obey, how endure, how must I quiet my mind! How I must hear of the seven and twelve mysteries, how must I groan! How must my mild Father's Word dwell among the creatures of the dark!" The prophet **Mani** was originally raised in a Mandean community, but sought to reform many of its ideas. Nevertheless, Manicheism and Mandean beliefs share many points in common.

**Mandrake** *Mandragora officinarum*, a plant with magical and supernatural associations. The mandrake is described in *The Book of Genesis* as an ingredient in love potions, and was similarly regarded by the Greek doctor Theophrastus (c. 370–328BCE) as both a soporific and an aphrodisiac. Always regarded as sinister because its roots resemble the form of a human being, it was associated in the Middle Ages with the bodies of executed criminals and was said to grow under the gallows and thrive on the dripping semen of men who had been hanged. It was alleged that when a mandrake was pulled from the ground its root would emit "wild shrieks" and drive anyone who heard these piteous screams insane. Mandrake contains the so-called "deliriant" alkaloids, scopolamine and hyoscyamine, and was an ingredient in medieval witches' ointments, especially those prepared as **love potions** and **flying ointments**.

**Manes** In ancient Rome, the spirits of the dead, who resided in the Under-world. Festivals were held three times a year in their honour, and on these occasions the manes could come back to haunt the world of the living. These spirits were ruled in the **Underworld** by **Mania**, a goddess associated with **Persephone**.

**Mangé** In **voodoo**, a sacrifice or feast. The expression *mangé moun* means to "eat someone", or to kill them by attacking them with evil spirits who "eat" them.

**Mani** (c. 216–c. 276CE). The son of a Babylonian prince of Persian descent, Mani (or Manichaeus) grew up in a **Mandean** community in Mesopotamia where **Gnostic** ideas were common. In c. 228, when he was twelve, he received a revelation from a celestial angel who appeared to him on behalf of "the king of the paradise of light". This angel urged him to forsake the Mandaeans and pursue a new moral quest. Mani was later shown "the mystery of the deep and the high; the mystery of light and darkness". At this stage, he was not required to make a public stand; but in c. 240 the angel advised him that the Lord had now selected him to be an apostle. He travelled to India, where he became interested in Buddhism, and later visited Babylonia and Persia. The Persian king Shapur gave him three audiences and was favourably impressed by Mani's teachings on light and darkness, instructing his local authorities to protect the "new religion". However, Mani later attracted hostility from a Zoroastrian named Karter, who supervised the fire temples, and he was opposed by the **Magi** in general, who were consolidating their place as the dominant religious group in Persia. As Mani's missionary zeal continued, he began to refer to himself increasingly as "an apostle of Jesus Christ", further alienating himself from traditional Persian religion. Meanwhile, Shapur died in 273 and was succeeded by his son Hormizd I, who was favourably disposed to Mani. However, Hormizd died after

**MAJOR ARCANA**  Four cards from the Major Arcana in the Marseilles Tarot deck. Clockwise from the upper left, they are: *The Charioteer*, *The Star*, *Judgment* and *The Hermit*.

only a year and was succeeded by his brother Bahram I (reigned 274–277). Bahram was a supporter of Karter and the Zoroastrian cause, and he asked Mani why revelations should have been given to him as a prophet rather than to himself as king. Mani replied that it was God's will. This answer was not well received and Mani was imprisoned, with heavy chains around his neck and ankles. After a month of fasting, Mani's strength was exhausted and he died.

The doctrine of **Mani** is known as Manicheism. Mani believed in the absolute duality of light and darkness and held that the world had been created by Saklas – the ruler of darkness. Mani maintained that Adam and Eve were the offspring of two demons, Asqalun and Namrael, and that his role as a spiritual leader was to awaken light in humankind in the same way that Ohrmazd-Jesus had done before him. Mani believed that true Gnostic Christianity had disappeared quite early on in the historical process and that the Paraclete, or Spirit of Truth, had called on him to restore it. The orthodox Church Fathers differed from Mani on this point and suppressed his teachings c. 600. The influence of Manicheism continued, however, and was a strong influence on the **Bogomils**, **Cathars**, and other medieval heretical sects. See also **Heresy**.

**Mania** In ancient Rome, the goddess of the dead, sometimes referred to as "Mother of ghosts". She ruled over the lares and the manes in the **Underworld**.

**Manicheism** See Mani.

**Manipura** In Kundalini yoga, the chakra or energy centre located in the region of the solar plexus. The manipura chakra is activated by using an appropriate mantra while meditating on the tattva symbol of fire, *tejas*.

**Manitou** Among the Algonquins and other North American Indians, supernatural **spirits** said to reside everywhere in nature, representing a great source of magical power. **Shamans** and **medicine men** would often contact the manitou in their rituals. Some Indian tribes referred to the Great Manitou as the supreme being.

**Mannaz** See Man.

**Man of High Degree** A term used generally to describe an Australian Aboriginal shaman or medicine man.

**Manqueira, Exú** In Macumba a surrogate of Exú. See Exú.

**Mansions of the Moon** In astrology, the twenty-eight divisions of the moon's journey through the 360-degree cycle of its orbit. Each mansion represents approximately one day's travel of the moon, the cycle commencing at zero degrees Aries (the first house).

**Mantic** From the Greek *mantis*, "a prophet", anything related to prophecy or divination.

**Mantichora** Also, **Manticore**. Mythic beast that took its name from the Persian *mardkhora*, a man-eating tiger. The mantichora had a lion's body and the tail of a scorpion. Its head was human except that it had a triple row of teeth in both its upper and lower jaw. The mantichora could fire the spines in its tail as if they were arrows, and had a fondness for eating children.

**Manu** See Man.

**Mara** An Old English word meaning a female **demon** – especially with reference to elf-women who would appear to men during a **nightmare** or dream. See also **Elves**.

**Marax** see Morax

**Marbas** In the Goetia, the fifth spirit, a great president who appears in the form of a lion but who can also assume human shape. Marbas can cause disease but also cure illness. He can change humans into other forms and is able to provide true information about things hidden or secret. He governs 36 legions of spirits.

**Marble** In alchemy, a symbol for the "white stone" that is able to transmute base metals into pure silver. This stone is created at the alchemical stage known as albedo.

**Märchen** A German folktale, fable or fairytale.

**Marchosias** In the Goetia, the 35th spirit, a powerful marquis who appears in the form of a wolf with the wings of a griffin. He has a serpent's tail, and fire spews from his mouth. At the command of the magician he will assume human form. A strong fighter, he is also truthful and will answer all questions put to him. According to magical tradition, Marchosias expects to return to the "Seventh Throne of King Solomon" after 1,200 years. Marchosias governs 30 legions of spirits.

**Marduk** Originally a deity of fertility and agriculture, Marduk became the Babylonian high god after defeating Tiamat. Marduk was a solar deity and maintained the forces of order in the universe. He was popular in Assyria between the fourteenth and seventh centuries BCE, but was subsequently displaced by the tribal war god, Assur.

**Marijuana** See Hashish; Hemp, Indian.

**Mark, Devil's** See Devil's Mark.

**Marrngit** Among the Murngin Aborigines of Arnhem Land in northern Australia, a medicine man who has powers of healing and psychic dissociation. The Marrngit can read other people's thoughts and "see" what is happening a long way away. He can also locate a sorcerer who has stolen someone else's soul.

**Mars** (1) In Roman mythology, the god of war. With Jupiter, Mars was one of the most notable gods in the Roman pantheon; and his cause was furthered by Emperor Augustus, who built two temples in his honour. March 15 (the month which derives its name from him) was a festival day, put aside to celebrate the marriage of Mars; and in the northern hemisphere this day represented the official beginning of spring.

**Mars** (2) The planet named after the Roman war god. In astrology, Mars represents a tendency towards violent or hostile acts, aggression, and strong willpower. Those with Mars strongly aspected in their chart are inclined to be pugnacious and single-minded in their actions and are said to be generally lacking in refinement. However, seen in a more positive light, the "Martian" person can differentiate truth from falsehood and may demonstrate great moral courage, being willing to take a stand against a tide of vacillating popular opinion. The sign of the zodiac most compatible with Mars is Aries, the ram.

**Martello, Leo Louis** (1931–2000) An American hypnotist, occultist, and Wiccan, and founder of the Witches Anti-Defamation League, one of the first pagan civil rights organizations in the United States. He was also director of Witches International Craft Association and a pastor of the Temple of Spiritual Guidance. His books include *It's in the Stars*; *It's in the Cards*; *Weird Ways of Witchcraft*; and *How to Prevent Psychic Blackmail*.

**Marthim** See Bathin.

**Martinism** The esoteric teaching of Martinez de Pasqually, who drew on various mystical traditions, including Gnosticism, the Kabbalah, and *The Hermetica*. De Pasqually believed that one could only attain salvation by contacting the divine source of all being and by participating in an initiatory ceremony invoking one's holy guardian angel. Once the latter had been achieved, one could go through life in a "reintegrated" way. There were Martinist orders in Foix, Bordeaux, Paris, and Lyons; but the movement declined after the death of de Pasqually in 1774.

**Mary's bath** See Bain-Marie.

**Masculine Planets** In astrology, the sun (planet of light); Mars (associated with war and destruction); Jupiter (wealth and abundance); Saturn (aloofness and solitude); and Uranus (spiritual intuition). Compare Feminine Planets.

**Masculine Principle** In mystical cosmologies there is an interplay between masculine and feminine forces. Of these, the masculine principle is usually regarded as positive, outward going, dynamic, and solar. It is also intellectual rather than intuitive. See also Chokmah; Yang. Compare with Binah; Feminine Principle; Lunar Goddesses; Yin.

**Mask** A facial covering, often used in magical and religious ceremonies to allow a practitioner to assume the role of an invoked deity or spirit, or to frighten away demons and hostile forces.

**Master** In occultism and mysticism, a great adept or illuminated being. Masters are often said to be invisible or discarnate, influencing the world through the charismatic leaders of occult sects and groups. See also Illuminati.

**Master of the Animals** In Native American tradition, a general term used to refer to the supernatural ruler or master who protects animals of a particular species and who may offer them up to the hunter, or withhold them from being slain.

**Master of the Divine Name** In Jewish mysticism, the title given to those who possessed the knowledge of the sacred name of God and who knew how to use the sacred formulae for mystical or magical purposes. Such people were called **Ba'al Shem**, a term which predates the medieval **Kabbalah**.

**Master Therion** The magical name assumed by the ceremonial magician Aleister Crowley in 1915 when he attained the magical grade of **Magus** in the **Argenteum Astrum**.

**Maté** The name given to the dried leaves of the yerba maté (*Ilex paraguayensis*), which is widely used in magical rituals in Brazil, Paraguay, and Argentina and is also drunk as a tea-like infusion. Yerba maté is a large evergreen shrub with tubular orange-scarlet flowers. The Guaraní Indians believe that the plant contains a spirit who appears in the form of a beautiful young woman. Those who yield to her enticing call will be swept into the forest forever. Nevertheless, the Guaraní also maintain that the plant protects those who respect it.

**Materia Prima** In alchemy, the "first substance" or "Universal First Cause" from which all other substances were said to have come forth. For base metals to be transmuted into silver or gold, they had to first be reduced to their materia prima, and then reconstituted as one of the "noble" metals that had an immediate link with God. See also **Transmutation**.

**Material Plane** See Matter and compare Astral Plane.

**Math** See Gwydion.

**Mathers, Moina** (1865–1928) The sister of the French philosopher Henry Bergson, Moina Bergson married the influential English occultist **MacGregor Mathers** in 1890 and spent most of her married life with him in Paris. After his death in 1918 she became head of the Alpha-Omega Temple of the **Hermetic Order of the Golden Dawn** and a rival to **Dion Fortune**. Moina Mathers is remembered, rightly or wrongly, primarily for the claims made against her by Dion Fortune, who maintained that Mrs Mathers attacked her magically on the **astral plane** in the form of a huge cat. Dion Fortune also accused Mrs Mathers of the "psychic murder" of Alpha-Omega member Netta Fornario, whose naked body was found on the island of Iona accompanied by a Golden Dawn cloak and a silver chain. See Magical Attack.

**Mathers, Samuel Liddell MacGregor** (1854–1918) A key figure in the **Hermetic Order of the Golden Dawn**, MacGregor Mathers developed the rituals that formed the basis of the order and also translated a number of medieval magical works into English, including **Christian Knorr von Rosenroth**'s *Kabbalah Denudata* (*The Kabbalah Unveiled*); Solomon Trismosin's alchemical treatise *Splendor Solis*; and several grimoires, including *The Sacred Magic of Abra-Melin the Mage*, *The Key of Solomon*, and *The Grimoire of Armadel*. Mathers spent much of his time in the British Museum reading room, studying and translating ancient texts. As the Golden Dawn grew in importance, Mathers – who had taken a senior rank and begun to claim inspiration from the **secret chiefs** – became increasingly autocratic. After moving to Paris with his wife, **Moina Mathers**, in 1892, he demanded financial support from Golden Dawn members while he translated occult texts at his leisure, and schisms soon began to appear in the order. Serious rifts appeared around 1903 with the defection of key order members like R.W. Felkin and A.E. Waite, although other members, like J.W. Brodie-Innes, remained loyal to him. Mathers died in Paris in 1918. The probable cause was Spanish influenza, but according to Mather's wife it resulted from a transcendental encounter with the secret chiefs which no mortal could survive.

**Matrona** In the Kabbalah, the female aspect of God, also known as **Shekhinah**.

**Matter** In many occult and Gnostic

systems, the antithesis of **spirit** and the grossest emanation of the **godhead** in the process of creation. Occultists generally believe that matter is animated by an inner, vibrant force that provides life and dynamism in the universe and that this energy is identical, in essence, to God. Matter is not regarded as "reality" in and of itself, but as the outer form of an inner, transcendent process. Among the Gnostics, matter was regarded as evil because of its "distance" from the spirit.

**Matthews, Caitlín** A well-known English writer, singer and harpist who has contributed widely to shamanic and Celtic research through her many books, lectures, and experiential workshops. An ordained minister of the Circle of the Sacred Earth, she has also written extensively on the western esoteric tradition, soul work, and the divine feminine and has a shamanic counselling practice in Oxford. Her books include *Singing the Soul Back Home*; *Shamanism in Daily Life*; *The Elements of the Celtic Tradition*; *Sophia – Goddess of Wisdom*; *Celtic Spirit*; *The Encyclopedia of Celtic Myth and Legend*; and *The Western Way* – the last two of these co-authored with her husband **John Matthews**.

**Matthews, John** (1948– ) Currently based in Oxford, England, Matthews has spent more than thirty years researching Celtic mythology, the Grail legends and other aspects of the western esoteric traditions. Well known on both sides of the Atlantic for his lectures and workshops, Matthews is the author or editor of over fifty books, among them *The Celtic Seers' Sourcebook*; *The Druid Sourcebook*; *Elements of the Arthurian Tradition* and – co-authored with his wife **Caitlín Matthews** – *The Encyclopedia of Celtic Myth and Legend* and *The Western Way*.

**Matutine** From Latin *matutinus*, "of the morning". In **astrology**, the situation where the **moon**, **Mercury**, or **Venus** rise in the morning before the sun. The planet is matutine until it reaches its first station, the point in its orbit where it becomes retrograde.

**Mauve Zone** In the cosmology of the Typhonian Order of the Outer Ones, a branch of the **Ordo Templi Orientis** headed by tantric magician **Kenneth Grant**, a synonym for the **Abyss** or **Great Gulf** represented on the kabbalistic **Tree of Life** by the sephirah **Daath**. The Mauve Zone is also known as the Crimson Emptiness, the Night of Pan, and the Desert of Set.

**May Day** An ancient pre-Christian festival of rebirth and renewal celebrated in the northern hemisphere on 1 May and associated with the pagan Celtic festival of **Beltane**. In Britain the ceremonies of May Day include the choosing of a **May Queen**. Young people bring garlands of flowers to the ceremony and there is much merriment and dancing around the **maypole**. The Morris men also perform their colourful dances at this time. See also **Walpurgis Night**.

**May Eve** See Beltane.

**Mayim** In the **Kabbalah**, the Hebrew term for "water". It is also the element corresponding to the letter mem.

**Mayomberos** In Santería, practitioners who have contact with demons, deal in black magic, or *brujeria*, and who specialize in magical retribution and necromancy. See also **Magic, Black**.

**Maypole** A tall pole with streamers that is central to the traditional celebrations and dances performed on **May Day**. The maypole itself is in origin a symbol of the phallus, an important motif in the May Day ceremonies, which honour fertility and the regeneration of nature.

**May Queen** In folk tradition, a girl chosen to personify the powers of fertility and natural abundance in **May Day** festivities, which celebrate the beginning of summer in the northern

hemisphere. In **Wicca**, the May Queen is the representative of the earth goddess.

**Maz** In Enochian magic, the sixth Aethyr. The meanings associated with Maz include creative power and the ability to act without incurring karmic consequences. Maz is associated with **Aquarius, Taurus**, and **Leo** and its magical number is 105.

**Mazdaism** The worship of **Ahura Mazdah**. See also **Zarathustra**.

**Maze** A mythic symbol that characterizes the wandering path of life, with its seemingly never-ending dead-ends, false turns, obstructions, and multiple choices. The most famous example of a maze is the mythical **Labyrinth** at the palace of Knossos.

**Mbasaoka** See Iboga.

**M.C.** In astrology, the standard abbreviation for *medium coeli*, or **midheaven**.

**Mead, G.R.S.** (1863–1933) One-time secretary to **Madame Helena Blavatsky** in the London branch of the **Theosophical Society**, Mead was a scholar who specialized in studies of **Gnosticism** and *The Hermetica*. In 1909 he founded an esoteric group known as the Quest Society, which published the magazine *The Quest* and held meetings for those interested in aspects of the western mystery tradition. Mead is best known for his editions of the *Pistis Sophia* (1896) and *Thrice Greatest Hermes* (1906). His other books include *Fragments of a Faith Forgotten* (1900); *Apollonius of Tyana* (1901); *Echoes of the Gnosis* (1907); and *The Subtle Body* (1919).

**Mead Moon** See Esbats.

**Medea** In Greek mythology, the witch who was in love with the hero Jason, and used magic enchantments to enable him to steal the Golden Fleece. When Jason deserted her, she killed their two children

– Mermerus and Pheres – and fled to Athens, where she married King Aegeus. Medea was a niece of **Circe**, another notorious witch and enchantress.

**Medicine** (1) In alchemy, a term for the **Philosopher's Stone** and its fluid counterpart the **Elixir of Life**. This alchemical "medicine" could cure the "diseases" (also known as **leprosy**) of the so-called "imperfect metals".

**Medicine** (2) In Native American religion, a general term for supernatural or sacred power. Such power often emanates from a protector spirit.

**Medicine Bag** In Native American religion, a sack made from animal skin in which a clan may keep objects of sacred power such as bones, claws, hooves, feathers, and so on.

**Medicine Man** In Native American and other indigenous societies, the **witch-doctor**, **shaman**, or **priest** responsible for divining illness and preparing effective magical remedies. He protects the community from **witchcraft** and **black magic**; and, through trance and incantations, holds regular discourse with the gods and spirits.

**Medicine Pipe** In Native American religion, a sacred ceremonial pipe. See also **Sacred Pipe**.

**Medicine Woman** The female counterpart of a medicine man.

**Medium** In spiritualism, one who acts as a medium between the world of spirits and **discarnate** entities and the everyday world of normal reality.

**Medium Coeli** See Midheaven.

**Medmenham Abbey** The meeting place in Buckinghamshire, England, of the notorious Hell Fire Club. See **Dashwood, Sir Francis**.

**Medusa** See Gorgons.

**Megaliths** From the Greek *megas* ("great") and *lithos* ("stone"), a term applied to ancient sacred monuments found in various parts of the world and consisting of large, roughly hewn stones. The best known megaliths are found in Britain and Brittany and appear to have been constructed for religious or funerary purposes. Most megaliths in western Europe date from c. 2000–c. 1500BCE. Megaliths have been categorized by archaeologists under four main headings: the single standing stone, or **menhir**; the chamber tomb, or **dolmen**, consisting of two or more upright stone slabs that in turn support a capstone or "table" (probably originally covered in earth, now eroded); the stone row; and the stone circle. A circle of standing stones, like those found at Stonehenge, is known as a **cromlech**.

**Melampus** According to *The Odyssey* and *The Aeneid*, a famous soothsayer from Argos, who was able to predict the future and understand the languages of all animals.

**Melusine** A water spirit or mermaid. According to medieval French legend, Melusine was a young woman but every Saturday transformed into a serpent from the waist down. She married the count of Lusignan, and made him promise never to see her on Saturday; but one Saturday the count hid and saw her metamorphosis. In some versions she fled, fated to wander the earth forever. Sometimes shown with two tails, the melusine features in heraldry and is depicted on the arms of the house of Lusignan. Several other European families, among them the houses of Luxembourg, Rohan, and Sassenaye, have claimed descent from such a mermaid, and have actually altered their pedigrees to this effect.

**Mem** The Hebrew letter ascribed to the path linking **Hod** and **Geburah** on the Tree of Life. Mem has a numerical value of 40. In modern magical visualization and **pathworkings** the Tarot card

associated with this path on the Tree is
*The Hanged Man*.

**Memory, Cosmic** See Akashic Records.

**Mendes, Goat of** Form in which the
Devil was said to manifest during the
medieval Witches' Sabbath. Here the
Devil assumed a form that was half-goat
and half-human, and sat cross-legged
upon the altar with an inverted
pentagram inscribed upon his forehead
and a blazing torch between his horns.
The goat was male but had female breasts.
The Goat of Mendes takes its name from
the sacred goat kept captive in the
Egyptian city of the same name. Here,
women were supposed to mate with the
goat in the same way that medieval
witches had ritual intercourse with the
Devil. The Goat of Mendes features on
the Tarot card *The Devil*.

**Menhir** From the Breton *men* ("stone")
and *hir* ("high"), a prehistoric stone
monolith. See Megaliths.

**Menorah** A Jewish candle holder used
during the eight days of the festival of
Chanukah (Hanukah), symbolizing the
Tree of Life and the Four Worlds of
creative manifestation.

**Menstruum** In alchemy, the mercurial
solvent which dissolved metals into the
prima materia with a view to subsequently transmuting them into perfect
gold or silver.

**Mephistopheles** From a Greek
expression meaning "one who does not
like light", the demon to whom Faust is
said to have sold his soul. In Goethe's
celebrated drama, *Faust*, Mephistopheles
is said to have been able to change his
form into that of a dog, and he also
appeared before Faust as the Devil
himself.

**Mercurius** In alchemy, the transforma-
tive substance which allowed the process
of transmutation to occur. Mercurius was
sometimes known as philosophical

mercury as distinct from ordinary
mercury. Mercurius represented the
divine spirit of life and the prima
materia and was formed through the
union of sulphur and argent vive, or
quicksilver. It was considered the mother
of all metals – the mother from which all
other metals were created. Mercurius was
thought to contain both male and female
"seeds" and it was essential for this
mediating principle to be present if the
chemical wedding of King Sol and
Queen Luna was to take place. Mercurius
was also known as aqua permanens,
divine water, or aqua vitae.

**Mercury (1)** In classical mythology, the
Roman counterpart (in Latin Mercurius)
of the Greek god Hermes.

**Mercury (2)** In astrology, the planet
that traditionally represents logical or
rational human qualities, together with
scholarship and learning. It also
represents the ability to discriminate or
observe objectively, and the acts of
arranging, ordering, and purifying. In
the same way that Mercury, or Hermes,
was the messenger of the gods in ancient
classical mythology, people with Mercury
well aspected in their charts are said to
be highly skilled in communications and
could make their careers in one of the
media professions, in trade, or in
politics. The zodiac sign most
compatible with Mercury is Gemini.

**Mercury (3)** See Argent Vive;
Mercurius.

**Merkabah** A Jewish mystical tradition
centred on the Merkabah, or throne-
chariot of God, described in *The Book of
Ezekiel*. The Merkabah could ascend or
descend through the different heavenly
halls or palaces known as the Hekhaloth
– the last of which revealed the divine
glory of God. During the period of the
Second Temple, the vision of Ezekiel was
interpreted as a mystical flight to heaven,
and the kabbalistic mystics evolved a
technique of using the symbol of the
chariot as a meditative focus. The mystic

would make a visionary journey to the seven palaces and use secret magic names to ensure safe passage through each of these palaces in turn. Until recently, these mystical procedures and formulae were little known except to kabbalistic scholars. However, the relevant texts from the *Greater Hekhaloth* – the key work of the Merkabah mystics – have been published in English in an important book titled *Meditation and Kabbalah* (1982) by **Aryeh Kaplan**.

**Merlin** A wizard and Druid who features prominently in the Arthurian legends. The persona of Merlin may ultimately derive from a bard and seer known as Myraddin, or Myrddin, who was said to have lived in what is now southern Scotland and assisted the British chieftain Ambrosius Aurelianius near the Solway Firth. His magical spells are said to have caused the Battle of Arderydd near Carlisle, but a vision from the heavens transformed him into a raving lunatic who thereafter lived a rambling existence in the forests of the Scottish lowlands. The Merlin of myth was of fairy birth, born of a virgin – a "demon" child. While still only a child, Merlin became well known for his magical powers of prophecy and visited the court of Vortigern, another British king, when he was five years old. The king was puzzled by a curse that was affecting the construction of his fortress on Salisbury Plain. Astrologers had told the monarch that the blood of a young child was required to counteract the curse, but Merlin maintained that the trouble lay with two mighty dragons – one white and the other red – that were locked in ferocious combat beneath the earth. Merlin predicted that the white dragon would prove victorious and that the death of the red monster would herald the death of Vortigern himself. When these events came to pass, Merlin became famous as a wizard and served the next king, Uther Pendragon, assisting in the construction of the new castle at Carlisle, which housed the mystical Round Table. Merlin also tutored the young future king, Arthur, who obtained the magical sword Excalibur from the Lady in the Lake and was protected by it in battle. In due course Merlin found his match in the enchantress **Vivian**, with whom he fell in love. One day, while walking in the forest of Broceliande, Vivian entreated Merlin to tell her his most powerful spell – a spell which would enable a witch to trap any man and subject him to her command. Merlin was so infatuated by Vivian that he parted with his secret formula of enchantment and she in turn trapped him with the spell when he fell asleep in the forest.

**Mermaids** Legendary, bewitching creatures usually depicted as beautiful naked women with tails of fishes. Mermaids were said to dwell on craggy rocks, holding a comb and mirror, and singing alluring and enchanting songs that would draw sailors and their vessels to their doom. Their male counterparts are called **mermen**. See also **Elementals; Water Spirits**.

**Mermen** See Mermaids.

**Mescal Buttons** See Peyote.

**Mescaline** The psycho-active ingredient in the **peyote** cactus, a hallu-cinogenic plant which is used as a sacrament by the Huichol Indians in Mexico and among the Plains Indians of the southwestern United States. Mescaline attracted widespread attention. after the publication of Aldous Huxley's two books on his visionary psychedelic experiences: *The Doctors of Perception* (1954) and *Heaven and Hell* (1956). In fact, mescaline had been synthesized long before this – possibly as early as 1919. The first scientific paper on peyote was earlier still – dating from 1888 – and had been written by Ludwig Lewin following his experiments with the effects of the drug on animals. Havelock Ellis and William James were early pioneers of mescaline experience and wrote personal accounts of the visionary

effects of the drug. See also
Hallucination.

**Metals, Planetary** In alchemy and
astrology, symbolic correlations exist
between the planets (which traditionally
include the sun and moon) and certain
metals. These correlations are a follows:
Saturn (lead), Jupiter (tin), Mars (iron),
the sun (gold), Venus (copper), Mercury
(quicksilver), and the moon (silver).

**Metatron** A heavenly angel who
features prominently in the apocryphal
*Book of the Visions of Ezekiel* (fourth
century) and various other visionary
tracts and apocalypses associated with
the Hekhaloth school of Jewish
mysticism. In one Talmudic text,
Metatron is referred to as the "lesser
YHVH"; and he is also identified with
Enoch, who in Genesis "walked with
God", and in *The Book of Enoch*
ascended into heaven, and was later
changed into the angel. Occultists regard
Metatron as the archangel governing
Kether, the supreme sephirah on the
kabbalistic Tree of Life. See also
Kabbalah.

**Michael** In western magic, the
archangel said to govern the southern
quarter. He rules the element fire, and is
invoked during the banishing ritual of
the Lesser Pentagram. Michael is
regarded by occultists as the archangel
governing Hod on the kabbalistic Tree of
Life. See also Pentagram.

**Microcosm** See Macrocosm and
Microcosm.

**Microprosopus** In the Kabbalah, the
so-called "Lesser Countenance of God".
See also Macroprosopus;
Tetragrammaton.

**Middle Pillar** In the Kabbalah, the
central "pillar" on the Tree of Life. The
Tree, which consists of ten sephiroth, or
emanations of God, can be viewed as
being aligned in three columns headed
by Kether, Chokmah, and Binah,

respectively. The Middle Pillar is the
column headed by Kether and is
regarded by occultists as the magical
equivalent of the mystical "Middle Way".
The sephiroth that lead to Kether on the
Middle Pillar are, in order of ascent:
Malkuth, Yesod, Tiphareth, and
Daath.

**Midgard** In Scandinavian mythology,
one of the Nine Worlds located on the
World Tree, Yggdrasil. Midgard – or
Middle Earth – is the realm inhabited by
humans.

**Midgard Serpent** In Scandinavian
mythology, a huge serpent that was the
offspring of Loki and Angerboda. Odin
threw him into the sea and he lay in the
depths, encircling the world. Thor tried
to catch him without success, but at
Ragnarok finally killed him with his
hammer. However, Thor himself
perished in this contest – a victim of the
serpent's venom.

**Midheaven** In astrology, the so-called
south point, or cusp of the tenth house.
It should not be equated with the tenth
house as a whole, however, and is
sometimes confused with the zenith,
which is the point opposite the nadir.

**Midpoint** In astrology, an unoccupied,
unaspected degree of the horoscope that
lies between, and equidistant from, two
other planets. See also Aspects.

**Mighty King** In alchemy, the "red
stone". See Rubedo.

**Miko** In Japan, the shamanic medium
who acts as a mouthpiece for the kami,
or spirit ancestor.

**Minggah** Among the Australian
Aborigines of western New South Wales,
a tree haunted by spirits. The friendly
spirits that reside in the tree are regarded
by the local medicine-man as his magical
allies and he is able to take refuge in the
Minggah at a time of danger.

**Minor Arcana** In the Tarot, the 56 minor cards. These are arranged in four suits, each linked to one of the four elements: fire – wands; water – cups; air – swords; earth – pentacles or discs. The following broad areas of human activity can also be assigned to each of the four Tarot suits : Wands are associated with growth, energy and personal enterprise and also new ideas and creativity. Their counterpart in the modern deck of playing cards is the suit of clubs. Cups symbolize love, happiness and the emotions and by extension are linked to fertility and beauty. In reflecting the dynamics of the psyche, cups refer to the subconscious mind and natural instincts rather than to intellect or reason. Their modern-day equivalent is the suit of hearts. Swords represent aggression, force, ambition, struggle and animosity. They equate with spades in the modern deck. Pentacles are associated with property and financial interests – in some decks the pentacles, or discs, are shown as coins. The coins in turn represent the fruits of one's labour in everyday life. Pentacles correspond to diamonds in the modern deck.

There are also sixteen so-called "court" cards in the Minor Arcana, a king, queen, knight, and page of each suit. The court cards reflect the different qualities of fire, water, air and earth. The king represents the air aspect through all four suits, the queen the water aspect, the knight the fire aspect and the page the earth aspect. The allocation of air to the king and fire to the knight may seem to be contradictory but in medieval times the knights were the aggressors and warriors and the king more commonly the administrator or ruler. The medieval creators of the Tarot also recognized that each of the four elements has its most rarefied aspects (represented by air) and its densest or most material aspects (represented by earth), while water represented their fluid qualities and fire their dynamic properties.

The court cards combine the elements in different ways. For example,

| | |
|---|---|
| King of Wands | = Air of Fire |
| Queen of Wands | = Water of Fire |
| Knight of Wands | = Fire of Fire |
| Page of Wands | = Earth of Fire |

and so on through the other three suits.

Unlike the Major Arcana, the Minor Arcana has no specific application as a meditative device, but plays an important role in Tarot divination. See also Major Arcana.

**Minotaur** In Greek mythology, a famous monster with a human body and the head of a bull. The minotaur was kept in the Labyrinth at the palace of King Minos and was fed on the bodies of human victims – seven boys and seven girls selected each year in Athens as a ritual sacrifice. The beast was eventually slain by the Athenian hero Theseus.

**Mirror, Magic** See Magic Mirror.

**Mistletoe** A plant with magical associations. Celtic Druid priests used to distribute mistletoe to worshippers after a white bull had been sacrificed to the beneficent spirits, and this mistletoe was taken home and hung from the ceiling to frighten away evil forces. Among the Romans, mistletoe was similarly regarded as a protection against the Devil and enabled one to speak to ghosts. However, in Scandinavian mythology, mistletoe had a more unfortunate mythic association, for the sun god Balder was slain by a branch of mistletoe gathered by the jealous Loki.

Couples kiss beneath the mistletoe at Christmas time to ensure fertility, but the plant is not allowed within a church because of its pagan associations.

**Mithra** or **Mithras** An ancient Persian god of light who, according to the Avesta, would appear before sunrise and watch over the earth and firmament while riding in a chariot drawn by four white horses. Mithra was regarded as the all-knowing god, and as a deity of fertility and abundance. He was also the untiring opponent of evil, and would ruthlessly destroy wickedness wherever he discovered it. Following the expeditions of Alexander the Great and the fusion of Greek and eastern religious beliefs that followed his conquests, Mithra became associated with **Helios**, the Greek god of light. The cult of Mithra was introduced into the Roman empire when Pompey returned to Rome after capturing Jerusalem in 63BCE, bringing captives with him who were devotees of the Persian religion. By the end of the first century, the cult of Mithra was well established, especially among Roman soldiers, and by 250CE it had become a major rival to Christianity.

Mithra was lord of the four **elements** – which are symbolized by his four horses – and came to be regarded as a mediator between the common people and the "unknowable" God who transcended existence. In this respect Mithra was like a demiurge. Always linked to **astrology**, Mithra was associated with the constellation of **Taurus**, which, as the sun entered it, heralded the beginning of spring. Mithra was often depicted overcoming the bull (Taurus), which had been the first animal created by **Ohrmazd**. In Mithraic cosmology, the useful herbs and plants of nature were said to have sprung from the carcass of the bull slain by Mithra, thus identifying the bull as a source of fertility, new life, and abundant crops. The blood of the bull also represented the life-force which would nourish the earth and its people.

**Mizraim** An ancient name for Egypt, still used in **Freemasonry**.

**Moabi** See Iboga.

**Mohin Degadlus** In Hasidism, the Hebrew expression for mystical ecstasy.

**Moly** In *The Odyssey* by Homer, a magical herb given to **Odysseus** by Hermes to protect him from the magical spells of **Circe**.

**Monastery of the Seven Rays** See Bertiaux, Michael.

**Monkshood** *Aconitum napellus*, a poisonous herb said in Greek legend to have come forth from the saliva that dripped from the mouth of the monster **Cerberus**. Monkshood was used by medieval witches in **flying ointments** and "love potions", but it is one of the most poisonous and dangerous of all magical herbs, often causing death when consumed.

**Monoceros** A mythical creature described by Pliny as resembling a horse with a stag's head, elephant's feet, and the tail of a boar. It had a single short black horn in the centre of its forehead (monoceros is Greek for "one horn"), and resembled a **unicorn**.

**Moon** (1) In alchemy, a reference to **Queen Luna**.

**Moon** (2) In **astrology**, perhaps the most important celestial body after the sun, since it moves through all the signs of the **zodiac** and therefore has a profound influence on one's **horoscope**. The moon is regarded by astrologers as a strong influence on individual emotions and moods, and people with the moon strongly aspected in their natal chart are regarded as sensitive and intuitive. However, they may also be impressionable and easily influenced. This interpretation of the moon's influence derives from the fact that the moon enters a new sign of the zodiac approximately every two and a half days, whereas the sun changes signs only twelve times every year. See also **Eye of Horus**; **Thoth**; and individual deities referred to under **Lunar Goddesses**.

**Moonchild** A concept advanced by ceremonial magician Aleister Crowley. Crowley believed that the human foetus does not have a **soul** during its first three months in the womb. He thought therefore that it was possible to incarnate a "moonchild", a non-human being like an **elemental** or a planetary spirit that embodied specific metaphysical qualities or paranormal abilities. To achieve this result the parents of the foetus would have to engage in sex magic at astrologically favourable times. This theme is explored in Crowley's novel *Moonchild*, published in London in 1929. See **Magic, Sexual**.

**Moonstone** In Wicca, a magical stone assigned to the ritual celebration of **Litha**. See also **Magical Stones**.

**Moon, The** In the Tarot, a card in the **Major Arcana** that symbolizes the processes of biological and spiritual evolution. A lobster, representing an early form of life, emerges from the waters; while on land we see two dogs – one an aggressive wolf, and the other a more domesticated and "evolved" form: both of these animals look upwards towards the moon, to which the dog is sacred. The element **water** predominates in the symbolism of *The Moon*, and the card is affiliated with the lunar sphere **Yesod**, which is associated on the kabbalistic **Tree of Life** with sexuality and the cycles of fertility. *The Moon* represents the path from **Malkuth** to Yesod on the Tree.

**Morax** In the Goetia, the 21st spirit, a great earl and president who appears in the form of a bull with a human face. Extremely well-versed in the virtues of herbs and precious stones, Morax offers the magician a profound knowledge of astronomy and can provide excellent familiar spirits should they be required. Morax governs 30 legions of spirits and is also known as Marax or Forfax. He is referred to as Foraii by the sixteenth-century demonologist **Johannes Wier**.

**Morgan le Fay** In Arthurian legend and Celtic folklore, the sister or half-sister of King Arthur – for whom she had strong feelings of hatred – and, in some accounts, the mistress of the wizard **Merlin**. Possibly connected to the Celtic goddess **Morrigan**, Morgan le Fay ("le Fay" is Old French for "the Fairywoman") was sometimes depicted as a hag and sometimes as an enchantress. In *Sir Gawain and the Green Knight* she is portrayed as the hag in the castle of the Green Knight who planned to overthrow the Round Table. But she is also the Green Knight's beautiful wife, who sought to seduce Gawain.

**Morning Glory** *Rivea corymbosa*, a well-known flowering vine containing ergot alkaloids related to d-lysergic acid diethylamide — better known as LSD. Intake of the seeds can produce a sensation of bright lights and colour patterns, feelings of euphoria, and often profound states of peace and relaxation. This morning glory species was known to the Aztecs as ololiuhqui, and they regarded the plant as a divinity. It is possible that the Aztec god of flowers, Xochipilli, had a link with ololiuhqui, because he was considered the "patron deity of sacred hallucinogenic plants" and the "flowery dream". The ritual use of morning glory among the Aztecs was suppressed after the Spanish conquest, but the Aztecs continued to hide the seeds in secret locations to avoid detection and persecution. Ironically, as if to redeem their "satanic" associations in the minds of the Spanish conquerors, the Zapotecs of Oaxaca now refer to the morning glory seeds in Christian terms, calling them "Mary's herb" or "the seed of the Virgin".

**Morrígan** or **Morrígu** A shapeshifting Celtic deity who appears in Irish myth. The Morrígan ("Phantom Queen" or "Great Queen") could transform herself magically into the shape of a deer, raven or crow, as well as changing her appearance from a young maiden into a hag. She was the goddess of war and death and would be seen hovering over the field of battle. She was said to have intercourse with the **Dagda**, the father god of the **Tuatha De Danann**, on the feast of **Samhain**. She may be related to the Arthurian figure of **Morgan le Fay**. See also **Nemain**.

**Mort Bon Dieu** In voodoo, "a call from God" – a natural death as opposed to one caused by harmful magic.

**Mortification** In alchemy, the so-called "death" of the metal which occurred when it was dissolved into the **prima materia**. The process of mortification released the "soul" of the metal from its putrefying body.

**Mortuary Magic** See Magic, Mortuary.

**Moss Folk** In German and Scandinavian folklore, fairy creatures who lived in the forests and had occasional contact with people. They would sometimes borrow domestic goods or foods, but would always repay gifts many times over. On occasion the moss folk would beg for human breast milk to feed their sick children, but this aroused fear and superstition among local mothers, who viewed the moss folk with apprehension.

**Mother** In Wicca, the second of the threefold aspects of the **Great Goddess**. The Mother represents maturity and fulfilment. The two other aspects of the Great Goddess venerated in Wicca are the **Maid** (representing youth and enchantment) and the **Crone** (representing old age and wisdom). These phases of womanhood are particularly important in the "women's mysteries" of feminist Wicca groups.

**Mother Goddess** A goddess who personifies the force of nature and the cycles of fertility. Often the mother goddess is considered to be the mother of the manifested universe: it is from her womb that creation comes forth. The mother goddess appears in every primitive religion in which fertility rites have an important role, and she is also important in the ancient Greek mysteries of Eleusis. In the Tarot, the archetype of the mother goddess is presented as *The Empress*. See also Great Goddess; Triple Goddess.

**Mother Letters** In the Kabbalah, a designation for the Hebrew letters **aleph**, **mem**, and **shin** in the Sepher Yetzirah.

**Muinn** In the Celtic tree alphabet, the ogham representing the mulberry and the letter "m". Muinn is also linked to the titmouse and the colour purple.

**Muladhara** In Kundalini yoga, the chakra or energy centre at the base of the spine where the kundalini serpent energy lies "coiled", ready to be awakened. The muladhara chakra is activated by using an appropriate mantra while meditating on the Tattva symbol of Earth, **prithivi**. see also Chakra; Tantric.

**Multiplier** In alchemy, a person believed to have the skills to transmute base metal into silver or gold. The term was also used with reference to people who produced counterfeit coins as part of an alchemical deception.

**Mumford, Jonn** (1937– ) Born in Windsor, Ontario, and now based in Sydney, Australia, Dr Mumford is widely regarded as one of the world's leading authorities on tantric magic. After training in chiropractice in Portland, Oregon, and later in Sydney, he specialized for many years in the treatment of muscular and skeletal disorders. However, he always had a deep interest in metaphysics and eastern mysticism and in 1973 he was initiated by Paramahansa Swami Satyananda Saraswati of Bihar, India, and now conducts international workshops and lectures on relaxation, sexuality, **tantra**, and yoga. His best known books include *Ecstasy Through Tantra*; *Karma Manual*; and *Psychosomatic Yoga*.

**Mummification** The ancient Egyptian practice of embalming human bodies and also the bodies of sacred animals. In Egypt, the body was considered to be a vital part of the human identity and survival in the afterlife was not possible without it. When a person died, the intestines and other organs were removed and the body cavities filled with preserving incenses and bitumen. The organs that had been removed were separately bandaged and preserved in "canopic jars". These jars and the mummified body were then interred together. Mummification was well established at the time of the compilation of the Pyramid Texts (c. 2400BCE) and continued until the fourth century CE, when it was replaced by Christian burial practices.

**Mundane Aspect** In astrology, an aspect in a **horoscope** that is indicated by a **planet** occupying a **cusp**.

**Mundane Astrology** See **Astrology, Mundane**.

**Mundification** In alchemy, the act of purifying putrefied material to reach the stage of **albedo**. See **Ablution**.

**Murmur, Murmus,** or **Murmux** In the **Goetia**, the 54th spirit, a great duke and earl who appears in the form of a warrior riding on a **griffin**. He wears a ducal crown upon his head and is preceded by his ministers, who are playing trumpets. Murmur teaches perfect philosophy and constrains the souls of the dead to appear before the magician to answer questions as required. Murmur commands 30 legions of spirits.

**Murray, Margaret A.** (1862–1963) An English Egyptologist and anthropologist who maintained that witchcraft was a remnant of an ancient religion centred around the **Mother Goddess** and the **Horned God**, and that this tradition had existed in secret through all ages, up to the present. Murray's book, *The Witch-Cult in Western Europe* (1921), "reconstructed" the "Old Religion" and put forward the view that the witches had been unfairly persecuted as a rival religion to Christianity. Most modern scholars reject the idea of a linear witchcraft tradition, but the concept has had a strong romantic appeal for some contemporary practitioners of **Wicca**.

**Muryans** In Cornish folk legend, fairies who were originally larger than human beings in size but who, year by year, grew smaller in size until they became ants and died.

**Muses, The** In Greek mythology, the personifications of creative inspiration. The Muses were the nine daughters of **Zeus** and Mnemosyne (Memory), and each had a different specialization: Calliope (epic poetry); Clio (history); Erato (love poetry); Euterpe (music and lyric poetry); Melpomene (tragedy); Polyhymnia (hymns and sacred music); Terpsichore (dance); Thalia (comedy); and Urania (astronomy).

Homer, Hesiod, and Virgil wrote invocations to the Muses, as did many English poets, among them Spenser, Milton, **William Blake**, and Byron.

**Mushroom, Sacred** See *Amanita muscaria*; *Psilocybe*; Soma.

**Music of the Spheres** A concept introduced by **Pythagoras** (c. 572–479BCE), who related the mathematical relationship between tones on the musical scale to the orbits of the planetary spheres. The symbolic links between celestial bodies and music also interested such Renaissance mystics as **Marsilio Ficino**, who sought to correlate the different stars and constellations with musical tones.

**Muspellheim** In Scandinavian mythology, one of the **Nine Worlds** located on the World Tree, **Yggdrasil**. Muspellheim is the realm of cosmic fire.

**Mutable Signs** In astrology, the changeable signs of the **zodiac**: Gemini, Sagittarius, Virgo, and Pisces. There are distinguished from the **cardinal signs** and the **fixed signs**. See also **Double-Bodied Signs**.

**Mute Signs** In astrology, those signs of the zodiac which have as their motif a creature that emits no sounds: **Cancer, Scorpio,** and **Pisces**.

**Myraddin, Myrddin** See Merlin.

**Myrrh** A transparent aromatic gum, yellow-brown in colour, from the bark of a tree of the genus *Commiphora*. Myrrh was one of the three gifts (together with gold and frankincense, or **olibanum**) brought by the **Magi** to honour the infant Jesus. In ancient Egypt myrrh was used both as a ritual offering to the sun god **Ra**, and also to embalm corpses. In western magic it is associated with the planet Saturn, symbolic of death.

**Myrtle** An evergreen plant symbolically associated with love and marriage. The ancient Egyptians consecrated it to **Hathor**, and in ancient Greece it was sacred to **Aphrodite** – both goddesses of love. Similarly, in ancient Rome, where the goddess **Venus** ruled love and fertility, brides wore wreaths of myrtle blossom on their wedding day.

**Mystagogue** One who, in the role of adept, initiates a **neophyte** into an esoteric or occult teaching or practice. See also **Initiation**.

**Mystères** In voodoo, a collective term for the **loa**.

**Mysteria Mystica Maxima** The British lodge of the **Ordo Templi Orientis**, founded by the ceremonial magician **Aleister Crowley** in 1912. Its leading member was **Victor Neuburg**. Crowley later amalgamated the **Mysteria Mystica Maxima** with the **Argenteum Astrum**.

**Mystery** From the Greek *myein*, "to keep one's mouth closed", a secret or occult truth not to be disclosed to the uninitiated.

**Mystery Religion** In ancient Greece and Rome, a cult whose initiatory rites and ceremonies and inner teachings and practices were secret. There were famous mystery cults at **Eleusis** and on the island of Samothrace. The deities honoured in the mystery religions included **Demeter** and **Persephone**, **Attis** and **Cybele**, **Dionysus**, **Isis**, **Serapis**, and **Mithra**.

**Mystic** One who through contemplation, meditation, or self-surrender seeks union with the **godhead**; and who believes in the attainment of universal wisdom, cosmic consciousness, or spiritual transcendence. Mystics are generally differentiated from occultists as being less interested in psychic powers, mental abilities, or ceremonial activities. Occultists who practise western **magic** and use the kabbalistic **Tree of Life** as their framework for spiritual growth sometimes maintain that the mystic path to the godhead is more direct than the occult route. In the **Kabbalah** it is represented by the ascent of the **Middle Pillar** on the Tree (the "Middle Way" through **Malkuth**, **Tiphareth**, and **Kether**), as distinct from the occult journey through each of the ten **sephiroth**. See also following entry.

**Mysticism** The act of seeking union with the **godhead**. It has been defined by St Thomas Aquinas as "the knowledge of God through experience"; and by Evelyn Underhill as "the art of union with reality". Mystics believe that the godhead or supreme being sustains the manifested universe and is responsible for all aspects of existence and consciousness.

**Mystic Union** In mysticism and theurgy, union with the **godhead** through contemplation and prayer. Mystic union is sometimes regarded as a type of spiritual marriage with the creator.

**Myth** A story or fable, often relating to a deity or a supernatural being. In popular usage the word also has the negative connotation of something illusory or false. However researchers like **Dr Carl Jung** and Joseph Campbell have suggested that mythic images are present at a deep level of the unconscious mind and may be viewed as an expression of the archetypes of the **collective unconscious**. To this extent, the various deities of myth and legend personify common human attributes or universal principles in nature and the cosmos. Myths often express the spiritual values of a culture and provide a framework of meaning within which members of a society live and function. Occultists sometimes adapt myths for ceremonial purposes and invoke different gods and goddesses in ritual to enhance their spiritual awareness and personal growth.

**Mythological Correspondences** See Magical Correspondences.

**Mythology** The collective myths of a culture. See also Myth.

# N

**Naberius** In the Goetia, the 24th spirit, a valiant marquis who appears in the form of a black crane. He speaks with a hoarse voice but is nevertheless highly skilled in rhetoric and can also impart a vast knowledge of all the arts and sciences. Naberius governs 19 legions of spirits.

**Nadir** In astrology, the point opposite the zenith: the lowest point below the earth. It should not be confused with the imum coeli.

**Nag Hammadi Library** A collection of mostly **Gnostic** writings discovered in 1945 in an ancient cemetery near Nag Hammadi in southern Egypt. The Nag Hammadi library parallels the discovery of the Dead Sea Scrolls in importance and offers an illuminating perspective on religious beliefs current during the formative years of Christianity. The library consists of thirteen volumes containing over 50 texts written in Coptic, including *The Gospel of Truth*, *The Gospel of Thomas*, *The Sophia of Jesus Christ*, and several apocalypses. There are also a couple of Hermetic works. The texts are especially significant because the Gnostic philosophy had previously been known to scholars primarily through the writings of such Church spokesmen as Irenaeus, Clement, Hippolytus, and Tertullian, who were critical of Gnostic beliefs. The texts of the Nag Hammadi library present Gnosticism on its own terms. The library was first published in English in 1977.

**Nagual** Also, **Nawal**. In Central American **magic** and folk belief, a **witch** who is able to transform into an animal, often for a sinister or evil purpose. The term is sometimes used to mean a "companion spirit" or alter ego; and if harm befalls the nagual, this rebounds on the body of the witch or sorcerer who is travelling in animal form on the **spirit-**

journey. See also Lycanthropy; Shamanism; Sorcery.

**Naiads** Also, Naiades. In Greek mythology, nymphs of the rivers, streams, and fountains.

**Name, Divine** In many religions, God has a sacred name and its pronunciation is jealously guarded as an esoteric teaching. In Judaism, the Tetragrammaton, or four-letter name of God, YHVH, was considered too sacred to be vocalized and was replaced with Adonai, or "Lord". For some Jews, even Adonai is too sacred to be spoken, and is replaced with ha-Shem – "the Name". There was also a version known as the **Shem ha-Meforash** consisting of 216 letters. See also God-Name.

**Name, Magical** See Magical Name.

**Names of Power** Magical conjurations and ritual formulae, which include sacred god-names, deemed to have a strong magical effect. In ancient Egypt these formulae were called **hekau**. See also God-Name; Tetragrammaton; Words of Power.

**Nanna** The Sumerian moon god and counterpart of the Babylonian Sin.

**Nanta** – In Enochian magic, the sacred name of the spirit of earth. Nanta (pronounced *Nah-en-tah*) is assigned to the North and is represented by the colour black. See also Exarp; Hcoma; Bitom.

**Naphula** See Vapula.

**Nastrond** In Scandinavian mythology, a hell-region located in the depths of Niflheim – the cold north – which was said to be a dark abode, far from the sun, with walls formed of wreathing, venomous snakes. It was surrounded by the serpent monster **Nidhoggr**, who tormented the dead. It was in Nastrond that **Loki** was chained to a rock.

**Natal Astrology** See Astrology, Natal.

**Natal Horoscope** See Horoscope, Natal.

**Natema** Among the Jivaro Indians of Ecuador, a sacramental, hallucinogenic beverage made from the leaves of the banisteriopsis vine. Jivaro shamans drink the brew in order to have initiatory visions. See also Ayahuasca; Hallucination; Initiation; Tsentsak.

**Nativity** See Horoscope, Natal.

**Natural Magic** See Magic, Natural.

**Nature Spirit** A popular name for a sprite or elemental. Occultists regard nature spirits as "energy-beings" who sustain nature and personify the life processes in plants, flowers, and trees. Dryads, elves, fairies, naiads, and pixies belong in this category.

**Nature Worship** The worship of life-sustaining forces of nature personified by the cycles of the seasons, which inevitably return to the rebirth of spring and new life. Nature worship relates also to fertility and sexuality and is usually associated with deities of the earth and moon. Nature worship is practised in modern witchcraft, which draws heavily on the Celtic mystical tradition. See also Celts; Eleusis; Horned God; Lunar Goddesses and deities referred to under Earth Goddesses.

**Nauthiz** See Nyd.(Rune letter).

**Navushieip** Among the Shoshoni Indians, a dream or vision. The word is also used to refer to the "dream-soul", the soul that has these visionary experiences.

**Nawal** See Nagual.

**Nazps** In Enochian magic, the angelic word for a ritual sword. It is pronounced *nah-zod-peh-seh.*

**Neck** See Crow's Beak.

**Necklace, Witch's** In Wicca, a necklace worn by women witches in ritual workings. The traditional Wiccan priestess's necklace is made of alternate beads of amber and jet, symbolizing solar/lunar and male/female polarities in perfect balance.

**Necromancy** From the Greek *nekros*, "dead", and *manteia*, "divination", a form of **divination** in which the spirits of the dead are summoned to provide omens relating to future events. The Bible describes how the witch of Endor summoned the spirit of Samuel to answer Saul's questions (1 Samuel 28); and Lucan, in his *Pharsalia*, describes a ritual of necromancy in which the witch Enrichtho used the body of a dead soldier and other hideous ingredients in her rites. In more recent times, the French occultist **Eliphas Lévi** endeavoured to summon the spirit of **Apollonius of Tyana** by calling on **Hermes, Asklepios,** and **Osiris,** and then finally Apollonius himself. An account of this bizarre conjuration is given in Lévi's *Dogme et Rituel de la Haute Magie*, which describes the results as follows: "Three times and with closed eyes I invoked Apollonius. When I again looked forth there was a man in front of me, wrapped from head to foot in a species of shroud...he was lean, melancholy and beardless." The ghostly figure disappeared as Lévi brandished his ritual sword in front of it, but it later reappeared. Lévi says that "the apparition did not speak to me, but it seemed that the questions I had designed to ask, answered themselves in my mind."

**Necronomicon, The** A work containing blasphemous magical incantations ascribed to a wizard called Abdul Alhazred but actually invented by the renowned American fantasy author **H.P. Lovecraft.** Lovecraft provided a brief history of this imaginary book in an essay titled "History of the *Necronomicon*", written in 1927. Alhazred is said to have wandered from Babylon through Egypt and thence to the southern desert of Arabia, where he learned the metaphysical secrets of the universe. Later, in Damascus, he composed a work known as *Al Azif* – *azif* being an Arabic word associated with the howling of demons. This book subsequently became known as the *Necronomicon*. Lovecraft's bizarre vision has inspired several other works bearing the same title, each claiming to be authentic.

**Necrophilia** Sexual intercourse with the dead. This is sometimes committed by psychopathic murderers who believe their victims to be still alive. Necrophilia is also a feature of the most debased forms of black magic; see **Magic, Black.**

**Nectar** In Greek mythology, the drink of the gods. It was poured by the cupbearers Hebe (Ganymeda) and Ganymede.

**Nefesh** See Nephesch.

**Neither-Neither** A theory of magical paradox developed by **Austin Osman Spare.** Spare believed that through paradoxical thinking the sorcerer was able to experience a fecund instant in which he perceived the unlimited realization of his true self. Spare's idea of "Neither-Neither" parallels the paradoxical *koan* in the Zen Buddhist tradition (such as the famous "What is the sound of one hand clapping?"), which was regarded as a bridge to *satori*, or enlightenment.

**Nemain** In Irish Celtic mythology, the aggressive and vengeful aspect of the **Morrígan** who hovered over the battlefield in the form of a raven or crow, urging bloodlust. Nemain was also known as Nemon.

**Nemesis** In Greek mythology, the goddess of anger and vengeance who punished those who broke the moral code. It became her role to encourage moderation in society and she therefore sought to eliminate pride and arrogance. Nemesis was the daughter of **Erebus** and Nyx.

**Nemo** In Enochian magic, an angel "like a young man, dressed in white linen robes" who appears during the call of the thirteenth **Aethyr, Zim.**

**Nemon** See Nemain.

**Neopaganism** A general term used to describe followers of **Wicca,** goddess worship, **nature worship,** and contemporary forms of **shamanism** and earth-based rituals. Neopagans venerate the life-force and sacred cycles of Mother Nature and pay homage through a variety of eclectic rituals, most of which derive from contemporary forms of **witchcraft.**

**Neophyte** One who is a candidate for initiation. In the **Hermetic Order of the Golden Dawn** the probationary grade of Neophyte was not attributed to the **Tree of Life,** but was nevertheless intended to provide candidates with a glimpse of the Light that they would aspire to in subsequent ceremonial workings. Accordingly, the Neophyte grade was regarded by these occult practitioners as highly symbolic and significant.

**Neoplatonism** A school of philosophy that blended the ideas of Plato and various Near Eastern religions. Neoplatonism was developed in the third century by **Plotinus** and his successors Iamblichus, Porphyry, and Proclus. According to this philosophy, all material and spiritual existence emanated from the One – the transcendent **godhead –** through the actions of the divine mind, or **logos,** and the **world soul.** Neoplatonism was banned by the emperor Justinian I in 529CE, but was revived in the Renaissance by such mystics as **Pico della Mirandola** and **Marsilio Ficino.**

**Nepenthe** A magic drink that was said to relieve sorrow and grief. According to *The Odyssey,* Polydama, the queen of Egypt, entertained Helen of Troy and gave her the drink to banish her melancholy.

**Nephelomancy** A form of **divination** by interpreting the formation and direction of clouds.

**Nephesch** In the **Kabbalah,** the animal instincts. Some practitioners of western magic ascribe Nephesch to the tenth sephirah, **Malkuth,** on the **Tree of Life.** However, it is more appropriately linked to the ninth sephirah, **Yesod,** which is the symbolic energy centre for sexuality, fertility, and the more primeval aspects of human consciousness. Yesod is also the sphere of the moon. It can be argued that some types of contemporary **neopaganism** are a form of Nephesch-worship.

**Nephthys** In Egyptian mythology, a goddess associated with death. She was married to **Set,** but gave birth to **Anubis** as the result of an affair with **Osiris** in which she disguised herself as **Isis.** Nephthys had magical powers and was able to transform people into animals in order to defend them. She could also restore the dead to life. Nephthys protected the deceased in the Osirian **Judgment Hall.**

**Neptune** (1) The Roman counterpart of the Greek god **Poseidon,** lord of the sea, and brother of **Zeus.**

**Neptune** (2) In astrology, the planet that symbolizes divine principles and which is equated with "the spirit of God that moved upon the waters". Symbolically, Neptune is the infinite ocean from which the universe came forth, and is therefore associated with spiritual consciousness and wisdom. Astrologers usually classify Neptune as a feminine planet, despite its male connotation in Roman mythology. In the western magical tradition, water is regarded as a feminine element.

**Nereids** In Greek mythology, 50 sea nymphs who were the daughters of Nereus, a sea god, and Doris, the daughter of **Oceanus,** another sea deity. See also **Oceanids.**

**Nereus** In Greek mythology, a sea god who in some accounts was the son of the primal deities Pontus (the sea) and **Gaea** (the earth). He was therefore older even than **Poseidon** (**Neptune**) and was known as the "Old Man of the Sea". He could change shape at will. He married Doris, one of the **Oceanids** (daughters of Oceanus), who bore the **Nereids**.

**Neschamah** In the Kabbalah, the spiritual dimension of the soul: one's higher spiritual self. It is identified with the three supernals on the **Tree of Life**: Kether, Chokmah, and Binah.

**Nest** In **alchemy**, a name for the alchemical vessel in which the "egg of the philosophers" – the **Philosopher's Stone** – was generated or "hatched".

**Netzach** or **Netsah** A Hebrew word meaning "victory "or "endurance", the seventh emanation or sephirah on the kabbalistic **Tree of Life**. In western **magic**, Netzach is regarded as the sphere of creativity, subjectivity, and the emotions – a very clear contrast to the sphere of **Hod**, which represents intellect and rational thought. Netzach is the sphere of love and spiritual passion and is therefore associated by occultists with such deities as **Aphrodite, Venus, Hathor**, and any other goddesses who personify these qualities.

**Neuburg, Victor** (1883–1940) A poet and occultist, who for a time was **Aleister** Crowley's homosexual partner in rites of sexual magic. Neuburg shared Crowley's belief that the perfect symbolic human form was the heavenly **androgyne** – a figure containing both sexual polarities – and he became involved in Crowley's magical orders, the **Argenteum Astrum** and the **Mysteria Mystica Maxima**. Neuburg went with Crowley to the Algerian desert in 1909 and there they summoned the so-called 30 **Aethyrs** of **Enochian magic**: powerful conjurations derived from the work of **Dr John Dee** and **Edward Kelley**. Crowley focused meditatively on a large topaz while

making the conjurations, and Neuburg transcribed his trance utterances. The results of this ceremonial working are included in Crowley's *Vision and the Voice* (1929) and in Jean Overton Fuller's biographical work *The Magical Dilemma of Victor Neuburg* (1965). Neuburg avoided Crowley later in his life and moved away from the occult altogether. In the literary world he is remembered as an inspirational force in the careers of Pamela Hansford Johnson and Dylan Thomas. See also **Magic, Sexual**.

**New Aeon** An expression used by the magician **Aleister Crowley** and his devotees to describe the 2,000-year cycle that commenced in 1904 following his illumination through the entity **Aiwaz**, who dictated *The Book of the Law*. Crowley claimed that his new magical cosmology replaced Christianity and he installed himself as the personification of the magical child, **Horus**. The New Aeon is thus referred to by Crowley's followers as the **Aeon of Horus**.

**New Forest Coven** The coven in Hampshire where **Gerald Gardner** claimed he was initiated in September 1939, just after the beginning of World War Two. Gardner was initiated by the head of the coven, Dorothy Clutterbuck, whose magical name was Daffo or Dafo.

**New Isis Lodge** A Lodge of the Ordo Templi Orientis operated by tantric magician **Kenneth Grant** for seven years between 1955 and 1962. Its aim was to explore the sexual dynamism created by the celestial ("Nu") and terrestrial ("Isis") currents which, according to Grant, incarnated "cosmic forces of superhuman potential". The lodge functioned for exactly seven years, seven being the number of **Set** and the "primal goddess of the seven stars".

**Ngetal** In the Celtic tree alphabet, the ogham representing juniper and broom and the sound "ng". Ngetal is also linked to the goose and the colour light yellow-green.

**Nia** In Enochian magic, the 24th Aethyr. The meanings associated with Nia include freedom, movement, and travel. It is associated with **Scorpio**, **Sagittarius**, and **Taurus** and its magical number is 116.

**Nibelungs** In Scandinavian and northern European mythology, a band of dwarfs who lived below the earth in Niflheim and guarded precious treasure. In due course the hero Sigurd, or Siegfried, overcame them.

**Nidhoggr** In Scandinavian mythology, the serpent monster who constantly gnawed at the roots of the world tree, Yggdrasil, attempting to destroy the earth's foundations. He dwelt near Nastrond in the icy depths of Niflheim.

**Niflheim** In Scandinavian mythology, one of the **Nine Worlds**, specifically the **Underworld** of cold and darkness in the north. It was here that a stream of cosmic ice encountered its fiery counterpart flowing from **Muspellheim**, which in turn caused an outpouring of energy crystallizing into the giant **Ymir** and the great cow Audhumbla. Niflheim was the domain of the souls of the dead and the monstrous serpent **Nidhoggr** dwelt there. See also **Hel**; **Nibelungs**.

**Night Houses** In astrology, the first six houses, which lie below the horizon. See also **House**.

**Nightmare** A terrifying or disturbing dream. Nightmares were traditionally thought to have been caused by attacks by evil spirits or demons during the night, crouching on their victims and causing a sensation of suffocation. The term may be derived from the myth of the Teutonic mare-headed goddess Mara – bringer of terror dreams – who was said to change herself into a white mare while visiting male sleepers at night. However it is also possibly related to the Old Germanic *mare*, meaning a goblin, spectre, or hag. See also **Incubus**; **Succubus**; **Hag Stone**.

**Night of Pan** See Mauve Zone.

**Night Rider** A supernatural entity like an **incubus** or **succubus** who "rides" its unsuspecting victim during the night, causing a sensation of suffocation, terror, or magical attack. See also **Nightmare**.

**Nightshade, Deadly** See Deadly Nightshade.

**Nigredo** The first stage of the **opus alchymicum**, in which the impure metal is "killed", putrefies, and is subsequently dissolved within the **prima materia**. The nigredo is associated with the colour black, which signifies the "death" of the impure metal.

**Nimahenan** A term used by the Cheyenne Indians to refer to the sacred arrows used by shamans to inflict injuries on their enemies. The keeper of the sacred arrows is the **shaman** holding the highest rank among those shamans who have served as ritual priests at one of the major ceremonial occasions. See also **Eehyom**.

**Nine** In numerology, this number denotes cosmic significance (nine is the number of the spheres in medieval cosmology). As the "highest" of the numbers (because ten = 1 + 0 which equates with one, and so on), nine symbolizes spiritual achievement and is the number of initiation.

**Nine Worlds** In Scandinavian mythology, the nine mythic realms located on the World Tree, **Yggdrasil**. These worlds included **Asgard**, the realm of the gods located at the crown of the tree; **Ljossalfheim**, the realm of the elves; **Midgard**, or Middle Earth – the realm inhabited by humans; **Niflheim**, the realm of cold and darkness; **Muspellheim**, the realm of cosmic fire; **Vanaheim**, the home of the **Vanir**, the peaceful nature and fertility gods; **Jotunheim**, the world of the giants; **Svartalfheim**, the world of the dark elves or dwarves; and **Hel**, the realm of the dead.

**Nirang** In Zoroastrianism, consecrated bull's urine. It is drunk by the priest and rubbed on his body during the *bareshnum* purification ceremony. The urine is believed to bestow spiritual and mystical power.

**Nisimon** Among the Cheyenne Indians, a shaman's guardian spirit or personal helper spirit.

**Nixie** In Scandinavian folk belief, a water spirit hostile to people. The female nixie was like a **Siren** and would sometimes lure men to their death by drowning; the male nixie was depicted either as an elderly dwarf or as a **centaur** with cloven feet.

**Nixie Pae** Among the Cashinahua Indians of Peru, spirit creatures with bows and arrows who appear to the **shaman** when he consumes the sacramental **banisteriopsis** beverage. The nixie pae are accompanied by coloured snakes, trumpeting armadillos, and singing frogs.

**Nodens** An ancient Romano-British healing deity, about which little is known, although he is probably related to the Welsh mythological figure of Llud. Nodens is also the name of a mysterious deity – the god of the great deep – mentioned in the macabre fantasy writings of **Arthur Machen** and H.P. Lovecraft. Machen referred to him in his novel *The Great God Pan* and Lovecraft calls him the "only named Elder God" in his short story *The Gable Window*.

**Nodes of the Planets** In astrology, the points at which the orbits of the planets intersect the ecliptic.

**Norns** In Scandinavian mythology, the three goddesses who guarded the world tree, **Yggdrasil**, and ordained the fate of humankind. Their names were Verdandi (the present), Urd (the past), and Skuld (the future). They are the equivalent of the Roman **Fates**.

**North** In western ceremonial magic, the direction associated with the element earth. It is said to be ruled by the archangel **Uriel**. See also **Four Directions**.

**Northern Signs** In astrology, the signs of the zodiac from **Aries** through to **Virgo**. See also **Commanding Signs**.

**North Point** In astrology, the imum coeli or cusp of the fourth house.

**Norton, Rosaleen** (1917–1979) An Australian witch and occult artist, whose trance-based paintings and drawings parallel those of **Austin Osman Spare**. Norton had fantasy visions as a child and was expelled from high school for allegedly corrupting the other children with her "pagan" influence. Norton later became an art student and also studied the writings of **Carl Jung, Eliphas Lévi, Dion Fortune,** and **Aleister Crowley**. She began experimenting with trance techniques and came to believe that the ancient gods could be contacted on the inner planes. Several deities – including **Pan, Jupiter,** and **Hecate** – feature in her art, which was the subject of controversial obscenity charges in the Sydney courts during the 1950s. A book describing her philosophy and drawings, *The Art of Rosaleen Norton* (originally issued as a limited edition), was republished in 1982. Her biography, *Pan's Daughter*, by Nevill Drury, was first published in 1988 and subsequently reissued in 2002 in a revised edition titled *The Witch of Kings Cross*.

**Nose** In alchemy, the tubular section of the **alembic**, the beaked vessel used as the upper part of the distillation apparatus.

**Nostradamus** (1503–1566) The magical pseudonym of Michel de Nostre Dame, who became Catherine de Medici's favourite astrologer. A Provençal Jew, Nostradamus wrote in archaic French and Latin as well as in his regional tongue and published his famous predictive writings, *The*

*Centuries*, in 1555. The book has been in print ever since. Nostradamus at times seems to have had a remarkable foresight into the events of the French Revolution, and some have discerned references in his writings to Mussolini and Hitler. According to Nostramus the "King of Terror" was scheduled to appear in July 1999, heralding the end of the world, but he failed to appear. The problem with Nostradamus is that his writings are often heavily symbolic and are presented in a jumbled sequence: the year 1999 was one of the few specific references in his writings. Personal interpretations of his predictive writings vary considerably.

**Notarikon** In the Kabbalah, a technique of abbreviating Hebrew words and god-names in order to disguise esoteric knowledge. There are two forms: in the first method a new word is formed by taking the first and final letters of another word or words; in the second, the letters in a word represent the first and final letters of each word in a sentence. See also **Gematria**; **Temura**.

**No-Thing** That which is no particular thing and therefore encompasses everything. From this perspective one can formulate the concept which is found both in Christianity and Jewish mysticism, that the world was created out of nothing (i.e. from Infinity). In the Kabbalah, the name for the infinite light, or godhead, is **Ain Soph Aur**.

**Notosa** See Angelica.

**Noumenon** In ancient Greek philosophy, the true and essential nature of being, as distinct from the illusory perceptions of the senses.

**Nous** A Greek word, used by Aristotle to describe the divine aspect of the mind or soul.

**November Eve** In contemporary witchcraft, an alternative name for **All Hallows' Eve**, or Halloween, which falls on 31 October.

**Nox** The Roman goddess of night, the counterpart of the Greek goddess Nyx.

**Nudity, ritual** See Skyclad.

**Nuin** In the Celtic tree alphabet, the ogham representing the ash and the letter "n". Nuin is also linked to the snipe and the colour blue-green.

**Nuit** See Nut.

**Numbers, Magical** See **Magical Numbers**.

**Numerology** The study of the sacred and divinatory value of numbers. The esoteric and symbolic significance of numbers are as follows:

### One

This is the beginning, and it is therefore associated with creative power, individuality, initiative, and unity. People whose ruling number is one are said to be independent and single-minded in their purpose. One is the primary number from which all other numbers arise. It is the number which represents the One God and the true Self.

### Two

This number represents duality in all its forms – duplication, reflection, receptivity, alternation, antagonism and so on. It is associated with polar opposites like night and day, positive and negative, male and female, good and evil. Because, by its very nature, duality is not resolved, the number two represents creativity unfulfilled.

### Three

This is a number associated with growth, expansion, ambition, and development. In its classic application a mother and father produce a child through their union, so symbolically two begets three. The Holy Trinity – Father, Son, and Holy Ghost – are the three different faces of the divine in Christian tradition, and the number three reflects the three-fold nature we all share as human beings: body, mind, and spirit.

## Four

The number four is symbolized by a square or cube and represents order, logic, classification, and measurement. It also represents the material universe and physical reality because when the sacred trinity gives rise to the universe, three then becomes four. For this reason four is also the number associated with hard work and practicality. According to the kabbalists, four is the number of memory.

## Five

The number five has several meanings. It embodies the idea of many forces operating at once – perhaps at odds with each other – and for this reason is linked to change and uncertainty. It is also the number of versatility. The number five is also associated with human aspiration because the five-pointed star or **pentagram** represents the head, arms, and legs of a human being. When the Pentagram points upwards it is a symbol of positive, spiritual aspiration (white magic) and when it points downwards it is a symbol of materialism and evil (black magic).

## Six

Six represents balance, harmony, symmetry, equilibrium, beauty, loyalty, and love. It is also the number associated with marriage and motherhood. Six is sometimes represented by the six-sided cube – a symbol of solidity. In the Jewish spiritual tradition the **Seal of Solomon** is the six-pointed star consisting of two intersecting triangles, one triangle representing spirit and the other material form, or earth. It epitomizes the ideal of heaven on earth.

## Seven

This number represents perfection, security, completeness, safety, victory and rest (because God rested on the seventh day of creation). It is also the mystic number symbolizing wisdom. There are seven notes on the musical scale, seven colours in the rainbow, and in traditional **astrology** there are seven planets.

## Eight

The number eight represents strength of character, and individuality of purpose. It is associated with justice, health, balance, progress, and independent thought. On the kabbalistic **Tree of Life**, the eighth sphere, **Hod**, is the centre for rational intellect.

## Nine

This is the culmination of all the numbers which have preceded it (ten, which follows nine, consists of 1 + 0, so numerologically equals one) so nine represents completion, attainment, and fulfilment. With specific reference to spiritual attainment nine is also the number of initiation.

## Ten

This number represents the end of the cycle and a return to the beginning (1 + 0 = 1). It is therefore known as the number which symbolizes "perfection through completion". On the kabbalistic Tree of Life, the tenth and final emanation from God is the physical world – the kingdom of the spirit.

**Nun** The Hebrew letter ascribed to the path linking **Tiphareth** and **Netzach** on the kabbalistic **Tree of Life**. Nun has a numerical value of 50 (and as a final letter, 700). In modern magical visualization and **pathworkings** the **Tarot** card associated with this path on the Tree is *Death*.

**Nut** or **Nuit** In ancient Egypt, the sky goddess. She and her brother Geb were the parents of **Osiris, Isis, Set,** and **Nephthys**. Nut was often represented as a woman with an elongated body that arched across the sky so that only her fingertips and toes touched the earth.

**Nyame** Among the Ashanti, the sky god and ruler of storms and lightning. Nyame created the moon, sun, and rain. See also **Ananse**.

**Nyd** In the Germanic **Elder Futhark**, the rune letter representing the number ten.

Nyd corresponds to the letter "n" and is the rune of need and necessity. Nyd demands that we make the best out of our situation in difficult circumstances. Also known as Nauthiz.

**Nyipij** Among the Shoshoni Indians, the so-called "Wind Master" – the spirit who controls the winds.

**Nymphs** In folk legends, the general name given to nature spirits who reside in different locations or **elements**. In ancient Greece these were known as follows: **dryads** and **hamadryads** (nymphs who lived in trees); **naiads** (nymphs of the rivers and streams); **Nereids** and **Oceanids** (nymphs of the sea); **oreads** (nymphs of the mountains). Oceanids, oreads, and naiads were immortal; but dryads would die with their trees.

**Nynymbi** A term used by the Shoshoni Indians to refer to evil dwarf spirits who carry bows and arrows and shoot lone travellers who are vulnerable to attack. The victims fall from their horses and are then found to have a lung haemorrhage. The Shoshoni Indians also blame the nynymbi for causing tuberculosis.

**Nyujo** A Japanese term for the state of cataleptic trance in which the **soul** is believed to separate from the body. It can also refer to a state of suspended animation.

**Nyx** The Greek goddess of Night, who was both the sister and wife of **Erebus**, god of darkness. Both were born of **Chaos** (1).

**Nzambi** Among the Bantu, the supreme god who created humankind. The first man created was evil and hostile, so Nzambi buried him and created another in his place. His wife was fashioned from wood, and this couple were the ancestors of the human race.

**Nzame** In Santería, the god who created the stars, planets, vegetation and the animal world and who then created an immortal man named **Omo Oba** to rule over all of creation. Omo Oba later fell from grace and Nzame, together with **Olofi** and **Baba Nkawa**, created a mortal man named **Obatalá** to rule the earth in his place.

# O

**Oak** A tree with ancient mythical and magical associations. It was sacred to the Jews because Abraham had encountered an angel of God beneath its branches; and the devotees of the Phoenician god **Baal** made sacrificial offerings "under every leafy oak" (Ezekiel 6.13). An **oracle** to Zeus at Dodona in northeastern Greece was located in a grove of oaks; and Socrates regarded the oak as the "oracle tree". The oak was also sacred to the Roman god **Jupiter**; while among the **Druids** no rite took place without the assistance of the oak and **mistletoe**. Among the pre-Christian Irish, the oak was the sacred tree of the high god **Dagda**; and in Scandinavia, where it was considered the "thunder tree", it was dedicated to **Thor**.

**Oak King** See Holly King.

**Oak Moon** See Esbats.

**Oannes** A Babylonian deity, part fish, part man, who became identified with **Ea**.

**Oath** A pronouncement or promise made in the name of truth that also summons supernatural forces to invoke punishment should the utterance prove to be incorrect or broken. Christians may make an oath on the Bible, invoking God; while a Muslim may make an oath in the name of Allah. In the occult tradition, an oath of secrecy may form part of an initiation ceremony; and should this oath be broken and secret truths subsequently revealed, it is believed that a "psychic current" rebounds upon the practitioner in question by way of punishment.

**Oath, Wiccan** The binding oath of secrecy and loyalty made by every candidate for entry into a Wiccan **coven**.

**Ob** A Hebrew word for serpent. It is thought to be the root of the word **obeah**, a form of African and West Indian sorcery which similarly involves the worship of the serpent.

**Oba** In **Macumba**, ministers or devotees of **Xangô**, god of fire and thunder.

**Obá** In **Macumba**, the goddess of the River Obá. She is one of **Iemanjá**'s many children and is identified with St Catherine.

**Obaluaé** In **Macumba**, the god of disease and disfigurement. Obaluaé hides his face and body behind veils of straw because his appearance is so loathsome.

**Obatalá** (1) In **Macumba**, one of the two orìsàs, or deities, created by the Yoruba god of creation, **Olorun**. Obatalá, a male deity, represented by the pure sky. The other orìsà was his consort.

**Obatalá** (2) In **Santería**, the mortal man created by Nzame, Olofi, and Baba Nkawa to rule the earth after the spiritual demise of **Omo Oba**. Obatalá is a god of peace and purity and is symbolized by the colour white.

**Obeah** A word used in the West Indies to denote supernatural and magical power. This power is also believed to reside in certain ritual objects, such as balls of graveyard earth mixed with feathers, hair, and human or animal remains. The magicians, known as obeah-men and obeah-women, use evil spells and enchantments to counteract the hostile world and develop prestige for themselves within their own community. See also **Ob**; **Spell**; **Voodoo**.

**Obelisk** A tall, four-sided monolith, tapered and forming a pyramid-like point at its apex. In ancient Egyptian religion, the obelisk was generally associated with the worship of the sun god **Ra**.

**Object Intrusion** In native religions around the world, the idea that disease is due to the intrusion into the body of a spirit or an object like a **magical dart** that has been sent by a sorcerer.

**Obsidian** Vitreous lava or glassy volcanic rock, which in certain parts of the world has magical significance. Among the Aztecs it was sacred to the sky god **Tezcatlipoca** and was fashioned into mirrors which were used by diviners for skrying. It was also used for the eyes of the idols in the temple of **Quetzalcoatl**. Obsidian also had ceremonial and initiatory uses among the North American Indians. In **Wicca**, Obsidian is assigned to the ritual celebration of Yule.

**Occult Hierarchy** In Theosophy, the Great White Lodge. Many occult groups, especially those with ceremonial grades, have been inclined to believe in a hierarchy of occult adepts on the "inner planes". In the **Hermetic Order of the Golden Dawn**, these were known as the secret chiefs.

**Occultism** From the Latin *occulere*, "to hide", the term "occult" was originally used to suggest a secret and hidden tradition of esoteric knowledge. Occultism is now used generally to include the study of **magic, mysticism, Theosophy**, and **spiritualism**. It may also be used with reference to secret societies like the **Rosicrucians** and **Freemasonry**.

**Occultist** A term used variously to describe a practitioner of any one of the "secret" mystic arts within the traditions of **magic, Theosophy, mysticism**, or **spiritualism**. See also **Occultism**.

**Oceanids** In Greek mythology, the nymphs of the ocean. There were 3,000 such nymphs, all of them the daughters of the Titan **Oceanus** and his wife Tethys.

**Oceanus** In Greek mythology, the oldest of the twelve **Titans** and the husband of Tethys. Oceanus, who personified the great river Ocean that was believed to surround the world, was the father of the **Oceanids** and the grandfather of the **Nereids**.

**Och** According to *The Arbatel of Magick* there are seven different "Olympic spirits", appointed by God to rule the world. Och, the spirit of the sun, bestows good health and wisdom. He is able to convert "all things into most pure gold and precious stones" and has 36,536 legions of lesser spirits at his command.

**Ochosi** In Santería, the god of hunters and wild animals, symbolized by a bow and arrows. His Christian counterpart is St Isidro (Isidore).

**Octad** In numerology, the number eight. See also **Ogdoad**.

**Octinomos** From a Greek expression meaning "he who has an eight-lettered name". In occult tradition, the master magician has an eight-lettered name; thus **Aleister Crowley** took the magical name Baphomet when he assumed leadership of the **Ordo Templi Orientis** in 1922.

**Odal** In the Germanic **Elder Futhark**, the rune letter representing the number 24. Odal corresponds to the letter "o" and refers to ancestral influences, ancestral property, and the concept of inheritance generally. This rune is used to call on ancestral powers, to guard family fortunes, and to enhance personal power. Odal suggests pride in ancestral traditions and the sense of returning to one's mythic homeland. It represents the culmination of the journey – the home of the sacred self, a place of well-being and personal fulfilment. Also known as Othala.

**Oddudúa** In Macumba and Santería, the wife of **Obatalá**. A mother goddess, she is often depicted as a black woman breastfeeding an infant. Oddudúa and Obatalá had two children, a son named Aganyú and a daughter named Yeramayá. They in turn married producing a handsome son Orungán, who subsequently had an incestuous relationship with his mother, the goddess of the moon. Yeramayá cursed her son, who died. She then climbed a mountain and gave birth to fourteen gods conceived with her son. After this dramatic multiple birth Yeramayá died and the waters from her burst abdomen gave rise to the Flood. The place of her tragic death became the site for the sacred city of Ile Ife. See also **Odudua.**

**Odin** In Scandinavian mythology, the supreme god and All-Father who lived in Valhalla with the spirits of fallen heroes. While he was the god of war and the dead, he was also believed to have set the **sun** and **moon** on their courses at the beginning of the world, and had a positive role as god of inspiration, ecstasy, **magic,** and poetry. King of the **Aesir,** Odin was informed about events in the world by two ravens. He rode an eight-legged horse named Sleipnir and owned the magical ring **Draupnir.** Odin often travelled among the heroes in the form of an old man with one eye. It was said that he had sacrificed his other eye in return for sacred knowledge, and that this eye was hidden in the **Underworld** in the well of Mimir, god of inland waters and the springs of wisdom. Odin was finally overcome by the monstrous wolf **Fenris** during the cataclysm of **Ragnarok.** See also **Wotan.**

**Odudua,** In Yoruba mythology, the goddess of the less pure realm of the earth. See also **Oddudúa.**

**Odum** In Macumba, the pattern of cowrie shells used in **divination.**

**Odysseus** In Greek mythology, the son of Laertes and Anticlea. Odysseus was the king of Ithaca and one of the leading Greek heroes during the Trojan War. He features in Homer's epic *The Iliad* and is the main character in *The Odyssey.* He was known to the Romans as Ulysses.

**Odyssey, The** An epic ancient Greek poem attributed to Homer (eighth century BCE), which describes the wanderings of the hero **Odysseus** after the fall of Troy, as he journeys home to Ithaca. It is divided into 24 books, the first twelve of which describe Odysseus's travels on the sea, the second those on land.

**Ofanim** or **Ophanim** In the Jewish mystical tradition, wheel-shaped angelic beings that accompany the throne of God, as described in *The Book of Ezekiel.* They are often identified as the angelic beings known as "thrones".

**Officer** See Fetch.

**Ogdoad** Especially in ancient Egyptian religion, a group of eight deities. The cosmogony of Hermopolis in Upper Egypt was an account of four pairs of gods: Nun and his female consort Naunet; Huh and Hauhet; Kut and Kauket; and **Amon** (Amun) and Amaunet. In this system the second name in each pair is the feminine form of the first, masculine form. The names mean, respectively: water; infinity; darkness; and air/spirit. The term Ogdoad was also used in the **Gnostic** system of **Valentinus,** which was based on eight mystical emanations. In the beginning was the Abyss (masculine), from which came forth Silence (feminine). These gave rise to Mind (masculine) and Truth (feminine), who then projected Word (masculine) and Life (feminine). From their union Man (masculine) and the Church (feminine) were born.

**Ogham** A Celtic divinatory system featuring 25 characters associated with trees and shrubs. They are: the birch, rowan, alder, willow, ash, hawthorn, oak, holly, hazel, apple, grapevine, ivy, reed, blackthorn, elder, silver fir, furze, heather, white poplar, yew, spindle, honeysuckle, pine, and beech. An additional character in the system is "grove", representing a collection of trees and "the totality of knowledge". Each tree character is represented by a stave and is associated with specific physical, mental, and spiritual qualities. Of Irish origin and sometimes referred to as the "alphabet of the trees", ogham was also a practical system of writing involving vertical and oblique strokes of different lengths, used for inscriptions on memorial stones and other monuments. See also **Ogma**.

**Ogma** In Irish Celtic mythology, the son of **Dagda** and **Boann** and one of the **Tuatha de Danann**. He was the god of learning and poetry and was said to have been the creator of **ogham** – the famous Irish "tree alphabet".

**Ogoun** In voodoo, the "lord of the thunderbolt" – the **loa** of fire and war. He is the patron of warriors and also the ironsmiths who produce weapons of war. By extension Ogoun represents power, strength, and authority. Compare **Ogum**.

**Ogre** In medieval **folklore**, a hideous and frightening man-eating giant.

**Ogum** or **Ogun** Among the Yoruba and devotees of **Macumba**, the warrior god and lord of iron. His colour is red and he includes Mars among his subservient spirits. In some areas Ogum is associated with St George and in others with St Anthony (Santo Antonio). Compare **Ogoun**.

**Ohn** also **Onn**. In the Celtic tree alphabet, the **ogham** representing furze, ash, and gorse and the letter "b". Ohn is also linked to the colour gold.

**Ohrmazd** An alternative form of the name of **Ahura Mazdah**, the Zoroastrian lord of Wisdom.

**Oimelc** See **Imbolc**.

**Ointments, Flying.** See **Flying Ointments**.

**Oir** In the Celtic tree alphabet, the **ogham** representing the spindle tree and the sound "oi". Oir is also linked to the colour red.

**Ojas** A Sanskrit term for magical energy used by members of the **Typhonian Order of the Outer Ones**, a branch of the **Ordo Templi Orientis**.

**Okê** In Macumba, one of the sons of **Iemanjá**. He is the god of hills and mountains.

**Olam** In the Jewish mystical tradition, the Hebrew term for "world". See also **Malkuth**.

**Old Religion** An expression used by contemporary devotees of **Wicca** to describe witchcraft. The term has acquired special significance since the publication of **Margaret Murray**'s influential book *The Witch-Cult in Western Europe* (1921), which described witchcraft as an ancient fertility cult.

**Old Shuck** See **Black Shuck**.

**Olibanum** A fragrant gum resin, also known as frankincense, used since ancient times in sacred rituals.

**Olive** A tree sacred to the Greek goddess Athena, who was said to have first caused it to bear fruit. According to legend, Athena's original olive tree on the Acropolis was burnt by Xerxes when he conquered Athens in 480BCE, but the tree reappeared, as if through an act of **magic**. The olive is also a Christian symbol of peace and divine blessings because a **dove** brought a sprig of olive to Noah, indicating that dry land had appeared and that the Flood was therefore subsiding.

**Olodumare** In Santería, the founder god of creation, the counterpart of the voodoo supreme being **Gran Maître**. From Olodumare came forth three deities: **Nzame**, **Olofi**, and **Baba Nkwa**.

**Olofi** In Santería, a deity associated with Jesus Christ. See **Nzame**.

**Olokun** In Yoruba religion, the sea god embodying the primordial ocean. It was from this ocean that **Olorun** came forth. Olokun is the Yoruba equivalent of **Neptune** and lives in the depths of the sea.

**Ololiuhqui** A hallucinogenic variety of the plant species *Rivea corymbosa* (**morning glory**), whose seeds were used by the Aztecs as an intoxicant. It is also used as a shamanic sacrament by the Zapotec Indians of Mexico. Ololiuhqui causes vivid hallucinations characterized by bright colours and patterns, and was popular during the psychedelic era of the 1960s. See also **Hallucination**.

**Olorun** In Yoruba religion and **Macumba**, the creator god and ruler of heaven who was born from the primordial ocean, **Olokun**. According to the Yoruba tradition, Olorun created two orìsàs, or deities – **Obatalá**, a male deity, who represented the pure sky, and his consort **Odudua**, goddess of the earth. Olorun is a remote deity and is not actively worshipped.

**Olosi** See Omo Oba.

**Olympians, The Twelve Great** The twelve great deities of classical Greek mythology: **Zeus, Hera, Poseidon, Demeter, Apollo, Artemis, Hephaestus, Pallas Athena, Ares, Aphrodite, Hermes**, and **Hestia**. Sometimes **Hades** (**Pluto**) is also added to the list.

**Olympic Spirits** In the medieval grimoire *The Arbatel of Magick*, the seven planetary spirits of Olympus appointed by God to rule the world. They were **Aratron** (Saturn); **Bether** (Jupiter); **Phalec** (Mars); **Och** (sun); **Hagith** (Venus); **Ophiel** (Mercury); and **Phul** (moon). With the exception of Saturn, who has no counterpart among the Twelve Great Olympians, the classical Greek deities who correlate with these spirits are: **Zeus** (Bether), **Ares** (Phalec), **Apollo** (Och), **Aphrodite** (Hagith), **Hermes** (Ophiel), and **Artemis** (Phul).

**Olympiodorus** An early Greek alchemist (c. 400CE) who sought to connect the practice of **alchemy** with cosmological theory. He was the author of a tract on the visions of the Egyptian alchemist **Zosimos**, who lived a century earlier.

**Olympus, Mount** In ancient Greek mythology, the home of the gods and goddesses. Mount Olympus (elevation 9,794 feet) is the highest peak on the Greek peninsula and is located in Macedonia, close to the border of Thessaly. See also **Olympians, The Twelve Great**.

**Omen** A sign relating to some future event. Omens may be favourable or unfavourable and can occur spontaneously or be sought as a result of the many different methods of **divination**. See also **Augur; Prophecy**.

**Omo Oba** In Santería, the immortal human being created by the deities **Nzame, Olofi** and **Baba Nkwa** to rule over the world. Omo Oba became arrogant, fell from grace, and was forced to hide deep undergound. Changing his name to Olosi he then resurfaced in the world like a fallen angel, or **devil**, trying to tempt human beings to break God's laws and commands. Omo Oba was replaced as ruler of the earth by the mortal **Obatalá**.

**Omulu** In Macumba, the god of sickness and cemeteries. According to Brazilian spiritualist Pedro McGregor, Omulu heads one of seven major lines of **Umbanda** spirits. Omulu rules the demons of the graveyard and through his association with St Lazarus also has a connection with **Shapanan**, the god of smallpox.

**One** In **numerology** the symbol of unity, often associated with God, the supreme being and origin of everything in the universe. Those whose ruling number is one are said to be dominating, independent, jealous of rivals, and single-minded in purpose.

**Oneiromancy** A form of divination by interpreting the symbolic or prophetic contents of dreams. In many ancient cultures, dreams have been viewed as portents of the gods, a perspective reformulated by the psychologist Carl Jung, who believed that dreams often reveal spiritual archetypes from the collective unconscious. See also Archetype.

**Oni** In Japanese folk belief, demons with claws and horns that in many ways resemble the devils of medieval sorcery. See Demon.

**Onn** See Ohn.

**Onniont** A term used by the Huron Indians of eastern Canada to refer to a potent magical charm. Said to resemble a serpent or armoured fish, the charm is capable of penetrating anything that stands in its way – trees, bears, or rocks – and cannot be stopped by anything else.

**Onocentaur** A medieval variant on the classical centaur, it was half man, half ass. Dedicated at all costs to preserving its own liberty, it would starve itself to death if captured.

**Onomancy** A form of divination by means of interpreting the letters in a person's name, with particular reference to the numbers of vowels and the numerical total of the letters. Compare Gematria.

**Onychomancy** A form of divination by interpreting fingernails. The practitioner would watch shadows cast on the fingernails of a young boy and interpret future omens by assessing the shadow shapes formed on the surface of the nails.

**Onyx** In Wicca, a magical stone assigned to the ritual celebration of Yule.

**Open and Shut** See Solve et Coagula.

**Open State** See Void (2).

**Ophidian Current** From the Greek *ophis*, "snake", sexual energies used in magical ceremonies, especially in the Ordo Templi Orientis. Here the symbolism of the snake parallels that of the kundalini serpent, which is aroused in the chakra at the base of the spine. See also Draconian Current; Tantra.

**Ophiel** According to *The Arbatel of Magick*, there are seven different "Olympic Spirits" appointed by God to rule the world. Ophiel is the spirit of Mercury, and is a teacher of all the magical arts. He can convert quicksilver into the Philosopher's Stone.

**Ophiolatry** From the Greek *ophis*, "snake", serpent worship. The symbolism of the snake often has a sexual connotation. See also Kundalini; Magic, Sexual; Ophidian Current; Tantra.

**Ophites** A Gnostic sect in Syria, members of which traced their descent from Seth, the third son of Adam and Eve, and worshipped the serpent (Greek *ophis*). The Ophites believed that the snake was really Sophia, the personification of divine wisdom, and the enemy of Ialdabaoth. The Ophites are sometimes known as Sethian-Ophites. See also Ophiolatry.

**Opifex** Latin, "maker of works". A term used by the kabbalist and Hermetic philosopher Agrippa to refer to God, the supreme creator of the world, whose presence could be evoked through celestial magic. See Agrippa von Nettesheim, Heinrich Cornelius.

**Opposition** In astrology, the situation that exists when two planets are separated by 180 degrees and are therefore opposite each other. Depending on the planets in question, an opposition could be deemed to be favourable or unfavourable.

**Ops** See Rhea; Saturn.

**Opus Alchymicum** or **Opus Circulatorium** In alchemy, a name given to the repeated process óf dissolutions and coagulations which occur as the base metal or matter is dissolved into the **prima materia** and then coagulated into a newer, purer form – culminating finally in a perfect blending of elements and the attainment of the **Philosopher's Stone**.

**Opus, Stages of the** In alchemy, the opus, or work, was divided into four main stages, each represented by a different colour. These stages were the **nigredo** (black); the **albedo** (white/silver); the **citrinitas** (yellow), and the **rubedo** (red/gold). After the fifteenth century, references to the citrinitas were gradually phased out and the opus then had three main stages.

**Oracle** A person serving as an intermediary between a supernatural being and those seeking counsel or **prophecy**. Often the oracle takes the role of a medium and becomes possessed by the god from whom the prophecy is sought. At the shrine of Delphi in ancient Greece, the Pythian oracle would enter a trance state and make oracular pronouncements that were said to be communications from **Apollo**, patron of the shrine. These often rather obscure statements were then interpreted and communicated by the officiating priests. See **Delphic Oracle**.

**Orb** In astrology, the space on a horoscope within which an **aspect** is deemed to be effective. Astrologers differentiate between "wide" or "exact" aspects.

**Ordeal by Water** See Swimming.

**Order of the Silver Star** See Argenteum Astrum.

**Order of the Temple** See Knights Templar.

**Ordo Rosae Rubeae et Aureae Crucis** The "Order of the Red Rose and the Golden Cross", the second, or inner,

order in the **Hermetic Order of the Golden Dawn**. Its initiatory grades – **Adeptus Minor, Adeptus Major,** and **Adeptus Exemptus** – corresponded to the spheres of **Tiphareth, Geburah,** and **Chesed** on the kabbalistic **Tree of Life**. See also **Kabbalah**.

**Ordo Templi Orientis (O.T.O.)** The "Order of the Temple of the East", a sexual magic order formed by **Karl Kellner** c. 1896. After Kellner died in 1905, leadership passed to **Theodor Reuss**, and then in 1922 to **Aleister Crowley**. There are now two organizations that bear the name O.T.O. The first of these is headed by the tantric **occultist Kenneth Grant** in England, and the second by the successors of Grady McMurtry in California. Members of the O.T.O. arouse sexual energy during their magical ceremonies and identify with the gods and goddesses who personify this principle.

**Oreads** In Greek mythology, mountain nymphs who attended **Artemis** on the hunt. The most famous of these was Echo.

**Orenda** (1) A term used by the Iroquois Indians to refer to the magical nature of power. It is this power that is found in all matter, as well as in the spiritual world, and it is by harnessing this power that the shaman is able to perform acts of healing and magical transformation.

**Orenda** (2) Among the Iroquois Indians, the term for the life-principle. Objects, animals, and human beings could possess it and medicine men could draw upon it as a source of magical power. It can be compared with **manitou** (Algonquin Indians, and wakan (Sioux Indians) and mana (Melanesia/ Polynesia). See also **Medicine Man**.

**Orgy** Sexual revelry and debauchery, associated in the occult tradition with such ceremonies as the medieval witches' sabbath, during which the **Horned God** was worshipped, and with the frenzied dancing and drunken rites held in classical Greece and Rome in honour of **Dionysus**, and **Bacchus** respectively.

**Orias** or **Oriax** In the Goetia, the 59th spirit, a powerful marquis who appears in the form of a lion, or a lion-faced man, riding on a strong horse. He has a serpent's tail and holds two hissing serpents in his right hand. Orias teaches the "virtues of the stars and the mansions of the planets" and is able to gain favours from friends and foes alike. He governs 30 legions of spirits and is also known as Oriax.

**Origen** (c. 185 – c. 284CE) One of the most influential theologians in the early Christian Church, Origen fell from favour because he advocated the pre-existence of the **soul** and its **reincarnation** in subsequent lifetimes. Although St Gregory of Nyssa called him "the prince of Christian learning in the third century", it is clear that Origen was strongly influenced by Platonic thought and inclined towards **Gnosticism**. His theology was condemned at the Church's fifth ecumenical council in 553, when the "Anathemas Against Pre-Existence" became part of Church doctrine.

**Orìsà** In Macumba, a god or goddess. The term means "master of the head". Compare **Orisha**.

**Orisha** In Yoruban magic and **Santeria**, a god or goddess – literally "master of the head". Sometimes called Orixá Compare **Orìsà**.

**Orishakô** In Macumba, the god of agriculture. Also considered a god of fertility by the Yoruba, he is celebrated at harvest time, or during the new moon – such occasions being regarded as a time for sexual license among his worshippers. Orishakô is one of the sons of the water goddess **Iemanjá**.

**Orixá** See Orìsà

**Orlog** In Scandinavian mythology, the term for destiny or fate. Orlog was determined by the **Norns** – the three goddesses Verdandi, Urd, and Skuld, who guarded the World Tree, **Yggdrasil**.

**Ornithomancy** A form of **divination** by interpreting the songs or flight patterns of birds. In ancient Rome this form of divination was part of the national religion. See also **Augury**.

**Orobas** In the Goetia, the 55th spirit, a great and mighty prince who appears initially in the form of a horse but who will assume a human form if so commanded. He discovers all things past, present, and still to come and can provide valuable information about the creation of the world and the nature of divinity. According to the Goetia, Orobas will remain faithful to the evoking magician and will not allow him to be tempted by any other spirit. Orobas governs 20 legions of spirits.

**Orphan** In alchemy, a term applied, somewhat ironically, to the **Philosopher's Stone**, which emerges as a result of the union and "death" of its parents – sulphur and argent vive.

**Orpheus** In Greek mythology, a musician who sang so beautifully and played his lyre so enchantingly that birds and animals came to listen to him. The son of Calliope, one of the **Muses**, and the Olympian god **Apollo**, Orpheus is associated with the region of Thrace in northern Greece. He is also famous in Greek mythology as one of the few living beings (like **Theseus**, **Heracles**, and **Odysseus**) who visited Hades. Orpheus descended to the **Underworld** to seek his wife Eurydice, who had been fatally bitten by a snake. His beautiful singing endeared him to Hades, who agreed to release Eurydice if Orpheus did not set eyes on her before they reached their home. But Orpheus could not resist turning to look at her and his wife was compelled to return to the Underworld.

**Orphic Cults** Cults in Hellenistic Greece and in the Roman empire which claimed affiliation with the legendary singer **Orpheus**. The so-called Orphic literature consists of numerous hymns, songs, and poems composed by various authors but attributed to Orpheus and incorporated into the mystery tradition. See also **Mystery Religion**.

**Orun** In Yoruba religion and **Macumba**, the sun. According to Yoruba mythology, Orun sprang forth from the womb of Iemanjá, the goddess of salt water, after she was raped by her son **Orungan**.

**Orungan** In Yoruba religion and Macumba, the son of Iemanjá and her brother, Aganjú. Orungan fell desperately in love with his mother and subsequently raped her. As she stumbled through the forest and fell on the ground, her breasts ripped apart to make twin rivers that became a lake, and from her womb sprang eleven orìsàs, as well as the sun and moon. See **Orìsà**.

**Orunmila** In Yoruba religion and Macumba, the god of knowledge and the deity identified with the body of knowledge known as the odú.

**Os** In the Germanic **Elder Futhark**, the rune letter representing the number four. Os corresponds to the letter "a". The word os means "god" or "deity" and is specifically linked to **Odin**. Os is associated with sacred power, wisdom, inspiration, good counsel, effective communication, and inheritance.

**Osculum Infame** Latin for the "kiss of shame".

**Ose** In the Goetia, the 57th spirit, a great president who appears initially in the form of a leopard but then transforms into human shape. He offers to provide truthful answers concerning sacred and secret things and to make one cunning in the knowledge of the liberal sciences. He is also able to change men into any shape the evoking magician may desire. Ose commands 30 legions of spirits and is also known as Voso.

**Oshú** In Yoruba religion and **Macumba**, the moon. According to Yoruba mythology, Oshú sprang forth from the womb of Iemanjá, the goddess of salt water, after she was raped by her son Orungan.

**Oshun** In Yoruba religion and Macumba, the goddess of the River Oshun and goddess of food. The daughter of Iemanjá, Oshun was also the second wife of Xangô, god of thunder and lightning. She is revered as "queen of the sweet water" and devotees appeal to her in times of need.

**Osiris** In ancient Egypt, a major deity associated with vegetation and fertility, who personified the principle of spiritual rebirth. Osiris was the son of Geb and Nut, the brother and husband of Isis, and the brother of Set. Set was jealous of Osiris and one day tricked him into climbing into a chest, which was later thrown into the Nile. Isis retrieved his dead body, but Set again discovered it and tore it into fourteen pieces, which he scattered around the kingdom. Isis again went in search of Osiris' body and through her magical skills reassembled and embalmed her husband and restored him to life for long enough for her to conceive the god Horus. (In another version, Isis found all the parts except the phallus, which had been swallowed by a crab in the Nile). Osiris then descended to the underworld as its ruler and lord of fertility and regeneration. See also **Judgment Hall; Mummification**.

**Ostara** In Wicca, the festival of the spring equinox. See **Sabbats, Lesser**.

**Othala** See Odal.

**O.T.O.** The initials of the **Ordo Templi Orientis**.

221

**Otz Chiim** In the Kabbalah, the Hebrew term for the Tree of Life.

**Oum'phor** See Hounfor.

**Our Lady of the Stars** In the Thelemite cosmology of the **Ordo Templi Orientis**, a reference to the Egyptian goddess Nuit or **Nut**. Nuit is the goddess of the night sky. Following his revelation in Cairo in 1904, ceremonial magician **Aleister Crowley** came to believe that he was an incarnation of Ra-Hoor-Khuit, the divine child of Nuit and **Hadit**, a Chaldean counterpart to **Set**, the Egyptian god of darkness. See also **Thelema**.

**Ouroboros** In Gnosticism and alchemy, a symbol depicting a snake devouring its own tail. It symbolizes the cycles of life and nature, the fusion of opposites, and the transcendence of duality. Also known as Uroboros.

**Outer Order** In the Hermetic Order of the Golden Dawn, the initiatory grades corresponding to the **sephiroth** of **Malkuth, Yesod, Hod,** and **Netzach** on the kabbalistic **Tree of Life**.

**Out-of-the-Body Experience (O.B.E.)** A dissociative experience characterized by the sensation that one's consciousness is separate and distinct from one's body, and at some distance removed. Numerous case histories exist of people who have claimed to float above their bodies or above rooftops, and even to pass through walls and other solid objects. The out-of-the-body experience is commonly referred to as **astral travel** (or astral projection), although the latter term is more correctly used when the O.B.E. is produced by will.

**Oval** See Egg; Alembic.

**Oven** In alchemy, the slow-burning furnace or **athanor**, used in the **opus alchymicum**.

**Overlooking** A word used to describe the act of cursing a victim with the **evil eye**.

**Owl** A nocturnal bird associated in many cultures with evil powers, death, and misfortune. The Romans regarded the owl as a sinister bird associated with omens of bad tidings, but also used it as a motif to combat the effects of the **evil eye**. In folk belief, the owl is also thought of as the bird of wisdom, possibly as a result of its link with the ancient Greek goddess **Athena**.

**Owl Shamans** Among the Kiowa Indians, shamans who derive their power from owls. Owls are linked to **sorcery** because they are considered to be the souls of the dead. They are also associated with evil whirlwinds that blow over people while they are asleep, causing paralysis. Owl shamans have the ability to summon spirits for divinatory and healing purposes. See also **Owl**.

**Oxalá** In Yoruba religion and **Macumba**, the supreme deity next to God himself. Sometimes identified with Christ, Oxalá is the god of the sky and the universe. He embodies purity and beauty and his sacred colour is white.

**Oxalis** A mystic emblem among the **Druids**. See also **Clover**.

**Oxo** In Enochian magic, the fifteenth **Aethyr**. The meanings associated with Oxo include joy, happiness, dances, songs, and music. It is associated with **Libra** and **earth** and its magical number is 460.

**Oxóssi** or **Oxôce** In Yoruba religion and **Macumba**, the god of hunting and the jungle. He is associated with St Sebastian and is depicted as a tortured young man with arrows piercing his body.

**Ôxun** In Yoruba religion and **Macumba**, the goddess of fresh water. Her name suggests she might once have been an aspect of **Oshun**, but Oxun –

whose name is sometimes spelt Oxum – has now become associated with Our Lady of the Conception.

**Oxzem** A term used by the Cheyenne Indians to refer to the spirit lance used by shamans to inflict injuries on their enemies. See also **Eehyom**.

**Oya** In Yoruba religion and **Macumba**, one of **Iemanjá**'s daughters and, like her sister **Oshun**, a wife of **Xangô**, the god of thunder and lightning. The goddess of violent rainstorms, she turned into the River Niger.

**Oyá** In Santería, the patroness of justice and favourite concubine of **Changó**, the god of fire, thunder, and lightning. Oyá also governs death and cemeteries. She is associated with St Theresa and St Catherine.

# P

**Pact** An agreement. In medieval magic, it was often taken to mean a pact with the **Devil** in which one bartered one's soul for worldly pleasures and supernatural powers. See also **Faust**.

**Paean** A song or chant of praise. According to Greek mythology, the first paean was sung by **Apollo** after he had killed the giant serpent **Python** at Delphi.

**Pagan** One who was not a Christian, Jew, or Muslim. The term was used derogatorily to describe a **heathen** or "unbeliever", but has now assumed a new currency among practitioners of **neopaganism**, **witchcraft**, and **magic**. The so-called neopagans or "new pagans" are dedicated to reviving the **Old Religion** and reestablishing the worship of nature and the lunar goddess. See also **Lunar Goddesses**.

**Pagan Federation Ethic** In Wicca, an expanded form of the **Wiccan Rede** issued by the Pagan Federation in London. It outlines a basic philosophy of life from a **pagan** or Wiccan point of view, as follows:
1. **Love for and kinship with nature** – rather than the more customary attitude of aggression and domination over nature; reverence for the life force and the ever-renewing cycles of life and death. 2. **The pagan ethic:** "Do what thou wilt, but harm none." This is a positive morality, not a list of thou-shalt-nots. Each individual is responsible for discovering his or her own true nature and developing it fully, in harmony with the outer world. 3. **The concept of goddess and god** – as expressions of the divine reality; an active participation in the cosmic dance of goddess and god, female and male, rather than the suppression of either the female or the male principle.

**Paganing** In neopaganism and Wicca, a ritual of dedication which commits a person to study and practise paganism. It includes a vow of allegiance to the "old ways" and to the gods and goddesses worshipped in pagan traditions.

**Pagao, Exú** In Macumba a surrogate of Exú.

**Paimon** In the Goetia, the ninth spirit, a great king who is "very obedient unto Lucifer". Paimon rides on a dromedary – a single-humped Arabian camel – and wears a crown on his head. He is accompanied by a host of spirits in human form, blasting forth with trumpets, cymbals, and other musical instruments. Paimon roars with a loud voice, which can be alarming, but he is nevertheless highly skilled in all the arts and sciences, including the potentials of the mind. Observed towards the West, he rules 200 legions of spirits. Those evoking Paimon must make him an offering but the magician will then be granted familiar spirits.

**Pakht** In ancient Egypt, a goddess who had the head of a lion and was sometimes identified with Bast. Compare Sekhmet.

**Palindrome** A word or phrase that has the same spelling when read forwards or backwards, e.g. "radar". Palindromes are sometimes used in magic squares and are believed to have considerable potency as magical formulae.

**Palingenesis** Rebirth or regeneration, a term sometimes used to refer to the rebirth or transmigration of the human soul after death. The medieval alchemist Paracelsus believed that when a physical form was destroyed its astral counterpart remained and he speculated that plants could be brought back to life from their ashes.

**Pan** In ancient Greek mythology, sometimes said to be the son of Hermes and Dryope. Pan was the god of flocks and shepherds, but also had a more far-reaching role as lord of nature and all forms of wildlife. He was depicted as half man, half goat, and played a pipe with seven reeds. Ever lecherous, he had numerous love affairs with the nymphs, notably Echo, Syrinx, and Pithys. Pan's name means "All", and among practitioners of witchcraft he is regarded as a high god. See also Pan-Pipe; Pantheism.

**Pan-Pipe** The seven-reeded pipe played by the Greek god Pan. It was also known as a syrinx, because the nymph Syrinx had been transformed into the reed from which Pan fashioned his first pan-pipe.

**Pantheism** The religious and mystical doctrine that the whole universe is God and that every part of the universe is an aspect or manifestation of God. The term is also used to describe the worship of all the gods of a pantheon, and is sometimes applied generally to mean "nature worship." See also Neopaganism; Wicca.

**Pantheon** A group of gods·and goddesses who are worshipped collectively. Ancient Greece, Rome, and Egypt provide prime examples of civilizations where a pantheon of deities has been worshipped. See also Ennead; Ogdoad; Olympians, Twelve Great.

**Papa** In voodoo, a reference to Legba in his role as the "guardian of the gates". For some practitioners of voodoo, Legba has become linked with St Peter, to whom Christ gave the keys to the kingdom of heaven.

**Paphia** In ancient Greek mythology, the name for Aphrodite in her role as goddess of sexual love. The name derives from her shrine at Paphos and in turn gives rise to the word paphian.

**Paphian** Sexual, illicit love, sometimes used to describe acts of prostitution. The term derives from Paphia, which was one of the names for the goddess of love, Aphrodite.

**Papus** (1865–1916) A Spanish-born physician who lived in Paris, published a number of occult works, and contributed significantly to the literature on the Tarot. Papus, whose real name was Gérard Encausse, was influenced by **Theosophy** and spent much of his time delving into Hermetic, kabbalistic, and alchemical texts. A member of the kabbalistic Order of the Rosy Cross, Papus believed that esoteric knowledge was transmitted by a secret line of occult adepts and counted himself among their number. He acquired a reputation as a necromancer and, on one occasion in 1905, was summoned to the Russian imperial palace where he performed a ceremony to summon the spirit of Tsar Alexander III. Like Eliphas Lévi, Papus was best known for his writings on the Tarot and for connecting the cards of the *Major Arcana* to the Hebrew alphabet. His most significant work in English is ~*The Tarot of the Bohemians* (reissued 1970), but he published widely in French. His other books include *Traité Méthodique de Science Occulte* (1891); *La Kabbale* (1892); *Le Diable et l'Occultisme* (1895); and *La Magie et l'Hypnose* (1897). See also **Alchemy**; *Hermetica, The*; Kabbalah; Necromancy; Rosicrucians.

***Papyri Graecae Magicae*** "Greek Magical Papyruses", a collection of magical spell-books from Graeco-Roman Egypt, dating from the second century CE. Like modern cooks, magical practitioners preserved their painstakingly accumulated secrets in their private notebooks, which contained specific hints, notes, and ideas – some of them borrowed or adapted, some independently developed. Many of these secret writings were handed down from father to son.

**Paracelsus** (1493–1541) Pseudonym of one of the most illustrious of the medieval metaphysicians. He was born Theophrastus Bombastus von Hohenheim at Einsiedeln, near Zurich in Switzerland. He spent his childhood at Villach in Carinthia, and is thought to have pursued medical studies under the direction of his father, who was a physician. Nothing else is known of his early medical training, but it is thought that he received his doctorate from the medical school at the university of Ferrara in northern Italy, c. 1515. He then travelled to Rome, Naples, Spain, Portugal, Paris, London, Moscow, Constantinople, and Greece. He subsequently accepted a position as city physician and professor of medicine at Basle in 1526. He only stayed in Basle for eleven months, however, and then became an itinerant physician for the rest of his life, living in many different places in Austria and Germany.

Paracelsus was highly regarded as a physician, specializing in bronchial illnesses and developing the first comprehensive treatment for syphilis, but he also denounced earlier medical pioneers like Avicenna, Galen, and Rhasis for being pedantic and too theoretical. Paracelsus believed that medicine was based on four distinct foundations: a sound philosophical approach; astronomy (by which he really meant medical **astrology**); **alchemy**; and the moral purity of the physician himself. He wrote extensively on the connections between medicine and astrology and was interested in the possible links between weather and illness. Paracelsus emphasized the Hermetic doctrine of the **macrocosm and microcosm**, believing that each human being was a mirror of the universe, and he also developed the so-called "doctrine of signatures" which he had inherited from **Albertus Magnus**. This concept is based on the principle that every part of the human organism (the microcosm) corresponds to a part of the macrocosm, or spiritual universe, and the connection is then established through some similarity in colour or form – which is its essential "signature". Paracelsus regarded disease as a form of imbalance, and maintained that a healthy person combined the three alchemical constituents of **sulphur** (male), **mercury** (female), and **salt**

ALTERIVS NON SIT, QVI SVVS ESSE POTEST.

LAVS DEO, PAX VIVIS, REQVIES ÆTERNA SEPVLTIS.

OMNE DONVM PERFECTVM A DEO, IMPERE A DIABO.

AVREOLVS PHILIPPVS THEOPHRASTVS

PARACELSUS  Perhaps the most famous of all medieval alchemists, Paracelsus believed that human beings were mirrors of the universe. He also claimed knowledge of the Philosopher's Stone.

(neutral) in perfect harmony. He also subscribed to the idea that each of the **elements** was governed by elemental spirits (he called the spirits of fire *acthnici*; the spirits of air *nenufareni*; the spirits of water *melosinae;* and the spirits of earth *pigmaci*). Basically, Paracelsus believed what many holistic practitioners and naturopaths continue to believe today. As he expressed it: "Medicine is founded upon nature, nature herself is medicine, and in her only shall men seek it. And nature is the teacher of the physician, for she is older than he." In addition to his training and work as a physician, Paracelsus also studied with Johannes Trithemius, abbot of Sponheim, who had instructed **Cornelius Agrippa** in the magical traditions. In *The Archidoxes of Magic* Paracelsus writes: "Some will think that I write **witchcraft**, or some such like things, which are far absent from me. For this I certainly affirm, that I write nothing here which is supernatural and which is not wrought and effected by the power of nature and celestial influences." Nevertheless, he did believe that sacred names, magical motifs, and astrological symbols could be inscribed on lamens (magical talismans; see **Lamen**) and then hung around the patient's neck at the appropriate astrological time as part of an effective medical cure. By way of explanation, Paracelsus wrote: "Characters, letters and signs have several virtues and operations, wherewith also the nature of metals, the condition of heaven, and the influence of the planets, with their operations, and the significations and proprieties of characters, signs and letters, and the observation of the times, do concur and agree together. Who can object that these signs and seals have not their virtue and operations?"

Like Cornelius Agrippa, Paracelsus considered his magical and medical knowledge compatible with the teachings of the Christian tradition, for he continues: "All this is to be done by the help and assistance of the father of all medicines, our Lord Jesus Christ, our only Saviour." The main works of Paracelsus are contained in the two-volume edition *The Hermetic and Alchemical Writings of Paracelsus* (edited by A.E. Waite, 1894) and *The Archidoxes of Magic* (reissued 1975).

**Paramahansa** In Hinduism, the highest grade of spiritual enlightenment and the equivalent of the grade of **Ipsissimus** on the kabbalistic **Tree of Life**. The ceremonial magician **Aleister Crowley** claimed this grade by describing himself as a *Paramahansa* in his book *Eight Lectures in Yoga* published by the **Ordo Templi Orientis** in 1939.

**Parcae** The Latin name by which the three **Fates** were known.

**Parergon** In alchemy, the left eye of the soul, which is directed towards time. The right eye of the soul – the **ergon** – looks toward eternity.

**Paroketh** In the **Kabbalah**, the "veil" that separates **Tiphareth** from the lower spheres on the **Tree of Life**. The mystic has to pass through Paroketh to receive the solar rebirth-initiation of Tiphareth.

**Parsons, Jack** (1914–1952) Born Marvel Whiteside Parsons but known to his friends as John or Jack, Parsons was one of the pioneers of American rocket science. He helped create the Jet Propulsion Laboratory in Pasadena, California, and founded the company that today makes the solid-fuel boosters used on the NASA Space Shuttle. Parsons' link to the magical world arose through his connection with **Aleister Crowley**. Crowley visited the United States and Canada in 1915 and in Vancouver he met briefly with an expatriate Englishman named Wilfred Talbot Smith, an associate of **Frater Achad**. Smith moved to Los Angeles in 1930 and opened the **Agapé Lodge** of the **Ordo Templi Orientis**, dedicated to the practice of Crowleyan magic and the **Law of Thelema**. In 1939 Jack Parsons attended a performance of the **Gnostic Mass**, Crowley's magical alternative to the Roman Catholic Mass, and in 1941 Parsons and his wife Helen were initiated into the Lodge, at the same time becoming members of the **Argenteum Astrum**. In 1945 Parsons met **L. Ron Hubbard** – who later founded Scientology – and subsequently shared some of the O.T.O. rituals with him, thereby breaking his oath of secrecy. In January 1946 Parsons and Hubbard began an experiment titled the **Babalon Working** in which they sought to use **Enochian magic** and goetic incantations from *The Lesser Key of Solomon* to manifest an air elemental who could become the mother of a **moonchild**. This moonchild would in turn be a spirit manifestation of Babalon, goddess of the New Aeon. In February 1946 Parsons wrote to Crowley – for whom the **Whore of Babalon** was a central figure – announcing that the "elemental" had arrived in the form of Marjorie Elizabeth Cameron, a woman with red hair and slanting green eyes as specified in the ritual. Cameron subsequently became Parsons' lover and magical partner. In 1948 Parsons took a magical oath seeking to cross the magical **Abyss**, and continued his ritual activities. On 17 June 1952 he died in a mysterious explosion, while experimenting in his garage. Some have speculated that he was trying to create a **homunculus**, or artificial intelligence. See also **Aeon of Horus; Moonchild**.

**Partzufim** From the Hebrew, "veils", "faces". In the kabbalistic teachings of **Isaac Luria**, a term relating to different aspects of the **godhead**, YHVH. Luria correlated these letters with the terms "Vast Face" (God without attributes), "Ancient Father", "Ancient Mother", and "Small Face" (God in the manifested world). They also correspond to the **Four Worlds** in the **Kabbalah**.

**Pasqually, Martinez** See Martinism.

**Pathworkings** In modern western magic, a **guided imagery** technique in which the subject is led along "inner pathways" of consciousness in order to experience archetypal visions. Pathworkings often make use of the symbolism of the **Major Arcana** of the **Tarot**, and are designed to trigger a personal experience of the gods and goddesses of the magical **pantheon**. Pathworkings may be regarded as inner magical journeys that make use of active imagination. Among the most detailed descriptions of pathworkings in contemporary occult literature are *The Shining Paths* (1983) by **Dolores Ashcroft-Nowicki** and *The Tarot Workbook* (2004) by Nevill Drury.

**Pautiwa** Among the Zuni Indians, the chief of the **Kachina** priests.

**Paz** In **Enochian Magic**, the fourth **Aethyr**. The meanings associated with Paz include love, positive relationships, and the attraction of opposites. Paz is associated with **Leo, Taurus**, and Caput

Draconis and its magical number is 24.

**Pe** In **voodoo**, the altar stone located in the **hounfor**, or temple. The pe is covered with candles as well as small **govi** vessels thought to contain the spirits of the ancestors.

**Peacock's Tail** In alchemy, the stage in the **opus alchymicum** which occurs straight after the **nigredo** – the black, "deathly" phase – and just before the pure white phase, or **albedo**. According to alchemical tradition, when the dark impurities of the nigredo were washed away, they were replaced by a vivid and colourful display which resembled the tail of a peacock. This may have been caused by the iridescence sometimes observed on the surface of molten metals.

**Pearl** In Wicca, a magical stone assigned to the ritual celebration of **Litha**.

**Pedro, Don Juan Felipe** The Spanish **voodoo** priest and former slave after whom the **Petro** rites are named.

**Pegasus** In Greek mythology, the legendary winged horse which emerged from the blood of the gorgon Medusa when Perseus cut off her head. It was when mounted on Pegasus that the Corinthian hero Bellerophon killed the monstrous **Chimera**. See also **Gorgons**.

**Peh** The Hebrew letter ascribed to the path linking **Hod** and **Netzach** on the **Tree of Life**. Peh has a numerical value of 80 (and, as a final letter, 800). In modern magical visualization and **pathworkings** the Tarot card associated with this path on the Tree is *The Tower*. Also Pey.

**Peji** In Macumba, the inner sanctuary of the **terreiro**, or temple. This is where the sacred implements associated with the deities are kept and where special ritual offerings are made.

**Peladan, Sar Josephin** (1858–1918) A

French astrologer, **magician**, and novelist who became a fashionable aesthete in the Rosicrucian salons in Paris during the 1890s. Peladan took the title "La Sar Merodack" after the kings of Babylon, and wore a full, Assyrian-style beard for effect. Sar Peladan was a friend and occult colleague of **Stanislas de Guaita** and assisted him in the **magical attack** against **Joseph-Antoine Boullan**. See also **Rosicrucians**.

**Pelican** In alchemy, a circulatory still with a dome at the top of its belly and tubes leading back into the bottom of the still allowing distilled liquid to be retained. It was so called because it resembled a pelican holding its beak to its breast.

**Pemba** In Macumba, ritual chalk used ceremonially to draw *pontos riscados*, or magical diagrams. See **Ponto Riscado**.

**Penates** Roman household deities, similar to the **lares**. The penates were literally the gods of the pantry, and every household had a shrine with figurines of these dieties.

**Pendderwen, Gwydion** See Faery Tradition.

**Pentacle** In Wicca, a circular disc of metal – usually copper – which represents the element **earth**. It typically features inscriptions of a **pentagram**, the waxing and waning moon-crescents of the **Great Goddess**, and a symbol of the **Horned God**. The pentacle is a centrepiece for the ceremonial altar. Together with the chalice, the pentacle represents the female polarity in ritual workings.

**Pentacles** In the Tarot, one of the four suits – the others being **cups, wands,** and **swords** – Pentacles represent the feminine element **earth**. See also Pentacle.

**Pentagram** A five-pointed star. The pentagram is an important symbol in western **magic** and represents the four

elements surmounted by the **spirit**. It is regarded as a symbol of human spiritual aspirations when the point faces upwards; but is a symbol of bestiality and retrograde evolution when facing down. The pentagram is inscribed in the air at the four quarters during the banishing ritual of the Lesser Pentagram, a ceremonial purging of negative influences from the magical temple.

**Peorth** In the Germanic **Elder Futhark**, the **rune** letter representing the number fourteen. Peorth corresponds to the letter "p" and is associated with change, coincidence, and fate. By extension this rune is also connected to the idea of receiving unexpected help from an external and unknown source. Peorth suggests that mysterious forces are always at play in our lives and we should not depend too much on the "reality" of external appearances. Also Perthro.

**Perfumes, Magical** See Magical Perfumes.

**Periapt** From the Greek *periapton*, "an object fastened around", an **amulet** or charm worn as a protection against spells and the **evil eye**.

**Periplus** Literally a voyage around a coast, a circumnavigation. The term is also used to refer to the concept of progressive initiation, whereby participants have to move from one sacred location to another, as on a pilgrimage. Visits to such holy sites represent stages along the path to spiritual illumination. See also **Illumination; Initiation**.

**Peristyle** In architecture, a range of columns around the outside of a building, courtyard, or square, often supporting a covered walkway, as in a cloister. Peristyles are common features of Egyptian and Graeco-Roman temples. In **voodoo**, the term is applied to the roofed, unwalled area where most ceremonies take place. See also **Hounfor**.

**Persea** A species of wild laurel tree sacred to the ancient Egyptians and considered to be a symbol of eternal fame. Thoth, the Egyptian god of wisdom, and Safekh, the goddess of knowledge, were said to write the names of pharaohs and high priests on its leaves to ensure that they were remembered forever.

**Persecution of Witches** See Burning Times.

**Persephone** In Greek mythology, the goddess of spring. Persephone was the daughter of Zeus and Demeter and is the archetypal "Divine Maiden". Persephone was picking flowers on the Nysian plain when she was overwhelmed by the beauty of a narcissus. At this moment the earth opened and Hades rushed forth in his chariot, snatching Persephone down into the bowels of the earth. She became queen of the Underworld; but after an angry Demeter appealed to Zeus, Persephone was able to spend two-thirds of the year above the ground and only a third (the winter) below. Persephone was the personification of the wheat grain, and symbolized the cyclic patterns of nature. She was a central deity in the mystery religion of Eleusis. Persephone was also known as Kore ("Maiden"), and her Roman counterpart was Proserpina.

**Perthro** See Peorth.

**Petro** A branch of voodoo. The Petro rites have a Caribbean rather than African origin and originated in Haiti during the period of slavery. Thought to be named after Don Juan Felipe Pedro, a Spanish voodoo priest and former slave, the Petro rites are more violent than the African Rada ceremonies and reflect the violence and rage associated with slavery. In Petro rites the colour red is used both on the face and on ceremonial clothing, the drumming is more upbeat, and the loas are more aggressive. In Petro ceremonies pigs are sacrificed to honour the gods.

**Pey** See Peh.

**Peyote** A cactus used in shamanic ceremonies because of its psychedelic properties. The Huichol Indians conduct a ritual hunt for this sacred plant after the rainy season in the early spring, and subsequently consume around a dozen "buttons" each during the night. After approximately an hour, exhilarating effects occur – colour and sound are intensified and subjects experience heightened awareness and perception. Peyote cactus contains eight isoquinoline alkaloids, one of which – mescaline – produces vivid hallucinations. Also known as Mescal Buttons. See also Shamanism.

**Phaeton** See Chariot of Phaeton.

**Phagos** In the Celtic tree alphabet, the ogham representing the witch hazel and beech and the sound "ae". Phagos is also linked to the colours black and white. Also known as Emancoll.

**Phalec** According to the medieval grimoire *The Arbatel of Magick*, there are seven different Olympic Spirits, appointed by God to rule the world. Phalec is the spirit of Mars and governs all activities relating to war.

**Phallus** The male sexual organ. The paramount male symbol in all creeds and practices based on fertility and sexual worship, the phallus is represented by such diverse forms as the maypole, the magician's wand, and the snake. The phallus is known in yoga as the lingam. In tantric yoga the procreative sexual union of Shiva and Shakti gives rise to the entire universe.

**Phantom** From the Latin *phantasma*, an apparition or ghost presumed to be the spirit of a deceased person.

**Phial** See Vial.

**Phillips, Julia** An Australian Wiccan high priestess and author, Phillips' formal study of the occult dates from 1971 when she began attending lectures at the Society of Psychical Research in London. In 1991 she founded the Australian Pagan Alliance and its magazine *Pagan Times*. She is the author of *Witches of Oz* (1994), a guide to the practice of Wicca in the southern hemisphere, and has also contributed to several other magical anthologies.

**Philosopher** In alchemy, the alchemist himself. Many alchemists regarded their pursuit of gold as a quest for "truth", perfection, and mystical union with God, and not simply as the pursuit of material wealth and fortune.

**Philosopher's Stone** In alchemy, the stone of perfection, a substance which could transmute base, "imperfect" metals into gold and which could transform the ordinary unenlightened person into one "illuminated" by spiritual wisdom and truth. While many medieval alchemists sought the Philosopher's Stone in their laboratories, it is clear that the essential idea behind it is a mystical one. It is a central symbol for the essence of life and the oneness of creation. The hexagram is also associated with the Philosopher's Stone, and characteristically it too represents the interrelatedness of matter and spirit. Also called Lapis Philosophorum. See also **Aurum Potabile**.

**Philosophical Bird** See Bird of Hermes.

**Philosophical Child** In alchemy, the "child" born of the union of King Sol and Queen Luna following their coniunctio, or chemical wedding. This child is therefore the Philosopher's Stone itself.

**Philosophical Lead** In alchemy, a term not for common lead but for the prima materia. The expression was also used to denote the "unclean body" that had the potential, through subsequent alchemical processes, to yield perfect gold once its blackness and "corruption" had been purged.

**Philosophical Mercury** In alchemy, mercury that has been prepared by the alchemist's art and which is made from the union of sulphur and argent vive. It was distinguished from the common element mercury and was also known as Mercurius.

**Philosophical Salt** In alchemy, the unifying principle in metals. Philosophical salt is not ordinary salt but an abstract principle relating to the qualities of matter. Philosophical salt keeps matter together by providing its fixed qualities and firmness.

**Philosophical Sulphur** In alchemy, the fiery, masculine, hot dry active seed of metals. Philosophical sulphur is not ordinary sulphur but an abstract principle relating to the qualities of matter. Philosophical sulphur provides its structure or form as well as its combustibility, and also represents the principle of growth.

**Philosophical Tree** Medieval alchemists sometimes represented the opus alchymicum by using the image of a tree. The tree could represent the prima materia itself – it was capable of transformation and refinement and "developed" through various stages. In such cases the tree would be shown growing inside the earth's crust. At other times it is shown as a golden tree located on an island surrounded by the ocean. The tree has seven branches representing the seven planetary metals, and its roots and trunk are nourished by the waters of the mercurial sea.

**Philosophus** In the Hermetic Order of the Golden Dawn, the ritual grade associated with the magical initiation of Netzach, the seventh sphere on the kabbalistic Tree of Life.

**Philtre** A magical potion, intended to arouse love or sexual passion. See also Love Potion.

**Phlegma** A term used by the medieval

alchemist **Paracelsus** to describe **Philosophical Mercury**. Phlegma was one of the three principles of matter (the other two being fat, or **Philosophical Sulphur**, and ash, or **Philosophical Salt**). See also **Mercurius**.

**Phoenix** (1) In the **Goetia**, the 37th spirit, a great marquis who appears in the form of the bird of that name, singing sweet songs with a child's voice. Phoenix will transform into a human shape at the magician's bidding and can provide information on all of the sciences as well as being skilled in the poetic arts. According to magical tradition, Phoenix hopes to return to the seventh throne of King **Solomon** after 1,200 years. Phoenix governs 20 legions of spirits.

**Phoenix** (2) A mythical bird resembling an eagle, which appears in the mythology of many countries. The phoenix is traditionally associated with the **sun**, and in Arabian legend sits in a nest that is ignited by solar rays. In this account, the phoenix is consumed by flames and reduced to ashes; but a worm emerges from the ashes and from it, in turn, arises a new phoenix. In China, the phoenix was similarly associated with the sun and was regarded as an envoy from the heavens, appearing during times when the gods were benevolent. In medieval Europe, it featured both in Christian cosmology – as a symbol of resurrection and the triumph of life over death – and in **alchemy**, where it repre-sented both the **Philosopher's Stone** and the **Elixir of Life**. The phoenix also has a parallel in the solar **Bennu** bird of Egyptian mythology. See also **Rebirth**.

**Phrygian Mysteries** See **Cybele**.

**Phul** According to the medieval grimoire *The Arbatel of Magick*, there are seven different **Olympic Spirits**, appointed by God to rule the world. Phul is the spirit of the **moon** and governs the spirits of the element **water**. He is able to change all metals into silver and can make people live to an age of 300 years.

**Phylacteries** Small leather bags containing sacred texts or magical **words of power** or spells. They were worn or carried like an **amulet**.

***Picatrix, The*** An eleventh-century magical text, which drew heavily on the Greek mystery tradition and was studied by such Renaissance mystics as **Marsilio Ficino** and **Cornelius Agrippa**. *The Picatrix* includes **cosmology**, **astrology**, and formulae for invoking planetary spirits. A German-language edition was published in 1962; it has not been translated into English. Compare *The Arbatel of Magick*.

**Pickingill, George** (1816–1909) A founding figure in modern British **witchcraft**, Pickingill was born in Hockley, Essex, and claimed to be descended from a line of hereditary witches dating back to the eleventh century. Pickingill is alleged to have derived some of his magical ideas – like **ritual nudity**, **drawing down the moon** and the **charge of the goddess** – by reading ancient texts such as Apuleius. He may also have been influenced by the British occultist **Francis Barrett**, author of *The Magus* (1801). Pickingill is believed to have founded nine witchcraft covens, one of which – located in the New Forest region of Hampshire – was the coven into which **Gerald Gardner** was initiated. Pickingill was contacted in the 1850s by a group of Freemasons who later founded the **Societas Rosicruciana in Anglia**, a precursor of the **Hermetic Order of the Golden Dawn**. As a result, he helped develop some of the S.R.I.A. ceremonies with the Rosicrucian enthusiast Hargrave Jennings, who became one of his followers. It is thought that another of Pickingill's magical pupils was **Allan Bennett**, who in turn had a strong influence on **Aleister Crowley**.

**Pico della Mirandola, Giovanni** (1463–1494) A Renaissance philosopher and mystic who was well-versed in the **Kabbalah** and understood Greek and

Latin as well as Hebrew. A disciple of the Jewish teacher Jochanum, he arrived in Rome at the age of 24, armed with some 900 propositions relating to logic, mathematics, physics, and the Kabbalah, and proclaimed – somewhat surprisingly – that the Kabbalah could be employed to convert Jews to Christianity. Pico advocated invocation of the archangels associated with the Tree of Life, and also believed in the alchemical transmutation of base metals into gold and silver, which he claimed to have witnessed at first hand. Pico was imprisoned by the Inquisition on the grounds of heresy, although many of his beliefs were theologically sound. He once wrote: "We may more easily love God than comprehend him or speak of him"; and he considered religion, rather than philosophy, to be the path to enlightenment. His kabbalistic and Neoplatonic inclinations, however, always drew the suspicions of the authorities. See also Neoplatonism.

**Pierre Tonnerre** In voodoo, magical thunderstones created by the spirits. They are believed to have mystical healing qualities.

**Pillar of Mildness** See Pillars of Manifestation.

**Pillar of Severity** See Pillars of Manifestation.

**Pillars of Manifestation** In the Kabbalah, the three "pillars" or vertical configurations applied to the Tree of Life. The Pillar of Severity is symbolically negative. It is headed by Binah and includes Geburah and Hod. The Pillar of Mildness is symbolically neutral and is also known as the Middle Pillar. It is headed by Kether and includes Daath, Tiphareth, Yesod and Malkuth. The Pillar of Severity is symbolically positive, is headed by Chokmah, and also includes Chesed and Netzach.

**Pine** See Fir and Pine.

**Pingala** In Kundalini yoga, the

positively charged solar current that circles around the central axis of the nervous system, **sushumna**. It counterbalances the negatively charged lunar current known as **ida**.

**Pisces** In astrology, the sign of the zodiac for those born between 20 February and 20 March. A water sign, ruled by Jupiter (or, according to some astrologers, by Neptune), Pisces is symbolized by the motif of two fish, facing in opposite directions. People born under the sign of Pisces are said to be patient and sensitive, but often lack personal direction. They may be artistic, but are often impractical and worry a lot. Charity work, nursing, art, and archaeology are careers associated with Pisces.

**Planes** In mystical and occult cosmology, the universe is often described as consisting of different planes of manifestation. It is common in mystical literature to find references to the spiritual, etheric, mental, astral, and physical planes, which are said to be characterized by increasing "density". The psychical or earth plane equates with the material, tangible world of waking consciousness; and the astral plane can be compared to the domain of the lower unconscious. The mental plane is characterized by archetypal images; while the etheric and spiritual planes reflect the universal life force and people's inherent divinity. See also Emanation.

**Planetary Metals** Metals linked symbolically to the planets in medieval cosmology and alchemy. The correlations were: sun (gold); moon (silver); Mercury (quicksilver); Venus (copper); Mars (iron); Jupiter (tin); and Saturn (lead).

**Planetary Spirits** See *Arbatel of Magick, The*.

**Planets, Seven** In traditional astrology, the following planets: Saturn, Jupiter, Mars, sun, Venus, Mercury, and the moon.

**Plato** (c. 427–347BCE) One of the most important of the classical Greek philosophers and a thinker who has profoundly influenced the development of mystical and esoteric thought. Plato, a disciple of **Socrates**, founded his famous Academy for the study of philosophy in Athens. Plato developed his theory of ideal forms, which differentiated the realm of the senses from reality itself. According to Plato, impressions received by the senses were impermanent and ever-changing; whereas the world of forms (or ideals) was eternal and changeless and the source of true knowledge. Plato's cosmology is described in his major book, *The Republic*, and provides a model of the universe as a spherical structure encompassing the fixed stars and the seven planets. The three **Fates** (Clotho, Lachesis, and Atropos) guide human destiny, but allow freedom of choice; thus people are ultimately responsible for the good and evil in their own lives. Plato was initiated in the temple at **Eleusis** and may have been influenced by his visionary experiences in formulating his theory of ideal forms, or **archetypes**. See also **Neoplatonism**.

**Pleasure** In the trance magic of visionary artist and sorcerer **Austin Osman Spare**, the blissful state achieved when the magician realises his intent. For Spare, true pleasure was a rapturous and transcendent state of non-duality, a state of union with the spiritual self.

**Pleroma** From a Greek word meaning "fullness", a **Gnostic** term used to signify the world of light – the Universal Soul. It was also the abode of the heavenly aeons. See also **Aeon**.

**Plotinus** (205–270CE) An Egyptian-born Greek philosopher who was the founding figure of **Neoplatonism**. He studied at Alexandria, became a pupil of Ammonius, and finally settled in Rome in 244, establishing a school of philosophy. Inspired by **Plato**, Plotinus believed that the ultimate goal was to discover the one-ness underlying manifested existence and that this task involved transcending philosophy itself. According to **Porphyry**, a close friend and disciple, Plotinus attained the mystical vision of unity at least four times in his life.

**Pluto** (1) The most distant of the known planets within the solar system. Pluto was discovered only in 1930 and consequently plays no role in traditional **astrology**. Some contemporary occultists believe, however, that Pluto should be recognized as the **ruler** of **Scorpio**.

**Pluto** (2) In Roman mythology, the ruler of the **Underworld** and the counterpart of the Greek **Hades**. He was also identified with **Dis**.

**Pneuma** The Greek word for "air", "breath", and "spirit" and closely associated with life itself. Compare **Prana**.

**Po'i-uhane** A type of Hawaiian **shaman** who is said to be able to see the souls of living persons. These shamans are allegedly capable of imprisoning human souls in a calabash or, alternatively, catching them in their hands and squeezing them to death.

**Poimandres** "*The Shepherd of Men*", the title of the main tractate in *The Hermetica*. It is usually referred to as *The Divine Pymander of Hermes Trismegistus* (English-language edition, 1923).

**Point of Love** In astrology, the position of the planet **Venus** in the solar **horoscope**. The point of love is always located in the first, second, eleventh, or twelfth **house**.

**Pointing** In ancient tribal practice, the act of directing one's magical will against others. Among the Australian Aborigines, for example, the **Kadaitja man**, or sorcerer, can condemn an enemy to death by "pointing the bone". Similarly the Malaysian magician, or pawang, points his kriz, or dagger which then begins to drip with blood.

**Polytheism** The belief in, and worship of, more than one god. Polytheism may be compared to **monotheism**, which is the belief in one god. See also Pantheism; Pantheon.

**Poma-Cira** In Macumba a surrogate of Exú.

**Pön** See Bön.

**Ponto Cantado** In Macumba, a ritual chant.

**Ponto Riscado** In Macumba, a magical diagram used to summon a god or goddess. Compare Vevers.

**Pop** In Enochian magic, the nineteenth Aethyr. The meanings associated with Pop include change and struggle. It is associated with **Leo** and **Libra** and its magical number is 48.

**Pope, Black** See La Vey, Anton Szandor.

**Porphyry** (c. 232–305CE) A disciple and friend of **Plotinus** and a leading figure in the philosophical school of Neoplatonism. Porphyry studied demonology and the magical incantations and formulae for overcoming evil spirits. However, he was also an important philosopher and produced a handbook of logic, *The Isagoge*, which was very influential in the Middle Ages. He edited and compiled Plotinus's writings under the title *The Enneads*.

**Portent** An omen relating to future events. See also Divination.

**Poseidon** In Greek mythology, the god of the sea, and one of the twelve great Olympians. In classical Greek cosmology, the universe was divided among the three sons of **Cronus** and **Rhea**, with **Zeus** being given rulership of the sky; **Hades** the Underworld; and Poseidon the sea. The earth was common to all three. Poseidon's Roman counterpart is **Neptune**. See Olympians, The Twelve Great.

**Poshayanki** See Beast Gods.

**Possession** An emotional and mental state in which a subject feels "possessed" by a **spirit** or **discarnate** entity, which takes over aspects of the personality totally or in part, and appears to operate independently of the person concerned. Spirit possession is a feature of **voodoo** and **spiritualism**, and also resembles some forms of schizophrenia.

**Postulant** In Wicca, a neophyte who has not yet received initiation in the coven. See First Initiation.

**Poteau Mitan** or **Poteau Legba** In voodoo, the centre post of the **peristyle**, the roofed but open-sided courtyard area outside the main temple where the ceremonies take place. Usually made of wood, the poteau mitan is the cosmic axis along which the **loa** rise to enter the ceremonies. The poteau mitan is also known as the Poteau Legba – the "wood of justice", or Legba Tree-of-the-Good.

**Potency** In alchemy, the power of the transmuting agent – the **stone** or **tincture** used to produce the alchemical transformation from imperfection

**Powder of projection** See Projection.

**Power Animal** In shamanism, a creature which appears on the **spirit journey** of the **soul** while the shaman is in a state of trance. The power animal usually resembles an actual species but may sometimes be a mythical or imaginary creature. It is invariably regarded as a personification of magical power and may be summoned in rituals and ceremonies. See also Familiar.

**Power Objects** In indigenous and native cultures, sacred objects imbued with magical power that have special significance for a **shaman** or **medicine man**. They include power stones, feathers, claws, bones, and other special objects used in healing ceremonies and initiations. Gifts provided by spirits during a vision quest may also fall into this category. For the shaman these objects are a tangible representation of his magical power and vitality. Native American shamans store their power objects in a **medicine bag**, or medicine bundle, and accord them great respect.

**Power Stones, Native American** See Tunkan.

**Practicus** In the Hermetic Order of the Golden Dawn, the ritual grade associated with the magical initiation of **Hod**, the eighth sphere on the kabbalistic **Tree of Life**.

**Prana** A Sanskrit word denoting "breath" or "life force". It can be used to describe specific vital fluids or energy in the body, and can also be used in a more general and all-encompassing way to denote the principle underlying life itself. See also **Chakra**; **Kundalini**; **Pneuma**.

**Prayer** The act of addressing a **deity** or **spirit**, often in praise, to make a request, or to acknowledge a personal failing. Praying usually takes a ceremonial form (e.g. with head inclined downwards and the hands held together).

**Precession of the Equinoxes** In **astrology**, a situation that refers to the slow revolution of the earth's pole around the ecliptic once every 26,000 years – which in turn changes the relationship of the signs of the **zodiac** to the constellations. Approximately 2,000 years are spent by the vernal point of the equinox in each constellation. The present era is the Age of Pisces, and it will be followed by the **Aquarian Age**.

**Prediction** See **Divination**; **Prophecy**.

**Predictive Astrology** See **Astrology, Predictive**.

**Pretos Velhos** In Macumba, black ancestor spirits who represent wisdom and experience and who provide counsel to human beings. They are not gods.

**Priapus** In Greek mythology, the son of **Aphrodite** and a god, sometimes said to be **Dionysus** or **Pan**. Like Pan, Priapus was a lustful god of fertility and vegetation. The protector of farmers and shepherds, he had an enormous erect phallus, hence the word "priapic".

**Pricking** In medieval English witchcraft, a test employed by witch-accusers in order to establish whether witches were guilty of practising **magic** and **sorcery**. The witch was pricked all over in order to detect the so-called **Devil's Mark** – an initiation mark allegedly provided by the **Devil** and said to be insensitive to pain.

**Priest** In Wicca, an initiated male witch. See also **High Priest**.

**Priestess** In Wicca, an initiated female witch. See also **High Priestess**.

**Priestess, High** See **High Priestess**.

**Priest, High** See **High Priest**.

**Priest, Priestess** In organized religions, the officially recognized mediator or "channel or inspiration" between the deity and the devotees of the faith. The priest performs acts of ceremonial sacrifice and **prayer**, makes offerings, and provides spiritual guidance to the worshippers. The priest may be differentiated from the **shaman**, whose role is individual communication with the god or gods, often in a state of **trance**, and who is associated more with tribal and hunter-gatherer societies than cultures with formalized religious expression.

**Prima Materia** In alchemy, the so-called "first matter" or original substance from which the universe was created. Base metals had to first be reduced to the prima materia from which they originated and finally, after all stages of the **opus alchymicum** were satisfactorily carried out these base metals could be transmuted into perfect gold.

**POWER ANIMAL** Native shamans summon their power animals, or spirit-helpers, to assist them on the visionary journey. Drawing by Martin Carey (courtesy of *Aquarian Angel*).

**Prime Qabalah** See Rankine, David.

**Primum Mobile** In kabbalistic cosmology, the first "swirlings" of the Infinite Light as it moved through the darkness of chaos, manifesting in **Kether** on the **Tree of Life**. The traditional Hebrew term is *Rashith ha- Galgalim*.

**Prince of Darkness** In demonology and occultism, the Devil – known variously as **Satan, Lucifer, Beelzebub,** and **Mephistopheles.**

**Prison** In alchemy, a term used for the putrefaction of matter in the stage known as **nigredo**. The putrefying matter is "trapped" in the **alembic,** or distillation vessel, and this is like being trapped in a dungeon or prison.

**Prithivi** In Hinduism and Western magic, the element Earth, symbolized by a yellow square. See **Tattvas.**

**Procel** In the Goetia, the 49th spirit, a powerful duke who appears in the form of an angel. Procel speaks mystically of hidden things, teaches the art of geometry and on command can create "great noises like the rushings of many waters, although there be none". He can also warm water if so required. He rules over 48 legions of spirits and is also known as Crocell or Pucel.

**Profane** That which is not **sacred** or religious in nature. It may also be used to describe the act of being disrespectful or irreverent in a sacred place or debasing sacred objects in a blasphemous way. The **Black Mass** performed by satanists involves profane ceremonies which parody Christian services and the partaking of the host.

**Projection** In alchemy, the final phase of the **opus alchymicum**. Here the alchemist's tincture is sprinkled over the base metal, transmuting it into silver or gold. According to alchemical tradition, the **white stone,** or tincture, had the power to transmute base metals into

pure silver and the **red stone** was able to transmute them into gold. The white stone was the tincture created by the **albedo,** or lunar transformation process, and the red stone was the prized **Philosopher's Stone** itself.

**Promise of the Cycle** In Wicca, a reference to the constant cycle of change, the promise of progress and development, and the gift of rebirth and renewal. Most Wiccans believe in **reincarnation.**

**Prophecy** From the Greek *prophetes*, "one who speaks before", a prediction made as the result of divine guidance or intervention. Biblical prophecies have become part of Jewish and Christian doctrine. See also **Divination; Eschatology.**

**Prosperpina, Prosperpine** See **Persephone.**

**Protean Soul** In occultism and magic, the **astral body,** which can be shaped by the imagination to form a vehicle for journeys on the **astral plane.** It is this body which can be used in sorcery for **magical attack.** See also **Nagual; Proteus.**

**Protective Magic** See Magic, Protective.

**Proteus** (1) In Greek mythology, an ancient god of the sea – the son of **Oceanus** and **Tethys.** Proteus had the gift of prophecy and was able to assume different shapes and forms at will, hence the term "protean".

**Proteus** (2) In alchemy, one of many names applied to the volatile and elusive **Mercurius,** or **philosophical mercury.** See **Proteus** (1).

**Psilocybe Mushrooms** The most important species of shamanic mushrooms in Mexico is *Psilocybe mexicana*, a species of "magic mushroom" which grows in wet pasture lands. Psilocybe mushrooms provide a state of intoxication characterized by vivid and colourful hallucinations and also unusual auditory effects. It is for the latter reason that the Mazatecs say, respectfully, that "the mushrooms speak". Mazatec shamans only utilize the sacred mushrooms to diagnose disease – to contact the spirits causing illness. If there is nothing wrong, there is no reason to eat them, and the mushrooms are not taken recreationally.

The Aztecs were in such awe of them that they called the mushrooms *teonanacatl*, which translates as "divine flesh". Today they are used ritually not only by the Mazatecs, but also by the Nahua Indians of Puebla and the Tarascana of Michoacan – specifically in religious and divinatory rites. In all cases the mushrooms are taken at night in rituals accompanied by chants and invocations. Interestingly, although psychoactive mushrooms also grow in South America, they appear not to enjoy the same ritual usage there as they do in Mexico.

**Psilocybin** A psychedelic synthesized by Dr Albert Hofmann from the hallucinatory mushroom *Psilocybe mexicana*, which is regarded as a sacrament by the Mazatec Indians of Mexico. The mushroom is used by both healers and sorcerers because of its intoxicating properties. See also **Sabina, Maria; Shamanism**.

**Psychagogues** Necromancers, who invoke the spirits of the dead. See also **Lévi, Eliphas; Necromancy; Peladan, Sar Josephin**.

**Psyche** A Greek word meaning "mind", "consciousness", "spirit", and "soul" – originally used to denote the state of being alive, and the life force itself. It is used in modern psychology to mean the mental faculties, encompassing both the conscious and unconscious mind.

**Psychedelic** From the Greek *psyche*, "soul" or "mind", and *delos*, "evident", a substance that stimulates the contents of the unconscious mind to become manifest. The word was coined by the

Canadian psychiatrist Dr Humphry Osmond and is generally used with reference to the hallucinogenic drug LSD and related chemicals. See also **Hallucination**.

**Psychic** One who possesses paranormal powers of **extrasensory perception**: precognition, clairvoyance, mental telepathy, an ability to see and diagnose the **aura**.

**Psychic Attack** See **Magical Attack**.

**Psychopomp** From the Greek meaning "guide of souls", a term used of the god Hermes in his role as a guide for the dead in the **Underworld**. The term is sometimes used by anthropologists to refer to the **shaman** in his role as a "guide of souls".

**Ptah** In one ancient Egyptian creation account, Ptah was the creator of the universe. Ptah's cult had its centre at Memphis, where he was worshipped along with his wife Sekhmet, the lion goddess.

**Pucel** See **Procel**.

**Puffer** Also Souffler. In alchemy, a person who made excessive use of the bellows to keep the fire going in the **athanor**, or furnace. The term was also used in a derogatory way to refer to amateur alchemists and quacks who mistakenly believed that the more fire they could create, the quicker would be the process of transmutation from base metal into gold.

**Puha** A term used by the Shoshoni Indians to denote supernatural power and also the **guardian spirit** who grants this power.

**Puhagan** Among the Shoshoni Indians, a **medicine man** or **medicine woman** who possesses supernatural magical power, granted to them by a **guardian spirit**.

**Pumpkin** In alchemy, a term used for the alchemical distillation vessel otherwise known as the **cucurbite**.

**Purple Tincture** In alchemy, an alternative term for the red tincture or **red stone**, which could transmute all base metals into gold. See also **Philosopher's Stone**.

**Purson** In the **Goetia**, the 20th spirit, a great king who appears in the form of a man but with the face of a lion. He holds a viper in his hand and is riding on a bear as he makes his grand entrance, attended by the rapturous sound of trumpets. Purson has the ability to discover hidden treasure and also has a knowledge of all things, past, present and future. He can change his appearance from an earthly to ethereal form and can provide authentic information on secret and sacred phenomena, including the creation of the world. Purson governs 22 legions of spirits, some drawn from the order of Virtues and others from the order of Thrones. He is also known as Curson.

**Putrefaction** In alchemy, the "death and decay" of a substance like an imperfect metal leading to its dissolution within the **prima materia**. Putrefaction was characteristic of the **nigredo**, the first stage of the **opus alchymicum**.

**Pwin** In voodoo, magical power evoked by a sorcerer. Such power can be used for good or evil.

**Pylon** A term used by members of the **Temple of Set** to refer to a regional branch of the main temple. The Temple of Set currently has pylons in a number of towns and cities across the United States as well as in Australia, Britain, Germany, and Finland. The extent of their membership is not publicly revealed. See **Temple of Set**.

**Pymander** See *Poimandres, The*.

**Pyramid** In alchemy, a symbolic representation of the "black earth" which gave alchemy its name (from the Egyptian word *chem* or *qem*, meaning "black"). The four signs of the elements are all pyramids, or triangles. An upright triangle represents **fire**; an upright triangle with a horizontal line through it represents **air**; an inverted triangle represents **water**; and an inverted triangle with a horizontal line through it represents **earth**.

**Pyramid, Great** One of the most massive (though not the highest) buildings in the world, with a base covering fourteen acres (0.6 hectares) and including 90 million cubic feet (2.5 million cubic metres) of stone, the Great Pyramid is located at Giza in Egypt and was built for the pharaoh Khufu (Cheops) in the third millennium BCE. The Great Pyramid is aligned exactly to magnetic north. In ancient times it had a polished limestone face that could reflect light like a beacon: the word "pyramid" itself translates as "glorious light" (from the Greek *pyros*, "fire").

**Pyromancy** A form of divination involving fire. The practitioner seeks prophetic guidance while throwing leaves, twigs, or incense into the flames of a fire. Change in the colour of the flames, and their shape and intensity, are interpreted as an omen of things to come.

**Pythagoras** (c. 572–479BCE) A Greek philosopher, mathematician, and **mystic**, born in Samos. He travelled in Egypt and then settled in Croton, southern Italy, where he established a religious brotherhood. Pythagoras taught several mystical doctrines, including the immortality of the **soul** and its **transmigration**, and the value of the contemplative life. A gifted mathematician, he related the orbits of the planets to the musical scale and originated the concept of the "music of the spheres".

**Pythia, Python** See **Delphic Oracle**.

# Q

**Qabalah** See Kabbalah.

**Qabalah, Prime** See Rankine, David.

**QBL** A Hebrew root meaning "from mouth to ear" and thereby signifying a secret oral tradition. It provides the core meaning for the Qabalah or Kabbalah, the secret tradition of Jewish mysticism.

**Qesheth** In the Kabbalah, the rainbow located above Malkuth in the form of a veil. It takes its name from the letters of the three paths on the Tree of Life which it bisects: Qoph, Shin, and Tau.

**Qlippoth** or **Kelipoth** In the Kabbalah, the negative or "impure" shells of existence, which formed during creation. In modern western magic, they are taken to be the spheres of the Tree of Evil, the obverse image of the Tree of Life.

**Qoph** or **Kuf** The Hebrew letter ascribed to the path linking Malkuth and Netzach on the Tree of Life. Qoph has a numerical value of 100. In modern magical visualization and pathworkings the Tarot card associated with this path on the Tree is *The Moon*.

**Qopine** Among the Winnebago Indians, a term used to describe the mysterious and magical nature of power. It equates with the Iroquois term **orenda**.

**Quadrants** In astrology, the four quarters of the horoscope or zodiac. The quadrants of the horoscope are the houses one to three; four to six; seven to nine; and ten to twelve. In the zodiac, they are the signs Aries to Gemini; Cancer to Virgo; Libra to Sagittarius; and Capricorn to Pisces.

**Quadrupedal Signs** In astrology, the signs of the zodiac represented by four-footed creatures: Aries, Taurus, Leo, Sagittarius, and Capricorn.

**Quadruplicities** In astrology, the classification of the signs of the zodiac into three groups of four, namely cardinal signs, fixed signs, and mutable signs. The quadruplicities are Aries, Cancer, Libra, and Capricorn (cardinal); Taurus, Leo, Scorpio, and Aquarius (fixed); and Gemini, Virgo, Sagittarius, and Pisces (mutable).

**Quartz Crystal** In Wicca, a magical stone assigned to the ritual celebration of Litha. On the kabbalistic Tree of Life it is assigned to the sephirah Yesod.

**Quaternity** In Theosophy and numerology, a union of four intrinsic components. Theosophists divide people into four bodies (physical, etheric, astral, and the self); and astrology includes many combinations of four; including the four signs of the zodiac, which make up each of the three "crosses": the so-called mutable, fixed, and cardinal signs. See Quadruplicities.

**Queen Luna** In alchemy, the embodiment of the receptive female qualities of "cold and moist" which give rise to the albedo, or white elixir, which can transmute base metal into silver.

**Queen of Elphame** In Wicca, a traditional name for the Queen of the Sabbat, the high priestess of the coven. The name Elphame refers to the Land of Faerie.

**Queen of the Sabbat** See High Priestess; Queen of Elphame.

**Queen, White** In alchemy, the white elixir or white stone produced by the albedo phase of the opus alchymicum. This tincture could transmute all base metals into silver.

**Querent** In astrology or divination, one who asks questions of the seer or fortune teller.

**Quert** In the Celtic tree alphabet, the ogham representing the wild apple tree and the letter "q". Quert is also linked to the hen and the colour apple-green.

*Quest* See Green, Marian.

**Quest, Quinary** In numerology, astrology, and mysticism, a combination of five within a system. In astrology there are five planets beyond the orbit of the earth around the sun; and in Kundalini yoga, there are five "elemental" chakras (muladhara – earth; svadhisthana – water; manipura – fire; anahata – air; and vishuddha – spirit, or akasha). In modern western magic, human beings are symbolized by the five-pointed star, or pentagram, See also Elements; Tattvas.

**Quest Society** An esoteric group established in 1909 by the Theosophical scholar G.R.S. Mead to study the western mystery tradition.

**Quetzalcoatl** Toltec diety who featured prominently in the Aztec Pantheon as god of the wind, fetility and wisdom. Personified as a feathered serpent, he was said to have invented the science of agriculture and also the calendar, and was associated with the Morning Star. According to Aztec mythology, Quetzalcoatl ruled during the golden age and then disappeared. When Hernando Cortez landed in Mexico with his conquistadors in 1519, the Aztecs at first thought Quetzalcoatl had returned to them. See also Tezcatlipoca; Xoloti.

**Quicksilver** See Mercury and Argent Vive.

**Quimbanda** See Macumba.

**Quincunx** In astrology, an aspect characterized by an angle of 150° between the planets.

**Quintessence** From Latin *quinta essentia*, "fifth essence, or element". In Pythagorean mysticism, the "fifth element", spirit, that fills the universe and gives it life and vitality (the other four elements being earth, water, fire, and air). In Hinduism, the fifth element is akasha; and in alchemy it is the transcendental Philosopher's Stone. The quintessence is the "pure essence."

# R

**R'lyeh** In *The Necronomicon*, the city beneath the sea where **Cthulhu**, Great Priest of the Deep Ones, bides his time.

**Ra** or **Re** In ancient Egyptian religion, the creator sun god. In one account, the sky goddess **Nut** carried Ra on her back to the heavens and he became lord and creator of the world. He subsequently became identified as a god of birth and **rebirth** because he would be reborn with the new dawn each day. The centre for the worship of Ra was at Heliopolis, and he was regarded as the main **deity** in the Ennead. See also **Amon**; **Ra Harakhte**; **Ra-Hoor-Khuit**.

**Rackham, Arthur** (1867–1939) An English book illustrator renowned for his pictures of **fairies, elves, goblins,** and water **nymphs**. Many of his best fairy-tale illustrations are included in his editions of *Rip Van Winkle* (1905), *A Midsummer Night's Dream* (1908), *The Rhinegold and the Valkyrie* (1910), and *Peter Pan in Kensington Gardens* (1912).

**Rad** or **Raidho** In the Germanic **Elder Futhark**, the **rune** letter representing the number five. Rad corresponds to the letter "r" and is the rune associated with riding and travel and specifically with going "the right way". By extension rad is connected with reason, rationality, and progress.

**Rada** A branch of **voodoo**. The Rada rites are of Dahomean origin and emphasize the positive aspects of the loas, or deities. Devotees wear all-white clothing at their ceremonies. See also **Loa**; **Petro**.

**Radical** In **astrology**, that which pertains to the **radix**.

**Radical Position** In astrology, the position of a planet in a birth chart. See Horoscope, Natal.

**Radix** In astrology, the **horoscope** drawn up for the moment of birth. See also **Horoscope, Solar Revolution**.

**Ragnarok** In Scandinavian mythology, the cataclysm in which nearly all of the gods, the universe, and living things were destroyed. After the death of Balder, the great god **Odin** led an army forth from **Valhalla** to fight the **giants** and the forces of evil. Finally, the heavens fell and the world was totally destroyed. However, it was believed that the holocaust of Ragnarok in turn gave rise to a new breed of people and gods. Odin's son, **Vidar**, was among the survivors who would lead the resurgence and herald a Golden Age.

**Ra-Hoor-Khuit** In the cosmology of ceremonial magician **Aleister Crowley**, the Egyptian god of force and fire. He is the divine child of **Nut** or Nuit, the sky goddess, and **Hadit**, a Chaldean counterpart to **Set**, the Egyptian god of darkness. Following a revelation from a semi-invisible entity named **Aiwaz** in Cairo in 1904, Crowley came to believe that he had been chosen to be the Lord of the New Aeon. The **Aeon of Horus** succeeded the matriarchal Aeon of Isis and the patriarchal Aeon of Osiris. Crowley was now the incarnation of Ra-Hoor-Khuit and his representative in the Aeon of Horus. The cosmic union of Nuit and Hadit proclaimed in the 1904 revelation also heralded the arrival of the Law of **Thelema**, whose main dictum was "Do what thou wilt, love is the law, love under will". For the rest of his magical career, this would be Crowley's principal message to the world.

**Ra-Horakhte** or **Ra-Harakhte** In ancient Egyptian religion, the title of Ra, the sun god, in his form as a falcon bearing the solar disc. The designation "Horakhte" means "Horus of the Horizon." See also **Horus**.

**Raidho** See Rad.

**Rainbow** In alchemy, the stage of the opus alchymicum between the nigredo and the albedo also known as the "peacock's tail".

**Rais, Gilles de** (1404–1440) A French marshal who fought alongside Joan of Arc at Orleans, Gilles de Rais is remembered primarily, however, as the murderer of at least 140 children whose hearts, hands, eyes, and blood he used in appalling demonic rituals. After a trial before the bishop of Nantes, he was sentenced to death and hanged.

**Randolph, Pascal Beverley** (1825–1871) An American Rosicrucian, Freemason, and medium who founded several groups. Randolph was a member of the Societas Rosicruciana in Anglia – an important predecessor to the Hermetic Order of the Golden Dawn. He became interested in sexual magic and is believed to have taught Karl Kellner a number of techniques which subsequently emerged as teachings within the Ordo Templi Orientis. See also Magic, Sexual; Rosicrucians.

**Rankine, David** The British ceremonial magician David Rankine has been studying and practising magic since the 1970s and has been involved with different Golden Dawn, kabbalistic and Thelemic groups during that time. In the 1980s and 1990s he edited the magazines *Evohe!* and *Dragon's Brew*, as well as contributing articles to many other magazines like *Chaos International*, *Nuit-Isis*, and *Talking Stick*. Rankine is well known in Britain for his lectures and workshops on Kabbalah, ceremonial magic, witchcraft, Egyptian magic and Thelema. In recent times he has been working with author Stephen Skinner on research into unpublished magical material from the Renaissance, resulting in the publication in 2004 of *The Practical Angel Magic of Dr John Dee's Enochian Table*, the first in a series of co-authored works. Rankine's other publications include *Magick Without Peers: A Course in Progressive Witchcraft*

for *Solitary Practitioners* (co-authored with Ariadne Rainbird); *Crystals - Healing & Folklore*; and *Becoming Magic* which contains many of the ideas and techniques he has worked with and created over the years. These include his system of English gematria using prime numbers, which he has named Prime Qabalah.

**Raphael** (1) An archangel of God. Not mentioned in the canonical Bible, Raphael features prominently in the apocryphal *Book of Tobit*, and is linked with healing. He also plays an important role in modern western magic where he is invoked in the East as the archangel of air. He is associated with the sphere of Tiphareth on the kabbalistic Tree of Life.

**Raphael** (2) The astrological pseudonym of Robert Cross Smith (1795–1832), who gave his name to the original *Raphael's Astronomical Ephemeris*. This publication is still issued annually and gives listings of planetary positions at noon and midnight for each day of the year, as well as other information useful for astrologers. There have been many "Raphaels" since Smith, ensuring the continuity of the *Ephemeris*. See also Astrology.

**Rarefaction** In alchemy, the act of purifying or refining the matter used in the operation. See also Distillation.

**Raum** In the Goetia, the 40th spirit, a great earl who appears in the form of a crow but who will assume a human form when commanded. Raum specializes in stealing treasure from the king's houses and carrying it off to another location, on the instruction of the magician. He destroys cities but can create love between friends and enemies alike. He also has a knowledge of all things – past, present, and future. Raum commands 30 legions of spirits and is also known as Raym.

**Rav** A Hebrew word meaning a "master", as in the expression Rav ha-Hasid, "a master of devotion."

**Raven** See Raven's Head.

**Raven's Head** In alchemy, a symbol of the first stage of the alchemical work, the stage of dissolution or "death" known as the nigredo. The Raven's Head was also referred to as the "Crow's Head".

**Raym** See Raum.

**Re** See Ra.

**Rebirth** A mystical term which can refer either to **reincarnation** or the act of spiritual awakening or **enlightenment**. See also **Initiation; Transmigration**.

**Receiver** In alchemy, a vessel, generally made of glass and used to receive the substance formed through distillation. See Distillation.

**Rectification** In astrology, the process of clarifying an uncertain birth-time by evaluating known personal characteristics or events in one's life, and relating them back to characteristics of a natal horoscope that matches these factors. See Horoscope, Natal.

**Red Earth** In alchemy, the name for philosophical gold – the reddish material from which **red elixir** – the Philosopher's Stone which can transmute all base metals into gold – is made.

**Red Elixir** In alchemy, the universal healing medicine which cures all forms of disease, provides longevity, and ensures that those who have died will be resurrected and granted eternal life. It equates with the **Philosopher's Stone**.

**Red Lily** See Red Elixir.

**Red Lion** In alchemy, a representation of sulphur – the hot, dry, active "seed" of metals. It is the male principle associated also with the sun and King Sol.

**Red Man** In alchemy, a representation

of sulphur. See Red Lion and Philosophical Sulphur.

**Red Powder** In alchemy, the red tincture attained at the final stage of the opus alchymicum known as the rubedo. When sprinkled over base "imperfect" metal this red powder transmutes the metal into perfect gold. See also **Red Earth; Red Elixir; Red Rose**.

**Red Rose** In alchemy, a symbol of the red tincture attained through the final stage of the opus alchymicum known as the rubedo. The red stone was able to transmute all base metals into gold. See also **White Rose**.

**Red Rose and the Cross of Gold, Order of the** See Ordo Rosae Rubeae et Aureae Crucis.

**Red Work** In alchemy, the conversion of impure base metals into gold – the final stage of the opus alchymicum.

**Redcap** In Scottish folklore, an evil spirit who took the form of an old man with long nails and a red cap stained with blood. Often found lurking in the peel-towers on the Scottish border, he could be driven away by the sign of the cross or by reciting verses from the Bible.

**Regardie, Dr Francis Israel** (1907–1985) An English-born authority on ritual magic who lived most of his life in the United States. Regardie was at one time personal secretary to **Aleister Crowley** and became a member of the **Stella Matutina**, a magical group descended from the **Hermetic Order of the Golden Dawn**. Regardie attracted considerable controversy in occult circles when he published the complete rituals of the order (1937–1940), but this four-volume source work, *The Golden Dawn*, is now regarded as the bible of practising ceremonial occultists. Regardie is widely considered to have been the foremost authority on modern western **magic**. His most important books included *The Tree of Life* (1932; republished 1969); *The*

*Philosopher's Stone* (1938; republished 1970); *The Art of True Healing* (1964); and *Ceremonial Magic* (1982). His biography of Aleister Crowley, *The Eye in the Triangle* (1970), is one of the major works on the celebrated ceremonial magician.

**Reincarnation** The belief that one's identity survives physical death and may · be reborn in different physical bodies, in a succession of future lives. Belief in reincarnation is commonly associated with the concept of spiritual evolution. In Hinduism and Buddhism, the **karma** earned in the present lifetime has a direct bearing on the subsequent incarnation. Reincarnation is an important part of Hindu and Buddhist belief, and has also been central in the western **mystery** tradition. Many influential thinkers, including **Pythagoras**, **Plato**, **Plotinus**, Hegel, Emerson, and William James have embraced it; and it is an accepted teaching among most adherents of modern **Theosophy**, **spiritualism**, and **occultism**. See also **Transmigration**.

**Relic** An object venerated because of its connection with an important spiritual figure or saint.

**Religion** A system of beliefs and practices relating to the worship of supernatural beings, deities, spirits, or God. Religions can broadly be of two sorts: **monotheism**, which entails belief in a single god or divine entity; or **polytheism**, in which more than one deity or spirit is worshipped.

**Religious Liberties Lawyers Network** See **Curott, Phyllis**.

**Resh** The Hebrew letter ascribed to the path linking **Yesod** and **Hod** on the kabbalistic **Tree of Life**. Resh has a numerical value of 200. In modern magical visualization and **pathworkings** the **Tarot** card associated with this path on the Tree is *The Sun*.

**Resurrection** The concept that the dead may return to life. Although a belief in resurrection is most commonly associated with Christianity, followers of **Osiris** in ancient Egypt and of **Attis** in Phrygia similarly believed in a resurrected god, and there are numerous other examples. According to **Mircea Eliade**, a leading authority on comparative religion, belief in resurrection is characteristic of a culture with a linear **cosmology** (creation–life–death–final judgment); whereas **reincarnation** – a related, but distinctly different concept – is more characteristic of "cyclic" cosmologies, such as Hinduism and Buddhism, which place less emphasis on the origin of the world and the concept of a final judgment.

**Retort** In alchemy a globe-shaped vessel, usually made of glass, with a long bent neck. It was used for the process of **distillation**.

**Retrograde** In astrology, a term applied to the apparent backward motion of a planet in relation to the **zodiac**. Retrograde movements occur when planets decrease in longitude as viewed from the earth.

**Reuss, Theodor** (1855–1923) A German **occultist** who succeeded **Karl Kellner** as head of the **Ordo Templi Orientis**. Reuss dispensed charters of membership to several prominent occultists, including **Papus** and **Rudolf Steiner**. In 1922 he resigned from the order, appointing **Aleister Crowley** his successor.

**Revelation** From the Latin *revelare*, "to reveal", "unveil". Something that has been revealed; in **mysticism**, this is often a sacred or esoteric truth revealed by a divine being. See also **Apocalypse**.

**Revenant** From the French *revenir*, "to return", a ghost or **discarnate** being who has returned from the dead, often for a specific purpose: to avenge a wrongdoing, or to make contact with a loved one. See also **Necromancy**.

**Rhabdomancy** A form of divination by using a rod. The term is generally associated with dowsing, but also applies to divination by interpreting the flight of arrows. See also **Hazel**.

**Rhapsodomancy** A form of divination in which one opens a sacred book and interprets as prophetic the first line that comes to view.

**Rhea** In Greek mythology, the sister and wife of **Kronos** and the mother of the gods. Her children included **Demeter**, **Hades**, **Poseidon**, and **Zeus**. She was sometimes identified with **Cybele** and was known to the Romans as Ops.

**Rhiannon** A Celtic fertility goddess who appears in *The Mabinogion*. In Welsh her name probably means "Great Queen", and she was presented as a goddess associated with horses. She may be related to the ancient Celtic horse goddess Epona.

**Right-Hand Path** In mysticism and occultism, the esoteric path associated with spiritual **illumination**, virtue, and positive aspirations. It is the path of light, as distinct from the so-called **left-hand path** of darkness, which runs counter to spiritual evolution and equates with **evil**, bestiality, and black magic. See also **Magic, Black** and **Magic, White**.

**Rii** In Enochian magic, the 29th **Aethyr**. The meanings associated with Rii include judgment, purification, decision, and justice. It is associated with **Pisces** and **Sagittarius** and its magical number is 220.

**Ring-Pass-Not** A mystical expression relating to the "circle of bounds", which limits the consciousness of an **occultist** who has not yet attained a higher state of spiritual unity.

**Rings, Magic** See Magic Rings.

**Ripening of Metals** The medieval alchemists believed that metals "ripened" inside the earth's crust and were living organisms just like plants and trees. "Imperfect" or "impure" metals like iron, copper, tin, and lead were thought to grow inside the womb of the earth and in time they would eventually "ripen" into pure gold, nourished by the rays of the sun. The alchemists worked in their laboratories to hasten this natural process of growth and perfection. See **Alchemy**.

**Rising Sign** In astrology, the sign rising on the eastern horizon at the moment of birth. It is usually referred to as the **ascendant**.

**Rites of Passage** Rites of **initiation** in which a **neophyte** undergoes a symbolic ceremony that leads from one status to another. Rites of passage are often associated with significant life changes (birth, puberty, marriage, death).

**Ritual** A prescribed form of religious or magical ceremony, often designed to invoke or placate a **deity**. Rituals are characterized by symbolic attire and formalized behaviour, and may involve imitating the deity in a ceremonial context in order to obtain supernatural power, spiritual **illumination**, or other specific blessings from the deity being worshipped.

**Ritual Magic** See Magic, Ceremonial.

**Ritual Nudity** See Skyclad.

**Robes** Ceremonial costumes worn by the priests of religious denominations and also by ritual magicians. They usually have symbolic significance, their colour and design indicating a season, a **deity**, or motifs of cosmological importance.

**Robin Goodfellow** In British folklore, a name for the **hobgoblin** Puck, who was noted for his mischievous tricks and his habit of misleading travellers. He was also able to change shape.

**Roc** or **Rukh** In Arabian myth, an enormous bird, which resembled an eagle and was believed to feed on young elephants and serpents. It is described in *The Arabian Nights*: on one occasion, Sinbad the Sailor climbed onto its huge foot and was carried away by it. However, he alighted safely and discovered the Valley of Diamonds. The Roc bears some resemblance to both the **griffin** and the Garuda bird.

**Rods** See Wands.

**Rollright Stones** A group of prehistoric standing stones in the English Cotswolds near Long Compton. Thought to be older than Stonehenge, the Rollright Stones are located in an area long associated with witches' meetings and sabbats. See also **Megaliths**.

**Roneve** See Ronobe.

**Ronobe** In the Goetia, the 27th spirit, a great marquis and earl who appears in the form of a monster. He imparts the skills associated with rhetoric and languages. Ronobe commands 19 legions of spirits. He is also known as Ronove and Roneve.

**Ronove** See Ronobe.

**Rosae Rubeae et Aureae Crucis, Ordo** See Ordo Rosae Rubeae et Aureae Crucis.

**Rose Cross** or **Rosy Cross** A golden cross with a rose at its centre: the emblem of the **esoteric** order of the Rosicrucians.

**Rosemary** A plant with mythic and magical associations. It was believed to ward off evil **spirits**, witches, and **fairies**, and was also a protection against storms. At funerals, sprigs of rosemary symbolize remembrance.

**Rosenkreuz** or **Rosencreutz, Christian** See Rosicrucians.

**Rosenroth, Christian Knorr von** (1636–1689) A German baron who travelled widely in western Europe, acquiring a strong interest in both Christian and kabbalistic **mysticism**. He is best known for translating the main books of the *Zohar* into Latin, under the title *Kabbala Denudata* (*The Kabbalah Unveiled*). This work, published in two volumes (1677–1684), gave many readers access to the *Zohar* for the first time, and until the late nineteenth century it remained the major non-Jewish source work for the **Kabbalah**. Rosenroth's translation was rendered into English by **MacGregor Mathers** in 1887.

**Rosicrucians** The name used by many occult groups who have claimed inspiration from a figure called **Christian Rosenkreuz** or Rosencreutz. The origin of the Rosicrucians (who take their name from Rosenkreuz, which means "Rose Cross" or "Rosy Cross") dates from the publication c. 1614–1616 of three books purporting to emanate from an occult order, the Brotherhood of the Rosy Cross (Fraternitas Rosae Crucis) – it is likely, however, that all three were written by **Johann Valentin Andreae**. The first of these publications, *Fama Fraternitatis*, described how a certain Christian Rosenkreuz met the "Wise Men of Damcar", and subsequently translated the mystical book *Liber M* into Latin. The second, *Confessio Fraternitatis R.C.*, provided more details about Christian Rosenkreuz and invited members of the public to join the order. The third, *Chymische Hochzeit Christiani Rosenkreuz* (*The Chymical Wedding of Christian Rosenkreuz*) was a Hermetic allegory in which the central figure witnesses a royal marriage and later discovers the king's "secret books of wisdom". The Rosicrucian myth has been a strong influence on several mystical groups, including the **Hermetic Order of the Golden Dawn** (who incorporated Rosicrucian elements into the **initiations** of their second order, the **Ordo Rosae Rubeae et Aureae Crucis**). Similarly, **Franz Hartmann** started a Rosicrucian order in Germany; and **Sar Josephin Peladan** ran a fashionable Rosicrucian salon in Paris. Competing Rosicrucian orders of questionable authenticity now market the **esoteric** wisdom of Christian Rosenkreuz in the United States.

**Rosy Cross** See Rose Cross, Rosicrucians.

**Rowan** A tree with mythic and magical associations. The rowan, or mountain ash, was sacred among the **Druids** and was regarded in the Middle Ages as protection against **witchcraft** and the forces of **evil**. Rowan Tree Witch Day was celebrated at the Celtic festival of **Beltane**.

**Royal Art** A term applied to medieval alchemy. The **Philosopher's Stone**, a symbol of perfection and purity, was born of the **chemical wedding** between King Sol and Queen Luna and therefore had a noble lineage. By contrast with the "impure" metals – tin, copper, lead, and iron – gold was considered "royal" and alchemy, the means by which gold could finally be obtained, was similarly regarded as a "royal art". See also **Ripening of Metals**.

**Royal Water** See Aqua Regia.

**R.R. et A.C.** See Ordo Rosae Rubeae et Aurae Crucis.

**Ruach** In the Kabbalah, that part of the soul that lies between the **Neschamah** and the **Nephesch**. Referred to by magicians as the "higher astral soul", the Ruach corresponds to the spiritual realm between, and including, **Chesed** and Hod on the **Tree of Life**.

**Ruach Elohim** In the Jewish mystical tradition, the spirit of God.

**Ruach ha-Qadesh** In the Jewish mystical tradition, the Holy Spirit. See also **Ruach; Ruach Elohim; Shekinah**.

**Rubedo** The final stage of the opus

alchymicum, characterized by the reddening of the white matter of the stone which has already been purified by the lunar **albedo** process. In the **coniunctio** or **chemical wedding** between **King Sol** and **Queen Luna**, the white stone is now ready to be reunited with the spirit and is given form through a reddening process or "rubification" which the alchemists referred to as "blushing". The **Philosopher's Stone** has now been attained.

**Rubification** See Rubedo.

**Ruby** In Wicca, a magical stone assigned to the ritual celebrations of **Samhain** and **Ostara**. On the kabbalistic Tree of Life the ruby is assigned to the sephirah **Geburah**.

**Rue** *Ruta graveolens*, a shrubby herb with greenish-yellow flowers and blue-green leaves. Rue is native from the Mediterranean to eastern Siberia. The leaves of rue have a strong odour and are used in flavourings, beverages, and herbal vinegars as well as in the preparation of cosmetics and perfumes. In classical Rome rue was associated with the lunar goddess **Diana** and her daughter **Aradia** and as a plant it has a long association with **witchcraft**. Pagan followers of Diana honoured rue and used it in magical love charms, while in the Middle Ages the act of burning rue or hanging it in one's house was thought to protect against witchcraft. In symbolic terms, rue is associated with grace, repentance, and memory – Shakespeare refers to it in *Richard II* as the "sour herb of grace". See also **Syrian Rue**.

**Ruis** In the Celtic tree alphabet, the ogham representing the elder tree and the letter "r". Ruis is also linked to the rook and the colour red.

**Ruler** In astrology, a planet that is said to dominate a particular sign of the zodiac. The modern astrological ascriptions (including **Pluto**) are as follows: Mars (**Aries**); **Venus** (**Taurus** and **Libra**);

Mercury (Gemini); moon (Cancer); sun (Leo); Mercury (Virgo); Pluto (Scorpio); Jupiter (Sagittarius); Saturn (Capricorn); Uranus (Aquarius); and Neptune (Pisces).

**Runa-Raven Press** See Flowers, Stephen Edred.

**Rune-Gild** See Flowers, Stephen Edred.

**Rune Numbers** In the Germanic Elder Futhark of 24 letters, the runes are divided into three groups of eight, known respectively as Freyr's Aett (runes 1–8); Haegl's Aett (runes 9–16), and Tyr's Aett (runes 17–24 ). See Futhark, Elder; Runes.

**Runes** From the Old English and Old Norse *run*, meaning "a secret" or "mystery", an alphabet which the ancient peoples of northern Europe used for both secular and spiritual purposes, including divining the future. According to one tradition the Scandinavian god Odin hung for nine days and nights on the World Tree and paid with one of his eyes for his knowledge of the runes. See Futhark, Younger and Futhark, Elder and individual listings.

**Runic Alphabet** See Futhark, Younger; Futhark, Elder; Runes.

**Run-Wita** In the Anglo-Saxon poem *Beowulf*, a privy counsellor of royalty or, more specifically, a wise person (*wita*) who knew how to interpret the secrets of the Runes.

**Rusalki** In Slavonic folk belief, elementals who were commonly said to be the spirits of girls whose deaths were the result of drowning. The rusalki (singular, rusalka) were mischievous spirits and were regarded as the divinities of streams, rivers, and forests.

**Russell, George William** (1867–1935) Better known by his pen-name, "A.E.", Russell was born in northern Ireland and later met William Butler Yeats at Dublin Art School. They became good friends and shared many mystical and cultural interests. Both had affiliations with the Theosophical Society, and both became important figures in the so-called Irish literary renaissance. A natural mystic, Russell knew both the ascent of the soul towards light and also its plunge into despair and doubt. A superbly lyrical writer, he is best known for his classical book *The Candle of Vision* (1918). His other books include *Song and its Fountains; Homeward Songs by the Way;* and *The Avatars.* Russell was also a talented artist and produced mystical paintings comparable in style to those of Odilon Redon.

# S

**Sabazius** A Phrygian deity sometimes identified with **Dionysus, Zeus,** and **Jupiter** and worshipped in Athens in the late fifth century BCE. Symbolized by a snake, he was often portrayed bearing the thunderbolt of Zeus.

**Sabbatic Goat** A term applied to Baphomet.

**Sabbats, Greater** In Wicca, the celebrations of **Candlemas** (2 February), **May Eve** (30 April), **Lammas** (1 August) and **All Hallows' Eve** (31 October). The traditional Celtic/Druidic names for these celebrations are respectively **Imbolc** or Oimelc, **Beltane, Lughnassadh,** and **Samhain.**

**Sabbats, Lesser** In Wicca, the celebrations held at the time of the midsummer and midwinter solstices, and the equinoxes in spring and autumn.

**Sabbats, Witches'** See Sabbats, Greater; Sabbats, Lesser.

**Sabnack** In the Goetia, the 43rd spirit, a mighty marquis who appears in the form of an armed soldier with a lion's head. He rides on a pale-coloured horse and can build high towers, castles, and cities and furnish them with armour. He can also afflict men with wounds and sores. Sabnack commands 50 legions of spirits and is also known as Saburac or Savnok.

**Saburac** See Sabnack.

**Sacrament** A ritual or object that has special ceremonial significance and is regarded as the outward, visible sign of inner spiritual grace. In Christianity, the host and wine taken in communion are sacraments because for the devotee they are the body and blood of Christ. In certain pre-literate and tribal societies, especially those involving **shamanism,** a

god may be identified with a mushroom or sacred plant that is eaten to provide communion with the spirit world.

**Sacred** That which is holy, or dedicated to a god. The opposite of **profane.**

**Sacred Alphabet** See Alphabet of Desire.

**Sacred Food** In Wicca, the cakes and wine which symbolize the flesh and blood of the goddess and god in ritual. They are ceremonially blessed by the **high priest** and **high priestess** of the coven.

***Sacred Magic of Abra-Melin the Mage, The*** See Abraham the Jew.

**Sacrifice** An offering made to a **deity,** often upon an altar. Sacrifices are performed ritually to placate the god and to offer blood – which is symbolic of the life force and invariably associated with fertility. Some magicians believe that the ritual slaughter of a sacrificial animal releases life energy, which can be tapped magically and used to attune the magician to the god invoked in ritual (e.g. doves are symbolic of the goddess **Venus**). In many pre-literate and tribal societies, the sacrificed animal may become the "scapegoat" for infringements of taboos by members of that group. Here the act of sacrificing the creature ceremonially has a purgative effect, eliminating potential harm and evil.

**Safed** A town in northern Galilee (now Israel), to which many Jewish religious scholars and mystics moved following the expulsion of Jews from Spain in 1492. In the sixteenth century Safed became the spiritual center of the Jewish world, and it was here that **Kabbalah** reached the peak of its influence.

**Sagittarius** In astrology, the sign of the zodiac for those born between 23 November and 21 December. A fire sign, ruled by **Jupiter,** Sagittarius is symbolized by the **centaur** – half horse, half man – which represents the conflict between the intellect and the animal instincts. Those born under the sign of Sagittarius are said to be often rebellious and strong-willed, but honest and trustworthy. They are generous, artistic, and musical and make excellent organizers. For this reason they are ideally suited to professional administrative roles, provided they can curb their naturally independent instincts.

**Sahasrara** In Kundalini yoga, the **Chakra** located at the crown of the head.

**Sahu** In ancient Egyptian **magic** and religion, the "highest" of the five human bodies, sometimes known as the "spiritual body". It is through the sahu that the magician or priest perceives the transcendental gods and undergoes spiritual transformation. See also **Aufu, Ka, Haidit,** and **Khu.**

**Saile** In the Celtic tree alphabet, the **ogham** representing the willow and the letter "s". Saile is also linked to the hawk and the colour yellow-pink.

**Saint-Germain, Comte de**
(1710–1780) A famous Rosicrucian **adept** who claimed to be immortal. Said to be the son of Prince Rakoczy of Transylvania, the count was educated at the University of Siena and later visited several European courts, where he masqueraded under many grandiose titles. He was also known variously as Comte Bellamarre, Marquis de Montserrat, and Chevalier Schoening, and could speak several languages. He enticed his audience with his extravagant claims, including the tale that he had received the magical "wand of Moses" from King Cyrus in Babylon, thereby maintaining that he was one of the **Illuminati**. The Comte de Saint-Germain was said to have derived his wealth from his knowledge of **alchemy** and his discovery of the secret of the **Philosopher's Stone**. Notwithstanding his flamboyant claims, he is certainly among the most remarkable of all occult writers

and his initiatory book *The Most Holy Trinosophia* is a significant contribution to the western mystical tradition

**Saladera** In South America, illness associated with continuing misfortune in the such areas as love, work, or family matters. It is often thought to result from **witchcraft** or **sorcery** initiated by an envious or vengeful individual intent on causing harm. See also **Daño**.

**Salamander** In medieval alchemy and magic, the spirit of the element fire. The mythic salamander is a lizard that was believed to dwell within the flames and be nourished by fire. It bears no resemblance to the real species of amphibians known as *Caudara*.

**Salem Witches** Salem (now renamed Danvers), Massachusetts, became notorious in 1692 as the result of a **witchhunt** that culminated in a dramatic trial. Two young girls, Elizabeth Parris and Abigail Williams, accused a Carib Indian house slave named Tituba, and two other women – **Sarah Good** and Sarah Osburn – of being witches and harassing them with magic spells. Tituba "confessed" to these crimes, and a feeling of hysteria and fear quickly spread among the local Puritan inhabitants. Many others were accused of being witches, and people became frightened of venturing out at night in case **Satan** or evil forces ensnared them. In due course, 200 people were arrested in New England and 34 – including Sarah Good – went to the gallows. The Salem witchcraft incident bears comparison with the Loudon and Aix-en-Provence demonic hysteria cases although it is now thought to have been caused by ergot poisoning, which induces vivid hallucinations. See also **Aix-en-Provence Nuns; Grandier, Urbain; Witchcraft.**

**Saleos** or **Sallos** In the Goetia, the 19th spirit, a great and mighty duke who appears in the form of a gallant soldier riding on a crocodile. He is wearing a crown on his head and comes in peace.

He can bring men and women together in love and commands 30 legions of spirits.

**Salt** In alchemy, the symbol of **earth** and the body, personified as female. Salt was regarded by the alchemists as one of the three vital ingredients of nature, the other two constituents being **sulphur** and **mercury**, representing the **spirit** and **soul** respectively.

**Salute, Fivefold** See Fivefold Kiss.

**Salve** See Flying Ointments; Unguent.

**Samael** In the Jewish religious tradition, a fallen angel and a chief force of evil.

**Samedi, Baron** See Baron Samedi.

**Samekh** The Hebrew letter ascribed to the path linking **Yesod** and **Tiphareth** on the kabbalistic **Tree of Life**. Samekh has a numerical value of 60. In modern magical visualization and **pathworkings** the Tarot card associated with this path on the Tree is *Temperance*.

**Samhain** A major Wiccan sabbat, also known as **All Hallows' Eve** and Halloween and celebrated on 31 October. An ancient Celtic festival, Samhain is a celebration to honour the dead. The name is Irish and means "summer's end", and it is a time of grieving, as the dying sun passes into the nether world. However, the festival is regarded as both an ending and a beginning – for the sun god will be reborn with the passage of the seasons. Samhain is said to be the time of the year when the thin veil between the everyday and netherworlds is most transparent – allowing Wiccans to communicate more readily with the spirits of the departed. Samhain is also a time to reflect on one's own mortality. Mythologically, this is the season during which the dying god goes to sleep in the underworld awaiting rebirth in spring. At the same time the seed of new life gestates within the womb of the Great Mother – who in this cycle is regarded as the queen of darkness. See also **Great Goddess; Sabbats, Greater**.

**Samigina** See Gamygyn.

**San Pedro Cactus** Dating back at least 3,000 years as a ritual sacrament, the San Pedro cactus (*Trichocereus pachanoi*) is one of the most ancient magical plants of South America. The Spanish noticed shamans in Peru drinking a beverage made from its sap and, essentially, this process still continues today. The cactus is cut into slices, boiled for around seven hours in water, and then consumed to bring on visions. In Peru it is known simply as San Pedro, in Bolivia as achuma. Purchased by shamans at the markets, the cactus contains mescaline and initially produces drowsiness and a state of dreamy lethargy. However, this is followed by a remarkable lucidity of mental faculties. Finally, one may experience "a telepathic sense of transmitting oneself across time and matter". Shamans in Peru and Bolivia use the cactus to contact spirits, to treat illness, to counteract the dangers of **witchcraft**, and for **divination**.

**Sand Bath** In alchemy the bath, or balneum, within the **alembic** containing warmed sand. This allowed the material to be heated gently and evenly in the furnace.

**Sandalphon** In modern western **magic**, the **archangel** ascribed to the sphere of **Malkuth** on the kabbalistic **Tree of Life**. Sandalphon is thus the archangel who protects the physical world.

**Sanders, Alex** (1916–1988) An English witch who, with **Gerald Gardner**, is acknowledged as a central figure in the modern **witchcraft** revival. Sanders maintained that he came from a family in which witchcraft had been practised for generations, and that he was initiated into the **Craft** by his grandmother.

Sanders became highly visible in the

media during the 1970s – especially with his **high priestess**, Maxine – and has been the subject of several books and a film. In his later years he combined magical ritual with spirit possession and claimed to be a trance medium. His tradition of witchcraft is often referred to as "Alexandrian", a play on the words of his name, which suggests a certain antiquity in his rituals. **Janet and Stewart Farrar** were members of Alex Sanders' coven in London. See also **Sanders, Maxine**.

**Sanders, Maxine** (1946 – ) An influential British **witch** and former wife of **Alex Sanders**. Born Maxine Morris, she was educated at a convent in Manchester and introduced to Sanders by her mother while she was still a child – her mother had befriended him at a local hospital. Maxine later met him again through a Subud group that her mother belonged to. Maxine Morris was initiated into the **Craft** in 1962 at the age of sixteen and three years later entered into several **handfasting** ceremonies with Alex Sanders. They were legally married in 1968 and for several years were highly visible as representatives of the British witchcraft revival. They divorced in 1973 but Maxine continues in her active dedication to the Craft. She has since remarried.

**Santeras, Santeros** Respectively female and male practitioners of **Santería**.

**Santería** A magical tradition similar to **Voodoo** and **Macumba** found in several regions of the Caribbean, especially Jamaica and Cuba. Here the worship of African deities, mostly from the Yoruba peoples of West Africa, has been fused with homage to the Christian saints following a process of forced religious conversion. The term "santería" derives from the Spanish word *santo*, meaning a saint. Santería is also widely practised in Hispanic communities in various regions of the United States.

**Sapientia** In alchemy, divine wisdom – the goal of the alchemical quest – born of the **coniunctio** between **King Sol** and **Queen Luna**.

**Satan** The personification of evil, also known variously as the **Prince of Darkness**, **Lucifer**, and the **Devil**, among other names. Satan takes his name from the Hebrew word *satan*, "adversary", and in the Bible is depicted as the great adversary of God and the tempter of humankind. In John 8.44, Jesus describes the god worshipped by the Jews as the Devil; and in 2 Corinthians 4.4, Paul identifies the Devil, or Satan, as "the god of this world ... who has blinded the minds of them which believe not". In the Middle Ages, the **Knights Templar** were accused of worshipping Satan in the form of **Baphomet**; and **witchcraft** and various heretical sects – including the Cathars and Waldenses – were also charged with satanic practices. While these accusations were clearly misguided, there have existed from time to time various sects and groups whose purpose has been to mimic and profane the Christian mass and the spiritual principles it represents. The best known contemporary example is provided by Anton La Vey's **Church of Satan** in San Francisco, California. See also **Satanism**.

**Satanic Mass** In satanism, a blasphemous ritual that parodies the Christian mass, invokes the powers of darkness, and sometimes employs the use of a naked woman as an altar. See **Black Mass**; **Church of Satan**; **Satanism**.

**Satanism** The worship of Satan. See also **Satanist**.

**Satanist** A worshipper of **Satan**; a devotee of **satanism**. To the extent that Satan is a personification of evil and the powers of darkness, satanists can be regarded as practitioners of black magic, although the term is not synonymous with satanism. See also **Left-Hand Path**; **Magic, Black**.

**Saturn** (1) In Roman mythology, the god of agriculture and the harvest, whose attribute was a scythe. The husband of Ops, he is the Roman counterpart of the Greek god **Kronos**, the god of time, and with his scythe came to be associated with death – the "grim reaper". His festival, the **Saturnalia**, was held annually in December. See also **Saturnus**.

**Saturn** (2) In **astrology**, a planet that casts an inhibiting or limiting **aspect** on one's life and career. Saturn inclines towards solitude rather than friendship and social conviviality, and is regarded as a generally negative planet. In fact, with **Mars**, it is one of the two **malefics**. A person who has a dour, gloomy, or morose temperament as a result of the influence of Saturn is referred to as "saturnine".

**Saturnalia** A great midwinter festival held in ancient Rome to honour **Saturn**, the god of agriculture. The Saturnalia, which ran from 19 December for a week, was characterized by freedom and equality: slaves were allowed to ridicule their masters, gifts were exchanged, war could not be declared, and rejoicing and debauchery were the accepted custom. It is likely that the Church decided to celebrate Christmas around this time in order to Christianize the popular pagan festival.

**Saturnine** See Saturn (2).

**Saturnus** In alchemy, the term Saturnus – the Roman name of the god Saturn – was used to connote putrefaction. The god, otherwise known as the "grim reaper", was closely associated with the deathly phase of the **nigredo** – the first stage of the **opus alchymicum** in which the impure metal was "killed", putrefied, and subsequently "dissolved" within the **prima materia**. This death process was thought to release the "soul" of the metal from its putrefying body.

**Satyrs** In Greek and Roman mythology, woodland deities. They resembled men, but had the lower bodies of goats, and short horns on their heads. The

attendants of **Dionysus** (Bacchus), and Pan, they were renowned for their sexual orgies and lasciviousness.

**Savnok** See Sabnack.

**Scales, The** See Libra.

**Scarab** In ancient Egyptian mythology, the symbol of **Khepera** – the sun god in his aspect as lord of **rebirth** and **immortality**. The female scarab beetle rolls excrement into a ball with her hind legs and encloses her larvae in it. In Egyptian religion, the scarab became identified with the sun because it flew during the hottest part of the day and was said to roll its dung ball from east to west. Khepera was depicted rolling the sun from the eastern horizon across the sky in much the same fashion.

**Scarlet Woman** See Whore of Babalon.

**Sceptres** See Wands.

**Scholem, Gershom** (1897–1982) A leading authority on the medieval **Kabbalah**, which he believed was a form of Jewish **Gnosticism**. Having gained his doctorate at the University of Berlin, he studied at the Jena, Berne, and Munich and in 1923 joined the Hebrew University of Jerusalem. From 1933 until his retirement in 1965 he was professor of Jewish **mysticism** and Kabbalah there. His works include *Major Trends in Jewish Mysticism*; *Origins of the Kabbalah*; *On the Kabbalah and its Symbolism*; *Jewish Gnosticism*; *Merkabah Mysticism and Talmudic Tradition*; and *On the Mystical Shape of the Godhead*.

**Schure, Edouard** (1841–1929) A French Theosophist and **mystic** whom **Rudolf Steiner** considered to be "one of the best guides for finding the path to the spirit in our day". Schure believed that divinely illuminated beings have appeared in each epoch to guide humankind towards higher spiritual knowledge. These include **Rama, Krishna, Moses, Hermes, Orpheus,**

Pythagoras, and **Pluto**. Schure's approach to the **mystery** tradition is romantic rather than scholarly, and the once fashionable occult concept of an ancient lineage of mystical adepts holds less sway today. Nevertheless, Schure's writings are of continuing interest. His main books are *The Great Initiates* and *From Sphinx to Christ*. See also **Illuminati**.

**Scorpio** In **astrology**, the sign of the zodiac for those born between 23 October and 22 November. A **water** sign, ruled by **Mars**, Scorpio is symbolized by the scorpion or asp. Those born under the sign of Scorpio are said to have great strength of character, and to be watchful and naturally cautious. They are resourceful and make excellent friends, although the "sting" in the scorpion's tail indicates that passionate friendships and love affairs can sometimes turn bitter and become tragic or violent. Careers in science, medicine, and diplomacy are associated with Scorpio; and many occultists – especially those who thrive on secrecy – are found under this sign.

**Scourge** In **Wicca**, a symbolic ritual implement widely used in ceremonial initiations. It typically has eight tails with five knots in each tail and is applied gently by the initiator using light strokes that will not harm the candidate, but nevertheless provide a sense of symbolic reinforcement.

**Scox** See Shax.

**Scrying** See Skrying.

**Scucca** In ancient Anglo-Saxon **sorcery**, a demon. See also **Black Shuck**.

**Scylla** In Greek mythology, a squid-like monster with six heads, eighteen rows of teeth, and twelve feet. Scylla was originally a water-nymph, but she was transformed by **Circe** into a fearsome creature. Thereafter, she turned her attention to devouring seamen as they passed by in their sailing vessels.

**Seal of Solomon** A hexagram consisting of two interlocking triangles, one facing up, the other down. See also **Magen David**.

**Seance** see Spiritualism.

**Sear** See Seere.

**Seax-Wica** A tradition of contemporary **witchcraft** founded in the United States in 1973 by British-born occultist **Raymond Buckland**, a former Gardenerian high priest. Seax-Wica draws on the Saxon tradition. Unlike contemporary Wicca, Seax-Wica has only one degree of initiation and not three and the **high priest** and **high priestess** are regarded as equal in status.

**Second Degree** See Second Initiation.

**Second Initiation** In Wicca, the initiation undertaken so that the first-degree **coven** member may become a **high priestess** or **high priest**. Some covens require at least three years of ritual work before granting the second degree to one of their members. Candidates are asked to find an opposite-sex partner with whom they can work compatibly in partnership and the second-degree rite is essentially a journey into the depths of the mythic unconscious. An important feature of this initiation is a mystery play titled *The Legend of the Descent of the Goddess* in which the candidate and other coven members enact the descent of the **Great Goddess** into the Underworld. Here the goddess encounters the God in his role as the dark lord of death. According to Wiccan high priestess **Vivianne Crowley**, the purpose of the second initiation is different for a man and a woman. For a man, in order to discover his true self he must encounter the divine feminine. For a woman, the ritual highlights her need to overcome passivity and to actively seek a far-ranging experience of life. The second degree in Wicca is essentially about overcoming fear and encountering the opposite sexual polarity within the psyche. Many practitioners take a new magical name after attaining the second degree. See also **First Initiation; Third Initiation.**

**Secret Chiefs** In modern western magic, especially with reference to the **Hermetic Order of the Golden Dawn,** high-ranking spiritual beings who are believed to provide guidance and inspiration to the leaders of the inner order. In the Golden Dawn, the Secret Chiefs were said to reside above the **Abyss,** in the transcendental regions of the **Tree of Life.** They were the magical equivalent of the Theosophical **Masters** or **Mahatmas.**

**Secret Tradition** The occult concept of a line of mystical and magical adepts who have passed their **esoteric** knowledge from generation to generation since earliest times. At all times this knowledge has been jealously guarded by **initiates.** See also **Adept.**

**Secret Wisdom** A general term for traditional occult knowledge, especially that associated with the western **mystery** tradition, which many believe to have passed down through adepts and initiates of different secret orders (e.g. the Rosicrucians, **Freemasonry,** and the **Illuminati**). The existence of an unbroken lineage of occult adepts was challenged by the great occult scholar A.E. **Waite,** and remains a matter of controversy. See also **Adept.**

**Sedna** The Inuit sea goddess who ruled over the sea animals and determined how many could be slain as food or used for fuel or clothing. Inuit shamans would journey to the bottom of the sea to determine how prosperous the future hunt would be and to see whether Sedna required placation. The goddess would advise the shamans whether breaches of taboos had occurred. See also **Shaman.**

**Seed Moon** See **Esbats.**

**Seer** One who "sees" or prophesies the future or who is gifted with second sight. See also **Divination; Oracle.**

**Seere** In the **Goetia,** the 70th spirit, a mighty prince who serves under Amaymon, King of the East. He appears in the form of a beautiful man riding upon a winged horse. He can "pass over the whole earth in the twinkling of an eye" and can advise on the location of hidden treasure and all sorts of theft. It is said that he will willingly undertake anything desired by the evoking magician. Seere rules over 26 legions of spirits and is also known as Sear or Seir.

**Seidkona** In ancient Norse culture, another name for **Volva,** meaning a divinatory priestess. According to Norse tradition, the first seidkona was the fertility goddess **Freyja.**

**Seir** See **Seere.**

**Sekhmet** or **Sekhet** In Egyptian mythology, the wife of **Ptah.** Sekhmet was depicted with the head of a lioness. She is regarded by the tantric occultist **Kenneth Grant** as the personification of "solar-phallic or sexual heat…considered by the ancients as the divine inspirer or breather, the spirit of creation". To this extent she is the Egyptian counterpart of the Hindu **Shakti.** Compare **Pakht.**

**Selene** or **Selena** In Greek mythology, the name for the lunar goddess in her waxing-moon aspect, as distinct from her waning-moon personification as Hecate. See also **Luna; Lunar Goddesses.**

**Self** In mysticism and occult philosophy, the divine essence of one's being. It may be contrasted to the ego which mystics regard as a transitory identity which disappears at death. The self, on the other hand, contains the spark of **godhead** and is the source of pure consciousness.

**Self-Realization** Knowledge of one's true, inner self: spiritual enlightenment.

**Semi-Sextile** In astrology, an aspect characterized by an angle of 30° between two planets. Compare **Sextile.**

**Sensation Body** A term used by occultists to describe the "etheric body", which they believe provides awareness through the senses when united with the physical body.

**Senses, Significators of the** In astrology, the significators of the different human faculties, or senses, are: Mercury (sight); Venus (touch); Mars (taste); Jupiter (smell); and Saturn (hearing).

**Separ** See Vepar.

**Sepher Yetzirah** The kabbalistic work known as *The Book of Creation*. The *Sepher Yetzirah* is the earliest metaphysical text in the Hebrew language, and describes God's revelations to Abraham. The visionary tract – which was originally passed down orally – describes the ten sephiroth of the Tree of Life, and the "22 letters and sounds which comprise the Foundation of all things". The *Sepher Yetzirah* is one of the most important books of the Kabbalah; but it does not represent the complete tradition, for it does not describe the Ain Soph Aur, Adam Kadmon, or the Shekhinah.

**Sephirah** See Sephiroth.

**Sephiroth** The ten spheres or emanations on the kabbalistic Tree of Life, a symbol which depicts the divine energy of creation proceeding like a "lightning flash" through ten different stages, culminating in physical manifestation. The sephiroth (singular, sephirah) represent levels of spiritual reality both in the cosmos and in people because the Tree, metaphorically, is the "body of God", and people are created in his image. The Tree is sometimes shown superimposed on the body of Adam Kadmon – the archetypal man. The ten sephiroth, in descending order, are Kether (the crown); Chokmah (wisdom); Binah (understanding); Chesed (mercy); Geburah (power); Tiphareth (beauty and harmony); Netzach (victory); Hod (splendour); Yesod (foundation); and Malkuth (the kingdom).

**Seraphim** In Hebrew and medieval Christian cosmologies, the highest of the nine orders of angels. The seraphim are guardians of God's throne and have three pairs of wings.

**Serapis** The Greek name for the sacred bull of Memphis in ancient Egypt. His worshippers believed he was an incarnation of Osiris. Serapis became the chief deity in Alexandria and a large temple called the Serapeum was built in his honour. Serapis was a god of the Underworld and was later worshipped in Greece and Rome alongside Zeus, Jupiter, and Dionysus.

**Serpent** In alchemy, a symbol for the potent and destructive power of Mercurius – or philosophical mercury – which was able to dissolve metals and return them to the prima materia.

**Serpent Power** A term used by magical practitioners of the Ordo Templi Orientis to describe the so-called Ophidian Current in its raw or primordial form. It is also connected to the ritual worship of Apep – the ancient Egyptian serpent deity – which plays a central role in the magic of the Typhonian Order of the Outer Ones.

**Servants of the Light** An international magical organization currently headed by Dolores Ashcroft-Nowicki. Based on magical techniques developed by Dion Fortune and her fellow practitioners in the Fraternity of the Inner Light, the S.O.L. currently has lodges in Australia, Britain, Canada, Mexico, the Netherlands, Sweden, and the United States and around 2,600 students scattered across 23 countries. Dolores Ashcroft-Nowicki periodically visits her S.O.L. members in these different countries and is able to manage the growth of the S.O.L. and its core magical procedures through the Internet and her own website. The S.O.L. remains one of the most prominent contemporary organizations dedicated to the exploration of visionary **magic** in the world today.

**Serviteur** In **voodoo**, a person who serves the **loa**.

**Set** or **Seth** In Egyptian mythology, the brother of **Osiris** and Isis. Set was jealous of his brother and tricked Osiris into climbing into a beautiful chest; Set and a group of conspirators then sealed and weighted it heavily, and cast it into the Nile. Isis recovered the body of Osiris and became pregnant by him with **Horus** through an act of magical conception. However, Set discovered Osiris once again and tore his body into fourteen pieces, which he scattered around the kingdom. In the Egyptian **pantheon**, as the adversary of Osiris – who symbolizes the renewal of life – Set is the dark god and the personification of evil. He was identified by the Greeks with **Typhon**.

**Sethians** A Gnostic sect that traced its ancestry to Seth, the third son of Adam and Eve. See **Ophites**.

**Setian** A member of the **Temple of Set**.

**Seven** In mythology and **numerology**, a number with mystic and supernatural connotations. There were seven planets in ancient astronomy; the world (according to Genesis) had been created in seven days; Joshua and the Israelites marched around Jericho for seven days; and each of the four phases of the **moon** lasts for seven days. There are seven notes on the musical scale and seven colours in the rainbow. Accordingly, seven is the number of completeness, wisdom, spiritual truth, and cosmic harmony. The seventh son of a seventh son is traditionally said to possess supernatural powers.

**Seven-Pointed Star** In Wicca, a star with its points marked by the astrological signs assigned to the different days of the week. The **sun** rules Sunday, the moon Monday, **Mars** Tuesday, **Mercury** Wednesday, **Jupiter** Thursday, **Venus** Friday and **Saturn** Saturday. Sometimes the seven-pointed star is worn as a magical pendant or **lamen** by the high priestess of the **coven**.

**Seven Stewards of Heaven** One of the names by which the seven **Olympic Spirits** are known. See also *The Arbatel of Magick*.

**Sextile** In astrology, an aspect characterized by an angle of 60° between two planets.

**Sexual Magic** See Magic, Sexual.

**Seymour, Charles R.F.** (1880–1943) A leading member of Dion Fortune's **Fraternity of the Inner Light**, Seymour was born in Ireland and came from a distinguished military family, rising to the rank of lieutenant colonel. He joined the Inner Light c. 1932 and in 1937 formed a close psycho-spiritual connection with Christine Thomson (later Hartley, but married at the time to Oscar Cook), connecting with her energetically on the **astral plane**. Together, over a period of several years, they explored a succession of past lives and richly detailed reincarnational memories, the transcripts of which are provided in Alan Richardson's *Dancers to the Gods* (1985). Seymour produced an important short work titled *The Old Religion* which was included under a pseudonym in *New Dimensions Red Book* by Basil Wilby (**Gareth Knight**) See also **Hartley, Christine**.

**Shaddai** A Hebrew word meaning "almighty". It is a common **god-name** in Jewish mystical writing, and is used as a formula of invocation in modern western **magic**.

**Shaddai El Hai** In the Kabbalah, the divine name associated with the sphere **Yesod** on the **Tree of Life**. It translates as "Almighty Living One" or "Divine Life Force". See also **Shaddai**.

**Shadows, Book of** See *Book of Shadows*.

**Shaitan** An ancient deity of the Yezidi, worshipped in lower Mesopotamia, and a counterpart to the Egyptian god **Set**, god of darkness. Shaitan does not equate directly with **Satan**.

**Shakuru** Among the Pawnee Indians, the sun god – honoured annually with colourful religious ritual and dances.

**Shaman** A sorcerer, magician, medicine man, or healer who is able to enter a trance state under will and who serves as an intermediary between people and the realm of gods and spirits. Shamans, who may be male or female, make use of drums, ritual objects, and ceremonial costume in identifying with the gods; and they often enter a state of trance in order to undertake a **journey of the soul**. The purpose of this spirit journey is to recover stolen spirits or to seek information from the deities relating to the availability of food and the likely outcome of the hunt. Associated with tribal and hunter-gatherer societies, the shaman may be distinguished from the spirit medium, who is possessed in trance but does not control the experience; and also from the **priest**, who conducts rituals but does not necessarily enter a state of trance.

**Shamaness** An alternative name for a female **Shaman**.

**Shamanic Visualization** A contemporary application of traditional shamanic practice in which a person undertakes a "spirit journey", or **journey of the soul**, in the mind's eye, usually to the accompaniment of a monotonous and regular drum beat. During this spirit journey the meditator may make contact with power animals, spirit helpers, or inner guides – all of whom may assist in processes of healing or self-renewal, or in some form of magical activity. See **Shaman**; **Spirit Helper**.

**Shamanism** A technique of gaining trance consciousness found in pre-literate and tribal societies, in which the shaman undertakes a **journey of the soul** in order to encounter the gods or **spirits**. The shaman may use the monotonous sound of a drum beat to "ride" into this trance state, and usually performs his ceremonies in darkness. Psychedelics are sometimes used to enhance the states of visionary consciousness. Shamanism is found principally in Siberia (where the word **shaman** itself comes from), North and South America, and Indonesia, and is characterized by trance states in which the shaman retains control of his experience – unlike states of **spirit possession**, where the gods or spirits dominate proceedings.

**Shamash** The Mesopotamian sun god and brother of the fertility goddess **Ishtar**. Shamash was the personification of light and righteousness and had the power to deliver oracles or prophecy. Compare **Apollo** and see also **Oracle**; **Prophecy**.

**Shamrock** The three-leafed clover, the national emblem of Ireland. Its threefold structure links it symbolically to the Christian Trinity but also to the much more ancient Celtic tradition of the **Triple Goddess**. The shamrock is also associated with the Celtic sun wheel and it was revered by the fairy folk of Ireland, the legendary sídhe or **Tuatha de Danann**.

**Shango** See Xangô

**Shapanan** In Macumba, the god of smallpox. See also **Omulu**.

**Shape-Shifting** The supernatural ability to transform one's shape into that of an animal, bird, or other creature. Shape-shifting is sometimes ascribed to witches, shamans, and sorcerers. See also **Lycanthropy**.

**Shax** In the Goetia, the 44th spirit, a powerful marquis who appears in the form of a dove or stork and who speaks with a hoarse voice. He destroys the faculties of sight and hearing on command of the magician, will steal money from the king's houses, and can also fetch horses when so instructed. Shax must first be commanded to enter the magic triangle for he will otherwise deceive the practitioner who evokes his presence. He rules 30 legions of spirits and is also known as Shaz, Chax, or Scox.

**Shaz** See Shax.

**Shedim** In the Kabbalah, demonic beings who confuse the mind of the mystic while the latter is engaged in meditation. See Demon.

**Shekhinah** In the Jewish mystical tradition, God's female aspect and immanent presence in the physical universe. Shekhinah, which is said to "dwell in exile", is associated with the sephirah Malkuth on the kabbalistic Tree of Life.

**Shem ha-Meforash** In the Jewish mystical tradition, the 72-syllable name of God, which consists of 216 letters. According to Jewish tradition, the source of this name may be found in Exodus 14.19–21, which contains three verses each containing 72 Hebrew letters. At a later stage, the Shem ha-Meforash was said to have been simplified to the form YHVH, known as the Tetragrammaton.

**Sheol** From the Hebrew *she'ol*, "a cave", the dark Underworld where departed spirits are thought to dwell after death. The word is sometimes used generally to mean hell, although Sheol is closer to Hades, and Gehenna is more akin to the western notion of hell.

**Shevarith ha-Kelim** Hebrew for "Shattering of the Vessels". In the kabbalistic teachings of Isaac Luria, a doctrine which asserts that at the moment of creation there was an explosion which shattered the totality into holy sparks, which will reunite over time.

**Shi Tenno** In traditional Japanese cosmology, the guardians of the four cardinal directions. Their names were Jikoku (east); Zocho (west); Bishamon (north); and Komoku (south). The Shi Tenno were powerful protectors against demons and evil spirits.

**Shield of David** See Seal of Solomon; Hexagram; Magen David.

**Shin** The Hebrew letter ascribed to the path linking Malkuth and Hod on the kabbalistic Tree of Life. Shin has a numerical value of 300. In modern magical visualization and pathworkings the Tarot card associated with this path on the Tree is *Judgment*.

**Shrine** A sacred location or object. Temples, chapels, tombs, and sacred groves often have special significance as shrines because of their historic connection with a holy personage and are venerated for this reason.

**Shuck, Black** See Black Shuck

**Sibyls** In ancient Greece and Rome, women who lived in caves and who were renowned for their gifts of prophecy. The most famous of the sibyls lived at Cumae near Naples, and guarded the temple of Apollo, near the reputed entrance to the Underworld. According to Varro, there were ten sibyls in all, the others residing in Persia, Libya, Delphi (the Delphic Sybil), Samos, Cimmeria, Erythrae, Tibur, Marpessa, and Phrygia.

**Sidereal Gods and Goddesses** From the Latin sidus, "star", Greek and Roman deities of the sky. They include Apollo, Artemis, Diana, Helios, Luna, Selene, Uranus, and Zeus.

**Sídhe** The fairy folk of ancient Ireland. See also Tuatha de Danann.

**Sighel** See Sigil (2).

**Sigil** (1) In the Germanic Elder Futhark, the rune letter representing the number sixteen. Sigil corresponds to the letter "s". It is a rune symbol of the sun and is associated with light, health, and vitality. Sigil also represents the positive transcendent power in the cosmos – the force of light overcoming darkness and chaos. It therefore symbolizes the higher self of the mystical seeker. Also known as Sowilo.

**Sigil** (2) An occult symbol that represents a specific supernatural being or entity. In medieval **magic**, sigils were used to summon **spirits** and angels. In recent times, the trance occultist **Austin Osman Spare** developed his own alphabet of magical sigils to release atavistic images from his unconscious mind.

**Sign** In astrology, one of the twelve divisions of the **zodiac**. The twelve signs, in their usual order, are: Aries, Taurus, Gemini, Cancer, Leo, Virgo, Libra, Scorpio, Sagittarius, Capricorn, Aquarius, and Pisces. The signs are each ascribed to the four elements, and are classified as cardinal, fixed, and mutable, as follows:

|       | *Cardinal* | *Fixed* | *Mutable* |
|-------|-----------|---------|-----------|
| Fire  | Aries     | Leo     | Sagittarius |
| Water | Cancer    | Scorpio | Pisces |
| Air   | Libra     | Aquarius | Gemini |
| Earth | Capricorn | Taurus  | Virgo |

**Signatures** A mystical concept of correspondences which holds that since plants were created by God for people to use, their shapes are indicators, or "signatures", of their function or character. In medieval **herbalism**, yellow flowers or roots were used to treat jaundice; while the **mandrake**, whose roots often have a human shape, were said to "scream" when pulled from the ground and to grow from the semen of men sent to the gallows to die.

**Significator** In astrology, the significator of a natal horoscope is the planet which is most strongly aspected: it is usually held to be the **ruler** of the **ascendant**. Significators can also be identified for the different astrological houses. See **Horoscope, Natal**; **Light, Collector.**

**Signs of the Elements** See Pyramid.

**Sileni** In Greek mythology, mythic creatures that resembled satyrs, except that they had the bodies of horses instead of goats. See also **Satyr**; **Silenus.**

**Silenus** In Greek mythology, the oldest of the satyrs. In the region of Phrygia, Silenus was a **deity** in his own right, but was later identified as the son of **Pan** or **Hermes.**

**Silvanus** or **Sylvanus** Roman god of fields, gardens, and woods, who was half man, half goat. He is often confused with Silenus, but was in fact one of the *numina* – the protective spirits of home and garden.

**Silver** A metal associated with the element **water** and with the **moon**. In western **magic** and the **tattvas**, the symbol of the moon is a silver crescent. In **alchemy**, silver symbolizes the **albedo**, the second stage of the **opus alchymicum**. This stage gave rise to the so-called **white stone**, the tincture that could transform base metals into silver.

**Silver Star, Order of the** See **Argenteum Astrum.**

**Simon Magus** A magician or sorcerer mentioned in Acts 8 who gathered a following among the Samaritans; many believed he had divine and magical powers and worshipped him as if he were a god. He was rebuked by the apostle Peter for trying to buy the gift of healing through the Holy Spirit, and consequently has a poor reputation in Christian tradition. According to one tradition, Simon learned the magical arts in Egypt and became an initiate in the sect of Dositheus. Another tradition had Simon as an antagonist of the apostle Peter in Rome. At different times Emperor Nero challenged Peter to prove that the power the apostle claimed through Jesus Christ was superior to that of Simon. A particular test proved conclusive: Nero ordered that a tower be raised in the Campus Martius, from which Simon Magus claimed he would "ascend into heaven". Simon, according to tradition, stretched forth his hands and began to fly, and Nero asked Peter whether this meant Jesus and his followers were deceivers. At this point Peter is said to have called on Christ to banish the angels of **Satan** supporting Simon in the air, whereupon the magician fell to earth in the Sacra Via, his body broken into four pieces.

**Simos, Miriam** See **Starhawk.**

**Simulacrum** A copy. The word is used to describe acts of imitative magic, where a simulacrum of a person may be injured with the intent of harming the person at a distance; and it is also used to describe the body image an **occultist** visualizes in attempting to project his or her consciousness onto the **astral plane**. See also **Magic, Black; Magic, Imitative.**

**Sin** In Mesopotamian religion, the moon god who personified goodness and kept a vigil against the forces of evil. Sin was a wise deity and advised the other gods on appropriate courses of action. He also marked the passage of time through each month. Sin was identified by the Sumerians with **Nanna.** See also **Shamash.**

**Sinister** From the Latin word meaning "left", that which is on the left-hand side. It has come to mean something undesirable or unfortunate; in **occultism** the **left-hand path** is associated with black magic and **sorcery.** See also **Magic, Black; Right-Hand Path.**

**Sipapu** See **Kiva.**

**Sirens** In Greek mythology, three notorious sea nymphs – part bird, part women – who lured sailors to their deaths on treacherous rocks by singing enchanting songs. Their names were Leucosia, Ligeia, and Parthenope. **Circe** warned **Odysseus** of their seductive powers, and he in turn instructed his companions to stuff their ears with wax

as they passed the island where the Sirens lived. When the song of the Sirens failed to have an effect on the crew, the three nymphs hurled themselves into the sea and perished.

**Sirius** The Dog Star – the brightest star in the sky and part of the constellation Canis Major (Greater Dog). It was named Sirius (from the Greek *seirios*, "scorching") because it rises in mid-July, the hottest time of the northern hemisphere year. Its rising heralded the annual Nile flood in Egypt, where the star was venerated as the goddess Sopdet (Sothis). Sirius has attracted renewed interest in recent years among cosmologists and ufologists interested in the origins of alien intelligence.

**Sistrum** A metal rattle used as a musical instrument by the ancient Egyptians in their worship of Isis. Used generally to describe a rattle used in dancing, the sistrum (plural, *sistra*) has its place in South American **shamanism**, where it often accompanies the drum as a sacred instrument. It also featured in the religious traditions of the Aztecs and Romans.

**Sitry** In the Goetia, the 12th spirit, a great prince who appears with a leopard's head and the wings of a **griffin** but who may by commanded by the magician to adopt a human form. Essentially a spirit of love and lust, Sitry is able to enflame "men with women's love and women with men's love" and can also compel them to appear naked "if it be desired". Sitry governs 60 legions of spirits. He is also known as Sytri.

**Six** In **numerology**, a number indicative of love, domesticity, family affairs, and loyalty. Six consists of the first masculine number (three) multiplied by the first feminine number (two) and therefore characterizes a productive and harmonious union.

**Skinner, Stephen** (1948– ) An Australian-born occultist, currently living near Singapore. Skinner, an authority on medieval **magic**, Enochian magic, geomancy and feng shui, established the Askin publishing house in 1972 to produce facsimile editions of magical writings by **Dr John Dee**, **Cornelius Agrippa**, and **Paracelsus**. In recent times he has been working with author **David Rankine** on research into previously unpublished magical material from the Renaissance, resulting in the publication in 2004 of *The Practical Angel Magic of Dr John Dee's Enochian Table*, the first in a series of projected works co-authored with Rankine. Skinner is also the co-author, with the late **Francis X. King**, of *Techniques of High Magic* (London, 1976), one of the most coherent books on practical techniques of modern magic ever written. His other magically oriented books include *The Oracle of Geomancy* (1977); *Terrestrial Astrology* (1980); and *The Living Earth Manual of Feng-Shui* (1982), as well as several editions of magical writings by **Aleister Crowley**. See also **Magic, Enochian**.

**Skrying** or **Scrying** A form of **divination** in which the practitioner gazes at a shiny or polished surface to induce a **trance** state in which scenes, people, words, or images appear as part of a **psychic** communication. The familiar **crystal ball** of the Gypsy fortune teller provides the best example; but mirrors, polished metal, coal or bone, and even cups of clear liquid, have also been used for skrying.

**Skuld** See Norns.

**Skyclad** In Wicca, being "skyclad" refers to the act of working naked in a ritual.

**Sleepy Nightshade** See Deadly Nightshade.

**Small Face** In the Kabbalah, the manifested God whose attributes are reflected in the **sephiroth** of the **Tree of Life**.

**Smaragdine Table** The fabled Hermetic *Tabula Smaragdina*. See **Emerald Tablet**.

**Smudging** The Native American practice of burning a herb and "washing" oneself and others in the smoke as a ritual purification. The act of smudging defines a particular point in the ceremony – from this point onwards everything performed in the ceremony is regarded as a sacred act. Traditionally four herbs are used in smudging: cedar, sweetgrass, sage, or wormwood.

**Snake Worship** See Ophiolatry.

**Sneezing Spice** See Hellebore.

**Snow Moon** See Esbats.

**Snuffs, Magical** See Magical Snuffs.

**"So Mote It Be"** In Wicca, the equivalent to the Christian expression "Amen".

**Societas Rosicruciana in Anglia** The Rosicrucian Society in England, founded by Robert Wentworth Little (1840–1878) in 1867, drawing on a system of grades employed by a Rosicrucian group in Edinburgh. The Societas Rosicruciana in Anglia was an important precursor of the **Hermetic Order of the Golden Dawn** and its members included **Dr William Wynn Westcott**, **Samuel Liddell MacGregor Mathers**, **Dr W.R. Woodman**, the occultist and clairvoyant **Frederick Hockley**, and the Freemason **Kenneth R.H. Mackenzie**, who may have helped Little adapt the Scottish grades used to create the society. In 1871 **Sir Edward Bulwer-Lytton** was voted in as honorary grand patron of the society but this was without his knowledge and he never attended any meetings.

**Sol** (1) "Sun", the Roman name for the sun god. His Greek counterpart was known variously as **Apollo**, **Helios**, **Hyperion**, and **Phoebus**. See also **Sun**.

**Sol** (2) In alchemy, a term referring either to the sun, gold, or the philosophical virtues of gold, for example perfection. Sol was said to be the "father" of the Philosopher's Stone. See also King Sol.

**Solar Gods** Traditionally, the sun has been regarded as a masculine force and the moon as feminine. Consequently, the sun is often personified as a male deity and is worshipped in this form. Many of the ancient pantheons featured solar gods. They include Ra (Egypt); Mithra (Persia); Apollo, Helios, and Hyperion, (Greece); and Sol (Rome). In China, the sun is the force behind all things that are yang, or masculine.

**Solar Plexus** A large network of nerves found behind the stomach. The solar plexus is regarded in yoga as the seat of the chakra or energy centre known as manipura. According to Carlos Castañeda, it is also the source of the magical power of the shaman.

**Solar Revolution Horoscope** See Horoscope, Solar Revolution.

**Solas** In the Goetia, the 36th spirit, a powerful prince who appears first in the form of a raven but who will then assume human form. Solas imparts a knowledge of astronomy and the virtues of herbs and precious stones. He commands 26 legions of spirits and is also known as Stolas or Stolos.

**Solitary** In Wicca, a practitioner who worships privately, outside a group or coven.

**Sol Niger** In alchemy, the so-called "black sun" – a reference to the death and putrefaction of the metal. See Nigredo.

**Solomon** The legendary biblical king of Israel, who probably reigned c. 975BCE. Solomon was the son of David and Bathsheba and was famed for his wisdom. He acquired considerable

wealth through trade and built his legendary temple in Jerusalem. Many works have been attributed to him, including the biblical books *Proverbs*, *Ecclesiastes*, and *The Song of Songs* and numerous apocryphal works; and in the Middle Ages he was claimed as the author of several magical grimoires including *The Lesser Key of Solomon* and *The Greater Key of Solomon*. See *Key of Solomon, The*.

**Solve et Coagula** In alchemy, a Latin term meaning "dissolve and coagulate" – the process whereby the "body" of the material intended for the Philosopher's Stone was dissolved or made soft, and fluid or "spirit" was congealed or made hard. The alchemical process required numerous cycles of dissolution and coagulation and with each cycle the material contained in the alembic, or alchemical distillation vessel, became purer. Also Open and Shut.

**Soma** A sacred plant that was used to make a narcotic drink, consumed in Vedic sacrificial rites held in honour of the warrior god Indra. Soma was said to be the drink of the gods and to bestow divinity upon mortals. It has been identified by some writers as the leafless plant *Sarcostemma acidum*, but the ethnomycologist R. Gordon Wasson has produced impressive evidence that soma was in fact *Amanita muscaria*, the hallucinogenic red- and white-spotted mushroom also known as fly agaric. See also Hallucination.

**Son of Light** An occult term for a practitioner of white magic. See Magic, White.

**Soothsayer** From the Old English *soth*, "truth", one who has the supernatural ability to divine future events. See also Divination; Prophecy.

**Sophia** Greek for "Wisdom". In Judaeo-Christian tradition and Gnosticism, the female personification of divine wisdom. For the Gnostic teacher Valentinus, she is an archetype of the Great Mother; and in some Gnostic cosmologies bears a resemblance to the Virgin Mary. Sophia is sometimes referred to as the female Logos.

**Sophic Hydrolith** In alchemy, "the waterstone of wisdom" – the Philosopher's Stone. See also **Hydrolith**.

**Sopdet** See Sirius

**Sorcerer, Sorceress** A magician, wizard, or shaman who uses magical spells and incantations to summon spirits, especially for evil purposes or to gain personal power. See also **Incantation; Sorcery; Spell**.

**Sorcerer's Herb** See Thornapple.

**Sorcery** The act of summoning super-natural powers or spirits through spells and incantations. The word is generally applied to black magic. See also **Goetia; Incantation; Magic, Black; Sorceror; Spell**.

**Sortilege** A form of divination by casting or drawing lots. It can take various forms: drawing straws from a cluster or a card from a pack; opening a book at random and taking the first passage one notices as an oracle; or simply throwing dice. See also **Urim and Thummim**.

**Sothis** See Sirius.

**Souffleurs** See Puffers.

**Soul** The eternal, immaterial, spiritual dimension of an organism, which animates its physical form and gives it life. In some mystical traditions animals, plants, and even inanimate objects such as rocks can have souls. The Greek philosopher **Plato** believed that the soul could exist independently of the body, although it was still part of God; and in many traditions the projection of the soul beyond the body (as in the spirit journey, or **journey of the soul**, of the

shaman) is taken as proof of immortality and the transitional nature of death. In Hinduism, Buddhism, and most branches of **occultism**, the soul is believed capable of **reincarnation** or **transmigration** into other human or animal forms. Sometimes the soul is regarded as a unified entity (as in Platonic thought), while at other times it is divided into different parts. In the **Kabbalah**, for example, the soul has three divisions: the **Neschamah**, the **Ruach**, and the **Nephesch**. Of these the first, or "higher soul", shares the spiritual qualities of the trinity (the three **sephiroth** above the **Abyss**), while the other divisions of the soul are less elevated.

In many shamanic cultures around the world there is a belief that human beings have more than one soul. The "free soul" is able to leave the body and journey to other realms, like the land of the dead or the spirit world. Loss of the free soul is linked to disease and malaise and retrieving it may require the services of a **shaman**. The free soul is distinguished from the "body soul", or "life soul", which is the force that animates the body, keeping it alive. See also **Self; Soul Loss; Spirit**.

**Soul Body** See Astral Body; and Soul.

**Soul, Free** See **Soul**.

**Soul, Life** See **Soul**.

**Soul Loss** In many forms of shamanism, soul loss is equated with loss of spirit, leading to greatly increased vulnerability to illness and magical attack. When a person experiences soul loss they are literally "dis-spirited" and they may require the skills and knowledge of a **shaman** or folk healer to retrieve their soul and regain their health and vitality.

**Soul Mates** Two individuals who believe they have a shared spiritual destiny together and who have possibly maintained a unique bond through many incarnations. See also **Reincarnation**.

**South** In western ceremonial **magic**, the direction associated with the element fire. It is said to be ruled by the archangel **Michael**. See also **Four Directions**. See also **Magic, Ceremonial**.

**Sovereign Grand Architect of the Universe, The** In Freemasonry, the name by which the **supreme being**, or God, is known. It is normal in Freemasonry to refer to God by an acronym made up of the initials of this title: T.S.G.A.O.T.U. Belief in **God** is a condition of membership for those seeking to be initiated as Freemasons.

**Sowilo** See Sigil (1).

**Spagyric Art** A term used to describe alchemy. It is thought to have been coined by **Paracelsus**.

**Spagyrist** A follower of the medieval alchemist **Paracelsus**.

**Spare, Austin Osman** (1886–1956) An English trance artist and magician whose magical concept of the relationship between **Zos** and **Kia** has been instrumental in the formation of "chaos magic". One of five children, Spare was born in Snow Hill, London, on 30 December 1886, the son of a policeman. The family later moved to south London and Spare attended St Agnes' School in Kennington Park; he would live in this area of the city, in modest circumstances, for most of his life. Spare showed artistic talent early on, and at the age of twelve began studying at Lambeth Evening Art School. In 1902, when he was sixteen, he won a scholarship enabling him to attend the Royal College of Art, South Kensington, and in 1905 examples of his work were exhibited at the Royal Academy.

Spare's art teems with magical imagery and he was briefly a member of both the **Argenteum Astrum** and the **Ordo Templi Orientis**. When he began to self-publish his illustrated magical books from 1905 onwards it became evident that his was an eccentric rather than a mainstream artistic talent, and there is little doubt that his unconventionality has pushed him to the sidelines of cultural history. He nevertheless remains a legendary figure in the 20th-century western esoteric tradition and is one of its truly original thinkers, his approach to **trance** states and his technique of **atavistic resurgence** representing a unique contribution to the study of magical consciousness. Spare postulated the existence of a primal, cosmic life force which he termed Kia, and he believed that the spiritual and occult energies inherent in Kia could be channelled into the human organism, which he called Zos. His technique of arousing these primal energies – an approach he termed atavistic resurgence – involved focusing the will on magical sigils, or potent individualized symbols, which in effect represented instructions to the subconscious. When the mind was in a "void" or open state – achieved, for example, through meditation or exhaustion, or at the peak of sexual ecstasy – this was an ideal condition in which to direct magical sigils to the subconscious. Here they could "grow" in the seedbed of the mind until they became "ripe" and reached back down into the conscious mind. In such a way one could learn to manipulate one's own "psychic reality".

Spare visited Egypt during World War One and was impressed by the magnetic presence of the ancient gods depicted in monumental sculpture. He also believed that the ancient Egyptians understood very thoroughly the complex mythology of the subconscious mind. For Spare, impressions from earlier human incarnations and potentially all mythic impulses could be reawakened from the subconscious mind. The gods themselves could be regarded as a form of internal impetus. "All gods have lived (being ourselves) on earth", he wrote, "and when dead, their experience of **karma** governs our actions in degree". However, while the classical gods of ancient Egypt made a marked impression on him, Spare learnt his actual technique of trance activation

**AUSTIN OSMAN SPARE** Self-portrait (1912) of renowned trance-artist and magician Austin Osman Spare, surrounded by his "atavisms".

from an elderly woman called Mrs
Paterson, who was a friend of his parents
and used to tell his fortune when he was
quite young. Mrs Paterson claimed a
psychic link with the **Salem witches** and
also appeared to have an extrasensory
ability to project thought-forms.
According to Spare, she was able to
transform herself in his vision from
being a "wizened old crone" to appearing
quite suddenly as a ravishing siren,
"creating a vision of profound sexual
intensity and revelation that shook him
to the very core".

The archetypal female image recurs in
all phases of Spare's artistic work – he
was a master at depicting the sensuous
naked female form – and the "universal
woman" would become a central image
in his mythology of the subconscious.
Spare employed a technique of ecstasy
which frequently combined active imagination and will with the climax of sexual
orgasm. Spare believed that his magical
sigils – representing symbols of the
personal will – could be directed to the
subsconscious mind during the peak of
sexual ecstasy since, at this special
moment, the personal ego and the
universal spirit, or Kia, were united in a
state of blissful, transcendent openness.
"At this moment, which is the moment
of generation of the Great Wish", writes
Spare, "inspiration flows from the source
of sex, from the primordial goddess who
exists at the heart of matter...inspiration
is always at a *void* moment." Undoubtedly,
one of Spare's major objectives in using
the trance state was to tap energies which
he believed were the source of genius.
According to Spare, "Ecstasy, inspiration,
intuition, and dream...each state taps the
latent memories and presents them in
the imagery of their respective
languages." And genius itself was "a
directly resurgent atavism" experienced
during the ecstasy of the "Fire Snake" –
Spare's term for magical sexual arousal.
See also **Magic, Chaos.**

**Speculum** Any object used in skrying
to focus one's gaze in entering a state of
**trance** consciousness. Examples include
the **crystal ball,** or any objects with
shiny, reflective surfaces that are used
for this purpose.

**Spell** An **incantation** or **invocation,**
performed by a **witch, wizard,** or
**magician,** which is believed to have a
tangible outcome – for either good or
evil. Spells can be a form of absent
healing, or can be used to inflict harm
to person or property. See also **Evil Eye;
Magic; Sorcery.**

**Spellcraft** In Wicca, the practice of
working magic spells. See **Spell.**

**Spence, James Lewis** (1874–1955) A
Scottish poet and politician best known
for his interest in **magic, mythology,**
and the occult. Spence was a sub-editor
of *The Scotsman* newspaper and later
one of the founder members of the
National Party of Scotland. But it is his
writings on mythology and **occultism**
that have secured his reputation. Spence
was generally sympathetic to occult
groups and societies while maintaining
a sense of distance from their more
extravagant claims. He had difficulty
accepting that the western esoteric
tradition provided a key to the "inner
sanctuary of Christianity" – a concept
championed by **Anna Bonus Kingsford**
in the Hermetic Society and **A.E. Waite**
in the **Hermetic Order of the Golden
Dawn** – but nevertheless believed
strongly in the value of authentic
**mysticism.** Spence was a prolific author
and wrote on a variety of occult
subjects. His other books include *The
History of Atlantis; The Magic Arts in
Celtic Britain;* and *The Fairy Tradition in
Britain.* His *Encyclopaedia of Occultism*
(London 1920), remains a standard
reference on the subject.

**Sperm** In alchemy, the seed or life
force of metals, associated with
**Mercurius.** Without this sperm the
union of **Sol** and **Luna** could yield no
offspring. See also **King Sol; Queen
Luna.**

**Spheres** In mystical cosmology, levels of spiritual awareness or specific celestial objects in the heavens (e.g. planetary spheres). See also **Music of the Spheres**. Compare with **Aeon**; **Emanations**; **Sephiroth**.

**Sphinx** A composite mythic creature consisting of a human head and breast, the body, feet, and tail of a lion, and sometimes the wings of a bird. The most famous example is the **Great Sphinx** at Giza, which represents **Horus** and has a king's head. At Karnak, there are also avenues of sphinxes with the head of a ram, representing the god **Amon**. The Greek Sphinx had a woman's head and breasts and was said to be the offspring of **Typhon** and **Echidna**. Travellers who came near her were devoured if they could not answer her question: "What creature goes on four legs in the morning, on two at noonday, and on three in the evening?" The answer to the riddle of the sphinx was "man" – who crawls as a baby on all fours, walks erect in maturity, and requires the use of a staff when bent over with old age. Oedipus successfully answered the Sphinx, who then threw herself off a cliff to her death.

**Spindle of Fate** In classical Greek mythology, the spindle turned by the three **Fates** in unfolding destiny.

**Spirit** The divine spark or "essence" within each person which, in mystical belief, unites that person with the **godhead**. It is the vital ingredient of life. See also **Prana**; **Soul**; **Spirits, Discarnate**.

**Spirit Beings** See Spirits, Discarnate.

**Spirit Helper** In shamanism, spiritualism, and **witchcraft**, a spirit being that acts as a guide, guardian, or **familiar**.

**Spirit Intrusion** In tribal and native religions around the world, the idea that disease is due to the intrusion into the body of a **spirit** or an object like a **magical dart**. See also **Macaiyoyo**.

**Spirit Journey** See Journey of the Soul.

**Spirit Possession** See Possession.

**Spirit Vision** A term used by occultists and trance magicians to describe the visionary nature of the **astral plane**, where encounters with spirits and other celestial and magical beings are experienced as an existential reality.

**Spirits, Discarnate** entities, often ancestors or **elementals**, who are believed to influence the world of the living. In hunter-gatherer and tribal societies, placating the spirits is usually considered necessary if life is to continue harmoniously, and if abundant crops and favourable hunting or harvesting conditions are to be guaranteed. In modern **spiritualism**, spirits are summoned by a **medium** during a seance for information relating to life in the afterworld and to provide reassurance that one's deceased relatives are still interested in temporal matters and can provide guidance to the living.

**Spirits of the Elements** See Elements.

**Spiritualism** The belief that the spirits of the dead can communicate with the living through a psychic **medium**. During a seance – a session conducted to summon a particular spirit – the medium enters a state of trance. The deceased spirit subsequently "possesses" the medium and either addresses the gathering directly or communicates through **automatic writing** or **automatic painting or drawing**. Spiritualists regard the phenomena occurring at seances as proof of life after death.

**Spodomancy** A form of divination in which the cinders taken from sacrificial fires are interpreted for omens.

**Sprenger, Jacob** (c. 1436–1495) A Swiss-born Dominican Inquisitor who, with **Heinrich Kramer**, compiled the notorious medieval source work on

De lanijs et phitonicis mu=
lieribus ad illustrissimum principem dominū Sigismūdum
archiducem austrie tracigrus pulcherrimus

SPELL   Medieval witches conjuring a hail-storm.

witchcraft, *Malleus Maleficarum*. Sprenger became prior of the convent of Cologne, and founded the Fraternity of the Rosary after being inspired by a religious vision. He rose in power and status and in 1481 became Inquisitor for the provinces of Cologne, Treves (Trier), and Mainz. It is generally considered that Sprenger was the more scholarly of the two authors, although Kramer did most of the compilation work on the *Malleus*. See also **Inquisition**.

**Sprite** A nature spirit. See also **Elementals; Elves; Fairies; Nymphs; Pixies**.

**Square** In astrology, an aspect characterized by an angle of 90° between two planets. Compare **Semi-Sextile; Sextile**.

**S.R.I.A.** See **Societas Rosicruciana in Anglia**.

**St Anthony's Fire** In medieval Europe, a name given to ergot poisoning. St Anthony was the patron saint of people afflicted by this disease.

**St John's Wort** A medium-sized herbaceous perennial of the genus *Hypericum* that grows in the grasslands and woods of Britain, Europe, and Asia, and which is traditionally regarded as an excellent source of healing oil for wounds and abrasions. In the Middle Ages, people would hang St John's wort in doors and windows on St John's Day (27 December) to keep away the **Devil** and evil spirits. The herb was also used in magic charms and talismans.

**Star Chamber** The meeting place of the reigning English monarch's councillors in the palace of Westminster in London, so named because of the stars painted on the ceiling. It became notorious because many charges of witchcraft were heard there, and strict punishments handed out – including lengthy prison sentences, floggings, and acts of mutilation like slicing off ears and noses. The influence of the court of the Star Chamber increased during the fifteenth century under the Lancastrian and Yorkist kings but it was finally abolished by Parliament in 1641.

**Star, Five-Pointed** See **Pentagram**.

**Starhawk** (1951– ) The magical name of the priestess and peace activist Miriam Simos, one of the leading advocates for Goddess-based spirituality in the United States since the late 1970s. An initiate of the Faery tradition, Starhawk burst onto the American neopagan scene in 1979 with the publication of her bestselling book *The Spiral Dance*, a handbook of ritual, mythology, spells, and inspirational reflections. At the time it was by no means clear whether Starhawk was advocating a similar approach to witchcraft as modern British Wiccan practitioners **Doreen Valiente** and **Janet Farrar**, or whether her own expression of feminist spirituality involved something potentially much broader and more comprehensive. When Starhawk was asked several years later what sort of witch she was, she replied: "A witch is somebody who has made a commitment to the spiritual tradition of the Goddess, the old pre-Christian religions of western Europe. So I am a witch in the sense that that is my religion, my spiritual tradition. I am an initiated priestess of the Goddess." Starhawk became a founding member of a community in the San Francisco Bay area called Reclaiming – a network of women and men working in the Goddess tradition to unify spirituality and politics – and she remains one of the most respected voices in modern Goddess- and earth-based spirituality. Starhawk is deeply committed to bringing the techniques and creative power of spirituality to political activism and she continues to travel internationally teaching **magic**, the tools of ritual, and the skills of political activism. Her award-winning *Webs of Power: Notes from the Global Uprising* (2002) explores these connections. See also **Great Goddess**.

**Star of David**  See Magen David; Hexagram; Seal of Solomon.

**Star Sapphire**  On the kabbalistic Tree of Life, a magical stone assigned to the sephirah Binah.

**Stars, Divination by the**  See Astrology.

**Star, Six-Pointed**  See Magen David; Hexagram; Seal of Solomon.

**Star, The**  In the Tarot, a card of the Major Arcana that depicts a beautiful naked woman kneeling by a pool and pouring water from flasks held in both hands. Regarded as a personification of the "white goddess" in her various forms – Isis, Hathor, or Aphrodite – she is considered to be a receptacle for the waters of the spirits which flow down upon the earth. In western **magic**, which combines the Tarot paths of the Major Arcana with the ten **sephiroth** on the Tree of Life, the path of *The Star* connects Yesod and Netzach.

**Station**  In astrology, the point in a planet's orbit where it becomes direct or retrograde. See also Matutine.

**Steinbrecher, Edwin**  An American metaphysician who developed the so-called "guide meditation" technique for contacting "the inner gods" and who founded the D.O.M.E. Foundation, now based in Los Angeles. The initials of Steinbrecher's organization derive from the Latin expression *Dei Omnes Munda Edunt* : "All the gods/goddesses bring forth the worlds". The Guide Meditation incorporates **Tarot** symbols – which "correspond to reality-creating images within all of us" – and **astrology** which "provides a map of the inner and outer worlds". However, the essence of the D.O.M.E. Foundation system involves inner contact with a "guide" similar to the magical ally called by a traditional **shaman**. The D.O.M.E. meditation technique utilizes a relaxed body posture with the back straight and both feet flat

on the floor. The hands rest on the thighs, the palms face upwards and the eyes are closed. The meditator imagines himself entering a cave and tries through an act of will to enhance the sense of its being moist or dry, dark or light. Steinbrecher believes that the meditator should retain the sense of being consciously within the body rather than watching an external body image, and in this respect the D.O.M.E method resembles identically the shamanic and magical concepts of transferring perceptual consciousness to the inner planes. Like the shaman, Steinbrecher has found it valuable to call for an animal ally who will in turn lead the meditator to the appropriate guide. On various occasions such animals as deer, lions, dogs, and cats have appeared and have led the way to the guide who, in Steinbrecher's experience, has initially always taken a male form. The D.O.M.E. method advocates focusing on and summoning the transcendent inner sun, which is the "archetype of the self" – "the inner life-centre". The basic intent is to "place spiritual authority back within the individual...its true and holy place".

In the guide meditation system, astrology is combined with the Tarot in order to identify dominating and conflicting archetypes within the self, so that the encounter process becomes a form of therapy. For example, Aries equates with *The Emperor* and Mercury with *The Magician*, Venus with *The Empress*, Gemini with *The Lovers* and Aquarius with *The Star*. According to Steinbrecher, we are able to analyze the **horoscope** in order to identify the "high energy" areas via squares, oppositions, and opposing zodiacal fields; "unions", or harmonizing forces, via the conjunctions, sextiles, parallels and quincunxes; and basic archetypes via the sun sign and ruler of the ascendant. The horoscope is thus a chart and symbolic guide to the individual cosmos of each meditator. In the final analysis, the aim of the guide meditation is self-integration, individuation, and a broader spiritual perspective.

As Steinbrecher writes: "Outer world perceptions become acute, and the world literally becomes *new*. The creative energy wells up from within and a knowledge of a *oneness* with all becomes a fact of being." See also **Inner Guide, Shamanic Visualization**

**Steiner, Rudolf** (1861–1925) An Austrian occultist, Theosophist, and scholar who founded the Anthroposophical Society after breaking away from **Theosophy**. Steiner was an authority on the German author Goethe, and his theories on education are still pursued in the many Steiner Waldorf schools throughout the world. However, he was also a clairvoyant and a highly knowledgeable occultist who investigated the myths of **Atlantis** and Lemuria and the development of occult faculties of consciousness. He was connected with several occult movements, including the **Ordo Templi Orientis** and Engel's Order of the **Illuminati**, and wrote prolifically on esoteric subjects. His works include *Occult Science*; *Christianity as Mystical Fact*; and *The Knowledge of Higher Worlds and Its Attainment*.

**Stella Matutina** A branch of the **Hermetic Order of the Golden Dawn** established in 1903 by a group of rebellious order members who wished to sever their connection with **MacGregor Mathers**. The outer order of the Golden Dawn was renamed the Stella Matutina (which means Morning Star) and in London a group of former Golden Dawn members, including **Dr R.W. Felkin**, formed the **Amoun Temple**. Following the break with Mathers, **A.E. Waite** joined forces with M.W. Blackden to continue the Isis-Urania Temple while changing its orientation away from ritual magic and more towards Christian mysticism, and **Dr J.W. Brodie-Innes** continued the Amen-Ra Temple in Edinburgh. The renowned ceremonial magician and author **Israel Regardie** joined the Stella Matutina in 1933 but after attaining the grade of **Theoricus Adeptus Minor**, left in December 1934.

Between 1937 and 1940, believing that the Stella Matutina was in a state of decline and that valuable esoteric material could be lost forever, Regardie published the definitive four-volume series of the Golden Dawn's rituals and teachings through the Aries Press in Chicago.

**Stichomancy** See Bibliomancy.

**Still** In an alchemical laboratory, the apparatus used for **distillation**.

**Stolas** See Solas.

**Stolistes** In the **Neophyte** grade of the **Hermetic Order of the Golden Dawn**, the bearer of the "Cup of Lustral Water". In this ceremonial working, the **magician** representing this role stands in the northern quarter of the temple.

**Stone** In alchemy, the **Philosopher's Stone** or the material being refined and purified in order to produce it.

**Stones, Magical** See Magical Stones.

**Storm Moon** See Esbats.

**Straif** In the Celtic tree alphabet, the ogham representing blackthorn, wild plum and willow, and the sound "str". Straif is also linked to the thrush and the colour orange-red.

*Strength* In the Tarot, a card of the **Major Arcana** that depicts a woman prying open the jaws of a lion. Symbolic of the triumph of intuition over brute animal strength, this card indicates the "victory" of the higher aspects of the soul (**Neschamah** and **Ruach**) over the lower or animal soul (**Nephesch**). In western **magic**, which combines the Tarot paths of the Major Arcana with the ten **sephiroth** on the **Tree of Life**, the path of *Strength* connects **Geburah** and **Chesed**. Very much a stabilizing force in the **psyche**, *Strength* is also associated with the spiritual consolidation required prior to the inner journey across the **Abyss**.

**Striges** In ancient Greece and Rome, shape-shifting female demons who preyed on sleeping men and children. Able to transform into monstrous birds of prey with sharp talons, they also had breasts bulging with poisonous milk. During the Middle Ages *striges* were associated with evil **witchcraft** and were regarded as the servants of **Satan**.

**Styx** In Greek mythology, one of the five rivers of **Hades**. The Styx circled Hades nine times and **Charon** was responsible for ferrying the souls of the dead across to the infernal regions.

**Sublimation** In alchemy, the process of purification of a material whereby the "volatile spirit" was extracted from the "impure" substance through heat. Vaporization was followed by cooling and condensation. The process of vaporization was known as sublimation and this was followed by **distillation**.

**Subtle Planes** In Theosophy, mysticism, and **occultism**, the "inner" or "higher" planes of being, which are regarded as more "subtle" than the plane of physical reality. In many cosmologies, the subtle planes are expressed as emanations from the **godhead** (the "grossest" and furthest removed from the divine centre being the level of the everyday world). See also **Emanation**.

**Succubus** A demon or **discarnate** spirit entity that takes the form of a woman and has sexual intercourse with a man. See also **Incubus; Hanon Tramp**.

**Sucking Shaman** A shaman who sucks on the skin of his patient to remove a magical object that has "intruded" itself into the body, thereby causing harm or disease. Sometimes sucking shamans use hollow bones, reeds or other tubular objects to extract these magical entities, rather than sucking directly on the surface of the skin. See also **Object Intrusion**.

**Sulia** Among the Coast Salish Indians of the American northwest, a powerful dream in which a **shaman** encounters **spirits** and receives power from them through a spirit song which is taught to him while he is dreaming.

**Sulphur** In alchemy, the male principle – the hot, dry active seed in metals. Sulphur was regarded by the alchemists as one of the three vital ingredients of nature, the other two constituents being **quicksilver** and **salt**, representing the soul and body respectively. See **Philosophical Sulphur**.

**Summerlands** In Wicca and **spiritualism**, the **heaven** where souls go after death.

**Summers, Montague** (1880–1948) An English author who wrote prolifically on **satanism**, **demonology**, black magic, and werewolves. Summers took the title "Reverend", although it is not known what religious orders he had been admitted to, and was a firm believer in the reality of the powers of **evil**. While obsessed with the dangers of black magic and satanism, and an advocate of the death penalty for the practice of **witchcraft**, he spent most of his life documenting these subjects and thereby stimulating interest in them. His books include *The History of Witchcraft and Demonology*; *The Vampire in Europe*; and *The Geography of Witchcraft*. He also translated the notorious medieval source book on witchcraft, *Malleus Maleficarum*, into English. See also **Magic, Black; Werewolf**.

**Summoner** See Fetch.

**Sun** The symbol of life and light, personified universally as a **deity** of goodness, spiritual **illumination**, and **rebirth**. As the symbolic centre of our immediate universe and the most dominant celestial orb, the sun has great mythological significance, being regarded variously as the eye of, for example, **Ra**; **Horus**, **Ahura Mazdah**, **Zeus**, and **Varuna**. As a giver of life and heat, the sun is usually regarded as masculine – in contrast to the moon, which is traditionally regarded as female. Among the most important sun gods in the occult mystery tradition are Ra, Osiris, Horus, and Khepera (Egypt); Helios and Apollo (Greece); Mithra (ancient Persia); and Sol (Rome).

In astrology, the sun is also the most important of the celestial bodies, and one of the most significant factors in a horoscope. The sun is associated with Leo, and considerable attention is paid by astrologers to both the sign and the house occupied by the sun at a given moment. The sun is said to define the basic temperament of a person, and to be the source of a person's vitality (i.e. "inner light"). See also Sun Sign.

**Sun Sign** In astrology, the sign of the zodiac through which the sun is passing at the moment of one's birth. The sun sign is identical with one's birth sign.

**Sun, The** In the Tarot, a card of the Major Arcana that depicts a young boy and girl dancing in a magical ring and holding hands. They represent innocence and the synthesis of opposite polarities, a common theme in the Tarot. However, they are usually shown with a barrier (e.g. a wall) between themselves and the light, indicating that they have not yet attained spiritual maturity. In western magic, which combines the Tarot paths of the Major Arcana with the ten sephiroth on the Tree of Life, the path of *The Sun* connects Yesod and Hod.

**Superior Planets** In astrology, those planets which lie outside earth's orbit: Mars, Jupiter, Saturn, Uranus, Neptune, and Pluto.

**Supernal Chariot** See Chariot, Heavenly.

**Supernal Form** In the Kabbalah, the sephiroth arranged in the form of Adam Kadmon, the primordial human being who represents "the body of God".

**Supernals** In the Kabbalah, the three sephiroth (Kether, Chokmah, and Binah) that lie above the Abyss. The supernals represent the most sacred domains of mystical consciousness symbolized by the Tree of Life, and are the kabbalistic equivalent of the Holy Trinity.

**Superstition** An irrational belief, often based on fear, which is accompanied by a strong belief in supernatural forces and powers affecting one's life. People who are superstitious often look for omens and have a special reverence for magic charms and amulets, which are believed to ward off evil influence. See also Amulet; Charm; Omen; Evil Eye.

**Supreme Being** In mysticism and occultism, the personification of ultimate reality: God. Not all mystical traditions believe in a "being" as such – in the Kabbalah and in Mahayana Buddhism, Infinite Light and the Void respectively are considered the supreme and absolute state of being.

**Sushumna** In Kundalini yoga, the primary nadi, or energy channel, in the body, corresponding with the spinal column. It is the only nadi that connects all the chakras, and is therefore regarded as the channel through which the kundalini is raised. Sushumna culminates in the supreme chakra, Sahasrara. Kundalini yoga plays a vital role in modern sexual magic as explored by the members of the Ordo Templi Orientis. See also Magic, Sexual; Tantra.

**Suster, Gerald** (1951–2001) A British writer whose work focused primarily on the magic of Aleister Crowley and related subjects. Educated at Trinity Hall, Cambridge, Suster produced over 30 books, including nine novels, a book on the magical legacy of Aleister Crowley and a study of the occult ideas of Adolf Hitler. However he is best known for his book *Crowley's Apprentice*, an overview of the life and ideas of the influential magical practitioner, Israel Regardie, who was a close friend. An obituary of Suster by fellow **Thelemite** G.M. Kelly described him as "a gentleman, and in today's occult community that made him stand out like a glowing star in an often otherwise dark universe". See also **Thelema**.

**Susto** In South American **shamanism** and folk healing, a term for **soul loss**, widely regarded as a source of illness and malaise.

**Svadhisthana** In Kundalini yoga, the chakra located below the navel in the sacral region.

**Svartalfheim** In Scandinavian mythology, one of the **Nine Worlds** located on the World Tree, **Yggdrasil**. Svartalfheim was the world of the dark elves or dwarves.

**Swan** In alchemy, a symbol of the so-called "white" stage of the **opus**. See **Albedo**.

**Swanassu** Among the Gitksan Indians of the Canadian northwest, a term used for a **shaman** or **medicine man**. It is one of two terms used, the other being halaait – a word used for a shaman who performs healing ceremonies in which patients are treated in a group.

**Swastika** A universal mythic symbol consisting of an equal-armed cross with four bent "arms", which appear to rotate in the same direction. Regarded by many as a type of "sun wheel", the swastika represents eternal movement and spiritual renewal. The counterclockwise swastika adopted by the Nazis is regarded as symbolizing movement "away from the **godhead**", and has become a contemporary motif of **evil**; while the clockwise swastika represents movement towards **God** and suggests a cosmic rhythm in tune with the universe.

**Sweat** In alchemy, the beads of liquid that gathered on the sides of the vessel during **distillation**.

**Sweat Lodge** In Native American religion, an act of ritual purification. Participants sit naked or scantily clad in total darkness within a chamber called a sweat lodge while heated rocks are brought into the lodge by the ceremonial leader, who then pours water over them. This generates a substantial amount of steam inside the sweat lodge. Sacred songs are sung, prayers offered, and spirits called to attend as part of the ritual purification process.

**Swimming** In medieval English witchcraft, a test employed by witch-accusers in order to establish whether witches were guilty of practising magic and sorcery. The witch was bound hand and foot and thrown into deep water. If she sank it was proof that God's water had accepted her and she was hauled ashore, often drowning in the process. If she "swam" (floated) she was considered guilty.

**Sword** In Wicca and western ritual **magic**, the sword is used to cast the magical circle. In Wiccan ritual it is sometimes replaced by the **athame**, but the sword is generally regarded as more authoritative. Together with the **wand**, the sword represents the male polarity in ritual workings.

**Swords** One of the four suits of the **Minor Arcana** of the **Tarot**. Swords are one of the two masculine suits (the other being **wands**), and are ascribed to the element **air**.

**Sycamore** A tree with mythic associations. Regarded in ancient Egypt as the **Tree of Life**, it was sacred to **Hathor**, the goddess of love, and **Nut**, the sky goddess, both of whom were also protectors of the dead.

**Sylph** An elemental, or spirit of the element **air**. See also **Elementals**.

**Symbol** A representation of an abstract quality. **Mysticism** and **occultism** abound with symbols that often point to a **transcendental** reality beyond conscious understanding (e.g. the Great Mother as the womb of the universe; the infinite ocean of the Spirit; the **Holy Grail** as a symbol of divine inspiration and spiritual renewal; and the personification of the sun as a symbol of illumination [discovery of the inner light] and mystical **initiation**).

**Symonds, John** An English occult author and novelist who is best known for his illuminating study of the magician **Aleister Crowley**, *The Great Beast* (1971). Symonds was appointed literary executor to Crowley's estate and, with **Kenneth Grant**, has edited a number of his more important magical writings, including *The Confessions of Aleister Crowley*; *The Magical Record of the Beast 666*; *Magick*; and *White Stains*. Symonds has also written a lucid account of the life of Madame Helena Blavatsky, titled *In the Astral Light* (1965).

**Sympathetic Magic** See Magic, Sympathetic.

**Synastry** In astrology, a technique of comparing the horoscopes of two or more people in order to determine the degree of personal compatibility and the likely outcome of the relationship between them. The technique can also be used to compare the destinies of political parties and national leaders, and even trends in international affairs. See also **Astrology, Mundane; Horoscope.**

**Synchronicity** A term used by the Swiss psychoanalyst **Carl Jung** to describe "meaningful coincidences". In Jung's view, it was not uncommon for symbols of the unconscious mind to coincide in dreams, or mystical experiences with events occurring in the waking world of physical reality. Jung believed that synchronicity provided a rationale for **astrology** and some forms of **divination** such as the Chinese classic, the *I Ching*.

**Syncretism** The merging of religious ideas and traditions. Examples include the Graeco-Egyptian deity **Serapis**, who is a Hellenistic form of **Osiris**; and the Roman and **Gnostic** deities **Mithra** and **Abraxas**, both of whom have Persian antecedents.

**Syrian Rue** *Peganum harmala*, a plant grown in several Mediterranean countries, the Middle East, and the Himalayan region. A bushy perennial plant with black roots, solitary white flowers, and globular fruit, the oil extracted from its seeds is used in Egypt and Turkey to produce incense which is burned to protect against the **evil eye**. In ancient Egypt, Syrian rue was associated with **Bes**, the ugly dwarf deity and god of pleasure and music who was considered a protector against evil. See also **Rue**.

**Sytri** See Sitry.

**Syzygy** In astrology, the "yoking together" of two celestial bodies, whether in **opposition** or **conjunction**. The term is often used to describe such a relationship between a planet and the sun.

# T

**Tables of Houses** In astrology, tables which show the degrees of the signs which occupy the cusps of all the houses, including details of midheaven and ascendant. The tables need to show the different latitudes for every degree of right ascension or for every four minutes of sidereal time.

**Tablets, Enochian** In Enochian magic, the sacred names of the spirits of each of the four elements. These names are Exarp – air, Hcoma – water, Nanta – earth, and Bitom – fire.

**Tabula Smaragdina** See Emerald Tablet.

**Tahuti** A form of the name Thoth.

**Talho** In Enochian magic, the angelic word for a ritual cup. It is pronounced *tah-leh-hoh*.

**Talisman** A magical object, like a charm, which is worn to attract good fortune. The talisman is often inscribed with a god-name or the image of a supernatural power believed to bring luck to the person wearing it. See also Abraxas; Amulet; Charm; Luck.

**Tambour Maringuin** In voodoo, a mosquito drum, associated with Guede, god of the dead.

**Tammuz** The Babylonian god of vegetation who died each winter and was reborn the following spring. Tammuz was the husband of Ishtar, goddess of love and fertility.

**Tan** In Enochian magic, the 17th Aethyr. Tan is associated with morality, ethics, harmony, and balance, and with Caput Draconis, Taurus, and Scorpio. Its magical number is 65.

**Tane** In Polynesia, the sky god and lord of fertility, who protected the birds and forests and created the first man out of red clay. Tane also protected those who worked in wood, and the popular tiki amulet symbolizes his creative power.

**Tanith** In the cosmology of the Typhonian Order of the Outer Ones, a branch of the Ordo Templi Orientis headed by tantric magician Kenneth Grant, Tanith is the "Typhonian Dragon of the Deep" and typifies the Draconian Current or Ophidian Current. See also Draconian Cult; Typhon.

**Tantra** A form of Kundalini yoga in which the divine female energy, or Shakti, is aroused through ceremonial sexual union. The orgasm is resisted by self-control, however, so that the energy generated may stimulate the arousal of the kundalini from the muladhara chakra. Tantrics regard the universe as the divine play of Shakti and Shiva, and believe that liberation may be attained by enjoyment. In the western magical tradition, Tantra has had a profound influence on the development of rites of sexual magic, as practiced in the Ordo Templi Orientis. See also Magic, Sexual.

**Tarantula, Astral** See Bertiaux, Michael.

**Tarot** A pack of 78 cards, often regarded as the precursor of modern playing cards, and commonly used in divination. The Tarot pack is divided into the Major Arcana (22 cards) and the Minor Arcana (56 cards). The latter consists of four suits – wands, swords, cups, and pentacles – which approximate to the four suits of the modern pack (clubs, spades, hearts, and diamonds respectively). The Major Arcana, on the other hand, has archetypal significance, and the cards are regarded by occultists as symbolic meditative pathways that can be correlated with the kabbalistic Tree of Life. The Major Arcana card are as follows: *The World; Judgment; The Moon; The Sun; The Star; The Tower; The Devil; Death; Temperance; The*

*Hermit; Justice; The Hanged Man; The Wheel of Fortune; Strength; The Charioteer; The Lovers; The Hierophant; The Emperor; The Empress; The High Priestess; The Magus;* and *The Fool* (see individual listings). Tarot card divination is a form of **cartomancy**.

**Tartarus** In Greek mythology, the lowest region of **Hades**, where the wicked were punished. Darker than the darkest night, it was surrounded – according to Virgil – by a river of fire.

**Tasseography** Divination by reading tea-leaves. The dregs of a cup of tea are swirled round three times inside the cup, and the cup is then inverted on its saucer. The **seer** then takes the cup and interprets the patterns of leaves inside it. The leaves closer to the rim are said to relate to events about to pass, while those at the bottom represent the distant future. The following patterns are each taken as an **omen**: stars (success); triangles (good fortune); squares (protection); bird-like shapes (an important message); and dagger shapes (personal misfortune).

**Tatari** A Japanese term for a curse inflicted on a human being by an angry **kami** or ghost.

**Tattvas** In Hinduism and visionary western **magic**, the four elements. The tattvas are **prithivi** (**earth**, symbolized by a yellow square); **Apas** (**water**, symbolized by a silver crescent); **tejas** (**fire**, symbolized by a red triangle); and **vayu** (**air**, symbolized by a blue hexagram). Sometimes the fifth element **akasha** (**spirit**, symbolized by a black egg) is also included among the tattvas. See also **Chakra; Quintessence**.

**Tau** Also Tav. The Hebrew letter ascribed to the path linking **Malkuth** and **Yesod** on the **Tree of Life**. Tau has a numerical value of 400. In modern magical visualization and **pathworkings** the **Tarot** card associated with this path on the Tree is *The World*.

**Taurobolium** A ritual associated with the cults of **Cybele** and **Mithra** in the Roman empire. The ritual was essentially a rebirth ceremony in which neophytes would be baptized in the blood of the sacred bull. The blood – in itself regarded as a symbol of life force – bestowed special powers of mystical renewal.

**Taurus** In astrology, the sign of the zodiac for those born between 21 April and 20 May. An **earth** sign, ruled by **Venus**, Taurus is symbolized by the bull. This animal was associated by the Babylonians with the beginning of spring, and by the Greeks with the transformation of **Zeus**. Apis (or **Serapis**) was also venerated as an incarnation of **Osiris** in the form of a bull. While those born under the sign of Taurus are often considered to be practical, obstinate, and even lazy, they are also said to be excellent friends, fond of music, and generous with money. Taureans make faithful lovers and reliable, patient companions. They often gravitate towards careers in handicrafts, building, or music.

**Tav** See Tau.

**Tea-Leaf Reading** See Tasseography.

**Tears** In alchemy, a term for the beads of liquid that gathered on the sides of the vessel during **distillation**.

**Teish, Luisah** An American voodoo priestess, Dianic goddess worshipper and author, Teish was born in New Orleans of mixed African, Haitian, Native American, and French ancestry. Raised as a "Louisiana Catholic" – a voodoo devotee with a Christian veneer – she has inherited two magical traditions: New Orleans voodoo and the Lucumi Yoruba religion of Nigeria. She is a priestess of **Oshun**, the Yoruba counterpart of the Roman goddess **Venus**, and maintains that the goddess lies asleep within the crown **chakra**, or energy centre, in the head. Magical herbs and songs arouse

TALISMAN  A medieval Jewish childbirth talisman. The hexagram, or Star of David, is a central feature.

the spirit, making it possible for the initiate to be possessed by the goddess. Teish is the author of two books, *Jambalaya: The Natural Woman's Book of Personal Charms and Practical Rituals*, and a work on seasonal celebrations, *Jump Up*.

**Tejas** In Hinduism and western **magic**, one of the **tattvas** or symbols of the **elements**. Tejas is symbolized by a red triangle and represents the element fire. It is associated with the **chakra** known as **manipura**.

***Temperance*** In the Tarot, the card of the **Major Arcana** that shows the archangel **Michael** standing with one leg in a stream (a symbol of **water**), the

other on dry land (a symbol of **earth**). With him, and at his command, are an **eagle** (a symbol of **air**), and a **lion** (a symbol of **fire**) – so in this capacity the archangel unites the four **elements** in harmony. Above Michael in the sky shines a rainbow – representative of God's covenant with humankind – and the light of new day can be seen rising in the distance over a mountain peak. *Temperance* personifies the process of spiritual **illumination** and **initiation**, for it reveals the inner light that may potentially develop within each person. The tempering, or balancing, qualities of the path are in accord with **Carl Jung's** principle of individuation – the process of acquiring harmony and "wholeness" within the inner self. In western **magic**,

TAROT Four people playing *tarocchi*. These 15<sup>th</sup> century cards were possibly a precursor of the Tarot deck as we know it today.

which combines the Tarot paths of the Major Arcana with the ten **sephiroth** on the **Tree of Life**, the path of *Temperance* connects **Yesod** and **Tiphareth** and is an intregral part of the mystic journey up the **Middle Pillar**.

**Templars** See Knights Templar.

**Temple** A building erected and dedicated to the worship of a **deity** or deities, and often thought to be the dwelling place of the deity to whom it is consecrated. In western **magic**, the temple is a sacred location (often a room within a house) in which ceremonial rites and magical invocations are performed. It usually has a **magic circle** inscribed upon the floor and is adorned to reflect the symbolism of the invoked deity. Meeting places of other occult or mystical groups are also sometimes called temples.

**Temple of Ara** See Curott, Phyllis.

**Temple of Set** An organization founded in 1975 by former members of Anton LaVey's **Church of Satan**. In early 1975, LaVey gave notice in his newsletter that all higher degrees of initiation issued through the Church of Satan would be available for contributions in cash, real estate, or valuable objects of art. This had a major impact among his followers and in June 1975 an act of mass desertion took place. Headed by leading defector **Michael Aquino**, key members of the priesthood resigned from the Church of Satan, at the same time making it clear that they were not leaving the priesthood itself but taking it with them. In a subsequent magical ceremony, Aquino summoned the **Prince of Darkness**, "to tell us what we may do to continue our quest". The result, according to Aquino, was an act of

**automatic writing** – "a communication from a god to a human being". In a document known as *The Book of Coming Forth by Night*, Satan is said to have revealed himself as the ancient Egyptian god Set, or Seth, and named Michael Aquino as LaVey's replacement. Aquino was also described in the script as the successor to **Aleister Crowley**, and Magus (fifth degree), of the new Aeon of Set. Set also announced in this communication that the sacred magical word for the new era would be "xeper", meaning "to become". See also **La Vey, Anton**.

**Temple of the Flesh** An occult and mystical term for the physical body.

**Temple of the Sacred Earth** See **Curott, Phyllis**.

**Temura** Also Temurah. Kabbalistic technique of modifiying the sequence of letters to achieve a particular effect. The first half of the Hebrew alphabet is written in reverse order and located above the remaining section so that the letters forrm vertical pairs.

```
k  y  th ch z  v  h  d  g  b  a
l  m  n  s  o  p  th q  r  sh t
```

in this code k=l, y=m, th=n, and so on. A given word is disguised in temura by substituting the code letter in each case, so that completely new words are formed. Compare with **Gematria**; **Notarikon**. See also **Kabbalah**.

**Teonanacatl** The name given by the Nahuatl Indians of Mexico to a variety of mushrooms used in religious worship prior to the arrival of the Spanish. Used to describe a number of agaric mushrooms, including silocybe, the word "teonanacatl" translates as "flesh of the gods" – a reference to the sacred visions arising from the hallucinatory qualities of the mushrooms. See also **Hallucination**; **Psilocybin**.

**Terreiro** In Macumba, the temple where ceremonial worship takes place and offerings are made to the gods.

**Teth** The Hebrew letter ascribed to the path linking **Geburah** and **Chesed** on the Tree of Life. Teth has a numerical value of 9. In modern magical visualization and **pathworkings** the Tarot card associated with this path on the Tree is *Strength*.

**Tetrad** In numerology, the number four.

**Tetragrammaton** In Judaism and Jewish mysticism, the sacred four-lettered name of God, rendered variously as IHVH, JHVH, YHWH, or YHVH. The name has been transcribed as Jehovah, and more recently as Yahweh; but the name itself is never uttered, sometimes not even written down, by devout Jews because it is considered too sacred to be spoken. It is often replaced by the word Adonai, meaning "Lord".

**Tex** In Enochian magic, the 30th Aethyr. The meanings associated with Tex include restriction, desire, silence, and fear. It is associated with Cauda Draconis, **Virgo**, and **earth** and its magical number is 413.

**Tezcatlipoca** The Aztec god of life and air who according to Aztec cosmology ruled as the sun of the first universe. Tezcatlipoca was, paradoxically, a god of darkness; and was represented by a dark obsidian mirror that was believed to reflect the future of humankind. He is often depicted struggling with the serpent god **Quetzalcoatl**.

**Thanatos** In Greek mythology, the god of death. His Roman counterpart is Mars.

**Thaumaturge** From the Greek *thaumatourgos*, "one who works wonders", a miracle worker or **magician**. See also **Thaumaturgy**.

**Thaumaturgy** Magic, or the working of wonders or miracles by calling on supernatural powers. See also **Thaumaturge**.

**Theism** From the Greek *theos*, "a god", the belief in gods or God. The belief in a single God who transcends the universe, but is also immanent within it, is known as **monotheism**; belief in a plurality of gods is known as **polytheism**. The distinction between monotheism and polytheism is less marked in cosmologies where individual gods are regarded as an **emanation** of the transcendent **godhead**, as in some forms of Egyptian religion and Gnosticism.

**Thelema** The Greek word for "will", which the ceremonial magician Aleister Crowley used to define one's true, occult purpose. Crowley formulated the magical axiom "Do what thou wilt shall be the whole of the law". However, he did not interpret this to mean self-indulgence, believing as he did that the **magician** was obliged to discover his true will, or inner purpose in life, and to have communion with the **holy guardian angel**. As Crowley's disciple Kenneth Grant has written, "The purpose of magick is to unveil the True Will and reveal the Hidden Light".

**Thelemite** A follower of the ceremonial magician Aleister Crowley and his doctrine of Thelema.

**Themis** In Greek mythology, the daughter of Uranus and Gaea and the mother of the three Fates. Themis was one of the twelve **Titans** and was said to have been the first Greek goddess to have had a temple erected in her honour.

**Theocrasy** The uniting, or "mingling", of several gods or divine attributes within one composite personality. The word is also used to describe the mystical union with God.

**Theogony** From the Greek *theogonia* meaning "begetting of the gods", an account of the origin and genealogy of the gods and goddesses in a **pantheon** See also **Olympians, The Twelve Great; Titans.**

**Theojas** A term coined by the American voodoo magician **Michael Bertiaux** to refer to the ultimate form of Ojas, or magical energy.

**Theolithos** See **Lapis Judaicus**.

**Theomachy** A combat with, or among, the gods; opposition to divine will. The account of the fall of **Lucifer** from grace provides an example of a contest of this sort.

**Theophagy** The practice of "eating the god" during a sacred or sacrificial ceremony. The animal- or food-offering personifies the god, and the act of partaking of the sacrifice confers supernatural power upon the devotees.

**Theophany** The manifestation or appearance of a deity or god before humankind.

**Theoricus (Theoricus Adeptus Minor)** In the Hermetic Order of the Golden Dawn, the ritual grade associated with the magical initiation of Yesod on the kabbalistic Tree of Life. See also **Adeptus Minor; Kabbalah.**

**Theosophical Society** A mystical and occult organization founded in New York in 1875 by Madame **Helena Blavatsky** and Colonel H. S. Olcott. The society had three basic aims: 1. The brotherhood of man – without distinction of race, colour, religion, or social position. 2. The serious study of the ancient world religions for purposes of comparison and the selection therefrom of universal ethics. 3. The study and development of the latent divine powers in people. The Theosophical Society has been influential in cultural and political affairs ever since, attracting such members as **William Crookes**, Thomas Alva Edison, **William Butler Yeats**, and **Rudolf Steiner** (Steiner in due course broke away, founding the Anthroposophical Society.) Mahatma Gandhi first studied *The Bhagavad Gita* with Theosophists; and the influential Dr Annie Besant, who became the second president of the Theosophical Society in 1891, worked tirelessly in favour of Indian home rule, believing it to be the will of the supernatural powers formulating the "Great Plan". While the Theosophical Society has drawn primarily on Buddhism and Hinduism for its religious teachings, its members generally believe in a universal wisdom-teaching or **esoteric** tradition which has been available in all cultures and which draws on perennial and universal truth.

**Theosophy** (1) From the Greek *theos*, "a god" and *sophia* "wisdom", divine wisdom. The term is used to describe a number of **esoteric** and mystical systems that describe the relationship of human beings to the universe and the **godhead** (e.g. **Gnosticism, Neoplatonism, Kabbalah**). Usually, these belief systems describe emanations from the infinite God, or **supreme being**, who reveals different aspects of **transcendent** reality through various intermediary deities, spirits, "intelligences", and levels of **manifestation**. See also **Aeon; Archon; Deity; Emanation; Subtle Planes**.

**Theosophy** (2) The teaching and doctrines of the **Theosophical Society**.

**Therion** See **Master Therion**.

**Theurgy** From the Greek *theourgia*, "divine work", the working of miracles through supernatural aid. Among the Neoplatonists, miraculous effects were believed to result from magical invocations to gods and **spirits**, and the word theurgy has come to mean "divine magic" or white magic. This interpretation of magic has been succinctly defined by **Israel Regardie** in his major work *The Tree of Life* (1932), where he writes: "the object of magic...is the return of man to the gods". See also **Invocation; Magic, High; Magic, White; Neoplatonism;**

**Third Degree** See **Third Initiation**.

**Third Initiation** In Wicca, an initiation which celebrates the profound

and sacred bond between the **high priestess** and the **high priest** in a **coven**. Only practitioners who are themselves third-degree **coven** members are allowed to participate as initiators. The third degree initiation is bestowed upon a couple together and involves what is known in Wicca as the Great Rite. The ritual itself is essentially a sacred marriage – the ritual union of the Goddess and the God. During the first part of the ritual, the Goddess and the God are invoked into the high priestess and high priest by their initiators. However, in the second part they are acting as **incarnate** deities so that the marriage is not between two individual people but between the Goddess and the God themselves. The Great Rite is a ritualized act of sexual union. If it is enacted symbolically by plunging the **athame**, or ritual dagger, into the **chalice**, it is said to be performed *in token*. If the sexual union is enacted physically it is said to be performed *in true*. Usually the partners in the ritual bestow the initiation upon each other, the high priest offering the third degree to his partner in token, and the high priestess returning it to him in true. In Wicca the Great Rite is regarded as a sacred act. It is performed in private after other coven members have left the circle.

**Third Order** In the **Hermetic Order of the Golden Dawn**, the initiatory grades corresponding to the **sephiroth Binah, Chokmah**, and **Kether** on the kabbalistic **Tree of Life**. This was also the realm of the so-called **Secret Chiefs** – the mysterious inspirational beings who were believed to guide the order. See also **Kabbalah**.

**Thirty Aethyrs** The magical invocations employed by the occultists **Aleister Crowley** and **Victor Neuburg** during their remarkable ceremonial workings in Algeria in 1909. The invocations were based on the Enochian magic system of **Dr John Dee** and **Edward Kelley**, and included the conjuration of the demon of chaos, **Choronzon**. Crowley also invoked two of the Aethyrs in Mexico in 1900. See also **Aethyr**.

**Thirty-Two Paths** In the Kabbalah, the ten sephiroth on the **Tree of Life** and the 22 interconnecting paths that join them. The **Sepher Yetzirah** refers to them collectively as "thirty-two wondrous paths of wisdom".

**Thor** In Scandinavian mythology, the god of the sky and thunder. The son of **Odin**, Thor was depicted as a strong but friendly man with a red beard, who aided farmers and sailors. However, he was the sworn enemy of the giants and demons who threatened to overturn the forces of order in the world. Thor possessed a famous hammer, which he used to break the winter ice and make possible the arrival of spring. At **Ragnarok**, Thor and the **Midgard Serpent** destroyed one another.

**Thorn** In the Germanic Elder Futhark, the **rune** letter representing the number three. Thorn is the rune of the will, associated with the sky god **Thor** and his hammer. Thorn corresponds to the sound "th", and is associated with force, will, protection, and the ability to make good decisions in the face of the enemy. Also known as Thurisaz.

**Thornapple** *Datura stramonium*, a comparatively rare plant with white or pale lavender funnel-shaped flowers and spiny fruit, or "apples". Thornapple is an annual and is classified as a hallucinogen and hypnotic – its active constituents include scopolamine, hyoscyamine, and atropine. The highest alkaloid concentrations are found in the seeds. Regarded by medieval witches as a "love drug", Thornapple was one of the herbs used in preparing **flying ointments**. Thornapple was introduced to eastern North America by European colonists and was used as a herb by some British soldiers in Jamestown, Virginia, in 1676. After consuming large quantities of the plant some of these soldiers "turn'd fools...for several days...one would blow up a

feather in the air... another stark naked was sitting in a corner, like a monkey." In the United States, thornapple is frequently referred to as **Jimson weed**, a reference to this Jamestown incident, and in Europe it is sometimes referred to as "sorcerer's herb".

**Thoth** In ancient Egyptian mythology, the god of wisdom and **magic**. Thoth was the scribe of the gods, invented numbers and writing, and measured time. He was also a moon god. Together with this consort **Maat**, Thoth was present in the **Judgment Hall**, where the hearts of the deceased were weighed against the feather of truth. Thoth recorded the judgments on the dead, and the first month of the Egyptian year was named after him. Depicted as an **ibis**, an ibis-headed man, or as a baboon, he was identified by the Greeks with **Hermes**, messenger of the gods.See also **Tahuti**.

**Thought-Form** A mental image that forms on the **astral plane** as a result of willed intent. The ability to "hold pictures in the imagination" has a magical application, because occultists believe it is possible to transfer consciousness to thought-forms and use them as "magical bodies" on the inner or **subtle planes**. Thought-forms can also personify the collective will of a magical group. See also **Astral Projection**; **Egrigor**; **Shape-Shifting**; **Simulacrum**. Sometimes known as Tahuti.

**Three** A number widely regarded as spiritual and creative. In Christianity, it is the number of the Holy Trinity; and in the Kabbalah, three sephiroth (**Kether**, **Chokmah**, and **Binah**) lie above the **Abyss**. Among the **Pythagoreans**, three was considered a perfect number because it had a beginning, a middle, and an end. On the level of popular **numerology**, three symbolizes intelligence, vitality, artistic ability, and ambition. It is also a lucky number and is regarded as a popular choice for a love **charm**.

**Three Principles** In alchemy, the collective term for philosophical mercury, philosophical salt, and philosophical sulphur – the core constituents of the manifested world.

**Throne** In astrology, a planet is described as being "on its throne" when it is located in the sign of which it is the ruler (e.g. sun in Leo).

**Throne Mysticism** See Merkabah.

**Thundering Rod** In ceremonial magic, the magical wand of the magician or sorcerer. The wand is one of several "magical weapons" used in western magic and is ascribed to the sephirah Hod on the kabbalistic Tree of Life. It is associated with Mercury and the element air.

**Thurible** A shallow dish mounted on three legs and used in witchcraft. The thurible is placed on the altar and used to mix herbs and burn incense. See also Censer.

**Thurisaz** See Thorn.

**Ti Bon Ange** In voodoo, the conscience or spirit of a person, as distinct from their soul. Compare Gros Bon Ange.

**Tiamat** The Babylonian goddess of the sea. The personification of chaos and evil, Tiamat was depicted as a monstrous dragon. The warrior god Marduk finally slew her, and the two halves of her body formed heaven and earth.

**Tiferet, Tifereth** See Tiphareth.

**Tiki** A Polynesian amulet, usually worn around the neck. The tiki is a human figure and is usually made of wood and mother-of-pearl. It depicts the first man created by the sky god Tane.

**Tikkun** In the Jewish mystical tradition, the divine restoration of the cosmos. According to the nature of human

intent, each personal act either aids or impedes this process.

**Tincture** Literally, a dye or pigment that can cause a change of colour. In alchemy this image was transposed to the prized red and white elixirs and the Philosopher's Stone itself. See Red Rose, White Rose.

**Tinne** In the Celtic tree alphabet, the ogham representing holly and the letter "t". Tinne is also linked to the starling and the colour scarlet.

**Tiphareth** In the Kabbalah, the sixth mystical emanation on the Tree of Life. In the traditional Kabbalah it is the sphere of beauty, harmonizing the forces of mercy (Chesed) and judgment (Geburah), higher on the Tree. Occultists identify Tiphareth as the sphere of spiritual rebirth, and ascribe to it the solar deities of different pantheons – including Ra, Apollo, and Mithra – as well as the resurrected gods Osiris and Jesus Christ. In modern western magic, the Tarot path of *Temperance* identifies the direct mystical ascent to Tiphareth from Malkuth, the physical world. See also Solar Gods.

**Tisiphone** In Greek and Roman mythology, one of the three Erinyes or Furies – the avenging spirits. The other two were Alecto and Megaera.

**Titans** In Greek mythology, the twelve children of the primal deities Uranus and Gaea, who ruled the heavens and earth before the reign of the twelve Olympians. The Titans were the first race of gods and goddesses, and personified the violent side of nature. Their names were Oceanus, Hyperion, Crius, Coeus, Kronos, and Iapetus (male personifications respectively of the sea, sun, memory, moon, harvests, and justice); and their respective female counterparts: Tethys, Theia, Eurybia (or Mnemosyne), Phoebe, Rhea, and Themis. The rule of the Titans ended in in a great battle – the Titanomachy, or Battle of the Titans

– between Kronos and his followers and the Olympians – the latter were joined by all the female Titans and the male Titans Prometheus, Oceanus, and **Helios** (son of Hyperion and Theia). After their defeat Kronos and his allies were consigned to **Tartarus**. See also **Olympians, The Twelve Great.**

**Tiw** or **Tiwaz** See Tyr.

**Toad** In alchemy, a reference to the swelling and puffing nature of the **stone** in the **alembic** during the process of putrefaction associated with the **nigredo**. The image of a frog was also used.

**Tobacco** A shamanic intoxicant used in some parts of South America. The Campa Indians of the eastern Peruvian rainforest combine tobacco and **ayahuasca** as a shamanic sacrament but regard the tobacco in itself as a source of power. Used in nocturnal rituals, the combination of tobacco and **Banisteriopsis** produces an altered state of consciousness in which the **shaman**'s voice takes on an eerie quality. As he begins to sing, the shaman's soul may go to some distant place, but the words themselves are those of the spirits – the trance state allowing direct communication with the other world.

**Toé** or **Tohé** In South American shamanism and folk healing, a hallucinogenic plant, *Datura suavoleons*, which is mixed with other plant extracts like **ayahuasca** to produce a vision-inducing beverage.

**Tolkien, John Ronald Reuel** (1892–1973) Probably the most revered master of magical fantasy fiction in modern times, Tolkien was born in Bloemfontein, South Africa, and moved to Birmingham, England, as a child. An enthusiastic reader, he was influenced by the popular writers of the day, including G.K. Chesterton and H.G. Wells. Tolkien succeeded in obtaining a scholarship to Oxford University and studied philology – the study of words and language.

Fascinated by ancient languages in particular, he was greatly influenced by Icelandic, Norse, and Gothic mythology and some of the characters and place names in his most famous works – *The Lord of the Rings* and *The Hobbit* – are borrowed from ancient sagas. *The Hobbit*, the work that would make him famous, was first published in 1936 and became a bestseller. By now Tolkien was not only well known as a scholar but was also a distinguished member of an Oxford group known as the Inklings. Another leading member of this group was C.S. Lewis, who would remain one of Tolkien's best friends and admirers for many years. In the late 1930s, Tolkien began writing *The Lord of the Rings* – an enormous three-volume work that would take him over ten years to complete. It too was a huge publishing success and in recent years has since been made into an equally successful epic film series. Unfortunately Tolkien did not live long enough to taste this final triumph. He died in 1973 from pneumonia, not knowing that many years later his work would delight whole new generations of movie enthusiasts and fantasy readers around the world.

**Tools, Witches'** See Witches' Tools.

**Topaz** In Wicca, a magical stone assigned to the ritual celebration of **Lammas**. On the Kabbalistic Tree of Life it is assigned to the sephirah **Tiphareth**. See also **Magical Stones**.

**Tor** In Enochian magic, the 23rd Aethyr. The meanings associated with Tor include energy, force, labour, toil, and work. It is associated with **Leo**, **Libra**, and **Pisces** and its magical number is 133.

**Torah** A Hebrew word meaning "teaching" but often translated as "law". It refers specifically to the first five books of the Hebrew Bible – also known as the Pentateuch or the Law of Moses – which were said to have been dictated to Moses by God on Mount Sinai. In Judaism there is also said to be an "oral Torah", and this consists of learned opinions and discussions related to the written Torah.

**Totem** An animal, object, or mythic creature that symbolizes the unity of a clan or family group and is regarded as sacred. Native American totem poles depict totem animals, carved and painted in bright colours.

**Tower** In alchemy, the **athanor**, or furnace.

**Tower, The** In the Tarot, a card of the **Major Arcana** that depicts the arrogant attempt by people to scale the heights of heaven. The tower shown on this card reaches to lofty heights, but is fragmented by a blast of lightning from the **godhead**, dislodging the crown (i.e. **Kether**), which is its turret. Two human figures are also shown plummeting to earth. Regarded by occultists as a symbolic warning against pride on the mystic journey, the symbolism of *The Tower* is sometimes compared to the biblical Tower of Babel. Associated with the sexual sphere of the **Tree of Life**, *The Tower* is also in some degree a phallic symbol and the energy of the thunderbolt is the magical equivalent of the **kundalini**. There is a clear implication that the **magician** should balance personality and ambitions, and proceed on the inner journey with a "solid foundation" of humility and systematic endeavour. In western **magic**, which combines the Tarot paths of the Major Arcana with the ten **sephiroth** of the **Tree of Life**, the path of *The Tower* connects Hod and Netzach.

**Traditional Witches** Practitioners of witchcraft whose traditions existed prior to the post-war revival of **Wicca** and the establishment of **Gardnerian and Alexandrian witchcraft**. See also **Hereditaries**.

**Trance** An altered state of consciousness, induced by various means including rhythmic chanting, **dance** or the use of psychedelic sacraments, in which the subject enters a perceptual domain which is experientially distinct from the waking world. Shamans and spirit mediums employ trance states to contact **animal familiars, deities,** and the **spirits** of the dead. Shamans maintain their state of active awareness while in the trance realm and undertake what is often referred to as a "**journey of the soul**" or **spirit-journey**. They retain a memory of the events which occurred in trance after they return to the waking state. Trance mediums act passively and do not retain an active awareness of trance events either during the state of trance or after awakening from it. Instead they are possessed by the deities they have invoked and may act as trance oracles, conveying special information or "messages from the gods" to others who are present when the medium falls into a trance state. **Voodoo** represents an example of mediumistic trance. Here trance subjects are possessed and "ridden" by the **loa**, or divine horsemen. See also following entries and **Medium; Shaman; Voodoo**.

**Trance Medium** A psychic medium who is able to enter a state of trance, usually to communicate with the spirits of the dead. In modern **spiritualism**, the possessing entity is called a **control**.

**Trance, Mediumistic** In spiritualism and some forms of pre-literate religion, a type of **trance** state characterized by the withdrawal from the familiar behavioural patterns of the normal conscious personality and its replacement by a secondary personality, which acts as if it is another personality "possessing" the body of the **medium**. This secondary personality is referred to in spiritualism as the **control** and in pre-literate societies is often interpreted as a **deity** or one of the ancestral **spirits**. Mediums often have no recollection of their psychic "transformation" while in the trance state, and are usually unaware of specific utterances or pronouncements that have been made.

**Trance, Shamanic** In pre-literate religion, a type of **trance** state characterized by the **journey of the soul.** The **shaman** undertakes this journey in order to obtain information, and sometimes visionary insights, from the gods of creation whose rules and taboos govern society. The shaman enters the magical dimension in a state of sensory deprivation (usually, total darkness) and often uses percussive instruments to establish a rhythm that is used to propel him on his vision-quest. Shamanic trance differs from mediumistic trance to the extent that the shaman returns with full knowledge of his visionary journey and is able to report on his encounter with the gods. The deities do not "possess" the shaman as they do in mediumism, although in some shamanic initiations the body of the shaman is transformed by the gods in order to bestow supernatural powers. See also **Shamanism; Trance, Mediumistic.**

**Transcendent, Transcendental** That which exceeds the bounds of possible human experience and knowledge. It is often applied to the "unknowable" **God** who lies far beyond human comprehension. The concept of a transcendent **supreme being** may be compared with the idea of an immanent God who is omnipresent in nature and accessible to the senses.

**Transit** In astrology, the movement of a planet through a **sign** or **house.** The angles between planets on a **horoscope** are interpreted for their different aspects.

**Transitional Rites** See Rites of Passage.

**Transmigration** The belief that, after death, the **soul** can pass into another physical body – either human or animal. Transmigration is synonymous with metempsychosis, and similar to the idea of **reincarnation.**

**Transmutation** In alchemy, the process of converting one element or substance into another by using the **Philosopher's Stone** or a **tincture** attained through the **opus alchymicum.** The alchemists sought to transmute imperfect base metals into silver or gold. See **Red Stone; White Stone.**

**Tree Datura** See Angel's Trumpet.

**Tree of Life** In the Kabbalah, the multiple symbol known in Hebrew as the Otz Chiim. The Tree consists of ten spheres, or **sephiroth,** through which – according to mystical tradition – the creation of the world came about. The sephiroth are aligned in three columns headed by the **supernals** (**Kether, Chokmah,** and **Binah**) and together symbolize the process by which the "Infinite Light" **Ain Soph Aur** becomes manifest in the universe. Beneath the supernals are the "seven days of creation": **Chesed, Geburah, Tiphareth, Netzach, Hod, Yesod,** and **Malkuth.** Taken as a whole, the Tree of Life is also a symbol of the archetypal man **Adam Kadmon,** and the sephiroth have a role resembling that of the chakras in yoga. The mystical path of self-knowledge entails the rediscovery of all of the levels of one's being, ranging from Malkuth (physical reality) to the infinite Source. With this in mind, the medieval kabbalists divided the Tree of Life into three sections of the soul: **Nephesch** (the animal soul) corresponding to the sephirah Yesod; **Ruach** (the middle soul) corresponding to the sephiroth from Hod to Chesed; and **Neschamah** (the spiritual soul) corresponding to the supernals – especially Binah.

Practitioners of western **magic,** who use the Tree of Life as a glyph for the unconscious mind, sometimes distinguish the "magical" path (which embraces all ten sephiroth) from the "mystical" path of the **Middle Pillar,** which is an ascent from Malkuth through Yesod and Tiphareth to Kether on the central pillar of the Tree. Occultists also identify the 22 cards of the **Major Arcana** of the Tarot with the paths connecting the ten sephiroth, although this view is not accepted by traditional scholars of the Kabbalah. See also **Chakra**.

**Tria Prima** See Three Principles.

**Triangle** In western magic, a symbol of finite manifestation. In rituals, it is used for the purpose of evoking spirits. A talisman is placed in the centre of the triangle, together with the seal or sign of the entity to be summoned. Ceremonial magicians take considerable care to reinforce mentally the confines of the triangle in order to contain the evoked spirit. The triangle may be compared with the magic circle, which is a symbol of invocation. In this case, by contrast, the magician stands within the circle and summons supernatural forces, which may lead to his own spiritual transformation.

**Trine** In astrology, an aspect characterized by an angle of 120° between two planets.

**Triple Goddess** See Great Goddess.

**Trolls** In Scandinavian mythology, elemental spirits who lived in caves in the mountains and emerged after nightfall to steal women and substitute changelings for human offspring. Trolls took two forms – they were either giants or dwarfs – and they were regarded by country folk with extreme caution. They could be kept away by sprigs of mistletoe, large bonfires, or the sound of church bells.

**Trump** In the Tarot, a general term for any of the 22 cards of the Major Arcana.

**Trumpet, Angel's** See Angel's Trumpet

**Tuat** or **Duat** In ancient Egyptian mythology, the Underworld of darkness, which corresponded with the twelve hours of night (conceived of as twelve caverns or dungeons). The Egyptians conceived of the land of the living as being surrounded by a chain of mountains. The sun rose by emerging

through a hole in the eastern horizon and sank through a hole in the western horizon. Fairly close to these mountains, and beyond them, lay the Tuat. In other accounts, the Tuat was located not underground, but parallel with the mountains and on the same plane as the earth and sky, or within the sky. The sun god passed through the Tuat each day, safely protected from the forces of evil by an army of followers and magical formulae, or hekau, which enabled him to pass from one dungeon to the next. See also *Am Tuat*; Khepera; Osiris; Ra.

**Tuatha De Danann** In the Celtic mythology of Ireland, the race of gods and goddesses who became the rulers of the country after defeating the Fomorians. These deities – the people of Dana – took their name from the mother goddess Dana, whose consort, and the male leader of the Tuatha De Danann, was Dagda. The Tuatha De Danann were ousted as rulers of Ireland by the Milesians, or Gaels, but continued to live in a parallel "otherworld" – sometimes said to be underground – as the *sídhe* or fairy folk.

**Tuathal** See Widdershins.

**Tunkan** A term used by the Lakota Indians to refer to small round power stones which are believed to possess magical properties for healing and protection. Sometimes these stones are thought to be the gift of spirits. Tunkans are regarded as living objects and are cared for in a sacred manner. Many Native Americans wear such power stones in small leather pouches around their necks, and the famous Oglala chieftain Crazy Horse is said to have worn a power stone to protect both himself and his horse from enemy bullets.

**Tunraq** Among the Netsilik Inuit, the protector spirit given to the shaman during his initiation. According to traditional Inuit belief, it was possible for the shaman to acquire further tunraqs, either as gifts from other shamans or following the spirits' own volition. Tunraqs generally had an animal form or were ancestors of the dead. The famous Netsilik shaman Iksivalitaq, who died in 1940, was said to have had seven tunraqs – including the spirit of a dog with no ears, the spirit of a killer whale, and the ghost of his grandfather.

**Turning of the Wheel**  See Promise of the Cycle.

**Turquoise**  In Wicca, a magical stone assigned to the ritual celebration of Imbolc. On the kabbalistic Tree of Life it is assigned to the sephirah Chokmah.

**Twelve**  A number widely regarded as a symbol of completion and totality. There are twelve months in a year and twelve tribes of Israel; twelve labours of Heracles and twelve great Olympians. Jesus had twelve apostles, and there are traditionally twelve days of Christmas. Twelve is related to the number seven – another number of mystical significance – because seven consists of four *plus* three and twelve of four *times* three. See also Numerology; Olympians, The Twelve Great.

**Twin Souls**  See Soul Mates.

**Two**  A number associated with division and lack of harmony. As the opposite of one, it stands apart from God and is therefore considered by many to be evil. However, on the level of popular numerology, two is considered to be a number associated with the person who follows rather than leads; therefore, it has the attributes of gentleness and tact, although these qualities are often combined with indecision and hesitation.

**Typhon**  In Greek mythology, a monstrous, fire-breathing giant with a hundred dragon heads and a body covered with serpents. The youngest son of Gaea, Typhon was the father of many monsters in turn – including the Hydra of Lerna, the Chimera, and Cerberus. Typhon was finally struck by a thunderbolt from Zeus and despatched to

Tartarus, the lowest region of Hades.

**Typhonian Dragon of the Deep**  See Tanith.

**Typhonian Order of the Outer Ones**  A name used for the branch of the Ordo Templi Orientis headed by Kenneth Grant. Grant claims to head several organizations which serve as channels for the Typhonian Tradition.

**Typhonian Tradition**  In the magical cosmology of the Ordo Templi Orientis, a magical current associated with the ancient Egyptian Draconian Cult. According to tantric magician Kenneth Grant this magical current is also known as the Typhonian Tradition because Typhon – a fire-breathing monster from Greek mythology – could be considered "the Dragon or Reptile of the Deep". See also Draconian Cult; Typhonian Order of the Outer Ones.

**Tyr**  In the Germanic Elder Futhark, the rune letter representing the number seventeen. Tyr corresponds to the letter "t" and is the rune of courage, victory, and self-sacrifice. In Norse mythology Tyr (also known as Tiw or Tiwaz) is the god of war, and this rune is shaped like a spearhead. Tyr represents honour in battle, strength of purpose, and the power of the will to achieve great and noble things – not just for oneself, but collectively for the tribe or nation.

**Tyr's Aett**  In the Germanic Elder Futhark, rune numbers 17 to 24. See Futhark, Elder; Rune Numbers.

**Tyrian Purple**  See Purple tincture.

**Tyson, Donald**  A Canadian occultist from Halifax, Nova Scotia, Tyson was initially drawn to the world of science and was especially fascinated by astronomy. However he soon became disillusioned with the mechanistic world view and after studying English at university pursued a writing career. He now devotes his life "to the attainment of a complete gnosis of the art of magic in theory and practice". His numerous books include *Enochian Magic for Beginners; Ritual Magic, Familiar Spirits: A Practical Guide for Witches and Magicians;* and *Sexual Alchemy.*

**Tzaddi** The Hebrew letter ascribed to the path linking **Yesod** and **Netzach** on the **Tree of Life.** Tzaddi has a numerical value of 90 (and as a final letter 900). In modern magical visualization and **path-workings** the **Tarot** card associated with this path on the Tree is **The Star.**

# U

**Ualac** See Valac.

**Uathe** See Huathe.

**Uilleand** In the Celtic tree alphabet, the **ogham** representing the honeysuckle and the sound "ui". Uilleand is also linked to the colour doe red.

**Uli** In the Hawaiian **Kahuna** tradition, the god of **sorcery.** Kahuna sorcerers call on Uli and also on a variety of lesser deities and **helper spirits** to attack their enemies. See **Kahuna.**

**Ulysses** The Roman name of the Greek hero **Odysseus.**

**Umbanda** A term sometimes used incorrectly as a synonym for **Macumba,** especially in Rio de Janeiro. According to Brazilian spiritist author Pedro McGregor, while both Umbanda and Macumba relate to practices brought to Brazil by African slaves, and feature deities from the Yoruba **pantheon,** the term Umbanda refers specifically to a form of white magic influenced by the French spiritualist **Allen Kardec.** Another distinguishing factor is that practitioners of Umbanda never charge for their work. Compare with **Magic, White.** See also **Macumba.**

**Umbral Eclipse** In astrology, an eclipse of the moon, which occurs when the moon enters the shadow (Latin *umbra*) of the earth. The term is also used to describe an eclipse of the sun where the disc of the moon is fully contained within that of the sun.

**Unconscious, Collective** See Collective Unconscious.

**Unction** Anointing with oil, either as an act of consecration or in special rites to heal the sick. In magical ceremonies, practitioners may be anointed with "holy oil" to personify the sacred quest of theurgy. For example, ceremonial magicians following the tradition of the Hermetic Order of the Golden Dawn anoint the four points of the microcosm (Kether, Chesed, Geburah, and Malkuth, from the kabbalistic Tree of Life) upon the forehead, left and right shoulders, and solar plexus, respectively. The ointment consists of the oils of olive, myrrh, cinnamon, and galangual.

**Underhill, Evelyn** (1875–1941) An English poet, novelist, and mystic. Raised in an Anglican family, she had a religious visionary experience in 1906 that convinced her of the universal truth of the Church of Rome. She later taught philosophy of religion at Manchester College, Oxford, and gained an honorary doctorate in divinity from Aberdeen University. Notwithstanding her orthodox religious background, she was fascinated by the occult tradition and joined the Hermetic Order of the Golden Dawn in 1904. Her best known work is the classic *Mysticism*, first published in 1911.

**Underworld** In many ancient mythologies, a domain beneath the earth where the souls of the deceased went after death. In Greek mythology, the realm of Hades was located in the west, on the edge of the earth, beyond the great river Oceanus. Later, as Greek geographical knowledge increased, the lands of the dead were located underground, in the centre of the earth. There were said to be five rivers in the Underworld: Acheron (the river of woe); Cocytus (the river of waiting); Lethe (the river of forgetfulness); Phlegethon (the river of fire); and the Styx (by which the gods sealed their oaths). Charon ferried the souls of the dead to the entrance of the Underworld, which was guarded by Cerberus. The deceased were subsequently judged and either allowed entrance to the blessed Elysian Fields or condemned to a world of torment in Tartarus. In Scandinavian mythology, Niflheim was located in the icy north. See also Tuatha De Danann; Valhalla;

**Undine** A female elemental or sprite associated with water. See also Elementals; Nereids; Nymphs; Oceanids.

**Unfortunate Signs** In astrology, the so-called negative signs of the zodiac: Taurus, Cancer, Virgo, Scorpio, Capricorn, and Aquarius.

**Unguent** An ointment or salve. In the Middle Ages, hallucinatory unguents were prepared by witches to produce the visionary sensation of flight to the witches' sabbath. See also Flying Ointments.

**Unicorn** In mythology, folk legend, and heraldry, a creature with a single horn extending from its forehead. The unicorn ("one-horn") of European tradition basically takes the form of a horse, but unicorns in other parts of the world are also depicted with the body of a goat, rhinoceros, ram, or serpent. Portrayed as a pure white creature, the unicorn was usually regarded as a symbol of purity and spiritual unity, its horn being considered masculine and its body feminine. In medieval Europe, the unicorn had Christian associations – its single horn symbolizing the unity of God the Father, Son, and Holy Spirit – and it also featured in the tradition of courtly love, for only a virgin holding a mirror was able to tame it. In alchemy, the unicorn was associated with the male-female or androgynous Mercury – a motif indicating attainment of the Great Work. See also Monoceros.

**Unio Mystica** See Mystic Union.

**Union of Opposites** A mystical concept found in Indian yoga and also in the Kabbalah, western magic, and alchemy. In many traditions, the attainment of self-realization necessitates the transcendence of duality, and this includes the harmony of sexual opposites within a person. In kundalini yoga, the energy channels ida and pingala – representing the female and male polarities respectively – are united in the supreme chakra, sahasrara. Similarly, in alchemy the heavenly **androgyne** personifies the harmony of opposites. In the Kabbalah, the supreme and "neutral" sephirah **Kether** transcends **Chokmah** (the Great Father) and **Binah** (the Great Mother).

**Unity Consciousness** The experience of oneness with God. According to the mystical traditions this is all that really exists. See also **Mystic Union**.

**Universal Mind** In Theosophy, mysticism, and **occultism**, the mind of the **supreme being**, or God, which pervades the universe and gives order and meaning to all aspects of creation. See also **Cosmic Consciousness**.

**Universal Solvent** In alchemy, the universal substance from which all other specific constituents evolved; a name for the life force. See also **Elixir of Life**.

**Upper Light** In the Kabbalah, an alternative name for **Ain Soph Aur**.

**Ur** (1) In the Celtic tree alphabet, the **ogham** representing thorn and heather and the letter "u". Ur is also linked to the lark and the colour light green.

**Ur** (2) In the Germanic **Elder Futhark**, the **rune** letter representing the number two. Ur (also uruz) corresponds to the letter "u", and is associated with good fortune, strength, vitality, and a successful career.

**Uraeus** In ancient Egyptian mythology, the fire-breathing cobra or asp that protected the sun god Ra by destroying his enemies. The pharaoh, the gods' representative on earth, wore a uraeus diadem on his headdress or crown as a symbol of royal dominion and authority. The creature was often shown in combination with the solar disc.

**Urania** In Greek mythology, one of nine **Muses**. Urania governed astronomy and **astrology**, and was regarded by John Milton as the muse of poetry. She was also identified with **Aphrodite** in her role as goddess of spiritual love.

**Uranus** (1) or Uranos, Ouranos. In Greek mythology, the most ancient of the gods and father of the Titans. Uranus was the husband of **Gaea** and personified the sky and heavens. He was sometimes known as Father Sky. See also **Uranus** (2).

**Uranus** (2) In astrology, the planet associated with change and revolution – a reference to Uranus's overthrow by his son **Kronos** in classical Greek mythology. Uranus represents rebellion, independence, impatience, and new inventions and discoveries.

**Urd** See Norns.

**Uriel** The name of an **archangel** who is not mentioned in the Bible but appears in apocryphal writings. In modern western **magic**, Uriel is invoked in the **banishing ritual** of the Lesser Pentagram. He is summoned in the northern quarter and is ascribed to the element **earth**. His counterparts are **Raphael** (east: **air**); **Michael** (south: **fire**); and **Gabriel** (west: **water**).

**Urim and Thummim** According to Hebrew tradition, two objects – possibly flat discs – attached to the breastplate of the high priest of the temple of Jerusalem. The Urim and Thummim were consulted in **divination** to enable the high priest to learn the will of God. See also **Sortilege**.

**Uroboros** See Ouroboros.

**Ursuline Convent Possession** See Aix-en-Provence Nuns.

**Uruz** See Ur (2).

**Uti** In Enochian magic, the 14th Aethyr. The meanings associated with Uti include spiritual selfishness, egoism, a lack of caring, aloofness, and the absence of desire. Uti is associated with **Capricorn**, Caput Draconis, and **Sagittarius** and its magical number is 79.

**Uvall** See Vual.

# V

**Valac** In the Goetia, the 62nd spirit, a mighty president who appears in the form of a young child with angel's wings, riding on the back of a two-headed dragon. Valac can reveal where serpents may be seen and can also provide truthful answers in relation to hidden treasures. Valac rules over 38 legions of spirits and is also known as Volac, Valu, or Ualac.

**Valefor** In the Goetia, the sixth spirit, a mighty duke who appears in the form of a lion with a bellowing ass' head. Referred to as a "good familiar", he can reveal secrets and change men into animals. He is also in charge of magical medicine and can treat all complaints successfully. Valefor commands ten legions of spirits and is also known as Malaphar.

**Valentinus** (110–175CE) A leading Gnostic teacher and poet. Born in Egypt, Valentinus was possibly a disciple of **Basilides** and claimed to have access to St Paul's **esoteric** teachings through Theodas, one of Paul's followers. According to Valentinus, the **pleroma**, or **godhead**, encompassed 30 spiritual beings called aeons, with four major groupings: Abyss and Silence, Mind and Truth, Word and Life, Man and Church. The 30th aeon, **Sophia** (Wisdom), gave rise to matter and produced as her offspring **Ialdaboath** (a deity he claimed was mistaken by the Jews as the creator **Yahweh**). According to Valentinus, the role of Jesus was to restore Sophia to her status as part of the pleroma. Valentinian Gnosticism was not without its controversial features. According to its founder, the pairs of aeons were extremely sexual, and it was appropriate for sect members to imitate this. The Valentinian sex celebrations were held just prior to the Roman **Lupercalia** and led to fierce condemnation from Clement of Alexandria, Irenaeus, and other critics of the Gnostic sects. See also **Aeon** (2).

**Valhalla** In Scandinavian mythology, the hall of **Odin** where warriors and heroes killed in battle resided in the afterworld. Here Odin and his comrades drank and feasted, awaiting **Ragnarok** – the final encounter with the giants and forces of evil.

**Valiente, Doreen** (1922–1999) One of the leading figures in the international Wiccan community and sometimes referred to as the "mother of modern **paganism**", Valiente was born Doreen Dominy in London, in 1922. Brought up as a Christian, she escaped from the convent school to which she had been sent and never returned. Dominy worked as a secretary but also practised as a clairvoyant. In 1944 she married Casimiro Valiente, a refugee from the Spanish Civil War. Doreen Valiente was initiated into **witchcraft** in 1953 by **Gerald Gardner** and became **high priestess** of his **coven**. However, she broke with Gardner in 1957 when he ignored the coven's vows of secrecy by seeking publicity. Valiente was a gifted writer as well as a gifted ritualist and her text "The Charge of the Goddess" is now a central component in contemporary Wiccan ceremonies around the world. She also produced several influential books, including *Witchcraft for Tomorrow* and *The Rebirth of Witchcraft*, which have become standard references for neopagan practitioners. See also Wicca.

**Valkyries** In Scandinavian mythology, the battle-maidens of **Odin** who dwelt with him in the paradise of **Valhalla**. At Odin's bidding, the Valkyries rode into the fray to carry the fallen heroes to Valhalla, where they made them welcome with pork and mead.

**Valu** See Valac.

**Vama Marg** From a Sanskrit term which translates as "left path or way", the so-called **left-hand path** in magic, often associated with sexual magic and sorcery. According to tantric magician

Kenneth Grant, Vama Marg involves "the magical use of woman as the human embodiment of the Supreme Goddess". See also **Magic, Sexual**.

**Vampire** A bloodsucking **demon** that was believed to be a **revenant** corpse. Vampires – the word is of Slavonic origin – were usually of pale complexion and ice-cold to touch. They had gleaming eyes, pointed ears, and long fingernails, and were able to transform themselves into animals. The most famous vampire in folk legend and literature was Count Dracula. See also **Lycanthropy; Werewolf; Zombie**.

**Vanaheim** In Scandinavian mythology, one of the **Nine Worlds** located on the World Tree, **Yggdrasil**. Vanaheim is the home of the **Vanir** – the peaceful deities, who included the fertility goddess Freyja and Freyr, lord of the harvest.

**Vanir** In Scandinavian mythology, the peaceful gods who protected the crops and nature, and all living things. The Vanir deities, including **Freyr** and **Freyja**, feuded with the **Aesir** gods headed by Odin, until they were admitted to the citadel in the sky known as **Asgard**.

**Vapula** In the Goetia, the 60th spirit, a strong and mighty duke who appears in the form of a lion with the wings of a griffin. He provides skills in manual crafts and professions as well as in philosophy and other sciences. Vapula commands 36 legions of spirits and is also known as Naphula.

**Varengan** In Persian mythology, a magical bird whose feathers were regarded as a protection against curses and spells. Capable of flying as swiftly as an arrow, it was the fastest of all birds.

**Varuna** A Vedic sky god regarded as an omniscient lord of wisdom and later associated with the moon and the dead. It is thought that the Persian deity **Zurvan** and the **Gnostic** deity **Abraxas** derive at least in part from Varuna. He

may also be related to the Greek **Uranus**.

**Vase of the Philosophy** See Aludel.

**Vassago** In the Goetia, the third spirit, a mighty prince of "good nature" whose special ability is to "declare things past and to come" as well as locating things lost or hidden. He governs 26 legions of spirits.

**Vast Face** In the Kabbalah, the unmanifested God – a transcendent God completely without attributes. See also **Ain Soph Aur** and **Antiga**.

**Vau** See Vav.

**Vaughan, Thomas** (1622–1665) A noted Welsh hermeticist, alchemist, and mystic who wrote under the pseudonym of Eugenius Philalethes. Vaughan believed in the kabbalistic principle that "the spirit of man is itself the spirit of the living god" – accepting the concept of the **macrocosm and microcosm**. Vaughan's principal works include *Anthroposophia Theomagica*, a discourse on the nature of man and his state after death; *Magia Adamica*, a treatise on the antiquity of **magic**; *Coelum Terrae*, a work on heaven and chaos; *Lumen de Lumine*, a tract on **theurgy**; and *Euphrates*, a work on **alchemy**. His writings were compiled by **A.E. Waite** and published as *The Works of Thomas Vaughan* (London, 1919; reissued New York, 1968). See also *Hermetica, The*.

**Vaulderie** An expression used by members of the French **Inquisition** to describe the act of forming a satanic pact. Named after the hermit Robinet de Vaulse, who was accused of this crime, it became a familiar charge against witches. It was linked to the witches' **flying ointments** – which, according to the Inquisition, enabled devil worshippers to "fly wherever they wished to go…the devil [carrying] them to the place where they should hold their assembly." See also **Witches' Sabbath**.

**Vav** The Hebrew letter ascribed to the path linking Chokmah and Chesed on the Tree of Life. Vav has a numerical value of 6. In modern magical visualization and **pathworkings** the Tarot card associated with this path on the Tree is *The Hierophant*.

**Vayu** In Hinduism, one of the **tattvas**, or **elements**. Vayu is the symbol of **air**, and is represented by a blue hexagon. It is associated with the **chakra anahata** located near the thymus gland. See also **Kundalini**.

**Velada** Among the Mazatec Indians of Mexico, a healing ceremony involving the use of psilocybe mushrooms. Both the patient and the female **shaman** take the **psychedelic** mushroom·so both may hear the healing words which are revealed from the spirit world. The shaman, meanwhile, goes on a **spirit journey** to discover the cause of sickness and to seek the healing power from the gods. Among the Mazatecs, folk belief and Christianity have fused so that cures are attributed both to the sacred mushroom and also to "God the Father and God the Son." See also **Psilocybin**.

**Veneris Herba** Also known as Verbanaca, the Roman name for *Verbena officinalis*, a plant sacred to **Venus**. See Vervain.

**Venus** (1) In Roman mythology, the counterpart of the Greek goddess of love, **Aphrodite**. Venus personified sexuality, fertility, prosperity, and good luck. The Romans venerated her in late April and early May – the season for promiscuity.

**Venus** (2) In **astrology**, a planet associated with sexual love and desire, and relationships in general. Astrologers regard Venus as a beneficent planet, attracting harmony, affection, and love. Its particular location in the **horoscope** indicates sympathy and friendship and often a degree of sentimentality. According to some astrologers, a man

with the sun and Venus closely aspected is likely to be effeminate, while Venus in conjunction with **Saturn** or **Mercury** may indicate female domination.

**Vepar** In the **Goetia**, the 42nd spirit, a powerful duke who appears in the form of a mermaid. He governs the waters and guides ships laden with arms, armour and ammunition. At the magician's bidding he can create storms at sea. He can also putrefy wounds and cause worms to breed in them. Vepar commands 29 legions of spirits and is also known as Separ.

**Verbanaca** The Roman name for *Verbena officinalis*, a plant sacred to Venus. See **Vervain**.

**Verbena** See Vervain.

**Verdandi** See Norns.

**Vernal Equinox** The equinox that occurs on 21 March, the first day of spring. It equates with the entry of the sun into **Aries**, the first sign of the zodiac.

**Verser** In voodoo, the act of pouring drops of water, coffee or liquor on the ground as an offering to the **loa**.

**Vervain** *Verbena officinalis*, a sacred plant among the ancient Romans, who believed that vervain was able to repel the enemy in war. Accordingly, vervain was associated with **Mars** and was worn by ambassadors and heralds in their missions to other nations. Vervain was also sacred among the **Druids**, who used it in spells of enchantment. Also called Druid's Weed.

**Vesica Piscis** Latin for "fish's bladder", an almond-shape aureole or halo also called a mandorla, often shown in medieval art surrounding God the Father, Christ, or saints. Signifying transcendence and creative power, it may have originated as a symbol of the vulva. In the **Kabbalah**, the shape contains additional symbols and is ascribed to **Binah**, on the **Tree of Life**.

**Vestal Virgins** In ancient Rome, priestesses who dedicated themselves to serving Vesta, the goddess of the hearth. The Vestals were between six and ten years of age when they entered training – a process taking ten years. They then remained in service for another ten years: tending the sacred fire on the altar of Vesta so that it never went out; carrying water from the fountain known as Egeria; and serving as custodians of the Palladium from Troy. The Vestals finally spent another ten years instructing novices, and were then free to renounce their vow of celibacy, and marry if they wished. They were held in high regard in Rome, and it was said that the tradition was as old as Aeneas, who was believed to have selected the first Vestals. Rhea Silvia, the mother of Rome's legendary founders, Romulus and Remus, was herself a Vestal.

**Vevers** In **voodoo**, symbolic signs, resembling magical sigils, which are drawn on the ground to invoke the **loa**, or gods, in ritual ceremonies. Compare **Ponto Riscado**

**Via Mystica** Latin for "mystic way" or "mystic path", a reference to the spiritual path that leads to union with God. See also **Mystic Union**.

**Vial** In alchemy, a small spherical glass bottle with a slim straight neck used in the process of **distillation**. It is also called a phial or viol.

**Vidar** In Scandinavian mythology, the son of **Odin**, who slew the wolf **Fenris** and survived **Ragnarok** – becoming the deity who would herald the new Golden Age.

**Vine** In the Goetia, the 45th spirit, a powerful king and earl who appears in the form of a lion, or lion-headed man, riding on a black horse and bearing a viper in his hand. Vine can detect the presence of hostile witches and wizards and also has a knowledge of all things past, present, and future. He can construct towers, overthrow large stone walls, and create storms at sea. He governs 36 legions of spirits.

**Viol** See **Vial**.

**Violent Signs** In astrology, the signs Aries, Libra, Scorpio, Capricorn, and Aquarius.

**Viracocha** Among the Incas, the personification of life and creator of the universe. Viracocha was the lord of thunder and brought the sun, moon, and stars into existence. He was said to dwell in the depths of Lake Titicaca and received sacrificial offerings of children and animals.

**Virgin** In alchemy, a symbol of the feminine aspect of the **prima materia** and also the feminine nature of Mercurius, who is sometimes portrayed as hermaphroditic.

**Virginity** In mysticism and **magic**, a condition that symbolizes purity, innocence, and spirituality. In medieval folk legend only a virgin could tame the unicorn, itself a symbol of male and female polarity; and in the Tarot, the supreme male and female archetypes are the virgin male (*The Magician*) and the virgin female (*The High Priestess*). Among the great religions, both Jesus Christ and Gautama Buddha were each said to have been born of a virgin – symbolic of their pure spiritual being.

**Virgin's Milk** In alchemy, the pure white tincture created by the **albedo** and which could transform base metals into silver. It is also a term applied to the so-called mercurial water or "water of life" – the white **philosophical mercury** known as **Mercurius**. See **Mercurius**.

**Virgo** In astrology, the sign of the zodiac for those born between 23 August and 22 September. An **earth** sign, ruled

by **Mercury**, Virgo is represented by the
figure of the virgin. Those born under
the sign of Virgo are often analytical and
methodical in their day-to-day lives and
can appear reserved and cool in manner.
They have an excellent grasp of complex
details and often choose careers in
business. In their personal relationships
they are usually intensely loyal, but often
nervous and lacking in self-confidence.
They are also inclined to be self-centred
and critical of others. Virgos are traditionally associated with an interest in
food or drugs, and are often found in
careers linked to nutrition, analytical
chemistry, or pharmacology.

**Virote** In South American shamanism
and folk healing, a magical dart sent by
an evil **witch** or **sorcerer** in order to
cause harm.

**Vishuddha** In kundalini yoga, the
**chakra** associated with **akasha**
(symbolized by a black oval egg), the
**tattva** representing the element **spirit**.
The vishuddha chakra is located in the
region of the thyroid gland.

**Visionary** One who has the capacity to
see beyond the immediate. While for
many this implies a person who is
idealistic and impractical, it can also be
used to describe one who is gifted with
paranormal vision or who has profound
and universal insights into the human
condition. See also **Adept; Avatar;
Master.**

**Vision, Crystal** See Crystal Gazing;
Crystalomancy.

**Vision Quest** In Native American
religion, the ritual quest for a **guardian
spirit** undertaken by a young male or
female. The person goes to a lonely and
isolated location where the guardian
spirit is thought likely to appear in a
vision. A vision quest may take several
days and nights.

**Vision, Spirit** An altered state of consciousness in which sacred or magical

images dominate one's perception and
are accompanied by feelings of awe,
mystery, and transcendence. On a less
profound level, mental images and
visions may also appear during a state of
reverie, during **skrying**, or in meditative
sessions involving the use of **guided
imagery**. Visions of this sort frequently
have archetypal content and arise from
the spiritual areas of the **psyche**. See also
**Archetype; Collective Unconscious.**

**Vital Force** The life force, which resides
in all living things and which, in mystical
and occult traditions, is presumed to be
the source of health and vitality. If the
life force is blocked from the organism,
disease results and eventually death
ensues. The life force is known variously
as, for example, *ch'i* or *qi* (Chinese); *ki*
(Japanese); and *prana* (Sanskrit).

**Vitalism** The belief that living
organisms may be distinguished from
inorganic matter by virtue of the
presence of a **vital force**. This force,
sometimes known as *elan vital*, is capable
of existing independently of physical
form. See also **Nous.**

**Vivian** In Arthurian legend, the
enchantress who finally ensnared the
wizard **Merlin** by trapping him with his
own magical **spell**.

**Vodoun** See Voodoo.

**Void** (1), **The** A term used to describe
the supreme, **transcendent** reality which
lies beyond form and **manifestation**.
Often regarded as the "first cause", and
sometimes identified with the **godhead**,
the void is also characterized in some
cosmologies as **chaos** and formlessness.
**Ain Soph Aur** is the "Infinite Light" of
the **Kabbalah**; and *shunyata* is the
supreme void in Mahayana Buddhism.

**Void** (2) In the magic of trance occultist
**Austin Osman Spare**, an open state of
mind, achieved through meditation,
exhaustion or at the peak of sexual
ecstasy, which he used to arouse primal

energies from the cosmic life'force, which he named **Kia**. Spare focused his will on magical sigils and used them to direct instructions to his subconscious mind when it is was in a "void" or "open" state.

**Voiding the Coven** In Wicca, the situation where members of a new **coven** sever all practical working contact with the previous coven from which they have hived off. With the approval of the **high priestess** such coven members may sometimes continue social contact with each other but they no longer perform rituals with members of the original coven. See also **Hiving Off**.

**Volac** See Valac.

**Volatile** In alchemy, a term used to describe substances that vaporized when heat was applied to the vessel in which they were contained. This volatile substance had to be subsequently "captured" and "fixed" through the lengthy process **solve et coagula**.

**Volva** In ancient Norse culture, a priestess in the cult of **Freyja** whose principal functions included **divination** and **prophecy**. The term *volva* means "one who can foresee the future". Volvas entered trance states for their divinatory purposes and were sometimes regarded as an incarnation of the goddess Freyja herself.

**Voodoo** or **Vodoun, Vaudoux, Vondou**. Haitian magical practices involving chanting, drumming, singing, and dancing, and which lead to states of **dissociation, trance,** and **spirit possession**. The word voodoo derives from the West African word *vodun*, meaning "a god" or "spirit": the rites of voodoo were imported into Haiti and other parts of the Caribbean during the period of the slave trade, when Africans were brought across to work on the plantations. Voodoo rites include sexual sacrifices; snake dances; the ritual use of corpses; the evocation of **spirits**,

monsters, and **zombies**; and occasional cannibalism. In some voodoo ceremonies, practitioners are possessed by the **loa**, or gods. Among the principal deities are **Ogoun**, the warrior god: **Baron Samedi**, the god of cemeteries; and his other evil counterparts, Baron Cimitiere, Baron Piquant, and **Guede**, who rule the forces of evil with him .

**Voso** See Ose.

**Voval** See Vual.

**Vti** In Enochian Magic, the 25th **Aethyr**. The meanings associated with Vti include intuition, inspiration, insight, and humility. It is associated with **Capricorn**, Caput Draconis, and **Sagittarius** and its magical number is 133

**Vual** In the Goetia, the 47th spirit, a strong and mighty duke who appears initially in the form of a dromedary – a single-humped Arabian camel – but who will assume a human shape when so commanded by the magician. He speaks "in the Egyptian tongue", has a knowledge of things past, present, and future, and specializes in procuring the love of women. He can also establish love and friendship among enemies. Vual commands 37 legions of spirits and is also known as Uvall or Voval.

**Vulture** See Bird of Hermes.

# W

**Waite, Arthur Edward** (1857–1942) A noted occult historian and **mystic**. Born in Brooklyn, New York, Waite came with his mother to England when very young and spent most of his life in his adopted country. Influenced by the writings of **Madame Helena Blavatsky** and the French occultist **Eliphas Lévi**, Waite began to explore the western occult tradition in earnest and in due course became the leading occult scholar of his time. Waite rejected the notion of the Mahatmas and left **Theosophy** to join the **Hermetic Order of the Golden Dawn,** later (c. 1916) becoming leader of a splinter faction. Waite had been raised in a Roman Catholic environment and believed that the western occult tradition provided an esoteric **mystery** tradition that the orthodox Christian Church had either forgotten or never possessed. He attracted Christian figures like **Evelyn Underhill** and writer Charles Williams to the Golden Dawn, and was decidedly more a mystic than an occultist. Nevertheless, with artist Pamela Colman-Smith, he created the most popular **Tarot** deck – the so-called Rider Pack – and authored several books on western **magic**, including *Devil Worship in France* and *The Book of Ceremonial Magic*. His other books include *The Brotherhood of the Rosy Cross; The Real History of the Rosicrucians; The Holy Kabbalah; The Holy Grail; The Secret Tradition in Freemasonry;* and perhaps his most eloquent work on mysticism, *Azoth*. Waite also compiled and translated many of the esoteric writings of **Paracelsus** and Eliphas Lévi, as well as anthologizing the important works of alchemist **Thomas Vaughan**.

**Waititcani** A Zuni Indian ceremonial medicine bowl used in **divination**. See Macaiyoyo.

**Wakan** or **Wakan Tanka; Wakanda**. In traditional Lakota (Sioux) Indian belief, the supreme deity, the universal life force that permeates all aspects of nature and is a source of spiritual power.

**Walkerbeere** In early Germanic herbalism and mythology, the plant belladonna, or **deadly nightshade**. It was sacred to **Wotan**, the god of ecstasy. Wotan is the early counterpart of the Scandinavian god **Odin**. See **Deadly Nightshade**.

**Walpurgis Night** or **Walpurgisnacht** The German festival of **May Eve**, 30 April, traditionally regarded as a night when dark forces are afoot. In Germany, Walpurgis Night is associated with Mount Brocken in the Harz mountain range, where the witches were said to gather and hold their sabbath. It is named after St Walburga, whose feast fell on 1 May. See also **All Hallows' Eve; Witches' Sabbath**.

**Wand** In modern ceremonial **magic**, one of the four traditional implements, the others being the dagger or **sword**, the cup, and the **pentacle**. The wand is fashioned from **ash** or **hazel** and represents the element **fire** in ceremonial workings. See also **Magic, Ceremonial**.

**Wands** or **Rods** One of the four suits of the **Minor Arcana** of the **Tarot**. Wands is one of the two masculine suits (the other being **swords**) and is ascribed to the element **fire**.

**Wanga** In **voodoo**, a magical **charm** used for selfish purposes or to harm others.

**Warlock** The male counterpart of a female **witch**. The term is more commonly used to describe a **sorcerer** who is skilled in summoning supernatural evil forces and practising black magic. See **Magic, Black; Satanism**.

**Warren-Clarke, Ly** See De Angeles, Ly.

**Wasson, R. Gordon** (1898–1986) An American private researcher and ethnomycologist who, in the early 1950s, with his wife Valentina, began to explore the impact of psychoactive mushrooms on different cultures in Siberia, India, Europe, and North and South America. Wasson believed that visionary experiences associated with the use of psychedelic mushrooms have played a profound role in shaping religious beliefs. Wasson is best known for his suggestion – now seriously considered by academic specialists – that the sacred **soma** in Indian mythology was in fact *Amanita muscaria*. In his book *The Road to Eleusis* (1978), Wasson explored initiation in classical Greece and provided an analysis of *The Homeric Hymn to Demeter*. He suggested that the visions of the neophytes in the **Mysteries of Eleusis** were caused by the presence of **ergot** in the sacred ceremonial drink. Ergot is the parasitic fungus from which the psychedelic LSD was later synthesized. Wasson's other books include *Soma: The Divine Mushroom of Immortality* (1969); *Maria Sabina and the Mazatec Mushroom Velada* (1974); and *The Wondrous Mushroom* (1980).

**Watcher on the Threshold** A magical term for the accumulated karmic impressions amassed from past incarnations and which must be confronted on the path to transcendence. See **Karma**.

**Watchtowers** In Wicca, the guardians of the four cardinal points of the magical circle. Their protective presence is summoned at the commencement of many rituals to clear the sacred space of malevolent forces.

**Water** One of the four alchemical elements, the others being **earth, fire,** and **air**. The **spirits** of water are known as **undines** and **mermaids**, or **mermen**. The three astrological **water signs** are Cancer, Scorpio, and Pisces. See also **Water Sprites**.

**Water Bearer, The** In astrology, a popular name for **Aquarius**, the eleventh sign of the **zodiac**.

**Water Signs** In astrology, the signs Cancer, Scorpio, and Pisces, which characterize the element **water** in its cardinal, fixed, and mutable aspects respectively.

**Water Sprite** Nature spirits, or elementals, of water. In Greek mythology, these sprites were the **Oceanids** or **Nereids**. In medieval folklore they are the **mermaids, mermen**, and **undines**.

**Way of the Mystic** or **Way of the Messiah** In the Kabbalah, the path of mystical ascent using the Middle Pillar on the **Tree of Life**. It is also called the Way of the Messiah, because when the heart sephirah **Tiphareth** is awakened, the entire Tree lights up and the devotional love of the Messiah is experienced. See **Tiphareth, Middle Pillar.**

**Way of the Wizard** In kabbalistic magic, the path of mystical ascent which utilizes all of the **sephiroth** on the **Tree of Life**, not just those on the **Middle Pillar**, as in the Way of the Mystic.

**Weed, Druid's** See Vervain.

**Weed, Jimson** See Thornapple.

**Weighing of the Heart (Soul)** In ancient Egyptian mythology, when the deceased reached the **Judgment Hall**, he or she had to swear before **Osiris, Maat, Thoth** and 42 divine judges that they were free of a long list of sins. The deceased's heart was then weighed against the **feather** of truth. The soul was judged "true of voice" and sinless if the feather and heart balanced perfectly, and the deceased was admitted to paradise; but if the heart was heavy with sin, the deceased was condemned to oblivion. Thoth recorded the verdict.

**Weishaupt, Adam** (1748–1830) The Bavarian founder of the Order of the Illuminati.

**Well of Urd** In Scandinavian mythology, the spring of destiny which was said to well up among the roots of the world tree, Yggdrasil. The Norns, or goddesses of fate, resided near the Well of Urd.

**Weretiger** In traditional Malaysian folk belief, a man who is capable of transforming himself into a tiger. The local expression for this manifestation of lycanthropy is *jadi-jadian*. Compare Werewolf.

**Werewolf** In occult and folk belief, a person who can transform into the form of a wolf and eat human flesh. In other cultures, individuals are similarly believed to become other fierce animals, such as a jaguar or a tiger. Compare Vampire and see also Lycanthropy.

**West** (1) In alchemy, the direction associated with argent vive and the cold, moist dissolving aspects of the alchemical process. Compare East. See also Solve et coagula.

**West** (2) In western ceremonial magic, the direction associated with the element Water. It is said to be ruled by the archangel Gabriel. See also Four Directions. See Magic, Ceremonial.

**Westcott, Dr William Wynn** (1848–1925) An influential English occultist and Freemason. Westcott obtained a series of Masonic writings, which he asked MacGregor Mathers to develop into a series of graded magical rituals. In due course, these became the basis of the ceremonial practices of the Hermetic Order of the Golden Dawn, and both Westcott and Mathers held senior grades within the new order. Westcott's occult writings include *An Introduction to the Qabalah* (1910) and translations of the *Sepher Yetzirah* (1911), and Eliphas Lévi's *The Magical Ritual of the Sanctum Regnum* (1896). He was also the editor of an important series of occult monographs known as *Collectanea Hermetica*, published by the Theosophical Publishing House in London in the 1890s. See also Freemasonry.

**Western Esoteric Tradition** A commonly used phrase which refers to the western magical tradition with all its component strands and movements. The western esoteric tradition encompasses alchemy, Kabbalah, Wicca and Goddess worship, Freemasonry, Rosicrucianism, ritual magic, astrology, numerology, and various forms of divination like Tarot and geomancy – as well as drawing on practices derived from shamanism, yoga, tantra, and pre-Christian European pagan religions.

**Wheatley, Dennis** (1897–1977) An English adventure writer who wrote a number of novels dealing with satanism and black magic. Wheatley maintained that he had never taken part in magical ceremonies, although he knew many leading figures in the occult world. His best known books include *The Devil and All His Works* (a study of magic and the occult); *The Devil Rides Out; The Gates of Hell; To the Devil – a Daughter; They Used Dark Powers*; and *The Haunting of Toby Jugg*. See also Magic, Black.

**Wheel** See Opus Circulatorium.

**Wheel of Fortune, The** In the Tarot, the card of the Major Arcana that symbolizes the forces of fate and destiny. In the Kabbalah, words composed of similar letters (and therefore having the same numerical total according to gematria) are believed to have related meanings, and in this way the words Rota (Latin for "wheel"), Taro, and Ator are regarded by some occultists as being linked. According to American occultist Paul Foster Case, *The Wheel of Fortune* can be summarized by the pronouncement that "The Wheel (Rota) of Tarot (Taro) speaks the Law of Hathor (Ator)" – an interpretation that reflects Case's personal belief that the Tarot had an Egyptian origin. Other occultists see this card as a magical mandala, a symbol reflecting the mastery of opposite polarities within the psyche. On the kabbalistic Tree of Life, the path of *The Wheel of Fortune* links Netzach and

Chesed, the first of these being a feminine sphere, the second masculine.

**Wheel of the Year** In Wicca, the cycle of the seasons, or more specifically the cycle of nature's fertility. Wiccans celebrate both the lunar and solar cycles of nature. Esbats are monthly meetings of the **coven** held at the time of full moon, while the solar cycle is marked by eight sabbaths referred to collectively as the Wheel of the Year: these are the solstices, equinoxes, and the four points between. As American Wiccan author Margot Adler has observed, these meetings and festivals renew a sense of living communion with natural cycles, and with the changes in the seasons and the land. See **Esbats; Sabbats, Greater; Sabbats, Lesser.**

**White Elixir** In alchemy, the "medicine" attained in the lunar stage of the **opus alchymicum.** The white elixir had the power to transmute base metals into pure silver. It is identical to the white stone.

**White-Handled Knife** In Wicca, a practical implement also known as a **boline,** used for cutting or making marks on ritual objects. It is a working tool rather than a ritual object. See also **Altar; Athame.**

**White Hellebore** See **Hellebore.**

**White Magic** See **Magic, White.**

**White Rose** In alchemy, a symbol of the white tincture attained through the stage of the **opus alchymicum** known as the **albedo,** which occurs prior to the **rubedo.** The white stone was able to transmute all base metals into silver.

**White Stage** In alchemy, the lunar stage of the **opus alchymicum.** See **Albedo.**

**White Water** See **Mercurius.**

**White Woman** In alchemy, a represen-

tation of **argent vive,** or **mercury** – the cold, moist, receptive, female principle in metals associated also with the moon and **Queen Luna.** See **Philosophical Mercury.**

**White Work** In alchemy, the conversion of impure base metals into silver – a possibility following the attainment of the second stage of the **opus alchymicum.** See **Albedo.**

**Whore of Babalon** In the Thelemic cosmology of ceremonial magician **Aleister Crowley,** the magical partner of the **Great Beast 666.** Together, through their sexual union, they would herald the New Aeon, the **Aeon of Horus.** Many women temporarily filled this role, including Leah Hirsig, Mary d'Este Sturges, Roddie Minor, and the beautiful Australian violinist Leila Waddell. Crowley intentionally spelt the name Babalon rather than Babylon for numerological reasons. See also **Thelema.**

**Wicca** Modern **witchcraft** is often referred to as Wicca, from the Old English words *wicca* (masculine) and *wicce* (feminine) meaning "a practitioner of witchcraft". The word *wiccan,* meaning "witches" occurs in the Laws of King Alfred (c. 890CE) and the verb *wiccian* – "to bewitch" – was also used in this context. Some witches believe the words connote a wise person, and Wicca is sometimes known as the "Craft of the Wise".

Witchcraft, in essence, is a nature-based religion with the **Great Goddess** as its principal deity. She can take many forms: the Great Mother or Mother Nature, or more specifically **Astarte, Hathor, Isis Aphrodite, Artemis, Athena, Demeter, Persephone, Diana,** or **Venus,** – among many others. The **High Priestess** of the **coven** incarnates the spirit of the goddess in a ceremonial context when the **High Priest** "draws down the moon" into her body. In witchcraft, the High Priestess is the receptacle of wisdom and intuition and is symbolized by the cup, whereas her consort is represented by a short sword or dagger. Many witchcraft rituals feature the act of uniting dagger and cup as a symbol of sexual union, and there is also a comparable relationship in Celtic mythology between the sacred oak tree and Mother Earth. Accordingly the High Priest, or consort, is sometimes known as the Oak King – a reference to the oak of the Celts – and at other times as Cernunnos, "The Horned God". In witchcraft the Horned God personifies fertility, and in ancient Greece the great god Pan – the horned and goat-footed god – was a symbol of nature and the universal life force. There is no connection between the Horned God of witchcraft and the Christian horned Devil, although, since the witchcraft persecutions of the Middle Ages, this has been a common error.

Wiccan covens vary in size although traditionally the membership number is thirteen – consisting of six men, six women and the High Priestess. When the group exceeds this number, some members leave, or hive off, to form a new coven. Wiccans take special magical names which they use in a ritual context and they meet for their ceremonies at specific times of the year. These meetings, or sabbats, are related to the cycles of nature and the traditional times for harvesting crops. The four "Greater Sabbats" are: Candlemas (2 February), known by the Celts as Imbolc (celebrated on 1 August in the southern hemisphere); May Eve (30 April), or Beltane (celebrated on 31 October in the southern hemisphere); Lammas (1 August), or Lughnassadh (celebrated on 2 February in the southern hemisphere); and All Hallows' Eve (Halloween, Celebrated on 31 October), or Samhain (celebrated on 30 April in the southern hemisphere). In addition, there are four Lesser Sabbats – the two solstices at midsummer and midwinter, and the two equinoxes in spring and autumn.

In pre-Christian times, Imbolc was traditionally identified with the first signs of spring; Beltane was a fertility celebration when the sacred oak was burned, mistletoe cut, and sacrifices made to the gods; Lughnassadh, which was related to autumn and the harvesting of crops, celebrated both the gathering in of produce and the continuing fertility of the earth; and Samhain represented the transition from autumn to winter and was associated with bonfires to keep away the chilly winter winds. Samhain was also a time when the spirits of the dead could return to earth to be once again with their loved ones. Contemporary witches meet in their covens to celebrate these Celtic rites although, in the southern hemisphere – as detailed above – most Wiccan practitioners adjust the sabbats to equate with the appropriate season. Sabbats are a time for fellowship, ceremony; and initiation, and after the rituals have been performed there is feasting, drinking, and merriment.

Contemporary Wicca recognizes three initiations. The first initiation confers witch-status upon the neophyte, the second initiation promotes a first-degree witch to the position of High Priestess or High Priest, and the third initiation celebrates the bonding of the High Priestess and High Priest in the Great Rite: either real or symbolic sexual union.

There is also an emphasis in Wicca on the threefold aspect of the Great Goddess in her role as Maid (youth, enchantment), Mother (maturity, fulfilment), and Crone (old age, wisdom). This symbolic personification of the phases of womanhood is represented, for example, by the Celtic triad Brigit – Danu – Morrígan; the Greek goddess in her three aspects Persephone – Demeter – Hecate; or by the three Furies, Alecto (goddess of beginnings) – Tisiphone (goddess of continuation) – Megaera (goddess of death and rebirth), and these three-fold aspects are particularly emphasized by feminist Wicca groups in their development of "women's mysteries". As American neopagan Z. Budapest writes in her *Holy Book of Women's Mysteries*: "Images of the Mother Goddess, female principle of the universe and source of all life, abound...[for she is] the goddess of ten thousand names."

On a practical level, Wiccan ceremonies can involve spells of enchantment, invocations for healing, and initiations which lead a coven member from one grade of advancement to the next. Witches also conduct their own type of weddings known as "hand-fastings" – binding Wiccans for a specified time ranging from a year and a day to "eternity" – and also "wiccanings", the pagan counterpart of christenings. Coven members tend to become close friends and the group functions rather like a family, with the High Priestess and High Priest taking a caring, parental role over other members of the coven.

Witchcraft has frequently been confused in the popular imagination with black magic – that is to say, magic intended to cause harm to another person through injury, illness, or misfortune. However, this type of labelling is very misplaced and completely unfair. Most witches would regard their spiritual practices as a form of white magic – magic associated with healing, beneficial outcomes, and personal spiritual transformation. As Wisconsin-based Wiccan Selena Fox has put it: "We're working with the energies of the earth, and we're very much tuned into a love consciousness. We're seeking to do those kinds of things that religions around the world have as their essence, which is working with healing, working with love and working to achieve an inner balance." See also **Magic, White; Neopaganism.**

**Wiccan** A male or female practitioner of modern **witchcraft**, or Wicca.

**Wiccaning** In Wicca, the ritual blessing of a baby – the Wiccan equivalent of a baptism or christening. It does not commit the baby to follow the Wiccan path, which is an individual choice to be taken in adulthood.

**Wiccan Oath** See Oath, Wiccan.

**Wiccan Rede** In Wicca, a simple principle and statement of ethical conduct to which all Wiccans are asked to adhere: "And it harm none, do what you will."

**Widdershins** In Wicca, the act of moving in the opposite direction to that of the sun in a magical ritual. Widdershins is therefore anti-clockwise in the northern hemisphere and clockwise in the southern hemisphere. See also **Deosil.**

**Wier, Johannes** (1515–1588) Also called Wierius, a sixteenth-century German demonologist who chronicled the hierarchy of **hell** in his extraordinary work *Pseudomonarchia Daemonum.* Among the most prominent demons in Wier's compilation are **Beelzebub, Satan,** Euronymous, Moloch, **Pluto,** and **Baalberith.** Wier also listed **Proserpina** and **Astaroth** as arch-demonesses. Wier was a pupil and friend of the legendary occultist Cornelius Agrippa, and like him had a profound regard for magical cosmology.

**Wierius** See Wier, Johannes.

**Wilby, Basil** See Knight, Gareth.

**Will** In western **magic,** an important factor in the attainment of spiritual knowledge. Unlike eastern schools of devotional **mysticism,** which advocate the surrender of the ego to a higher spiritual reality, western magic emphasizes the will of the **magician** as the means of maintaining control over psychic and spiritual events. Acts of **invocation** and **evocation** are performed in such a way as to ensure the magician has control over the supernatural forces summoned.

**Will-o'-the wisp** A popular name for the flickering, ethereal light sometimes observed over graveyards, and tradition-ally associated with the spirits of the dead.

**Wilson, Monique** A Wiccan high priestess in the **coven** of **Gerald Gardner**. Wilson, known in magical circles as Lady Olwen, initiated **Raymond Buckland** into the **Craft** in 1964. It was Buckland who brought the Gardnerian tradition of modern witchcraft to the United States. Monique Wilson was one of the main beneficiaries of Gardner's estate and inherited Gardner's Witchcraft Museum in Castletown, on the Isle of Man, after Gardner's death in 1964.

**Wine Moon** See Esbats.

**Wireenum** Among the Aborigines of western New South Wales, a **medicine man** or **shaman**, who derives his magical powers from his contact with the great god **Baiame**.

**Wiringin** Among the Weilwan and Kamilaroi Aborigines, a **shaman** or **medicine man**, sometimes referred to simply as a "clever man".

**Wise Men, Three** See Magi.

**Wishing Well** A well where one makes an unspoken wish while dropping a coin into the well as a token offering. The **superstition** derives from the traditional folk belief that **spirits** or spirit beings resided in wells and could make wishes come true through their magic powers.

**Witch** A practitioner of **witchcraft**; one who has been initiated as a member of a **coven**. The term is more commonly used to describe female practitioners, but can also be used for males. A male witch is also known as a **warlock**. See also **Wicca**.

**Witch Balls** Glass balls hung in the home to avert harmful influences, especially those attributed to the **evil eye**. See also **Magic, Preventive**; **Spell**.

**Witchcraft** A term used to refer to both "modern witchcraft" – the magical and neopagan practices of modern revival movements such as **Wicca** – and its traditional European antecedents ("traditional witchcraft"). It is also used to refer to practices in pre-literate and tribal societies in which, for example, spells, enchantments, and evocations are used to cure disease and ward off evil influences. See **Medicine Man**; **Nature Worship**; **Neopaganism**; **Shaman**; **Witchcraft, Modern**; **Witchcraft, Traditional**; **Witch Doctor**.

**Witchcraft as a Science** A branch of Wicca established in the United States in 1955 by **Craft** initiate Laurie Cabot. Cabot, who is based in Salem, Massachusetts, maintains that witchcraft can be considered a science as well as a spiritual path and that it may be used to develop psychic potential. Focusing on the ethics of the **Wiccan Rede** as a moral philosophy, Cabot's approach to Wicca is eclectic and draws on **astrology**, anthropology, parapsychology, and the healing arts as well as traditional Craft teachings.

**Witchcraft, Modern** A neopagan movement strongly influenced by such figures as **Gerald Gardner, Alex Sanders, Doreen Valiente, Z. Budapest**, and **Starhawk**. Witchcraft is the worship of the "**Old Religion**", and focuses primarily on the **Great Goddess** in her many forms: **Aphrodite, Artemis, Astarte, Diana, Hecate** and so on. As such, it draws on many of the ancient pantheons, differing from modern western **magic** primarily in its emphasis on **lunar goddesses** rather than **solar gods**. In modern witchcraft, the women rather than the men play the paramount role; and members of the **coven** regularly meet at sabbaths to perform seasonal rituals. Witches perform rituals dressed in ceremonial regalia or "sky clad" (naked). These rituals invariably involve the invocation of the Goddess in one of her forms: and the ceremony of "**drawing down the moon**", in which the lunar energy is drawn into the body of the **high priestess** within the magic circle. See also **Wicca**.

**Witchcraft Persecution** See Burning Times.

**Witchcraft, Traditional** A medieval religious movement often – incorrectly – identified with **devil worship, satanism,** and black magic. Today, traditional witchcraft is regarded by most authorities as a folk religion that blended **superstition, fortune telling,** folklore, and **herbalism** with remnants of various pre-Christian religious beliefs (e.g. of the Celts and Druids). Witchcraft actually has more in common with the many forms of **nature worship** and fertility rituals found in pre-industrial societies, than with the diabolical and satanic practices of black magicians, whose main antagonist is the Christian Church. Nevertheless, in the Middle Ages most categories of **heathen, pagan,** and **heretic** were combined and uniformly persecuted by the Inquisition. The notorious book *Malleus Maleficarum* describes the persecutions meted out to medieval witches; and such figures as **Matthew Hopkins** and the officials engaged in the trials of the **Salem witches** characterize the ferocity of witchcraft persecutions prior to the modern era.

**Witch Doctor** In pre-literate societies, a practitioner of **magic** and **witchcraft** who uses his knowledge of spells, enchantments, and evocations to cure disease and ward off evil influences. Witch doctors are found in many primitive cultures in Africa, Australia, Melanesia, Polynesia, South and Central America, and Haiti. See also **Medicine Man; Shaman; Soul Loss.**

**Witches, Aberdeen** See Aberdeen Witches.

**Witches, Alexandrian** See Alexandrian Witches.

**Witches' Coven** See Coven.

**Witches, Dianic** See Dianic Witches.

**Witches, Gardnerian** See Gardnerian Witches.

**Witches' Sabbath** A meeting of a witches' coven, held in order to perform magical rites and ceremonies. The traditional witches' sabbath – which belongs more to folklore and popular imagination than to history – brought together a large number of witches and warlocks who would gather around a bonfire or cauldron, light black candles, and perform sacrifices. The goat-headed god (often confused with the Christian **Devil**) would be present, seated on a throne, and the sabbath would culminate in a sexual orgy. It now seems that these fantasies derive in part from visionary episodes brought on by **flying ointments,** psychedelic mixtures that cause sensations of flying and vivid sexual hallucinations. The modern witches' sabbath – more commonly spelt "sabbat" – is held at specific times of the year that mark transitions in the seasons. The main sabbats are **All Hallows' Eve** or Halloween (31 October), which represents the end of autumn and the beginning of winter, **Imbolc** (2 February), the first signs of spring; **Beltane** (30 April), an important celebration of fertility and **Lammas** (1 August), the beginning of the harvest. See **Wheel of the Year.**

**Witches, Salem** See Salem Witches.

**Witches' Tools** In Wicca, the tools used in rituals. They include the **sword,** the **athame,** the dagger, the **cup** or **chalice,** the **wand,** the **thurible** or **censer,** the **pentacle** or **disc,** the **candelabra,** the **scourge,** the altar cloth, ritual cords, the **besom** or **broomstick,** and the **cauldron.**

**Witches, Traditional** See Traditional Witches.

**Witch Finder** See Matthew Hopkins.

**Witch Hunt** The relentless persecution of witches was a characteristic of the Inquisition, and is described in the treatise *Malleus Maleficarum* (*The Hammer of the Witches*). Witch hunts were also conducted in England, most notoriously by the self-styled "Witch Finder General", Matthew Hopkins, in the 1640s; and at Salem, Massachusetts, in 1692 among the Puritan community. See also **Burning Times; Salem Witches.**

**Witching Hour** In Wicca, the hour of midnight on the night of the full moon, a time when the magical powers of the witch are at their peak.

**Witch Queen** In Wicca, a high priestess who has had at least two covens hive off from her orginal coven. See Hiving Off.

**Witch's Cup** A chalice used in witchcraft during the preparation of special philtres, and also to drink conse-crated wine. It usually takes the form of a goblet made of polished metal or horn.

**Witch's Hat** A black conical hat with a wide brim, associated primarily with modern caricatures of medieval witches. Most contemporary practitioners of Wicca and **neopaganism** are bareheaded in their rituals although the **high priestess** and **high priest** in a coven may sometimes wear ceremonial crowns or headbands representing the **Great Goddess** and **Horned God** respectively.

**Witch's Ladder** In Wicca, either a string of 40 beads or a cord with 40 knots, used rather like a Roman Catholic rosary as an aid to concentration.

**Witch's Mark** Additional protuberances – breasts, or nipples – upon the body of an accused witch, regarded by persecu-tors and Inquisitors as evidence that the witch was suckling a **familiar.**

**Witch's Rune** In Wicca, a chant to raise energy, accompanied by a ring dance in the **deosil** direction. The Witch's Rune that commences with the lines *Eko, Eko, Azarak, Eko, Eko, Zomelak* and which is used by both **Gardnerian witches** and **Alexandrian witches,** was written jointly by **Gerald Gardner** and **Doreen Valiente.** See also **Circle.**

**Withershins** See Widdershins.

**Wizard** From the Old English *wis,* meaning "wise", a sage, **adept,** or magician skilled in summoning super-natural powers. The most famous wizard in occult tradition is the legendary Merlin. See also **Sorcerer; Warlock.**

**Woden** See Odin, Wotan.

**Wolfbane** See Monkshood.

**Womb** In alchemy, an image used to describe the **alembic,** the beaked vessel used as part of the distillation apparatus. The stone was originally "conceived" in the alembic and like a child required protection and warmth.

**Woodharrow Institute** See Flowers, Stephen Edred.

**Woodman, Dr William Robert** (1828–1891) English Freemason and Rosicrucian who, with **Dr Wynn Westcott** and MacGregor Mathers, founded the influential magical group, the Hermetic Order of the Golden Dawn. Woodman was apparently a knowledgeable Hebrew scholar and an accomplished kabbalist, and many of his writings were said to be in the secret archive of the Second Order or **Ordo Rosae Rubeae at Aureae Crucis.** However, none of these works has ever been published and Woodman remains something of an enigmatic figure in occult history. See also **Freemasonry; Rosicrucians.**

**Word of the New Aeon** See Abrahadabra.

**Words of Power** Magical conjurations and invocations used in rituals and ceremonies for a specific result: to confer power upon the magician, to banish evil and darkness, or – in the case of the Egyptian sun god – to ensure safe passage through the dungeons of the Tuat. In western **magic,** words of power are usually Hebrew **god-names,** deriving

WITCHES' SABBATH   Etching by Albrecht Durer (c.1501) showing a witch riding on a
goat on her way to the Sabbath.

in the main from the **Kabbalah**. See also **Hekau**; **Magical Formulae**.

**Working** In Wicca, a magical ritual.

**Worlds, Four** See Four Worlds.

**World Soul** A theosophical concept of the immanent **godhead**, which structures and organizes the universe and provides it with vitality and purpose. See also **Neoplatonism**.

**World Tree** In **shamanism**, the axis which unites the upper and lower worlds with "Middle Earth". The shaman makes a trance journey to its upper branches, or ventures down through its roots to the lower world, in order to contact the gods and ancestor **spirits**. The symbol of the Tree occurs in several cosmologies. Notable examples include **Yggdrasil** in Scandinavian mythology and the **Tree of Life** in the **Kabbalah**. See also **Axis Mundi**; **Journey of the Soul**.

**World, The** In the **Tarot**, a card of the Major Arcana that shows a maiden dancing in a wreath of wheat grains. The card is reminiscent of the mythology of the Greek goddess **Persephone**, and represents the descent into the **Underworld** of the unconscious **psyche**. Persephone symbolized the wheat grain; but after her abduction by **Hades**, she also became queen of the Underworld. She thus came to represent both life and death and was an important figure in the **Mysteries of Eleusis**. The figure on *The World* appears to be feminine, but her genitals are hidden – she is in fact androgynous – reflecting the harmonizing or uniting aspects of the **Middle Pillar** on the kabbalistic **Tree of Life**. She is the personification of the **Shekhinah**, and the first "path" into the unconscious. In western **magic**, *The World* is regarded as a major initiatory path linking **Malkuth** and **Yesod** and also representing **Kether** on a lower plane: "as above, so below." See **Kabbalah**; **Macrocosm and Microcosm**.

**Wort Moon** See Esbats.

**Wotan** or **Wodan** The early Germanic predecessor of the Scandinavian god **Odin**. He was known as Woden by the pagan Anglo-Saxons, and Wednesday is named after him.

**Wraith** An **apparition**, of either a person who has recently died or one who is about to die.

**Wunjo** See Wyn.

**Wyn** In the Germanic **Elder Futhark**, the **rune** letter representing the number eight. Wyn corresponds to the letter "w" and is the rune of joy, happiness, and glory. From the runic viewpoint, happiness arises whenever hardship, tragedy, and sorrow are absent and we should learn to recognize those precious moments. Happiness can make us strong and bonds us with our friends and family.

**Wyrd** In ancient Anglo-Saxon **sorcery**, a way of being in which the universe was believed to fluctuate between the mystical polarities of fire and frost – a western magical equivalent of the Taoist concept of **yin** and **yang**. Everything within the Anglo-Saxon universe was regarded as interconnected, linked by a network of fibres like strands in a spider's web. This network of fibres allowed the **sorcerer** to access all aspects of the manifest universe through his ability to manipulate the life force.

**Wyvern** or **Wivern** In folk legend and heraldry, a flying serpent, resembling a **dragon**, with eagle's legs and a barbed tail.

# X

**Xangô** or **Shango** In Macumba, the god of thunder. Many practitioners of Macumba in Brazil identify Xangô with St Jerome, and he also bears resemblance to Thor and Jupiter. Devotees worship Xangô on Wednesdays and offer him dishes made from tortoise, goat, and cockerel.

**Xapáaliia** A term used by the Crow Indians to refer to sacred power objects, including all the objects stored by the shaman in his **medicine bag**. These include sacred stones, eagle feathers and objects used in healing ceremonies.

**Xatáùl** A term used by the Navajo Indians of the American southwest to refer specifically to ceremonies where healing chants are accompanied by rattles.

**Xeper** In the **Temple of Set**, the magical word of the New Aeon. Pronounced *khefer* and translated as "I have come into being", its associated symbols were the **scarab** beetle and the dawning sun. In a statement exploring the significance of xeper, Temple spokesman Don Webb has written that this word "generates the Aeon of Set, and is the current form of the Eternal Word of the Prince of Darkness". Webb describes xeper as "the experience of an individual psyche becoming aware of its own existence and deciding to expand and evolve that existence through its own actions".

**Xerion** An ancient Greek word meaning "dry powder for wounds". It was subsequently adopted into Arabic as *el-ixir*, from which the word **elixir** derives.

**Xibalba** Among the Maya of Central America, the **Underworld** land of the dead.

**Xiuhtecutli** The Aztec god of fire and ruler of the sun. In Aztec rituals, live sacrificial victims were cast into flames as an offering to him.

**Xoloti** In the Aztec pantheon, the twin of **Quetzalcoatl** and the patron god of magicians. He personified the planet **Venus** as the Evening Star, while Quetzalcoatl personified Venus as the Morning Star.

**Xudam** An Etruscan god, subsequently identified with the Roman Mercury.

**Xylomancy** A form of **divination**, of Slavic origin. The position and shape of dry pieces of wood found in one's path are interpreted for omens.

# Y

**Yagé** See Banisteriopsis.

**Yahweh** The God of Israel, whose name, written with the four letters YHVH, is regarded by devout Jews as too sacred to be pronounced. Yahweh guided Moses, and the Israelites believed he had made a special covenant with them, elevating them to the status of an elect people. Yahweh was considered the creator of the world and became identified among the Christians with the divine Father who had given his only son, Jesus Christ, as a redeemer to the world.

**Yaje** See Banisteriopsis.

**Yang** In Chinese esoteric tradition, the aspect of the universal life force – *ch'i* – which is active, positive, and "masculine". It is outward-looking in emphasis and radiates light in all directions. As such, it is the dynamic opposite of Yin. Yang embraces heaven, fire, and summer.

**Yaô** In Macumba, a recently initiated medium or "bride of the gods".

**Yasna** In Zoroastrianism, one of the three divisions of the sacred text known as the *Avesta*. It consists of 72 chapters and includes the hymns and songs known collectively as the *Gathas*.

**Yeats, William Butler** (1865–1939) The great Irish poet who, in his early 20s, became attracted to Theosophy and esoteric thought. He was a friend of mystical writer George Russell (better known as "A.E."), became a member of the Dublin Hermetic Society, and later made contact with Madame Helena Blavatsky, G.R.S. Mead, and MacGregor Mathers in London. Yeats became a member of the Isis-Urania Lodge of the Hermetic Order of the Golden Dawn in 1890, taking the magical name Daemon est Deus Inversus – "the Devil is the Reverse Side of God". When Mathers retired to Paris to translate occult manuscripts, Yeats became head of the order and soon afterwards had to ward off an attempt to challenge his authority from Aleister Crowley, who was keen to attain high magical office. In 1905, Yeats resigned from the order, together with his friend Arthur Machen and founder member Wynn Westcott. Yeats's experience of ceremonial magic and the visionary symbols of the Tarot nevertheless continued to influence his creative writing and he often incorporated Tarot images into his verse. As Kenneth and Steffi Grant wrote in their Carfax Monographs: "It was the Golden Dawn that taught Yeats to consolidate his visions and to create a magical vehicle that would carry his ambition towards name and fame." Yeats's international reputation as a poet was acknowledged when he was awarded the Nobel Prize for Literature in 1923.

**Yechidah** In the Jewish mystical tradition, union with the absolute. See also Ain Soph Aur.

**Yei** A term used by the Navajo Indians of the American southwest to refer to a specific class of spirits who feature in Navajo ceremonies and who are often represented by costumed dancers. Yei spirits are also represented in Navajo sand paintings. During a healing ceremony, a patient may have to walk around on a yei sand-painting in order to re-establish contact with the sacred forces guiding everyday life.

**Yemanja** See Iemanjá.

**Yeramayá** See Oddudúa.

**Yerba Maté** See Maté

**Yesod** The ninth emanation or sephirah on the kabbalistic Tree of Life. In western magic, Yesod is associated with the moon and the element water. Regarded as a female sphere, it is the seat of the sexual instinct and corresponds to the genital chakra on the archytypal man, Adam Kadmon. On the Tree of Life, Yesod has the function of channelling the energies of the higher planes down to the earth below (Malkuth). Occultists associated Yesod with the astral plane, because if the sephiroth above Malkuth are collectively regarded as a map of the unconscious psyche, Yesod is the most accessible area of the mind. There is no doubt that it was the aspect of the psyche first explored in psychoanalysis and it remains the key energy – nexus in Freudian thought. Because Yesod is the sphere of fertility and lunar imagery, it is identified with witchcraft and goddess worship. It is also the seat of the so-called "animal soul" known by the kabbalists as Nephesch. See also Kabbalah.

**Yetzirah** In the Kabbalah, the world of formation contains the sephiroth Chesed, Geburah, Tiphareth, Netzach, Hod, and Yesod. Yesod literally provides the "foundation" for all that has preceded it in the process of sacred emanation from the highest realms. Yetzirah is also the domain of ten divisions of angels, who are collectively ruled by the archangel Metatron. The orders of angels are as follows: Malachim, Arelim, Chajoth, Ophanim, Chashmalim, Elim, Elohim, Benei, Ishim, and Seraphim. See also Assiah; Atziluth; Briah; Four Worlds.

**Yezid** According to tantric magician Kenneth Grant, Yezid was a high priest among worshippers of Shaitan in ancient Sumer, and Aleister Crowley was an avatar, or incarnation, of this high priest. Grant maintains that Crowley fulfilled a prophecy made by Yezid when he received *The Book of the Law* from Aiwaz in Egypt in 1904.

**Yfrit** See Efreet.

**Yggdrasil** In Scandinavian mythology, the World Tree, a sacred ash tree which overshadowed the entire universe; its roots, branches, and trunk united

heaven, earth, and the nether regions. The roots of Yggdrasil lay in Hel, while the trunk ascended through Midgard – the earth. Rising through the mountain known as Asgard, it branched into the sky – its leaves were the clouds in the sky, and its fruit were the stars.

**YHVH** In Judaism, one rendering of the four-letter sacred name of God – the Tetragrammaton – vocalized, for example, as Yahweh and Jehovah. This sacred name was not pronounced and was often substituted by such lesser godnames as Adonai or Shaddai. YHVH is also written JHVH, IHVH, and YHWH.

**Yichud** In the Jewish mystical tradition, a meditation exercise utlilizing mental visualization and the ten sephiroth on the Tree of Life. This technique was developed by the sixteenth-century kabbalists in Safed.

**Yin** In Chinese esoteric tradition, that aspect of the universal life force – *ch'i* – which is passive, negative, and "feminine". It is inward-looking in emphasis and dark rather than bright. As such, it is the dynamic opposite of Yang. Yin embraces earth, moon, water, and winter.

**Yliaster** A term coined by the medieval alchemist Paracelsus with reference to the prima materia. It consisted of both body and soul but also contained all the "chaos" which existed prior to creation. Only later – with the blessing of the "supreme master" – did this "first body" or prime matter give rise to minerals, fluids, herbs, stones, and gems.

**Ymir** In Scandinavian mythology, a giant whose body formed in the mists of Niflheim when the universe was born, and who subsequently became the ancestor of the other giants. The earth, heavens, and sea formed his body; and after his defeat at the hands of Odin, the world tree Yggdrasil emerged from his body.

YHVH   The 72 sacred names of Yahweh, God of Israel.

**Yod** The Hebrew letter ascribed to the path linking **Tiphareth** and **Chesed** on the kabbalistic **Tree of Life**. Yod has a numerical value of ten. In modern magical visualization and **pathworkings**, the Tarot card associated with this path on the Tree is *The Hermit*.

**Yohimbé** *Corynanthe yohimbe*, a tree whose bark is used by African black magicians and fetish priests to brew love potions. These drinks are consumed as an aphrodisiac and to promote potency. Yohimbé is sometimes combined with **Iboga** during magical initiations.

**Yoni** The Hindu term for the vulva. In tantra, the phallic pillar, or lingam, and yoni symbolize the divine creative and generative powers and the fusion of male and female polarities in the universe. The yoni is often portrayed in art and sculpture as a stone circle, sometimes with the lingam rising from it.

**Yud** See Yod.

**Yule** A Wiccan sabbat celebrating the winter solstice held around 21–22 December to celebrate the death and rebirth of the sun god. The term Yule is thought to derive from the Norse word *Iul*, meaning "a wheel". Yule is one of the four so-called Lesser Sabbats, the others being celebrated at the summer solstice and on the dates of the spring and autumn equinoxes. See **Sabbats, Lesser**.

# Z

**Zaa** In Enochian magic, the 27th Aethyr. The meanings associated with Zaa include solitude, loneliness, separation, isolation, and emptiness. It is associated with **Leo** and **Taurus** and its magical number is 21.

**Zaddik** In the Jewish mystical tradition, the spiritual leader of a community who serves as an intermediary between the people and the world of the divine. The term translates as "pious one".

**Zagan** In the **Goetia**, the 61st spirit, a great king and president who appears at first in the form of a bull with **griffin's** wings and then assumes a human shape. Zagan is able to make men witty and fools wise. He can turn water into wine, blood into wine, and wine into water and he can also change any metal into the coins of the realm. Zagan governs 33 legions of spirits.

**Zain** The Hebrew letter ascribed to the path linking **Binah** and **Tiphareth** on the kabbalistic **Tree of Life**. Zain has a numerical value of seven. In modern magical visualization and **pathworkings**, the **Tarot** card associated with this path on the Tree is *The Lovers*.

**Zain, C.C.** (1882–1951) The pseudonym of Elbert Benjamin, who founded the First Temple of Astrology in the United States. This later became the Church of Light, an organization that offers courses on different aspects of the occult tradition. Zain maintained that he had been contacted by "The Brotherhood of Light" in 1909 and was instructed by secret adepts to prepare a complete occult system for teaching the religion of **astrology**. Zain also wrote a large book on the **Tarot**, which linked the symbolism to both the **Kabbalah** and ancient Egyptian symbolism (*The Sacred Tarot*, reissued Los Angeles, 1969).

**Zakhor** In the Kabbalah, the practice of repeating the sacred names of God. See also **God-Name**.

**Zarathustra** (c. 600BCE) In Greek, Zoroaster. A Persian prophet and founder of Zoroastrianism. At the age of fifteen he is said to have retreated to a mountain cave and had a vision of **Ahura Mazdah** (Ohrmazd) – the supreme being. Thereafter, he endeavoured to preach the gospel of the one god who overcomes evil. After a period of wandering through what is now Persia and Afghanistan and experiencing many mystical visions, Zarathustra gained only one convert, his cousin. However, he was given an audience with King Vishtaspa who requested a miracle as proof of his spiritual teachings. Zarathustra produced heavenly fire that could not be extinguished, but which nevertheless burned those who came near; and the king agreed to let the prophet stay at his court. Zarathustra subsequently earned considerable influence with the royal family and the king began to spread the faith, building fire temples for the worship of Ahura Mazdah.

Zarathustra divided the world into the Followers of Truth (Asha) and the Followers of the Lie (Druj). Although Ahura Mazdah transcended this division, the seeds were thereby sown for the dualistic thought that characterized later Zoroastrianism. Unlike **Gnosticism**, which held that the material world was evil, Zarathustra believed that the world was intrinsically good, because it had been created by Ahura Mazdah, but had since been corrupted by the Devil (**Ahriman**). People essentially had a choice of serving the two masters; fate in the afterworld was determined accordingly. Zarathustra is said to have written the *Gathas* – teachings which form part of the *Avesta*. The religion of Zoroastrianism survives among the Parsees.

**Zax** In **Enochian magic**, the tenth Aethyr – the so-called "accursed" Aethyr linked to the powerful demon of chaos,

Choronzon. The meanings associated with Zax include confusion, incoherence, madness, and insanity. Zax is associated with Caput Draconis, Taurus, and earth and its magical number is 415.

**Zayin** See Zain.

**Zelator** In the Hermetic Order of the Golden Dawn, the initiatory grade of ceremonial **magic** associated with the sphere of **Malkuth** on the kabbalistic Tree of Life. See also **Adeptus Minor**.

**Zell, Morning Glory** (1948– ) A noted American Goddess priestess and **neopagan**, Morning Glory Zell was born Diana Moore in Long Beach, California, and is of mixed Irish and Choctaw descent. After rejecting Christianity she explored Buddhism and Vedanta but then read a work by the English witch **Sybil Leek** which led her to believe that she too was a **witch**. After a **vision quest** in Big Sur, Zell initiated herself into the **Craft**. She changed her name to Morning Glory soon afterwards. Zell met her future husband Tim at the 1973 Gnosticon Aquarian festival in St Paul, Minnesota, and they both recognized each other as **soul mates**. They married the following year. In 1974 she became co-editor of the Church of All Worlds magazine *Green Egg* and in 1988 vice-president of the Church itself. Now known as Morning Glory Zell-Ravenheart, she is renowned for her fantasy fiction and her sculptures of ancient gods and goddesses.

**Zell, Otter** (1942– ) An influential American **neopagan**, Tim Zell (later, Otter Zell, later still Oberon Zell-Ravenheart) enrolled at Westminster Fulton College in St Louis, Missouri and it was here, in the early 1960s, that he met Richard Lance Christie. Their association led eventually to the establishment of the Church of All Worlds, one of the most important neopagan organizations in the United States. Zell and Christie originally established Atl – a group named after the

Aztec word for water – and the Church of All Worlds grew out of this. Formally chartered in 1968, the Church of All Worlds became the first neopagan establishment to be recognized in the United States as a church. In 1976 Zell undertook a mystical **vision quest** in the wilderness that had a profound impact on him and led to him becoming a self-initiated priest of **Gaea**. Zell married Morning Glory, his second wife, in 1974, and since 1988 they have co-edited the leading neopagan magazine *Green Egg*. Zell works as a sculptor and writer and now refers to himself as Oberon Zell-Ravenheart. He and Morning Glory live in northern California.

**Zell-Ravenheart, Morning Glory** See Zell, Morning Glory.

**Zell-Ravenheart, Oberon** See Zell, Otter.

**Zen** In Enochian magic, the eighteenth Aethyr. The meanings associated with Zen include sacrifice, crucifixion, and selfessness. It is associated with **Leo**, **Virgo**, and **Scorpio** and its magical number is 69.

**Zend-Avesta** The sacred writings of the Zoroastrians. Strictly, the *Avesta* is the body of texts, and the *Zend* is its translation and interpretation in Pahlavi.

**Zenith** In **astrology**, the "pole of the horizontal", or the point directly overhead. The closer a planet is to the zenith of a given position, the stronger is its influence.

**Zepar** In the Goetia, the sixteenth spirit, a great duke who appears wearing red apparel and armour. Zepar can bring women and men together in love but he can also make women barren. He governs 26 legions of spirits.

**Zephyr** In alchemy, a word used to describe the mercurial vapour which rose in the **alembic** during the **distillation** process. See also **Mercurius**.

**Zeus** In Greek mythology, the most powerful of the gods and ruler of heaven and earth. The son of **Kronos** and **Rhea**, Zeus had seven wives and numerous romances. He was capable of changing into different forms – a satyr, a white bull, a swan, a shower of gold – and became known as "the Father of Gods and Men". Zeus hurled the thunderbolts that caused storms and death, and was therefore also called "the Cloud-Gatherer". The oak tree and eagle were sacred to him. See also **Jove**; **Jupiter**.

**Zid** In Enochian magic, the eighth Aethyr. The meanings associated with Zid include truth, identity, reality, and sexual masculinity. Zid is associated with **Leo**, **Sagittarius**, and the element **spirit** and its magical number is 73.

**Zim** In Enochian magic, the thirteenth Aethyr. The meanings associated with Zim include service, duty, love, compassion, responsibility, and dedication to duty. Zim is associated with **Leo**, **Sagittarius**, and **Aquarius** and its magical number is 159.

**Zip** In Enochian magic, the ninth Aethyr. The meanings associated with Zip include bliss, ecstasy, and youthful feminity. Zip is associated with **Leo** and **Sagittarius** and its magical number is 78.

**Zivo** According to tantric magician Kenneth Grant, a corrupt form of **Oviz**, the god worshipped in ancient Sumer and identical with **Set** or **Shaitan**. Grant also equates Oviz with the Thelemite entity **Aiwaz** whom **Aleister Crowley** claimed as his Guardian Angel and who provided the inspirational basis for *The Book of the Law*. See also **Thelema**.

**Zoanthropy** From the Greek *zoon*, "an animal", the belief that a human being can transform into an animal, acquiring its characteristics. See also **Lycanthropy**; **Shape-Shifting**; **Werewolf**.

**Zodiac** In astrology, the twelve-fold division of the sky into signs. Zodiac means "circle of animals" and refers to the symbols of the twelve constellations. The so-called "northern" signs are the first six signs of the zodiac: **Aries, Taurus, Gemini, Cancer, Leo**, and **Virgo**; the "southern" signs are the remaining six: **Libra, Scorpio, Sagittarius, Capricorn, Aquarius**, and **Pisces**. The positions of each of the planets at birth is mapped in the chart of the heavens or **horoscope**, and significant aspects evaluated. The sign of the zodiac under which one is born is known as the **sun sign**, and it is regarded as a dominant factor in determining one's character and personal make-up.

**Zohar, The** More exactly, *Sepher Ha-Zohar, (The Book of Splendor)*, the principal work of the **Kabbalah**. It is thought to have been written by the Spanish mystic **Moses de León** and first circulated from his home in Guadalajara between 1280 and 1290. It includes commentaries on the **Torah**; a work titled *The Book of Concealment*; an account of the seven heavenly halls of God's chariot-throne (the **Merkabah**); and a commentary on *The Song of Songs*.

**Zombi Cadavre** In Haitian voodoo, a "zombie of the flesh", who can be put to work.

**Zombie** Among **voodoo** practitioners, especially in Haiti, a corpse that has allegedly been brought back to life through magical spells of enchantment. The zombie is said to act like a robot, and can be employed by its master in menial tasks of labour, having only negligible intelligence and no will of its own. According to folk belief, if zombies eat salt they are awakened from their condition of being "living dead" and hasten back to their graveyards to bury themselves in the earth. Belief in zombies is also found in the Caribbean and parts of West Africa.

**Zon** In Enochian magic, the third **Aethyr**. The meanings associated with Zon include creativity, control, and

mastery. Zon is associated with **Leo, Libra**, and **Scorpio** and its magical number is 129.

**Zoroaster** See Zarathustra.

**Zoroastrianism** The doctrines and teachings of **Zarathustra**, the Persian prophet known to the Greeks as Zoroaster.

**Zoroastrians** Followers of the prophet Zarathustra (Zoroaster). When Persia was conquered by the Arabs in 650CE, the majority of Zoroastrians fled to India and their descendants are now found mainly in the state of Bombay, where they number around 100,000. Zoroastrians are now known as Parsees and they continue their practice of praying to the sun as a symbol of life, commencing each day with a fire-worshipping ceremony.

**Zosimos** An early Egyptian alchemist and Gnostic philosopher from Panopolis (Akhmim) who lived in Alexandria c.300CE, compiled an alchemical encyclopedia consisting of 28 books – some fragments of which survive – and who documented a remarkable series of alchemical visions. In a work titled *On Virtue*, he describes how he fell asleep while reciting alchemical formulae. In his visions, some of which were very frightening, he experienced the themes of death and transformation found in medieval **alchemy** and came to understand that the alchemical process referred not only to the transmutation of metals but to the spiritual renewal of man himself.

**Zos Kia Cultus** The term used by English trance magician and visionary artist **Austin Osman Spare** to refer to the cult practice of **atavistic resurgence**. Devotees were required to accept Spare's *Book Of Pleasure* as their sacred book and were called to embrace the "path of ecstasy" as their magical path. They also had to acknowledge as their principal deity "The All-Prevailing Woman" ("And

I strayed with her, into the path·
direct…"). The principles of the Zos Kia
Cultus are contained in a document
titled the *Affirmation Creed of Zos vel
Thanatos*.

**Zostrianos** The title of the longest text
in the Gnostic **Nag Hammadi library**.
The author of the text is unknown but
must have lived prior to 268CE because
his writings were known to **Plotinus**.

**Zos vel Thanatos** The magical name of
the visionary English occultist and artist
**Austin Osman Spare**. He sometimes
referred to himself simply as Zos but also
used this shortened form to refer to the
body as a receptacle for the primal
energies of **Kia**.

**Zurvan** or **Zervan** A Persian god of
time who was the father of both **Ahura
Mazdah** and **Angra Mainyu** – personifications of good and evil respectively. In
Persian cosmology, time was measured
by the path of the sun, and this was
symbolized on statues of Zurvan by a
snake coiled around his body. Zurvan
·may derive from the Indian sky god
**Varuna**; he in turn contributed to the
symbolism of the Basilidean high god
**Abraxas**, who had serpentine coils
instead of legs. Zurvan was known as
**Aion** by the Neoplatonists. See also
**Basilides; Gnosticism; Neoplatonism.**

# Further Reading

Aaronson, B., and Osmond, H., *Psychedelics*, Doubleday Anchor, New York 1970

Abraham the Jew, *The Sacred Magic of Abra-Melin the Mage*, (trs. S.M. Mathers) De Laurence, Chicago 1932

Abraham, L., *A Dictionary of Alchemical Imagery*, Cambridge University Press, Cambridge 1998

Adams, A. and M., *The Learned Arts of Witches and Wizards*, Lansdowne, Sydney 1998

Adler, M., *Drawing Down the Moon*, Beacon Press, Boston 1988

Alvarado, L., *Psychology, Astrology and Western Magic: Image and Myth in Self-Discovery*, Llewellyn, St Paul, Minnesota 1991

Andrews, T., *Animal-Speak*, Llewellyn, St Paul, Minnesota 1993

*How to Meet and Work with Spirit Guides*, Llewellyn, St Paul, Minnesota 1992

*More Simplified Magic: Pathworkings and the Tree of Life*, Dragonhawk Publishing, Jackson, Tennessee 1998

*Simplified Qabala Magic*, Llewellyn, St Paul, Minnesota 2003

Aquino, M., *The Crystal Tablet of Set*, Temple of Set, San Francisco 1983

Ashcroft-Nowicki, D., *Highways of the Mind: The Art and History of Pathworking*, Aquarian Press, Wellingborough, England 1987

*The Shining Paths: An Experiential Journey through the Tree of Life*, Aquarian Press, Wellingborough, England 1983

Baker, A., *The Wizard: A Secret History*, Ebury, London 2003

Bardon, F., *The Practice of Magical Evocation*, Rudolf Pravica, Graz-Puntigam, Austria 1967

Barnstone, W. (ed.), *The Other Bible*, Harper & Row, San Francisco 1984

Barton, B., *The Secret Life of a Satanist*, Feral House, Los Angeles 1990

Bates, B., *The Way of Wyrd*, Century, London 1983

Best, M.R., and Brightman, F.H., *The Book of Secrets of Albertus Magnus*, Oxford University Press, New York 1973

Blacker, C., *The Catalpa Bow*, Allen & Unwin, London 1975

Bonner, J., *Qabalah*, Skoob Publishing, London 1995

Bracelin, J.L., *Gerald Gardner: Witch*, Octagon Press, London 1960

Bramly, S., *Macumba: The Teachings of Maria-José, Mother of the Gods*, St Martins Press, New York 1977

Buckland, R., *Witch Book: The Encyclopedia of Witchcraft, Wicca, and Neopaganism*, Visible Ink, Detroit 2001

*Buckland's Complete Book of Witchcraft*, Llewellyn, St Paul, Minnesota 1986

*Signs, Symbols, and Omens*, Llewellyn, St Paul, Minnesota 1988

Budapest, Z., *The Holy Book of Women's Mysteries*, Wingbow Press, Los Angeles, 1989

Budge, E.A. Wallis (ed.), *Lefefa Sedek: The Bandlet of Righteousness*, Luzac, London 1929

Buhner, S. H., *Sacred Plant Medicine*, Roberts Rinehart, Boulder. Colorado 1996

Burckhardt, T., *Alchemy*, Penguin Books, Baltimore 1971

Burkert, W., *Ancient Mystery Cults*, Harvard University Press, Cambridge, Mass. 1987

Burland, C.A., *The Arts of the Alchemists*, Weidenfeld & Nicolson, London 1967

Butler, W.E., *Magic and the Qabalah*, Aquarian Press, London 1964

Canizares, R., *Cuban Santería*, Destiny Books, Rochester, Vermont 1999

Case, P.F., *The Tarot*, Macoy Publishing Co., New York 1947

Castañeda, C., *The Teachings of Don Juan,* University of Caifornia Press, Berkeley 1968

Cavendish, R., *The Tarot*, Michael Joseph, London 1975

Christ, C.P., and Plaskow, J., (ed.), *Womanspirit Rising*, Harper & Row, San Francisco 1979

Churton, T., *The Gnostics*, Weidenfeld & Nicolson, London 1987

Colquhoun, I., *Sword of Wisdom*, Spearman, London 1975

Cooper, D.J., *Using the Runes*, Aquarian Press, Wellingborough, UK 1987

Couliano, I.P., *The Tree of Gnosis*, HarperCollins, San Francisco 1992

Crowley, A., *The Vision and the Voice*, Sangreal Foundation, Dallas 1972

*Magick in Theory and Practice*, Castle Books, New York (no date)

*Book Four* Sangreal Publishing, Dallas Texas 1972

*The Book of Thoth*, Weiser, New York 1969

Crowley, V., *Wicca: The Old Religion in the New Millennium*, Thorsons, London 1996

Crowther, P., *Lid off the Cauldron*, Muller, London 1981

Culling, L.T., *Sex Magick*, Llewellyn, St Paul, Minnesota 1988

Davis, W., *The Serpent and the Rainbow*, Simon and Schuster, New York 1985

Decker, R., Depaulis, T., and Dummett, M., *A Wicked Pack of Cards: The Origins of the Occult Tarot*, St Martin's Press, New York 1996

Deren, M., *Divine Horsemen: The Voodoo Gods of Haiti*, Thames & Hudson, London 1953

Dobkin de Rios, M., *Visionary Vine: Psychedelic Healing in the Peruvian Amazon*, Chandler, San Francisco 1972

Drury, N., *Magic and Witchcraft: From Shamanism to the Technopagans*, Thames & Hudson, London and New York 2003

*Sacred Encounters: Shamanism and Magical Journeys of the Spirit*, Watkins, London 2003

*Echoes from the Void: Writings on Magic, Visionary Art and the New Consciousness*, Prism Press, Dorset 1994

*The Elements of Shamanism*, Element, Dorset 1989

Edinger, E., *Ego and Archetype*, Penguin Books, London 1973

Eliade, M., *Cosmos and History*, Harper & Row, New York 1959

   *Shamanism*, Princeton University Press, New Jersey 1972

Elkin, A.P., *Aboriginal Men of High Degree*, University of Queensland

Emboden, W., *Narcotic Plants*, Studio Vista, London 1979

Epstein, P., *Kabbalah: The Way of the Jewish Mystic*, Doubleday, New York 1978

Farrar, J.& S., *The Witches' Goddess*, Hale, London 1987

   *The Witches' Bible*, Magickal Childe, New York 1985

   *The Witches' Way*, Hale, London 1984

Farrar, S., *What Witches Do*, Phoenix, Custer, Washington 1983

Feldman, D.H., *Qabalah: The Mystical Heritage of the Children of Abraham*, Work of the Chariot, Santa Cruz, California 2001

Ferguson, J, *An Illustrated Encyclopaedia of Mysticism and the Mystery Religions*, Thames & Hudson, London 1976

Fernando, D., *The Dictionary of Alchemy*, Vega/Chrysalis, London 2002

Fisdel, S.A., *The Practice of Kabbalah* , Jason Aronson Inc., Northvale, New Jersey 1996

Fortune, D., *Applied Magic*; Aquarian Press, London 1962

Frost, G. and Y., *Magic Power of White Witchcraft*, Prentice Hall Press, Englewood Cliffs, New Jersey 1999

   *Witch's Book of Magical Ritual*, Prentice Hall Press, Englewood Cliffs, New Jersey 2002

   *Witch's Magical Handbook*, Prentice Hall Press, Englewood Cliffs, New Jersey 2000

Fuller, J.O., *The Magical Dilemma of Victor Neuburg*, W.H. Allen, London 1965

Furst, P.T., (ed.) *Flesh of the Gods*, Allen & Unwin, London 1972

Gardner, G.B., *Witchcraft Today*, Rider, London 1954

Gettings, F., *Dictionary of Astrology*, Routledge & Kegan Paul, London and New York 1985

Giger, H.R., *Necronomicon*, Big O Publishing, London 1978 (republished by Morpheus International)

Gilbert, R.A. *Revelations of the Golden Dawn*, Quantum/Foulsham, London 1997

Gilchrist, C., *The Elements of Alchemy*, Element Books, Dorset 1991

Gottlieb, R.S. (ed.) , *A New Creation: America's Contemporary Spiritual Voices*, Crossroad, New York 1990

Graf, F., *Magic in the Ancient World*, Harvard University Press, Cambridge, Mass. 1997

Graf, S.J., *W.B. Yeats: Twentieth-Century Magus*, Weiser, York Beach, Maine 2000

Grant, K., *Hecate's Fountain*, Skoob, London 1992

   *The Magical Revival*, Muller, London 1972

Grant, R. (ed.), *Gnosticism – An Anthology*, Collins, London 1961

Gray, W.G., *Inner Traditions of Magic*, Weiser, Maine 1984

Green, M., *The Elements of Natural Magic*, Element Books, Dorset 1989

Greer, M.K., *Women of the Golden Dawn*, Park Street Press, Rochester, Vermont 1995

Guiley, R.E., *Encyclopedia of Witches and Witchcraft*, Facts on File, New York 1989

Halifax, J., (ed.) *Shamanic Voices*, Arkana, New York 1991

Hansen, H.A., *The Witch's Garden*, Unity Press, Santa Cruz, California 1978

Harner, M., *The Way of the Shaman*, Harper & Row, San Francisco 1980

Harper, G.M., *Yeats' Golden Dawn*, Macmillan, London 1974

Harvey, G., and Hardman, C. (ed.), *Paganism Today*, Thorsons, London 1996

Harvey, G., *Listening People, Speaking Earth*, Hurst, London 1997

Hoffman, E., *The Heavenly Ladder*, Harper & Row, New York 1985

*The Way of Splendor: Jewish Mysticism and Modern Psychology*, Shambhala, Boulder, Colorado 1981

Holmyard, E.J., *Alchemy*, Penguin Books, London 1957

Houston, J., *The Hero and the Goddess*, Ballantine, New York 1992

Howard, M., *The Wisdom of the Runes*, Rider, London 1985

Howe, E., *The Magicians of the Golden Dawn*, Routledge & Kegan Paul, London 1972

Hultkrantz, A., *Native Religions of North America*, HarperCollins, San Francisco 1987

Hume, L., *Witchcraft and Paganism in Australia*, Melbourne University Press, Melbourne 1997

Hutin, S., *Astrology: Science or Superstition?* Bay Books, Sydney 1972

Hutton, R., *The Triumph of the Moon*, Oxford University Press, Oxford 1999

Jacobs, L. (ed.), *The Jewish Mystics*, Kyle Cathie, London 1990

Jamal, M., *Shape Shifters*, Arkana, New York and London 1987

Jones, P., and Matthews, C. (ed.), *Voices from the Circle*, Aquarian Press, London 1990

Jordan, M., *Witches: An Encyclopedia of Paganism and Magic*, Kyle Cathie, London 1996

Jung, C.G., *Memories, Dreams, Reflections*, Random House, New York 1961

*Man and his Symbols*, Dell, New York 1968

Kalweit, H., *Dreamtime and Inner Space*, Shambhala, Boston 1988

Kaplan, A., *Meditation and Kabbalah*, Weiser, New York 1982

Kaplan, S.R. *Tarot Classic*, Grossett & Dunlap, New York 1972

Kelly, A., *Crafting the Art of Magic*, Llewellyn, St Paul, Minnesota 1991

Kieckhefer, R., *Magic in the Middle Ages*, Cambridge University Press, Cambridge 2000

King, F., (ed.) *The Secret Rituals of the O.T.O.*, C.W.Daniel, London 1973

(ed.) *Astral Projection, Magic and Alchemy*, Spearman, London 1971

*Ritual Magic in England*, Spearman, London 1970 (republished as *Modern Ritual Magic*, Prism Press, Dorset 1989)

*Sexuality, Magic and Perversion*, New English Library, London 1972

King, F., and Skinner, S., *Techniques of High Magic: A Manual of Self-Initiation*, C.W. Daniel, London 1976

King, F., and Sutherland, I., *The Rebirth of Magic*, Corgi, London 1982

Knight, G., *A History of White Magic*, Mowbray, London and Oxford 1978

Kraig, D. M., *Evocation of Spirits*, Llewellyn, St Paul, Minnesota 1995

*Modern Sex Magick*, Llewellyn, St Paul, Minnesota 1998

Langdon, E.J.M., and Baer, G., *Portals of Power: Shamanism in South America*, University of New Mexico Press, Albuquerque 1992

Langguth, A.J., *Macumba: White and Black Magic in Brazil*, Harper & Row, New York 1975

Larsen, S., *The Shaman's Doorway*, Harper & Row, New York 1976

LaVey, A., *The Satanic Rituals*, Avon, New York 1972

*The Satanic Bible*, Avon, New York 1969

Lévi, E., *The Key of the Mysteries*, Rider, London 1959

Lewis, J.R., (ed.), *Magical Religion and Modern Witchcraft*, State University of New York Press, Albany 1996

Loewe, M., and Blacker, C., (ed.) *Divination and Oracles*, Allen & Unwin London 1972

Luhrmann, T.M., *Persuasions of the Witch's Craft*, Harvard University Press, Cambridge, Massachusetts 1989

Lyon, W.S., *Encyclopedia of Native American Healing*, Norton, New York 1998

Lyons, A., *The Second Coming: Satanism in America*, Dodd-Mead, New York 1970

Mathers, S.L.(ed.), *The Grimoire of Armadel*, Routledge & Kegan Paul, London 1980

*The Lesser Key of Solomon*, De Laurence, Chicago 1916

Matt, D.C., *The Essential Kabbalah*, HarperCollins, New York 1995

Matthews C., *Celtic Spirit*, HarperCollins, San Francisco 1998

*Sophia – Goddess of Wisdom*, Mandala, London 1991

Matthews, C. and J., *Encyclopedia of Celtic Myth and Legend*, Lyons Press, Guilford, Connecticut 2004

*The Western Way*, Arkana, London 1994

Matthews, J., *The Celtic Seers' Sourcebook*, Blandford, London 1999

McGregor, P., *Jesus of the Spirits*, Stein and Day, New York 1967

Meyer, M.W. (ed.), *The Ancient Mysteries: A Sourcebook*, Harper & Row, San Francisco 1987

Murray, M., *The Witch-Cult in Western Europe*, Oxford University Press, New York 1971 (first published 1921).

O'Hare, G., *Pagan Ways*, Llewellyn, St Paul, Minnesota 1997

Pachter, H.M., *Paracelsus: Magic into Science*, Collier Books, New York 1961

Pagels, E., *The Gnostic Gospels*, Weidenfeld & Nicolson, London 1979

Papus *The Tarot of the Bohemians*, Rider, London 1919

Parker, D and J., *A History of Astrology*, Andre Deutsch, London 1983

Patai, R., *The Hebrew Goddess*, Wayne State University Press, Detroit 1990

Pinch, G., *Magic in Ancient Egypt*, British Museum Press, London 1994

Pollard, J., *Seers, Shrines and Sirens*, Allen & Unwin, London 1965

Rätsch, C., *The Dictionary of Sacred and Magical Plants*, Prism Press, Dorset 1992

Redgrove, H.S., *Alchemy: Ancient and Modern*, Rider, London 1922

Regardie, I., *The Eye in the Triangle: An Interpretation of Aleister Crowley*, Falcon Press, Pheonix, Arizona 1982

(ed.), *The Golden Dawn*, vols 1–4, Aries Press, Chicago 1937-40

*The Tree of Life: A Study in Magic* , Rider, London 1932

Richardson, A., *Dancers to the Gods: The Magical Records of Charles Seymour and Christine Hartley 1937-1939*, Aquarian Press, Wellingborough, UK 1985

*Priestess: The Life and Magic of Dion Fortune*, Aquarian Press, Wellingborough 1987

Robinson, J.M., (ed.) *The Nag Hammadi Library in English*, Harper & Row, San Francisco 1977

Russell, J.B., *A History of Witchcraft: Sorcerers, Heretics and Pagans*, Thames & Hudson, London and New York 1980

Scholem, G., *On the Mystical Shape of the Godhead*, Schocken, New York 1997

*Origins of the Kabbalah*, Princeton University Press, New Jersey 1990

*Major Trends in Jewish Mysticism*, Schocken, New York 1961

Schueler G. and B., *The Enochian Tarot*, Llewellyn, St Paul, Minnesota 1989

Schueler, G. J., *An Advanced Guide to Enochian Magick*, Llewellyn, St Paul, Minnesota 1987

Schultes, R.E., Hofmann, A., and Rätsch, C., *Plants of the Gods*, Healing Arts Press, Rochester, Vermont 1998

Seligmann, K., *Magic, Supernaturalism and Religion*, Pantheon, New York 1971

Shumaker, W., *The Occult Sciences in the Renaissance*, University of California Press, Berkeley, California 1979

Skinner, S., and Rankine, D., *Practical Angel Magic of Dr John Dee's Enochian Tables*, Golden Hoard Press, London 2004

Spare, A.O., *The Book of Pleasure*, privately published, London 1913

Starhawk, *The Spiral Dance*, Harper & Row, New York 1979

Suster, G., *The Legacy of the Beast*, Weiser, Maine 1989

Sutin, L., *Do What Thou Wilt: A Life of Aleister Crowley*, St Martins Press, New York 2000

Symonds, J. and Grant, K., (ed.), *The Magical Record of the Beast 666*, Duckworth, London 1972

(ed.) *The Confessions of Aleister Crowley*, Hill and Wang, New York 1969

Symonds, J., *The Great Beast*, Mayflower, London 1973

Taylor, F.S., *The Alchemists*, Paladin, London 1976

Teish, L., *Jambalaya: The Natural Woman's Book of Personal Charms and Practical Rituals*, HarperCollins, San Francisco 1987

Tyson, D., *Enochian Magic for Beginners*, Llewellyn, St Paul, Minnesota 1997

*Familiar Spirits: A Practical Guide for Witches and Magicians*, Llewellyn, St Paul, Minnesota 2004

*Ritual Magic*, Llewellyn, St Paul, Minnesota 1992

*Sexual Alchemy: Magical Intercourse with Spirits*, Llewellyn, St Paul, Minnesota 2000

Valiente, D., *Witchcraft for Tomorrow*, Hale, London 1978

Waite, A.E., *The Holy Kabbalah*, University Books, New York 1960

Walker, B., *Gnosticism: Its History and Influence*, Aquarian Press, Wellingborough 1983

Walker, D.P., *Spiritual and Demonic Magic: From Ficino to Campanella*, Sutton Publishing, Stroud, England 2000

Wasson, R.G., et.al *The Road to Eleusis*, Harcourt Brace Jovanovich, New York 1968

Widengren, G., *Mani and Manichaeism*, Holt, Rinehart and Winston, New York 1965

Wilby, B. (ed.) *The New Dimensions Red Book*, Helios, Cheltenham 1968

Wild, L.D., *The Runes Workbook*, Thunder Bay Press, San Diego, California 2004

Wilson, C., *Aleister Crowley: The Nature of the Beast*, Aquarian Press, Wellingborough, England 1987

Yates, F., *The Occult Philosophy in the Elizabethan Age*, Routledge, London and New York 2000

*The Rosicrucian Enlightenment*, Shambhala Publications, Boulder 1987